Lecture Notes in Computer Science 6013

Commenced Publication in 1973
Founding and Former Series Editors:
Gerhard Goos, Juris Hartmanis, and Jan van Leeuwen

Advanced Research in Computing and Software Science
Subline of Lectures Notes in Computer Science

T0223383

David S. Rosenblum
Gabriele Taentzer (Eds.)

Fundamental Approaches to Software Engineering

13th International Conference, FASE 2010
Held as Part of the Joint European Conferences
on Theory and Practice of Software, ETAPS 2010
Paphos, Cyprus, March 20-28, 2010. Proceedings

 Springer

Volume Editors

David S. Rosenblum
University College London
Department of Computer Science
London WC1E 6BT, UK
E-mail: d.rosenblum@cs.ucl.ac.uk

Gabriele Taentzer
Philipps-Universität Marburg
Fachbereich Mathematik und Informatik
35032 Marburg, Germany
E-mail: taentzer@mathematik.uni-marburg.de

Library of Congress Control Number: 2010921922

CR Subject Classification (1998): D.2, F.3, D.3, C.2, H.4, C.2.4

LNCS Sublibrary: SL 1 – Theoretical Computer Science and General Issues

ISSN   0302-9743
ISBN-10   3-642-12028-8 Springer Berlin Heidelberg New York
ISBN-13   978-3-642-12028-2 Springer Berlin Heidelberg New York

springer.com

© Springer-Verlag Berlin Heidelberg 2010
Printed in Germany

Typesetting: Camera-ready by author, data conversion by Scientific Publishing Services, Chennai, India
Printed on acid-free paper   06/3180   5 4 3 2 1 0

Foreword

ETAPS 2010 was the 13th instance of the European Joint Conferences on Theory and Practice of Software. ETAPS is an annual federated conference that was established in 1998 by combining a number of existing and new conferences. This year it comprised the usual five sister conferences (CC, ESOP, FASE, FOSSACS, TACAS), 19 satellite workshops (ACCAT, ARSPA-WITS, Bytecode, CMCS, COCV, DCC, DICE, FBTC, FESCA, FOSS-AMA, GaLoP, GT-VMT, LDTA, MBT, PLACES, QAPL, SafeCert, WGT, and WRLA) and seven invited lectures (excluding those that were specific to the satellite events). The five main conferences this year received 497 submissions (including 31 tool demonstration papers), 130 of which were accepted (10 tool demos), giving an overall acceptance rate of 26%, with most of the conferences at around 24%. Congratulations therefore to all the authors who made it to the final programme! I hope that most of the other authors will still have found a way of participating in this exciting event, and that you will all continue submitting to ETAPS and contributing to make of it the best conference on software science and engineering.

The events that comprise ETAPS address various aspects of the system development process, including specification, design, implementation, analysis and improvement. The languages, methodologies and tools which support these activities are all well within its scope. Different blends of theory and practice are represented, with an inclination toward theory with a practical motivation on the one hand and soundly based practice on the other. Many of the issues involved in software design apply to systems in general, including hardware systems, and the emphasis on software is not intended to be exclusive.

ETAPS is a confederation in which each event retains its own identity, with a separate Programme Committee and proceedings. Its format is open-ended, allowing it to grow and evolve as time goes by. Contributed talks and system demonstrations are in synchronised parallel sessions, with invited lectures in plenary sessions. Two of the invited lectures are reserved for 'unifying' talks on topics of interest to the whole range of ETAPS attendees. The aim of cramming all this activity into a single one-week meeting is to create a strong magnet for academic and industrial researchers working on topics within its scope, giving them the opportunity to learn about research in related areas, and thereby to foster new and existing links between work in areas that were formerly addressed in separate meetings.

ETAPS 2010 was organised by the University of Cyprus in cooperation with:

▷ European Association for Theoretical Computer Science (EATCS)
▷ European Association for Programming Languages and Systems (EAPLS)
▷ European Association of Software Science and Technology (EASST)

and with support from the Cyprus Tourism Organisation.

The organising team comprised:

General Chairs: Tiziana Margaria and Anna Philippou
Local Chair: George Papadopoulos
Secretariat: Maria Kittira
Administration: Petros Stratis
Satellite Events: Anna Philippou
Website: Konstantinos Kakousis.

Overall planning for ETAPS conferences is the responsibility of its Steering Committee, whose current membership is:

Vladimiro Sassone (Southampton, Chair), Parosh Abdulla (Uppsala), Luca de Alfaro (Santa Cruz), Gilles Barthe (IMDEA-Software), Giuseppe Castagna (CNRS Paris), Marsha Chechik (Toronto), Sophia Drossopoulou (Imperial College London), Javier Esparza (TU Munich), Dimitra Giannakopoulou (CMU/NASA Ames), Andrew D. Gordon (MSR Cambridge), Rajiv Gupta (UC Riverside), Chris Hankin (Imperial College London), Holger Hermanns (Saarbrücken), Mike Hinchey (Lero, the Irish Software Engineering Research Centre), Martin Hofmann (LM Munich), Joost-Pieter Katoen (Aachen), Paul Klint (Amsterdam), Jens Knoop (Vienna), Shriram Krishnamurthi (Brown), Kim Larsen (Aalborg), Rustan Leino (MSR Redmond), Gerald Luettgen (Bamberg), Rupak Majumdar (Los Angeles), Tiziana Margaria (Potsdam), Ugo Montanari (Pisa), Oege de Moor (Oxford), Luke Ong (Oxford), Fernando Orejas (Barcelona) Catuscia Palamidessi (INRIA Paris), George Papadopoulos (Cyprus), David Rosenblum (UCL), Don Sannella (Edinburgh), João Saraiva (Minho), Michael Schwartzbach (Aarhus), Perdita Stevens (Edinburgh), Gabriele Taentzer (Marburg), and Martin Wirsing (LM Munich).

I would like to express my sincere gratitude to all of these people and organisations, the Programme Committee Chairs and members of the ETAPS conferences, the organisers of the satellite events, the speakers themselves, the many reviewers, all the participants, and Springer for agreeing to publish the ETAPS proceedings in the ARCoSS subline.

Finally, I would like to thank the organising Chair of ETAPS 2010, George Papadopoulos, for arranging for us to have ETAPS in the most beautiful surroundings of Paphos.

January 2010   Vladimiro Sassone

Preface

This volume contains the papers accepted for presentation at FASE 2010, the 13th International Conference on Fundamental Approaches to Software Engineering, which was held in Paphos, Cyprus, in March 2010 as part of the annual European Joint Conference on Theory and Practice of Software (ETAPS). As with previous editions of FASE, this year's papers present foundational contributions and results on a broad range of topics in software engineering, including requirements engineering, software architectures, model-based and model-driven development, program analysis, testing, debugging, verification, and evolution.

This year we received 103 submissions, of which 25 were accepted by the Program Committee for presentation at the conference, resulting in an acceptance rate of 24.3%. The submissions comprise 96 research papers and 7 tool demonstration papers, and the Program Committee accepted 24 of the research papers and 1 of the tool demonstration papers. Each paper received a minimum of three reviews, and acceptance decisions were reached through email discussions conducted with the Program Committee. We used the free conference management system EasyChair to manage the paper submissions, reviews, and email communication with the authors and Program Committee.

We are also delighted to have welcomed Mark Harman of King's College London as the FASE keynote speaker at ETAPS 2010. Mark is well known as the pioneer of *search-based software engineering*, which employs heuristic search techniques such as genetic algorithms to find efficient solutions for a wide variety of complex problems in software engineering, as diverse as test suite minimization and software project staffing.

The success of a conference like FASE 2010 depends on the contribution and support of *many* people. First, we thank the authors for continuing to produce interesting and timely research in software engineering, ensuring that FASE remains a key venue for the most important research results in the field. We also extend a very warm thanks to our Program Committee, who worked very hard under a tight schedule to produce thorough, detailed reviews for the authors and to achieve consensus on paper acceptance decisions. We thank Marsha Chechik and Vladimiro Sassone, the respective Chairs of the FASE and ETAPS Steering Committees, for providing all the information and support we needed for our work as Chairs. We thank the sponsors of ETAPS and FASE, namely EACTS and EASST. We thank Stefan Jurack and Gerd Wierse for their expert help in assembling this proceedings, and also the staff at Springer for their helpful collaboration and quick turnaround on the proceedings. Finally, we extend our best wishes to the chairs of FASE 2011, Dimitra Giannakopoulou and Fernando Orejas. We sincerely hope you enjoy these proceedings!

January 2010

David S. Rosenblum
Gabriele Taentzer

Organization

Program Chairs

David S. Rosenblum   University College London (UK)
Gabriele Taentzer   Philipps-Universität Marburg (Germany)

Program Committee

Don Batory   University of Texas at Austin (USA)
Antonia Bertolino   ISTI-CNR (Italy)
Vittorio Cortellessa   Università dell'Aquila (Italy)
Alexander Egyed   Johannes Kepler University Linz (Austria)
Sebastian Elbaum   University of Nebraska – Lincoln (USA)
Serge Demeyer   University of Antwerp (Belgium)
José Fiadeiro   University of Leicester (UK)
Dimitra Giannakopoulou   Carnegie Mellon University and NASA Ames
                            Research Center (USA)

Holger Giese   Hasso Plattner Institute, Potsdam (Germany)
Reiko Heckel   University of Leicester (UK)
Paola Inverardi   Università dell'Aquila (Italy)
Jana Köhler   IBM Research Zurich (Switzerland)
Rainer Koschke   University of Bremen (Germany)
Juan de Lara   Universidad Autónoma de Madrid (Spain)
Emmanuel Letier   University College London (UK)
Tom Maibaum   McMaster University (Canada)
Tiziana Margaria   Universität Potsdam (Germany)
Gail Murphy   University of British Columbia (Canada)
Mauro Pezzè   University of Lugano (Switzerland) and
                            University of Milan Bicocca (Italy)
Leila Ribeiro   Federal University of Rio Grande do Sul
                            (Brazil)
Franco Raimondi   Middlesex University (UK)
Andy Schürr   Technische Universität Darmstadt (Germany)
Perdita Stevens   University of Edinburgh (UK)
Harald Störrle   Technical University of Denmark (Denmark)
Dániel Varró   Budapest University of Technology and
                            Economics (Hungary)
Heike Wehrheim   University of Paderborn (Germany)

External Reviewers

Anthony Anjorin
Shay Artzi
Marco Autili
András Balogh
Luca Berardinelli
Gábor Bergmann
Domenico Bianculli
Dénes Bisztray
Filippo Bonchi
Henning Bordihn
Artur Boronat
Roberto Bruni
Benedikt Burgstaller
Jordi Cabot
Jacques Carette
Yoonsik Cheon
Robert Clariso
Christophe Damas
Sylvain Degrandsart
Giovanni Denaro
Joachim Denil
Davide Di Ruscio
Zinovy Diskin
Adwoa Donyina
William Farmer
Marcelo Frias
Gregor Gabrysiak
Joris Van Geet
Iris Groher

Esther Guerra
László Gönczy
Roberto Lopez Herrejon
Stephan Hildebrandt
Ákos Horváth
Falk Howar
Niaz Hussein
Thierry Jéron
Sven Jörges
Wolfram Kahl
Anne Keller
Tamim Khan
Felix Klar
Jochen Küster
Bernard Lambeau
Ahmed Lamkanfi
Marius Lauder
Sven Lauder
Mark Lawford
Leonardo Mariani
Narciso Marti-Oliet
Maik Merten
Björn Metzler
Gergely Mezei
Patrick Mukherjee
Muhammad Naeem
Johannes Neubauer
Stefan Neumann
Fernando Orejas

Lucian Patcas
Lars Patzina
Patrizio Pelliccione
Gergely Pintér
Matteo Pradella
Zvonimir Rakamaric
Alexander Reder
Sebastian Rose
Thomas Ruhroth
Neha Rungta
István Ráth
Antonino Sabetta
Andreas Schaefer
Andreas Seibel
Quinten David Soetens
Monika Solanki
Christian Soltenborn
Kathryn Stolee
Nils Timm
Massimo Tivoli
Paolo Torrini
Catia Trubiani
Emilio Tuosto
Gergely Varró
Jan Vlegels
Thomas Vogel
Daniel Wonisch
Pingyu Zhang

Table of Contents

Modeling Concepts

Verification

Program Analysis

Testing and Debugging

Performance Modeling and Analysis

Why the Virtual Nature of Software Makes It Ideal for Search Based Optimization

Mark Harman

CREST, King's College London, Strand, London,
WC2R 2LS, United Kingdom

Abstract. This paper[1] provides a motivation for the application of search based optimization to Software Engineering, an area that has come to be known as Search Based Software Engineering (SBSE). SBSE techniques have already been applied to many problems throughout the Software Engineering lifecycle, with new application domains emerging on a regular basis. The approach is very generic and therefore finds wide application in Software Engineering. It facilitates automated and semi-automated solutions in situations typified by large complex problem spaces with multiple competing and conflicting objectives. Previous work has already discussed, in some detail, the advantages of the SBSE approach for Software Engineering. This paper summarises previous work and goes further, by arguing that Software Engineering provides the *ideal* set of application problems for which optimization algorithms are supremely well suited.

Keywords: SBSE, Search Based Optimization, Search Based Testing, Metaheuristic Search, Optimization Algorithms.

1 Introduction

We often speak of 'Software Engineering' without thinking too deeply about what it means to have a discipline of 'engineering' that considers the primary material to be 'software'. By considering both the 'engineering' aspects of 'Software Engineering' and also the unique properties of 'software' as an engineering material, this paper makes an argument that search based optimization techniques are ideally suited to Software Engineering.

That is, though all other engineering disciplines have also provided rich sources of application for search based optimization, it is in its application to problems in Software Engineering that these techniques can find greatest application. This acts as a secondary motivation for the field of SBSE. The primary motivation

---

[1] This paper is written to accompany the author's keynote presentation at Fundamental Approaches to Software Engineering (FASE 2010). The talk provides an overview of SBSE and its applications and motivation. The paper focuses on the argument that the virtual nature of software makes it ideal for SBSE, since other aspects of SBSE mentioned in the FASE keynote have been covered by the author's previous keynotes and invited papers.

D.S. Rosenblum and G. Taentzer (Eds.): FASE 2010, LNCS 6013, pp. 1–12, 2010.

for SBSE comes from the simple observation that these techniques do, indeed, apply well in other engineering disciplines and that, therefore, should we wish to regard Software Engineering as truly an engineering discipline, then it would only be natural to consider the application of search based optimization techniques. This form of advocacy for SBSE has been put forward by this and other authors before [CDH+03, HJ01, Har07b, Har07a, Har07c].

The acceptance of SBSE as a well-defined and worthwhile activity within the rich and diverse tapestry of Software Engineering is reflected by the increasing number of survey papers on SBSE [ABHPW10, ATF09, HMZ09, McM04, Räi09]. Further evidence for widespread interest and uptake, comes from the many special issues, workshops and conferences on the topic. However, this paper seeks to go a step further. It argues that Software Engineering is not merely an acceptable subject for the application of search based optimization, but that it is even better suited than all other areas of engineering activity, as a result of the very special properties of software as an engineering material.

2   Overview of SBSE

The existing case for SBSE in the literature rests upon the observation that

> "Software engineers often face problems associated with the balancing of competing constraints, trade-offs between concerns and requirement imprecision. Perfect solutions are often either impossible or impractical and the nature of the problems often makes the definition of analytical algorithms problematic." [HJ01]

The term SBSE was first used by Harman and Jones [HJ01] in 2001. The term 'search' is used to refer to the metaheuristic search–based optimization techniques. Search Based Software Engineering seeks a fundamental shift of emphasis from solution construction to solution description. Rather than devoting human effort to the task of finding solutions, the search for solutions is *automated* as a search, guided by a fitness function, defined by the engineer to capture *what* is required rather than *how* it is to be constructed. In many ways, this approach to Software Engineering echoes, at the macro level of Software Engineering artefacts, the declarative programming approach [DB77], which applies at the code level; both seek to move attention from the question of 'how' a solution is to be achieved to the question of 'what' properties are desirable.

Harman and Jones argued that SBSE could become a coherent field of activity that combines the expertise and skills of the Metaheuristic Search community with those of the Software Engineering community. Though there was previous work on the application of search based optimization to Software Engineering problems [CCHA94, JES98, TCM98, XES+92], the 2001 paper was the first to articulate SBSE as a field of study in its own right and to make a case for its wider study.

Since the 2001 paper, there has been an explosion of SBSE activity, with evidence for a rapid increase in publications on the topic [HMZ09]. For example, SBSE has been applied to testing [BSS02, Bot02, BLS05, GHHD05,

HHH+04, MHBT06, WBS01], bug fixing [AY08, WNGF09] design, [HHP02, MM06, SBBP05], requirements, [BRSW01, ZFH08], project management [AC07, ADH04, KSH02] and refactoring. [OÓ06, HT07]. There have been SBSE special issues in the journals Information and Software Technology (IST), Software Maintenance and Evolution (JSME) and Computers and Operations Research (COR) with forthcoming special issues in Empirical Software Engineering (EMSE), Software Practice and Experience (SPE), Information and Software Technology (IST) and IEEE Transactions on Software Engineering (TSE). There is also an established Symposium on Search Based Software Engineering (SSBSE), a workshop on Search Based Software Testing (SBST) and a dedicated track of the Genetic and Evolutionary Computation COnference (GECCO) on SBSE.

2.1 All You Need Is Love *of optimization*; You Already Have Representation and Fitness

Getting initial results from SBSE is relatively straightforward. This has made SBSE attractive to researchers and practitioners from the Software Engineering community. Becoming productive as a Search Based Software Engineer does not required a steep learning curve, nor years of apprenticeship in the techniques, foundations and nomenclature of Optimization Algorithms. It has been stated [Har07d, HJ01] that there are only two key ingredients required:

1. The choice of the representation of the problem.
2. The definition of the fitness function.

Of course, a Software Engineer is very likely to have, already at their disposal, a workable representation for their problem. Furthermore, Harman and Clark argue that

"Metrics are Fitness functions too"[HC04].

They argue that the extensive body of literature on metrics and software measurement can be mined for candidate fitness functions. This would allow Software Engineers to optimize according to software measurements, rather than merely to passively measure software artefacts. Though every metric may not be effective, because some may fail to measure what they claim to measure [She95], this need not be a problem. Indeed, one of the attractive aspects of metrics as fitness functions, is that such failings on the part of the metrics will become immediately evident through optimization. Harman and Clark show that there is a close connection between metrics as fitness functions and empirical assessment of the representation condition of software measurement.

2.2 Algorithms

The most widely used algorithms in SBSE work have, hitherto [HMZ09], been local search, simulated annealing genetic algorithms and genetic programming.

However, other authors have experimented with other search based optimizers such as parallel EAs [AC08], evolution strategies [AC05], Estimation of Distribution Algorithms (EDAs) [SL08], Scatter Search [BTDD07, AVCTV06, Sag07], Particle Swarm Optimization (PSO) [LI08, WWW07], Tabu Search [DTBD08] and Local search [KHC+05].

3   Why Software Engineering is the 'Killer Application' for Search Based Optimization

Previous work has considered the motivation for SBSE in terms of the advantages it offers to the Software Engineer. For instance it has been argued [HMZ09, Har07b] that SBSE is

1. **Scalable**, because of the 'embarrassingly parallel' [Fos95] nature of the underlying algorithms which can yield orders of magnitude scale up over sequential implementations [LB08].
2. **Generic**, due to the wide prevalence of suitable representations and fitness functions, right across the Software Engineering spectrum.
3. **Robust**, due to the ability of search based optimization to cope with noise, partial data and inaccurate fitness.
4. **Insight-rich**, as a result of the way in which the search process itself can shed light on the problems faced by decision makers.
5. **Realistic**, due to the way in which SBSE caters naturally for multiple competing and conflicting engineering objectives.

These five features of SBSE are important and have been described in more detail elsewhere [HMZ09, Har07b]. However, most are reasons for the use of search based optimization in general. They apply equally well to any class of optimization problems, both within and without the field of Software Engineering. This does not make them any less applicable to Software Engineering. However, it does raise the question as to whether there are any special software-centric reasons why SBSE should be considered to be an attractive, important and valuable field of study in its own right. That is, we ask:

> Are there features of Software Engineering problems that make search based optimization particularly attractive?

Perhaps unsurprisingly, the author's answer to this question is: 'yes'. The rest of this paper seeks to explain why.

In more traditional engineering disciplines, such as mechanical, biomedical, chemical, electrical and electronic engineering, search based optimization has been applied for many years [BW96, CHS98, LT92, PCV95]. These applications denote a wide spectrum of engineering activity, from well-established traditional fields of engineering to more recent innovations. However, for each, it has been possible and desirable, to optimize using search based optimization. This is hardly surprising. After all, surely engineering is all about optimization.

When we speak of finding an engineering solution, do we not include balancing competing practical objectives in the best way possible? It should not be surprising, therefore, that optimization algorithms play a very important role.

In all of these fields of engineering, the application of optimization techniques provides the engineer with a mechanism to consider many candidate solutions, searching for those that yield an acceptable balance of objectives. The advent of automatic high speed computation in the past sixty years has provided a huge stimulus to the optimization community; it has allowed this search to be automated. Guided by a fitness function, automated search is one of the most profitable and archetypal applications of computation. It allows a designer to focus on the desired properties of a design, without having to care about implementation details.

It is the advent of software and the platforms on which it executes that has facilitated enormous breakthroughs in optimization methods and techniques. However, it is only comparatively recently that Software Engineering has started to catch up with this trend within the wider engineering community. This seems curious, since search based optimization can be viewed as a software technology. Perhaps it reflects the comparatively recent realization that the activity of designing and building software-based systems is, indeed, an engineering activity and thus one for which an optimization-based world view is important.

When we speak of software we mean more than merely the code. We typically include requirements, designs, documentation and test cases. We also include the supporting logical infrastructure of configuration control, development environments, test harnesses, bug tracking, archives and other virtual information-based resources that form part of the overall system and its development history. The important unifying property of all of this information is that it is purely logical and without any physical manifestation. As every software engineer knows, software is different from every other engineering artefact; very different. One cannot see, hear, smell, touch nor taste it because it has no physical manifestation.

This apparently trite observation is *so* obvious that its importance can sometimes be overlooked, for it is precisely this *virtual* nature of software makes it even better suited to search based optimization than traditional engineering artefacts. The materials with which we perform the automated search are made of the same 'virtual stuff' as the artefacts we seek to optimize. This has profound implications for the conduct of search based optimization because it directly impacts the two key ingredients of representation and fitness (see Figure 1).

In traditional engineering optimization, the artefact to be optimized is often simulated. This is typically necessary precisely because the artefact to be optimized is a physical entity. For instance, if one wants to optimize an aircraft engine, one cannot search the space of real engines; building even a small subset of such candidate engine designs would be prohibitively expensive. Rather, one builds a *model* of the engine (in *software*), capturing, hopefully realistically and correctly, those aspects of performance that are of interest. Furthermore, in order to compute fitness, some form of simulation of the model is required. This

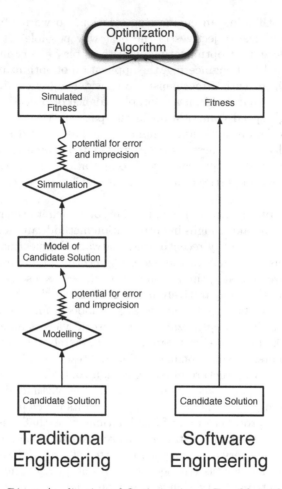

Fig. 1. Direct Application of Optimization is Possible with SBSE

allows us to explore the space of possible engine models, guided by a simulation of their likely real fitness.

Modeling and simulation create two layers of indirection and consequent potential for error. The model may not be entirely accurate. Indeed, if we are able to build a perfect model, then perhaps we would know so much about the engineering problem that we would be less likely to need to employ optimization. The fitness of each candidate model considered is calculated indirectly, in terms of the performance of the model with respect to some simulation of its real world behaviour. Once again, this introduces indirection and with it, the potential for error, imprecision and misunderstanding.

Contrast this traditional, physical engineering scenario with that of SBSE. For instance, consider the widely studied problem of finding test data. Suppose we wish to find test inputs that traverse a chosen branch of interest [ABHPW10, HMZ09, McM04]. For this problem there is no need for a model of the software to be tested nor the test case to be applied. Rather than modeling the test case, the optimization is applied directly to a vector which *is* the input to the program under test. Furthermore, in order to compute fitness, one need not *simulate* the execution, one may simply execute directly.

Of course, some instrumentation is required to facilitate fitness assessment. This can create issues for measurement if, for example, non–functional properties are to be optimized [ATF09, HMZ09]. These bear a superficial similarity to those present with simulations. The instrumented program is not the real program; it could be thought of as a kind of model. However, the instrumented program is clearly much closer to the original program under test than a simulation of an engine is to a real physical engine.

Furthermore, many software testing objectives, such as structural test adequacy criteria [ABHPW10, HMZ09, McM04], are entirely unaffected by instrumentation and so there is no indirection at all. This observation applies in many aspects of software engineering. The problem of finding suitable sets of requirements operates on the requirements sets themselves. This is also true for optimization of regression test sets and for optimization of project plans and architectures.

Of course, there are some aspects of software systems which are modeled. Indeed, there is an increasing interest in model driven development. When SBSE is applied to these models, at the design level [Räi09], it may be the case that search based optimization for Software Engineering acquires a closer similarity to search based optimization for traditional engineering. Nevertheless, there will remain many applications for which SBSE is ideally suited to the problem because the engineering artefact is optimized directly (not in terms of a model) and the fitness is computed directly from the artefact itself (not from a simulation thereof).

4   Conclusions

Search Based Software Engineering (SBSE) is a newly emergent paradigm for both Software Engineering community and the Metaheuristic Search and optimization communities. SBSE has had notable successes and there is an increasingly widespread application of SBSE across the full spectrum of Software Engineering activities and problems. This paper is essentially a 'position paper' that argues that the unique 'virtual' property of software as an engineering material makes it ideally suited among engineering materials for search based optimization. Software Engineers can build candidate Software Engineering artefacts with comparative ease and little cost compared to traditional engineers, faced with physical artefact construction and consequent cost. In general, the Software Engineer can also measure fitness directly, not in terms of a (possibly imprecise or misrepresented) simulation of real world operation.

5   Author Biography

Mark Harman is professor of Software Engineering in the Department of Computer Science at King's College London. He is widely known for work on source code analysis and testing and he was instrumental in the founding of the field of Search Based Software Engineering, the topic of this keynote. He has given 14 keynote invited talks on SBSE and its applications in the past four years. Professor Harman is the author of over 150 refereed publications, on the editorial board of 7 international journals and has served on 90 programme committees. He is director of the CREST centre at King's College London.

Acknowledgements

The author is grateful for ongoing discussion and collaboration with many other colleagues in the SBSE community, sadly too numerous to list by name here. His work is currently funded by the EPSRC project Software Engineering by Automated Search (EP/D050863, SEBASE, 2006-2011), for which the other principal investigators are John Clark (University of York) and Xin Yao (University of Birmingham) and by an EPSRC platform grant (EP/G060525, CREST, 2009-2014). He was also supported by the recently completed EU Specific Targeted Research Project: Evolutionary Testing (IST-33472, EvoTest, 2006-2009). This paper draws on work done by the author on these projects. Lorna Anderson kindly assisted with proof reading.

References

[ABHPW10] Ali, S., Briand, L.C., Hemmati, H., Panesar-Walawege, R.K.: A systematic review of the application and empirical investigation of search-based test-case generation. IEEE Transactions on Software Engineering (to appear, 2010)

[AC05] Alba, E., Chicano, F.: Testing with Evolutionary Strategies. In: Guelfi, N., Savidis, A. (eds.) RISE 2005. LNCS, vol. 3943, pp. 50–65. Springer, Heidelberg (2006)

[AC07] Alba, E., Chicano, F.: Software Project Management with GAs. Information Sciences 177(11), 2380–2401 (2007)

[AC08] Alba, E., Chicano, F.: Observations in using Parallel and Sequential Evolutionary Algorithms for Automatic Software Testing. Computers & Operations Research 35(10), 3161–3183 (2008)

[ADH04] Antoniol, G., Di Penta, M., Harman, M.: Search-based Techniques for Optimizing Software Project Resource Allocation. In: Deb, K., et al. (eds.) GECCO 2004. LNCS, vol. 3103, pp. 1425–1426. Springer, Heidelberg (2004)

[ATF09] Afzal, W., Torkar, R., Feldt, R.: A systematic review of search-based testing for non-functional system properties. Information and Software Technology 51(6), 957–976 (2009)

[AVCTV06] Ramón Alvarez-Valdes, E., Crespo, J.M.: A Scatter Search Algorithm for Project Scheduling under Partially Renewable Resources. Journal of Heuristics 12(1-2), 95–113 (2006)

[AY08] Arcuri, A., Yao, X.: A Novel Co-evolutionary Approach to Automatic Software Bug Fixing. In: Proceedings of the IEEE Congress on Evolutionary Computation (CEC 2008), Hongkong, China, June 1-6, pp. 162–168. IEEE Computer Society, Los Alamitos (2008)

[BLS05] Briand, L.C., Labiche, Y., Shousha, M.: Stress Testing Real-Time Systems with Genetic Algorithms. In: Proceedings of the 2005 Conference on Genetic and Evolutionary Computation (GECCO 2005), Washington, D.C., USA, June 25-29, pp. 1021–1028. ACM, New York (2005)

[Bot02] Bottaci, L.: Instrumenting Programs with Flag Variables for Test Data Search by Genetic Algorithms. In: Proceedings of the 2002 Conference on Genetic and Evolutionary Computation (GECCO 2002), New York, USA, July 9-13, pp. 1337–1342. Morgan Kaufmann Publishers, San Francisco (2002)

[BRSW01] Bagnall, A.J., Rayward-Smith, V.J., Whittley, I.M.: The Next Release Problem. Information and Software Technology 43(14), 883–890 (2001)

[BSS02] Baresel, A., Sthamer, H., Schmidt, M.: Fitness Function Design to Improve Evolutionary Structural Testing. In: Proceedings of the 2002 Conference on Genetic and Evolutionary Computation (GECCO 2002), New York, USA, July 9-13, pp. 1329–1336. Morgan Kaufmann, San Francisco (2002)

[BTDD07] Blanco, R., Tuya, J., Daz, E., Adenso Daz, B.: A Scatter Search Approach for Automated Branch Coverage in Software Testing. International Journal of Engineering Intelligent Systems (EIS) 15(3), 135–142 (2007)

[BW96] Bentley, P.J., Wakefield, J.P.: Generic representation of solid geometry for genetic search. Microcomputers in Civil Engineering 11(3), 153–161 (1996)

[CCHA94] Chang, C.K., Chao, C., Hsieh, S.-Y., Alsalqan, Y.: SPMNet: a Formal Methodology for Software Management. In: Proceedings of the 18th Annual International Computer Software and Applications Conference (COMPSAC 1994), Taipei, Taiwan, November 9-11, p. 57. IEEE, Los Alamitos (1994)

[CDH+03] Clark, J., Dolado, J.J., Harman, M., Hierons, R.M., Jones, B., Lumkin, M., Mitchell, B., Mancoridis, S., Rees, K., Roper, M., Shepperd, M.: Reformulating software engineering as a search problem. IEE Proceedings — Software 150(3), 161–175 (2003)

[CHS98] Cordón, O., Herrera, F., Sánchez, L.: Evolutionary learning processes for data analysis in electrical engineering applications. In: Quagliarella, D., Périaux, J., Poloni, C., Winter, G. (eds.) Genetic Algorithms and Evolution Strategy in Engineering and Computer Science, pp. 205–224. John Wiley and Sons, Chichester (1998)

[DB77] Darlington, J., Burstall, R.M.: A tranformation system for developing recursive programs. Journal of the ACM 24(1), 44–67 (1977)

[DTBD08] Díaz, E., Tuya, J., Blanco, R., Dolado, J.J.: A Tabu Search Algorithm for Structural Software Testing. Computers & Operations Research 35(10), 3052–3072 (2008)

[Fos95] Foster, I.: Designing and building parallel programs:Concepts and tools for parallel software. Addison-Wesley, Reading (1995)

[GHHD05] Guo, Q., Hierons, R.M., Harman, M., Derderian, K.: Constructing Multiple Unique Input/Output Sequences using Evolutionary Optimisation Techniques. IEE Proceedings - Software 152(3), 127–140 (2005)

[Har07a] Harman, M.: Automated test data generation using search based software engineering (keynote). In: 2nd Workshop on Automation of Software Test (AST 2007) at the 29th International Conference on Software Engineering (ICSE 2007), Minneapolis, USA (2007)

[Har07b] Harman, M.: The current state and future of search based software engineering. In: Briand, L., Wolf, A. (eds.) Future of Software Engineering 2007, pp. 342–357. IEEE Computer Society Press, Los Alamitos (2007)

[Har07c] Harman, M.: Search based software engineering for program comprehension (keynote). In: 15th International Conference on Program Comprehension (ICPC 2007), Banff, Canada (2007)

[Har07d] Harman, M.: The Current State and Future of Search Based Software Engineering. In: Briand, L., Wolf, A. (eds.) Proceedings of International Conference on Software Engineering / Future of Software Engineering 2007 (ICSE/FOSE 2007), Minneapolis, Minnesota, USA, May 20-26, pp. 342–357. IEEE Computer Society, Los Alamitos (2007)

[HC04] Harman, M., Clark, J.A.: Metrics Are Fitness Functions Too. In: Proceedings of the 10th IEEE International Symposium on Software Metrics (METRICS 2004), Chicago, USA, September 11-17, pp. 58–69. IEEE Computer Society, Los Alamitos (2004)

[HHH+04] Harman, M., Hu, L., Hierons, R.M., Wegener, J., Sthamer, H., Baresel, A., Roper, M.: Testability Transformation. IEEE Transaction on Software Engineering 30(1), 3–16 (2004)

[HHP02] Harman, M., Hierons, R., Proctor, M.: A New Representation and Crossover Operator for Search-based Optimization of Software Modularization. In: Proceedings of the 2002 Conference on Genetic and Evolutionary Computation (GECCO 2002), New York, USA, July 9-13, pp. 1351–1358. Morgan Kaufmann Publishers, San Francisco (2002)

[HJ01] Harman, M., Jones, B.F.: Search-based Software Engineering. Information & Software Technology 43(14), 833–839 (2001)

[HMZ09] Harman, M., Mansouri, A., Zhang, Y.: Search based software engineering: A comprehensive analysis and review of trends techniques and applications. Technical Report TR-09-03, Department of Computer Science, King's College London (April 2009)

[HT07] Harman, M., Tratt, L.: Pareto Optimal Search Based Refactoring at the Design Level. In: Proceedings of the 9th annual Conference on Genetic and Evolutionary Computation (GECCO 2007), London, England, July 7-11, pp. 1106–1113. ACM, New York (2007)

[JES98] Jones, B.F., Eyres, D.E., Sthamer, H.-H.: A Strategy for using Genetic Algorithms to Automate Branch and Fault-based Testing. Computer Journal 41(2), 98–107 (1998)

[KHC+05] Korel, B., Harman, M., Chung, S., Apirukvorapinit, P., Gupta, R., Zhang, Q.: Data Dependence Based Testability Transformation in Automated Test Generation. In: Proceedings of the 16th IEEE International Symposium on Software Reliability Engineering (ISSRE 2005), Chicago, Illinios, USA, November 2005, pp. 245–254. IEEE Computer Society, Los Alamitos (2005)

[KSH02] Kirsopp, C., Shepperd, M., Hart, J.: Search Heuristics, Case-based Reasoning And Software Project Effort Prediction. In: Proceedings of the 2002 Conference on Genetic and Evolutionary Computation (GECCO 2002), New York, July 9-13, pp. 1367–1374. Morgan Kaufmann Publishers, San Francisco (2002)

[LB08]   Langdon, W.B., Banzhaf, W.: A SIMD interpreter for genetic program-
         ming on GPU graphics cards. In: O'Neill, M., Vanneschi, L., Gustafson,
         S., Esparcia Alcázar, A.I., De Falco, I., Della Cioppa, A., Tarantino, E.
         (eds.) EuroGP 2008. LNCS, vol. 4971, pp. 73–85. Springer, Heidelberg
         (2008)
[LI08]   Lefticaru, R., Ipate, F.: Functional Search-based Testing from State Ma-
         chines. In: Proceedings of the First International Conference on Software
         Testing, Verfication and Validation (ICST 2008), Lillehammer, Norway,
         April 9-11, pp. 525–528. IEEE Computer Society, Los Alamitos (2008)
[LT92]   Labossiere, J.E., Turrkan, N.: On the optimization of the tensor polyno-
         mial failure theory with a genetic algorithm. Transactions of the Cana-
         dian Society for Mechanical Engineering 16(3-4), 251–265 (1992)
[McM04] McMinn, P.: Search-based Software Test Data Generation: A Survey.
         Software Testing, Verification and Reliability 14(2), 105–156 (2004)
[MHBT06] McMinn, P., Harman, M., Binkley, D., Tonella, P.: The Species per
         Path Approach to Search-based Test Data Generation. In: Proceedings
         of the 2006 International Symposium on Software Testing and Analysis
         (ISSTA 2006), Portland, Maine, USA, July 17-20, pp. 13–24. ACM, New
         York (2006)
[MM06]   Mitchell, B.S., Mancoridis, S.: On the Automatic Modularization of Soft-
         ware Systems using the Bunch Tool. IEEE Transactions on Software
         Engineering 32(3), 193–208 (2006)
[OÓ06]   O'Keeffe, M., Ó Cinnéide, M.: Search-based Software Maintenance. In:
         Proceedings of the Conference on Software Maintenance and Reengi-
         neering (CSMR 2006), Bari, Italy, March 22-24, pp. 249–260. IEEE
         Computer Society, Los Alamitos (2006)
[PCV95] Poli, R., Cagnoni, S., Valli, G.: Genetic design of optimum linear and
         nonlinear QRS detectors. IEEE Transactions on Biomedical Engineer-
         ing 42(11), 1137–1141 (1995)
[Räi09] Räihä, O.: A Survey on Search-Based Software Design. Technical Re-
         port D-2009-1, Department of Computer Sciences University of Tampere
         (March 2009)
[Sag07] Sagarna, R.: An Optimization Approach for Software Test Data Genera-
         tion: Applications of Estimation of Distribution Algorithms and Scatter
         Search. PhD thesis, University of the Basque Country, San Sebastian,
         Spain (January 2007)
[SBBP05] Seng, O., Bauer, M., Biehl, M., Pache, G.: Search-based Improvement of
         Subsystem Decompositions. In: Proceedings of the 2005 Conference on
         Genetic and Evolutionary Computation (GECCO 2005), Washington,
         D.C., USA, June 25-29, pp. 1045–1051. ACM, New York (2005)
[She95] Shepperd, M.J.: Foundations of software measurement. Prentice Hall,
         Englewood Cliffs (1995)
[SL08]   Sagarna, R., Lozano, J.A.: Dynamic Search Space Transformations for
         Software Test Data Generation. Computational Intelligence 24(1), 23–61
         (2008)
[TCM98] Tracey, N., Clark, J., Mander, K.: The Way Forward for Unifying Dy-
         namic Test-Case Generation: the Optimisation-based Approach. In: Pro-
         ceedings of the IFIP International Workshop on Dependable Computing
         and Its Applications (DCIA 1998), Johannesburg, South Africa, January
         12-14, pp. 169–180. University of the Witwatersrand (1998)

[WBS01] Wegener, J., Baresel, A., Sthamer, H.: Evolutionary Test Environment for Automatic Structural Testing. Information and Software Technology Special Issue on Software Engineering using Metaheuristic Innovative Algorithms 43(14), 841–854 (2001)

[WNGF09] Weimer, W., Nguyen, T.V., Goues, C.L., Forrest, S.: Automatically finding patches using genetic programming. In: International Conference on Software Engineerign (ICSE 2009), Vancouver, Canada, pp. 364–374 (2009)

[WWW07] Windisch, A., Wappler, S., Wegener, J.: Applying Particle Swarm Optimization to Software Testing. In: Proceedings of the 9th annual Conference on Genetic and Evolutionary Computation (GECCO 2007), London, England, July 7-11, pp. 1121–1128. ACM, New York (2007)

[XES^{+}92] Xanthakis, S., Ellis, C., Skourlas, C., Le Gall, A., Katsikas, S., Karapoulios, K.: Application of Genetic Algorithms to Software Testing. In: Proceedings of the 5th International Conference on Software Engineering and Applications, Toulouse, France, December 7-11, pp. 625–636 (1992)

[ZFH08] Zhang, Y., Finkelstein, A., Harman, M.: Search Based Requirements Optimisation: Existing Work & Challenges. In: Paech, B., Rolland, C. (eds.) REFSQ 2008. LNCS, vol. 5025, pp. 88–94. Springer, Heidelberg (2008)

A Formalisation of Constraint-Aware Model Transformations

Adrian Rutle[1], Alessandro Rossini[2], Yngve Lamo[1], and Uwe Wolter[2]

[1] Bergen University College, P.O. Box 7030, 5020 Bergen, Norway
{aru,yla}@hib.no
[2] University of Bergen, P.O. Box 7803, 5020 Bergen, Norway
{rossini,wolter}@ii.uib.no

Abstract. This paper introduces a formal approach to the definition of constraint-aware model transformations. The proposed approach is based on the Diagram Predicate Framework and extends graph transformations with the ability to handle constraints in the definition and execution of model transformations. In particular, it uses non-deleting rules that are typed over the metamodel of a joined modelling language which is constructed from the source and target languages. Furthermore, the application of transformation rules is formalised as a pushout construction that creates a model which is typed over the metamodel of the joined modelling language. Finally, the target model is obtained from the created model by a pullback construction.

1 Introduction and Motivation

Models are first-class entities of the software development process in Model-Driven Engineering (MDE) and undergo a complex evolution during their life cycles. In this regard, model transformation is one of the key techniques which is used to automate several model-based activities such as code generation, refactoring, optimisation, language translation etc. [23].

A general definition of model transformation given in [11] and further generalised in [15] is as follows. A *transformation* is the automatic generation of target models from source models, according to a transformation definition. A *transformation definition* is a set of transformation rules that together describe how a model in the source language can be transformed into a model in the target language. A *transformation rule* is a description of how one or more constructs in the source language can be transformed into one or more constructs in the target language.

Several classifications of model transformations are given in [4,15]. A first classification is based on whether the transformation is used to transform models specified by one modelling language, called *homogeneous* transformation, or models specified by different modelling languages, called *heterogeneous* transformation. The former class of transformations is suitable for model refactoring and optimisation [1], while the latter is suitable for language translation. A second classification is based on whether the target model is created from scratch, called *out-place*, or the source model is modified in order to obtain the target model, called *in-place*. A third classification is based on the

D.S. Rosenblum and G. Taentzer (Eds.): FASE 2010, LNCS 6013, pp. 13–28, 2010.

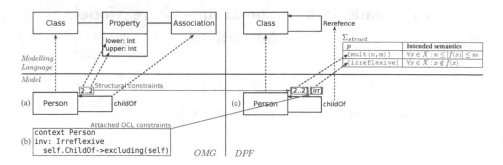

Fig. 1. Constraints in MOF-based modelling languages and DPF: (a) structural constraints in UML (b) attached OCL constraints (c) integration of constraints in DPF

underlying technique which is used to carry out the transformations, e.g. logic programming, functional programming, graph transformation, etc. The approach introduced in this paper is classified under heterogeneous, out-place and graph-transformation based transformation.

In the context of MDE, models are typically specified by means of modelling languages such as the Unified Modeling Language (UML) [17]. Each of these modelling languages has a corresponding metamodel – a model that defines the abstract syntax of models which can be specified by the modelling language. These metamodels, in turn, are specified by means of a metamodelling language called the Meta-Object Facility (MOF) [16]. MOF-based modelling languages allow the specification of simple constraints such as multiplicity and uniqueness constraints, hereafter called *structural constraints*. These constraints are usually specified by properties of classes in the metamodel of the modelling language. For instance, the requirement "a person is the child of exactly two parents" in a UML model can be forced by a multiplicity constraint which uses the properties `lower` and `upper` of the class `Property` of the UML metamodel (see Fig. 1a). Instances of the UML model should satisfy this multiplicity constraint. However, these structural constraints may not be sufficient to meet complex requirement's specifications. Hence, textual constraint languages such as the Object Constraint Language (OCL) are usually used to define complex constraints, hereafter called *attached OCL constraints*. For instance, the requirement "a person can not be a child of her/himself" in a UML model can only be forced by an OCL expression (see Fig. 1b).

While existing model transformation techniques always take into account structural constraints, they often ignore the attached OCL constraints [14,18]. This is because model transformation rules are defined over metamodel elements while attached OCL constraints are defined in a different technical space. This problem is closely related to the fact that the *conformance* relation between models and metamodels is not formally defined for MOF-based modelling languages [5,19], especially when OCL constraints are involved [2].

In this paper, a solution to this challenge is proposed. The solution is based on the Diagram Predicate Framework (DPF) [21,20,22] and reuses the diagrammatic formalisation of MOF-based modelling languages described in [21]. DPF provides a formal diagrammatic approach to (meta)modelling and model transformation based on

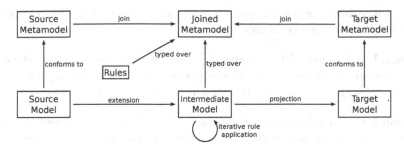

Fig. 2. Overview of the DPF-based approach to model transformation

category theory [9]. The proposed approach to model transformation provides an extension to the formal framework of graph transformations [8] in the sense that it can be used to transform models as well as attached OCL constraints. This is done by integrating structural constraints and attached OCL constraints in modelling formalisms which represent the formalisation of MOF-based modelling languages (see Fig. 1c for an intuition).

The DPF-based approach to model transformation introduces the concept of constraint-aware model transformation; i.e. a model transformation technique which supports specifying constraints in input and output patterns and using these constraints to control (i) which structure to create in the target model and (ii) which constraints to impose on the created structure. The first step in this approach consists of creating a joined modelling language which consists of a combination of the source and the target modelling languages; i.e. a joined metamodel is created (see Fig. 2). The second step consists of defining constraint-aware model transformation rules which are typed over the joined metamodel. The model transformation is applied in a final step as follows: extending a source model which conforms to the source metamodel to an intermediate model which is typed over the joined metamodel, iterative application of the transformation rules, and projection of a target model which conforms to the target metamodel.

A running example is used to illustrate our approach. It presents a transformation of an object-oriented structural model to a relational data model. In this example, the syntax used for the definition of the transformation rules is the same as the syntax used to specify the (meta)models.

The remainder of the paper is organised as follows. Section 2 reviews our diagrammatic formalisation of MOF-based modelling languages. Section 3 presents the details of our model transformation approach. In Section 4, a comparison of our approach with other graph transformation-based approaches to model transformation is given. Finally, in Section 5 some concluding remarks and ideas for future work are presented.

2   Diagram Predicate Framework

In DPF, models are formalised as *diagrammatic specifications*. A diagrammatic specification $S = (G^S, C^S)$ consists of an underlying graph G^S decorated by a set of constraints C^S. The graph represents the structure of the model, and predicates from a predefined *diagrammatic predicate signature* are used to impose constraints on the model. In this paper, we use the terms "model" and "specification" interchangeably. The formal definitions are as follows:

Definition 1 (Signature). *A (diagrammatic predicate) signature $\Sigma := (\Pi, \alpha)$ consists of a collection of predicate symbols Π with a mapping α that assigns a graph to each predicate symbol $p \in \Pi$. $\alpha(p)$ is called the arity of the predicate symbol p.*

Definition 2 (Constraint). *Given a signature $\Sigma = (\Pi, \alpha)$, a constraint (p, δ) on a graph G is given by a predicate symbol p and a graph homomorphism $\delta : \alpha(p) \to G$.*

Definition 3 (Σ-specification). *Given a signature $\Sigma = (\Pi, \alpha)$, a (diagrammatic) Σ-specification $S := (G^S, C^S)$ is given by a graph G^S and a set C^S of constraints (p, δ) on G^S with $p \in \Pi$.*

Example 1. Let us consider an information system for the management of employees and projects. At any state of the system the following requirements should be satisfied.

1. An employee must work for at least one department.
2. A department may have none or many employees.
3. A project may involve none or many employees.
4. A project must be controlled by at least one department.
5. An employee involved in a project must work in the controlling department.

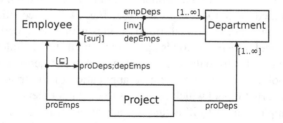

Fig. 3. A Σ_{struct}-specification $S = (G^S, C^S)$

Fig. 3 shows a Σ_{struct}-specification $S = (G^S, C^S)$ which specifies a structural model compliant with the requirements above. Table 1 shows the signature Σ_{struct}. Here we present how two of the above mentioned requirements are specified in S using the predicates from Σ_{struct}. In particular we present a requirement which can be specified by means of structural constraints in UML syntax; as well as a requirement which demands the usage of attached OCL constraints (see [21] for a comparison of the UML/OCL- and DPF-based models of a similar system). The requirement "an employee must work for at least one department" is forced in S by the predicate [mult(1,∞)] on the arrow empDeps. Furthermore, the requirement "an employee involved in a project must work in the controlling department" is forced in S by using the predicates [composition] and [subset] on the arrows proDeps;depEmps and proEmps.

Table 1. The signature Σ_{struct}

p	$\alpha_{struct}(p)$	Proposed visual.	Intended semantics
`[mult(n,m)]`	$1 \xrightarrow{f} 2$	$X \xrightarrow[\text{[n..m]}]{f} Y$	$\forall x \in X : n \leq |f(x)| \leq m$
`[irreflexive]`	$1 \circlearrowright f$	$\text{[irr]} \, X \circlearrowright f$	$\forall x \in X : x \notin f(x)$
`[injective]`	$1 \xrightarrow{f} 2$	$X \xrightarrow[\text{[inj]}]{f} Y$	$\forall x, x' \in X : f(x) = f(x')$ implies $x = x'$
`[surjective]`	$1 \xrightarrow{f} 2$	$X \xrightarrow[\text{[surj]}]{f} Y$	$f(X) = Y$
`[jointly-injective]`	$1 \xrightarrow{f} 2$, $1 \xrightarrow{g} 3$	$X \xrightarrow{f} Y$, $X \xrightarrow{g} Z$ [ji]	$\forall x, x' \in X : f(x) = f(x')$ and $g(x) = g(x')$ implies $x = x'$
`[inverse]`	$1 \underset{g}{\overset{f}{\rightleftarrows}} 2$	$X \underset{g}{\overset{f}{\rightleftarrows}} Y$ [inv]	$\forall x \in X, \forall y \in Y : y \in f(x)$ iff $x \in g(y)$
`[composition]`	$1 \xrightarrow{f} 2$, $1 \xrightarrow{h} 3$, $2 \xrightarrow{g} 3$	$X \xrightarrow{f} Y$, $X \xrightarrow{f;g} Z$, $Y \xrightarrow{g} Z$	$\forall x \in X : f;g(x) = \bigcup\{g(y) \mid y \in f(x)\}$
`[subset]`	$1 \underset{g}{\overset{f}{\rightrightarrows}} 2$	$X \underset{g}{\overset{f}{\rightrightarrows}} Y$ $\text{[}\subseteq\text{]}$	$\forall x \in X : f(x) \subseteq g(x)$

Note that, any OCL-constraint that can be seen as a "sort-wise" property; i.e. properties of sets, functions, or diagrams of sets and functions as a whole, can be specified in DPF. This is because DPF is based on category theory which is centred around sort-wise properties. A precise characterisation of non-sort-wise OCL-constraints is an open issue which is part of our current research.

In DPF, we distinguish between two types of conformance relations: *typed over* and *conforms to*. A model is typed over a metamodel if its underlying graph is typed over the underlying graph of the metamodel; i.e. each model element is assigned a type in the metamodel by a *typing morphism*. In contrast, a model is said to conform to a metamodel if it is typed over the metamodel and, in addition, it satisfies all the constraints of the metamodel [21].

The definition of typed Σ-specification depends on the definition of Σ-specification morphisms. These definitions will also be used in Section 3 in our approach to model transformation. A specification morphism between two Σ-specifications is a graph homomorphism which preserves constraints. In contrast, a typed specification morphism between two typed Σ-specifications is a specification morphism which respects the typing morphisms. The formal definitions are as follows:

Definition 4 (Σ**-specification Morphism**). *A Σ-specification morphism $f : S \to S'$ between two Σ-specifications $S = (G^S, C^S)$ and $S' = (G^{S'}, C^{S'})$ is a graph homomorphism $f : G^S \to G^{S'}$ preserving constraints, i.e. $(p, \delta) \in C^S$ implies $(p, \delta; f) \in C^{S'}$ for all constraints $(p, \delta) \in C^S$.*

Definition 5 (**Typed Σ-specification**). *An H-typed Σ-specification S, i.e. a Σ-specification typed over a graph H, is a Σ-specification S together with a graph homomorphism $t^S : G^S \to H$. t^S is called a typing morphism.*

Definition 6 (**Typed Σ-specification Morphism**). *A typed Σ-specification morphism between two H-typed Σ-specifications S and S' is a Σ-specification morphism $\psi : S \to S'$ such that $\psi; t^{S'} = t^S$.*

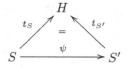

In DPF, each modelling language is formalised as a modelling formalism which is a triple $F = (\Sigma_2, S_2, \Sigma_3)$ [21]. The concepts of the modelling language are located in the Σ_3-specification S_2; and the constraining constructs which are available for the users of the modelling language are located in the signature Σ_2.

Definition 7 (**Modelling Formalism**). *A modelling formalism $F = (\Sigma_2, S_2, \Sigma_3)$ is given by signatures $\Sigma_2 = (\Pi_2, \alpha_2)$ and $\Sigma_3 = (\Pi_3, \alpha_3)$, and a Σ_3-specification $S_2 = (G^{S_2}, C^{S_2})$. S_2 is called the metamodel of F. An F-specification is a Σ_2-specification $S_1 = (G^{S_1}, C^{S_1})$ which conforms to S_2.*

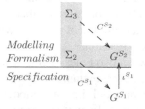

Predicates from the signature Σ_3 are used to add constraints to the metamodel S_2. This corresponds to metamodel definition. These constraints should be satisfied by F-specifications. Moreover, predicates from the signature Σ_2 are used to add constraints to F-specifications. This corresponds to model definition. These constraints should be satisfied by instances of the F-specifications, in the same way as the F-specifications should satisfy the metamodel constraints.

For a given modelling formalism, the semantics of nodes and arrows have to be chosen in a way which is appropriate for the corresponding modelling environment. For structural models in object-oriented development, it is appropriate to interpret nodes as sets and arrows $X \xrightarrow{f} Y$ as multi-valued functions $f : X \to \wp(Y)$. The powerset $\wp(Y)$ of Y is the set of all subsets of Y, i.e. $\wp(Y) = \{K \mid K \subseteq Y\}$. On the other hand, for relational data models it is appropriate to interpret nodes as sets and arrows as single-valued functions.

3 Model Transformation

This section describes the DPF-based approach to constraint-aware model transformation. The first step consists of creating a joined modelling formalism which enables the specification of both source and target models. One way to achieve this is to construct the disjoint union of the components of the source and target modelling formalisms.

Roughly speaking, given the source $F^S = (\Sigma_2^S, S_2, \Sigma_3^S)$ and the target $F^T = (\Sigma_2^T, T_2, \Sigma_3^T)$ modelling formalisms (see Fig. 4a and Fig. 4c, respectively), a joined modelling formalism $F^J = (\Sigma_2^J, J_2, \Sigma_3^J)$ will be created (see Fig. 4b). In more detail, the source and target metamodels are joined together to $J_2 := S_2 \uplus K_2 \uplus T_2$, and the source and target signatures are joined together to $\Sigma_2^J := \Sigma_2^S \uplus \Sigma_2^T$ and $\Sigma_3^J := \Sigma_3^S \uplus \Sigma_3^K \uplus \Sigma_3^T$, where $\uplus$ denotes the disjoint union operation (see Example 2). In J_2, the component K_2 represents the correspondence between S_2 and T_2. In most cases, the elements in K_2 will be arrows connecting nodes in S_2 and T_2. However, in some cases it may be convenient to have also auxiliary nodes in K_2 and arrows connecting these nodes with elements in S_2 and/or T_2. In Σ_3^J, the component Σ_3^K contains additional predicates which are used to constrain elements of J_2. The definitions of K_2 and Σ_3^K should be done manually by transformation designers.

Although the transformation designer is free to relate any elements of the source and target metamodels, there is a *projection condition* which should be satisfied by the joined metamodel J_2. The condition is that for any F^J-specification J_1, it should be possible to construct an F^S-specification S_1 and an F^T-specification T_1 by pullback

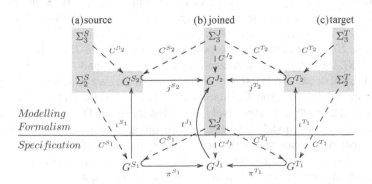

Fig. 4. Source, target and joined modelling formalisms

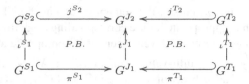

Fig. 5. Projection condition for the joined metamodel J_2

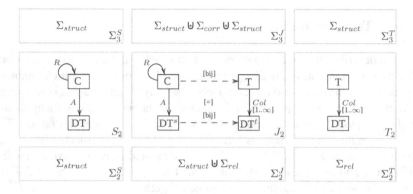

Fig. 6. Joining the modelling formalisms of structural models and relational data models

constructions as depicted in Fig. 5 (see [6] for a description and motivation for using pullbacks in model transformation). In order to satisfy the projection condition, J_2 must be constrained by predicates from the signature Σ_3^J.

In the next example, we present a joined modelling formalism and show the constraints of J_2 which are necessary to satisfy the projection condition.

Example 2. Fig. 6 shows a source modelling formalism $F^S = (\Sigma_2^S, S_2, \Sigma_3^S)$ for specifying structural models; a target modelling formalism $F^T = (\Sigma_2^T, T_2, \Sigma_3^T)$ for specifying relational data models; and their joined modelling formalism $F^J = (\Sigma_2^J, J_2, \Sigma_3^J)$. In particular, $\Sigma_3^S, \Sigma_3^T, \Sigma_2^S := \Sigma_{struct}$ (see the signature Σ_{struct} for structural models in Table 1); $\Sigma_2^T := \Sigma_{rel}$ (see part of the signature Σ_{rel} for relational data models in Table 2); $\Sigma_2^J := \Sigma_{struct} \uplus \Sigma_{rel}$; and $\Sigma_3^J := \Sigma_{struct} \uplus \Sigma_{corr} \uplus \Sigma_{struct}$ (see part of the signature Σ_{corr} for defining correspondence constraints in Table 3). In the source metamodel S_2, the arrows R and A stand for Reference and Attribute, respectively; and the nodes C and DT stand for Class and DataType, respectively. In the target metamodel T_2, the arrow Col stand for Column; and the nodes T and DT stand for Table and DataType, respectively. Note that the node DT is renamed to DT^s and DT^t in the joined metamodel J_2 by the disjoint union operation. The projection condition is satisfied by constraining the arrows in J_2 by the predicates [bijective] and [commutative]. This means that for each class, a corresponding table should be created. In addition, for each attribute belonging to a class, a corresponding column belonging to the corresponding table should be created.

Table 2. A part of the signature Σ_{rel}

p	$\alpha_{rel}(p)$	Proposed visual.	Intended semantics
[total]	$1 \xrightarrow{f} 2$	$\boxed{X} \bullet\!\!\xrightarrow{f} \boxed{Y}$	$\forall x \in X : |f(x)| = 1$
[primary-key]	$1 \xrightarrow{f} 2$	$\boxed{X} \xrightarrow[\text{[pk]}]{f} \boxed{Y}$	f is [total] and [injective]
[foreign-key]	$1 \xrightarrow{f} 2$, $\ 3 \xrightarrow{g} 2$	$\boxed{X} \xrightarrow{f} \boxed{Y}$, [fk], g, $\boxed{Z}$	$f(X) \subseteq g(Y)$
[image-equal]	$1 \xrightarrow{f} 2$, $\ 3 \xrightarrow{g} 2$	$\boxed{X} \xrightarrow{f} \boxed{Y}$, [ie], g, $\boxed{Z}$	$f(X) = g(Z)$
[join]	$1 \xrightarrow{f} 2$, $3 \xrightarrow{f'} 4$, g', g	$\boxed{X} \xrightarrow{f} \boxed{Y}$, g', [join], g, $\boxed{XZ} \xrightarrow{f'} \boxed{Z}$	$\forall x \in X , \forall z \in Z : (x,z) \in$ XZ iff $f(x) = g(z)$

3.1 Constraint-Aware Transformation Rules

The second step in our approach is the definition of constraint-aware transformation rules. In each transformation rule, the input pattern is included in the output pattern. The input and output patterns are Σ_2^J-specifications which are typed over G^{J_2}.

Definition 8 (Transformation Rules). *Given a joined modelling formalism $F^J = (\Sigma_2^J, J_2, \Sigma_3^J)$, a transformation rule $r : L \hookrightarrow R$ is a G^{J_2}-typed Σ_2^J-specification morphism between the input and output patterns L and R, with r being an inclusion.*

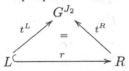

In the following example, we illustrate our approach to the definition of transformation rules. Note that the output patterns of the transformation rules are not only dependent on the structure of the input patterns, but also on the constraints.

Example 3. Building on Example 2, Table 4 outlines some of the transformation rules which are used for the transformation of structural models to relational data models. These rules are typed over the joined metamodel J_2 shown in Fig. 6. Note that (1:C) is a "user-friendly" notation for the typing assignment ($t : 1 \mapsto C$). In rule r_1, each

Table 3. A part of the signature Σ_{corr}

p	$\alpha_{corr}(p)$	Proposed visual.	Intended semantics
[commutative]	$1 \xrightarrow{f} 2$ $g\downarrow \quad\quad \downarrow g'$ $3 \xrightarrow{f'} 4$	$\boxed{X} \xrightarrow{f} \boxed{Y}$ $g\downarrow \quad [=] \quad \downarrow g'$ $\boxed{Z} \xrightarrow{f'} \boxed{Æ}$	$\forall x \in X : g'(f(x)) = f'(g(x))$
[bijective]	$1 \xrightarrow{f} 2$	$\boxed{X} \xrightarrow[\text{[bij]}]{f} \boxed{Y}$	f is [mult(1,1)], [injective] and [surjective]

class is transformed to a corresponding table. In rule r_2, for each attribute a column is created. The rules r_3 and r_4 are used to transform bidirectional references (or a pair of inverse functions) between two classes to foreign keys between two tables. Notice that the only difference between the input patterns of the rules r_3 and r_4 is the constraint forced by the predicate [mult(0,1)] on the arrow 2:R. This constraint affects the way in which a match of the input pattern is transformed to a match of the output pattern. More precisely, since in r_3 each 2:C is related to at most *one* 1:C, a foreign key column 3:Col will be created which will refer to 1:Col. However, in r_4 each 2:C may be related to many 1:C and vice versa. Therefore, a link table 3:T is created with two foreign key columns 3:Col and 4:Col. The contents of this link table may be seen as tuples (1:DT^t, 2:DT^t).

3.2 Application of Model Transformation

The last step in our approach is the application of model transformation. In this step categorical constructions [7,9] such as pushout and pullback are exploited. The application of a model transformation consists of iterative application of transformation rules.

Definition 9 (Application of Transformation Rules). *Given a source model J_1, an application $\langle r, m \rangle$ of a transformation rule $r : L \hookrightarrow R$ via a match $m : L \to J_1$, where m is a G^{J_2}-typed Σ_2^J-specification morphism, is given by the pushout*

$$
\begin{array}{ccc}
L & \xrightarrow{\quad r \quad} & R \\
{\scriptstyle m}\downarrow & P.O. & \downarrow{\scriptstyle m^*} \\
J_1 & \xrightarrow{\quad \langle r,m \rangle \quad} & J_1'
\end{array}
$$

In the following, the procedure for transforming a source model S_1 to a target model T_1 is outlined.

1. *Extension of the source model.* The source F^S-specification S_1 is extended to an intermediate G^{J_2}-typed Σ_2^J-specification J_1. This transformation is given by the composition $\iota^{S_1}; j^{S_2}$ (see Fig. 4) which leads to $J_1 = S_1 \uplus K_1 \uplus T_1$ with both K_1 and T_1 being empty specifications.

2. *Iterative application of the transformation rules.* Upon the application of a rule $r : L \hookrightarrow R$, for a match of the input pattern L in $J_1 = S_1 \uplus K_1 \uplus T_1$, the K_1 and T_1 parts will be extended by an appropriate copy of the new elements in R, i.e., by those elements in R that are not already in L.
3. *Obtaining the target model.* The iterative application of transformation rules may stop once an F^J-specification J_1 is constructed. The projection condition ensures then that the pullback of the span $G^{J_1} \rightarrow G^{J_2} \hookleftarrow G^{T_2}$ (see Fig. 5) constructs an F^T-specification T_1 which may be considered the target model.

In Table 4, we defined the transformation rules which were needed to transform structural models (with only structural constraints) to relational data models. What remains to show now is the ability to define transformation rules which enable transformation of more complex constraints such as the requirement 5 in Example 1.

Example 4. Building on Example 3, Fig. 7 shows the relational data model which is created by applying the rules in Table 4 and 5 to the Σ_{struct}-specification S in Fig. 3. Recall that arrows in Σ_{rel}-specifications are interpreted as single-valued functions. Hence, we do not need to add constraints to force single-valued functions.

Table 4. Rules for the transformation of structural models to relational data models

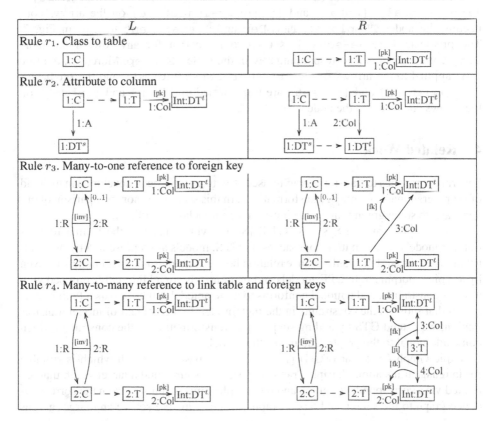

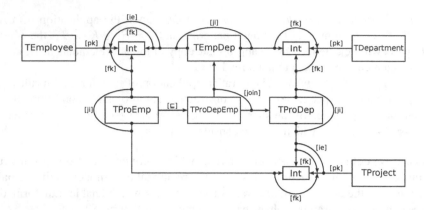

Fig. 7. The target Σ_{rel}-specification resulting from the transformation of the Σ_{struct}-specification presented in Fig. 3

However, we use the predicate [total] from Σ_{rel} to add constraints which force total functions whenever necessary, for example columns for which a value is required. The rule r_5 in Table 5 is applied to the arrows empDeps and depEmps, and the predicates [inverse] and [surjective] are transformed to [foreign-key], [image-equal], [total] and [jointly-injective] on the arrows connecting the nodes TEmployee, TEmpDep and TDepartment to Int in Fig. 7. The predicate [image-equal] is used to force that for any row in the table TEmployee there is a corresponding row in the table TEmpDep. Moreover, the rule r_6 is applied to the arrows proEmps and proDeps;depEmps, and the predicates [composition] and [subset] are transformed to [join] and [subset] on the arrows connected to the node TProDepEmp.

4   Related Work

Several approaches to transform graph-based structures have been developed in the field of graph grammars and graph transformations. In this section, a short comparison of our approach to some graph transformation-based approaches is outlined.

Graph Transformation Systems (GTS) [8] are widely used as the formal foundation for model transformation approaches. In GTS, models are represented by typed attributed graphs, and the conformance relation between models and metamodels is given by a typing morphism. In DPF, models and metamodels are additionally equipped with a set of constraints, and a model conforms to a metamodel if there exists a typing morphism that satisfies the constraints in the metamodel. In the context of model transformation, we extend GTS by adding support for transformation of the constraints which come additional to the graph structure of the models.

Triple Graph Grammar (TGG) [12,7] is a GTS-based approach which is suitable for language translation. A triple graph consists of a source and a target graph that are related via a correspondence graph and two graph homomorphisms from the correspondence graph to the source and target graphs. In this way, the source and target graphs

Table 5. Rules for the transformation of attached constraints

L	R
Rule r_5. [inverse] and [surjective] to [foreign-key], [image-equal], [total] and [jointly-injective]	

Rule r_5 diagram (L):
- $1{:}C \dashrightarrow 1{:}T \xrightarrow[1{:}Col]{[pk]} Int{:}DT^t$
- $1{:}R \xrightleftharpoons[{}]{[inv]} 2{:}R$, [surj]
- $2{:}C \dashrightarrow 2{:}T \xrightarrow[2{:}Col]{[pk]} Int{:}DT^t$

Rule r_5 diagram (R):
- $1{:}C \dashrightarrow 1{:}T \xrightarrow[1{:}Col]{[pk]} Int{:}DT^t$
- $1{:}R \xrightleftharpoons[{}]{[inv]} 2{:}R$, [surj]
- $3{:}Col$ [fk], $3{:}T$ [ji], $4{:}Col$ [fk], [ie]
- $2{:}C \dashrightarrow 2{:}T \xrightarrow[2{:}Col]{[pk]} Int{:}DT^t$

| **Rule r_6.** [composition] and [subset] to [join] and [subset] | |

Rule r_6 diagram (L):
- $1{:}C \dashrightarrow 1{:}T \xrightarrow[1{:}Col]{[pk]} Int{:}DT^t$, [fk]
- $8{:}Col$, $4{:}Col$ [fk], $4{:}T$ [ji], $6{:}T$ [ji]
- $3{:}R$, $1{:}R$, $1,2{:}R$
- $2{:}C \dashrightarrow 2{:}T \xrightarrow[2{:}Col]{[pk]} Int{:}DT^t$, $5{:}Col$ [fk], [⊑]
- $6{:}Col$ [fk], $5{:}T$ [ji], $7{:}Col$ [fk]
- $2{:}R$, $9{:}Col$
- $3{:}C \dashrightarrow 3{:}T \xrightarrow[3{:}Col]{[pk]} Int{:}DT^t$, [fk]

Rule r_6 diagram (R):
- $1{:}C \dashrightarrow 1{:}T \xrightarrow[1{:}Col]{[pk]} Int{:}DT^t$, [jk]
- $8{:}Col$, $4{:}Col$ [jk], $4{:}T$ [ji], $6{:}T$ [ji]
- $3{:}R$, $1{:}R$, $1,2{:}R$, u, [⊑] h, $f{:}T$
- $2{:}C \dashrightarrow 2{:}T \xrightarrow[2{:}Col]{[pk]} Int{:}DT^t$, $5{:}Col$ [jk], [io;h], v, [⊑]
- $6{:}Col$ [jk], $5{:}T$ [ji], $f{:}Col$ [jk]
- $2{:}R$, $9{:}Col$
- $3{:}C \dashrightarrow 3{:}T \xrightarrow[3{:}Col]{[pk]} Int{:}DT^t$, [jk]

are joined into a single structure thus providing a basis for consistent co-evolution of the graphs [7]. The use of correspondence graphs allows to relate a node (arrow) in the source graph with a node (arrow) in the target graph and to constrain these simple relations by means of OCL. Similar to TGG, in DPF a joined metamodel is used to describe relations between the source and target metamodels. The difference is however that we can define and constrain, in a diagrammatic way, arbitrary complex relations between source and target metamodel elements, e.g. the commutativity constraint in Fig. 6.

The Visual Modeling and Transformation System (VMTS) [13] is an n-layer meta-modelling environment which supports editing models according to their metamodels and allows specifying OCL constraints. VMTS provides a graph transformation-based approach to model transformations in which models are formalised as directed, labelled graphs. Moreover, OCL constraints are used to control the execution of transformations. The input and output patterns of transformation rules use metamodel elements; meaning that an instantiation of the input pattern must be found in the source graph instead of an isomorphic subgraph of the pattern. These patterns are guarded by pre- and post-conditions. Before the execution of each transformation rule, the pre-conditions are checked and used to narrow down the set of matches. After execution of each rule, the post-conditions are checked against the output of the rule. In this way, if a rule executes successfully it can be asserted that the transformation has resulted in the expected output. The DPF-based approach is different in that constraints are not used only for controlling the matches, but they can also be transformed from the source models to target models. In DPF terms, this means that VTMS can be seen as transforming the set of constraints C^{S_2} while ignoring C^{S_1}.

An approach to the analysis of graph transformation rules based on an intermediate OCL representation is presented in [3]. The semantics of rules together with their properties (such as rule applicability, conflict or independence) are transformed into OCL expressions. While these OCL expressions are combined with structural- and attached OCL constraints during the analysis process, the attached OCL constraints are not shown to be transformed. In the DPF-based approach attached OCL constraints and structural constraints are integrated in modelling formalisms, facilitating a uniform transformation of these constraints.

The approach proposed in [10] employs transformation rules to preserve the semantics of UML/OCL class diagrams when using the refactoring rule moveAttribute. The DPF-based approach is more generic in the sense that it can be used for the definition of transformation rules between constrained models which are specified by different modelling languages.

5 Conclusion and Future Work

This paper proposes a formal approach to the definition of constraint-aware model transformation which is applied to language translation. This is possible due to the diagrammatic formalisation of MOF-based modelling languages in which attached OCL constraints are integrated in modelling formalisms.

In this approach, the process of model transformation is organised into three steps. Firstly, the source and target modelling languages are joined together; i.e. a joined metamodel is created. Secondly, the transformation rules are declared as input and output patterns which are typed over the joined metamodel. The input and output patterns of the transformation rules are diagrammatic specifications; and the morphisms between input and output patterns as well as their matches are formalised as constraint- and type preserving specification morphisms. Hence, constraints can be added to the input patterns, and these constraints can be used to control (i) which structure to create in the target model and (ii) which constraints to add to the created structure. Thirdly, the model transformation is applied as follows. The source model is extended to an intermediate model which is typed over the joined metamodel. Next, the transformation rules are iteratively applied to the intermediate model. Finally, the target model is obtained by projection. The approach exploits existing machinery from category theory to formalise constraint-aware model transformations. More precisely, pushout construction is used for the application of transformation rules, and pullback construction is used for the projection of target models.

In a future study, we will analyse scheduling and controlling application of constraint-aware transformation rules building upon our previous work described in [22]. Furthermore, analysing to what extent our approach is suitable for bidirectional transformations is part of our current research.

References

1. Biermann, E., Ehrig, K., Köhler, C., Kuhns, G., Taentzer, G., Weiss, E.: EMF Model Refactoring based on Graph Transformation Concepts. ECEASST 3 (2006)
2. Boronat, A., Meseguer, J.: Algebraic Semantics of OCL-Constrained Metamodel Specifications. In: Oriol, M., Meyer, B. (eds.) TOOLS Europe 2009: 47th International Conference on Objects, Components, Models and Patterns. LNBIP, vol. 33, pp. 96–115. Springer, Heidelberg (2009)
3. Cabot, J., Clarisó, R., Guerra, E., de Lara, J.: Analysing Graph Transformation Rules through OCL. In: Vallecillo, A., Gray, J., Pierantonio, A. (eds.) ICMT 2008. LNCS, vol. 5063, pp. 229–244. Springer, Heidelberg (2008)
4. Czarnecki, K., Helsen, S.: Classification of Model Transformation Approaches. In: OOPSLA 2003: 2nd Workshop on Generative Techniques in the Context of MDA (2003)
5. Diskin, Z.: Mathematics of UML: Making the Odysseys of UML less dramatic. In: Practical foundations of business system specifications, pp. 145–178. Kluwer Academic Publishers, Dordrecht (2003)
6. Diskin, Z., Dingel, J.: A metamodel Independent Framework for Model Transformation: Towards Generic Model Management Patterns in Reverse Engineering. Technical Report 1/2006, ATEM 2006, Johannes Gutenberg Universität Mainz, Germany (October 2006)
7. Ehrig, H., Ehrig, K., Ermel, C., Hermann, F., Taentzer, G.: Information Preserving Bidirectional Model Transformations. In: Dwyer, M.B., Lopes, A. (eds.) FASE 2007. LNCS, vol. 4422, pp. 72–86. Springer, Heidelberg (2007)
8. Ehrig, H., Ehrig, K., Prange, U., Taentzer, G.: Fundamentals of Algebraic Graph Transformation. Springer, Heidelberg (2006)
9. Fiadeiro, J.L.: Categories for Software Engineering. Springer, Heidelberg (2004)
10. Fondement, F., Baar, T.: Making Metamodels Aware of Concrete Syntax. In: Hartman, A., Kreische, D. (eds.) ECMDA-FA 2005. LNCS, vol. 3748, pp. 190–204. Springer, Heidelberg (2005)
11. Kleppe, A.G., Warmer, J., Bast, W.: MDA Explained: The Model Driven Architecture: Practice and Promise. Addison-Wesley Longman Publishing Co., Inc., Boston (2003)
12. Königs, A., Schürr, A.: Tool Integration with Triple Graph Grammars – A Survey. ENTCS 148(1), 113–150 (2006)
13. Lengyel, L., Levendovszky, T., Charaf, H.: Constraint Validation Support in Visual Model Transformation Systems. Acta Cybernetica 17(2), 339–357 (2005)
14. Marković, S., Baar, T.: Refactoring OCL annotated UML class diagrams. Software and System Modeling 7(1), 25–47 (2008)
15. Mens, T., Gorp, P.V.: A Taxonomy of Model Transformation. ENTCS 152, 125–142 (2006)
16. Object Management Group: Meta-Object Facility Specification (January 2006), http://www.omg.org/cgi-bin/doc?formal/2006-01-01
17. Object Management Group: Unified Modeling Language Specification (February 2009), http://www.omg.org/cgi-bin/doc?formal/2009-02-04
18. Petter, A., Behring, A., Mühlhäuser, M.: Solving Constraints in Model Transformations. In: Paige, R.F. (ed.) ICMT 2009. LNCS, vol. 5563, pp. 132–147. Springer, Heidelberg (2009)

19. Poernomo, I.H.: A Type Theoretic Framework for Formal Metamodelling. In: Reussner, R., Stafford, J.A., Szyperski, C. (eds.) Architecting Systems with Trustworthy Components. LNCS, vol. 3938, pp. 262–298. Springer, Heidelberg (2006)

20. Rutle, A., Rossini, A., Lamo, Y., Wolter, U.: A Category-Theoretical Approach to the Formalisation of Version Control in MDE. In: Chechik, M., Wirsing, M. (eds.) FASE 2009. LNCS, vol. 5503, pp. 64–78. Springer, Heidelberg (2009)

21. Rutle, A., Rossini, A., Lamo, Y., Wolter, U.: A Diagrammatic Formalisation of MOF-Based Modelling Languages. In: Brakhage, H. (ed.) TOOLS Europe 2009: 47th International Conference on Objects, Components, Models and Patterns. LNBIP, vol. 33, pp. 37–56. Springer, Heidelberg (2009)

22. Rutle, A., Wolter, U., Lamo, Y.: A Diagrammatic Approach to Model Transformations. In: EATIS 2008: Euro American Conference on Telematics and Information Systems, pp. 1–8. ACM, New York (2008)

23. Sendall, S., Kozaczynski, W.: Model Transformation: The Heart and Soul of Model-Driven Software Development. IEEE Software 20(5), 42–45 (2003)

Formal Real-Time Model Transformations in MOMENT2

Artur Boronat[1] and Peter Csaba Ölveczky[2]

[1] Department of Computer Science, University of Leicester
[2] Department of Informatics, University of Oslo

Abstract. This paper explains how the MOMENT2 formal model transformation framework has been extended to support the formal specification and analysis of real-time model-based systems. We provide a collection of built-in timed constructs for defining the timed behavior of model-based systems that are specified with in-place model transformations. In addition, we show how an existing model-based system can be extended with timed features in a *non-intrusive* way (i.e, without modifying the class diagram) by using in-place *multi-domain* model transformations supported in MOMENT2. We give a real-time rewrite formal semantics to real-time model transformations, and show how the models can be simulated and model checked using MOMENT2's Maude-based analysis tools. In this way, MOMENT2 becomes a flexible, effective, automatic tool for specifying and verifying model-based real-time and embedded systems within the Eclipse Modeling Framework using graph transformation and rewriting logic techniques. We illustrate our approach on a simple round trip time protocol.

1 Introduction

In model-driven engineering (MDE), metamodels provide modeling primitives to represent software artifacts as models, and model transformations are the core technique to support software evolution in an automated manner [19]. These techniques have been applied to the development of real-time and embedded systems (RTES), such as automotive, avionics, and medical systems. Such RTES are often hard to design correctly, since subtle timing aspects impact system functionality, yet are safety-critical systems where a bad design can result in the loss of revenue and human lives. Therefore, there is a clear need for automated formal analysis of RTES designs.

Some of the MDE approaches to RTES, such as MARTE [12], provide modeling languages based on UML profiles, others, such as AADL [18], on domain-specific modeling languages. To enable formal analysis of designs, these languages typically have to be mapped in an *ad hoc* way onto *external* formalisms that support automated reasoning [1].

In contrast, the approach taken in the MOMENT2 project [6,3] is to formalize MOF metamodels in rewriting logic, providing for free (i) a formal semantics of the *structural* aspects of any modeling language with a MOF metamodel, and

D.S. Rosenblum and G. Taentzer (Eds.): FASE 2010, LNCS 6013, pp. 29–43, 2010.
© Springer-Verlag Berlin Heidelberg 2010

(ii) automated formal reasoning in the MOMENT2 tool, e.g., to analyze whether a given model conforms to its metamodel. To provide a generic formal framework for *dynamic* system aspect, MOMENT2 has been extended with in-place model transformations. In this framework, the static semantics of a system is given as a class diagram describing the set of valid system states, system states are represented as object diagrams, and the dynamics of a system is defined as an in-place model transformation where the application of a model transformation rule involves a state transition in the system. To the best of our knowledge, MOMENT2 is the first model transformation tool with both simulation and LTL model checking capabilities that is integrated into EMF.

This paper describes our extension of MOMENT2 to support the formal specification and analysis of *real-time* model transformations by providing:

- a simple and expressive set of constructs, defined in an EMF metamodel, for specifying real-time behaviors;
- a precise formal semantics of real-time model transformation systems as *real-time rewrite theories* [13];
- a methodology for formally simulating and model checking such systems using Maude as a hidden, back-end formal framework; and
- an approach for adding real-time features to model-based systems in a *non-intrusive* way, i.e., without modifying their metamodel.

We illustrate our techniques by specifying and analyzing a simple round trip time protocol. Although this protocol is a software system, we use metamodels for describing its structural semantics in order to show how our approach can be applied in the setting of an EMF modeling language.

Our work should be seen as a first step towards an automatic, executable formalization of systems defined with modeling languages with real-time features where a class diagram corresponds to a metamodel, an object diagram to a well-formed model and model transformations specify the behavior of the system. In this way, a software engineer can use MDA standards and Eclipse Modeling Framework (EMF) technology to formally define and analyze RTES.

This paper is organized as follows. Section 2 provides some background on rewriting logic and MOMENT2. Section 3 presents our approach for specifying real-time model transformations, as well as our example and the formal real-time rewrite semantics of such transformations. Section 4 shows how our transformations can be subjected to Maude-based formal analyses. Section 5 discusses related work and Section 6 gives some concluding remarks.

2   Preliminaries

2.1   Rewriting Logic, Maude, and Real-Time Maude

In rewriting logic [10], a concurrent system is specified as a rewrite theory $\mathcal{R} = (\Sigma, E, R)$ where:

- (Σ, E) is a *membership equational logic* (MEL) [11] theory where Σ is an algebraic signature[1], and E is a set of conditional *equations* $t = t'$ **if** *cond* and conditional *membership* axioms $t : s$ **if** *cond* stating that the term t has sort s when *cond* holds. (Σ, E) specifies the system's state space as an algebraic data type.
- R is a set of (possibly conditional) *rewrite rules* of the form $t \longrightarrow t'$ **if** *cond* that describe all the *local transitions* in the system; such a rule specifies a *one-step transition* from an instance of t to the corresponding instance of t', *provided* the condition holds.

Maude [7] is a high-performance implementation of rewriting logic that provides a set of formal analysis methods, including: *rewriting* for simulating *one* behavior of the system, *reachability analysis* for the verification of invariants, and *model checking* of linear temporal logic (LTL) properties. The Maude syntax is fairly intuitive. For example, a function symbol f is declared with the syntax op f : $s_1 \ldots s_n$ -> s, where $s_1 \ldots s_n$ are the sorts of its arguments, and s is its *sort*. Equations are written with syntax eq $t = t'$, and ceq $t = t'$ if *cond* for conditional equations, and rewrite rules are written with syntax rl [l] : t => t' and crl [l] : t => t' if *cond*. The mathematical variables in such statements are declared with the keywords var and vars. We refer to [7] for more details on the syntax of Maude.

We assume rewrite theories of the form $\mathcal{R} = (\Sigma, E \cup A, R)$, where A is a set of axioms, so that both the equations E and the rules R are applied *modulo* the axioms A. That is, we rewrite not just terms t but rather A-equivalence classes $[t]_A$. The axioms A of associativity, commutativity, and identity of set union define *multisets*, and rewriting modulo these axioms corresponds to *multiset rewriting* that is directly supported in Maude. Rewriting multisets of objects linked by (possibly opposite) references exactly corresponds to graph rewriting, a correspondence that is systematically exploited in MOMENT2.

The Real-Time Maude language and tool [14] extend Maude to support the formal specification and analysis of *real-time rewrite theories*. The rewrite rules are divided into ordinary, *instantaneous* rewrite rules that are assumed to take zero time, and *tick rules* of the form crl [l] : {t} => {t'} in time u if *cond*, where u is a term (that may contain variables), denoting the *duration* of the rewrite, and {_} is a new operator that encloses the global state to ensure that time advances uniformly in all parts of the system. Real-Time Maude extends the Maude simulation, reachability, and LTL model checking features to timed systems, e.g., by providing time-bounded versions of these analysis methods, and by providing a set of *time-sampling strategies* to execute time-nondeterministic tick rules (see [14]).

2.2   MOMENT2: MOF, Models, and Model Transformations

MOMENT2 provides formal support for model-driven engineering by formalizing metamodels, defined using the MOF standard [15] and implemented in

---

[1] i.e., Σ is a set of declarations of *sorts*, *subsorts*, and *function symbols*.

EMF, as membership theories [6], and by formalizing model transformations as rewriting logic theories in Maude [5]. That is, MOMENT2 provides a simple well-known interface to software engineers, while providing a variety of formal analysis methods to analyze models and model transformations.

The algebraic semantics of MOF is defined as a "parametric" membership equational logic theory $\mathbb{A}$, so that for each MOF meta-model $\mathscr{M}$, we have a MEL specification $\mathbb{A}(\mathscr{M})$, and so that a model M conforms to the meta-model $\mathscr{M}$ iff its Maude representation is a term of sort *Model* in $\mathbb{A}(\mathscr{M})$. The representation of models as algebraic terms has the form `<< OC >>`, where `OC` is a multiset of objects of the form `< O : C | PS >`, with `O` an object identifier, `C` a class name, and `PS` a set of attributes and references between objects. This representation is automatically generated by MOMENT2 from models in the Eclipse Modeling Framework (EMF) [8]. A detailed definition of the mapping $\mathbb{A}$ is given in [4].

MOMENT2 provides support for developing, executing, and analyzing multi-model transformations, where several models might be involved. A pair $(\mathscr{M}, \mathscr{T})$, of a set of MOF metamodels $\mathscr{M}$ and a MOMENT2 model transformation definition $\mathscr{T}$, represents a model transformation, whose semantics is formally defined by a *rewrite theory* $\mathbb{R}(\mathscr{M}, \mathscr{T})$ that extends the MEL theory $\mathbb{A}(\mathscr{M})$.

A model transformation is defined as a set of production rules. Each such rule l of the form

`rl` l `{ nac` dl $nacl$ `{` NAC `} such that` *cond* `;...`
      `lhs {` dl `{` L `} };   rhs {` dl `{` R `} };   when` *cond*`;...}`

has a left-hand side L, a right-hand side R, a set of (possibly conditional) negative application conditions NAC and a condition with the *when* clause. L, R, and NAC contain model patterns, where nodes are object patterns and unidirectional edges are references between objects. For instance, in the pattern `A : Class1 { a = V, r = B : Class2 { .. },.. }` an object `A` of type `Class1` has an attribute `a`, whose value is bound to the variable V[2], and has a reference `r` that points to an object B of type `Class2`. Several models can be manipulated with a single production rule in MOMENT2. To identify which model should be matched by a given model pattern, we use the notion of *domain* that associates an identifier dl to an input model. See Section 3.2 for examples of model transformation rules.

The semantics of model transformations in MOMENT2 is based on the *single-pushout approach* (SPO) for graph transformations [17]. A production rule is applied to a model when a match is found for the patterns in L, a match is *not* found for the patterns in NACs, and the *when* clause holds. When a rule is applied, objects and references in $L \setminus R$ are removed, objects and references in $R \setminus L$ are created and objects and references in $L \cap R$ are preserved. According to the SPO semantics, all dangling edges are removed. In this paper we focus on *in-place* (multi-)model transformations, which use the same (multi-)model both as input and as output of the transformation. Such models usually represent *system states*, and the application of production rules correspond to *state transitions*.

---

[2] Variables are declared without types. The type of the variable is inferred from the information in the metamodel.

3   Real-Time Model Transformations in MOMENT2

This section shows how *timed* behaviors can be added to behavioral specifications in MOMENT2. *Ecore* is the modeling language used in EMF to define metamodels, which we use to specify the static view of a system. We provide a collection of built-in types for defining *clocks*, *timers*, and *timed values* so that: (i) the Ecore model $\mathcal{M}$ of an RTES can be extended with such types, and (ii) a system state can contain clocks, timers, and timed values.

In our approach, a *timed behavioral specification* of a system is given as a triple $(\mathcal{M}, \mathcal{T}, \delta)$, where $\mathcal{M}$ is the structural specification of the system, given as an Ecore model extended with our built-in timed constructs, $\mathcal{T}$ is an in-place model transformation in MOMENT2 defining the dynamics of the system, and δ is the time sampling strategy used to decide whether each moment in a discrete time domain is visited, or only those moments in time when a timer expires.

Section 3.1 introduces the built-in timed constructs and their metamodel. Section 3.2 illustrates the use of these constructs on a small and simplified, but prototypical, real-time protocol for finding the message exchange round trip time between two (in our case neighboring) nodes in a network. Section 3.3 discusses how we can define real-time behaviors without having to modify the (possibly "untimed") metamodel of a system. Section 3.4 defines the formal real-time rewrite semantics of our model transformations as a mapping

$$\mathbb{R}_T : (\mathcal{M}, \mathcal{T}, \delta) \mapsto (\Sigma_T, E_T, R_T),$$

taking a timed specification $(\mathcal{M}, \mathcal{T}, \delta)$ to a real-time rewrite theory (Σ_T, E_T, R_T).

3.1   Constructs for Defining Real-Time Model Transformations

The metamodel for the basic built-in constructs provided by MOMENT2 to support the specification of real-time model transformations is given in Fig. 1. We below give an intuitive explanation of these constructs, whose formal semantics is given in Section 3.4, and their use. Timed constructs specialize the `TimedConstruct` class that has a reference to the `EObject` class from the Ecore metamodel. This reference allows our timed constructs to point to any construct in an EMF model so that time features can be added to system states in a non-intrusive way as explained in Section 3.3.

Timer. A `Timer` whose `on` attribute is `true` *decreases* its `value` according to the elapsed time. When the `value` reaches 0, time advance is blocked, forcing the use of a model transformation rule *which also modifies the timer* by either turning off the `Timer` (that is, the `on` attribute is set to `false`), or by resetting the `value` attribute to the time until the timer should expire the next time. In this way, a timer is used to force an action to happen at (or before) a certain time. The `value` of a `Timer` whose `on` attribute is `false` does *not* change when time advances; neither can such a turned off `Timer` block time advance.

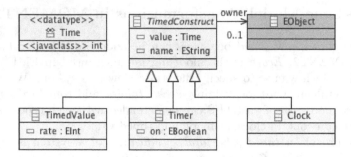

Fig. 1. Ecore metamodel of the predefined timed constructs

Clock. The `value` of a `Clock` is increased according to the elapsed time. A `Clock` with initial `value` 0, and whose value is not changed by a model transformation rule, therefore always denotes the current "model time."

Timed Value. The `TimedValue` construct is similar to the `Clock` construct. The difference is that, whereas the `value` of a `Clock` is increased by the amount of elapsed time, the `value` of a `TimedValue` object is increased by *the elapsed time multiplied with the* `rate`, which may be a negative number.

3.2   Example: A Round Trip Time Protocol

For an example that uses both clocks and timers, consider a very simple protocol for finding the *round trip time* between two neighboring nodes in a network; that is, the time it takes for a message to travel from source to destination, and back.

The initiator starts a round of this protocol by sending a *request* message to the other node and recording the time at which it sent the request. When the responder receives the request message, it immediately sends back a *reply* message. When the initiator receives the reply message, it can easily compute the round trip time using its local clock. Since the network load may change, and messages may get lost, the initiator starts a new round of the protocol *every* 50 time units. We assume that the message transmission time is between 2 and 8 time units; in addition, any message could be lost for some reason.

Figure 2 shows the structural model for this example as a class diagram, defined as an Ecore model in EMF. The attribute `rtt` of a `Node` denotes the latest computed round trip time value; `lastSentTime` denotes the time that the last request message was sent; `roundTimer` points to the timer upon whose expiration the node starts another round of the RTT protocol; and the `Clock` denotes the local clock of the node.

To model the fact that the transmission delay of a message is between 2 and 8 time units, each message has an associated clock (to avoid that the message is read too early) and a timer (to ensure that the message is not read too late).

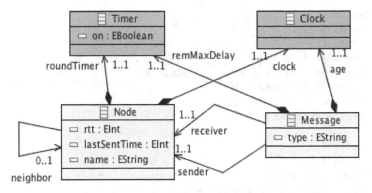

Fig. 2. Class diagram for the RTT example

The following rule models the transformation when an active round timer of a node A expires (that is, equals 0). As seen in the right-hand side of the rule, the node then sets the value of `lastSentTime` to the current time (as given by its local clock), resets its timer to expire in 50 time units, and generates a `request` message. The generated message sets its `age` clock to 0, and sets its timer to 8, ensuring that the message is read (or lost) within 8 time units[3]:

```
rl sendRequest {
   lhs { model {
      A : Node {
         clock = C : Clock { value = TIME },
         neighbor = B : Node { },
         roundTimer = RT : Timer { value = 0, on = true }  }
   }};
   rhs { model {
      A : Node {
         clock = C : Clock { value = TIME },
         neighbor = B : Node { },
         roundTimer = RT : Timer { value = 50, on = true },
         lastSentTime = TIME  }
      M : Message {
         age = MA : Clock { value = 0 },
         sender = A : Node {},
         receiver = B : Node { },
         remMaxDelay = RMD : Timer { value = 8, on = true },
         type = "request" }
   }};  }
```

The next rule models the reception (and consumption) of a `request` message. Since message transmission takes at least 2 time units, this can only happen when the `age` clock of the message is greater than or equal to 2. As a result of applying this rule, a `reply` message is created, and sent back to the node A:

---

[3] Variable names are capitalized in our model transformation rules.

```
rl replyRequest {
   lhs { model {
      B : Node { }
      M : Message {
         age = MA : Clock { value = MSGAGE },
         sender = A : Node { },
         receiver = B : Node { },
         type = "request" }
   } };
   rhs { model {
      B : Node { }
      NEW-MSG : Message {
         age = MA2 : Clock { value = 0 },
         sender = B : Node { },
         receiver = A : Node { },
         remMaxDelay = RMD : Timer { value = 8, on = true },
         type = "reply" }
   } };
   when MSGAGE >= 2; }
```

The following rule models the reception of the **reply** message. The receiver
A defines the round trip time **rtt** to be the difference between the current time
(as given by its local clock) and the value of **lastSentTime**:

```
rl getReplyAndComputeRtt {
   lhs { model {
      A : Node {
         lastSentTime = LASTTIME,
         clock = C : Clock { value = TIME } }
      M : Message {
         age = MA : Clock { value = MSGAGE },
         receiver = A : Node { },
         type = "reply" }
   } };
   rhs { model {
      A : Node {
         lastSentTime = LASTTIME,
         clock = C : Clock { value = TIME },
         rtt = TIME - LASTTIME }
   } };
   when MSGAGE >= 2; }
```

The last rule models the possibility of a message being lost in transition:

```
rl messageLoss {
   lhs { model { M : Message { } } };
   rhs { model { } }; }
```

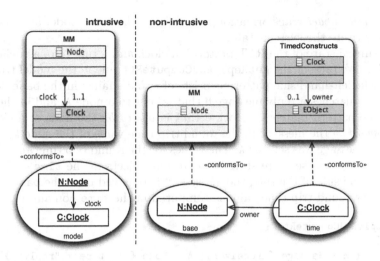

Fig. 3. Intrusive and non-intrusive approaches for adding time features

3.3   Non-intrusive Model-Based Real-Time Behavioral Specification

The presented approach might not seem the most suitable to specify a system that has been deployed, since it requires changing the structural design of the application, so that timer and clock objects can be defined in the state. We refer to this approach as *intrusive*. We therefore also provide a *non-intrusive* approach, in which the *user-defined* metamodel of the system is not modified. These two approaches are illustrated in Fig. 3 and explained below.

In the *intrusive* approach, the user-defined metamodel imports the built-in timed constructs. In this case, the extension of the system with time features is performed internally in the system by modifying the classes that constitute the static view of the system. For example, in the metamodel each node can have a clock. A state of such a system is a self-contained model that may contain time features. The behavioral specification can then be defined as an in-place model transformation with one single domain.

In the *non-intrusive* approach, the user-defined metamodel is not modified and remains agnostic from timed constructs. The extension of a system with time features is performed at the model level by defining an external model *time* that contains timed constructs. These timed constructs are related to objects in a model by means of **owner** external references. The timed behavioral specification of the system is defined with a *multi-model* transformation with two domains, one for the model and one for the time model that extends the initial model. Therefore, a system state consists of two separate model: *base* and *time*.

We next present a non-intrusive version of our round trip time protocol. Since the base system is not aware of time features, two steps are needed in order to attach real-time features to the objects: *(i)* a new independent model with timers and clocks extends the base model that corresponds to the initial state of the system; and *(ii)* the behavioral specification of the system is given as an in-place *multi-model* transformation, where both the base model and the time model constitute the system state.

In the initial state of the RTT protocol, a clock and a timer are associated to the sender. We present the `getReplyAndComputeRtt` rule in the model transformation. The left-hand side pattern consists of two domains: in the `base` domain the pattern matches a reply message M that is sent to a node A, and in the `time` domain the pattern matches a clock C that is *owned by* the node A, a clock MA that is *owned by* the message M, the round trip time value of the node A and the last time a message was sent by A. The values for the round trip time and the last time a message was sent are stored in external objects in the `time` domain. In the right-hand side of the rule, the message M is removed from the `base` domain and the new round trip time value is computed in the `time` domain:

```
rl getReplyAndComputeRtt {
   lhs {
      base { M : Message { receiver = A : Node { }, type = "reply" }}
      time { C : Clock { value = TIME, owner = A : Node{}}
       RTT : TimedConstruct { value = RTT, owner = A : Node{}}
       LST : TimedConstruct { value = LASTTIME, owner = A : Node{}}
       MA : Clock { value = MSGAGE, owner = M : Message { }}}};
   rhs {
      base { A : Node { } }
      time { C : Clock { value = TIME, owner = A : Node{}}
       RTT : TimedConstruct { value = TIME - LASTTIME, owner = A : Node{}}
       LST : TimedConstruct { value = LASTTIME, owner = A : Node{}}}};
   when MSGAGE >= 2 ; }
```

3.4   Formal Semantics of Real-Time Model Transformations

This section presents the formal *real-time rewriting logic* [13] semantics of real-time model transformations in MOMENT2. As mentioned, our semantics extends the (untimed) rewriting logic semantics of model transformations given in [5]. In particular, all data types and rewrite rules defining the semantics of model transformations are inherited. Those rewrite rules are now considered to be *instantaneous* rewrite rules modeling *instantaneous change*. The real-time rewrite semantics adds the single tick rule

```
crl [tick] : {<< OC >>} => {<< delta(OC, X) >>} in time X if X <= mte(OC)
```

where OC is a variable of the sort `ObjCol` denoting multisets of objects representing instances of classes in the rewrite semantics of model transformations, and X is a variable of the sort *Time* denoting the time domain.

Following the guidelines given in [14] for defining object-oriented real-time systems, the function `delta` defines the effect of time elapse on a system, and the function `mte` defines the *maximum time elapse* possible in a system before some action must be taken. These functions are defined as follows:

```
op delta : ObjCol Time -> ObjCol .

var OC : ObjCol .   var O : Oid .   var G : Int .   var PS : PropertySet .
vars T T' : Time .   var vTimer : Timer .   var vTDV : TimedValue .   var vClock : Clock.

eq delta(< O : vTimer | property : "value" = T', property : "on" = true, PS > OC, T) =
        < O : vTimer | property : "value" = (T' monus T), property : "on" = true, PS >
        delta(OC, T) .
```

The above equation defines the effect of the elapse of time T on a collection of objects consisting of a `Timer` object, whose `on` attribute is `true`, and other objects (captured by the variable OC). The effect of the time elapse is to decrease the `value` of the timer by T,[4] and to recursively apply the function `delta` to the remaining objects OC.

Likewise, the effect of the elapse of time T on a `Clock` object is to increase its `value` by T, and the effect of that time elapse on a `TimedValue` object with rate G is to increase the `value` by G * T:

```
eq delta(< O : vClock | property : "value" = T', PS > OC, T) =
        < O : vClock | property : "value" = (T' + T), PS > delta(OC, T) .

eq delta(< O : vTDV | property : "value" = T', property : "rate" = G, PS > OC, T) =
        < O : vTDV | property : "value" = (T' + (G * T)), property : "rate" = G, PS >
        delta(OC, T) .
```

The following equation matches "otherwise" (`owise`), that is, when none of the above equations can be applied. In those cases, time elapse has no effect on a collection of objects. In particular, time does not effect user-defined objects:

```
eq delta(OC, T) = OC [owise] .
```

The function `mte` should ensure that time does not advance beyond the expiration time of an active timer. Therefore, `mte` of a collection of objects returns the smallest `value` of the active `Timers` in the state (`INF` denotes "infinity"):

```
op mte : ObjCol -> TimeInf .
eq mte(< O : vTimer | property : "value" = T, property : "on" = true, PS > OC) =
        minimum(T, mte(OC)) .
eq mte(OC) = INF [owise] .
```

Although timed MOMENT2 model transformations have a real-time rewriting semantics, the current implementation of MOMENT2 is not based on the Real-Time Maude tool. Nevertheless, Real-Time Maude features such as, e.g., selecting the time sampling strategy with which to execute tick rules, and performing *time-bounded* reachability and LTL model checking analyses, *are* available in MOMENT2. For example, the tool allows the user to choose between advancing time by *one time unit* in each application of the tick rule, or advancing time until a timer expires.

---

[4] The function `monus` is defined by $x \text{ monus } y = \max(0, x - y)$.

4   Formal Analysis

The MOMENT2 tool provides a spectrum of formal analysis methods, in which a model transformation system can be subjected to Maude analyses such as simulation, reachability analysis, and linear temporal logic (LTL) model checking. Simulation explores *one* sequence of model transformations from an initial model. Reachability analysis analyzes *all* possible model transformation sequences from an initial model to check whether some model *pattern* can be reached, and LTL model checking analyzes whether all such sequences satisfy a given LTL formula.

Since the MOMENT2 implementation does not target Real-Time Maude, the above analysis methods are all *untimed*. Nevertheless, we can also easily perform *time-bounded* analyses by just adding a single unconnected `Timer`—whose initial value is the time bound—to the initial state. When this timer expires, time will not advance further in the system, since no rule resets or turns off the timer. The ability to perform time-bounded analysis is not only useful *per se*, but also makes (time-bounded) LTL model checking analysis possible for systems with an infinite reachable state space, such as our RTT example, that can otherwise not be subjected to LTL model checking.

4.1   Formal Analysis of the RTT Protocol

In MOMENT2, the model instance that corresponds to the initial state is used as input model for model transformations. To analyze our round trip time protocol specification, we have added a timer set to 500 to the initial model instance. The reachable state space is therefore restricted to those states that are reachable within 500 time units. Without such a restriction, the reachable state space would be infinite, since the clock values can grow beyond any bound.

We use MOMENT2's search command to verify the safety property that the recorded `rtt` value of a node is either 0 (reply message not yet received) or is some value in the interval $[4, 16]$. This property can be verified (for behaviors up to 500 time units) by searching for a reachable state where the recorded `rtt` value is *not* within the desired set of values; that is, by searching for a node `N : Node { rtt = RTT }` whose round trip time value is `RTT <> 0 and (RTT < 4 or RTT > 16)`. We search for one counterexample, and without any bound on the depth of the search tree (`[1,unbounded]`):

```
search [1,unbounded] =>*
          domain model { N : Node { rtt = RTT } }
              such that RTT <> 0 and (RTT < 4 or RTT > 16)
```

We use time-bounded LTL model checking to verify the stability property that once an `rtt` value in the desired range $[4, 16]$ has been recorded, the value of the `rtt` attribute stays in this interval. We first define a parametric state proposition `okRTTValue`, so that `okRTTValue(`*n*`)` holds in states where the recorded round trip time value of a node *n* is in the interval $[4, 16]$:

```
domain model { N : Node { rtt = RTT, name = ID } } |= okRTTValue(ID)
              = (RTT >= 4 and RTT <= 16) ;
```

We can then model check the following LTL formula to verify our desired stability property for node `"A"`:

```
[] (okRTTValue("A") -> [] (okRTTValue("A")))
```

5 Related Work

A prominent early work in the closely related field of timed *graph* transformations is the work by Gyapay, Varró, and Heckel in [9], where the authors define a model of timed graph transformations based on a timed version of Petri nets. In their model (the "GVH model"), each object has an associated time stamp, called *chronos*, denoting the last time the object participated in a transition. All transitions are *eager* and have durations.[5] This is quite different from our model, where transitions are non-eager and instantaneous, and where timeliness of desired actions is achieved by using timers. Another difference is that in the Petri-net-based semantics of the GVH model, executions may be *time-inconsistent* in that a transition firing at time t_1 may take place *after* a transition firing at a later time $t_2 > t_1$. However, in [9] it is shown that such time-inconsistent executions can be rearranged to "equivalent" time-consistent executions. Our real-time model transformations have a real-time rewrite theory semantics, where all computations are time-consistent [13]. Comparing the "timed" expressiveness of the two approaches is nontrivial. On the on hand, each GVH-execution cannot be "directly" simulated in our framework, since we cannot have time-inconsistent computations in real-time rewrite theories. Likewise, we do not know whether there exists a semantics-preserving encoding of our models as GVH-models.

Becker and Giese use a timed extension of graph transformation systems for verifying RTES [2], where clocks are used as attributes in graphs. Their work focuses on inductively verifying safety properties over all possible states in a system, as opposed to *automatically* verifying the system from a given initial state as in model checking approaches like ours, where more expressive linear temporal logic properties can be verified.

A recent paper by Rivera, Vicente-Chicote, and Vallecillo [16] also advocates the use of in-place model transformations to complement metamodels with timed behavioral specifications. However, the time models are completely different. In their approach, they do not add any explicit constructs for defining time behavior (so as not to modify metamodels); instead the transformation rules have time intervals denoting the duration interval of each local action. In our approach, timed constructs are included in the system state but their semantics is encoded in MOMENT2, providing a simpler setting in which time does not have to be explicitly manipulated in the behavioral specification of the system. Despite this simplicity, we have shown how our approach allows us to consider timed requirements in a non-intrusive way through multi-model transformations.

---

[5] Alternatively, one may view transitions as instantaneous transitions that apply at time Δ after becoming enabled.

In [20], Syriani and Vangheluwe model the PacMan as graph transformations extended with time. The timed behavior of their model is that the system remains in a state as long as specified by *time-advance* of that state, or until some input is received in some port. The system then performs a transition. This time behavior falls within our timed model, where *timed-advance* is simply modeled as a timer. The paper [20] presents no formal model of their framework, and the only form of analysis is simulation using a tool implemented in Python.

Using meta-models for Giotto and the E-Machine in the GME toolkit, Szemethy used the GReAT *untimed* graph rewrite system to transform time-triggered Giotto source code into schedule-carrying E-Machine code [21].

Several approaches use a model-driven development methodology for modeling real-time systems. For instance, AADL [18] and MARTE [12] are used for safety-critical avionics and automotive systems. These approaches only consider the specification of RTES, and formal analysis is provided by translating the model of a system into an external formalism with verification capabilities. Our work provides an automatic, direct mechanism to formalize and analyze model-based RTES by means of in-place model transformations in MOMENT2. MOMENT2 encodes the metamodels and model transformation into rewriting logic and leverages Maude verification techniques to analyze model transformations.

6   Concluding Remarks

This paper has shown how the formal model transformation specification and analysis tool MOMENT2 has been extended to real-time model transformations by providing a few simple and intuitive constructs for describing timed behavior. We have also shown how the multi-modeling capabilities of MOMENT2 can be exploited to define timed behaviors in a *non-intrusive* way; i.e., without changing the given metamodel to specify real-time behaviors. We have given a real-time rewrite semantics to real-time model transformation systems, and have shown how such systems can be subjected to (unbounded and time-bounded) reachability and LTL model checking analyses. We believe that our timed model is easy to understand and is suitable to define advanced real-time model transformations, as indicated by our example. In addition, and in contrast to most competing approaches, both simulation and LTL model checking are integrated into our tool. Furthermore, through MOMENT2, our methods can be automatically applied to EMF-based systems and modeling languages so that rewriting logic techniques are made available in mainstream model-driven development processes for analysis purposes.

Acknowledgments. We gratefully acknowledge financial support by The Research Council of Norway and by the EU project SENSORIA IST-2005-016004.

References

1. André, C., Mallet, F., de Simone, R.: Modeling time(s). In: Engels, G., Opdyke, B., Schmidt, D.C., Weil, F. (eds.) MODELS 2007. LNCS, vol. 4735, pp. 559–573. Springer, Heidelberg (2007)
2. Becker, B., Giese, H.: On Safe Service-Oriented Real-Time Coordination for Autonomous Vehicles. In: ISORC 2008. IEEE, Los Alamitos (2008)
3. Boronat, A., Meseguer, J.: Algebraic semantics of OCL-constrained metamodel specifications. In: TOOLS-EUROPE 2009. LNBIP, vol. 33. Springer, Heidelberg (2009)
4. Boronat, A.: MOMENT: a formal framework for MOdel manageMENT. PhD in Computer Science, Universitat Politènica de València (UPV), Spain (2007), http://www.cs.le.ac.uk/people/aboronat/papers/2007_thesis_ArturBoronat.pdf
5. Boronat, A., Heckel, R., Meseguer, J.: Rewriting Logic Semantics and Verification of Model Transformations. In: Chechik, M., Wirsing, M. (eds.) FASE 2009. LNCS, vol. 5503, pp. 18–33. Springer, Heidelberg (2009)
6. Boronat, A., Meseguer, J.: An Algebraic Semantics for MOF. In: Fiadeiro, J.L., Inverardi, P. (eds.) FASE 2008. LNCS, vol. 4961, pp. 377–391. Springer, Heidelberg (2008)
7. Clavel, M., Durán, F., Eker, S., Lincoln, P., Martí-Oliet, N., Meseguer, J., Talcott, C. (eds.): All About Maude - A High-Performance Logical Framework. LNCS, vol. 4350. Springer, Heidelberg (2007)
8. Eclipse Organization: The Eclipse Modeling Framework (2007), http://www.eclipse.org/emf/
9. Gyapay, S., Varró, D., Heckel, R.: Graph transformation with time. Fundam. Inform. 58(1), 1–22 (2003)
10. Meseguer, J.: Conditional rewriting logic as a unified model of concurrency. Theoretical Computer Science 96, 73–155 (1992)
11. Meseguer, J.: Membership algebra as a logical framework for equational specification. In: Parisi-Presicce, F. (ed.) WADT 1997. LNCS, vol. 1376, pp. 18–61. Springer, Heidelberg (1998)
12. Object Management Group: The official OMG MARTE Web site (2009), http://www.omgmarte.org/
13. Ölveczky, P.C., Meseguer, J.: Specification of real-time and hybrid systems in rewriting logic. Theoretical Computer Science 285, 359–405 (2002)
14. Ölveczky, P.C., Meseguer, J.: Semantics and pragmatics of Real-Time Maude. Higher-Order and Symbolic Computation 20(1-2), 161–196 (2007)
15. OMG: Meta Object Facility (MOF) 2.0 Core Specification, ptc/06-01-01 (2006)
16. Rivera, J., Vicente-Chicote, C., Vallecillo, A.: Extending visual modeling languages with timed behavioral specifications. In: XII Iberoamerican Conference on Requirements Engineering and Software Environments, IDEAS 2009 (2009)
17. Rozenberg, G.: Handbook of Grammars and Computing by Graph Transformation, vol. 1. World Scientific Publishing Company, Singapore (1997)
18. SAE: AADL (2007), http://www.aadl.info/
19. Schmidt, D.C.: Model-driven engineering. IEEE Computer 39(2), 25–31 (2006)
20. Syriani, E., Vangheluwe, H.: Programmed graph rewriting with time for simulation-based design. In: Vallecillo, A., Gray, J., Pierantonio, A. (eds.) ICMT 2008. LNCS, vol. 5063, pp. 91–106. Springer, Heidelberg (2008)
21. Szemethy, T.: Case study: Model transformations for time-triggered languages. ENTCS 152, 175–190 (2006)

Reusing Model Transformations
While Preserving Properties

Ethan K. Jackson[1], Wolfram Schulte[1],
Daniel Balasubramanian[2], and Gabor Karsai[2]

[1] Microsoft Research
{ejackson,schulte}@microsoft.com
[2] Vanderbilt University
{daniel,gabor}@isis.vanderbilt.edu

Abstract. Model transformations are indispensable to *model-based de-velopment* (MBD) where they act as translators between *domain-specific languages* (DSLs). As a result, transformations must be verified to ensure they behave as desired. Simultaneously, transformations may be reused as requirements evolve. In this paper we present novel algorithms to de-termine if a reused transformation preserves the same properties as the original, without expensive re-verification. We define a type of behavioral equivalence, called *lifting equivalence*, relating an original transformation to its reused version. A reused transformation that is equivalent to the original will preserve all compatible universally quantified properties. We describe efficient algorithms for verifying lifting equivalence, which we have implemented in our FORMULA [1, 2] framework.

1 Introduction

Model-based development (MBD) utilizes *domain-specific languages* (DSLs) and *model transformations* to support formal modeling [3–6] . DSLs are used to (1) capture vertical abstraction layers, (2) separately specify design concerns, and (3) provide convenient modeling notations for complex problem domains [7]. Model transformations act as bridges between DSLs in order to (1) incrementally refine models through abstraction layers, (2) compose models into a consistent whole or evolve them as requirements evolve [2], and (3) capture operational semantics as sequences of transformation steps [8].

Consequently, composition, verification, and reuse of DSLs/transformations are essential operations. Informally, a DSL X exposes an abstract syntax $S(X)$, and a model transformation τ is a mapping across syntaxes. A verified trans-formation is a mapping guaranteed to exhibit certain properties, such as every well-formed input yields a well-formed output. Transformations are reused when-ever a new transformation τ' is built from parts of an existing τ. We explore whether the properties of τ also hold in the reused transformation τ'.

For example, consider a DSL for a *non-deterministic finite state automa-ton* (NFA) abstraction. An important operation on NFAs is the synchronous product $\otimes$, which creates product NFAs where states have internal structure

D.S. Rosenblum and G. Taentzer (Eds.): FASE 2010, LNCS 6013, pp. 44–58, 2010.
© Springer-Verlag Berlin Heidelberg 2010

(i.e. pairs of product states). Let *ProdNFA* be the DSL for product NFAs, then the $\tau_\otimes$ transformation is a mapping from $S(NFA) \times S(NFA)$ to $S(ProdNFA)$. It can be verified that $\tau_\otimes$ has the property: $\forall x_1, x_2 \ \#states(\tau_\otimes(x_1, x_2)) = \#states(x_1) \times \#states(x_2)$, i.e. products grow combinatorially in size. This convenient transformation can be reused to create products of product NFAs: $\tau'_\otimes : S(ProdNFA) \times S(ProdNFA) \to S(ProdNFA)$. We would like to know if the previous property holds in the new context without reproving it.

In this paper we present a novel approach to avoid expensive re-verification when a model transformation is reused in a new context. Our approach is to fix an auxiliary class of transformations $\mathcal{T}_{rw}$, which we call *rewriting procedures*. Whenever a transformation is reused in a new context, an attempt is made to discover a rewriting procedure from the new to the old context. A reused transformation τ' *lifts* τ if it is equivalent to a rewriting procedure followed by an application of the original transformation τ. If this is the case, then all (compatible) *first-order universally quantified* properties of τ also hold for τ', but with dependencies on the rewriting procedures. Finally, for reasonable choices of $\mathcal{T}_{rw}$, these rewriting procedures can be eliminated from lifted properties resulting in an equivalent property that lives completely within the new context. We have implemented this approach in our FORMULA framework [2]: Static analysis automatically rejects reused transformations that should maintain properties, but for which lifting cannot be verified.

This paper is divided into the following sections: Section 2 describes related work. Section 3 presents a general formal framework. Section 4 explains our implementation of the general framework. We conclude in Section 5.

2   Related Work

Much work on transformation reuse is targeted at the automated or semi-automated evolution of transformations in response to either refactored models or language constructs. For instance, [9] describes how the evolution of models may break transformations intended to operate on these models. The solution is to capture model refactorings as transformations, which can then be used to upgrade transformations that are unaware of these refactorings. [10] deals the evolution of transformation context through user-defined rules relating the constructs in the original meta-models with those in the evolved meta-models. These rules are used to upgrade the transformation as much as possible.

Functional programming solves a related reuse problem: Given a function $f : X \to Y$, can f be applied to new recursive data structures containing data of type X? For example, if $f : \mathbb{Z} \to \mathbb{Z}$, determine a function $f' : Lists(\mathbb{Z}) \to \mathbb{Z}$ from lists of integers to integers that generalizes f. In this case, the lifted f' is not behaviorally equivalent to f, but may preserve properties of f depending on the choice of f'. The Bird-Meertens [11] formalism enumerates patterns of recursive data types that can be used to generalize f automatically. See [12] for a catalog of these recognizable patterns and the formal properties of these generalizations. The main application of this work has been to automatically parallelize functional programs [13].

There is also an important body of work on transformation verification. Verification of model transformations can be performed point-wise, on the input/output pairs of a transformation, or on the transformation itself. The former is known as *instance-based* verification. [14] describes an approach where each execution of the transformation is verified by checking whether the output model *bi-simulates* the input model. [15] uses a set of graph transformation rules to describe the operational semantics of a DSL and then generates a transition system for each well-formed model of the language. A model checker is used to provide formal verification and check dynamic properties of the models.

[16] is an example of verifying the action of a transformation τ over its entire domain. Here, it is assumed that the behaviors of source and target models are defined by simulation rules (which are also transformations). A transformation is correct/complete if for every input model the output model includes the behaviors of the input, and vice versa. This is verified by examining the effects of τ on the simulation rules. Modular verification of model refactorings is also described in [17, 18]. The authors show that once a behavioral semantics is fixed for models of a DSL (e.g. models may correspond to CSPs), then model refactorings can be shown to preserve behavior under certain conditions.

3   General Framework

3.1   Transformations and Reuse Scenarios

We begin with a general discussion of DSLs and transformations. For our purposes, a DSL X is an object providing a set $S(X)$, called the *abstract syntax of* X. A model x is instance of the abstract syntax; equivalently x is an element of $S(X)$. A *model transformation* τ is a map from n input models to m output models:

$$\tau : S(X_1) \times \ldots \times S(X_n) \to S(Y_1) \times \ldots \times S(Y_m) \tag{1}$$

The domain/range of τ form its context. A transformation is defined via a set of *rules R*, which match patterns in input models to build output models. A transformation *terminates* when no more rules can be applied. Rules are variously specified as graph-rewrite rules [3] [19], declarative relations [20], term-rewrites rules [21], logic programs [2], and even blocks of imperative code [22]. A set of rules R is converted to a mapping τ by a formal semantics $[\![\ ]\!]$, which also takes into account the input/output DSLs:

$$[\![R, \overline{X}, \overline{Y}]\!] \mapsto \tau, \text{ where } \overline{X} = [X_1, \ldots, X_n] \text{ and } \overline{Y} = [Y_1, \ldots, Y_m]. \tag{2}$$

Since rules operate on abstract syntax, the context $(\overline{X}, \overline{Y})$ is required to bind patterns in the rules with elements of the sytnax. We do not hypothesize on the framework-independent properties of $[\![\ ]\!]$, other than to assume that, when defined, τ is a *function* whose signature is given by (1). Later in the paper we investigate $[\![\ ]\!]$ for a particular transformation framework.

Using this notation, we study reuse scenarios where the rules R are interpreted in a new context $(\overline{X'}, \overline{Y'})$:

$$[\![R, \overline{X'}, \overline{Y'}]\!] \mapsto \tau', \text{ where } \overline{X'} = [X_1', \ldots, X_n'] \text{ and } \overline{Y'} = [Y_1', \ldots, Y_m']. \quad (3)$$

We provide static analysis to decide if τ' preserves the properties of τ without expensive re-verification. Several important scenarios are included in this definition:

Example 1. **Transformation Evolution.** A transformation is defined and verified, but changes in requirements necessitate changes in DSL syntax [10]. In this case τ evolves to τ', where each X_i' (or Y_j') is either the original X_i (or Y_j) or a modified version X_i^* (or Y_j^*).

$$X_i' = \begin{cases} X_i^* & \text{if requirements change} \\ X_i & \text{otherwise} \end{cases}, \quad Y_j' = \begin{cases} Y_j^* & \text{if requirements change} \\ Y_j & \text{otherwise} \end{cases}. \quad (4)$$

Example 2. **DSL Composition.** A DSL X may represent one *aspect* or *architectural facet* of a multi-faceted design problem. In this case, a complete abstraction is formed by composing X with another DSL X^* to obtain $X' = X \oplus X^*$. The DSL composition operator $\oplus$ varies across tools from *UML package merge* to *eBNF grammar composition* [23]. It is then necessary to reuse τ across composite DSLs.

$$X_i' = \begin{cases} X_i \oplus X_i^* & \text{if composed} \\ X_i & \text{otherwise} \end{cases}, \quad Y_j' = \begin{cases} Y_j \oplus Y_j^* & \text{if composed} \\ Y_j & \text{otherwise} \end{cases}. \quad (5)$$

3.2   Properties of Transformations

A *quantifier-free formula over* τ is a well-formed formula consisting of variables, function applications, and τ applications; the following pseudo-grammar provides a sketch:

$$\begin{aligned} expr & ::= Var \mid app \mid (expr). \\ app & ::= \tau(x_1, \ldots, x_n) \mid Func(expr_1, \ldots, expr_k). \\ Var & ::= \{u, v, w, x, y \ldots\}. \\ Func & ::= \{f, g, h, \wedge, \vee, \neg \ldots\}. \end{aligned} \quad (6)$$

(Note that τ applications are normalized so τ is only applied to variables.) Let $\varphi_\tau[V]$ be a quantifier-free formula containing one or more applications of τ; V is the set of variables appearing in φ. We refer to a (first-order) *universally quantified property of* τ as a statement of the form:

Definition 1. *Universally quantified property of* τ

$$\forall x_1 \in Q_1 \ldots \forall x_k \in Q_k \quad \varphi_\tau[x_1, \ldots, x_k]. \quad (7)$$

where every variable x_i is universally quantified over an input syntax $Q_i = S(X_j)$. We write $\tau \vdash p$ if property p can be deduced from τ. For the remainder of this paper we deal with this restricted class of properties, which encompasses a number of important examples:

Example 3. **Static Correctness.** As in traditional programming languages, an instance of DSL syntax $x \in S(X)$ is not guaranteed to be semantically meaningful. A compiler performs static analysis, e.g. type-checking, to check that x is meaningful. Let $check_X(\cdot)$ be a predicate evaluating to true when a model is statically correct. Then a transformation $\tau : S(X) \to S(Y)$ preserving static correctness has the following property [1]:

$$\forall x \in S(X), \ check_X(x) \Rightarrow check_Y(\tau(x)). \tag{8}$$

This property generalizes to transformations with multiple inputs/outputs. Let π_i be a projection operator; when applied to an n-tuple it returns the ith coordinate. Let τ be an transformation with n inputs and m outputs.

$$\begin{matrix} \forall x_1 \in S(X_1) \\ \vdots \\ \forall x_n \in S(X_n) \end{matrix} \quad \bigwedge_{1 \le i \le n} check_{X_i}(x_i) \Rightarrow \bigwedge_{1 \le j \le m} check_{Y_j}(\pi_j(\tau(x_1, \dots, x_n))). \tag{9}$$

Example 4. **Behavioral Correspondence.** Let $\sim \subseteq S(X) \times S(Y)$ be a simulation relation over models of X and Y. A transformation preserves *behavioral correspondence* [14] if the output simulates the input, whenever the input is meaningful.

$$\forall x \in S(X), \ check_X(x) \Rightarrow check_Y(\tau(x)) \wedge x \sim \tau(x). \tag{10}$$

Behavioral correspondence can also be generalized to multiple inputs/outputs according to a family of simulation relations.

In order to develop general theorems about property preservation, some assumptions on abstract syntaxes are required. We shall make the assumption that every $S(X)$ is disjoint from every other $S(Y)$. Under this assumption, a property p must satisfy simple *compatibility* conditions before it can be lifted to another context. Properties that are incompatible with a context do not hold there. Of course, when deeper knowledge about of syntax structure is available, then these compatibility conditions can be augmented appropriately.

Definition 2. *Compatible Properties. Let $\tau \vdash p$ where τ has context $(\overline{X}, \overline{Y})$. Let τ' be a reused transformation with context $(\overline{X'}, \overline{Y'})$. A property p is compatible with the context $(\overline{X'}, \overline{Y'})$ if whenever a variable x appears as the ith and j^{th} argument to a τ application then $X_i' = X_j'$.*

Example 5. Let $\tau : S(X) \times S(X) \to S(Y)$ and $\tau' : S(U) \times S(W) \to S(Z)$. Then the property $\forall x_1, x_2 \in S(X) \ \tau(x_1, x_2) = \tau(x_2, x_1)$ is not compatible in the new context because $S(U) \cap S(W) = \emptyset$.

3.3   A General Scheme for Property Preserving Reuse

We wish to determine if all compatible properties satisfied by τ are also satisfied by τ'. This is accomplished by establishing a behavioral equivalence between τ' and τ, which we call *lifting equivalence*. Assume $\tau : S(X) \to S(Y)$. We say τ' *lifts* τ if the following procedures are equivalent:

1. Calculate $y' = \tau'(x')$, and then rewrite $y' \in S(Y')$ to $y \in S(Y)$.
2. Rewrite $x' \in S(X')$ to $x \in S(X)$, and then calculate $y = \tau(x)$.

If τ' lifts τ, then τ' can be viewed as syntactic rewriting step followed by an application of τ. This scheme requires fixing a class $\mathcal{T}_{rw}$ of transformations, which we call *rewriting procedures*. Let $\mathcal{T}_{rw}(\overline{X'}, \overline{X})$ be the (possibly empty) subset of rewriting procedures from $\overline{X'}$ to $\overline{X}$. Formally, τ' lifts τ if for every rewriting procedure Λ on the inputs, there exists a rewriting procedure Γ on the outputs such that the diagram in Figure 1 commutes. In other words, there is no wrong choice for Λ. To simplify construction of rewriting procedures, $\mathcal{T}_{rw}$ must satisfy a decomposition criterion:

Definition 3. *Class of Rewriting Procedures.* *A class of rewriting procedures $\mathcal{T}_{rw}$ is a class of functions of the form $\Lambda : S(X'_1) \times \ldots \times S(X'_n) \to S(X_1) \times \ldots \times S(X_n)$. Every Λ can be decomposed into a direct product of unary rewrites:*

$$\Lambda = \langle \Lambda_1, \ldots, \Lambda_n \rangle \text{ and } \Lambda_i : S(X'_i) \to S(X_i) \in \mathcal{T}_{rw}. \tag{11}$$

In other words, $\Lambda(x'_1, \ldots, x'_n)$ can be calculated by point-wise rewriting each x'_i with Λ_i. The decomposition also agrees on how to perform rewrites: If components Λ_i and Λ_j have the same signature, then they are the same unary rewriting procedure.

Definition 4. *Lifting Equivalence.* *Let $\mathcal{T}_{rw}$ be a class of rewriting procedures. Then τ' lifts τ if both transformations have n-inputs/m-outputs and:*

$$\forall \Lambda \in \mathcal{T}_{rw}(\overline{X'}, \overline{X}) \; \exists \Gamma \in \mathcal{T}_{rw}(\overline{Y'}, \overline{Y}) \quad \tau \circ \Lambda = \Gamma \circ \tau'. \tag{12}$$

Claim. If $\tau \vdash p$, τ' lifts τ, and p is compatible with τ', then $\tau' \vdash p'$ where p' is constructed by the following procedure:

1. Pick any Γ and Λ satisfying Equation (12).
2. Replace every occurrence of $\tau(x_{c_1}, \ldots, x_{c_n})$ in p with $\Gamma(\tau'(x'_{c_1}, \ldots, x'_{c_n}))$.
3. Replace every remaining occurrence of x_i with $\Lambda_{x_i}(x'_i)$ where Λ_{x_i} is any well-typed unary rewrite from the decomposition of Λ.
4. Quantify each variable x'_i over a well-typed $Q'_i = S(X'_j)$, which must exist.

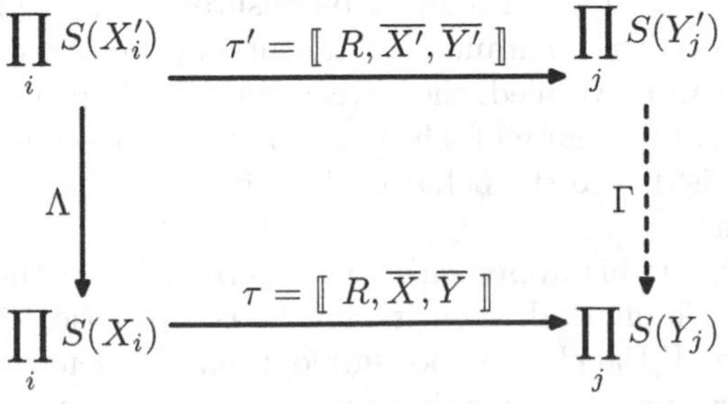

$$
\begin{array}{ccc}
\prod_i S(X'_i) & \xrightarrow{\;\tau' = [\![\, R, \overline{X'}, \overline{Y'} \,]\!]\;} & \prod_j S(Y'_j) \\[2mm]
\Big\downarrow{\scriptstyle \Lambda} & & \Big\downarrow{\scriptstyle \Gamma} \\[2mm]
\prod_i S(X_i) & \xrightarrow{\;\tau = [\![\, R, \overline{X}, \overline{Y} \,]\!]\;} & \prod_j S(Y_j)
\end{array}
$$

Fig. 1. A commuting diagram for lifting equivalence

We denote this replacement procedure by:

$$\forall x_1' \in Q_1', \ldots, \forall x_k' \in Q_k' \quad \varphi[x_1/\Lambda_{x_1}(x_1'), \ldots, x_k/\Lambda_{x_k}(x_k'), \tau/(\Gamma \circ \tau')]. \quad (13)$$

where $\varphi[x_1, \ldots, x_k]$ is the original formula appearing in p.

Example 6. **Lifting Static Correctness.** Given $\tau : S(X) \to S(Y), \tau' : S(X') \to S(Y')$. If τ' lifts τ and τ preserves static correctness, then p' becomes:

$$\forall x' \in S(X'), \; check_X(\Lambda(x')) \Rightarrow check_Y(\Gamma(\tau'(x'))). \quad (14)$$

Theorem 1. *Property lifting. If $\tau \vdash p$, τ' lifts τ, and p is compatible with τ, then $\tau' \vdash p'$ where p' is constructed according to (13). We say p' is a lifting of p.*

Proof. Observe that for every variable x_i quantified over Q_i there is at least one component $\Lambda_{x_i} : S(X') \to Q_i$. This is due to the compatibility condition (Definition 2) and the requirement that variables are quantified over input syntaxes (Definition 1). Since p holds for all values of x_i, replace every occurrence of x_i with $\Lambda_{x_i}(x_i')$ where x_i' is a fresh variable. Each x_i' is quantified over **dom** Λ_{x_i}, which we denote Q_i' yielding the property:

$$\forall x_1' \in Q_i', \ldots, \forall x_k' \in Q_k' \quad \varphi_\tau[x_1/\Lambda_{x_1}(x_1'), \ldots, x_k/\Lambda_{x_k}(x_k')]. \quad (15)$$

This property still has occurrences of τ. However, since the τ applications in p were normalized to $\tau(x_{c_1}, \ldots, x_{c_n})$, then every application in (15) has the form $\tau(\Lambda_{x_{c_1}}(x_{c_1}'), \ldots, \Lambda_{x_{c_n}}(x_{c_n}'))$. This can be rewritten $(\tau \circ \Lambda)(x_{c_1}', \ldots, x_{c_n}')$. Applying Equation (12), this is equivalent to $(\Gamma \circ \tau')(x_{c_1}', \ldots, x_{c_n}')$, which yields $\Gamma(\tau'(x_{c_1}', \ldots, x_{c_n}'))$. Thus, we obtain a property over τ' according to (13).   □

3.4   Summary of the Approach

Our approach relies on a class of rewriting procedures as a basis for comparing an original transformation with its reused version. Given τ' and τ, our algorithms characterize the set of rewriting procedures for reconciling the context of τ' with the context of τ. If no procedures can be found, then the contexts are too different and no guarantees can be provided about property preservation. If rewriting procedures exist, then it must be ensured that diagram 1 commutes for any choice of procedure, guaranteeing that lifted properties hold regardless of this choice. If this can be verified, then every compatible property p holding for τ also holds for τ' (in the sense of Theorem 1) even if p is not explicitly known to hold for τ. This is due to the behavioral equivalence that exists between the two transformations.

The effectiveness of this approach depends crucially on the choice for $\mathcal{T}_{rw}$. If the class is too complicated, then it may be computationally prohibitive to verify that τ' lifts τ. If the class is too simple, then either most contexts cannot be reconciled or occurrences of rewriting procedures cannot be eliminated from lifted properties. In other words, lifted properties may indirectly depend on the original context through the rewriting procedures. Fortunately, for some lifted properties it is possible to remove these occurrences, thereby obtaining an equivalent property with no dependency on the original context. For the remainder of this paper we show a reasonable choice for $\mathcal{T}_{rw}$ that leads to computationally efficient algorithms and to lifted properties where elimination of rewriting procedures can be automated.

4   Implementing Lifting Analysis

For the remainder of this paper we apply these techniques to strongly-typed rule-based systems where models are instances of recursive data types. We develop a useful class of rewriting procedures for algebraic data types, called *collapsing morphisms*.

4.1   Example: Reuse in FORMULA

We motivate the following sections by illustrating lifting analysis in our FORMULA framework, beginning with the classic *non-deterministic finite state automata* (NFA) abstraction specified with FORMULA. The left side of Figure 2 shows the syntax and static semantics for the NFA DSL. The domain keyword declares a DSL called NFA (line 1). DSL syntax is defined via a set of record constructors. For example, line 3 defines a record constructor State, which takes an integer ID and returns a State record with that ID. Record constructors can have more complex type constraints; e.g. the Transition constructor takes two State records an an Event record as input. Equality is defined over records; two records are the same if both were constructed by the same constructor using

```
1.  domain NFA                      16. domain ProdNFA
2.  {                               17. {
3.     State : (id: Integer).       18.    State    : (id: StateLbl).
4.     Event : (id: Integer).       19.    StateLbl : Integer + Pair.
5.     [relation]                   20.    Pair     : (p1: ProdLbl,
6.     Transition : (src: State,    21.                 p2: ProdLbl),
7.       trg : Event, dst: State).  22.    ProdLbl  : State + Pair.
8.     [relation]                   23.    Event    : (id: Integer).
9.     Initial    : (state: State). 24.    [relation]
10.                                 25.    Transition : (src: State,
11.    //At least one initial state.26.      trg : Event, dst: State).
12.    conforms :? i is Initial.    27.    [relation]
13. }.                              28.    Initial    : (state: State).
14.                                 29.    conforms   :? i is Initial.
15.                                 30. }.
```

Fig. 2. (Left) Simple automata DSL, (Right) Product automata DSL

the same arguments (i.e. structural equality). An instance x of DSL syntax is a finite set of finite records:

$$x = \{State(1), State(2), Event(3), Transition(State(1), Event(3), State(2))\} \tag{16}$$

A FORMULA specification also contains static semantics for the DSL. The annotations on lines 5, 8 require Transition and Initial records to behave like relations over states and events. Line 12 is an explicit conformance rule requiring at least one initial state (i.e. at least one Initial record).

The NFA DSL contains just enough elements to express the most basic of NFAs. For example, it is inconvenient to express products of NFAs, because the State constructor cannot hold the IDs of product states. The ProdNFA domain remedies this situation by defining states with more complex IDs (line 18). Now, IDs are instances of the StateLbl type, which is a union of the Integer and Pair types. In turn, a Pair constructor accepts either a State or another Pair. Consequently, State is a recursive data type permitting IDs such as:

$$State\bigg(Pair\big(Pair(State(1), State(2)), Pair(State(3), State(4))\big)\bigg) \tag{17}$$

At this point, the FORMULA compiler does not know that these two DSLs are related.

The two DSLs can be explicitly related by a transformation taking two NFAs and returning their synchronous product. Such a transformation has the signature:

```
transform SProd (NFA as in1, NFA as in2) returns (ProdNFA as out) {...}
```

The identifiers in1, in2, and out are special variables that hold the input and output models during execution of the transformation. Two NFAs can be composed with SProd, but further composition is not possible since SProd does not accept ProdNFA models as inputs. Intuitively, the rules defining SProd should behave similarly in the context $\overline{X'} = [\mathsf{ProdNFA}, \mathsf{ProdNFA}]$, $\overline{Y'} = [\mathsf{ProdNFA}]$. This intuition can be stated using the following one line declaration.

```
transform SProd2 lifts SProd overrides (ProdNFA as in1, ProdNFA as in2).
```

The SProd2 transformation interprets the rules from SProd in a new context according to the list of overrides. FORMULA accepts this declaration if it can be verified that SProd2 lifts SProd, in which case the lifted transformation also lifts properties. Otherwise, an error is emitted.

The lifting analysis employs a class of rewriting procedures that we call *collapsing morphisms*. This class allows automatic elimination of rewrites appearing in lifted properties. For example, we know that:

$$\forall x_1, x_2 \in S(NFA), \ \#states(SProd(x_1, x_2)) = \#states(x_1) \times \#states(x_2).$$

Assume SProd2 lifts SProd, then the lifted property is:

$$\forall x_1', x_2' \in S(ProdNFA), \ \#states(\Gamma(SProd2(x_1', x_2'))) = \frac{\#states(\Lambda_{x_1}(x_1'))\times}{\#states(\Lambda_{x_2}(x_2'))}.$$

If Γ and Λ are collapsing morphisms, then the rewrites can be immediately eliminated, yielding:

$$\forall x'_1, x'_2 \in S(ProdNFA),\ \#states(SProd2(x'_1, x'_2)) = \#states(x'_1) \times \#states(x'_2).$$

4.2   Collapsing Morphisms as Rewriting Procedures

Instances of algebraic data types with structural equality can be formalized as either *terms* over a *term algebra* or as *ordered trees* [24]. We describe the ordered tree representation as it simplifies description of algorithms. An ordered tree is a tree where the children of node v are ordered 1 to k_v. A record s instantiated by $f(s_1, \ldots, s_n)$ produces an ordered tree where the root is labeled by the constructor f and the ith child is the root of the ith subtree s_i. Syntactically, a model $x \in S(X)$ is a set of ordered trees; the left-hand side of Figure 3 shows the set of ordered trees corresponding to (16) from the previous section. (By convention children are drawn in order from left to right.) Note that every internal node must be labeled by a record constructor and every leaf node must be a value, such as the integer 3. (We treat nullary constructors as user-defined values.)

From this perspective, rewriting procedures must reconcile the legal trees of $S(X')$ with the legal trees of another syntax $S(X)$. Our approach is to preserve subtrees that are common to both syntaxes, while collapsing new types of subtrees from $S(X')$ into arbitrary values. The right side of Figure 3 illustrates this. On one hand, there is a complex **State** record from the ProdNFA domain. The rewriting procedure Λ transforms the root node into an equivalent node in the NFA domain, because the **State** constructor is common to both domains. However, the ID of the **State** record is rooted by a **Pair** node, which does not exist in the NFA domain. This entire subtree is collapsed into a single value $\sigma \in \Sigma_X$, where Σ_X is the set of all values that can appear in the trees of X. The result is a well-typed tree in the original syntax that preserves as much common structure as possible, and disguises foreign subtrees as values. A tree s is *legal* in $S(X)$ if $s \in \Sigma_X$ or s is rooted by the constructor f and its children satisfy the type-constraints of this constructor. Let $Trees(X)$ be the set of all legal finites trees of DSL X, then $S(X) = \mathcal{P}(Trees(X))$ is all finite sets of such trees.

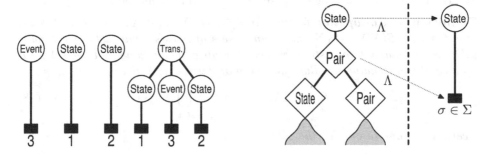

Fig. 3. (Left) Instance of syntax as set of ordered trees, (Right) Action of collapsing morphism Λ on trees

The motivation for this class of rewriting procedures is based on the following observation: Many transformation rules do not require full examination of record structure. Consider the rule for constructing product states; in pseudo-code:

Pattern: **Match** State s_1 from $input_1$, **match** State s_2 from $input_2$.
Action: For every match, **create** State(x) where x = Pair(s_1.id, s_2.id); add it to the output.

This rule uses the IDs to distinguish one state from another and to name product states, but the internal structural of the IDs is not important. Thus, we expect this rule to behave equivalently whether IDs are integers or trees of pairs. In fact, given two ProdNFA models as inputs, the product states could be calculated by first collapsing state IDs into distinct integers and then running the original SProd transformation. At the end replace these integers with their corresponding subtrees to obtain to correct result.

Rewriting procedures of this form do not exist between all pairs $(S(X'), S(X))$. It must be the case that: (1) Record constructors common to both syntaxes have the same arity, though type-constraints can differ. (2) Every legal finite tree in $S(X')$ can be rewritten into a legal finite tree in $S(X)$, taking into account collapsing of foreign subtrees. (3) For every *finite set* of legal finite trees the collapsing action must be in one-to-one correspondence. We formalize this in two parts by first characterizing morphisms over trees, and then generalizing these to finite sets of trees. Let $Cons(X)$ be the set of record constructors for DSL X.

Definition 5. *Collapsing Tree Morphism.* *Given X' and X such that common constructors agree on arity, then a collapsing tree morphism $\lambda : Trees(X') \to Trees(X)$ has the following properties:*

1. *Common values are fixed: $\lambda(s) = s$ if $s = \sigma \in (\Sigma_X \cap \Sigma_{X'})$.*
2. *A tree rooted with a shared constructor is preserved: $\lambda(s) = f(\lambda(s_1), \ldots, \lambda(s_n))$ if $s = f(s_1, \ldots, s_n)$ and $f \in (Cons(X) \cap Cons(X'))$.*
3. *All other trees are collapsed to a value: $\lambda(s) = \sigma$ and $\sigma \in \Sigma_X$ if neither (1) nor (2) apply.*

If collapsing tree morphisms exist, then trees from X' can always be rewritten to X. However, this does not guarantee that distinct trees can always be collapsed into distinct constants, which requires a finite inverse condition.

Definition 6. *Collapsing Morphism.* *Given X' and X, then a collapsing morphism $\Lambda : S(X') \to S(X)$ maps finite sets of trees so that distinct collapsed subtrees are mapped to distinct values. Specifically, applying Λ to a set x' is equivalent to extending a collapsing tree morphism over this set:*

$$\forall x' \in S(X') \; \exists \lambda_{x'}, \quad \Lambda(x') = \bigcup_{s \in x'} \lambda_{x'}(s). \tag{18}$$

Every $\lambda_{x'}$ is one-to-one for the subtrees of x':

$$\forall s_1, s_2 \in x' \; \forall t_1 \sqsubseteq s_1, t_2 \sqsubseteq s_2 \quad (\lambda_{x'}(t_1) = \lambda_{x'}(t_2)) \Rightarrow (t_1 = t_2), \tag{19}$$

where $t \sqsubseteq s$ indicates that t is an ordered subtree of s.

Collapsing morphisms establish global relationships between syntaxes, so it is not surprising that they can often be eliminated from lifted properties. In the interest of space, we present one example of this elimination. Given a DSL X, a counting function $\#f(x)$ counts the number of trees rooted by constructor $f \in Cons(X)$ occurring in the set x. (We already made use of the $\#State$ counting function.)

Theorem 2. Eliminating Rewrites from Counting Functions. *Given a subformula $\#f(\Lambda(x'))$, where $x' \in S(X')$ and Λ is a collapsing morphism from $S(X')$ to $S(X)$:*

$$\#f(\Lambda(x')) = \begin{cases} 0 \text{ if } f \notin Cons(X') \\ \#f(x') \text{ otherwise} \end{cases} \qquad (20)$$

As a final note, we have described unary collapsing morphisms. An arbitrary rewrite Λ is decomposable into a direct product of unary rewrites, so these results generalize immediately.

4.3   Calculating Collapsing Morphisms

We now turn our attention to calculating the set of collapsing morphisms, $CM(X', X)$, between DSLs X' and X. Our algorithm represents $CM(X', X)$ by a mapping from types declared in X' to type declarations compatible with X such that every collapsing tree morphism λ must respect this type map. If the algorithm fails to map every type in X', then no λ exists and $CM(X', X) = \emptyset$. The success of this algorithm guarantees the existence of λ's, but it does not guarantee the existence of a $\Lambda : S(X') \rightarrow S(X)$ satisfying the finite inverse condition. Fortunately, it can be constructively shown that Λ's exist by solving a *maximum bipartite matching problem* between a finite number of trees in $Trees(X')$ and $Trees(X)$.

A type declaration d can be any of the following: (1) A record constructor f: $(T_1, \ldots, T_n)$. (2) A finite enumeration of values e: $\{\sigma_1, \ldots, \sigma_n\}$. (3) A (non-disjoint) union of types u: $T_1 + \ldots + T_n$. Each T_i is the name of some type, and all DSLs share (order-sorted) infinite alphabets of values, e.g. $T_{integer}$, T_{string}. The type T_{basic} is the set of all values. Every type accepts a set of ordered trees, denoted $Trees(T)$. In our algorithms we use the fact that inclusion and equality testing between types is decidable and the type system is closed under union, intersection, and complement. In fact, every type is equivalent to a *tree automaton* that accepts exactly the set $Trees(T)$, so operations on types correspond to operations on tree automata [24]. (The details of tree automata algorithms are outside the scope of this paper.) Algorithm 1 tries to build a re-declaration map, called *redecl*, from type names in X' to declarations/alphabets compatible with X.

If Algorithm 1 succeeds, then *redecl* characterizes how every collapsing tree morphism behaves. Algorithm 2 ensures that the finite inverse condition can hold by checking if an invertible λ exists even under worst case conditions. The algorithm constructs a matching problem whenever a finite non-enumeration type T' must collapse into another finite type T. It succeeds if this matching

---

Algorithm 1. Compute Re-declaration Map

1: **for all** $f' \in (Cons(X') - Cons(X))$ **do**
2:    **update** $redecl(T_{f'}) := T_{\mathsf{basic}}$
3: **for all** $T' \in Types(X')$ where $T' \subseteq T_{\mathsf{basic}}$ **do**
4:    **if** T' is declared to be a finite enumeration $e' : \{\sigma_1, \ldots, \sigma_n\}$ **then**
5:       **update** $redecl(T') := e : \{\sigma_1, \ldots, \sigma_n\}$
6:    **else**
7:       **update** $redecl(T') := T_a$ // T' must be a built-in alphabet T_a
8: **for all** $f \in (Cons(X') \cap Cons(X))$ **do**
9:    **lookup** declarations $d' = f : (T'_1, \ldots, T'_n)$ and $d = f : (T_1, \ldots, T_n)$
10:    **for all** pairs (T'_i, T_i) **do**
11:       **for all** $T'' \in Types(X')$ where $T'' \subseteq T'_i$ and $T'' \not\subseteq T_i$ **do**
12:          **if** $T'' \subseteq T_{\mathsf{basic}}$ or $T'' = T_g$ where $g \in (Cons(X') \cap Cons(X))$ **then**
13:             **return false**
14:          **else if** $T'' = T_{g'}$ where $g' \in (Cons(X') - Cons(X))$ **then**
15:             **let** $T_{old} = redecl(T_{g'})$
16:                **update** $redecl(T_{g'}) := (T_{old} \cap T_i)$
17: **return true**

---

problem has a perfect matching, which is decidable in polynomial time (e.g. via the *Hopcroft-Karp* algorithm [25]). Note that $Values(X')$ is the set of all values that could appear as an argument to any constructor of X'. A full complexity analysis is outside the scope of this paper. However, the following theorem is immediate from the algorithm:

Algorithm 2. Check Finite Inverses

1: **update** $match := \{\}$ // Initialize a map called $match$ to the empty map.
2: **for all** (T', T) where $redecl(T') = T$ **do**
3:    **if** $|T'| > |T|$ **then**
4:       **return false**
5:    **if** T' is a finite non-enumeration type and T is a finite enumeration **then**
6:       **for** $s \in Trees(T')$ **do**
7:          **if** s is not in the domain of $match$ **then**
8:             **update** $match(s) := (Trees(T) - Values(X'))$
9:          **else**
10:             **let** $match_{old} = match(s)$
11:                **update** $match(s) := (Trees(T) \cap match_{old})$
12: **return** HasPerfectMatching($match$)

Theorem 3. *Construction of Collapsing Morphisms. The set of collapsing tree morphisms $CM(X', X)$ can be characterized with a polynomial number of type comparisons (e.g. tree automata operations) and a maximum bipartite matching problem of size $c(|Types(X')| + |Types(X)|)$ where c is the size of the largest finite enumeration.*

Surprisingly, the calculation of collapsing morphisms is the primary task to check if τ' lifts τ. After $CM(X', X)$ is calculated, static analysis determines if the diagram in Figure 1 commutes. This verification can be accomplished fairly easily, because the compiler knows that τ' and τ were generated by the same rule set. Static analysis examines the interpretation of each rule in the new and original contexts, and checks if any rule patterns are sensitive to the choice of Λ. All FORMULA rules are strongly typed during compile time, so a simple type comparison is required to test if a pattern might be sensitive to this choice.

5 Conclusion

We presented a novel framework for deciding if a reused transformation preserves properties. The key idea is to relate a reused transformation with its original version through an automatically deducible rewriting procedure. A reused transformation preserves compatible properties if it is behaviorally equivalent to a rewrite followed by the original transformation. We formalized a class of useful rewriting procedures, called collapsing morphisms, which can be automatically derived. Furthermore, properties lifted using collapsing morphisms are amenable to automatic elimination of rewrites. These procedures have been implemented in our FORMULA framework.

References

1. Jackson, E.K., Sztipanovits, J.: Formalizing the structural semantics of domain-specific modeling languages. Software and Systems Modeling (2008)
2. Jackson, E.K., Seifert, D., Dahlweid, M., Santen, T., Bjørner, N., Schulte, W.: Specifying and composing non-functional requirements in model-based development. In: Bergel, A., Fabry, J. (eds.) Software Composition. LNCS, vol. 5634, pp. 72–89. Springer, Heidelberg (2009)
3. Schürr, A.: Specification of graph translators with triple graph grammars. In: Mayr, E.W., Schmidt, G., Tinhofer, G. (eds.) WG 1994. LNCS, vol. 903, pp. 151–163. Springer, Heidelberg (1995)
4. Varró, D., Balogh, A.: The model transformation language of the VIATRA2 framework. Science of Computer Programming 68(3), 214–234 (2007)
5. Mens, T., Gorp, P.V.: A taxonomy of model transformation. Electr. Notes Theor. Comput. Sci. 152, 125–142 (2006)
6. Taentzer, G.: AGG: A tool environment for algebraic graph transformation. In: Münch, M., Nagl, M. (eds.) AGTIVE 1999. LNCS, vol. 1779, pp. 481–488. Springer, Heidelberg (2000)
7. Schmidt, D.C.: Guest editor's introduction: Model-driven engineering. IEEE Computer 39(2), 25–31 (2006)
8. de Lara, J., Vangheluwe, H.: Defining visual notations and their manipulation through meta-modelling and graph transformation. J. Vis. Lang. Comput. 15(3-4), 309–330 (2004)
9. Ehrig, H., Ehrig, K., Ermel, C.: Evolution of model transformations by model refactoring. In: Proceedings of the Eighth International Workshop on Graph Transformation and Visual Modeling Techniques, GT-VMT 2009 (2009)

10. Levendovszky, T., Balasubramanian, D., Narayanan, A., Karsai, G.: A novel approach to semi-automated evolution of dsml model transformation. In: 2nd International Conference on Software Language Engineering, SLE (2009)
11. Meertens, L.: Paramorphisms. Formal Aspects of Computing 4, 413–424 (1992)
12. Meijer, E., Fokkinga, M.M., Paterson, R.: Functional programming with bananas, lenses, envelopes and barbed wire. In: FPCA, pp. 124–144 (1991)
13. Achatz, K., Schulte, W.: Massive parallelization of divide-and-conquer algorithms over powerlists. Sci. Comput. Program. 26(1-3), 59–78 (1996)
14. Narayanan, A., Karsai, G.: Towards verifying model transformations. Electr. Notes Theor. Comput. Sci. 211, 191–200 (2008)
15. Varró, D.: Automated formal verification of visual modeling languages by model checking. Journal of Software and Systems Modeling 3(2), 85–113 (2004)
16. Ehrig, H., Ermel, C.: Semantical correctness and completeness of model transformations using graph and rule transformation. In: Ehrig, H., Heckel, R., Rozenberg, G., Taentzer, G. (eds.) ICGT 2008. LNCS, vol. 5214, pp. 194–210. Springer, Heidelberg (2008)
17. Bisztray, D., Heckel, R., Ehrig, H.: Verification of architectural refactorings by rule extraction. In: Fiadeiro, J.L., Inverardi, P. (eds.) FASE 2008. LNCS, vol. 4961, pp. 347–361. Springer, Heidelberg (2008)
18. Bisztray, D., Heckel, R., Ehrig, H.: Compositionality of model transformations. Electr. Notes Theor. Comput. Sci. 236, 5–19 (2009)
19. Balasubramanian, D., Narayanan, A., van Buskirk, C.P., Karsai, G.: The Graph Rewriting and Transformation Language: GReAT. ECEASST 1 (2006)
20. de Lara, J., Guerra, E.: Pattern-based model-to-model transformation. In: Ehrig, H., Heckel, R., Rozenberg, G., Taentzer, G. (eds.) ICGT 2008. LNCS, vol. 5214, pp. 426–441. Springer, Heidelberg (2008)
21. Rivera, J.E., Guerra, E., de Lara, J., Vallecillo, A.: Analyzing rule-based behavioral semantics of visual modeling languages with maude. In: Gašević, D., Lämmel, R., Van Wyk, E. (eds.) SLE 2008. LNCS, vol. 5452, pp. 54–73. Springer, Heidelberg (2009)
22. Cortellessa, V., Gregorio, S.D., Marco, A.D.: Using atl for transformations in software performance engineering: a step ahead of java-based transformations? In: WOSP, pp. 127–132 (2008)
23. Grönniger, H., Krahn, H., Rumpe, B., Schindler, M., Völkel, S.: Monticore: a framework for the development of textual domain specific languages. In: ICSE Companion, pp. 925–926 (2008)
24. Comon, H., Dauchet, M., Gilleron, R., Löding, C., Jacquemard, F., Lugiez, D., Tison, S., Tommasi, M.: Tree automata techniques and applications, http://www.grappa.univ-lille3.fr/tata (2007) (release October 12, 2007)
25. Hopcroft, J.E., Karp, R.M.: An $n^{5/2}$ algorithm for maximum matchings in bipartite graphs. SIAM J. Comput. 2(4), 225–231 (1973)

Are Popular Classes More Defect Prone?

Alberto Bacchelli, Marco D'Ambros, and Michele Lanza

REVEAL @ Faculty of Informatics - University of Lugano, Switzerland

Abstract. Traces of the evolution of software systems are left in a number of different repositories, such as configuration management systems, bug tracking systems, and mailing lists. Developers use e-mails to discuss issues ranging from low-level concerns (bug fixes, refactorings) to high-level resolutions (future planning, design decisions). Thus, e-mail archives constitute a valuable asset for understanding the evolutionary dynamics of a system.

We introduce metrics that measure the "popularity" of source code artifacts, *i.e.*, the amount of discussion they generate in e-mail archives, and investigate whether the information contained in e-mail archives is correlated to the defects found in the system. Our hypothesis is that developers discuss problematic entities more than unproblematic ones. We also study whether the precision of existing techniques for defect prediction can be improved using our popularity metrics.

1 Introduction

Knowing the location of future defects allows project managers to optimize the resources available for the maintenance of a software project by focusing on the problematic components. However, performing defect prediction with enough precision to produce useful results is a challenging problem. Researchers have proposed a number of approaches to predict software defects, exploiting various sources of information, such as source code metrics [1,2,3,4,5], code churn [6], process metrics extracted from versioning system repositories [7,8], and past defects [9,10]. A source of information for defect prediction that was not exploited so far are development mailing lists.

Due to the increasing extent and complexity of software systems, it is common to see large teams, or even communities, of developers working on the same project in a collaborative fashion. In such cases e-mails are the favorite media for the coordination between all the participants. Mailing lists, which are preferred over person-to-person e-mails, store the history of inter-developers, inter-users, and developers-to-users discussions: Issues range from low-level decisions (*e.g.*, bug fixing, implementation issues) up to high-level considerations (*e.g.*, design rationales, future planning).

Development mailing lists of open source projects are easily accessible and they contain information that can be exploited to support a number of activities. For example, the understanding of software systems can be improved by adding sparse explanations enclosed in e-mails [11]; the rationale behind the system design can be extracted from the discussions that took place before the actual implementation [12]; the impact of changes done on the source code can be assessed by analyzing the effect on the mailing

D.S. Rosenblum and G. Taentzer (Eds.): FASE 2010, LNCS 6013, pp. 59–73, 2010.

list [13]; the behavior of developers can be analyzed to verify if changes follow discussion, or vice-versa; hidden coupling of entities that are not related at code level can be discovered if often mentioned together in discussions.

One of the challenges when dealing with mailing lists as a source of information is to correctly link an e-mail to the source code entities it discusses. In previous work we specifically tackled this issue [14], and using a benchmark of a statistically significant size, we showed that lightweight grep-based techniques reach an acceptable level of precision in the linking task.

Why would one want to use e-mails for defect prediction? The source code of software systems is only written by developers, who must follow a rigid and terse syntax to define abstractions they want to include. On the other hand of the spectrum, mailing lists, even those specifically devoted to development, archive e-mails written by both programmers and users. Thus, the entities discussed are not only the most relevant from a development point of view, but also the most exploited during the use of a software system. In addition, e-mail are written using natural language. This does not require the writer to carefully explain all the abstractions using the same level of importance, but easily permits to generalize some concepts and focus on others. For this reason, we expect information we extract from mailing lists to be independent from those provided by the source code analysis. Thus, they can add valuable information to software analysis.

We present "popularity" metrics that express the importance of each source code entity in discussions taking place in development mailing lists. Our hypothesis is that such metrics are an indicator of possible flaws in software components, thus being correlated with the number of defects. We aim at answering the following research questions:

- *Q1: Does the popularity of software components in discussions correlate with software defects?*
- *Q2: Is a regression model based on the popularity metrics a good predictor for software defects?*
- *Q3: Does the addition of popularity metrics improve the prediction performance of existing defect prediction techniques?*

We provide the answers to these questions by validating our approach on four different open source software systems.

2 Methodology

Our goal is first to inspect whether popularity metrics correlate with software defects, and to study whther existing bug prediction approaches can be improved using such metrics. To do so, we follow the methodology depicted in Figure 1:

   - We extract e-mail data, link it with source code entities and compute popularity metrics. We extract and evaluate source code and change metrics.

   - We extract defect data from issue repositories and we quantify the correlation of popularity metrics with software defects, using as baseline the correlation between source code metrics and software defects.

   - We build regression models with popularity metrics as independent variables and the number of post-release defects as the dependent variable. We evaluate the performance of the models using the Spearman's correlation between the predicted and the

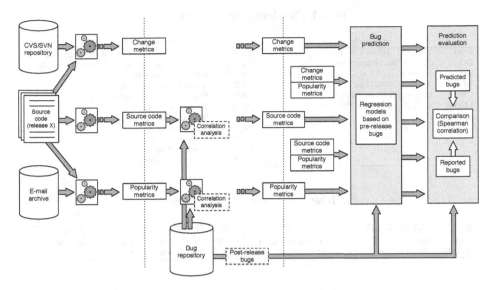

Fig. 1. Overall schema of our approach

reported bugs. We create regression models based on source code metrics [3,4,5,10] and change metrics [7,8] alone, and later enrich these sets of metrics with popularity metrics, to measure the improvement given by the popularity metrics.

Modeling. Using the tool inFusion[1], we extract FAMIX-compliant object-oriented models of the source code of the systems we want to analyze. FAMIX is a language independent meta-model of object oriented code [15].

Computing Source Code Metrics. Once we obtain the FAMIX model of a software system, we compute a catalog of object oriented metrics, listed in Table 1. The catalog includes the Chidamber and Kemerer (CK) metrics suite [16], which was already used for bug prediction [1,17,3,4], and additional object oriented metrics.

Computing Change Metrics. Change metrics are "process metrics" extracted from versioning system log files (CVS and SVN in our experiments). Differently from source code metrics which measure several aspects of the source code, change metrics are measures of how the code was developed over time. We use the set of change metrics listed in Table 2, which is a subset of the ones used in [7].

To use change metrics in our experiments, we need to link them with source code entities, *i.e.,* classes. We do that by comparing the versioning system filename, including the directory path, with the full class name, including the class path. Due to the file-based nature of SVN and CVS and to the fact that Java inner classes are defined in the same file as their containing class, several classes might point to the same CVS/SVN file. For this reason, we do not consider inner Java classes.

---

[1] http://www.intooitus.com/inFusion.html

Table 1. Class level source code metrics

CK metrics		Other OO Metrics	
WMC	Weighted Method Count	FanIn	Number of other classes that reference the class
DIT	Depth of Inheritance Tree	FanOut	Number of other classes referenced by the class
RFC	Response For Class	NOA	Number of attributes
NOC	Number Of Children	NOPA	Number of public attributes
CBO	Coupling Between Objects	NOPRA	Number of private attributes
LCOM	Lack of Cohesion in Methods	NOAI	Number of attributes inherited
		LOC	Number of lines of code
		NOM	Number of methods
		NOPM	Number of public methods
		NOPRM	Number of private methods
		NOMI	Number of methods inherited

Table 2. Class level change metrics

NR	Number of revisions	NREF	Number of times file has been refactored
NFIX	Number of times file was involved in bug-fixing	NAUTH	Number of authors who committed the file
CHGSET	Change set size (maximum and average)	AGE	Age of a file

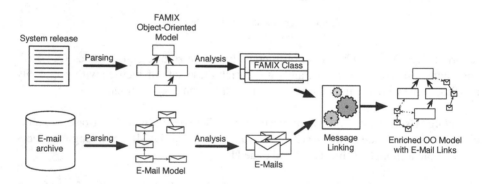

Fig. 2. Linking mails and classes

Computing Popularity Metrics. The extraction of popularity metrics, given a software system and its mailing lists, is done in two steps: First it is necessary to link each class with all the e-mails discussing it, then the metrics must be computed using the links obtained. In the following, we briefly present the technique to link e-mails to classes, then we discuss the popularity metrics we propose to answer our research questions. Figure 2 shows the process used to prepare the data for evaluating the popularity metrics.

First, we parse the target e-mail archive to build a model according to an e-mail meta-model we previously defined [14]. We model body and headers, plus additional data about the inter messages relationships, *i.e.,* thread details. Then, we analyze the FAMIX model of the target source code release to obtain the representation of all the classes. Subsequently, we link each class with any e-mail referring it, using lightweight linking techniques based on regular expressions, whose effectiveness was validated in a previous work [14]. We obtain an object-oriented FAMIX model enriched with all the connections and information about classes stored in the e-mail archive. Through this model we can extract the following popularity metrics:

POP-NOM (Number of E-Mails): To associate the popularity of a class with discussions in mailing lists, we count the number of mails that are mentioning it. Since we are considering development mailing lists, we presume that classes are mainly mentioned in discussions about failure reporting, bug fixing and feature enhancements, thus they can be related to defects. Thanks to the enriched FAMIX model we generate, it is simple to compute this metric. Once the mapping from classes to e-mails is completed, and the model contains the links, we count the number of links of each class.

POP-NOCM (Number of Characters in Mails): Development mailing lists can also contain other topics than technical discussions. For example, while manually inspecting part of our dataset, we noticed that voting about whether and when to release a new version occurs quite frequently in Lucene, Maven and Jackrabbit mailing lists. Equally, announcements take place with a certain frequency. Usually this kind of messages are characterized by a short content (*e.g.,* "yes" or "no" for voting, "congratulations" for announcements). The intuition is that e-mails discussing flaws in the source code could present a longer amount of text than mails about other topics. We consider the length of messages taking into account the number of characters in the text of mails: We evaluate the POP-NOCM metric by adding the number of characters in all the e-mails related to the chosen class.

POP-NOT (Number of Threads): In mailing lists discussions are divided in *threads*. Our hypothesis is that all the messages that form thread discuss the same topic: If an author wants to start talking about a different subject she can create a new thread. We suppose that if developers are talking about one defect in a class they will continue talking about it in the same thread. If they want to discuss about an unrelated or new defect (even in the same classes) they would open a new thread. The number of threads, then, could be a popularity metric whose value is related to the number of defects. After extracting e-mails from mailing lists, our e-mail model also contains the information about threads. Once the related mails are available in the object-oriented model, we retrieve this thread information from the messages related to each class and count the number of different threads. If two, or more, e-mails related to the same class are part of the same thread, they are counted as one.

POP-NOMT (Number of Mails in Threads): Inspecting sample e-mails from the mailing lists which form our experiment, we noticed that short threads are often characteristic of "announcements" e-mails, simple e-mails about technical issues experimented by new users of the systems, or updates about the status of developers. We hypothesize that longer threads could be symptom of discussions about questions that raise the interest of the developers, such as those about defects, bugs or changes in the code. For each class in the source code, we consider the thread of all the referring mails, and we count the total number of mails in each thread. If a thread is composed by more than one e-mail, but only one is referring the class, we still count all the e-mails inside the thread, since it is possible that following e-mails reference the same class implicitly.

POP-NOA (Number of Authors): A high number of authors talking about the same class suggests that it is subject to broad discussions. For example, a class frequently mentioned by different users can hide design flaws or stability problems. Also, a class discussed by many developers might be not well-defined, comprehensible, or correct,

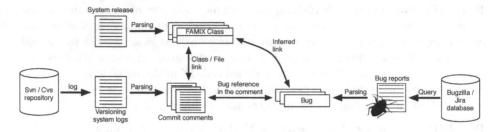

Fig. 3. Linking bugs, SCM files and classes

thus more defect prone. For each class, we count the number of authors that wrote in referring mails (*i.e.,* if the same author wrote two, or more, e-mails, we count only one).

Extracting Bug Information. To measure the correlation of metrics with software defects, and to perform defect prediction, we need to link each problem report to any class of the system that it affects. We link FAMIX classes with versioning system files, as we did to compute change metrics, and the files with bugs retrieved from a Bugzilla[2], or Jira[3], repository. Figure 3 shows the bug linking process.

A file version in the versioning system contains a developer comment written at commit time, which often includes a reference to a problem report (*e.g.,* "fixed bug 123"). Such references allow us to link problem reports with files in the versioning system, and therefore with source code artifacts, *i.e.,* classes. However, the link between a CVS/SVN file and a Bugzilla/Jira problem report is not formally defined, and to find a reference to the problem report id we use pattern matching techniques on the developer comments, a widely adopted technique [18,10]. Once we have established the link between a problem report and a file version, we verify that the bug has been reported before the commit time of the file version.

To measure the correlation between metrics and defects we consider all the defects, while for bug prediction only post-release defects, *i.e.,* the ones reported within a six months time interval after the considered release of the software system[4]. The output of the bug linking process is, for each class of the considered release, the total number of defects and the number of post-release defects.

3 Experiments

We conducted our experiment on the software systems depicted in Table 3.

We considered systems that deal with different domains and have distinct characteristics (*e.g.,* popularity, number of classes, e-mails, and defects) to mitigate some of the threats to external validity. These systems are stable projects, under active development, and have a history with several major releases. All are written in Java to ensure that all the code metrics are defined identically for each system. By using the same

---

[2] http://www.bugzilla.org
[3] http://www.atlassian.com/software/jira
[4] Six months for post release defects was also used by Zimmermann *et al.* [10].

Table 3. Dataset

System URL	Description	Classes	Mailing lists			Bug Tracking Systems	
			Creation	E-Mails		Time period	Number of defects
				Total	Linked		
Equinox eclipse.org/equinox	Plugin system for the Eclipse project	439	Feb 2003	5,575	2,383	Feb 2003 - Jun 2008	1,554
Jackrabbit jackrabbit.apache.org	Implementation of the Content Repository for Java Technology API (JCR)	1,913	Sep 2004	11,901	3,358	Sep 2004 - Dec 2008	674
						Sep 2004 - Aug 2009	975
Lucene lucene.apache.org	Text search engine library	1,279	Sep 2001	17,537	8,800	Oct 2001 - May 2008	751
						Oct 2001 - Sep 2009	1,274
Maven maven.apache.org	Tool for build automation and management of Java projects	301	Nov 2002	65,601	4,616	Apr 2004 - Sep 2008	507
						Apr 2004 - Aug 2009	616

parser, we can avoid issues due to behavior differences in parsing, a known issue for reverse engineering tools [19].

Public development mailing lists used to discuss technical issues are available for all the systems, and are separated from lists specifically thought for system user issues. We consider e-mails starting from the creation of each mailing list until the date of each release considered. Messages automatically generated by bug tracking and revision control systems are filtered out, and we report the resulting number of e-mails and the number of those referring to classes according to our linking techniques. All systems have public bug tracking systems, that were usually created along with the mailing lists.

3.1 Correlations Analysis

To answer the research question Q1 "*Does the popularity of software components correlate with software defects?*", we compute the correlation between class level popularity metrics and the number of defects per class. We compute the correlation in terms of both the *Pearson's* and the *Spearman's* correlation coefficient (r_{prs} and r_{spm}, respectively). The Spearman's rank correlation test is a non-parametric test that uses ranks of sample data consisting of matched pairs. The correlation coefficient varies from 1, *i.e.*, ranks are identical, to -1, *i.e.*, ranks are the opposite, where 0 indicates no correlation. Contrarily to Pearson's correlation, Spearman's one is less sensitive to bias due to outliers and does not require data to be metrically scaled or of normality assumptions [20]. Including the Pearson's correlation coefficient augment the understanding about the results: If r_{spm} is higher than r_{prs}, we might conclude that the variables are consistently correlated, but not in a linear fashion. If the two coefficients are very similar and different from zero, there is indication of a linear relationship. Finally, if the r_{prs} value is significantly higher than r_{spm}, we can deduce that there are outliers inside the dataset. This information first helps us to discover threats to construct validity, then put in evidence single elements that are heavily related. For example, a high r_{prs} can indicate that, among the classes with the highest number of bugs, we can find also the classes with the highest number of related e-mails.

We compute the correlation between class level source code metrics and number of defects per class, in order to compare the correlation to a broadly used baseline. For lack of space we only show the correlation for the source code metric LOC, as previous research showed that it is one of the best metrics for defect prediction [4,21,22,23].

Table 4. Correlation coefficients

System	POP-NOM		POP-NOCM		POP-NOT		POP-NOTM		POP-NOA		LOC	
	r_{spm}	r_{prs}	r_{spm}	r_{prs}	r_{spm}	r_{prs}	r_{spm}	r_{prs}	r_{spm}	r_{prs}	r_{spm}	r_{prs}
Equinox	.52	.51	.52	.42	**.53**	**.54**	.52	.48	.53	.50	.73	.80
Jackrabbit	.23	.35	.22	.36	**.24**	**.36**	.23	-.02	.23	.34	.27	.54
Lucene	.41	.63	.38	.57	.41	.57	**.42**	**.68**	.41	.54	.17	.38
Maven	.44	.81	.39	.78	**.46**	.78	.44	**.81**	.45	.78	.55	.78

Table 4 shows the correlation coefficients between the different popularity metrics and the number of bugs of each system.

We put in bold the highest values achived for both r_{spm} and r_{prs}, by system. Results provides evidence that the two metrics are rank correlated, and correlations over 0.4 are considered to be strong in fault prediction studies [24]. The Spearman correlation coefficients in our study exceed this value for three systems, *i.e.*, Equinox, Lucene, and Maven. In the case of Jackrabbit, the maximum coefficient is 0.24, which is similar to value reached using LOC. The best performing popularity metric depends on the software system: for example in Lucene, POP-NOTM, which counts the length of threads containing e-mails about the classes, is the best choice, while POP-NOT, number of threads containing at least one e-mail about the classes, is the best performing for other systems.

3.2 Defect Prediction

To answer the research question Q2 "*Is a regression model based on the popularity metrics a good predictor for software defects?*" , we create and evaluate regression models in which the independent variables are the class level popularity metrics, while the dependent variable is the number of post-release defects per class. We create regression models based on source code metrics and change metrics alone, as well as models in which these metrics are enriched with popularity metrics, where the dependent variable is always the number of post-release defects per class. We then compare the prediction performances of such models to answer research question Q3 "*Does the addition of popularity metrics improve the prediction performance of existing defect prediction techniques?*" We follow the methodology proposed by Nagappan *et al.* [5] and also used by Zimmermann *et al.* [24], consisting of: Principal component analysis, building regression models, evaluating explanative power and evaluating prediction power.

Principal Component Analysis is a standard statistical technique to avoid the problem of multicollinearity among the independent variables. This problem comes from intercorrelations amongst these variables and can lead to an inflated variance in the estimation of the dependent variable. We do not build the regression models using the actual variables as independent variables, but instead we use sets of principal components (PC). PC are independent and do not suffer from multicollinearity, while at the same time they account for as much sample variance as possible. We select sets of PC that account for a cumulative sample variance of at least 95%.

Building Regression Models. To evaluate the predictive power of the regression models we do cross-validation: We use 90% of the dataset, *i.e.,* 90% of the classes (training set), to build the prediction model, and the remaining 10% of the dataset (validation set) to evaluate the efficacy of the built model. For each model we perform 50 "folds", *i.e.,* we create 50 random 90%-10% splits of the data.

Evaluating Explanative Power. To evaluate the explanative power of the regression models we use the adjusted R^2 coefficient. The (non-adjusted) R^2 is the ratio of the regression sum of squares to the total sum of squares. R^2 ranges from 0 to 1, and the higher the value is, the more variability is explained by the model, *i.e.,* the better the explanative power of the model is. The adjusted R^2, takes into account the degrees of freedom of the independent variables and the sample population. As a consequence, it is consistenly lower than R^2. When reporting results, we only mention the adjusted R^2. We test the statistical significance of the regression models using the F-test. All our regression models are significant at the 99% level ($p < 0.01$).

Evaluating Prediction Power. To evaluate the predictive power of the regression models, we compute Spearman's correlation between the predicted number of post-release defects and the actual number. Such evaluation approach has been broadly used to assess the predictive power of a number of predictors [21,22,23]. In the cross-validation, for each random split, we use the training set (90% of the dataset) to build the regression model, and then we apply the obtained model on the validation set (10% of the dataset), producing for each class the predicted number of post-release defects. Then, to evaluate the performance of the performed prediction, we compute Spearman's correlation, on the validation set, between the lists of classes ranked according to the predicted and actual number of post-release defects. Since we perform 50 folds cross-validation, the final values of the Spearman's correlation and adjusted R^2 are averages over 50 folds.

Results. Table 5 displays the results we obtained for the defect prediction, considering both R^2 adjusted values and Spearman's correlation coefficients.

The first row shows the results achieved using all the popularity metrics defined in Section 2. In the following four blocks, we report the prediction results obtained through the source code and change metrics, first alone, then by incorporating each single popularity metric, and finally incorporating all the popularity metrics. For each system and block of metrics, when popularity metrics augment the results of other metrics, we put in bold the highest value reached.

Analyzing the results of the sole popularity metrics, we notice that, in terms of correlation, Equinox and Maven still present a strong correlation, *i.e.,* higher than .40, while Lucene is less correlated. The popularity metrics alone are not sufficient for performing predictions in the Jackrabbit system. Looking at the results obtained by using all the metrics, we first note that Jackrabbit's results are much lower if compared to those reached in other systems, especially for the R^2, and partly for the R_{spm}. Only change metrics reach a good R_{spm} value in this system.

Going back to the other systems, the R^2 adjusted values are always increased and the best results are achieved when using all popularity metrics together. The increase, with respect to the other metrics, varies from 2%, when other metrics already reach high values, up to 107%. Spearman's coefficients also increase by using the information

Table 5. Defect prediction results

Metrics	$R^2 adj$					$R_{spearman}$				
	Equinox	Jackrabbit	Lucene	Maven	Avg	Equinox	Jackrabbit	Lucene	Maven	Avg
All Popularity Metrics	.23	.00	.31	.55	.27	.43	.04	.27	.52	.32
All Change Metrics	.55	.06	.43	.71	.44	.54	.30	.36	.62	.45
All C.M. + POP-NOM	.56	.06	.43	.71	.44	.53	**.32**	.38	**.69**	**.48**
All C.M. + POP-NOCM	.58	.06	.43	.70	.44	.57	.31	**.43**	.60	.48
All C.M. + POP-NOT	.56	.06	.43	.71	.44	.54	.31	.39	.59	.46
All C.M. + POP-NOMT	.56	.06	.43	.70	.44	.53	.29	.41	.60	.46
All C.M. + POP-NOA	.56	.06	.43	.70	.44	**.58**	.29	.37	.43	.42
All C.M. + All POP	**.61**	**.06**	**.45**	**.71**	**.46**	.52	.30	.38	.43	.42
Improvement	*11%*	*0%*	*+5%*	*0%*	*+4%*	*+7%*	*+7%*	*+19%*	*+11%*	*+11%*
Source Code Metrics	.61	.03	.27	.42	.33	.51	.17	.31	.52	.38
S.C.M. + POP-NOM	.62	.03	.33	.59	.39	.53	.14	.35	.52	.38
S.C.M. + POP-NOCM	.62	**.04**	.32	.56	.38	.51	.15	.36	.60	.41
S.C.M. + POP-NOT	.61	.03	.31	.57	.38	.49	.15	**.38**	.52	.38
S.C.M. + POP-NOMT	.62	.03	.35	.60	.40	.55	.14	.33	.43	.36
S.C.M. + POP-NOA	.61	.04	.30	.56	.38	.53	.12	.38	**.70**	**.43**
S.C.M. + All POP	**.62**	.03	**.37**	**.61**	**.41**	**.58**	.14	.32	.52	.39
Improvement	*+2%*	*+25%*	*+37%*	*+45%*	*+27%*	*+14%*	*-12%*	*+23%*	*+35%*	*+15%*
CK Metrics	.54	.01	.39	.28	.31	.51	.13	.36	.60	.40
CK + POP-NOM	.56	.02	.40	.54	.38	.48	.13	.35	**.69**	**.41**
CK + POP-NOCM	.57	.02	.40	.50	.37	.50	**.17**	.33	.42	.35
CK + POP-NOT	.56	.01	.40	.51	.37	**.53**	.13	.34	.52	.38
CK + POP-NOMT	.57	.01	.40	.56	.39	.52	.14	.25	.49	.35
CK + POP-NOA	.56	.02	.40	.51	.37	.52	.14	**.41**	.53	.40
CK + All POP	**.57**	**.02**	**.42**	**.58**	**.40**	.51	.16	.30	.52	.37
Improvement	*+6%*	*+50%*	*+8%*	*+107%*	*+43%*	*+4%*	*+31%*	*+14%*	*+15%*	*+16%*
All Source Code Metrics	.66	.04	.44	.45	.40	.48	.15	.35	.36	.33
All S.C.M. + POP-NOM	.67	.04	.45	.60	.44	**.59**	.15	.34	**.62**	**.43**
All S.C.M. + POP-NOCM	.66	.04	.45	.56	.43	.51	.16	.30	.31	.32
All S.C.M. + POP-NOT	.66	.04	.44	.57	.43	.50	.14	**.35**	.52	.38
All S.C.M. + POP-NOMT	.67	.04	.44	.62	.44	.53	.14	.35	.34	.34
All S.C.M. + POP-NOA	.66	.04	.44	.57	.43	.51	.15	.34	.43	.36
All S.C.M. + All POP	**.67**	.04	**.46**	**.63**	**.45**	.51	**.16**	.33	.52	.38
Improvement	*+2%*	*0%*	*+5%*	*+40%*	*+12%*	*+23%*	*+7%*	*+0%*	*+72%*	*+26%*

given by popularity metrics: Their values augment, on average, more than fifteen percent. However, there is not a single popularity metric that outperforms the others, and their union does not always give the best results.

4   Discussion

Popularity of software components do correlate with software defects. Three software systems out of four show a strong rank correlation, *i.e.,* coefficients ranging from .42 to .53, between defects of software components and their popularity in e-mail discussions. Only Jackrabbit is less rank correlated with a coefficient of .23.

Popularity can predict software defects, but without major improvements over previously established techniques. In the second part of our results, consistently with the correlation analysis, the quality of predictions done by Jackrabbit using popularity metrics are extremely low, both for the R^2 adjusted values and for the Spearman's correlation coefficients. On the contrary, our popularity metrics applied to the other three systems lead to different results: Popularity metrics are able to predict defects. However, if used alone, they do not compete with the results obtained through other metrics. The best average results are shown by the Change Metrics, corroborating previous works stating the quality of such predictors [7,8].

Popularity metrics do improve prediction performances of existing defect prediction techniques. The strongest results are obtained integrating the popularity information into other techniques. This creates more reliable and complete predictors that significantly increase the overall results: The improvements on correlation coefficients are, on average, more than fifteen percent higher, with peaks over 30% and reaching the top value of 72%, to those obtained without popularity metrics. This corroborates our initial assumption that popularity metrics measure an aspect of the development process that is different from those captured by other techniques. Our results put in evidence that, given the considerable difference of the prediction performance across different software projects, bug prediction techniques that exploit popularity metrics should not be applied in a "black box" way. As suggested by Nagappan *et al.* [5], the prediction approach should be first validated on the history of a software project, to see which metrics work best for predictions for the system.

5   Threats to Validity

Threats to construct validity. A first construct validity threat concerns the way we link bugs with versioning system files and subsequently with classes. In fact, the pattern matching technique we use to detect bug references in commit comments does not guarantee that all the links are retrieved. We also made the assumption that commit comments do contain bug fixing information, which limits the application of our bug linking approach only to software projects where this convention is used. Finally, a commit that is referring to a bug can also contain modifications to files that are unrelated to the bug. However, this technique is the current state of the art in linking bugs to versioning system files, widely used in literature [18]. The noise affecting issue repositories constitutes another construct validity threat: Even though we carefully removed all the issue reports not marked as "bug" (*e.g.,* "New Feature", "Improvement", "Task") from our dataset, Antoniol *et al.* showed that a relevant fraction of issues marked as "bugs" in Bugzilla (according to their severity) are not actually related to corrective maintenance [25]. As part of our future work, we plan to apply the approach proposed by Antoniol *et al.* to filter "non bugs" out. Another threat concerns the procedure for linking e-mails to discussed classes. We use linking techniques whose effectiveness was measured [14], and it is known that they cannot produce a perfect linking. The enriched object-oriented model can contain wrongly reported links or miss connections that are present. We alleviated this problem manually inspecting all the classes that showed an uncommon number of links, *i.e.,* outliers, and, whenever necessary, adjusted the regular expressions composing the linking techniques to correctly handle such unexpected situations. We removed from our dataset any e-mail automatically generated by the bug tracking system and the revision control system, because they could bias the results.

Threats to statistical conclusion validity. In our experiments all the Spearman correlation coefficients and all the regression models were significant at the 99% level.

Threats to external validity. In our approach we analyze only open-source software projects, however the development in industrial environment may differ and conduct to different comportments in the developers, thus to different results. Another external validity threat concerns the language: all the software systems are developed in Java. Although this alleviates parsing bias, communities using other languages could have different developer cultures and the style of e-mails can vary. To obtain a better generalization of the results, in our future work, we plan to apply our approach to industrial systems and other object-oriented languages.

6 Related Work

Mining Data From E-Mail Archives. Li *et al.* first introduced the idea of using the information stored in the mailing lists as an additional predictor for finding defects in software systems [26]. They conducted a case study on a single software system, used a number of previously known predictors and defined new mailing list predictors. Mainly such predictors counted the number of messages to different mailing lists during the development of software releases. One predictor *TechMailing*, based on number of messages to the technical mailing list during development, was evaluated to be the most highly rank correlated predictor with the number of defects, among all the predictors evaluated. Our works differs in genre and granularity of defects we predict: We concentrate on defects on small source code units that can be easily reviewed, analyzed, and improved. Also Li *et al.* did not remove the noise from the mailing lists, focusing only on source code related messages. Pattison *et al.* were the first to introduce the idea of studying software entity (function, class etc.) names in emails [13]. They used a linking based on simple name matching, and found a high correlation between the amount of discussions about entities and the number of changes in the source code. However, Pattison *et al.* did not validate the quality of their links between e-mails and source code. To our knowledge, our work [14] was the first to measure the effectiveness of linking techniques for e-mails and source code. This research is the first work that uses information from development mailing lists at class granularity to predict and to find correlation with source code defects. Other works also analyzed development mailing lists but extracting a different kind of information: social structures [27], developers participation [28] and inter-projects migration [29], and emotional content [30].

Change Log-based Defect Prediction Approaches use information extracted from the versioning system to perform defect prediction. Nagappan and Ball performed a study on the influence of code churn (*i.e.,* the amount of change to the sytem) on the defect density in Windows Server 2003 [6]. Hassan introduced a measure of the complexity of code changes [31] and used it as defect predictor on 6 open-source systems. Moser *et al.* used a set of change metrics to predict the presence/absence of bugs in files of Eclipse [7]. Ostrand *et al.* predict faults on two industrial systems, using change and previous defect data [9]. The approach by Bernstein *et al.* uses bug and change information in non-linear prediction models [8].

Single-version Defect Prediction Approaches employ the heuristic that the current design and behavior of the program influence the presence of future defects, assuming that changing a part of the program that is hard to understand is inherently more risky than changing a part with a simpler design. Basili *et al.* used the CK metrics on 8 medium-sized information management systems [1]. Ohlsson *et al.* used several graph metrics including the McCabe cyclomatic complexity on a telecom system [2]. Subramanyam *et al.* used the CK metrics on a commercial C++/Java case study [3], while Gyimothy *et al.* performed a similar analysis on Mozilla [4]. Nagappan *et al.* used a catalog of source code metrics to predict post release defects at the module level on five Microsoft systems, and found that it was possible to build predictors for one individual project, but that no predictor would perform well on all the projects [5]. Zimmermann *et al.* applied a number of code metrics on the Eclipse IDE [10].

Other Approaches. Ostrand *et al.* conducted a series of studies on the whole history of different systems in order to analyze how the characteristics of source code files can predict defects [21,22,23]. On this basis, they proposed an effective and automatable predictive model based on such characteristics (*e.g.,* age, lines of code) [23]. Zimmermann and Nagappan used dependencies between binaries to predict defect [24]. Marcus *et al.* used a cohesion measurement based on LSI for defect prediction on C++ systems [32]. Neuhaus *et al.* used a variety of features of Mozilla to detect vulnerabilities, a subset of bugs with security risks [33]. Wolf *et al.* analyzed the network of communications between developers (*i.e.,* interactions) to understand how they are related to issues in integration of modules of a system [34]. They conceptualized communication as based on developer's comments on work items. Finally, Sarma *et al.* proposed a tool to visually explore relationships between developers, issue reports, communication (based on e-mail archives and comments and activity on issue reports), and source code [35].

7 Conclusion

We have presented a novel approach to correlate popularity of source code artifacts within e-mail archives to software defects. We also investigated whether such metrics could be used to predict post-release defects. We showed that, while there is a significant correlation, popularity metrics by themselves do not outperform source code and change metrics in terms of prediction power. However, we demonstrated that, in conjunction with source code and change metrics, popularity metrics increase both the explanative and predictive power of existing defect prediction techniques.

Acknowledgments. We gratefully acknowledge the financial support of the Swiss National Science foundation for the project "DiCoSA" (SNF Project No. 118063).

References

1. Basili, V.R., Briand, L.C., Melo, W.L.: A validation of object-oriented design metrics as quality indicators. IEEE Transactions on Software Engineering 22(10), 751–761 (1996)
2. Ohlsson, N., Alberg, H.: Predicting fault-prone software modules in telephone switches. IEEE Transactions on Software Engineering 22(12), 886–894 (1996)
3. Subramanyam, R., Krishnan, M.S.: Empirical analysis of CK metrics for object-oriented design complexity: Implications for software defects. IEEE Transactions on Software Engineering 29(4), 297–310 (2003)

4. Gyimóthy, T., Ferenc, R., Siket, I.: Empirical validation of object-oriented metrics on open source software for fault prediction. IEEE Transactions on Software Engineering 31(10), 897–910 (2005)
5. Nagappan, N., Ball, T., Zeller, A.: Mining metrics to predict component failures. In: Proceedings of the ICSE 2006, 28th International Conference on Software Engineering, pp. 452–461. ACM, New York (2006)
6. Nagappan, N., Ball, T.: Use of relative code churn measures to predict system defect density. In: Proceedings of ICSE 2005, 27th International Conference on Software Engineering, pp. 284–292. ACM, New York (2005)
7. Moser, R., Pedrycz, W., Succi, G.: A comparative analysis of the efficiency of change metrics and static code attributes for defect prediction. In: Proceedings of ICSE 2008, 30th International Conference on Software Engineering, pp. 181–190 (2008)
8. Bernstein, A., Ekanayake, J., Pinzger, M.: Improving defect prediction using temporal features and non linear models. In: Proceedings of the International Workshop on Principles of Software Evolution, Dubrovnik, Croatia, pp. 11–18. IEEE CS Press, Los Alamitos (2007)
9. Ostrand, T.J., Weyuker, E.J., Bell, R.M.: Predicting the location and number of faults in large software systems. IEEE Transactions on Software Engineering 31(4), 340–355 (2005)
10. Zimmermann, T., Premraj, R., Zeller, A.: Predicting defects for eclipse. In: Proceedings of PROMISE 2007, 3rd International Workshop on Predictor Models in Software Engineering, p. 9. IEEE Computer Society, Los Alamitos (2007)
11. Antoniol, G., Canfora, G., Casazza, G., Lucia, A.D., Merlo, E.: Recovering traceability links between code and documentation. IEEE Transactions on Software Engineering 28(10), 970–983 (2002)
12. Lucia, A.D., Fasano, F., Grieco, C., Tortora, G.: Recovering design rationale from email repositories. In: Proceedings of ICSM 2009, 25th IEEE International Conference on Software Maintenance. IEEE CS Press, Los Alamitos (2009)
13. Pattison, D., Bird, C., Devanbu, P.: Talk and Work: a Preliminary Report. In: Proceedings of MSR 2008, 5th International Working on Mining Software Repositories, pp. 113–116. ACM, New York (2008)
14. Bacchelli, A., D"Ambros, M., Lanza, M., Robbes, R.: Benchmarking lightweight techniques to link e-mails and source code. In: Proceedings of WCRE 2009, 16th IEEE Working Conference on Reverse Engineering, pp. 205–214. IEEE CS Press, Los Alamitos (2009)
15. Demeyer, S., Tichelaar, S., Ducasse, S.: FAMIX 2.1 — The FAMOOS Information Exchange Model. Technical report, University of Bern (2001)
16. Chidamber, S.R., Kemerer, C.F.: A metrics suite for object oriented design. IEEE Trans. Software Eng. 20(6), 476–493 (1994)
17. Emam, K.E., Melo, W., Machado, J.C.: The prediction of faulty classes using object-oriented design metrics. Journal of Systems and Software 56(1), 63–75 (2001)
18. Fischer, M., Pinzger, M., Gall, H.: Populating a release history database from version control and bug tracking systems. In: Proceedings of ICSM 2003, 19th International Conference on Software Maintenance, pp. 23–32. IEEE CS Press, Los Alamitos (2003)
19. Kollmann, R., Selonen, P., Stroulia, E.: A study on the current state of the art in tools-upported uml-based static reverse engineering. In: Proceedings WCRE 2002, 9th Working Conference on Reverse Engineering, pp. 22–32 (2002)
20. Triola, M.: Elementary Statistics, 10th edn. Addison-Wesley, Reading (2006)
21. Ostrand, T.J., Weyuker, E.J.: The distribution of faults in a large industrial software system. SIGSOFT Software Engineering Notes 27(4), 55–64 (2002)
22. Ostrand, T.J., Weyuker, E.J., Bell, R.M.: Where the bugs are. In: Proceedings of ISSTA 2004, ACM SIGSOFT International Symposium on Software testing and analysis, pp. 86–96. ACM, New York (2004)

23. Ostrand, T.J., Weyuker, E.J., Bell, R.M.: Automating algorithms for the identification of fault-prone files. In: Proceedings of ISSTA 2007, ACM SIGSOFT International Symposium on Software testing and analysis, pp. 219–227. ACM, New York (2007)

24. Zimmermann, T., Nagappan, N.: Predicting defects using network analysis on dependency graphs. In: Proceedings of ICSE 2008, 30th International Conference on Software Engineering, pp. 531–540. ACM, New York (2008)

25. Antoniol, G., Ayari, K., Penta, M.D., Khomh, F., Guéhéneuc, Y.G.: Is it a bug or an enhancement?: a text-based approach to classify change requests. In: Proceedings of CASCON 2008, Conference of the center for Advanced Studies On Collaborative research, pp. 304–318. ACM, New York (2008)

26. Li, P.L., Herbsleb, J., Shaw, M.: Finding predictors of field defects for open source software systems in commonly available data sources: A case study of openbsd. In: Proceedings of METRICS 2005, 11th IEEE International Software Metrics Symposium, p. 32. IEEE Computer Society, Los Alamitos (2005)

27. Bird, C., Gourley, A., Devanbu, P., Gertz, M., Swaminathan, A.: Mining Email Social Networks. In: Proceedings of MSR 2006, 3rd International Workshop on Mining software repositories, pp. 137–143. ACM, New York (2006)

28. Mockus, A., Fielding, R.T., Herbsleb, J.D.: Two case studies of open source software development: Apache and Mozilla. ACM Transactions on Software Engineering and Methodology 11(3), 309–346 (2002)

29. Bird, C., Gourley, A., Devanbu, P., Swaminathan, A., Hsu, G.: Open Borders? Immigration in Open Source Projects. In: Proceedings of MSR 2007, 4th International Workshop on Mining Software Repositories, p. 6. IEEE Computer Society, Los Alamitos (2007)

30. Rigby, P.C., Hassan, A.E.: What can oss mailing lists tell us? a preliminary psychometric text analysis of the apache developer mailing list. In: Proceedings of MSR 2007, 4th International Workshop on Mining Software Repositories, p. 23. IEEE Computer Society, Los Alamitos (2007)

31. Hassan, A.E.: Predicting faults using the complexity of code changes. In: Proceedings of ICSE 2009, 31st International Conference on Software Engineering, pp. 78–88 (2009)

32. Marcus, A., Poshyvanyk, D., Ferenc, R.: Using the conceptual cohesion of classes for fault prediction in object-oriented systems. IEEE Transactions on Software Engineering 34(2), 287–300 (2008)

33. Neuhaus, S., Zimmermann, T., Holler, C., Zeller, A.: Predicting vulnerable software components. In: Proceedings of CCS 2007, 14th ACM Conference on Computer and Communications Security, pp. 529–540. ACM, New York (2007)

34. Wolf, T., Schroter, A., Damian, D., Nguyen, T.: Predicting build failures using social network analysis on developer communication. In: Proceedings of ICSE 2009, 31st International Conference on Software Engineering, pp. 1–11. IEEE Computer Society, Los Alamitos (2009)

35. Sarma, A., Maccherone, L., Wagstrom, P., Herbsleb, J.: Tesseract: Interactive visual exploration of socio-technical relationships in software development. In: Proceedings of ICSE 2009, 31st International Conference on Software Engineering, pp. 23–33 (2009)

Operation-Based, Fine-Grained Version Control Model for Tree-Based Representation

Tung Thanh Nguyen, Hoan Anh Nguyen, Nam H. Pham, and Tien N. Nguyen

Electrical and Computer Engineering Department, Iowa State University, USA

Abstract. Existing version control systems are often based on text line-oriented models for change representation, which do not facilitate software developers in understanding code evolution. Other advanced change representation models that encompass more program semantics and structures are still not quite practical due to their high computational complexity. This paper presents OperV, a novel operation-based version control model that is able to support both coarse and fine levels of granularity in program source code. In OperV, a software system is represented by a project tree whose nodes represent all program entities, such as packages, classes, methods, etc. The changes of the system are represented via edit operations on the tree. OperV also provides the algorithms to differ, store, and retrieve the versions of such entities. These algorithms are based on the mapping of the nodes between versions of the project tree. This mapping technique uses 1) divide-and-conquer technique to map coarse- and fine-grained entities separately, 2) unchanged text regions to map unchanged leaf nodes, and 3) structure-based similarity of the sub-trees to map their root nodes bottom-up and then top-down. The empirical evaluation of OperV has shown that it is scalable, efficient, and could be useful in understanding program evolution.

1 Introduction

Software development is a dynamic process in which the software artifacts constantly evolve. Understanding code evolution is crucial for developers in the development process. However, most of the existing version control tools are text line-oriented which report the changes in term of added, deleted, or modified text regions. Those line-oriented models for changes disregard the logical structure of a program file. However, programmers, as well as compilers and program analysis tools, generally view a program as a structure of program elements, especially the fine-grained entities such as classes, methods, statements, expressions, etc. When a programmer modifies a program, (s)he always maintains in his/her mind the intention to change such elements. Therefore, reporting the changes in term of lines in existing version control tools would be less useful in analysis and understanding the program's evolution. A versioning tool that can support *change operations* on *fine-grained* program entities is desirable.

Recognizing that importance, researchers have proposed several models and tools for version control of fine-grained program entities [11–14]. Those

D.S. Rosenblum and G. Taentzer (Eds.): FASE 2010, LNCS 6013, pp. 74–90, 2010.

approaches, however, do not scale well because they generally rely on *total versioning* [16], which requires to store all versions of any entity for its own version history. In total versioning, a version of a compound entity refers to the versions of its constituent entities. Thus, as a new version is created for an entity, the corresponding new versions for all of its ancestors need to be created as well. Because fine-grained entities usually have many ancestors and are modified frequently, the versioning tools might need to create a huge number of versions of their ancestors. For example, when a variable is renamed, the enclosing statement(s), block(s), method, class, and package(s) are also considered as changed, and the new versions for all of them need to be created. This problem, called *version proliferation*, though might not involve physical copying, creates cognitive overhead and makes fine-grained versioning complicated. Consequently, it terribly affects the scalability of those fine-grained versioning tools [16].

Fortunately, version proliferation could be avoided using *project versioning* approach [2, 5, 16]. In project versioning, instead of storing the history of individual entity, the versioning tool stores only the history of the entire project. Any change committed to the repository will create a new version of the entire project. Then, the project's history is used to re-construct the histories of only requested entities. This improves the scalability over total versioning since the tool does not waste time and space for versions of non-involved entities.

In this paper, we propose OperV, a novel *operation-based* version control model that is able to support both *coarse* and *fine levels of granularity* in program source code. The key idea is the combination of *project versioning* and *operation-based* approaches. In OperV, a system is represented by a *tree-based hierarchy* (called *project tree*) of logical entities, such as packages, classes, methods, expressions, statements, etc. Changes to the system are represented via *tree edit operations* on the project tree. Only the project tree and its changes are stored. Versions and changes of the finer entities are re-constructed on demand.

To do those tasks, OperV provides the algorithms for identifying, differencing, storing, and retrieving the versions of program entities. All of those algorithms are based on the basis task: mapping the nodes of two versions of the project tree. Since a project tree is too large to be efficient for general tree edit script algorithms, we designed a mapping algorithm using several *divide-and-conquer* techniques specialized toward source code. The first technique is to separate between processing coarse- and fine-grained entities. The coarse-grained entities are processed first. Then, each coarse entity is considered as an independent subtree and is used for mapping of the finer-grained entities. The second technique is the mapping process with bottom-up and top-down phases, in which two nodes are considered as the candidates for mapping only if they have mapped descendants or ancestors. Candidate nodes are compared based on the structural similarity to find the mapped ones. The third technique is the localization of the mappings of leaf nodes based on their texts. The observation is that the leaf nodes belonging to an unchanged text region is considered as unchanged. Therefore, OperV maps a leaf node to the corresponding leaf node (in the other tree) if they belong to the corresponding changed or un-changed text regions.

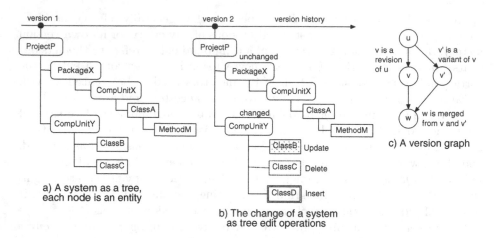

Fig. 1. OperV Concepts

The key contributions of our paper include

1. A scalable version control model that combines project versioning and operation-based approaches to support version control for both fine-grained and coarse-grained entities in a software system,

2. The associated algorithms for identifying, differencing, storing, and retrieving the versions of the system and the entities, and

3. An empirical evaluation to show the quality of OperV and its algorithms.

Section 2 describes the formulation of our model. Sections 3 and 4 present the details of the algorithms in OperV. Sections 5 discusses the evaluation. Section 6 presents related work and conclusions appear last.

2   Formulation

2.1   Concepts

Entity and Project Tree. In OperV, a software system is modeled as a *project*. A project is a hierarchical tree-based structure of *packages* and *compilation units*. A package could consist of other packages and/or compilation units. Each compilation unit is also a hierarchical structure of classes, methods, and other program units as in an abstract syntax tree (AST). The entities within a compilation unit are called *fine-grained*, and the other entities are *coarse-grained*. Thus, a system is represented by an *ordered, attributed tree*, called **project tree**, in which each node represents an **entity** and the parent-children relation of the nodes represents the containment relation between them. Figure 1a) shows an example of the project tree, the coarse-grained and fine-grained entities are illustrated with round and normal rectangles, respectively.

The properties of the entities and the structure of the project tree are represented by the *attributes* of the nodes. Among the attributes, Id is a unique and persistent identification of the corresponding entity. Parent, Right, and Children

Table 1. Tree Edit Operations

Operation	Description
Insert(u, v, k)	Insert u as the kth child of v
Move(u, v, k)	Move u as the kth child of v
Delete(u)	Delete u and insert its children as the new children of its parent node
Update(u, a, x)	Change the attribute a of u with new value x

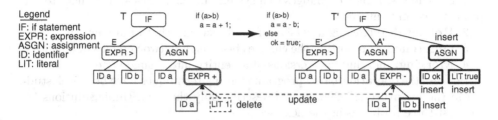

Fig. 2. Edit Operations on AST

respectively refer to the parent node, the right sibling node, and the ordered set of children nodes of the entity. Type is the type of the entity (e.g. *Class, Method,* etc). Content is the attribute representing the associated content of the entity. For example, if the entity is a *variable*, its Content contains the variable's name.

Change, Operation, and Version. The system and its entities evolve over time. In OperV, the **change** to a system is represented as tree edit **operations** on the project tree. Table 1 shows the list of operations including inserting, deleting, moving, and updating an attribute of a node (e.g. Content). Figures 1a) and b) illustrate such a change with corresponding operations. Figure 2 illustrates the similar operations on fine-grained entities in a program.

An entity is considered to be *changed* if and only if that entity or one of its descendants is affected by the operations of the changes. In other words, if any node of the sub-tree is affected by an operation, the entity corresponding to its root node is considered to be changed. A change of an entity is represented as the operations on the nodes of the corresponding sub-tree. The states of an entity between changes are called its **versions** and the changes are called **deltas**. In OperV, a delta is represented as a sequence of operations, i.e. an editing **script**.

Version Relation and Version Graph. The versions of an entity (including entire project tree) have the following relations:

1) *revision-of:* v is a revision of u if v is modified from u as in a sequential line of evolution.

2) *variant-of (branch-of):* v' is a variant of v if v' is interchangeable and differ with v in some aspects of function, design, or implementation.

3) *merge-from:* w is a merge from v if w is created by merging v with another version v'. The merge of versions is used in the situation that different changes made to the same version need to be combined.

The versions of an entity and their relations are represented via its **version graph**, in which the nodes represent versions and the edges represent the changes between the versions. Figure 1c) shows an example of a version graph.

2.2   Problems

OperV needs to provide the algorithms for the following problems:

1. **Storage:** storing the changes to a system, i.e. all states and changes to the project tree and entities.

2. **Retrieval:** retrieving a version of a project and that of any entity.

3. **Differencing:** reporting the changes between any two versions of an entity.

4. **Merging:** merging two versions of an entity into a single one.

Because the operation-based program merging techniques have been well studied in the literature [27–29], we will describe only the algorithmic solutions for the first three problems in the next sections.

3   Mapping Entities on Project Tree

Because OperV is based on project versioning, any change(s) to one or multiple entities committed to the repository will create a new version of entire project. Only the changes and states (i.e. the version graph) of the project, however, are stored. The version graph of other entities will be re-constructed and processed on demand, using the stored version graph of the project tree. Therefore, the basis task to solve the aforementioned problems is to compute the changes of the project tree. This is in fact the *tree editing problem,* i.e. the problem of mapping the nodes of two project trees representing two consecutive versions of the system and deriving an edit script that transforms one tree into the other.

Since the project tree is huge, optimal tree editing algorithms are too computationally expensive. In [19], we developed Treed, a tree editing algorithm to compute an editing script for two ASTs representing for any two cloned fragments. In this paper, we generalize it to work for two project trees. In general, the algorithm has two steps. First, it determines a one-to-one mapping between the nodes of two project trees, in which any two mapped nodes represent two versions of the same entity and unmapped nodes represent deleted/inserted entities. Then, it derives the editing operations based on the recovered mapping.

This section presents the mapping step. Section 4 discusses how edit scripts are derived and used to solve the problems of storage, retrieval, and differencing.

3.1   Mapping Strategy

In Treed, the mapping step is designed based on the following observations:

O1) Leaf nodes of ASTs belonging to unchanged text regions are unchanged.

O2) If two nodes u and v are mapped, their ancestors and descendants are likely to be mapped.

O3) Two versions of a compound entity generally have similar structures. Thus, if the sub-tree rooted at u is highly similar to the sub-tree rooted at v, then u and v are likely to be mapped.

To measure the structural similarity of the (sub)trees, Treed uses Exas [1] characteristic vectors, which are shown in our previous work to be efficient and accurate in capturing the structure of trees and graphs. Using Exas, each tree is assigned an occurrence-counting vector of its structural features, such as the label sequences of its paths. For any two trees with two vectors x and y, their structural similarity is defined as $1 - \frac{2\|x-y\|}{\|x\|+\|y\|}$. That is, the smaller their vector distance is, the more similar they are. Larger trees (i.e. having large vectors) are allowed to have a larger distance within the same level of similarity. More details on Exas could be found in [1].

We customize Treed to work on the project tree with the following divide-and-conquer principle. That is, instead of processing the whole project tree, we divide it into two levels: coarse-grained and fine-grained levels. The mapping will be first applied for the parts of project trees containing only coarse-grained entities. Then, each pair of mapped coarse-grained entities is then processed independently to map their finer-grained entities. In practice, the coarse-grained entities, i.e. compilation units and packages, are generally stored as source files and directories. Therefore, this strategy would facilitate the storage of both coarse-grained and fine-grained entities in a conventional file system.

Nevertheless, two mapping processes for coarse-grained and fine-grained entities have the same phases: 1) initial mapping, 2) bottom-up mapping, and 3) top-down mapping. First, OperV initially maps as many tree nodes at the lowest level as possible (file/directory nodes at the coarse granularity level and leaf nodes at the fine granularity level). Then using such initial mapping, OperV maps the nodes at higher levels in a bottom-up manner, using the above observations to find the candidates and to choose mapped nodes based on their structural similarity. After going up to the root node, the algorithm goes top-down, trying to map the unmapped descendants of the mapped nodes, based on the similarity of their structure or contents.

3.2   Initial Mapping

Initial mapping for coarse-grained entities is based on name and location. Two coarse-grained entities (e.g. file, directory) having the same name and the same location in the tree will be mapped, i.e. be considered as the two versions of the same entity. For finer-grained entities, the initial mapping is much more complex because OperV does not directly store them (due to the huge size of the project tree). To map the finer-grained entities in two versions of a compilation unit, the corresponding source files are first parsed into ASTs. Then, the initial mapping is applied for the leaf nodes of those ASTs based on observation O1 in Section 3.1. This observation suggests the use of text-based differencing to divide the text un-parsed from an AST into the changed and unchanged text segments and to map leaf nodes into only the nodes in the corresponding segments. Therefore, the initial mapping for ASTs works in the two following steps:

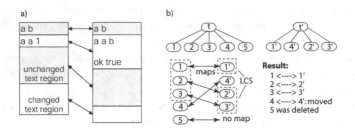

Fig. 3. Initial Mapping and Top-Down Mapping

Map Leaf Nodes of Unchanged Text Segments. First, two ASTs are un-parsed into text-based versions. (Treed uses the unparsed text instead of the original text to discard the differences in formatting and other cosmetic changes). Then, text-based differencing, with the longest common subsequence (LCS) al-gorithm, is applied to compare two sequences of text lines in order to detect and align the unchanged text lines. The alignment of unchanged text lines will partition the text lines into (un)changed segments as in Figure 3a). If Content of a leaf node belongs to more than one segment, those segments will be joined. The joined segment will be considered as changed if it is joined from a changed segment. With this process, each leaf node will belong to only one segment.

Then, Treed traverses two trees, exports their sequences of leaf nodes, and marks the leaf nodes belonging to unchanged segments as "unchanged". Such unchanged leaf nodes in two sequences are mapped one-by-one in order. In Fig-ure 2, two sequences of leaf nodes are $[a, b, a, a, 1]$ and $[a, b, a, a, b, ok, true]$. Be-cause the first two nodes of those sequences belong to an unchanged text line (if (a > b)), they are mapped one to one: $a \rightarrow a, b \rightarrow b$.

Map Leaf Nodes of Changed Text Segments. Next, Treed maps the leaf nodes belonging to the changed text segments. Such segments contain *all changed leaf nodes* and might contain *unchanged leaf nodes*. For example, in Figure 3, two sequences of nodes $[a, a, 1]$ and $[a, a, b, ok, true]$ correspond to changed text segments. However, the first node a is unchanged in the statement a = a + 1.

To find the mapped nodes, for each pair of the aligned segments of changed lines in the two versions, Treed finds the LCS between the corresponding se-quences of leaf nodes. Two nodes are considered as matched if they have the same Type and Content. The matched nodes of resulting subsequences are mapped to each other as unchanged leaf nodes. In the above sequences, Treed finds the common subsequences $[a, a]$ and maps the corresponding nodes $[a, a]$.

3.3 Bottom-Up Mapping

Treed maps the inner nodes in the bottom-up manner as follows. If an inner node u has a descendant u_1 mapped to v_1, u will be compared to any *ancestor* of v_1. Then, u will be mapped to a candidate node v if the subtrees rooted at u and v are sufficiently similar in structure and type (measured via Exas method, see Section 3.1). If no such v exists, u is considered as unmapped. For example, In Figure 2, both E' and T' contain the mapped nodes to the nodes in E. However, because E is identical to E', they are mapped to each other. Similarly, A is mapped to A', although they are not identical in structure.

3.4   Top-Down Mapping

The bottom-up process might be unable to map some nodes, such as the relocated nodes and renamed identifier ones. Thus, after bottom-up mapping, Treed examines the two trees in the top-down fashion and maps those not yet mapped nodes based on the already mapped nodes. Given a pair of mapped nodes u and v from the bottom-up pass, Treed proceeds the mapping between their descendant nodes by the following mechanism:

Firstly, Treed performs a greedy algorithm to find additional mapped nodes between the children nodes of u and v. The already mapped nodes are kept. If unmapped children nodes are inner ones, their descendants are compared based on Exas structural similarity as in the previous step. If they are unmapped leaf nodes, Treed computes their similarity based on their attributes. For AST leaf nodes, since their Contents are generally identifiers and literals, such attributes are first separated as the sequences of words, using well-known naming conventions such as Hungarian or Camel. For example, "getFileName" is separated into "get", "file", and "name". The similarity of two words is computed via the Levenshtein distance, a string-based similarity measure.

After the children nodes are mapped, the LCS algorithm is run on those two sequences of mapped nodes. The mapped nodes not belonging to the resulting LCS are considered to be moved, such as node 4 in Figure 3.

3.5   Complexity Analysis

Given two trees T_1 and T_2, let $|T|$ be the number of nodes and $n = max(|T_1|, |T_2|)$. The above mapping algorithm contains the following sequential steps. First, building the text lines from the leaves of the trees takes $O(|T_1| + |T_2|)$, which is $O(n)$. Then, the unchanged lines are located using the longest common subsequence algorithm between two lists of lines. Thus the complexity of this step is $O(m_1 m_2) < O(n^2)$, where m_i is the number of lines built from tree T_i, respectively. Mapping the leaf nodes on those (un)changed lines takes at most $O(n^2)$ because of the use of the longest common subsequence algorithm between two lists of nodes. Computing characteristic vectors for all AST nodes is done incrementally from the leaf nodes to the root node, therefore it takes $O(n)$ [1]. Note that the accessing and comparing time of those vectors do not depend on the size of the tree since the features are extracted using n-paths in Exas, in which the lengths of vectors depend only on the number of AST nodes' types and the maximum size of the n-paths [1].

In the bottom-up mapping, each node v in one tree has at most $l_v h$ candidate nodes to map in the other tree, where l_v is the number of children of v and h is the maximum height of T_1 and T_2. Therefore, the complexity of this step is $O(\sum_{v_1 \in T_1} l_{v_1} h + \sum_{v_2 \in T_2} l_{v_2} h) = O(h \sum_{v_1 \in T_1} l_{v_1} + h \sum_{v_2 \in T_2} l_{v_2}) = O(h|T_1| + h|T_2|) = O(hn)$. In the top-down mapping, for each pair of mapped nodes v_1 and v_2, the matching between the two lists of their children can be done with $O(l_{v_1} l_{v_2})$. Since a node in one tree is mapped to only one node in the other tree, the complexity of this step is $O(\sum_{v_1 \in T_1} l_{v_1} l_{v_2}) = O(\sum_{v_1 \in T_1} l_{v_1} \sum_{v_2 \in T_2} l_{v_2}) = O(|T_1||T_2|) = O(n^2)$. Finally, traversing the trees to derive the editing script is in $O(n)$. In total, the complexity of the mapping algorithm is $O(n^2)$.

4   Differencing, Storage, and Retrieval

4.1   Deriving Editing Script from Mapping

After having the mapping for all nodes of the project tree, Treed could derive the edit operations for each node. For example, if a node is not mapped into any node in the new (old) version, it is *deleted* (*inserted*). If it is mapped but has different location with the mapped node, it is considered to be *moved*. If its attributes change, it is considered to be *updated*. Then, the editing script for the project tree could be generated via a top-down traversal. At each node, OperV exports the Update, Move, Delete, and Insert operations on its children, and then, derives *recursively* the editing script for its mapped children.

Treed is able to find the changes not only to fine-grained entities but also to coarse-grained ones. For example, by top-down mapping from the root node of the project tree, Treed could find two files having different names but identical structures, and determine them to be two versions of a renamed file. Note that due to the divide-and-conquer technique which separates between processing coarse-grained and finer-grained entities, Treed does not detect the moving operations across coarse-grained entities.

4.2   Storage

OperV uses the *backward delta* mechanism [16] to store the version graph of the system. That is, only the latest versions of all the branches in the version graph (i.e. sink nodes), together with all editing scripts (i.e. edges of the version graph) are stored. Note that, the individual changes of other entities are not stored. Because of the backward delta storage, an editing script is the script that transforms the later version of the project tree into an earlier one.

As a new version v_{n+1} of the project is *committed* to the repository, OperV first maps and computes the difference of v_{n+1} to the current version v_n. It stores the computed script, and then replaces v_n by v_{n+1} as the latest version. Along with the editing script, it stores also the set of changed, coarse-grained entities (called a *change set*) for efficiency of future retrieval tasks.

4.3   Retrieval

The retrieval requests could 1) check out a version of the entire project; 2) retrieve a version of an entity; or 3) retrieve the history (i.e. version graph) of an entity.

Type 1: From the stored (latest) version of the project, OperV will gradually apply the backward deltas as the editing scripts on the current project tree to re-construct the previous versions. In other words, OperV re-constructs and traverses the version graph of the project from its sink nodes (i.e. latest versions) and edges (i.e. deltas) to the desired version.

Types 2 and 3: OperV re-constructs the version graph of a requested entity in a similar way. The process is as follows. First, OperV extracts the latest version v of the requested entity e from the project tree. Then, OperV gradually processes the backward deltas until a requested version. For each delta d, OperV checks whether e was changed, i.e. affected by d. If e is a coarse-grained entity, OperV checks the corresponding change set (i.e. the set of changed, coarse-grained entities), which was stored along with d. If e is a fine-grained entity, OperV checks whether d contains any operation on e or a descendant of e.

Then, if e is unchanged, OperV continues processing the next delta. Otherwise, the operations of d affecting on e and its descendants will be applied on v. If such operation involves another entity u, e.g. an operation moving a variable node from a statement v to another statement u, the current version of u will be requested to be extracted. After all operations are applied on v, OperV has the previous version of e, and the next delta will be processed using that version. Note that, when extracting or editing a version of an entity, OperV builds only the part of the project tree related to that entity. For example, if the entity is a method, OperV parses only the source file containing that method, rather than parsing all files to build the entire project tree. This on-demand scheme enables an efficient version retrieval for any fine-grained entities.

4.4   Tool Implementation

We have implemented a prototype of OperV with all aforementioned algorithms. In the implementation, logical entities are mapped to physical files in a file system: projects and packages are mapped to directories, classes are mapped to files. Finer-grained entities (corresponding to the AST nodes of a class) are parsed from source files. The tool provides the following functions:

1. Check-out the entire system at a version (this involves version retrieval),
2. Commit a new version of the entire system (this task involves version identification, differencing, and storage),
3. Display a version of a fine-grained entity (this involves version retrieval),
4. Display the version log of an entity in term of its version graphs, and
5. Compute and display the change of any two versions of an entity (i.e. differencing). If the entity is coarse-grained, the change is displayed in term of the file/directory operations. For a fine-grained entity in an AST, the change is

shown as AST operations. This function is done via mapping and differencing algorithms on the sub-trees corresponding to two versions of that entity.

5   Empirical Evaluation

5.1   Scalability and Efficiency in Differencing

To evaluate our tree editing algorithm, we compared it to one of the state-of-the-art optimal algorithms proposed by Zhang and Shasha [21, 23]. Two algorithms were run on a set of changed source files in a range of revisions of subject systems (Table 2). Then, the lengths of the output edit scripts and running time of two algorithms were compared. All experiments were carried out on a Windows XP computer with Intel Core 2 Duo 2Ghz CPU, 3GB RAM, and 80GB HDD.

Table 2 shows the results. Column *Revision* is the range of revisions of subject systems in our experiments. Column *File* is the number of modified files under processing (the added and deleted files were not processed since they are of trivial cases). Columns *Size* and *Size** show their average sizes in term of AST nodes before and after the changes, respectively. In this experiment, we set the limit for the file size of less than 2,000 nodes due to the scalability problem in the optimal algorithm. Columns L_{OperV} and L_{opt} show the average lengths of the output scripts of our algorithm and the optimal one, respectively. The columns labelled with Δ show the percentages of the cases in which the differences in the lengths of scripts are zero, between 1 and 3, and more than 3 operations, respectively. Columns T_{OperV} and T_{opt} show the average running time for each pair of files in two algorithms.

The result implies that, our algorithm outputs the scripts with the optimal lengths in 70-85% cases. In half of the remaining cases, the scripts are a bit longer with a few operations. Such little sacrifice in accuracy brings large saving on time efficiency. It could be seen that, the saving ratios are from 50 - 500 times.

5.2   Scalability in Storing

Table 3 shows the result of our experiment on the scalability of OperV the storing task. In this experiment, since only OperV was operated, we did not set the limit for file sizes, and we ran on wider ranges of revisions. For each subject system, we stored the initial version, continuously committed the successive versions and measured the total processing time (including parsing, differencing, and storing)

Table 2. Comparison to Optimal Algorithm on Running Time and Script Length

Project	Revision	File	Size	Size*	L_{OperV}	L_{opt}	$\Delta=0$	$\Delta=1\text{-}3$	$\Delta >3$	$T_{OperV}(s)$	$T_{opt}(s)$
ArgoUML	5000-5100	135	422	417	21	20	84%	6%	10%	0.19	13.1
Columba	200-300	208	513	516	45	43	73%	14%	13%	0.11	15.3
GEclipse	1800-2000	138	624	647	53	50	69%	10%	21%	0.13	25.3
jEdit	4000-4100	158	921	931	39	37	70%	13%	17%	0.13	50.3
ZK	5000-5400	284	272	277	16	15	85%	8%	7%	0.13	20.7

Table 3. Time and Space Costs

Project	Revision	File	MaxSize	Time (s)	Project(MB)	Delta(MB)	Delta/version
ArgoUML	5000-6000	1297	19044	0.7	14.7	8.1	0.06%
Columba	200-300	1549	4081	0.4	12.1	1.2	0.10%
GEclipse	1000-2000	779	10563	0.2	9.2	12.6	0.14%
jEdit	4000-5000	394	24660	1.7	7.8	16.1	0.21%
ZK	5000-6000	991	8287	0.3	8.3	2.9	0.03%

[Columba v252-v253] LocalCalendarStoreTest.java

Event model = new Event();
model.setSummary("summary");
model.setDescription("description");
String uuid = new UUIDGenerator().newUUID();
storage.add(model);
	String uuid = new UUIDGenerator().newUUID();
	Event model = new Event(uuid);
	model.setSummary("summary");
	model.setDescription("description");
	storage.add(model);

Fig. 4. Example of Change in Object Usage

[Columba v213-v214] TittleBar.java

g2.setPaint(firstHalf);
g2.fillRect(0, 0, w, h);
	if (active) {
	...
	  g2.setPaint(firstHalf);
	  g2.fillRect(0, 0, w, h);
	} else {
	  g2.setColor(fillColor);
	  g2.fillRect(0,0,w,h);

Fig. 5. Example of Change in Control Flow

and storage space. In the table, Column *Time* shows the average processing time for each revision. Columns *Project* and *Delta* show the total space for the initial version and all deltas, respectively. Column *MaxSize* shows the maximum file size in term of AST nodes on each system.

It could be seen that OperV is highly scalable. Processing time of each version generally costs less than 1 second on large-scale systems which could contain thousands of files with the sizes up to tens of thousands of nodes. For jEdit, although the number of files is less than in the other projects, the sizes of its files are generally larger. This makes processing time for jEdit a bit longer because OperV's differencing algorithm has a quadratic complexity on file size.

The storage cost is reasonable. For example, at revision 4000, jEdit has size of 7.8MB. After checking-in 1,000 versions, OperV needs extra 16.1MB to store 1,000 deltas. Thus, on average, each delta costs about 0.21% of the project size.

5.3   Anecdotal Evidence of Usefulness

Figure 4 shows an interesting example that OperV reported when running on Columba v252-v253. In this case, a developer moved the initialization statement for uuid, and used uuid as a parameter of a constructor call for an Event object. This example shows that OperV is able to detect the change in the usage of objects, which is one kind of semantic change. Thus, it provides more useful information for developers to understand code evolution than text-based changes.

OperV is also able to detect changes in a control flow. For example, in Figure 5, it was able to report the addition of branching to a block of code. Similarly, it found another case in which the statement `if (services.length > 1)` was changed to `if ((services != null) && (services.length > 1))`. It was able to report the insertion of that new control condition.

In another example in `WorkflowJobEditPart.java` of GEclipse v1803-v1804, OperV reported the renaming of two variables: `workflowJobNameFigure0` to `workflowJobNameFigure` and `workflowJobDescriptionFigure1` to `workflowJobDescriptionFigure` several times. This result suggests that OperV could be used as a foundation for the "renaming" refactoring recovery tools.

6   Related Work

The source code versioning and differencing approaches could be classified based on the abstraction level in the program representations of their tools. Generally, they could be classified into lexical (text-based), structural (often tree-based), syntactical (AST-based), or semantic approaches.

Traditional version control tools (CVS [3], RCS [4], SVN [5]) use the **text-based** differencing approaches (such as *text diff* [6]), which consider a program as a set of text lines and often use the longest common subsequence technique to calculate the inserted, deleted, and modified lines. Ldiff [7] was built upon text *diff* to track the changes to lines including line addition, removal, or moving. This type of approaches does not work well when developers care more about the changes in code structure. Moreover, the reported changes in term of text lines do not fit well with automated program analysis tools for software evolution.

Structural versioning and differencing tools assume that software documents are stored in a fine-grained and structural manner (e.g. XML). Algorithms for such structural differencing include [8–10]. POEM [11] provides tree-based version control for functions and classes [16]. The principles of the tree-based COOP/Orm framework [12] include the sharing of unchanged tree nodes among versions and change propagation. Unified Extensional Versioning Model [13] supports fine-grained versioning for a tree-structured document by composite/atomic nodes and links. Each atomic node is represented by a text file. In Coven [14], a versioned fragment could be entire method for C++ and Java programs, or text paragraph in LATEX documents. In Ohst's model [15], fine-grained changes are managed within contexts of UML tools and design transactions. Maletic and Collard [39] also used text `diff` to locate changed entities in an XML representation of code. However, their goal was not to derive edit scripts.

In general, those approaches heavily rely on the total versioning scheme with the technical drawback of the version proliferation problem [16] as described earlier. In contrast, the generic tree-based differencing algorithms [20–22] are too computationally expensive for source code evolution because they consider two arbitrary trees as the inputs, rather than two revisions of the same program [17].

OperV uses project versioning to avoid version proliferation and Treed makes it efficient due to its specialization toward source code with the divide-and-conquer strategy. SVN [5] also uses project versioning but with a text-based approach.

Our tree edit algorithm, Treed, belongs to the **syntactical** category. Treed is similar in nature to ChangeDistiller [17], a tree-based differencing and code change extracting tool. However, the first key departure point is the *divide-and-conquer* approach that helps Treed reduce the complexity of mapping the corresponding nodes in two versions. It takes into account the fact that the alignment of unchanged text regions between two revisions will partition the texts of two revisions into smaller and corresponding segments. Thus, it could apply its mapping procedure on smaller segments. ChangeDistiller does not use the alignment of un-changed texts in two versions for divide-and-conquer. Another key difference is the use of Exas [1], a vector-based structure similarity measure for trees. Exas [1] has been shown to perform better than the subtree similarity measure used in Chawathe *et al.* [18], which was also used in ChangeDistiller. Exas' characteristic features capture the structure via the paths in a tree, while Chawathe's approach relies only on the number of matched nodes in two trees.

Other syntactical, tree-based differencing approaches were also used in program differencing and merging tools [24, 25]. Their goals were not to detect editing operations. The tree matching techniques for AST were used in tree-based clone detection tools as well [19, 30–32]. Those algorithms include suffix tree [30], maximum common subtree isomorphism [31], or dice coefficient [32].

Our model is the first to combine the strength of both project versioning and operation-based approaches for fine-grained versioning. Operation-based model represents the changes between versions as explicit operations. However, similar to other syntactical approaches, OperV requires software artifacts to be parseable. Robbes and Lanza [26] advocate for an approach to analyze software evolution using semantic changes. Our work is similar to their analysis tool with the use of tree edit operations for change representation. They define semantic changes as well. The key difference is that OperV is a complete version model that combines versioning for entire project with the operation-based approach. Their evolution analysis approach will benefit from versioning tools built from OperV. Operation-based approach had also been used in software merging [27–29]. Ekman and Asklund [29] presented a refactoring-aware versioning system.

Semantic-based program versioning and differencing approaches often rely on graph-based techniques. They represent the behavior of a program via a graph (e.g. program dependence graph, program slice as in [33], control flow graph as in [34], semantic-graph as in [35]), and detect the changed entities in the graph. Those approaches provide more semantic information than OperV, however, they are more computationally expensive.

There exists version control models that are change-based ([36–38]). That is, in change-based models, the changes are first-class entities with unique identifiers that are used to compose the system at different time. Comparing to change-based models, OperV is still state-based because the revisions have identifiers and the changes (as operations) are computed via our tree edit script algorithm.

7 Conclusions

This paper presents OperV, a novel operation-based, fine-grained version control model and tool for source code. The key idea is the combination between project versioning and operation-based approaches. In OperV, a software system is represented by a project tree whose nodes represent all program entities at both coarse-grained and fine-grained levels. The changes of the system are represented via edit operations on the tree. OperV also provides the algorithms for storing, retrieving, and differencing between the versions of such entities. These algorithms are designed based on several heuristics to improve scalability and efficiency. The empirical evaluation of the model showed that OperV is scalable, efficient, and could be useful for developers in understanding of code evolution.

Acknowledgment. We thank reviewers for their very insightful feedbacks. The first author was partially funded by a grant from Vietnam Education Foundation.

References

1. Nguyen, H.A., Nguyen, T.T., Pham, N.H., Al-Kofahi, J.M., Nguyen, T.N.: Accurate and efficient structural characteristic feature extraction for clone detection. In: Chechik, M., Wirsing, M. (eds.) FASE 2009. LNCS, vol. 5503, pp. 440–455. Springer, Heidelberg (2009)
2. Nguyen, T.N., Munson, E.V., Boyland, J.T., Thao, C.: An Infrastructure for Development of Multi-level, Object-Oriented Config. Management Services. In: ICSE 2005, pp. 215–224. ACM, New York (2005)
3. Morse, T.: CVS. Linux Journal 1996(21es), 3 (1996)
4. Tichy, W.: RCS - A System for Version Control. Software - Practice and Experience 15(7), 637–654 (1985)
5. Subversion.tigris.org., http://subversion.tigris.org/
6. Hunt, J.W., Szymanski, T.G.: A fast algorithm for computing longest common subsequences. Communication of ACM 20(5), 350–353 (1977)
7. Canfora, G., Cerulo, L., Di Penta, M.: Ldiff: An enhanced line differencing tool. In: ICSE 2009, pp. 595–598. IEEE CS, Los Alamitos (2009)
8. Myers, E.W.: An O(nd) Difference Algorithm and Its Variations. Algorithmica 1, 251–266 (1986)
9. Tichy, W.F.: The string-to-string correction problem with block moves. ACM Trans. Comput. Syst. 2(4), 309–321 (1984)
10. Wang, Y., DeWitt, D.J., Cai, J.Y.: X-Diff: An Effective Change Detection Algorithm for XML Documents. In: ICDE 2003, pp. 519–530. IEEE CS, Los Alamitos (2003)
11. Lin, Y., Reiss, S.: Configuration management with logical structures. In: ICSE 1996, pp. 298–307 (1996)
12. Magnusson, B., Asklund, U.: Fine-grained revision control of Configurations in COOP/Orm. In: 6th Software Configuration Management Workshop (SCM-6), pp. 31–47. Springer, Heidelberg (1996)
13. Asklund, U., Bendix, L., Christensen, H., Magnusson, B.: The Unified Extensional Versioning Model. In: 9th Software Configuration Management Workshop (SCM-9). Springer, Heidelberg (1999)

14. Chu-Carroll, M.C., Wright, J., Shields, D.: Supporting aggregation in fine grained software configuration management. In: FSE 2002, pp. 99–108. ACM Press, New York (2002)
15. Ohst, D., Kelter, U.: A fine-grained version and configuration model in analysis and design. In: ICSM 2002. IEEE CS, Los Alamitos (2002)
16. Conradi, R., Westfechtel, B.: Version models for software configuration management. ACM Computing Surveys (CSUR) 30(2), 232–282 (1998)
17. Fluri, B., Wuersch, M., Pinzger, M., Gall, H.: Change distilling: Tree differencing for fine-grained source code change extraction. IEEE Transactions on Software Engineering 33(11), 725–743 (2007)
18. Chawathe, S.S., Rajaraman, A., Garcia-Molina, H., Widom, J.: Change detection in hierarchically structured information. In: SIGMOD 1996, pp. 493–504. ACM, New York (1996)
19. Nguyen, T.T., Nguyen, H.A., Pham, N.H., Al-Kofahi, J.M., Nguyen, T.N.: Clone-aware Configuration Management. In: The 24th ACM/IEEE International Conference on Automated Software Engineering (ASE 2009). IEEE CS Press, Los Alamitos (2009)
20. Bille, P.: A survey on tree edit distance and related problems. Theor. Comput. Sci. 337(1-3), 217–239 (2005)
21. Zhang, K.: Algorithms for the constrained editing distance between ordered labeled trees and related problems. Pattern Recognition 28, 463–474 (1995)
22. Selkow, S.: The tree-to-tree editing problem. Info. Processing Letters 6(6), 184–186 (1977)
23. Zhang, K., Shasha, D.: Simple fast algorithms for the editing distance between trees and related problems. SIAM Journal of Computing 18, 1245–1262 (1989)
24. Asklund, U.: Identifying conflicts during structural merge. In: Proceedings of the Nordic Workshop on Programming Environment Research (1994)
25. Westfechtel, B.: Structure-oriented merging of revisions of software documents. In: Proceedings of Workshop on Software Configuration Management, pp. 68–79. ACM, New York (1991)
26. Robbes, R., Lanza, M., Lungu, M.: An Approach to Software Evolution Based on Semantic Change. In: Dwyer, M.B., Lopes, A. (eds.) FASE 2007. LNCS, vol. 4422, pp. 27–41. Springer, Heidelberg (2007)
27. Lippe, E., van Oosterom, N.: Operation-based merging. In: SDE-5, pp. 78–87. ACM Press, New York (1992)
28. Edwards, W.: Flexible Conflict Detection and Management in Collaborative Applications. In: Proceedings of UIST (1997)
29. Ekman, T., Asklund, U.: Refactoring-aware versioning in Eclipse. Electronic Notes in Theoretical Computer Science 107, 57–69 (2004)
30. Gode, N., Koschke, R.: Incremental Clone Detection. In: CSMR 2009, pp. 219–228. IEEE CS, Los Alamitos (2009)
31. Sager, T., Bernstein, A., Pinzger, M., Kiefer, C.: Detecting similar Java classes using tree algorithms. In: MSR 2006, pp. 65–71. ACM, New York (2006)
32. Baxter, I.D., Yahin, A., Moura, L., Sant'Anna, M., Bier, L.: Clone detection using abstract syntax trees. In: ICSM 1998, pp. 368–377. IEEE CS, Los Alamitos (1998)
33. Horwitz, S.: Identifying the semantic and textual differences between two versions of a program. In: PLDI 1990, pp. 234–245. ACM, New York (1990)
34. Apiwattanapong, T., Orso, A., Harrold, M.J.: Jdiff: A differencing technique and tool for object-oriented programs. Automated Software Engg. 14(1), 3–36 (2007)

35. Raghavan, S., Rohana, R., Leon, D., Podgurski, A., Augustine, V.: Dex: A semantic-graph differencing tool for studying changes in large code bases. In: ICSM 2004, pp. 188–197. IEEE, Los Alamitos (2004)
36. Lie, A., Conradi, R., Didriksen, T., Karlsson, E., Hallsteinsen, S., Holager, P.: Change oriented versioning. In: Proceedings of the Second European Software Engineering Conference (1989)
37. Cronk, R.: Tributaries and deltas. BYTE, pp. 177–186 (January 1992)
38. Zelller, A., Snelting, G.: Unified versioning through feature logic. ACM Transaction on Software Engineering and Methodology 6, 397–440 (1997)
39. Maletic, J., Collard, M.: Supporting Source Code Difference Analysis. In: ICSM 2004. IEEE CS, Los Alamitos (2004)

A Method for Analyzing Code Homology in Genealogy of Evolving Software

Masatomo Hashimoto[1] and Akira Mori[2]

[1] AIST Tokyo Waterfront, 2-3-26 Aomi, Koto-ku, Tokyo 135-0064, Japan
m.hashimoto@aist.go.jp
[2] AIST Tokyo Akihabara Site, 1-18-13 Sotokanda, Chiyoda-ku,
Tokyo 101-0021, Japan
a-mori@aist.go.jp

Abstract. A software project often contains a large amount of "homologous code", i.e., similar code fragments distributed in different versions or "species" sharing common ancestry. Code homology typically arises when the code is inherited, duplicated, and patched. In this paper, we propose an automated method for detecting and tracking homologous code in genealogy of evolving software using fine-grained tree differencing on source code. Such a tool would help software developers/ maintainers to better understand the source code and to detect/prevent inconsistent modifications that may lead to latent errors. The results of experiments on several large-scale software projects are reported to show the capability of the method, including BIND9 DNS servers, a couple of Java software systems jEdit and Ant, and the entire Linux device driver subsystem.

1 Introduction

A large software system often contains a large number of similar code fragments across many versions or branches. They are typically introduced when the code is inherited from previous versions, duplicated for programming convenience, and patched to correct common defects. We call such correspondence in the code descended from a common ancestry *homology* of code, by analogy with biology [1].

Homologous code fragments or *homologues* may evolve in uniform or divergent manner as the development proceeds. If the evolution is uniform, it is likely that there exists a common programming logic and extra maintenance efforts are necessary [2] since further changes must be replicated on each code fragment to keep the system consistent. Even when the evolution is divergent, common characters of the code remain in later developments [3].

Locating homologous code and tracking their course of change would help software developers/maintainers to better understand the source code and to detect/prevent inconsistent modifications that may lead to latent errors. The task can be difficult even when a versioning system such as CVS is in place to record change descriptions since such information is too coarse to compare and

D.S. Rosenblum and G. Taentzer (Eds.): FASE 2010, LNCS 6013, pp. 91–106, 2010.
© Springer-Verlag Berlin Heidelberg 2010

usually not associated with reference to concrete source code entities such as functions and methods [2].

The analysis of *code clones* is a well-researched topic related to code homology. Many algorithms and tools have been proposed for detecting code clones [4]. However, those methods are not well-suited for analyzing how clone regions evolve over time since maintaining clone relations is difficult when regions go through different modifications and do not remain the same. Clone detection must be performed on each version and discovered clone regions must be tracked in the later versions. To distinguish newly introduced clone regions from those lasting from previous versions involves an awkward task of adjusting similarity thresholds by heuristics [3]. The method for tracking cloned code is relatively less explored with several exceptions [5,3,6,7,8] despite its practical importance.

In this paper, we propose an automated method for detecting and tracking homologues in genealogy of evolving software using a fine-grained tree differencing tool called Diff/TS[9] for source code. Tree differencing is used for calculating edit sequences on abstract syntax trees that transform one revision into another. It also computes node mappings up to relabeling for tracking source code entities across revisions. The method allows us to identify inconsistent changes on homologues by comparing semantic change histories reconstructed from raw edit sequences.

By following ideas from biology, we classify homology into three categories: *orthology*, *paralogy*, and *xenology*. Orthology describes homology arising from branching activity, xenology from exchange of code across different branches, and paralogy from duplication in a single branch. See Fig. 1 for illustration.

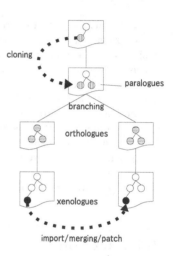

Fig. 1. Types of Code Homology

According to the classification, we implemented procedures for analyzing homologues. To show the capability of the method, the results of experiments on several large-scale software are reported including BIND9 DNS servers, a couple of Java software systems jEdit and Ant, and Linux device drivers. Xenology is investigated with BIND9 and paralogy is investigated with jEdit, Ant, and Linux device drivers.

The results shows that the proposed method is efficient enough to analyze the entire device driver subsystems in 32 versions of Linux from 2.6.0 to 2.6.31, each of which consists of millions of lines of source code. Several inconsistencies in Linux serial drivers have been detected that violate a crucial development policy change concerning kernel locking. It is also shown that the method produces better analysis results compared to existing code clone trackers. In fact, the system could track not only all clone regions reported in the previous literature [5,6,3,7,8], but also regions that escaped from previous analysis [6].

To summarize, the contributions of the paper are:

- proposal of the notion of code homology to categorize similar code in genealogy of evolving software,
- development of an automated method for detecting and tracking homologues, and
- development of an automated method for reconstructing and comparing fine-grained change histories for homologues.

The rest of the paper is organized as follows. Prerequisites for tree differencing used in code homology analysis are explained in Sect. 2. Section 3 describes the method for code homology analysis. The results of the experiments is reported in Sect. 4. After related work is reviewed in Sect. 5, we conclude in Sect. 6.

2   Tree Differencing

We regard a version of a software system as a set of abstract syntax trees (ASTs) which correspond to source files (compilation units) and also as a directory tree which consists of source files. Tree differencing plays an important role in code homology analysis, which consists of three steps: detecting homologous code, tracking homologous code, and tracking changes of homologous code. We enumerate below the required functions in each step, whose details are explained in Sect. 3. Tree differencing is responsible for 1-(a), 1-(b), 2-(a), and 3-(a) in code homology analysis.

1. Homologous code detection
   (a) discovering common structures between a pair of ASTs — for orthologues
   (b) differencing a pair of ASTs — for xenologues
   (c) detecting code clones — for paralogues
2. Code fragment tracking
   (a) mapping nodes in one AST to corresponding nodes in another AST
   (b) detecting cloning activities
   (c) mapping line ranges in source code to the corresponding sub-ASTs and vice versa
3. Change history reconstruction
   (a) deriving higher level descriptions from low level descriptions for changes between a pair of ASTs

A fundamental function of a tree differencing algorithm is to calculate a sequence of *edit operations* (called *edit sequences*) that transforms T_1 into T_2 for a given pair of trees T_1 and T_2. The basic edit operations include 1) relabeling, 2) deletion, and 3) insertion of nodes, and 4) moves of subtrees. An edit sequence between two ASTs may be regarded as difference or similarity between them. Tree differencing also computes a set of matched pairs of nodes between target trees. We call such a set of matched pairs of nodes a *node map*, which may be regarded as a (partial) finite mapping. Note that labels of a matched pair of nodes do not necessarily coincide. Node maps are constrained to preserve the structure of target trees up to relabeling. A common part of a pair of ASTs T_1 and T_2 with respect to a node map M between them is defined as a pair of sets of nodes $(\mathrm{dom}(M), \mathrm{cod}(M))$, where $\mathrm{dom}(X)$ and $\mathrm{cod}(X)$ denote domain and codomain of mapping X, respectively.

We can use any tree differencing algorithms or tools that satisfy the requirements for code homology analysis described above. In this study, we used a tree differencing system called Diff/TS [9]. Diff/TS approximates and extends an optimal tree comparison algorithm with heuristics driven control configurable for multiple programming languages. Diff/TS is capable of processing Python, Java, C and C++ projects, and provides all required functions but 3-(a). In order to reconstruct higher level description of source code changes from low level edit sequences computed by tree differencing, we developed a module for classifying changes in C programs into approximately 80 change types following the ideas of Fluri and Gall [2]. Change types are defined according to edit operations and syntactical information embedded in ASTs. For example, a change type **function call inserted** is defined as insertion of a subtree corresponding to function call and **return value changed** as some edit operation(s) on AST node(s) in a subtree corresponding to a return value.

3   Code Homology Analysis

This section presents procedures for detecting and tracking homologous code in a given set of branches. An overview of our key techniques for code homology analysis is also provided.

The tree differencing algorithm allows us to distinguish between the preserved portion (up to relabeling) and the added/deleted portion between a pair of versions, and to compute edit operations which transform the one into another. We employ a "double-differencing" technique to identify xenologues. First, we pairwise compute preserved portions between relative versions and conclude that the preserved portion found closest to the most recent common ancestor represents orthologues. Then, we compute differences between preserved portions to identify added code fragments as xenologues. See Fig. 2 for illustration, where version A branches into versions B and C, which then evolve into $B1$ and $C1$, respectively. A vertical dashed line denotes difference, in which a black triangle represents code addition and a white triangle represents code deletion. A horizontal dashed line denotes common code segments, i.e., homologues between relative versions. Segments that have been newly added in the homologues suggest existence of merged or patched code, which we call xenologues (e.g., a shaded black triangle in Fig. 2). Other segments that have disappeared from the homologues suggest existence of individually modified code. In general, we cannot decide whether xenologues are originated from code exchange or simultaneous patch application without manually inspecting available documents such as change-logs or development histories.

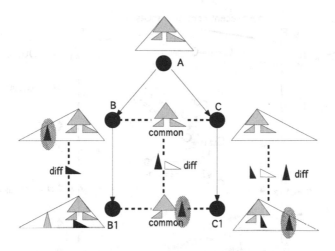

Fig. 2. Double-Differencing Between Branches

Paralogues, that is, code clones or duplicated code, are detected in a different manner. For the (given) initial version of the software, we apply existing code clone detection tools and accept the outputs as clone groups generated before the first version. For identifying cloning activities after the first version, we first compute added code fragments by tree differencing, and then find its potential duplication origins in the previous versions. A common token sequence matching algorithm is used for this.

We introduce several notations and terms needed for the rest of the paper. The set of nodes in A is denoted by $\mathcal{N}(A)$. By $\mathcal{I}(A)$, we denote the set of post-order indexes of an AST A. We identify nodes with their post-order indexes. Let v be a version of software system. We denote the set of ASTs corresponding to source files contained in v by $\mathcal{A}(v)$. For a tree A and $S \subseteq \mathcal{N}(A)$, $A|_S$ denotes the tree obtained from A by removing all nodes that do not belong to S. We introduce two wrapper functions of Diff/TS denoted by Δ for ASTs and Δ_d for directory trees. For ASTs A_1 and A_2, $\Delta(A_1, A_2)$ computes a triple (M, D, I), where M denotes a node map such that $M \subseteq \mathcal{I}(A_1) \times \mathcal{I}(A_2)$, D a set of deleted components, and I a set of inserted components. For versions v_1 and v_2, $\Delta_d(v_1, v_2)$ computes (M, D, I), where M denotes a node map such that $M \subseteq \mathcal{A}(v_1) \times \mathcal{A}(v_2)$, D a set of deleted source files, and I a set of inserted source files. Note that internal nodes (directories) are omitted from M. We extend the domain of Δ to the set of versions: $\Delta(v_1, v_2) = \{(A_1, A_2, M, D, I) | (M, D, I) = \Delta(A_1, A_2)$, where $(A_1, A_2) \in M_d, (M_d, D_d, I_d) = \Delta_d(v_1, v_2)\}$.

In order to detect homologues, we compute *common code structures* (CCSs) between versions. A CCS between two ASTs A_1 and A_2 with respect to a node map M, denoted by $\mathrm{CCS}_M(A_1, A_2)$, is defined as a pair of trees (S_1, S_2) where $S_1 = A_1|_{\mathrm{dom}(M)}$ and $S_2 = A_2|_{\mathrm{cod}(M)}$. A CCS between two versions is defined as a set of CCSs between ASTs which corresponds to source files matched

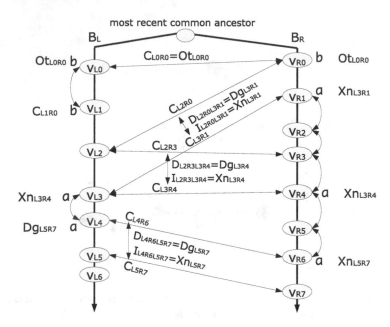

Fig. 3. Detecting Homologues

by Δ_d. We can compute a CCS between versions v_1 and v_2 by first computing $(M_d, D_d, I_d) = \Delta_d(v_1, v_2)$, and then computing $(M, D, I) = \Delta(A_1, A_2)$ and
$(A_1|_{\text{dom}(M)}, A_2|_{\text{cod}(M)})$, for each $(A_1, A_2) \in M_d$.

3.1   Detecting Homologues

An orthologue is defined between versions of different branches. For a pair of
branches B_L and B_R diverged from a common ancestor, an orthologue between
the oldest versions of B_L and B_R is defined as a CCS between the oldest versions. See Fig. 3, where C_{L0R0} and Ot_{L0R0} denote a CCS and an orthologue
between versions v_{L0} and v_{R0} of branches B_L and B_R. Once we have obtained
an orthologue between the oldest versions, orthologues between other versions
of B_L and B_R is obtained by tracking the oldest orthologue. Our method of
tracking code fragments is described in Sect. 3.2.

In order to detect xenologues, we must perform differencing one more time
on CCSs. Let B_L and B_R be branches that stem from a common ancestor (See
Fig. 4). For versions v_{Lb} and v_{Rb}, we compute $\text{Xn}(v_{Lb}, v_{Rb})$ which denotes the set
of xenologues between v_{Lb} and v_{Rb}. We let $\Delta_d(v_{Lb}, v_{Rb}) = (M_{LbRb}, D_{LbRb}, I_{LbRb})$
where $M_{LbRb} = \{(1,1), (5,3)\}$, where nodes are indicated by indexes (by post-
order traversal). Similarly, for (v_{La}, v_{Ra}), (v_{La}, v_{Lb}), and (v_{Ra}, v_{Rb}), we let
$M_{LaRa} = \{(1,1), (3,3)\}$, $M_{LaLb} = \{(1,2), (3,5)\}$, and $M_{RaRb} = \{(3,3)\}$. Among
the pairs contained in M_{LbRb}, only $(5,3) = (A_{Lb5}, A_{Rb3})$ is able to form a com-
mutative diagram consisting of dashed arrows in Fig. 4. Similarly in M_{LaRa}, only
(A_{La3}, A_{Rb3}) form a diagram. We apply Δ to (A_{Lb5}, A_{Rb3}) and (A_{La3}, A_{Ra3}) to

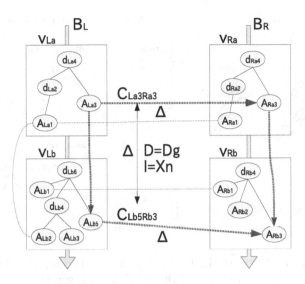

Fig. 4. Differencing Common Code Structures

obtain CCSs for them. Let $M_b = M_{Lb5Rb3}$ and $M_a = M_{La3Ra3}$ be node maps obtained from the applications, respectively. By definition, $\mathrm{CCS}_{M_b}(A_{Lb5}, A_{Rb3})$ $= (A_{Lb5}|_{\mathrm{dom}(M_b)}, A_{Rb3}|_{\mathrm{cod}(M_b)})$ and similarly we have $\mathrm{CCS}_{M_a}(A_{La3}, A_{Ra3})$ $= (A_{La3}|_{\mathrm{dom}(M_a)}, A_{Ra3}|_{\mathrm{cod}(M_a)})$. We let $C_{Lb5Rb3} = A_{Lb5}|_{\mathrm{dom}(M_b)}$ and $C_{La3Rb3} = A_{La3}|_{\mathrm{dom}(M_a)}$. Finally, we apply Δ to C_{La3Rb3} and C_{Lb5Rb3}. Let $(M, D, I) = \Delta(C_{La3Rb3}, C_{Lb5Rb3})$. I corresponds to $\mathrm{Xn}(A_{Lb5}, A_{Rb3})$ and D "degenerated" homologues between A_{Lb5} and A_{Rb3}, denoted by $\mathrm{Dg}(A_{Lb5}, A_{Rb3})$. Note that we can choose $A_{Rb3}|_{\mathrm{cod}(M_b)}$ for C_{Lb5Rb3} or $A_{Ra3}|_{\mathrm{cod}(M_a)}$ for C_{La3Ra3} since we ignore the difference of node labels in the node maps.

As mentioned in the beginning of Sect. 3, it is impossible to determine the origin of xenologues in general. For example, in Fig. 3, suppose that there exists some $a \in \mathrm{Xn}_{L3R4}$ and it also exists v_{L3} through v_{L4}, and v_{R1} through v_{R6}. We can not decide whether a is introduced by simultaneous patch application to v_{L3} and v_{R1} or by copying some part from a revision between v_{R1} and v_{R6} to v_{L3}.

We use existing tools for identifying paralogues (code clones) in the initial version of the given software versions. For the versions descending from the initial versions, we use a code tracking method described in the next section for detecting cloning activities.

3.2   Tracking Code Fragments

Once the occurrence of a homologue is discovered, we look into a *code continuum* to inspect developments in the subsequent versions. A code continuum is a data structure created by composing differencing results across versions to record entire lifetime of a source code entity. A code continuum can be illustrated by a set of *node continua*, that is, threads representing the lifetime of AST nodes

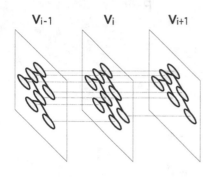

Fig. 5. Code Continuum

Alg. 1. Continuum Construction

```
1:  procedure CONSTCTM(⟨T₀, T₁, . . . Tₙ⟩, K)
2:      K ← ∅
3:      for 0 ≤ i ≤ n − 1 do
4:          Mᵢ = M(Tᵢ, Tᵢ₊₁)
5:          Mapped ← ∅
6:          for k = ⟨N₀, . . . , Nₗ⟩ ∈ K do
7:              k ← ⟨N₀, . . . , Nₗ, Mᵢ(Nₗ)⟩
8:              Mapped ← Mapped ∪ {Nₗ}
9:          end for
10:         for x ∈ dom(Mᵢ) do
11:             if x ∉ Mapped then
12:                 K ← K ∪ {⟨ε, . . . , ε, x, Mᵢ(x)⟩}
                                  ‾‾‾‾‾‾‾
                                  i times
13:             end if
14:         end for
15:     end for
16: end procedure
```

over time as in Fig. 5, where the beginning and the ending of a thread indicate the introduction and the removal of the AST node, respectively.

A node continuum is constructed for each AST node. For the same reason as we perform directory tree differencing, we construct a *file continuum* for each source code file. Each node/file continuum stores trace information of an AST node and a source file, respectively. A continuum for versions $v_0, \ldots, v_n$ is represented by a sequence of names $\langle N_0, \ldots, N_n \rangle$, where $N_i (0 \leq i \leq n)$ is a name of the node/file in version v_i. The node name is given by its index in post-order traversal and the file name by its path name. Non-existence of the node/file is represented by an empty name ϵ for convenience. An algorithm for constructing continua is shown in Alg. 1. In the description of continuum construction algorithm, $\mathcal{M}$ denotes a wrapper function of Diff/TS. For a pair of trees T_1 and T_2, $\mathcal{M}(T_1, T_2)$ computes a tree map between T_1 and T_2. The result is stored in K.

Since our AST nodes contain location information such as file names, line numbers, column positions and file offsets, continua make various analysis tasks easy including tracking corresponding source code entities on texts and reconstructing change sequences for a given code segment according to the results of source code tree differencing.

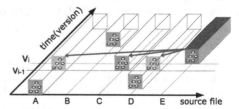

Fig. 6. Cloning Activity Detection

3.3   Detecting Cloning Activities

While traditional clone detection tools can discover code clones among given sets of software versions, they do not support tracking discovered code clones in the subsequent versions of software. To cope with the problem, we utilize code continua for identifying cloning activities by looking for the original code of cloning in the previous version by way of token based sequence matching.

Suppose that we analyze a sequence $v_0, v_1, v_2, \ldots, v_n$ of software versions. Clones that exist already in the initial version v_0 are marked using existing tools such as SimScan[1] for Java code and CCFinder [10] for C code. Cloning activities taking place between v_{i-1} and v_i ($i \geq 1$) are identified by the following procedure:

1. collect node continua starting from v_i to form a tree T included in the AST of v_i,
2. convert T into a sequence p of tokens by pre-order traversal,
3. compare p with token sequences obtained from ASTs in v_{i-1} by pre-order traversal using an O(ND) algorithm [11],
4. compute a score for each match by (number of matched tokens)/(number of tokens in p),
5. select the maximum score s and if it exceeds the pre-defined threshold, concludes that T is cloned from v_{i-1}.

The procedure is illustrated in Fig. 6. Note that code continua is collected to align pre-defined boundaries such as functions, methods, and classes to form subtrees.

3.4   Constructing and Comparing Change Histories

A change history for a code fragment is a sequence of change types obtained by accumulating change types whose locations are contained in the range of the fragment. In order to detect inconsistent changes, we define a *similarity score* between change histories as $2m/t$, where m is the number of matches calculated by a sequence matching algorithm and t is the total number of change types in both histories. We regard a pair of code fragments as inconsistently modified if and only if either of the change histories is non-empty and the similarity score between the change histories is less than a specified *similarity threshold*.

4   Experiments

In this section, we present the results of code homology analysis on several open source software projects including BIND9 daemon (for xenologue detection), a couple of Java projects, jEdit[2] and Ant[3] (for paralogue detection and tracking), and the Linux kernel driver subsystem (for change history construction). The experiments are conducted in the following manner:

---

[1] http://www.blue-edge.bg/simscan/simscan_help_r1.htm
[2] http://www.jedit.org/
[3] http://ant.apache.org/

Table 1. Sample Projects

	lang.	# of ver.	versions	# of src files	kSLOC
BIND9	C	26	9.0.0 - 9.5.0-P2	767 - 1,186	153 - 260
jEdit	Java	56	3.2.2 - 4.3.0pre17	279 - 532	55 - 108
Ant	Java	41	1.1 - 1.7.1	87 - 1,220	9 - 125
Linux	C	32	2.6.0 - 2.6.31	12,424 - 23,752	3,626 - 7,337
(drivers)				(3,285 - 8,116)	(1,778 - 4,106)

1. Fill the local software repository with revisions of target software.
2. Xenologues are calculated by double-differencing (BIND9 only) and paralogues are calculated by backward code matching. Code clones detected in the first version are also treated as paralogues.
3. Paralogues are checked for inconsistent changes descending from the origin of the paralogues, which often account for latent bugs. Checking is done at the level of change type sequences described in Sect. 2 (except BIND9).
4. Discovered homologues and change histories go through human inspection for validation.

We used a PC with a pair of quad-core Intel Xeon CPU (3.0GHz) with 16GB RAM running under Linux kernel 2.6.24 for these experiments.

The programming languages used for the software, the numbers and the ranges of analyzed versions, the numbers of source files, and kSLOC (ignoring comments and blank lines) of the initial and the latest versions of the target systems are shown in Table 1. For Linux, data for **drivers** subsystem are shown in parentheses.

4.1 BIND9

The main purpose of this experiment is to ascertain that our analysis can actually detect xenologues corresponding to merged or patched code fragments. ISC BIND (Berkeley Internet Name Domain) is an implementation of the Domain Name System (DNS) protocols. As of October, 2008, three release branches of BIND9, namely 9.2.x, 9.3.x, and 9.4.x are actively maintained. We selected 26 versions for analysis and our system detected 215 orthologues. We found that about 30% of them are degenerating, that is, decreasing in size. This indicates that 30% of commonly inherited code was modified in one or more branches and 70% of it is stable for generations. The system also detected 8,948 xenologues most of which (98.27%) are relatively small in size (< 64 nodes).

In the case of BIND9, it is likely that xenologues are introduced by patch applications such as security patches since multiple releases have been maintained in parallel. For example, a modification "Query id generation was cryptographically weak." (RT#16915) is commonly included in **CHANGES** files contained in releases 9.2.8-P1, 9.3.4-P1, and 9.4.1-P1. As we expected, several xenologues in **dispatch.c**, out of 34 xenologues among 9.2.8-P1, 9.3.4-P1, and 9.4.1-P1, appear to be strongly related to that modification.

4.2   jEdit and Ant

We collected 56 versions of jEdit from release 3.2.2 to 4.3pre17, and 41 versions of Ant from release 1.1 to 1.7.1. First, we compare the paralogue (code clone) tracking ability of our method with that of Duala-Ekoko and Robillard [6]. They implemented a system called CloneTracker which is capable of tracking code clones detected by clone detection tools. It identifies clone regions at the granularity of code blocks using heuristics based on the structural properties, lexical layout, and similarities of the clone region. They provided case studies of jEdit and Ant. A clone detection tool called SimScan was used to detect code clones in the initial versions. Then, they selected five clone groups, which were tracked across the subsequent versions. They also manually inspected changes made in the tracked clone groups.

We have tracked the clone groups detected by SimScan including the five clone groups above and reconstructed change histories for them by our method. We used SimScan with the same settings as that of Duala-Ekoko and Robillard's experiment, namely volume=medium, similarity=fairly similar, and speed=fast. Our tracking results were consistent with their results except for a clone region that they could not track. Our system was able to track the clone region up to the most recent version. All reported changes collected by their manual inspection were automatically reconstructed by our change history construction method briefly described in Sect. 3.4.

We also pairwise compared reconstructed change histories of code fragments in tracked clone groups. We set the similarity threshold to 0.5. For lack of space, we only report the results of Ant. 537 clone pairs out of 1,078 initial clone pairs detected by SimScan were inconsistently modified without disappearing before the latest version, while 340 pairs disappeared before the latest version. Our system also detected 1,247 additional clone pairs after the initial version. Among them, 272 pairs were inconsistently modified (excluding 369 disappeared clone pairs). Note that detected inconsistent changes do not immediately account for bugs. There is a possibility that clones are intentionally modified differently [12]. It took our system 60 and 70 minutes to complete the whole analysis of jEdit and Ant, respectively.

In our system, cloning activities can be visualized using continua. Figures 7 and 8 show file and code (MiscUtilities.java) continua for jEdit. Each horizontal line represents a file (node) continuum and each polygon a group of file (node) continua that begin at the same version. In each polygon, continua are sorted by terminating versions and colors represent the percentage of continua generated by cloning activities in the corresponding group. We can see that a couple of versions introduced numerous clones.

4.3   Linux Device Drivers

A case study is reported, in which investigation of inconsistent changes detected by our system has led to a certain contribution to an open source community. We collected and analyzed 32 versions of Linux 2.6 kernel source code from 2.6.0

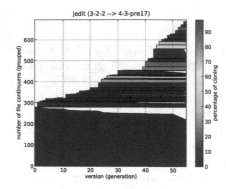

Fig. 7. File Continua of jEdit

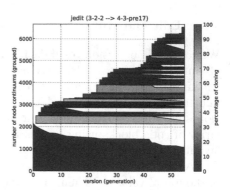

Fig. 8. Node Continua of jEdit
(MiscUtilities.java)

to 2.6.31. We first detected and tracked the paralogues in the entire kernel source code. Then we constructed fine-grained change histories for the paralogues in the **drivers** subsystem and inspected the histories to detect inconsistent changes. The **drivers** subsystem itself is a large code base as it occupies more than 70% of modern operating systems in volume and accounts for the vast majority of bugs as reported by Chou and others [13].

In order to detect initial clones in the initial version 2.6.0, we used CCFinder with the default setting. After CCFinder had detected 2,851 clone pairs, we set the similarity threshold between change histories to 0.9999 and ran the system. It took three days to detect additional clone pairs and to track all paralogues. It then took two more days to construct change histories for paralogues in the **drivers** subsystem. The system detected 814 additional clone pairs (cloning activities) after version 2.6.0, and 1,441 and 385 inconsistently modified pairs out of the initial and the additional clone pairs, respectively. After automated analysis is completed, we manually inspected inconsistent changes with similarity scores more than or equal to 0.9. It should be noted that overlooking changes such as **argument deleted** and **parameter type changed** leads to compiler errors, and hence immediate regression faults. Overlooking protocol changes such as **function call inserted**, however, often causes latent errors difficult to detect. Thus we focused on insertion of statements.

We were able to find approximately 10 inconsistent changes involving insertions of function calls to `lock_kernel` that remained in the latest version 2.6.31. An inconsistent change involving `lock_kernel` detected by the system is shown in Fig. 9, where a clone pair in `synclinkmp.c` and `synclink_cs.c` was inconsistently modified. Their change type sequences were mostly the same, which means that they almost consistently co-evolved, but differ in only one change. In this experiment, we observed a number of clone pairs that evolved almost consistently. Among them, a pair of change histories that shares 178 change types in common with a similarity score of 0.98 was discovered.

By further inspection, we found that the inconsistency relates to similar inconsistencies observed in Linux serial drivers violates a development policy

```
*** detected pair [1482] (historical similarity: 0.972973) ***
ORIGIN: "linux-2.6.0/drivers/char/synclinkmp.c":1129-1172 --
        "linux-2.6.0/drivers/char/pcmcia/synclink_cs.c":2616-2659
LATEST: "linux-2.6.31/drivers/char/synclinkmp.c":1052-1096 --
        "linux-2.6.31/drivers/char/pcmcia/synclink_cs.c":2439-2481
total significance of history1: 32 (max=4)
total significance of history2: 30 (max=4)

--- 1 changes found only in "linux-2.6.0/drivers/char/synclinkmp.c":1129-1172:

@"linux-2.6.25/drivers/char/synclinkmp.c":1109-1151
@"linux-2.6.26/drivers/char/synclinkmp.c":1111-1155
[statement inserted] (significance=2)
[Statement.Expression(Expression.Call()){lock_kernel}[(<call>(lock_kernel,<args>))]]
@Definition(wait_until_sent)(1108L,0C-1167L,0C(30773-32316))
@Definition(wait_until_sent)(1124L,1C-14C(31088-31101))
```

Fig. 9. An Example of Inconsistent Change

concerning kernel locking known as BKL (big kernel lock) pushdown. The BKL was introduced to make the kernel work on multi-processor systems. The role of the BKL, however, has diminished over years since fine-grained locking has been implemented throughout the kernel for better throughput. Although some attempts to entirely remove the BKL have been made, progress in that direction has been slow in recent years.

It was not long before the BKL accounted for a performance regression. At last, some of the developers decided to go a step further in versions 2.6.26 and 2.6.27. They began with serial drivers. In order to remove upper-level acquisition of the BKL in the control flows, they attempted to push the acquisition down to the device specific code level, where they expected BKL removal to be achieved. Indeed, numerous lock_kernel calls were (almost blindly for safety) inserted into serial driver code including synclinkmp.c at version 2.6.26, and then the upper-level call (in fs/char_dev.c) was removed at version 2.6.27. However, during the pushdown, synclink_cs.c was left unchanged, which led to an inconsistent change detected by our system.

Although the inadvertency itself does not cause errors, we could promote the BKL pushdown policy. In response to our report on the inconsistent change, the author of synclinkmp.c pointed out that the lock_kernel calls in the driver can be safely removed. We submitted a patch removing the BKL related calls from synclinkmp.c and its variations. It was acknowledged by the author of the driver.

5 Related Work

There is a large body of studies on code clones and related detection tools [4]. Code clone detection and source code differencing are two complementary techniques for analyzing relationship among software products. Although code clone detection tools may well be able to discover homologous code, they may not be suitable for precisely tracking life cycles of such code in the long evolution of the software as it requires consistently identifying changed and unchanged parts. It usually takes awkward steps of taking difference by way of clone detection. Since code clone detection methods can analyze clones across different and unrelated software products, it would be an interesting topic to combine these two methods. One idea is to use clone detection tools first to reduce the size and the scope of the problem, and then to apply tree differencing tools for detailed analysis.

Kim and others [7] proposed a method for inferring high-level description of structural changes based on the first-order logic in order to determine method level matches between versions of Java programs. While their method is specialized for Java programs, their idea of aggregating low-level description of changes seems applicable to our system. Kim and Notkin apply clone detection techniques to understand evolution of code clones [5] in Java software. They rely on location overlapping relationship to track code snippets across multiple versions of a program. While their analysis is simple and fast, it may not be able to extract how such code snippets changes over time from the source code. Duala-Ekoko and Robillard [6] proposes a code tracking method tailored for Java. Although the method is driven by heuristics and suitable for interactive use, the lack of precision in syntactic analysis may limit the ability of the tool. Godfrey and Zou [14] developed a set of techniques for detecting merging/splitting of functions and files in software systems. They presented a set of merge/split patterns and employed call relationships to aid in detecting their occurrence, which are also useful for our analysis. Aversano and others [15] proposed a method of investigating how clones are maintained over time. In order to derive evolution patterns of clones, they rely on fast but coarse line-by-line differencing to track clones.

In Sect. 3, we implicitly assumed that the genealogies of target software systems are given. However, without any development history or any explicit record of tagging or version copying operations, it may be difficult to determine the origin of branching, notably the version from which a development branch is duplicated. In such situations, we can reconstruct the genealogies by utilizing tree differencing and tools for phylogeny [9].

6   Conclusion

We have proposed an automated method for analyzing code homology in genealogy of evolving software based on fine-grained tree differencing. Homologues can be introduced through various activities: branching/forking in software projects (orthologues), code exchange between neighboring branches such as code import/merging and common bug-fix patches (xenologues), and code duplication within branches (paralogues or code clones). As the development proceeds, homologues can incur additional maintenance efforts. We have developed a method for detecting and tracking such distinctive pieces of code by exploiting fine-grained tree differencing. Detecting and tracking homologues along evolution branches enable us to reconstruct and to compare change histories of homologues, which leads us to detect inconsistent changes. Results of experiments conducted on several large-scale software including BIND9 DNS servers, a couple of Java software jEdit and Ant, and Linux device drivers have been reported to show the capability of the method. Having scalable and precise tree differencing engines helped us to analyze a large-scale software project such as the Linux kernel consisting of several millions of SLOC.

Future work includes the following:

1. to improve processing speed by further exploiting parallelism and by eliminating redundant computation,
2. to build a database for efficiently storing and retrieving various (intermediate) results computed by the system, together with comprehensive graphical user interface, and
3. to apply our analysis to:
   (a) change pattern mining and future modification prediction,
   (b) language-aware merging, and
   (c) the concrete problem of generating generic patches [16] that cover wide range of Linux device drivers.

References

1. Fitch, W.: Homology a personal view on some of the problems. Trends in Genetics 16(5), 227–231 (2000)
2. Fluri, B., Gall, H.C.: Classifying change types for qualifying change couplings. In: ICPC 2006: Proceedings of the 14th IEEE International Conference on Program Comprehension, pp. 35–45. IEEE Computer Society, Los Alamitos (2006)
3. Kim, M., Notkin, D.: Program element matching for multi-version program analyses. In: MSR 2006: Proceedings of the 2006 international workshop on Mining software repositories, pp. 58–64. ACM, New York (2006)
4. Roy, C.K., Cordy, J.R., Koschke, R.: Comparison and evaluation of code clone detection techniques and tools: A qualitative approach. Science of Computer Programming 74(7), 470–495 (2009)
5. Kim, M., Sazawal, V., Notkin, D., Murphy, G.: An empirical study of code clone genealogies. In: ESEC/FSE-13: Proceedings of the 10th European software engineering conference held jointly with 13th ACM SIGSOFT international symposium on Foundations of software engineering, pp. 187–196. ACM, New York (2005)
6. Duala-Ekoko, E., Robillard, M.P.: Tracking code clones in evolving software. In: ICSE 2007: Proceedings of the 29th International Conference on Software Engineering, pp. 158–167. IEEE Computer Society, Los Alamitos (2007)
7. Kim, M., Notkin, D., Grossman, D.: Automatic inference of structural changes for matching across program versions. In: ICSE 2007: Proceedings of the 29th international conference on Software Engineering, pp. 333–343. IEEE Computer Society, Los Alamitos (2007)
8. Reiss, S.P.: Tracking source locations. In: ICSE 2008: Proceedings of the 30th international conference on Software engineering, pp. 11–20. ACM, New York (2008)
9. Hashimoto, M., Mori, A.: Diff/TS: A tool for fine-grained structural change analysis. In: WCRE 2008: Proceedings of the 15th Working Conference on Reverse Engineering, pp. 279–288. IEEE Computer Society, Los Alamitos (2008)
10. Kamiya, T., Kusumoto, S., Inoue, K.: Ccfinder: A multilinguistic token-based code clone detection system for large scale source code. IEEE Transactions on Software Engineering 28(7), 654–670 (2002)

11. Myers, E.W.: An O(ND) difference algorithm and its variations. Algorithmica 1(2), 251–266 (1986)
12. Kapser, C., Godfrey, M.W.: "Cloning considered harmful" considered harmful. In: WCRE 2006: Proceedings of the 13th Working Conference on Reverse Engineering, pp. 19–28. IEEE Computer Society, Los Alamitos (2006)
13. Chou, A., Yang, J., Chelf, B., Hallem, S., Engler, D.: An empirical study of operating systems errors. In: SOSP 2001: Proceedings of the eighteenth ACM symposium on Operating systems principles, pp. 73–88. ACM, New York (2001)
14. Godfrey, M.W., Zou, L.: Using origin analysis to detect merging and splitting of source code entities. IEEE Transactions on Software Engineering 31(2), 166–181 (2005)
15. Aversano, L., Cerulo, L., Di Penta, M.: How clones are maintained: An empirical study. In: CSMR 2007: Proceedings of the 11th European Conference on Software Maintenance and Reengineering, pp. 81–90. IEEE Computer Society, Los Alamitos (2007)
16. Padioleau, Y., Lawall, J.L., Muller, G.: Understanding collateral evolution in linux device drivers. In: EuroSys 2006: Proceedings of the 1st ACM SIGOPS/EuroSys European Conference on Computer Systems 2006, pp. 59–71. ACM, New York (2006)

Dynamic Resource Scheduling in Disruption-Prone Software Development Environments

Junchao Xiao[1,2], Leon J. Osterweil[2], Qing Wang[1], and Mingshu Li[1,3]

[1] Laboratory for Internet Software Technologies, Institute of Software,
Chinese Academy of Sciences, Beijing 100190, China
[2] Department of Computer Science University of Massachusetts,
Amherst, MA 01003-9264 USA
[3] Key Laboratory for Computer Science, Institute of Software,
Chinese Academy of Sciences, Beijing 100190, China

Abstract. Good resource scheduling plays a pivotal role in successful software development projects. However, effective resource scheduling is complicated by such disruptions as requirements changes, urgent bug fixing, incorrect or unexpected process execution, and staff turnover. Such disruptions demand immediate attention, but can also impact the stability of other ongoing projects. Dynamic resource rescheduling can help suggest strategies for addressing such potentially disruptive events by suggesting how to balance the need for rapid response and the need for organizational stability. This paper proposes a multi-objective rescheduling method to address the need for software project resource management that is able to suggest strategies for addressing such disruptions. A genetic algorithm is used to support rescheduling computations. Examples used to evaluate this approach suggest that it can support more effective resource management in disruption-prone software development environments.

Keywords: Disruption, rescheduling, multi-objective, genetic algorithm.

1 Introduction

Software development processes are highly dependent upon human resources [1, 25]. Thus a key problem in software project management is appropriate human resource scheduling. Effective resource scheduling should ensure that assigned resources have the capability and capacity to execute their assigned tasks, that resource contention is minimized, project efficiency is maximized, and that organizational value and customer satisfaction are increased [3, 28, 29].

But disruptive events such as requirements changes, needs for fixing important bugs, incorrect or unexpected process execution, and staff turnover can create uncertainty that complicates resource scheduling [13, 21]. A particularly vexing aspect of this problem is how to balance the need to respond effectively to disruptive events against the need to be sure that this response does not create other (perhaps even more severe) disruptions by destabilizing other ongoing projects. There are risk management approaches that suggest how to anticipate and address some kinds of such disruptive events, but unexpected events simply cannot be predicted with sufficient accuracy, thus suggesting the need for a dynamic rescheduling approach.

D.S. Rosenblum and G. Taentzer (Eds.): FASE 2010, LNCS 6013, pp. 107–122, 2010.
© Springer-Verlag Berlin Heidelberg 2010

Answers to the following four questions are needed to support this approach:

(1) Under what circumstances should a rescheduling be executed? That is, how can the problems caused by disruptions and the current state of the process execution be used to suggest when a rescheduling should be undertaken?

(2) Which activities should be covered by the rescheduling? That is, what activities should be within the scope of the rescheduling when rescheduling is undertaken?

(3) How can the approach to rescheduling be tailored to accommodate different kinds of disruptions? What kinds of measures can be used to support finding a balance between dealing with current disruptions and avoiding the creation of excessive new disruptions in doing so?

(4) What kind of scheduling algorithm should be used? Which algorithm can provide as optimal a scheduling result as possible for costs in time and computing power that are as minimal as feasible?

This paper proposes a software process rescheduling method to address the issues of software project management in these kinds of dynamic disruption-prone environments. Articulate process and resource models are used to support this method. The value obtained from proposed reschedulings is computed using a function that weights both how well the rescheduling addresses the disruption (utility) and how little it creates new disruptions (stability). To address the problems posed by the high degree of complexity of such a rescheduling problem, a genetic algorithm (GA) [14] is adopted as the basis for our rescheduling approach.

The paper provides the following contributions:

(1) **A procedure for performing resource rescheduling in response to the occurrence of disruptive events** that assumes pre-specified responses to disruptions, and tackles the problems caused by executing these responses.

(2) **A multi-objective value function for evaluating rescheduling results** that takes into consideration the need for both high stability and high utility.

(3) **A GA based rescheduling method that seems to be effective** both in delivering good results and efficient in keeping costs modest.

Section 2 analyzes uncertainties and process change in software development, and describes the rescheduling approach we use to address disruptions. Section 3 presents the models used as the bases for both the rescheduling and the evaluation of the multi-objective function used to evaluate the rescheduling. Section 4 provides an initial demonstration of this method. Section 5 describes some related work, and section 6 presents conclusions and suggests future work.

2   A Rescheduling Approach to Responding to Dynamic Change

Software development managers need to make resource rescheduling decisions to respond to disruptions [15] such as:

(1) Requirement velocity: Requirements continually change during process executions [12, 16]. To address these changes, new activities may be inserted into development processes, requiring assigning resources to these activities.

(2) Sudden arrival of urgent activities: New activities may be needed to address urgent problems (e.g. serious bugs in delivered software) [20]. Although such events might not be unexpected, it may be hard to predict when they occur, and thus the changes they require may cause disruption to schedule or cost [5].

(3) Deviations in process execution: Inaccuracies in project cost estimates, incorrect performance of tasks by project personnel, the unexpected need for rework, or the occurrence of process exceptions may cause a project to fail to proceed as planned thus necessitating the rescheduling of project resources.

(4) Staff turnover: The software industry experiences high personnel mobility and staff turnover that create disruptions that typically require rescheduling [7].

This paper presents a resource rescheduling method designed to tackle the impact of these kinds of disruptions in dynamic environments. The first step in our method entails determining the changes to process execution needed to respond to the occurrence of disruptive events. These changes may include either the insertion of new process activities, the deletion of activities that were present in the initial process, or the addition or deletion of resources that had been in the initial resource set. Any of these changes triggers resource rescheduling.

The second step entails determining the scope of the resource rescheduling, namely identification of the activities and resources to be involved in a rescheduling. There are a number of reasons why rescheduling does not necessarily entail reconsideration of all the activities and resources in an entire software organization. One such reason is that process changes may occur in only one project or even in only a part of one project, and the needed resource scheduling adjustments might be readily restricted to this range. Moreover, we note that if rescheduling spans the entirety of a long term process, the rescheduling might itself introduce more disruptions than it addresses. In this paper the scope of a rescheduling is restricted to only a subset of the projects being performed by an organization at the time of the rescheduling.

Third, we construct the constraints and value objectives for rescheduling. The goal of rescheduling is to obtain optimal organizational value while conforming to various constraints. Since resource scheduling decisions are usually made under conflicting goals, a value function that can balance the goals is needed in rescheduling. This paper uses as an example addressing the conflicting goals of stability and utility.

Fourth, we seek value function optimization by using GA. This optimization problem has a high level of complexity, so we use GA as the scheduling approach, hoping to achieve near-optimal results at acceptable costs.

Section 3 describes our approaches to the problems arising in doing these steps.

3 Multi-objective Resource Rescheduling Using a GA

3.1 Project, Activity and Resource Models Used in Scheduling

3.1.1 Project Model

Software organizations are usually performing a group of projects, each described by basic information, constraints, and its value objectives. Thus we define a project as:

Definition 1. $P = (BasicAttr, ConSet, PWSet)$, **where,**

- *BasicAttr* describes such basic attributes as name, generation, descriptions, etc.
- *ConSet* is the set of all project level constraints (e.g. cost and time). Violation of each constraint will incur some quantified penalty.
- *PWSet* is a preference weight set. Each project in a multi-project environment is assigned a priority weight relative to the other projects. This weight is used to evaluate the importance of the resource requirements of each project. Note that this weight may change dynamically (e.g. to emphasize the importance of responding to the need to fix an important bug).

3.1.2 Activity Model

Precision and specificity in evaluating competing resource schedules are enhanced through the use of a project specification notation that is more precise and detailed. Thus, the Little-JIL process definition language [26] is used in this paper to define software development project activities, their dependencies upon each other, and their needs for resources. This language offers simplicity, semantic richness and expressiveness, and a formal and precise, yet graphical, syntax.

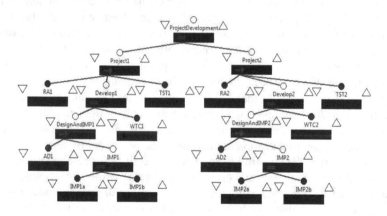

Fig. 1. Project development process described by Little-JIL

Fig. 1 shows a Little-JIL definition of a process for carrying out two software development projects in parallel. The "=" sign in the "ProjectDevelopment" root step indicates that its substeps (Project1 and Project2) are performed in parallel. Projects are decomposed into requirement analysis (RA), development (Develop), and testing (TST), which are executed sequentially (represented by "→" sign). Development is further decomposed into design (AD), implementation (IMP), and write test case (WTC). WTC is executed parallel with AD and IMP, which are executed sequentially.

Requests for resources are represented iconically by the dot atop the step, and are described as required skills, skill levels, and required quantities of skills.

Fig. 2 shows an example of how an activity may be added to a process to respond to a disruption. Thus Project3 executes RA, IMP, and TST sequentially to realize a changed requirement and Project4 and Project5 use IMP and TST sequentially to

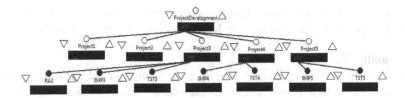

Fig. 2. Combine new project activities with initial project development process

realize urgent bug fixing. All are executed in parallel with Project1 and Project2. This process definition is used to select the activities that will be included in the scope of the rescheduling. This is done using graph searching algorithms whose details are omitted due to space constraints. In the work described here, all steps that are fewer than some previously fixed number of steps beyond the currently executing step(s) are included in the rescheduling. Details of how this is done can be found in [27]. Other criteria could be used to determine the steps in this rescheduling "window".

3.1.3 Resource Model

The human resource model proposed in [29] is used to describe human resources. Each human resource is described by its identification (ID), executable activity type set (EATS), skill set (SKLS), experience data (EXPD), schedulable time and work-load (STMW), together with salary per person-hour (SALR). EATS, SKLS and EXPD are capability attributes, and STMW is the capacity attribute.

Resources available for the rescheduling are preserved in a resource repository. The set of resources that are candidates to perform a step are those such that 1) the work type of the step is included in the EATS attribute of the resource, 2) the skills described in the step's requirements are also in the resource's SKLS attribute, and 3) the resource has a higher skill level than is required by the step. Note that when there is resource turnover, the resource repository is changed accordingly.

3.2 Multi-objective Value Measure of Rescheduling

A rescheduling may have different objectives that conflict with each other. Thus, for example, attaching a high priority to fixing a bug in one project indicates that this bug fix will return high value to the organization. But this may require using the resources of a different project, causing disruption to that project and loss of value to the organization. Thus rescheduling must be measured against a possible multiplicity of objectives. Assume a rescheduling has n objectives, $o_1, o_2, ..., o_n$, each having weight w_i, then the value of the rescheduling is defined to be $MO = \sum_{i=1}^{n} w_i * o_i$

Note that each objective in this function can be further decomposed into sub-objectives, each having its own importance weight. This paper presents, as an example, two resource rescheduling objectives to define the value function. The first (stability) weights the importance of keeping the rescheduled process similar to the initial process. The second (utility) weights the importance of responding to the disruption. Though the examples in this paper assume the existence of only two objectives, the approach scales up to consideration of any number of objectives.

3.2.1 Stability Value

Process stability is measured using two factors, change in the scheduling of each activity and change in human resource assignments to each of the activities. Schedule changes can reduce project commitment and customer satisfaction. Resource assignment changes can necessitate more communication effort, more training time, and waste of previous preparations, reducing the value of a project.

Schedule deviation is measured by the differences between initial process and rescheduled process start times and end times. Let the start time before and after rescheduling of an activity ACT be ts_{ACT} and ts'_{ACT} respectively, the end time of ACT be te_{ACT} and te'_{ACT} respectively. Since impact of start time and end time deviations may differ, let impact coefficients be α and β respectively. Then the deviation of ACT is defined to be $\alpha*|ts_{ACT} - ts'_{ACT}| + \beta*|te_{ACT} - te'_{ACT}|$, and the total deviation of the activities in $ActivitySet$ due to rescheduling is:

$$SDeviation = \sum_{ACT \in ActivitySet} (\alpha*|ts_{ACT} - ts'_{ACT}| + \beta*|te_{ACT} - te'_{ACT}|)$$

Note that in this example only the activities in the initial process are used to compute schedule deviation. Section 3.1.2 suggest how these activities are identified, and more complete details can be found in [27]. Other measures can also be defined.

To measure human resource changes, workload changes for each human resource scheduled to an activity are accumulated. Assume a human resource set HRS represents all the human resources assigned to an activity ACT in either the initial or the rescheduled process. For each hr $\in$ HRS, assume the workload allocated to ACT before rescheduling is E_{hr}^b, and after rescheduling is E_{hr}^a. If hr is not in ACT before rescheduling, E_{hr}^b is zero. If hr is not in ACT after rescheduling, E_{hr}^a is zero. Then total human resource changes are defined to be: $HRDeviation = \sum_{hr \in HRS_{ACT}} |E_{hr}^b - E_{hr}^a|$

Schedule deviation and resource change may have different impacts on stability, and so HC, a coefficient of human resource change is used to compute total deviation.

$$Deviation = \sum_{ACT \in ActivitySet} (\alpha*|ts_{ACT} - ts'_{ACT}| + \beta*|te_{ACT} - te'_{ACT}| + HC*\sum_{hr \in HRS_{ACT}} |E_{hr}^b - E_{hr}^a|)$$

The goal of stable rescheduling is to minimize the above stability loss. Therefore, total stability value is *StabilityValue = C-DP*Deviation*, where DP is the deviation penalty coefficient and constant C causes the stability value to be positive.

3.2.2 Utility Value

Utility describes the value obtained from a project that satisfies its constraints at its conclusion. If the project succeeds and satisfies its constraints, benefits will be obtained. If the project is delayed, penalties are incurred. The schedule utility of a project is defined by comparing the actual finishing date to the constraint finishing date. Let the actual finishing date and the constraint finishing date of a project be *AFD* and

CFD respectively. Let benefit of finishing one day ahead the constraint be *SB*, and the penalty for a one day delay be *SP*. The schedule utility is defined to be:

$$SUtility = SB * \max\{(AFD - CFD), 0\} - SP * \max\{(CFD - AFD), 0\}$$

Since the cost of developers is the primary cost in software development, our method only takes human resource cost into consideration. This cost is the total over all activities of the product of the salary rate of each human resource multiplied by the workload required. Assume the cost of a project is *CST* and cost constraint of this project is *CCST*, then cost utility of this project is: $CUtility = CCST - CST$

Weighting schedule and cost preference by coefficients *SWeight* and *CWeight* respectively, project utility is: $PU = SWeight * SUtility + CWeight * CUtility$

The preference weights of projects vary. For example, an urgent bug fix project may be very important and should have a high priority for resources. Thus a project preference weight (PPW) is set for each project and the utility value for all projects in an organization is defined by: $UtilityValue = \sum_{P \in ProjectSet} (PPW_P * PU_P)$

Now finally, assume the stability and utility objectives for a scheduling are given weights w_s and w_u respectively. Then a rescheduling's value is computed by:

$$Value = w_s * StabilityValue + w_u * UtilityValue$$

3.3 Rescheduling Using a GA

3.3.1 Encoding and Decoding

The first step in using GA as a problem solver is to represent the problem as a chromosome. In the activity model described by Little-JIL, non-leaf steps are used to represent scopes and to group certain kinds of activities, but only leaf steps represent actual project performance activities. Thus, once the scope of rescheduling has been determined as described in section 3.1.2 (and in more detail in [27]), only the leaf steps in that scope are selected for GA encoding. Assume the *N* steps, $S_1, S_2, ..., S_N$ are selected, and the human resources capable of executing step S_i are $HR_{i,1}, HR_{i,2}, ..., HR_{i,ti}$. We construct a resource queue $HR_{1,1}, HR_{1,2}, ..., HR_{1,t1}, ..., HR_{N,1} ..., HR_{N,tN}$, consisting of all resources that are schedulable to activities in the rescheduling scope. The first part of the chromosome (shown as the left part of Fig. 3) is generated by creating a gene for each step, as just described. The length of this part is: $T = \sum_{i=1}^{N} t_i$.

Once GA has run, if a gene has value "1" the corresponding human resource has been scheduled to the corresponding step. The value "0" means the corresponding human resource is not scheduled to the step.

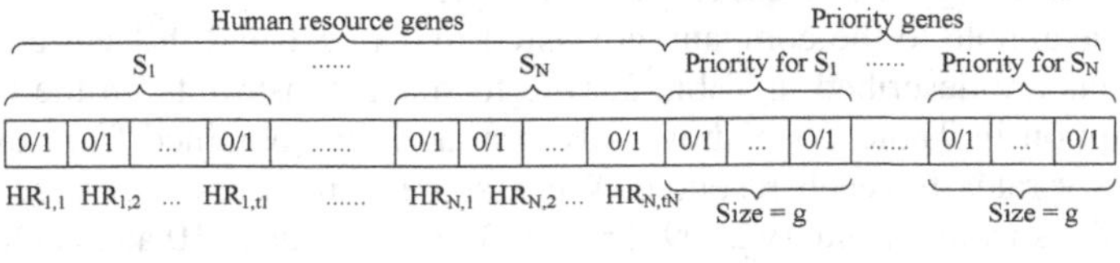

Fig. 3. Structure of the Chromosome

The chromosome also contains priority genes (shown on the right of Fig. 3) to represent the priority weight of each project. A priority weight is a binary number. If the GA assigns a human resource to more than one step, the step with highest priority value is assigned the human resource. Therefore, the length of the chromosome is:

$CL = T + N * g$, where g is the base 2 logarithm of the maximum priority level.

After GA has been run, a chromosome is decoded into a schedule as follows. First, sort all the steps involved in the rescheduling into a queue. In this queue, steps that precede others are placed in front of those that follow. If steps do not have a precedent/succedent relationship, steps with higher priority are placed in front of those with lower priority. Second, assign each resource whose gene has the value "1" to the corresponding step in the queue. If a step requires only a certain number of resources, then at most that number of resources are assigned. Third, allocate the schedulable workload of the assigned resources to each step and update the availability state of the resources. Finally, set the start time of the step so that it is the earliest time that is not earlier than the end time of all of its preceding steps.

Constraint satisfaction: Rescheduling constraints are built into the encoding and decoding process. During encoding, candidate resources for each step are determined to have the capability to execute the step. In the decoding process, only resources that have available workload are scheduled, and they are scheduled only at times when they are available and when the activity is actually executable. Other constraints could also be defined and used to assure that more qualified resources (e.g. those with higher skill levels) are favored for assignment over less qualified resources.

3.3.2 Running GA

The initial population of the GA is generated by creating chromosomes as described above. Evolution is realized by using predefined crossover and mutation rates, for each population generation. The fitness of each chromosome is evaluated by the value function presented in section 3.2 and chromosomes with higher fitnesses are selected for each succeeding generation. Evolution continues for a predetermined number of generations, and the chromosome with the highest fitness in the last generation is selected as the solution. Full details of the steps used in executing GA are omitted here due to space limitations. These details can be found, however, in [28].

4 Demonstration of the Use of This Approach

To evaluate our method, we used it to simulate the allocation of resources by a software company engaged in two different projects. We hypothesize that each of the two projects is addressing requirements for a group of modules, and that both are doing so by performing the process shown in Fig. 1.

Resources available to the company are listed in Table 1 and the leaf activities of the two projects are described in Table 2. Due to space constraints, in the human resource description in Table 1 we show only productivity (obtained from experience data) and salary rates for each resource. We assume human resources are available only on workdays from 1 January 2009 through 31 December 2010 and each workday

Table 1. Human resource information of initial process

Human resource	Executable activity and corresponding productivity (KLOC/Person-Hour)	Salary rate (RMB)	Human resource	Executable activity and corresponding productivity (KLOC/Person-Hour)	Salary rate (RMB)
HR1	RA/0.06	60	HR8	IMP/0.025	40
HR2	RA/0.04	45	HR9	IMP/0.02	35
HR3	RA/0.05	50	HR10	IMP/0.015	35
HR4	AD/0.06	60	HR13	WTC/0.05; TST/0.04	45
HR5	AD/0.05	60	HR14	WTC/0.045; TST/0.035	45
HR6	AD/0.05	50	HR15	WTC/0.035; TST/0.03	45
HR7	IMP/0.03	45	HR16	WTC/0.03; TST/0.03	40

Table 2. Activity information of initial process

Activity	Candidate resources	Size (KLOC)	Initial allocated resources	[Start, End]
RA1	HR1, HR2, HR3	20	HR1, HR2	[2009-05-01, 2009-06-05]
AD1	HR4, HR5, HR6	20	HR4, HR5	[2009-06-08, 2009-07-08]
IMP1a	HR7, HR8, HR9, HR10	12	HR7, HR8	[2009-07-09, 2009-08-17]
IMP1b	HR7, HR8, HR9, HR10	8	HR9, HR10	[2009-07-09, 2009-08-18]
WTC1	HR13, HR14, HR15, HR16	20	HR13, HR14	[2009-06-08, 2009-07-23]
TST1	HR13, HR14, HR15, HR16	20	HR13, HR14	[2009-08-19, 2009-10-5]
RA2	HR1, HR2, HR3	16	HR1, HR3	[2009-05-21, 2009-06-24]
AD2	HR4, HR5, HR6	16	HR5, HR6	[2009-06-25, 2009-07-30]
IMP2a	HR7, HR8, HR9, HR10	10	HR7, HR8	[2009-08-18, 2009-09-17]
IMP2b	HR7, HR8, HR9, HR10	6	HR9, HR10	[2009-08-19, 2009-09-17]
WTC2	HR13, HR14, HR15, HR16	16	HR15, HR16	[2009-06-25, 2009-08-11]
TST2	HR13, HR14, HR15, HR16	16	HR15, HR16	[2009-09-18, 2009-11-4]

has 8 person-hour workloads available. In the activity description shown in Table 2, we show only the candidate resources, size, initial allocated resources, and the start and end time for each activity execution. The candidate resources are identified by matching activity resource requests to human resource capabilities.

We now assume that after resources have been scheduled to the projects' activities three new requirements are issued. One is an upgrade requirement that is addressed by the process specified as Project3 in Fig. 2, and the other two are to address the sudden arrival of urgent bug fixing requests to be done as specified by Project4 and Project5 in Fig. 2. Leaf activities of these projects are described in Table 3.

Table 3. Activity information of added process

Activity	Candidate resources	Size (KLOC)
RA3	HR1, HR2, HR3	14
IMP3	HR4, HR5, HR6	14
TST3	HR13, HR14, HR15, HR16	14
IMP4	HR7, HR8, HR9, HR10	10
TST4	HR13, HR14, HR15, HR16	10
IMP5	HR7, HR8, HR9, HR10	8
TST5	HR13, HR14, HR15, HR16	8

Rescheduling is required in order to provide resources to address these new requirements. For this example we assume that rescheduling parameters of the multi-objective value function are set as shown in Table 4 and parameters used for computing project utility are set as shown in Table 5.

Table 4. Parameters of multi-objective value function

$\alpha/ \beta/$ HC	1 / 1 / 1
C	600,000
DP	300

Table 5. Parameters of projects used for computing utility

	Project1	Project2	Project3	Project4	Project5
Constraint start and finish date	[2009-05-01, 2009-10-30]	[2009-05-21, 2009-11-31]	[2009-06-01, 2009-8-31]	[2009-07-01, 2009-9-20]	[2009-08-01, 2009-10-30]
Constraint cost	200000	150000	120000	90000	90000
Schedule benefit/penalty	100 / 200	100 / 200	200 / 400	200 / 400	200 / 400
Schedule/Cost weight	1 / 1	1 / 1	2 / 1	2 / 1	2 / 1
Project weight	1	1	2	3	4

For the GA examples presented here, we set population scale to 60, crossover rate to 0.8, mutation rate to 0.02, and generation number to 500.

4.1 The Need for Rescheduling

We begin by computing an initial resource assignment plan for Project1 and Project2 assuming that there will be no disrupting events. This plan is shown in Fig. 4.

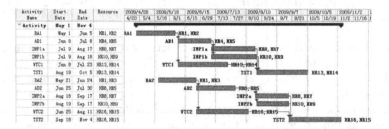

Fig. 4. Initial scheduling result

We then hypothesize the need to provide resources for Project3 starting on 1 June 2009. Activity RA3 has three candidate resources, and let us assume that it is decided that HR1 and HR2 are to be allocated to it. Thus its execution would require 18 work-days, from June 1 to June 24. Then IMP3 would need to be executed starting on June 25. IMP3 has four candidate resources and let us further assume that HR7 and HR8 are selected. Thus IMP3's execution would require 32 workdays, from June 25 to August 7. Finally, TST3 would need to be executed starting on August 8. However, note that from June 1 to June 5, HR1 and HR2 are occupied by RA1 and from June 1 to June 24, HR1 and HR3 are occupied by RA2, thus RA3 could not obtain the resources it needs without disrupting other projects. In addition, from July 9 to September 17, all resources able to execute IMP3 are occupied performing Project1 and Project2. Thus either Project3 must wait or other projects must be disrupted. Organizational value is lost in either case. Therefore, a rescheduling is indicated.

Once the scope of rescheduling has been determined, all the activities in this scope will be encoded in the chromosome, and used in the GA based rescheduling.

4.2 Results under a Specific Stability and Utility Weight Configuration

We start exploring the efficacy of our approach by examining the consequences of two rescheduling approaches, where stability is the only objective, and where utility is the only objective. Fig. 5 shows the rescheduling plan where stability is the only consideration (stability and utility weights are set to 1 and 0 respectively). The start/end times of activities in Project1 and Project2 are not changed, nor are scheduled human resources. The new added activities are executed only when resources are available, causing delay and low utility for Project3.

Fig. 6 shows the rescheduling plan where only utility value is considered (the stability and utility weights are set to 0 and 1 respectively). This schedule causes Project3 to have higher utility, but the start/end times and scheduled resources of most activities in Projects 1 and 2 are changed causing substantial reduction in organizational value. This case study and others not shown due to space constraints indicate that our approach supports scheduling resources to address stability and utility objectives. We now suggest how this capability can help project managers.

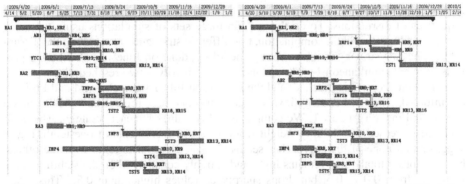

Fig. 5. Rescheduled plan when stability is 1   **Fig. 6.** Rescheduled plan when stability is 0

4.3 Results under Different Stability and Utility Weights

Using a multi-objective value function to evaluate rescheduling can help support exploring the way that different balances between stability and utility can affect organizational value. To demonstrate this we varied the stability and utility weights for a series of reschedulings. Fig. 7 shows the different values of the schedules obtained. As expected increasing the stability weight causes a consequent increase in stability value while utility value decreases. Conversely increasing the utility weight causes utility value to increase while decreasing stability value. Of perhaps more interest, however, is that the maximum total of the two values is obtained over a broad range of stability weights, and dips only when the stability weight is near either 0 or 1. This suggests that moderation in addressing disruption is likely to be the best course of

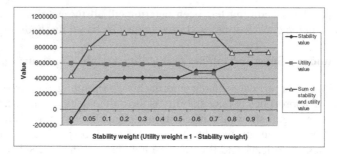

Fig. 7. Stability and utility value under different stability and utility weights (results are averages of 10 different simulations)

action, but the precise relatively weighting of the importance of stability and utility may not be particularly important.

4.4 A Series of Reschedulings to Tackle Multiple Disruptions

The foregoing suggests that our approach could help in deciding how to deal with a single disruptive event. But most software organizations experience a continuing flow of disruptions. Thus next we used our approach to seek a strategy for dealing with such sequences of disruptions. To do this we ran three sets of simulations using the same stability and utility weight combination, but different strategies for handling the disruptions. The first strategy involves one rescheduling, done on June 1, with all three projects initiated simultaneously. The second strategy involves two reschedulings, one on June 1 when Project3 is initiated; and the second on July 1 when Project4 and Project5 are initiated. The third strategy involves initiating one new project on June 1, one on July 1, and one on August 1. We computed utility values for each strategy, where for each we increased the stability weight from 0 to 1 in increments of one tenth. Fig. 8 suggests that none of the approaches seems to offer clear advantages over the others, but that for all total value remains high, and roughly constant when the stability value increases from 0.0 to 0.5, but drops sharply at values higher than 0.5. This result

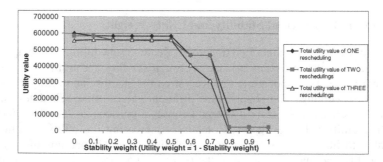

Fig. 8. Utility value curves for three different rescheduling strategies (results are averages of 10 different simulations)

seems to confirm the importance of responding promptly to disruptions, but also suggests that a "drop everything" approach seems to offer little advantage over a more measured response.

More generally, this case study seems to us to indicate that our rescheduling approach offers promise of being a useful tool in formulating and analyzing various strategies for dealing with various kinds and scenarios of disruption.

4.5 Discussion

The above case studies show that our proposed method can provide useful rescheduling results using different combinations of objectives, some of which might entail conflicts. Project managers can compare these results and use them to support their resource allocation decisions by suggesting alternatives to decisions the might have been planned by the human manager.

Currently our method still has some limitations. Some of them are:

The scale of the scheduling problem affects the running time and may make it impractical or impossible to obtain optimal results. If the problem is too large, dividing it into several smaller ones might help.

Different GA parameter settings affect whether optimal or near-optimal rescheduling results can be obtained. Different scheduling problems may suggest the use of different GA parameters.

Additional types of constraints could be used to improve the quality of schedules.

5 Related Work

Researchers have observed that software development project disruptions can be due to uncertainties in requirements, process execution, and human resources. Ebert et al. [1] analyze requirement uncertainties and provide problems that are caused by them. Li et al. [16] use rough set analysis to solve problems caused by requirement uncertainties. Pfahl et al. [22] and Liu et al. [17] use simulation to explain some effects arising from requirements volatility. Cass et al. [8] indicate that rework is an ongoing problem in software development. Melo et al. [19] point out that resource change is a key factor in maintenance schedule postponement and cost overrun. Dynamic rescheduling is not suggested as a way to deal with any of these different kinds of uncertainties.

Software process scheduling has been explored by quite a few researchers. Some methods provide schedules that are based upon the assumption of accurate human resource specifications, such as skills, productivity, and availability, and are thus able to satisfy constraints and obtain optimal scheduling values [3, 6, 9, 11]. However, these methods only address scheduling problems that arise in response to specifically anticipated activities and resource changes. Unlike our approach, they cannot dynamically respond during actual process execution to disruptions caused by unanticipated events.

To address uncertainties in software development and maintenance processes, Antoniol et al. [4] present a scheduling method that combines a genetic algorithm and queue simulation. Though the method realizes scheduling under some uncertainties, issues such as stability are not taken into account. Other methods tackle uncertainties by introducing probability into scheduling. Liu et al. [18] suggest a probability based two stage scheduling method. Though the method uses probability of commitment satisfaction in scheduling, dynamic changes still lead schedule disruption.

There are a lot of rescheduling methods in the manufacturing domain [2, 10, 23, 24]. These methods use rescheduling to achieve both makespan and stability value. However, the resources in manufacturing are usually machines, which do not pose problems such as volatility and skill level change that are characteristics of human resources. This limits the applicability of this work to software development

6 Conclusions and Future Work

This paper has presented a multi-objective software process resource rescheduling method using a GA. We identified some conditions that can necessitate rescheduling and introduced models to describe projects, activities, and resources. We then used these models to define some rescheduling problems, and presented a multi-objective value function that weights stability and utility to compute rescheduling value. The evaluation of our method shows that this multi-objective value function can be used to guide rescheduling, and might help managers to balance potentially conflicting objectives in making resource rescheduling decisions.

Future work
Continuous rescheduling: In our case study, we used examples for which relatively accurate parameter estimates are available. However, such estimates usually change during process execution. Thus process delay and activity completion date changes happen frequently. In future work, such continuous changes and reschedulings will be taken into consideration.

More constraints: This paper only models capability constraints, availability constraints, and activity execution order constraints in scheduling. Other constraints, such as different activities needing the same resource, will be modeled in future work.

Analysis of different objectives and their importance: The activities on a critical path have more impact on the stability of a project. Thus it seems more critical to schedule these activities than to schedule other activities. Furthermore, there are many other kinds of objectives in rescheduling. In future work, more objectives and more details of these objectives will be analyzed and used in rescheduling.

Acknowledgments. This paper was supported by the National Natural Science Foundation of China under grant No. 90718042, the 863 Program of China under grant No. 2007AA010303, 2007AA01Z186, as well as the 973 program under grant No. 2007CB310802. This work was also supported by the National Science Foundation under Awards No. CCR-0205575, CCR-0427071, and IIS-0705772. Any opinions, findings, and conclusions or recommendations expressed in this publication are those of the author(s) and do not necessarily reflect the views of the National Science Foundation.

References

1. Acuña, S.T., Juristo, N., Moreno, A.M.: Emphasizing Human Capabilities in Software Development. IEEE Software 23(2), 94–101 (2006)
2. Adibi, M.A., Zandieh, M., Amiri, M.: Multi-objective scheduling of dynamic job shop using variable neighborhood search. Expert Systems with Applications 37(1), 282–287 (2009)
3. Alba, E., Chicano, J.F.: Software Project Management with GAs. Journal of Information Sciences 177(11), 2380–2401 (2007)
4. Antoniol, G., Penta, M.D., Harman, M.: A Robust Search–Based Approach to Project Management in the Presence of Abandonment, Rework, Error and Uncertainty. In: Proceedings of the 10th International Symposium on Software Metrics, pp. 172–183 (2004)
5. Antoniol, G., Penta, M.D., Harman, M.: Search–Based Techniques Applied to Optimization of Project Planning for a Massive Maintenance Project. In: Proceedings of the 21st International Conference on Software Maintenance, pp. 240–249 (2005)
6. Barreto, A., Barros, M.d.O., Werner, C.M.L.: Staffing a software project: A con-straint satisfaction and optimization-based approach. Computer & Operations Research 35(10), 3073–3089 (2008)
7. Boehm, B.: Software risk management: principles and practices. IEEE Software 8(1), 32–41 (1991)
8. Cass, A.G., Sutton Jr., S.M., Osterweil, L.J.: Formalizing Rework in Software Processes. In: Oquendo, F. (ed.) EWSPT 2003. LNCS, vol. 2786, pp. 16–31. Springer, Heidelberg (2003)
9. Chang, C.K., Jiang, H.-y., Di, Y., Zhu, D., Ge, Y.: Time-line based model for software project scheduling with genetic algorithms. Information and Software Technology 50(11), 1142–1154 (2008)
10. Cowling, P., Johansson, M.: Using real time information for effective dynamic scheduling. European Journal of Operational Research 139(2), 230–244 (2002)
11. Duggan, J., Byrne, J., Lyons, G.J.: Task Allocation Optimizer for Software Construction. IEEE Software 21(3), 76–82 (2004)
12. Ebert, C., Man, J.D.: Requirements Uncertainty: Influencing Factors and Concrete Improvements. In: Proceedings of the 27th International Conference on Software Engineering, pp. 553–560 (2005)
13. Erdogmus, H., Favaro, J., Halling, M.: Valuation of Software Initiatives Under Uncertainty: Concepts, Issues, and Techniques. In: Biffl, S., Aurum, A., Boehm, B., Erdogmus, H., Grünbacher, P. (eds.) Value-Based Software Engineering, pp. 39–66 (2005)
14. Holland, J.H.: Adaptation in natural and artificial systems. MIT Press, Cambridge (1992)
15. Li, M., Yang, Q., Zhai, J., Yang, G.: On Mobility of Software Processes. In: Wang, Q., Pfahl, D., Raffo, D.M., Wernick, P. (eds.) SPW 2006 and ProSim 2006. LNCS, vol. 3966, pp. 105–114. Springer, Heidelberg (2006)
16. Li, Z., Ruhe, G.: Uncertainty Handling in Tabular-Based Requirements Using Rough Sets. In: Ślęzak, D., Yao, J., Peters, J.F., Ziarko, W.P., Hu, X. (eds.) RSFDGrC 2005. LNCS (LNAI), vol. 3642, pp. 678–687. Springer, Heidelberg (2005)
17. Liu, D., Wang, Q., Xiao, J., Li, J., Li, H.: RVSim: A Simulation Approach to Predict the Impact of Requirements Volatility on Software Project Plans. In: Wang, Q., Pfahl, D., Raffo, D.M. (eds.) ICSP 2008. LNCS, vol. 5007, pp. 307–319. Springer, Heidelberg (2008)

18. Liu, X., Yang, Y., Chen, J., Wang, Q., Li, M.: Achieving On-Time Delivery: A Two-Stage Probabilistic Scheduling Strategy for Software Projects. In: Wang, Q., Garousi, V., Madachy, R., Pfahl, D. (eds.) ICSP 2009. LNCS, vol. 5543, pp. 317–329. Springer, Heidelberg (2009)

19. de Melo, A.C.V., de J. Sanchez, A.: Bayesian Networks in Software Maintenance Management. In: Vojtáš, P., Bieliková, M., Charron-Bost, B., Sýkora, O. (eds.) SOFSEM 2005. LNCS, vol. 3381, pp. 394–398. Springer, Heidelberg (2005)

20. Moratori, P., Petrovic, S., Vazquez, A.: Match-Up Strategies for Job Shop Rescheduling. In: Nguyen, N.T., Borzemski, L., Grzech, A., Ali, M. (eds.) IEA/AIE 2008. LNCS (LNAI), vol. 5027, pp. 119–128. Springer, Heidelberg (2008)

21. Ozdamar, L., Alanya, E.: Uncertainty Modelling in Software Development Projects (With Case Study). Annals of Operations Research 102, 157–178 (2001)

22. Pfahl, D., Lebsanft, K.: Using Simulation to Analyze the Impact of Software Requirements Volatility on Project Performance. Information and Software Technology 42(14), 1001–1008 (2000)

23. Pfeiffer, A.S., Kadar, B., Monostori, L.S.: Stability-oriented evaluation of rescheduling strategies, by using simulation. Computers in Industry 58(7), 630–643 (2007)

24. Rangsaritratsamee, R., F Jr., W.G., Kurz, M.B.: Dynamic rescheduling that simultaneously considers efficiency and stability. Computers & Industrial Engineering 46(1), 1–15 (2004)

25. Wang, Q., Xiao, J., Li, M., Nisar, M.W., Yuan, R., Zhang, L.: A Process-Agent Construction Method for Software Process Modeling in SoftPM. In: SPW/ProSim 2006, Shang-hai China, pp. 204–213 (2006)

26. Wise, A.: Little-JIL 1.5 Language Report Department of Computer Science, University of Massachusetts, Amherst UM-CS-2006-51 (2006)

27. Xiao, J., Osterweil, L.J., Wang, Q., Li, M.: Dynamic Scheduling in Systems with Complex Resource Allocation Requirements. Department of Computer Science at the Uni-versity of Massachusetts Amherst. Technical report: UM-CS-2009-049 (2009)

28. Xiao, J., Wang, Q., Li, M., Yang, Q., Xie, L., Liu, D.: Value-based Multiple Software Projects Scheduling with Genetic Algorithm. In: Wang, Q., Garousi, V., Madachy, R., Pfahl, D. (eds.) ICSP 2009. LNCS, vol. 5543, pp. 50–62. Springer, Heidelberg (2009)

29. Xiao, J., Wang, Q., Li, M., Yang, Y., Zhang, F., Xie, L.: A Constraint-Driven Human Resource Scheduling Method in Software Development and Maintenance Process. In: Proceedings of 24th International Conference on Software Maintenance, pp. 17–26 (2008)

Incremental Service Composition Based on Partial Matching of Visual Contracts

Muhammad Naeem[1], Reiko Heckel[1,*], Fernando Orejas[2,**],
and Frank Hermann[3]

[1] Department of Computer Science, University of Leicester, United Kingdom
{mn105,reiko}@mcs.le.ac.uk
[2] Departament de L.S.I., Universitat Politècnica de Catalunya, Barcelona, Spain
orejas@lsi.upc.edu
[3] Fakultät IV, Technische Universität Berlin, Berlin, Germany
frank.hermann@tu-berlin.de

Abstract. Services provide access to software components that can be discovered dynamically via the Internet. The increasing number of services a requester may be able to use demand support for finding and selecting services. In particular, it is unrealistic to expect that a single service will satisfy complex requirements, so services will have to be combined to match clients' requests.

In this paper, we propose a visual, incremental approach for the composition of services, in which we describe the requirements of a requester as a *goal* which is matched against multiple *provider offers*. After every match with an *offer* we decompose the *goal* into satisfied and remainder parts. We iterate the decomposition until the *goal* is satisfied or we run out of *offers*, leading to a resolution-like matching strategy. Finally, the *individual offers* can be composed into a single *combined offer* and shown to the requester for feedback.

Our approach is based on visual specifications of pre- and postconditions by graph transformation systems with loose semantics, where a symbolic approach based on constraints is used to represent attributes and their computation in graphs.

1 Introduction

Service-oriented Architecture (SOA)[1] supports dynamic discovery and binding based on matching requesters' requirements with providers' offers. Both requirements and offers can be expressed as specifications of the (expected or given) semantics of a service's operations in terms of their pre- and postconditions. At a *technical level* this is supported by semantic web technologies (e.g. OWL-S [2], WSML [3]), at *modeling level* visual contracts have been suggested to describe service semantics [4].

---

* Partially supported by the project Sensoria IST-2005-016004.
** Partially supported by the MEC project (ref. TIN2007-66523), the MEC grant PR2008-0185, the EPSRC grant EP/H001417/1 and a Royal Society travel grant.

D.S. Rosenblum and G. Taentzer (Eds.): FASE 2010, LNCS 6013, pp. 123–138, 2010.

However, expecting to find a single service for each requirement is unrealistic. Often services need to be combined to satisfy the demands of clients. For example, let us consider a scenario, where a requester is looking to book a trip for attending a conference. The requester may be interested in flight and hotel reservation. Rather than using a single service, the requester may have to use two separate service providers.

In this paper we propose an incremental approach for service composition, where we assume that the requirements are expressed by a *single goal* stating pre- and postconditions. A variety of *offers* could contribute to the *goal*, each described by pre- and postconditions as well. We propose a notion of partial matching of *offers* with *goal*. After every partial match we compute the remaining requirements by decomposition of the *original goal* into the *satisfied subgoal* and its *remainder*. We iterate this process until the goal is achieved or we do not have any more *offers*.

As a result of this procedure we produce a *combined offer* which can be visualized and reviewed by the client. Our approach thus supports semi-automatic service composition.

2   Related Work

As motivated above, we work on the assumption that it is unrealistic to expect a single offer to be sufficient to satisfy a goal, i.e., several offers will have to be combined. This raises the first three of the following questions to serve as criteria for approaches to dynamic service composition. The fourth question derives from the desired integration into mainstream modelling techniques such as the UML, which use diagrammatic languages to specify software. For service specification to be integrated into standard software engineering processes, they have to use compatible visual notations.

- **Partial Match:** Does the approach support partial matching of an offer with a goal, or is full satisfaction of all requirements necessary for each match?
- **Flexibility:** Does the approach allow to match offers in flexible order or does it follow a given control flow?
- **Completeness:** Is the approach decidable, i.e., does it provide a complete and terminating procedure to find out if there are combinations of offers satisfying a goal?
- **Visualisation:** Does the approach provide a visual language for service specification and feedback on the result of the matching?

While there are many approaches to composition of services, we limit our discussion to semantics-based approaches using pre- and postconditions, disregarding process or workflow-based orchestration, see [5,6] for a more complete picture. We summarise the results of our analysis in Table 1.

In [7] the authors propose a semi-automatic approach for filtering and composition of services using OWL and DAML-S. An inference engine performs an exact match with available services and shows the resulting list to the user who

Table 1. How existing approaches realize the proposed requirements

Approach of:	Language	Partial Match	Flexibility	Completeness	Feedback
[7]	OWL, DAML-S	✓	✗	✗	✓
[8]	DAML-S, SHOP-2	✓	✓	✓	✗
[9]	FOL	✓	✓	✗	✗
[10]	WSML	✓	✓	✓	✗
Our Approach	Graph Theory, GTS	✓	✓	✓	✓

selects the ones to be composed. The approach is highly dependent on user input and so avoids the need for a decidable composition procedure required for automation. In contrast, we would require feedback on the end result of the automated composition only.

In a number of works, AI planning models are used to construct process models from goals and operations described by pre- and postconditions. For example, [8] is based on DAML-S. Their approach is decidable for a finite number of services / operations. Partial matching is possible based on the semantic description. The main difference with our approach is the use of logic-based (rather than visual) descriptions, which makes it difficult to provide feedback on the result of the composition to domain and business experts.

The work in [9] is representative of approaches based on first-order specification of goals and services. It allows partial matching and flexibility in ordering in addition to *goal templates* which abstract from the actual input parameters for invoking services and can thus be matched at design time. Our goals are at the level of goal templates in [9] in that they are generic with regard to the actual parameters.

Approaches such as [10] use semantic service web markup languages such as WSML-MX that are both specialised for the task of service description and matching and limited in expressiveness to guarantee computability.

3 Graphical Service Specification and Matching

Following [4,11], in this section we review the basic notions of service specification and matching used in the rest of the paper.

Visual Service Specification. According to [12], a web service describes a collection of operations that are network accessible, each specified by a pre- and a postcondition. As usual, a precondition denotes the set of states where that operation is applicable and the postcondition describes how any state satisfying the given precondition is changed by the operation. In our case the states can be seen as typed attributed graphs. This means graphs that may include values (the attributes) in their nodes or edges, all typed by a fixed type graph. For instance, Fig. 1 describes the type graph of the running example of a travel agency that we will use along the paper and Fig. 3 is an example of an attributed (instance) graph typed over that type graph after booking a flight.

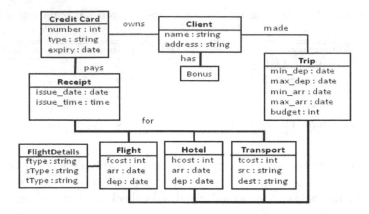

Fig. 1. Type Graph

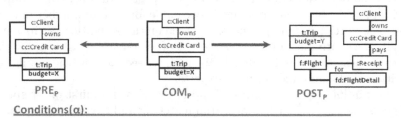

<u>Conditions(α):</u>

t.min_dep < f.dep < t.max_dep, t.min_arr < f.arr < t.max_arr, Y = X - f.fcost.

Fig. 2. *BookFlight* Operation for Travel Agency (Provider)

In [4,11] the specification of an operation Op, denoted $Op : PRE \Rightarrow POST$ is given by typed attributed graphs, PRE and $POST$ related by an injective partial graph morphism represented as a pair of injective morphisms, $pre : COM \rightarrow PRE$ and $post : COM \rightarrow POST$. Here COM provides the intersection of PRE and $POST$, and pre, $post$ are the corresponding injections into PRE and $POST$. Usually, attributed graphs PRE, $POST$ and COM include variables, values or complex expressions as attributes. However, in this paper attributes will be restricted to variables and basic values only, ruling out complex expressions. These will be captured, together with other constraints, by a formula α which constrains the possible values of the variables occurring as attributes in a graph G and we call (G, α) a constrained graph. In our case the graphs of an operation have a common condition α relating the variables occurring in PRE and $POST$. Hence, an operation specification is denoted by a pair $\langle PRE \Rightarrow POST, \alpha \rangle$ (or $\langle PRE \overset{pre}{\leftarrow} COM \overset{post}{\rightarrow} POST, \alpha \rangle$ if we are interested in the intersection COM). For instance, Fig. 2 describes an operation $BookFlight$ for booking a flight with a travel agency service.

In the example, graphs PRE_P and $POST_P$ are the pre- and postconditions for operation $BookFlight$ whereas graph COM_P represents the intersection of PRE_P and $POST_P$. Condition α constrains the operation to be flexible enough to choose the departure date $f.dep$ within the range of $t.dep\_min$ and $t.dep\_max$ as well as the arrival date $f.arr$ within $t.arr\_min$ and $t.arr\_max$. This way of dealing with attributed graphs, introduced in [13], has proved essential in order to support the declarative (as opposed to computational) description of attribute operations appropriate to the use of graphs as pre- and postconditions (rather than rewrite rules only). In particular, we allow attributed graphs representing states to include variables and conditions on attributes, rather than just values, thus providing a symbolic representation where not all the attributes are fully evaluated. We refrain from the use of application conditions [14] in the specification of operations to keep the presentation simple, but believe that they would not add an essential difficulty.

The semantics of the operation $\langle PRE \stackrel{pre}{\leftarrow} COM \stackrel{post}{\rightarrow} POST, \alpha \rangle$ is described using graph transformation. More precisely, given an attributed graph $\langle G, \alpha' \rangle$ representing the current state and given a matching morphism $m : PRE \rightarrow G$ such that α' implies $m(\alpha)$, with $m(\alpha)$ the formula obtained by replacing each variable X in α by its image $m(X)$, the result will be the attributed graph $\langle H, \alpha' \rangle$ with H defined by the following double pushout:

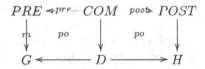

Intuitively, graph D is obtained by deleting from G all the elements (nodes, edges, or attributes) which are matched by an element that is present in PRE but not in COM. Then, the graph H is obtained adding to D all the elements which are present in $POST$, but not in COM. For instance, if we apply the operation $BookFlight$ to graph G in the left of Fig. 3, the result will be the graph H in the right of Fig. 3. Notice that, for readability, these graphs include some values, such as 200, instead of a variable X and the equality $X = 200$ included in the associated formula.

A requester looking for a service must specify the operations they want to use. Requester specifications have the same form as provider specifications. They are seen as inquiries that the requester is making, with the aim of entering into a contract with the provider. In particular, PRE would denote the data and resources that the requester would accept to provide and $POST$ would describe the expected result of the operation. In this use case, the semantics of these

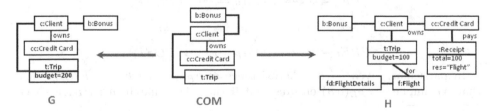

Fig. 3. Transformation due to $BookFlight$ of Travel Agency

specifications is a different one because the requester may not (need to) know all the details of the provider state and cannot thus describe completely all the changes caused by the operation. Such a semantics has been studied for graph transformations in terms of double pullbacks [15]. More precisely, given an attributed graph $\langle G, \alpha' \rangle$ and a matching morphisms $m : PRE \rightarrow G$ such that α' implies $m(\alpha)$, a graph H is the result of a double pullback transition if we can build a double pullback diagram of the same shape like the double pushout above, but replacing the *po* by *pb* squares.

Intuitively, in a double pullback transition, the rule $PRE \Rightarrow POST$ describes a lower bound to the effects the operation should cause when applied to G. This means, if an element a is present in PRE but not in COM, then $m(a)$ must be deleted from G, and if a is present in $POST$, but not in COM, then it must be added to G. And if a is present in COM, then it must remain unchanged. However, G may suffer other changes not specified by the operation. For instance, if the specification of the operation *BookFlight* in Fig. 2 would be part of a requester specification, then applying that operation to the graph G in Fig. 3 could yield the graph H in Fig. 3 as a result of a double pullback transition.

Matching Visual Contracts. In order to match the requirements for an operation $Op_R = \langle PRE_R \Rightarrow POST_R, \alpha_R \rangle$ of a requestor against a description $Op_P = \langle PRE_P \Rightarrow POST_P, \alpha_P \rangle$ supplied by a provider, we have to guarantee that all effects required by Op_R are implemented by Op_P. More precisely, assuming that $\langle G, \alpha \rangle$ represents the given state, the following conditions must be satisfied:

a) Whenever a transition for Op_R can take place, a corresponding transformation associated to Op_P must be possible.
b) If Op_R prescribes that some element must be deleted from the current state, that element must also be deleted by Op_P.
c) If Op_R prescribes that some element must be added to the current state, that element must also be added by Op_P.
d) If Op_R prescribes that some element remain in the current state, that element should be part of COM_P.

Technically, this means to ask for the existence of three injective morphisms $h_{PRE} : PRE_P \rightarrow PRE_R$, $h_{COM} : COM_R \rightarrow COM_P$, and $h_{POST} : POST_R \rightarrow POST_P$, such that α_R implies $h_{PRE}(\alpha_P)$, h_{PRE} and pre_R are jointly surjective[1], diagram (1) commutes, and diagram (2) is a pullback.

$$PRE_R \xleftarrow{pre_R} COM_R \xrightarrow{post_R} POST_R$$
$$\uparrow h_{PRE} \quad (1) \quad \downarrow h_{COM} \quad (2) \quad \downarrow h_{POST}$$
$$PRE_P \xleftarrow{pre_P} COM_P \xrightarrow{post_P} POST_P$$

In particular, given $\langle G, \alpha \rangle$, the existence of $h_{PRE} : PRE_P \rightarrow PRE_R$ such that α_R implies $h_{PRE}(\alpha_P)$ ensures that if there is a match $m : PRE_R \rightarrow G$

---

[1] This means that every element in PRE_R is the image of an element in COM_R or of an element in PRE_P.

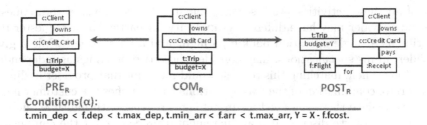

Fig. 4. *BookFlight* Operation of Requester

such that α implies $m(\alpha_R)$ then we also have a corresponding match $h_{PRE} \circ m$: $PRE_P \to G$ such that α implies $h_{PRE}(m(\alpha_P))$. In addition if an element is in PRE_R but not in COM_R, that element should also be in PRE_P, because h_{PRE} and pre_R are jointly surjective, but not in COM_P since diagram (1) commutes. Then, according to both rules, Op_R and Op_P, that element must also be deleted. If an element is in $POST_R$ but not in COM_R then that element should also be in $POST_P$ but not in COM_P because diagram (2) is a pullback. Finally, if an element is in COM_R its image through h_{COM} would also be in COM_P.

In our example the specification in Fig. 2 matches the specification in Fig. 4. All the elements in PRE_P, COM_R, and $POST_R$ have an image in PRE_R, COM_P, and $POST_P$ respectively. So there exist three injective morphisms [16,14] between PRE_P and PRE_R, COM_P and COM_R, and $POST_R$ and $POST_P$.

We have discussed how to match a request with a service offered by a provider in an *ideal* situation, where the granularity of requirements and offered services coincide and the matching is complete. However, such a lucky outcome is unlikely in practice.

On one hand, as seen above, a service precondition must describe the data and resources that may be needed to run that service (and, in addition, through the associated condition α_R, it may also describe the conditions under which a given service is considered to be acceptable, e.g. its cost). This means to assume that the requester knows, a priori, all the data and resources that may be required to satisfy his needs. This may be unrealistic in many cases. For instance, when booking a trip, the requester may describe in its precondition some basic data, like their name, date and destination of the travel, credit card or bank account number, etc. In addition, the requester may specify an overall budget for the travel. However the provider may also need to know the age of the traveller, to see if some discount applies, or whether the requester has a discount bonus that would be consumed when using the service.

On the other hand, the postcondition describes the effect of using a given service. In this sense, the requester will describe everything they expect to get when binding to a certain service. However, there may be two problems here. First, there may not be a single provider that offers a service covering all the requester needs. For instance, the requester for a travel may want, not only to book a flight and a hotel, but also to get tickets for a play and to have a dinner in a well-known restaurant. Then, there may be no travel agency that can take care of all these activities. And, second, the specification level of the requester and the provider may have different granularity. In particular, a requester may describe as a single operation booking a flight and a hotel room, while a given provider, in his specifications, may consider these two bookings as independent operations. Then, matching this request would mean for that provider finding an appropriate combination of the two operations that satisfies the customer needs.

So, we believe there is a need for matching a request with multiple offers. In the next section we discuss such an incremental procedure for the composition of services, where we will discuss the partial match of single *requester operation* with multiple *provider offers*.

4   Incremental Service Composition

Given a *goal* of a requester as well as a set of provider *offers*, both expressed by pre- and postconditions, first we select an offer providing a partial match of the goal. Then, we compute the remainder of the goal with respect to this offer, containing all the requirements not yet satisfied, and post the result as a new goal. We iterate these steps until all requirements are satisfied or we run out of offers to match. Finally, we compose all offers used into one global offer summarising the overall effect of the combined services. Next we describe this approach in detail.

Partial Matching. Given a request $\langle PRE_R \Rightarrow POST_R, \alpha_R \rangle$ a *partial match* with a provided description $\langle PRE_P \Rightarrow POST_P, \alpha_P \rangle$ is given by a partial embedding of PRE_P into PRE_R and of a partial embedding of $POST_R$ into $POST_P$. Following the previous discussion, the idea is that, on the one hand, not everything included in the provider's precondition needs to be present in the requester's precondition, since the latter may have to be completed later. On the other hand, not everything in the requester's postcondition needs to be present in the provider's postcondition, since not every effect demanded by the requester may be covered by a single provided operation.

Definition 1. *(partial match, common suboperation) Given requester and provider operations* $Op_R = \langle PRE_R \overset{pre_R}{\leftarrow} COM_R \overset{post_R}{\rightarrow} POST_R, \alpha_R \rangle$ *and* $Op_P = \langle PRE_P \overset{pre_P}{\leftarrow} COM_P \overset{post_P}{\rightarrow} POST_P, \alpha_P \rangle$ *a partial match* m *consists of embeddings:*

$$
\begin{array}{ccccc}
PRE_R & \xleftarrow{\ pre_R\ } & COM_R & \xrightarrow{\ post_R\ } & POST_R \\
\uparrow{\scriptstyle m_{PRE_R}} & (1) & \uparrow{\scriptstyle m_{COM_R}} & (2) & \uparrow{\scriptstyle m_{POST_R}} \\
PRE_C & \xleftarrow{\ pre_C\ } & COM_C & \xrightarrow{\ post_C\ } & POST_C \\
\downarrow{\scriptstyle m_{PRE_P}} & (3) & \downarrow{\scriptstyle m_{COM_P}} & (4) & \downarrow{\scriptstyle m_{POST_P}} \\
PRE_P & \xleftarrow{\ pre_P\ } & COM_P & \xrightarrow{\ post_P\ } & POST_P
\end{array}
$$

such that diagram (3) commutes, and diagrams (1), (2), and (4) are pullbacks.

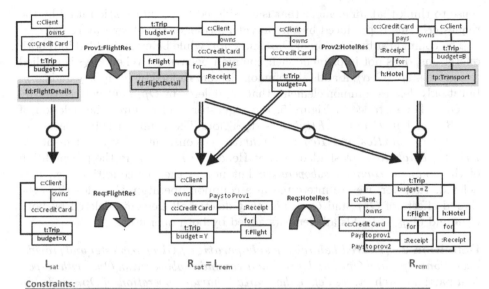

Constraints:

h.dep = f.dep, t.min_dep ≤ f.dep ≤ t.max_dep, t.min_dep ≤ h.dep ≤ t.max_dep, h.arr = f.arr, t.min_arr ≤ f.arr ≤ t.max_arr, t.min_arr ≤ h.arr ≤ t.max_arr, Y = X - f.fcost, Z = Y − h.hcost, B = A - h.hcost - tp.tcost.

Fig. 5. Requester goal jointly matched by two consecutive offers

The operation $Op_C = \langle PRE_C \overset{prec}{\leftarrow} COM_C \overset{postc}{\rightarrow} POST_C, \alpha_C \rangle$, where α_C is a condition such that α_R and α_P imply $m_{PRE_R}(\alpha_C)$ and $m_{PRE_P}(\alpha_C)$, respectively, is called a common suboperation of the provider and the requester operations, since it can be considered to be embedded in both operations. For example, the common suboperation is shown by unshaded background in Fig. 5 in both embeddings, where the circled arrows denote the partial embeddings between the providers and requesters pre and postconditions.

The condition α_C is obtained from α_P when some of its free variables are not present. In particular, α_C may be $\exists X \alpha_P$ or some stronger condition, where X is the set of variables included in the provided operation which are not present in the common suboperation. The fact that we do not ask diagram (3) to be a pullback, while we ask diagrams (1), (2), and (4) to be so, is a consequence of the fact that we want to express the condition that Op_P implements partially the effects of Op_R on their common elements. This means, on one hand, that if a common element is deleted by Op_P then that element must also be deleted by Op_R, but not necessarily the other way round. Conversely, this means that every common element preserved by Op_R must also be preserved by Op_C (and hence by Op_P), which means that (1) is a pullback. However, the fact that not every common element preserved by Op_P must also be preserved by Op_R means that (3) is not necessarily a pullback. On the other hand, (2) and (4) are pullbacks, because we consider that if a common element in $POST_C$ is produced by Op_P, then it should also be produced by Op_R, and vice versa, That is, it makes no sense to think that an element that is considered to be information used by the requester's rule is produced by the provider's rule, or the other way round.

The common suboperation of Op_P and Op_R, while being embedded into both operations, does not implement their common behaviour. When Op_C is applied to a given state $\langle G, \alpha \rangle$, it adds all common elements added by both Op_P and Op_R, but it only deletes common elements that are deleted by Op_R, but not necessarily by Op_P. For instance in Figure 5, the requestor goal requires the deletion of $b : Bonus$ but $Prov1 :: FlightRes$ does not. The common suboperation of $Prov1 :: FlightRes$ and $Req :: FlightRes$ is constituted by all elements of $Prov1 :: FlightRes$ not shaded in grey. Hence, $b : Bonus$ is in the precondition of the common *common suboperation* but not in the postcondition, i.e., it is deleted. However, we are interested in a common operation that describes the shared effects of Op_P and Op_R, i.e., that deletes all elements deleted by both Op_P and Op_R and adds all elements added by both operations.

Definition 2. *(shared behaviour suboperation) Given requester and provider operations Op_R and Op_P, and given their common suboperation Op_C with respect to a partial match m, we define the shared behaviour operation of Op_R and Op_P with respect to m as $Op_{SB} = \langle PRE_C \overset{pres_B}{\leftarrow} COM_{SB} \overset{post_{SB}}{\rightarrow} POST_{SB}, \alpha_C \rangle$, where COM_{SB} and $POST_{SB}$ are given by the following pullback and pushout diagrams:*

$$
\begin{array}{ccc}
PRE_C & \xleftarrow{\ pres_B\ } & COM_{SB} \\
\downarrow^{m_{PRE_P}} & pb & \downarrow^{m_{COM_{SB}}} \\
PRE_P & \xleftarrow{\ pre_P\ } & COM_P
\end{array}
\qquad
\begin{array}{ccc}
COM_C & \xrightarrow{\ post_C\ } & POST_C \\
\downarrow^{m_{COM_C}} & po & \downarrow^{m_{POST_C}} \\
COM_{SB} & \xrightarrow{\ post_{SB}\ } & POST_{SB}
\end{array}
$$

with m_{COM_C} defined by the universal property of the pullback defining COM_{SB}.

Intuitively, COM_{SB} includes the elements which are shared by PRE_P and PRE_R and are not deleted by Op_P, and $POST_{SB}$ includes all the elements of $POST_C$ plus the elements that are not deleted by Op_{SB}. Fig. 6 depicts the *shared behaviour suboperation* based on the requestor goal and $Prov1 :: FlightRes$ and their common sub operation (shown in Fig. 5).

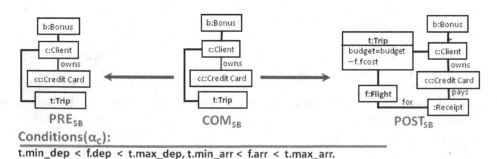

Conditions(α_c):

t.min_dep < f.dep < t.max_dep, t.min_arr < f.arr < t.max_arr.

Fig. 6. Shared behaviour operation of goal and Prov1::FlightRes of Fig. 5

We may consider several special kinds of partial matches which are of interest.

Definition 3. *(classes of partial matches) Given a partial match m as above:*

- *m provides* positive progress *if $post_C$ is not an isomorphism (or, equivalently, if $post_{SB}$ is not an isomorphism).*
- *m provides* negative progress *if pre_{SB} is not an isomorphism.*
- *m provides* progress *if m provides positive progress or negative progress.*
- *m is* demanding *if m_{PRE_P} is not an isomorphism.*
- *m is* weakly complete *if m_{POST_R} is an isomorphism.*
- *m is* complete *if diagram (3) is a pullback, m_{PRE_R} and pre_R are jointly surjective, and m_{POST_R} is an isomorphism.*

Two completely unrelated rules may be bound by a trivial partial match. For instance, a partial match where the common rule is empty, or if the precondition and the postcondition of the common rule coincide. In this sense, the first three cases describe partial matches where the provider's rule satisfies partially some of the goals of the requester. In particular, if m provides positive progress this means that the provider's rule produces some of the elements that the requester asks to be produced. Similarly, if m provides negative progress then the provider's rule consumes some of the elements that the requester asks to be consumed. Finally, m provides progress if it provides any progress at all.

If m is weakly complete then this means that the provider's rule produces all the elements that are asked by the requester but it may not consume all the elements that are specified to be consumed. If m is complete and not demanding this means that the provider's rule fully satisfies the requester's needs, i.e. m is a match. A partial match is demanding if the provider's rule demands the requester to strengthen its precondition. Conversely, this means that if m is not demanding then the provider's precondition is embedded in the requester's precondition, which means that the former can be considered stronger than the latter. This kind of situation may be part of a negotiation between the provider and the requester: the contract defined by the requester has specified some resources to satisfy his needs, but the provider is answering that, to satisfy this needs more resources are needed. If m is weakly complete then the provider's rule produces everything that the requester's rule asks to be produced. So this means that the requester's postcondition is embedded in the provider's postcondition. However, notice that this not necessarily means that the provider's rule consumes everything that the requester's rule asks to be consumed. This only happens if, in addition, diagram (3) is a pullback and m_{PRE_R} and pre_R are jointly surjective, i.e. m is complete. In particular, the condition that diagram (3) is a pullback ensures that a common element cannot be preserved by Op_P and be deleted by Op_R, and the condition that m_{PRE_R} and pre_R ensures that there are no elements in PRE_R which are deleted by Op_R and which are not common elements (and, hence, cannot be deleted by Op_P).

Remainder of Requester Operation. If the match is not complete, then we may want to know what remains to be done to satisfy the rest of the requester's needs. In particular, the provider may want to use other operations to satisfy their requirements. This can be done by computing what we call the *remainder* of the requester's rule with respect to the shared behaviour rule.

Definition 4. *(Remainder of an operation) Given operation specifications* $Op_R = \langle PRE_R \Rightarrow POST_R, \alpha_R \rangle$ *and* $Op_P = \langle PRE_P \Rightarrow POST_P, \alpha_P \rangle$, *we define the remainder of* Op_R *with respect to* Op_P *and a partial match* m *as the operation* $\langle PRE_{Rem} \Rightarrow POST_R, \alpha_R \rangle$, *where* PRE_{Rem} *is the result of applying the operation* Op_{SB} *to* PRE_R *with match* m_{PRE_R}.

The idea is quite simple. We know that PRE_R denotes the class of states where Op_R is expected to be applicable, but also that Op_{SB} specifies the shared behaviour of Op_P and Op_R, i.e., all the deletions and additions which are shared by both operations. Then, PRE_{Rem} would describe the states after these deletions and additions, and $\langle PRE_{Rem} \Rightarrow POST_R, \alpha_R \rangle$ would specify the effects that are yet to be implemented by another provider operation.

For example in Fig. 5, the left-hand side PRE_{Rem} of the remainder rule is obtained by applying the *shared behaviour suboperation* (shown in Fig. 6) to the left-hand side PRE_R of the goal, while the remainder's postcondition is $POST_R$. Op_{Rem} may be matched with $Prov2 :: HotelRes$ in the same way, leaving empty remainder.

It is not difficult to prove that the remainder is the trivial operation, i.e. $PRE_{Rem} = POST_R$, if and only if the match m is complete. Moreover, we

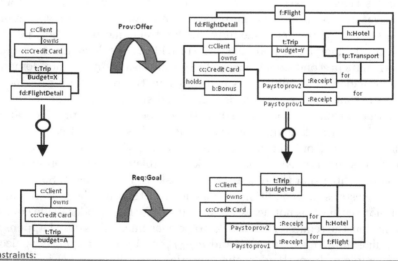

Constraints:
h.dep = f.dep, t.min_dep ≤ f.dep ≤ t.max_dep, t.min_dep ≤ h.dep ≤ t.max_dep, h.arr = f.arr, t.min_arr ≤ f.arr ≤ t.max_arr, t.min_arr ≤ h.arr ≤ t.max_arr, Y=X-f.fcost-h.hcost-tp.tcost, B=A-h.hcost-f.fcost.

Fig. 7. Composed Operation of both Provider Offers

can also prove that if a provider operation Op_P^1 can be partially matched via m_1 to a request Op_R leaving Op_{Rem} as a remainder, and if another provider operation Op_P^2 can be partially matched via m_2 to Op_{Rem} leaving as a new remainder Op'_{Rem}, then we can compose Op_P^1 and Op_P^2 to form a new operation $Op_P^3 = \langle PRE_P^3 \Rightarrow POST_P^3, \alpha_P^3 \rangle$ that can be partially matched to Op_R via m_3, which is built from m_1 and m_2, directly leaving as a remainder Op'_{Rem}. This means that the global effect of this new operation is the same one as the sequential application of Op_P^1 and Op_P^2. In particular, this means that if m_2 is complete then m_3 is also complete.

The operation Op_P^3 is built analogously to the so-called concurrent rule for the consecutive application of two graph transformation rules [16]: Intuitively, PRE_P^3 is the union of PRE_P^1 and (PRE_P^2 minus $POST_P^1$) and $POST_P^3$ is the union of $POST_P^2$ and ($POST_P^1$ minus PRE_P^2), where in each case elements from different graphs are identified if they are mapping to the same elements of the requester specification. As for conditions, α_P^3 is the conjunction of α_P^1, α_P^2, and all equations $x_1 = x_2$, for all variables x_1 from α_P^1 and x_2 from α_P^2 which are bound to the same variable x from α_R via m_1 and m_2, respectively. For our example, Fig. 7 shows the resulting composed operation.

Finding Complete Solutions. We describe a resolution-like procedure for building a complete match to a requester specification. This procedure is terminating, correct and complete, i.e., given a requester operation Op_R, if at all possible this procedure will combine suitable provider operations into a single composed one which forms a complete match for the requestor's goal. Moreover, this is done in a finite number of steps. The procedure is presented as an inference rule whose application is non-deterministic, although in practice we could use heuristics to guide the search and to produce first the results which are considered better according to some criteria.

Let us describe this procedure in detail. We describe the computation states of our procedure as 3-tuples $\langle Op_P, m, Op_{Rem} \rangle$, where Op_P is a provider operation (perhaps built from more basic operations), m is a partial match from Op_P to Op_R, and Op_{Rem} is the remainder associated to m. Intuitively, Op_P represents the partial solution that we have built up to that point, m is the partial match that tells us in which way Op_P partially satisfies the request, and Op_{Rem} is the the part of the request that we still have to satisfy. In this context, we consider that the initial state is the 3-tuple $\langle Triv, triv, Op_R \rangle$, where $Triv$ is the trivial (empty) operation, $triv$ is the trivial empty match and, obviously, the remaining part to satisfy is the whole request. Then, the procedure is based on the following inference rule:

$$\frac{\langle Op_P^1, m_1, Op_{Rem}^1 \rangle}{\langle Op_P^2, m_2, Op_{Rem}^2 \rangle}$$

If there is a provider operation Op_P^3, and a partial match m_3 from Op_P^3 to Op_{Rem}^1, such that m_3 provides progress, Op_{Rem}^2 is the remainder associated to m_3, and Op_P^2 and m_2 are, respectively, the composition of Op_{Rem}^1 and Op_{Rem}^3 and the associated partial match from Op_P^2 to Op_R.

An execution of this procedure is a sequence:

$$\langle Triv, triv, Op_R \rangle \Longrightarrow \langle Op_P^1, m_1, Op_{Rem}^1 \rangle \Longrightarrow \ldots \Longrightarrow \langle Op_P^n, m_n, Op_{Rem}^n \rangle$$

where, for each i, $\langle Op_P^{i+1}, m_{i+1}, Op_{Rem}^{i+1} \rangle$ can be inferred from $\langle Op_P^i, m_i, Op_{Rem}^i \rangle$. Then, an execution is successful if the final match m_n is complete.

It is not difficult to show that the above procedure is correct, complete and terminating. In particular, it is sound in the sense, for every i, m_i is a partial match from Op_P^i to Op_R, and Op_{Rem}^i is the corresponding remainder. It is complete in the sense that if there is a way of satisfying completely the request by applying a sequence of provider operations then there exists an execution that will return a composed operation, together with a complete match. Finally the procedure is terminating, i.e. there are no executions of infinite length and, moreover, there is a finite number of executions, provided that the graphs involved are finite and that there is a finite number of provider operations. This is due to the fact that the number of additions and deletions requested in a goal is finite. Since we are assuming that all the matchings involved provide progress, the length of each execution is bounded by the number of additions and deletions specified in the request. Moreover, with a finite number of provider operations and finite graphs only, there is a finite number of partial matches between requester operation and provider operations.

5   Conclusion

In this paper, we have proposed an approach to the incremental composition of services using visual specifications of pre- and postconditions. The procedure is based on the repeated partial matching of provider offers with a requestor goal, which is reduced in the process until all requirements are satisfied or there are no more offers to consider. As a result, the procedure constructs a combined offer, which can be presented to the requestor to confirm if it is acceptable.

The formalization of these notions and constructions is provided in the appendix for information. In summary, the main theoretical results are as follows.

1. A definition of partial matching allowing the comparison of individual offers of services with the global goal of the requestor.
2. An incremental matching procedure based on the construction of a remainder of a goal with respect to a chosen partial match. Assuming a finite number of offers, the incremental matching procedure terminates. Thus, partial matching is decidable.
3. Each combined offer constructed as result of the matching has the same overall effect as executing the sequence of offers from which the combined offer is derived. That means, for each sequence of applications of individual offer rules there exists an application of the combined offer rule with the same effect, and vice versa.

In general, there will be several combined offers computed for a given request. These could be presented to the client to let them choose the most suitable one. Alternatively, the selection could be automated based on a specification of preferences (non-functional properties) by the client. Once an offer is computed it can be stored in the repository of services, such that new requests can be served more quickly, matching them against existing combined offers. Future work will address the use of non-functional requirements for the selection of offers, as well as a proof-of-concept implementation of the approach.

References

1. Papazoglou, M.P.: Service-oriented computing: Concepts, characteristics and directions. In: Fourth International Conference on Web Information Systems Engineering (WISE 2003), Roma, Italy, December 2003, IEEE Computer Society, Los Alamitos (2003)
2. Kim, I.W., Lee, K.H.: Describing semantic web services: From UML to OWL-S. In: IEEE International Conference on Web Services ICWS 2007, Salt Lake City, UT, USA, July 2007, pp. 529–536. IEEE Computer Society, Los Alamitos (2007)
3. de Bruijn, J., Lausen, H., Polleres, A., Fensel, D.: The web service modeling language WSML: An Overview. In: Sure, Y., Domingue, J. (eds.) ESWC 2006. LNCS, vol. 4011, pp. 590–604. Springer, Heidelberg (2006)
4. Hausmann, J.H., Heckel, R., Lohmann, M.: Model-based development of web service descriptions: Enabling a precise matching concept. International Journal of Web Services Research 2(2), 67–84 (2005)
5. Peltz, C.: Web services orchestration and choreography. Computer, 46–52 (2003)
6. van der Aalst, W.: Don't go with the flow: Web services composition standards exposed. IEEE Intelligent Systems 18(1), 72–76 (2003)
7. Sirin, E., Hendler, J., Parsia, B.: Semi-automatic composition of web services using semantic descriptions. In: Workshop on Web Services: Modeling, Architecture and Infrastructure, pp. 17–24 (2002)
8. Wu, D., Parsia, B., Sirin, E., Hendler, J.A., Nau, D.S.: Automating DAML-S web services composition using SHOP2. In: Fensel, D., Sycara, K., Mylopoulos, J. (eds.) ISWC 2003. LNCS, vol. 2870, pp. 195–210. Springer, Heidelberg (2003)
9. Stollberg, M., Keller, U., Lausen, H., Heymans, S.: Two-phase web service discovery based on rich functional descriptions. In: Franconi, E., Kifer, M., May, W. (eds.) ESWC 2007. LNCS, vol. 4519, pp. 99–113. Springer, Heidelberg (2007)
10. Klusch, M., Kaufer, F.: Wsmo-mx: A hybrid semantic web service matchmaker. Web Intelli. and Agent Sys. 7(1), 23–42 (2009)
11. Heckel, R., Cherchago, A.: Structural and behavioral compatibility of graphical service specifications. Journal of Logic and Algebraic Programming 70(1.1), 15–33 (2007)
12. Kreger, H.: Web services conceptual architecture, IBM Software Group (2001), http://www.ibm.com
13. Orejas, F.: Attributed graph constraints. In: Ehrig, H., Heckel, R., Rozenberg, G., Taentzer, G. (eds.) ICGT 2008. LNCS, vol. 5214, pp. 274–288. Springer, Heidelberg (2008)

14. Ehrig, H., Ehrig, K., Prange, U., Taentzer, G.: Fundamentals of Algebraic Graph Transformation. Monographs in Theoretical Computer Science. An EATCS Series. Springer, Heidelberg (2006)
15. Heckel, R., Llabrés, M., Ehrig, H., Orejas, F.: Concurrency and loose semantics of open graph transformation systems. Mathematical Structures in Computer Science 12, 349–376 (2002)
16. Rozenberg, G. (ed.): Handbook of graph grammars and computing by graph transformation. Concurrency, parallelism, and distribution, vol. 3. World Scientific Publishing Co., Inc., River Edge (1999)

Formal Analysis and Verification of Self-Healing Systems*

Hartmut Ehrig[1], Claudia Ermel[1], Olga Runge[1],
Antonio Bucchiarone[2], and Patrizio Pelliccione[3]

[1] Institut für Softwaretechnik und Theoretische Informatik
Technische Universität Berlin, Germany
{ehrig,lieske,olga}@cs.tu-berlin.de
[2] FBK-IRST, Trento, Italy
bucchiarone@fbk.eu
[3] Dipartimento di Informatica Università dell'Aquila, Italy
patrizio.pelliccione@di.univaq.it

Abstract. Self-healing (SH-)systems are characterized by an automatic discovery of system failures, and techniques how to recover from these situations. In this paper, we show how to model SH-systems using algebraic graph transformation. These systems are modeled as typed graph grammars enriched with graph constraints. This allows not only for formal modeling of consistency and operational properties, but also for their analysis and verification using the tool AGG. We present sufficient static conditions for self-healing properties, deadlock-freeness and liveness of SH-systems. The overall approach is applied to a traffic light system case study, where the corresponding properties are verified.

1   Introduction

The high degree of variability that characterizes modern systems requires to design them with runtime evolution in mind. Self-adaptive systems are a variant of fault-tolerant systems that autonomously decide how to adapt the system at runtime to the internal reconfiguration and optimization requirements or to environment changes and threats [1]. A classification of modeling dimensions for self-adaptive systems can be found in [2], where the authors distinguish *goals* (what is the system supposed to do), *changes* (causes for adaptation), *mechanisms* (system reactions to changes) and *effects* (the impact of adaptation upon the system). The initial four self-* properties of self-adaptive systems are self-configuration, self-healing[1], self-optimization, and self-protection [4]. Self-configuration comprises components installation and configuration based on some high-level policies. Self-healing deals with automatic discovery of system

---

* Some of the authors are partly supported by the European Community's Seventh Framework Programme FP7/2007-2013 under grant agreement 215483 (S-Cube) and the Italian PRIN d-ASAP project.
[1] Following [3] we consider self-healing and self-repair as synonymous.

D.S. Rosenblum and G. Taentzer (Eds.): FASE 2010, LNCS 6013, pp. 139–153, 2010.
© Springer-Verlag Berlin Heidelberg 2010

failures, and with techniques to recover from them. Typically, the runtime behavior of the system is monitored to determine whether a change is needed. Self-optimization monitors the system status and adjusts parameters to increase performance when possible. Finally, self-protection aims to detect external threats and mitigate their effects [5].

In [6], Bucchiarone et al. modeled and verified dynamic software architectures and self-healing (SH-)systems (called self-repairing systems in [6]), by means of hypergraphs and graph grammars. Based on this work, we show in this paper how to formally model (SH-)systems by using algebraic graph transformations [7] and to prove consistency and operational properties. Graph transformation has been investigated as a fundamental concept for specification, concurrency, distribution, visual modeling, simulation and model transformation [7,8].

The main idea is to model SH-systems by typed graph grammars with three different kinds of system rules, namely normal, environment, and repair rules. Normal rules define the normal and ideal behavior of the system. Environment rules model all possible predictable failures. Finally, for each failure a repair rule is defined. This formalization enables the specification, analysis and verification of consistency and operational properties of SH-systems. More precisely, we present sufficient conditions for two alternative self-healing properties, deadlock-freeness and liveness of SH-systems. The conditions can be checked statically for the given system rules in an automatic way using the AGG^2 modeling and verification tool for typed attributed graph transformation systems.

Summarizing, the contribution of this paper is twofold: (i) we propose a way to model and formalize SH-systems; (ii) we provide tool-supported static verification techniques for SH-system models. The theory is presented by use of a running example, namely an automated traffic light system controlled by means of electromagnetic spires that are buried some centimeters underneath the asphalt of car lanes.

The paper is organized as follows: Section 2 motivates the paper comparing it with related work. Section 3 presents the setting of our running example. Section 4 introduces typed attributed graph transformation as formal basis to specify and analyze SH-systems. In Section 5 we define consistency and operational system properties. Static conditions for their verification are given in Section 6 and are used to analyze the behavior and healing properties of the traffic light system. We conclude the paper in Section 7 with a summary and an outlook on future work. For full proofs of the technical theorems and more details of our running example, the reader is referred to our technical report [9].

2   Motivation and Related Work

Focusing on modeling approaches for SH-systems, the *Software Architecture* approach (SA) [10], has been introduced as a high-level view of the structural organization of systems. Since a self-healing system must be able to change at runtime, *Dynamic Software Architectures* (DSAs) have shown to be very useful

---

^{2} AGG (Attributed Graph Grammars): http://tfs.cs.tu-berlin.de/agg.

to capture SA evolution [11,12,13]. Aiming at a formal analysis of DSAs, different approaches exist, either based on graph transformation [6,14,15,16,17,18,19] or on temporal logics and model checking [20,21,22]. In many cases, though, the state space of behavioral system models becomes too large or even infinite, and in this case model checking techniques have their limitations. Note that static analysis techniques, as applied in this paper, do not have this drawback. In addition to graph transformation techniques, also Petri nets [23] offer static analysis techniques to verify liveness and safety properties. But in contrast to Petri nets, graph transformation systems are well suited to model also reconfiguration of system architectures which is one possible way to realize system recovery from failures in self-healing (SH-)systems.

In the community of Service Oriented Computing, various approaches supporting self-healing have been defined, e.g. triggering repairing strategies as a consequence of a requirement violation [24], and optimizing QoS of service-based applications [25,26]. Repairing strategies could be specified by means of policies to manage the dynamism of the execution environment [27,28] or of the context of mobile service-based applications [29].

In [30], a theoretical assume-guarantee framework is presented to efficiently define under which conditions adaptation can be performed by still preserving the desired invariant. In contrast to our approach, the authors of [30] aim to deal with *unexpected* adaptations.

In contrast to the approaches mentioned above, we abstract from particular languages and notations. Instead, we aim for a coherent design approach allowing us to model important features of SH-systems at a level of abstraction suitable to apply static verification techniques.

3 Running Example: An Automated Traffic Light System

In an automated Traffic Light System (TLS), the technology is based upon electromagnetic spires that are buried some centimeters underneath the asphalt of car lanes. The spires register traffic data and send them to other system components. The technology helps the infraction system by making it incontestable. In fact, the TLS is connected to cameras which record videos of the violations and automatically send them to the center of operations. In addition to the normal behavior, we may have failures caused by a loss of signals between traffic light or camera and supervisor. For each of the failures there are corresponding repair actions, which can be applied after monitoring the failures during runtime. For more detail concerning the functionality of the TLS, we refer to [9].

The aim of our TLS model is to ensure suitable self-healing properties by applying repair actions. What kind of repair actions are useful and lead to consistent system states without failures? What kind of safety and liveness properties can be guaranteed? We will tackle these questions in the next sections by providing a formal modeling and analysis technique based on algebraic graph transformation and continue our running example in Examples 1 – 6 below.

4   Formal Modeling of Self-Healing Systems by Algebraic Graph Transformation

In this section, we show how to model SH-systems in the formal framework of algebraic graph transformation [7]. The main concepts of this framework which are relevant for our approach are typed graphs, graph grammars, transformations and constraints. Configurations of an SH-System are modeled by typed graphs.

Definition 1 (Typed Graphs). *A graph $G = (N, E, s, t)$ consists of a set of nodes N, a set of edges E and functions $s, t : E \to N$ assigning to each edge $e \in E$ the source $s(e) \in N$ and target $t(e) \in N$.*

A graph morphism $f : G \to G'$ is given by a pair of functions $f = (f_N : N \to N', f_E : E \to E')$ which is compatible with source and target functions.

A type graph TG is a graph where nodes and edges are considered as node and edge types, respectively. A TG-typed, or short typed graph $\overline{G} = (G, t)$ consists of a graph G and a graph morphism $t : G \to TG$, called typing morphism of G. Morphisms $f : \overline{G} \to \overline{G'}$ of typed graphs are graph morphisms $f : G \to G'$ which are compatible with the typing morphisms of G and G', i.e. $t' \circ f = t$.

For simplicity, we abbreviate $\overline{G} = (G, t)$ by G in the following. Moreover, the approach is also valid for *attributed* and *typed attributed graphs* where nodes and edges can have data type attributes [7], as used in our running example.

Example 1 (Traffic Light System). The type graph TG of our traffic light system TLS is given in Fig. 1. The initial state is the configuration graph in Fig. 2 which is a TG-typed graph where the typing is indicated by corresponding names, and the attributes are attached to nodes and edges. The initial state shows two traffic lights (TL), two cameras, a supervisor, and a center of operations, but no traffic up to now.

The dynamic behavior of SH-systems is modeled by rules and transformations of a typed graph grammar in the sense of algebraic graph transformation [7].

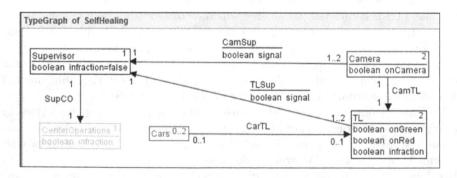

Fig. 1. TLS type graph TG

Definition 2 (Typed Graph Grammar)

A typed graph grammar $GG = (TG, G_{init}, Rules)$ *consists of a type graph TG,
a TG-typed graph G_{init}, called* initial graph, *and a set Rules of graph transformation rules. Each rule $r \in Rules$ is given by a span $(L \leftarrow I \rightarrow R)$, where L, I
and R are TG-typed graphs, called* left-hand side, right-hand side *and* interface,
*respectively. Moreover, $I \rightarrow L$, $I \rightarrow R$ are injective typed graph morphisms where
in most cases I can be considered as intersection of L and R. A rule $r \in Rules$
is applied to a TG-typed graph G by a* match morphism $m : L \rightarrow G$ *leading to
a* direct transformation $G \overset{r,m}{\Longrightarrow} H$ *via (r, m) in two steps: at first, we delete the
match $m(L)$ without $m(I)$ from G to obtain a context graph D, and secondly,
we glue together D with R along I leading to a TG-typed graph H.*

*More formally, the direct transformation
$G \overset{r,m}{\Longrightarrow} H$ is given by two* pushout diagrams
(1) and (2) in the category $\mathbf{Graphs_{TG}}$ *of TG-
typed graphs, where diagram (1) (resp. (2))
corresponds to gluing G of L and D along I
(resp. to gluing H of R and D along I).*

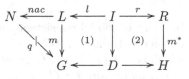

*Note that pushout diagram (1) in step 1 only exists if the match m satisfies a
gluing condition w.r.t. rule r which makes sure that the deletion in step 1 leads to
a well-defined TG−typed graph D. Moreover, rules are allowed to have* Negative
Application Conditions *(NACs) given by a typed graph morphism $nac : L \rightarrow N$.
In this case, rule r can only be applied at match $m : L \rightarrow G$ if there is no injective morphism $q : N \rightarrow G$ with $q \circ nac = m$. This means intuitively that r cannot
be applied to G if graph N occurs in G. A transformation $G_0 \overset{*}{\Longrightarrow} G_n$ via Rules
in GG consists of $n \geq 0$ direct transformations $G_0 \Longrightarrow G_1 \Rightarrow ... \Rightarrow G_n$ via rules
$r \subset Rules$. For $n \geq 1$ we write $G_0 \overset{+}{\Longrightarrow} G_n$.*

Example 2 (Rules of TLS). A rule $r = (L \leftarrow I \rightarrow R)$ of TLS with NAC
$nac : L \rightarrow N$ is given in Fig. 3 (interface I is not shown and consists of the
nodes and edges which are present in both L and R, as indicated by equal
numbers). For simplicity, we only show the part of the NAC graph N which
extends L. All graph morphisms are inclusions. Rule r can be applied to graph
G in Fig. 2 where the node (1:TL) in L is mapped by m to the upper node TL in

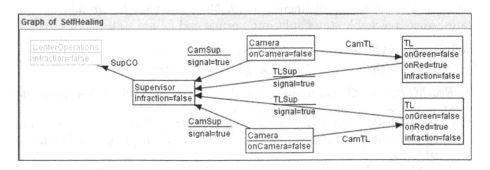

Fig. 2. TLS initial state G_{init}

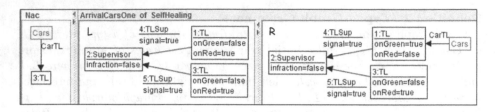

Fig. 3. TLS rule *ArrivalCarsOne*

G_{init}. This leads to a graph H where the attributes of TL are changed and the node Cars of R is attached to TL. Altogether, we have a direct transformation $G \stackrel{r,m}{\Longrightarrow} H$.

In order to model consistency and failure constraints of an SH-system, we use graph constraints. A *TG-typed graph constraint* is given by a TG-typed graph C which is *satisfied by a TG-typed graph* G, written $G \models C$, if there is an injective graph morphism $f : C \to G$. Graph constraints can be negated or combined by logical connectors (e.g. $\neg C$). Now we are able to define SH-systems in the framework of algebraic graph transformation (AGT). An SH-system is given by a typed graph grammar where four kinds of rules are distinguished, called *system*, *normal*, *environment* and *repair* rules. Moreover, we have two kinds of TG-typed graph constraints, namely *consistency* and *failure* constraints.

Definition 3 (Self-healing System in AGT-Framework)
A Self-healing system (SH-system) is given by $SHS = (GG, C_{sys})$, where:

- $GG = (TG, G_{init}, R_{sys})$ *is a typed graph grammar with type graph TG, a TG-typed graph G_{init}, called* initial state, *a set of TG-typed rules R_{sys} with NACs, called* system rules, *defined by $R_{sys} = R_{norm} \cup R_{env} \cup R_{rpr}$, where R_{norm} (called* normal rules*), R_{env} (called* environment rules*) and R_{rpr} (called* repair rules*) are pairwise disjoint.*
- C_{sys} *is a set of TG-typed graph constraints, called* system constraints, *with $C_{sys} = C_{consist} \cup C_{fail}$, where $C_{consist}$ are called* consistency constraints *and C_{fail}* failure constraints.

For an SH-system, we distinguish *reachable, consistent, failure* and *normal* states, where reachable states split into normal and failure states.

Definition 4 (Classification of SH-System States)
Given an SH-system $SHS = (GG, C_{sys})$ as defined above, we have

1. *$Reach(SHS) = \{G \mid G_{init} \stackrel{*}{\Longrightarrow} G$ via $R_{sys}\}$, the* reachable states *consisting of all states reachable via system rules,*
2. *$Consist(SHS) = \{G \mid G \in Reach(SHS) \wedge \forall C \in C_{consist} : G \models C\}$, the* consistent states, *consisting of all reachable states satisfying the consistency constraints,*
3. *$Fail(SHS) = \{G \mid G \in Reach(SHS) \wedge \exists C \in C_{fail} : G \models C\}$, the* failure states, *consisting of all reachable states satisfying some failure constraint,*

4. $Norm(SHS) = \{G \mid G \in Reach(SHS) \land \forall C \in C_{fail} : G \not\models C\}$, *the normal states, consisting of all reachable states not satisfying any failure constraint.*

Example 3 (Traffic Light System as SH-system). We define the Traffic Light SH-system $TLS = (GG, C_{sys})$ by the type graph TG in Fig. 1, the initial state G_{init} in Fig. 2, and the following sets of rules and constraints:

- $R_{norm} = \{ArrivalCarsOne, ArrivalCarsTwo, RemoveCarsOne, Remove\text{-}CarsTwo, InfractionOn, InfractionOff\}$,
- $R_{env} = \{FailureTL, FailureCam\}$,
- $R_{rpr} = \{RepairTL, RepairCam\}$,
- $C_{consist} = \{\neg allGreen, \neg allRed\}$,
- $C_{fail} = \{TLSupFailure, CamSupFailure\}$.

The normal rule *ArrivalCarsOne* is depicted in Fig. 3 and models that one or more cars arrive at a traffic light (1:TL) while all of the crossing's lights are red. The NAC in Fig. 3 means that in this situation, no cars arrive at the other direction's traffic light (3:TL). Applying this rule, the traffic light in the direction of the arriving cars (1:TL) switches to green. Rule *ArrivalCarsTwo* (see Fig. 4) models the arrival of one or more cars at a red traffic light (2:TL) where no cars have been before, while at the same time the traffic light for the other direction (3:TL) shows green and there are already cars going in this direction. This rule causes a change of the traffic light colors in both directions.   Rules *RemoveCarsOne* and *RemoveCarsTwo* are the inverse rules (with L and R exchanged) of the arrival rules in Fig. 3 and 4, and model the reduction of traffic at a traffic light. Rule *InfractionOn* is shown in Fig. 5 and models the situation that a car is passing the crossroad at a red light: the signal *infraction* of both the supervisor and the center of operations is set to true and the corresponding camera is starting to operate. The rule ensures that the corresponding camera is connected, using the edge attribute signal = true for edge 13:CamSup. Rule *InfractionOff* (not depicted) models the inverse action, i.e. the infraction attribute is set back to false, and the camera stops running.

The environment rules are shown in Fig. 6. They model the signal disconnection of a traffic light and a camera, respectively. The repair rules (not depicted) are defined as inverse rules of the environment rules and set the signal attributes back to true.

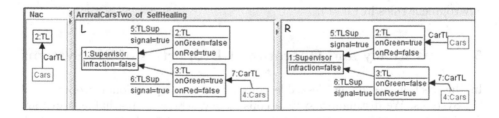

Fig. 4. TLS rule *ArrivalCarsTwo*

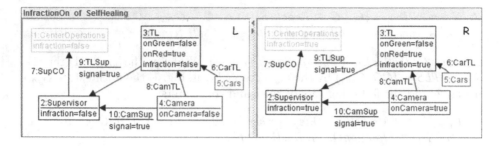

Fig. 5. Normal rule *InfractionOn* of *TLS*

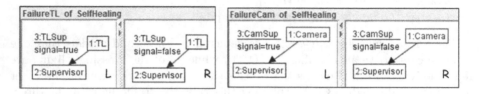

Fig. 6. Environment rules *FailureTL* and *FailureCam* of *TLS*

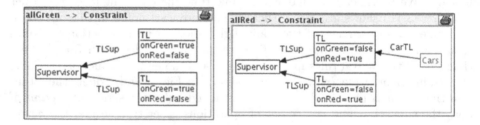

Fig. 7. Consistency constraint graphs of *TLS*

The consistency constraints model the desired properties that we always want to have crossroads with at least one direction showing red lights ($\neg$ *allGreen*) and avoiding all traffic lights red when there is traffic ($\neg$ *allRed*). The corresponding constraint graphs (without negation) are shown in Fig. 7. The failure constraints *TLSupFailure* and *CamSupFailure* express that either a traffic light or a camera is disconnected (the constraint graphs correspond to the right-hand sides of the environment rules in Fig. 6).

5   Consistency and Operational Properties of SH-Systems

In this section, we define desirable consistency and operational properties of SH-Systems. We distinguish system consistency, where all reachable states are consistent, and normal state consistency, where the initial state G_{init} and all states reachable by normal rules are normal states. Environment rules, however, may lead to failure states, which should be repaired by repair rules. We start with consistency properties:

Definition 5 (Consistency Properties). *An SH-System SHS is called*

1. *system consistent, if all reachable states are consistent, i.e.*
   $Reach(SHS) = Consist(SHS);$
2. *normal state consistent, if the initial state is normal and all normal rules preserve normal states, i.e.*
   $G_{init} \in Norm(SHS)$ *and* $\forall G_0 \xRightarrow{p} G_1$ *via* $p \in R_{norm}$
   $[\ G_0 \in Norm(SHS) \Rightarrow G_1 \in Norm(SHS)\ ]$

Example 4 (Consistency Properties of TLS) The SH-System TLS is system consistent, because for all $C \in C_{consist}$ $G_{init} \models C$ and for all $G_0 \xRightarrow{p} G_1$ via $p \in R_{sys}$ and $G_0 \in Consist(SHS)$ we also have $G_1 \in Consist(SHS)$. Similarly, TLS is normal state consistent, because $G_{init} \in Norm(SHS)$ and for all $G_0 \xRightarrow{p} G_1$ via $p \in R_{norm}$ for all $C \in C_{fail}$ $[\ G_0 \not\models C \Rightarrow G_1 \not\models C\ ]$. In both cases this can be concluded by inspection of the corresponding rules, constraints and reachable states. Moreover, there are also general conditions, which ensure the preservation of graph constraints by rules, but this discussion is out of scope for this paper.

Now we consider the operational properties: one of the main ideas of SH-Systems is that they are monitored in regular time intervals by checking, whether the current system state is a failure state. In this case one or more failures have occurred in the last time interval, which are caused by failure rules, provided that we have normal state consistency. With our self-healing property below we require that each failure state can be repaired leading again to a normal state. Moreover, strongly self-healing means that the normal state after repairing is the same as if no failure and repairing would have been occurred.

Definition 6 (Self-healing Properties). *An SH-System SHS is called*

1. *self-healing, if each failure state can be repaired, i.e.*
   $\forall G_{init} \Rightarrow^* G$ *via* $(R_{norm} \cup R_{env})$ *with* $G \in Fail(SHS)$
   $\exists\ G \Rightarrow^+ G'$ *via* R_{rpr} *with* $G' \in Norm(SHS)$
2. *strongly self-healing, if each failure state can be repaired strongly, i.e.*
   $\forall G_{init} \Rightarrow^* G$ *via* $(p_1 \ldots p_n) \in (R_{norm} \cup R_{env})^*$ *with* $G \in Fail(SHS)$
   $\exists\ G \Rightarrow^+ G'$ *via* R_{rpr} *with* $G' \in Norm(SHS)$ *and*
   $\exists\ G_{init} \Rightarrow^* G'$ *via* $(q_1 \ldots q_m) \in R_{norm}^*,$
   where $(q_1 \ldots q_m)$ *is subsequence of all normal rules in* $(p_1 \ldots p_n)$.

Remark 1. By definition, each strongly self-healing SHS is also self-healing, but not vice versa. The additional requirement for strongly self-healing means, that the system state G' obtained after repairing is not only normal, but can also be generated by all normal rules in the given mixed sequence $(p_1 \ldots p_n)$ of normal and environment rules, as if no environment rule would have been applied. We will see that our SH-System TLS is strongly self-healing, but a modification of TLS, which counts failures, even if they are repaired later, would only be self-healing, but not strongly self-healing.

Another important property of SH-Systems is deadlock-freeness, meaning that no reachable state is a deadlock. A stronger liveness property is strong cyclicity, meaning that each pair of reachable states can be reached from each other. Note that this is stronger than cyclicity meaning that there are cycles in the reachability graph. Strong cyclicity, however, implies that each reachable state can be reached arbitrarily often. This is true for the TLS system, but may be false for other reasonable SH-Systems, which may be only deadlock-free. Moreover, we consider "normal deadlock-freeness" and "normal strong cyclicity", where we only consider normal behavior defined by normal rules.

Definition 7 (Deadlock-Freeness and Strong Cyclicity Properties). *An SH-System SHS is called*

1. *deadlock-free, if no reachable state is a deadlock, i.e.*
   $\forall G_0 \in Reach(SHS) \; \exists \; G_0 \xoverset{p}{\Longrightarrow} G_1 \; via \; p \in R_{sys}$
2. *normal deadlock-free, if no state reachable via normal rules is a (normal) deadlock, i.e. $\forall G_{init} \Rightarrow^* G_0 \; via \; R_{norm} \; \exists \; G_0 \xoverset{p}{\Longrightarrow} G_1 \; via \; p \in R_{norm}$*
3. *strongly cyclic, if each pair of reachable states can be reached from each other, i.e. $\forall G_0, G_1 \in Reach(SHS) \; \exists \; G_0 \Rightarrow^* G_1 \; via \; R_{sys}$*
4. *normally cyclic, if each pair of states reachable by normal rules can be reached from each other by normal rules, i.e.*
   $\forall G_{init} \Rightarrow^* G_0 \; via \; R_{norm} \; and \; G_{init} \Rightarrow^* G_1 \; via \; R_{norm} \; we \; have \; \exists \; G_0 \Rightarrow^* G_1$
   via R_{norm}

Remark 2. If we have at least two different reachable states (rsp. reachable by normal rules), then "strongly cyclic" (rsp. "normally cyclic") implies "deadlock-free" (rsp. "normal deadlock-free"). In general properties 1 and 2 as well as 3 and 4 are independent from each other. But in Thm. 3 we will give sufficient conditions s.t. "normal deadlock-free" implies "deadlock-free" (rsp. "normally cyclic" implies "strongly cyclic" in Thm. 4).

6   Analysis and Verification of Operational Properties

In this section, we analyze the operational properties introduced in section 5 and give static sufficient conditions for their verification. The full proofs of our theorems are given in [9].

First, we define direct and normal healing properties, which imply the strong self-healing property under suitable conditions in Thm. 1. In a second step we give static conditions for the direct and normal healing properties in Thm. 2, which by Thm. 1 are also sufficient conditions for our self-healing properties. Of course, we have to require that for each environment rule, which may cause a failure there are one or more repair rules leading again to a state without this failure, if they are applied immediately after its occurrence. But in general, we cannot apply the repair rules directly after the failure, because other normal and environment rules may have been applied already, before the failure is monitored. For this reason we require in Thm. 1 that each pair (p, q) of environment rules p

and normal rules q is sequentially independent. By the Local Church-Rosser theorem for algebraic graph transformation [7](Thm 5.12) sequential independence of (p, q) allows one to switch the corresponding direct derivations in order to prove Thm. 1. For the case with nested application conditions including NACs we refer to [31]. Moreover, the AGG tool can calculate all pairs of sequential independent rules with NACs before runtime.

Definition 8 (Direct and Normal Healing Properties). *An SH-System SHS has the*

1. *direct healing property, if the effect of each environment rule can be repaired directly, i.e.* $\forall G_0 \stackrel{p}{\Longrightarrow} G_1$ *via* $p \in R_{env} \; \exists \; G_1 \stackrel{p'}{\Longrightarrow} G_0$ *via* $p' \in R_{rpr}$
2. *normal healing property, if the effect of each environment rule can be repaired up to normal transformations, i.e.* $\forall G_0 \stackrel{p}{\Longrightarrow} G_1$ *via* $p \in R_{env} \; \exists \; G_1 \Rightarrow^+ G_2$ *via* R_{rpr} *s.t.* $\exists \; G_0 \Rightarrow^* G_2$ *via* R_{norm}

Remark 3. The direct healing property allows one to repair each failure caused by an environment rule directly by reestablishing the old state G_0. This is not required for the normal healing property, but it is required only that the repaired state G_2 is related to the old state G_0 by a normal transformation. Of course, the direct healing property implies the normal one using $G_2 = G_0$.

Theorem 1 (Analysis of Self-healing Properties). *An SH-System SHS is*

  I. *strongly self-healing, if we have properties 1, 2, and 3 below*
 II. *self-healing, if we have properties 1, 2 and 4 below*

1. *SHS is normal state consistent*
2. *each pair* $(p, q) \in R_{env} \times R_{norm}$ *is sequentially independent*
3. *SHS has the direct healing property*
4. *SHS has the normal healing property*

In the following Thm. 2 we give static conditions for direct and normal healing properties. In part 1 of Thm. 2 we require that for each environment rule p the inverse rule p^{-1} is isomorphic to a repair rule p'. Two rules are isomorphic if they are componentwise isomorphic. For $p = (L \leftarrow I \rightarrow R)$ with negative application condition $nac : L \rightarrow N$ it is possible (see [7] Remark 7.21) to construct $p^{-1} = (R \leftarrow I \rightarrow L)$ with equivalent $nac' : R \rightarrow N'$. In part 2 of Thm. 2 we require as weaker condition that each environment rule p has a corresponding repair rule p', which is not necessarily inverse to p. It is sufficient to require that we can construct a concurrent rule $p *_R p'$ which is isomorphic to a normal rule p''. For the construction and corresponding properties of inverse and concurrent rules, which are needed in the proof of Thm. 2 we refer to [7].

Theorem 2 (Static Conditions for Direct/Normal Healing Properties)

1. *An SH-System SHS has the direct healing property, if for each environment rule there is an inverse repair rule, i.e.* $\forall p \in R_{env} \; \exists \; p' \in R_{rpr}$ *with* $p' \cong p^{-1}$

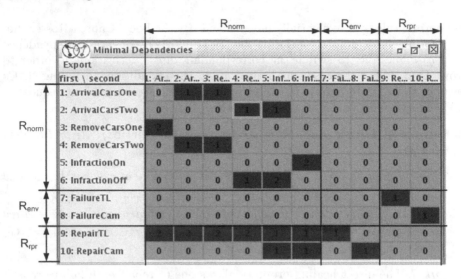

Fig. 8. Dependency Matrix of TLS in AGG

2. *An SH-System SHS has the normal healing property if for each environment rule there is a corresponding repair rule in the following sense:*
$\forall p = (L \leftarrow K \rightarrow R) \in R_{env}$ *we have*
   a) *repair rule $p' = (L' \leftarrow^{l'} K' \rightarrow^{r'} R')$ with l' bijective on nodes, and*
   b) *an edge-injective morphism $e : L' \rightarrow R$ leading to concurrent rule $p *_R p'$, and*
   c) *normal rule $p'' \in R_{norm}$ with $p *_R p' \cong p''$*

Remark 4. By combining Thm. 1 and Thm. 2 we obtain static conditions ensuring that an SH-System SHS is strongly self-healing and self-healing, respectively.

Example 5 (Direct Healing Property of TLS). TLS has direct healing property because "RepairTL" rsp. "RepairCam" are inverse to "FailureTL" resp. "Failure-Cam" and each pair $(p, q) \in R_{env} \times R_{norm}$ is sequentially independent according to the dependency matrix of TLS in Fig. 8.

In the following Thm. 3 and Thm. 4 we give sufficient conditions for deadlock-freeness and strong cyclicity which are important liveness properties. Here we mainly use a stepwise approach. We assume to have both properties for normal rules and give additional static conditions to conclude the property for all system rules. The additional conditions are sequentially and parallel independence and a direct correspondence between environment and repair rules, which should be inverse to each other. Similar to sequential independence, also parallel independence of rules (p, q) can be calculated by the AGG tool before runtime.

Theorem 3 (Deadlock-Freeness). *An SH-System SHS is deadlock-free, if*

1. *SHS is normally deadlock-free, and*

2. *Each pair $(p,q) \in (R_{env} \cup R_{rpr}) \times R_{norm}$ is sequentially and parallel independent.*

Theorem 4 (Strong Cyclicity). *An SH-System SHS is strongly cyclic, given*
  I. properties 1 and 2, or
  II. properties 1, 3 and 4 below.

1. *For each environment rule there is an inverse repair rule and vice versa.*
2. *For each normal rule there is an inverse normal rule.*
3. *SHS is normally cyclic.*
4. *Each pair $(p,q) \in (R_{env} \cup R_{rpr}) \times R_{norm}$ is sequentially independent.*

Remark 5. In part I of Thm. 4, we avoid the stepwise approach and any kind of sequential and parallel independence by the assumption that also all normal rules have inverses, which is satisfied for our TLS.

Example 6 (Strong Cyclicity and Deadlock-Freeness of TLS)
We use part I of Thm. 4 to show strong cyclicity. Property 1 is satisfied because "FailureTL" and "RepairTL" as well as "FailureCam" and "RepairCam" are inverse to each other. Property 2 is satisfied because "ArrivalCarsOne(Two)" and "RemoveCarsOne(Two)" as well as "InfractionOn" and "InfractionOff" are inverse to each other. Moreover, deadlock-freeness of TLS follows from strong cyclicity by remark 2. Note that we cannot use part II of Thm. 4 for our example TLS, because e.g. ("RepairTL", "ArrivalCarsOne") is not sequentially independent.

7   Conclusion

In this paper, we have modeled and analyzed self-healing systems using algebraic graph transformation and graph constraints. We have distinguished between consistency properties, including system consistency and normal state consistency,

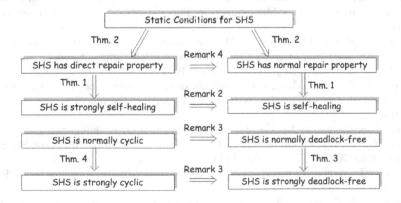

Fig. 9. Operational properties of self-healing systems

and operational properties, including self-healing, strongly self-healing, deadlock-freeness, and strong cyclicity. The main results concerning operational properties are summarized in Fig. 9, where most of the static conditions in Thms. 1- 4 can be automatically checked by the AGG tool.

All properties are verified for our traffic light system. Note that in this paper, the consistency properties are checked by inspection of corresponding rules, while the operational properties are verified using our main results. Work is in progress to evaluate the usability of our approach by applying it to larger case studies. As future work, we will provide analysis and verification of consistency properties using the theory of graph constraints and nested application conditions in [31]. Moreover, we will investigate how far the techniques in this paper for SH-systems can be used and extended for more general self-adaptive systems.

References

1. Brun, Y., Marzo Serugendo, G., Gacek, C., Giese, H., Kienle, H., Litoiu, M., Müller, H., Pezzè, M., Shaw, M.: Engineering self-adaptive systems through feedback loops. In: Software Engineering for Self-Adaptive Systems, pp. 48–70 (2009)
2. Andersson, J., Lemos, R., Malek, S., Weyns, D.: Modeling dimensions of self-adaptive software systems. In: Cheng, B.H.C., de Lemos, R., Giese, H., Inverardi, P., Magee, J. (eds.) Software Engineering for Self-Adaptive Systems. LNCS, vol. 5525, pp. 27–47. Springer, Heidelberg (2009)
3. Rodosek, G.D., Geihs, K., Schmeck, H., Burkhard, S.: Self-healing systems: Foundations and challenges. In: Self-Healing and Self-Adaptive Systems, Germany. Dagstuhl Seminar Proceedings, vol. 09201 (2009)
4. Kephart, J.O., Chess, D.M.: The vision of autonomic computing. Computer 36(1), 41–50 (2003)
5. White, S.R., Hanson, J.E., Whalley, I., Chess, D.M., Segal, A., Kephart, J.O.: Autonomic computing: Architectural approach and prototype. Integr. Comput.-Aided Eng. 13(2), 173–188 (2006)
6. Bucchiarone, A., Pelliccione, P., Vattani, C., Runge, O.: Self-repairing systems modeling and verification using AGG. In: WICSA 2009 (2009)
7. Ehrig, H., Ehrig, K., Prange, U., Taentzer, G.: Fundamentals of Algebraic Graph Transformation. EATCS Monographs in Theor. Comp. Science. Springer, Heidelberg (2006)
8. Ehrig, H., Engels, G., Kreowski, H.J., Rozenberg, G. (eds.): Handbook of Graph Grammars and Computing by Graph Transformation. Applications, Languages and Tools, vol. 2. World Scientific, Singapore (1999)
9. Ehrig, H., Ermel, C., Runge, O., Bucchiarone, A., Pelliccione, P.: Formal analysis and verication of self-healing systems: Long version. Technical report, TU Berlin (2010), http://www.eecs.tu-berlin.de/menue/forschung/forschungsberichte/2010
10. Perry, D., Wolf, A.: Foundations for the Study of Software Architecture. SIGSOFT Softw. Eng. Notes 17(4), 40–52 (1992)
11. Kramer, J., Magee, J.: Self-managed systems: an architectural challenge. In: FOSE, pp. 259–268 (2007)
12. Floch, J., Hallsteinsen, S., Stav, E., Eliassen, F., Lund, K., Gjorven, E.: Using architecture models for runtime adaptability. IEEE Software 23(2), 62–70 (2006)

13. Garlan, D., Schmerl, B.: Model-based adaptation for self-healing systems. In: WOSS 2002, pp. 27–32. ACM, New York (2002)
14. Becker, B., Giese, H.: Modeling of correct self-adaptive systems: A graph transformation system based approach. In: Soft Computing as Transdisciplinary Science and Technology (CSTST 2008), pp. 508–516. ACM Press, New York (2008)
15. Bucchiarone, A.: Dynamic software architectures for global computing systems. PhD thesis, IMT Institute for Advanced Studies, Lucca, Italy (2008)
16. Becker, B., Beyer, D., Giese, H., Klein, F., Schilling, D.: Symbolic invariant verification for systems with dynamic structural adaptation. In: Int. Conf. on Software Engineering (ICSE). ACM Press, New York (2006)
17. Baresi, L., Heckel, R., Thone, S., Varro, D.: Style-based refinement of dynamic software architectures. In: WICSA 2004. IEEE Computer Society, Los Alamitos (2004)
18. Hirsch, D., Inverardi, P., Montanari, U.: Modeling software architectures and styles with graph grammars and constraint solving. In: WICSA, pp. 127–144 (1999)
19. Métayer, D.L.: Describing software architecture styles using graph grammars. IEEE Trans. Software Eng. 24(7), 521–533 (1998)
20. Kastenberg, H., Rensink, A.: Model checking dynamic states in groove. In: Valmari, A. (ed.) SPIN 2006. LNCS, vol. 3925, pp. 299–305. Springer, Heidelberg (2006)
21. Aguirre, N., Maibaum, T.S.E.: Hierarchical temporal specifications of dynamically reconfigurable component based systems. ENTCS 108, 69–81 (2004)
22. Rensink, A., Schmidt, A., Varr'o, D.: Model checking graph transformations: A comparison of two approaches. In: Ehrig, H., Engels, G., Parisi-Presicce, F., Rozenberg, G. (eds.) ICGT 2004. LNCS, vol. 3256, pp. 226–241. Springer, Heidelberg (2004)
23. Reisig, W.: Petri Nets: An Introduction. EATCS Monographs on Theoretical Computer Science, vol. 4. Springer, Heidelberg (1985)
24. Spanoudakis, G., Zisman, A., Kozlenkov, A.: A service discovery framework for service centric systems. In: IEEE SCC, pp. 251–259 (2005)
25. Canfora, G., Penta, M.D., Esposito, R., Villani, M.L.: An approach for qos-aware service composition based on genetic algorithms. In: GECCO, pp. 1069–1075 (2005)
26. Zeng, L., Benatallah, B., Dumas, M., Kalagnanam, J., Sheng, Q.Z.: Quality driven web services composition. In: WWW, pp. 411–421 (2003)
27. Baresi, L., Guinea, S., Pasquale, L.: Self-healing BPEL processes with Dynamo and the JBoss rule engine. In: ESSPE 2007, pp. 11–20. ACM, New York (2007)
28. Colombo, M., Nitto, E.D., Mauri, M.: Scene: A service composition execution environment supporting dynamic changes disciplined through rules. In: ICSOC, pp. 191–202 (2006)
29. Rukzio, E., Siorpaes, S., Falke, O., Hussmann, H.: Policy based adaptive services for mobile commerce. In: WMCS 2005. IEEE Computer Society, Los Alamitos (2005)
30. Inverardi, P., Pelliccione, P., Tivoli, M.: Towards an assume-guarantee theory for adaptable systems. In: SEAMS, pp. 106–115. IEEE Computer Society, Los Alamitos (2009)
31. Ehrig, H., Habel, A., Lambers, L.: Parallelism and Concurrency Theorems for Rules with Nested Application Conditions. In: EC-EASST (to appear, 2010)

Stochastic Simulation of Graph Transformation Systems

Paolo Torrini[1], Reiko Heckel[1], and István Ráth[2]

[1] Department of Computer Science, University of Leicester
pt95,reiko@mcs.le.ac.uk
[2] Department of Measurement and Information Systems
Budapest University of Technology and Economics
rath@mit.bme.hu

1 Introduction

Stochastic graph transformation systems (SGTS) [1] support integrated modelling of architectural reconfiguration and non-functional aspects such as performance and reliability. In its simplest form a SGTS is a graph transformation system (GTS) where each rule name is associated with a rate of an exponential distribution governing the delay of its application. However, this approach has its limitations. Model checking with explicit states does not scale well to models with large state space. Since performance and reliability properties often depend on the behaviour of large populations of entities (network nodes, processes, services, etc.), this limitation is significant. Also, exponential distributions do not always provide the best abstraction. For example, the time it takes to make a phone call or transmit a message is more likely to follow a normal distribution.

To counter these limitations, *generalised* SGTS [2] allow for general distributions dependent on rule - match pairs (rather than just rule names). Generalised semi-Markov processes provide a semantic model for such systems, supporting stochastic simulation. Rather than model checking, simulations provide a more flexible tradeoff between analysis effort and confidence in the result and so allow to verify soft performance targets in large-scale systems.

We present a tool called GraSS, for Graph-based Stochastic Simulation, to enable the analysis of such processes. The tool is developed in Java-Eclipse, extending the VIATRA model transformation plugin with a control based on the SSJ library for Stochastic Simulation in Java. The main performance challenge, in finding, at each state of the simulation, all matches for all rules, is alleviated by VIATRA's RETE-style incremental pattern-matching approach [3], which stores precomputed matching information and updates it during transformation. We illustrate and evaluate the application of the tool by the simulation of the original P2P reconfiguration model as well as an improved and scaled-up version.

2 A P2P Network Model

As a test case we use an example of a SGTS modelling reconfigurations in a P2P network [1]. Generating the state space of the model for up to seven peers,

D.S. Rosenblum and G. Taentzer (Eds.): FASE 2010, LNCS 6013, pp. 154–157, 2010.

in [1] we used stochastic model checking to analyse, e.g., the probability of the network being fully connected, so that each participant can communicate with every other one.

The GTS below models basic P2P network reconfigurations. Rule *new* on the left adds a new peer, registers it and links it to an existing peer. Rule *kill* deletes a peer with all links attached. Predicate *disconnected* checks if there are two nodes that are not connected by a path of links labelled *l*.

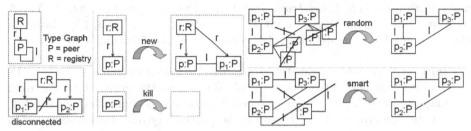

The two rules on the right create redundant links to increase reliability in case a peer is lost. Rule *random* creates a link between $p2$ and $p3$ unless there is one already or the number of additional connections of either $p2$ or $p3$ is greater than two. Rule *smart* creates a link if there is no two-hop path between $p2$ and $p3$ apart from the one via $p1$. We consider two families of systems, $SGTS_{random,x}$ and $SGTS_{smart,x}$. The former has rules $\{new, kill, random\}$ and rates $\sigma(new) = \sigma(kill) = 1$ and $\sigma(random) = x$. In the latter, *random* is replaced by *smart* with $\sigma(smart) = x$. In both cases x ranges from 1 to 10,000 to test different ratios between basic and redundancy rules.

3 Simulating Stochastic Graph Transformations

In order to define a general interface between the stochastic control component of the simulation and existing graph transformation tools used for executing rules, we define SGTS for a generic notion of graph transformation. Refining [4], a *graph transformation approach* is given by a class of graphs $\mathcal{G}$, a class of rules $\mathcal{R}$, and a $\mathcal{R} \times \mathcal{G}$-indexed family of sets of *rule matches* $\mathcal{M}_{r,G}$ for rule r into graph G. Transformation is defined by a family of partial functions $\Rightarrow_{r,m}: \mathcal{G} \to \mathcal{G}$, such that $\Rightarrow_{r,m}(G)$ is defined if and only if $m \in \mathcal{M}_{r,G}$. This captures the idea that rule application is well-defined and deterministic if m is a match for r in G.

For a set of rules R, $\mathcal{E}_R$ is the set of *events*, i.e., compatible pairs $\langle r, m \rangle$. $\mathcal{S} = \langle R, G_0, F \rangle$ is a *stochastic graph transformation system* with set of rules R, initial graph G_0, and $F : \mathcal{E}_R \to (\mathbf{R} \to [0,1])$ assigning each event a continuous distribution function such that $F(e)(0) = 0$.

We encode SGTS into generalised semi-Markov schemes (GSMS), a generalisation of Markov chains associated with generalised semi-Markov processes [5]. Here transitions are independent of past states, but unlike Markov chains they may depend on the time spent in the current one, i.e., interevent times may be non-exponentially distributed. Formally, a GSMS is a structure

$$\mathcal{P} = \langle\, S,\ E,\ act : S \to \wp(E),\ trans : S \times E \to S,\ \delta : E \to (\mathcal{R} \to [0,1]),\ init : S \,\rangle$$

where S is a set of states (given by all graphs reachable in $\mathcal{S}$), E is a set of events (the rule matches $\mathcal{E}_R$), *init* is the initial state (graph G_0), *act* gives the set of events (rule matches) enabled in a state (graph), *trans* is the transition function (given by $trans(G, \langle r, m \rangle) = \Rightarrow_{r,m}(G)$), and δ defines the probability distribution for each event (given by F).

The simulation component uses VIATRA as a graph transformation tool to implement the elements of the GSMS that depend on the representation of states and events, notably $S, E, act, trans, init$, i.e., GTSs are represented as a VIATRA models. Definitions of distributions F are loaded from an XML file. Based on this data, a GSMS simulation in GraSS consists of the following steps

1. Initialisation — the simulation time T is initialised to 0 and the set of the enabled matches (active events) is obtained from the graph transformation engine. For each active event, a scheduling time t_e is computed by a random number generator (RNG) based on the probability distribution assigned to the event. Timed events are collected as a list ordered by time (state list).
2. At each simulation step
   (a) the first element $k = (e, t)$ is removed from the state list
   (b) the simulation time is increased to t
   (c) the event e is executed by the graph transformation engine
   (d) the new state list s' is computed, by querying the engine, removing all the elements that have been disabled, adding to the list an event for each newly enabled match m with time $t = T + d$, where d is provided by the RNG depending on $F(m)$, and reordering the list with respect to time

GT rules with empty postconditions are used as probes — statistics about occurrence of precodition patterns are computed as SSJ tally class reports, giving average values over runs. One can specify the number of runs per experiment (esp. useful to reduce the biasing effect of runs truncated by deletion of all elements) and their max depth (either by number of steps or simulation time).

4   Evaluation

In order to validate the correctness and scalability of the tool we run a number of experiments based on the P2P model of Section 2. We do not expect to replicate exactly the results reported in [1] because (1) we remove the restriction to 7 nodes that was used to guarantee a finite (and manageable) state space; (2) unlike in [1] where states and transitions were presented up to isomorphism, our simulation deals with concrete graphs and transitions. A detailed comparison of the underlying mathematical models is beyond the scope of this paper, but it appears that, since the Markov chain is constructed from a more abstract transition system in [1], the two are not in stochastic bisimulation. Thus, evaluating the same properties on both models may lead to different results. As in [1] we run experiments with 10 different models, 5 versions each of using *random* and *smart* rules, with rates ranging through $x \in \{1, 10, 100, 1000, 10000\}$.

We perform 5 runs each with a simulation time bound of 10s for each experiment — i.e. no run exceeds 10s regardless of the number of steps. The table below gives the output of an experiment, indicating the version of the model (1st column) followed by the percentage of disconnected states encountered, the average number of steps performed per run, the average maximal extension of the network, and the average time taken for each run.

Model: P2P	Disconnected	Number of steps	Max number of peers	Runtime
random:1	0.46	33	6	5
random:10	0.62	71	8	8
random:100	0.55	86	8	7
random:1000	0.89	284	20	10
random:10,000	0.46	116	8	9
smart:1	1.33	18	5	1
smart:10	0.01	90	8	4
smart:100	0.00	3561	48	10
smart:1000	0.00	998	24	10
smart:10,000	0.00	62	8	3

Such results confirm the inverse dependency observed in [1] between the rate of the *smart* rule and the probability of being disconnected, whereas for the *random* rule an increased rate does not lead to any significant change in reliability — as confirmed by the average number of disconnections modulo square of node number (not shown). The performance (number of simulation steps per sec) is limited by the complexity of pattern *disconnect* which, in a network of n peers, checks for (non-) existence of n^2 paths. This can be hard due to transitive closure. As a simpler reliability measure, the proportion of peers with at least two connections (hence less vulnerable to loss of connectivity) can do. A simulation of 5 runs with a time limit of 10s has always been carried out in less than a minute. Reliance on incremental pattern matching means model size only affects simulation up to number of RNG calls, whereas increase in number and complexity of the rules can add to the cost of graph transformation, too.

References

1. Heckel, R.: Stochastic analysis of graph transformation systems: A case study in P2P networks. In: Van Hung, D., Wirsing, M. (eds.) ICTAC 2005. LNCS, vol. 3722, pp. 53–69. Springer, Heidelberg (2005)
2. Khan, A., Torrini, P., Heckel, R.: Model-based simulation of VoIP network reconfigurations using graph transformation systems. In: Corradini, A., Tuosto, E. (eds.) ICGT 2008. El. Com. EASST, vol. 16, pp. 1–20 (2008)
3. Bergmann, G., Ökrös, A., Ráth, I., Varró, D., Varró, G.: Incremental pattern matching in the Viatra model transformation system. In: GRaMoT 2008, pp. 25–32. ACM, New York (2008)
4. Kreowski, H.J., Kuske, S.: On the interleaving semantics of transformation units - a step into GRACE. In: Cuny, J., Engels, G., Ehrig, H., Rozenberg, G. (eds.) Graph Grammars 1994. LNCS, vol. 1073, pp. 89–106. Springer, Heidelberg (1996)
5. D'Argenio, P.R., Katoen, J.P.: A theory of stochastic systems part I: Stochastic automata. Inf. Comput. 203(1), 1–38 (2005)

Prescriptive Semantics for Big-Step Modelling Languages

Shahram Esmaeilsabzali and Nancy A. Day

Cheriton School of Computer Science
University of Waterloo
Waterloo, Ontario, Canada, N2L 3G1
{sesmaeil,nday}@cs.uwaterloo.ca

Abstract. A big-step modelling language (BSML) is a language in which a model can respond to an environmental input via a sequence of small steps, each of which may consist of the concurrent execution of a set of transitions. BSMLs are a popular class of modelling languages that are regularly reincarnated in different syntactic and semantic variations. In our previous work, we *deconstructed* the semantics of many existing BSMLs into eight high-level, conceptually intuitive *semantic aspects* and their *semantic options*, which together constitute a semantic design space for BSMLs. In this work, we describe a parametric semantic definition schema based on this deconstruction for defining formally the semantics of a wide range of BSMLs. A semantic definition in our framework is *prescriptive* in that the high-level semantic aspects of a BSML are manifested clearly as orthogonal parts of the semantic definition. Our goal is to produce a formal semantic definition that is accessible to various stakeholders of the semantics.

1 Introduction

In this paper, we describe a formal framework to define the semantics of *Big-step Modelling Languages* (BSMLs) [1,2]. BSMLs are a popular, effective class of behavioural modelling languages in which a modeller can specify the reaction of a system to an environmental input as a *big step*, which consists of a sequence of *small steps*, each of which may contain a set of concurrent transitions. There is a plethora of BSMLs, many with graphical syntax (e.g., statecharts variants [3, 4] and Argos [5]), some with textual syntax (e.g., Reactive Modules [6] and Esterel [7]), and some with tabular format (e.g., SCR [8,9]).

In our previous work, we *deconstructed* the semantics of BSMLs into eight mainly orthogonal *semantic aspects* and their corresponding *semantic options* [1, 2]. The semantic aspects distill the semantic concerns of different BSMLs into high-level semantic concepts. The combinations of the semantic options establish a semantic design space that includes the semantics of many existing BSMLs, as well as new BSML semantics. Our deconstruction is conceptually intuitive because the semantic aspects characterize a big step as a whole, rather than only considering its constituent transitions operationally.

D.S. Rosenblum and G. Taentzer (Eds.): FASE 2010, LNCS 6013, pp. 158–172, 2010.

Our contribution in this paper is the formalization of a wide range of BSML semantics in a manner that follows our deconstruction. Our semantic definition framework consists of a *semantic definition schema*, which has a set of *parameters*. By instantiating the parameters of the semantic definition schema, an operational BSML semantics is derived. The semantic definition schema, its parameters, and the values of the parameters are specified in standard logic and set theory. The semantic aspects of BSMLs correspond to disjoint parameters of the semantic definition schema, and the semantic options of each semantic aspect correspond to the possible values for the parameters. Thus, we achieve a formal semantics without sacrificing the intuitiveness achieved in our deconstruction.

A key insight in our formalization is the recognition, and separation, of the distinct roles in the formal definition for the semantic aspects of *concurrency*, *small-step consistency*, *preemption*, and *priority*. We call these parameters *structural parameters*, because they affect the meaning of the hierarchial structure of a model. Structural parameters are distinct from the more common *dynamic parameters* found in other formalizations, which specify how the state of the model changes from one small step to the next. We believe we are the first to separate these structural parameters disjointly in a manner that matches the factoring into aspects from our high-level deconstruction of the semantics of BSMLs.

In formal semantics, there are two approaches in using formalism: *descriptive* vs. *prescriptive* [10, 11]. Our semantic definition framework is a prescriptive approach to define BSML semantics. A prescriptive semantic definition uses the formalism in an active role, to prescribe a semantics that is already known to the semanticist. A descriptive semantic definition uses the formalism in a passive role to describe, what seems like, the discovery of a semantics in the world of all possible semantics. A prescriptive semantic method can provide insights and guidance about what is a *good* semantics, whereas a descriptive semantics cannot. For example, BNF is a prescriptive method for defining syntax, as opposed to pre-BNF methods, which were descriptive [10]. "In general, the descriptive approach aims for generality even at the expense of simplicity and elegance, while the prescriptive approach aims for simplicity and elegance even at the expense of generality." [11, p.284]. A semantic definition produced by our semantic definition schema is prescriptive in that the high-level semantic aspects of a BSML chosen by its various stakeholders are manifested clearly as orthogonal parts of the semantic definition. A result of our semantic deconstruction and its formalization is a clear scope for the BSML family of modelling languages.

The remainder of the paper is organized as follows. In Section 2, we first describe the common syntax that we use for BSMLs, and then describe our deconstruction of BSML semantics using a feature diagram. In Section 3, we describe our semantic definition schema, by presenting its common elements, its structural and dynamic parameters, and their possible values. We also specify the scope of BSML semantics that our framework covers. In Section 4, we consider the related work, comparing our work with other semantic definition frameworks, including those used in tool-support generator frameworks. In Section 5, we conclude our paper and discuss future work.

2   Background

In Section 2.1, we describe our normal form syntax for BSMLs, and in Section 2.2, we describe our deconstruction of BSML semantics [1,2]. We adopt few syntactic definitions from Pnueli and Shalev's work [12].

2.1   Normal Form Syntax

As is usual when studying a class of related notations, we introduce a *normal form syntax* [13], which is expressive enough for representing the syntax of many BSMLs [1,2]. In our normal form syntax, a model consists of: (i) a *hierarchy tree* of *control states*, and (ii) a set of *transitions* between the control states. Fig. 1 shows the BNF for the hierarchy tree of a model and its transitions, which permits an arbitrary hierarchy of *And* and *Or* control states, with *Basic* control states appearing at the leaves.[1] The symbol "transitions" in the rules is a set of transitions. The highest level control state in a hierarchy tree is called the *root*, which is an *Or* control state with an empty set of transitions.

$$
\begin{array}{ll}
\langle \text{root} \rangle & \to \langle \text{Orstate} \rangle \\
\langle \text{Orstate} \rangle & \to \textbf{Or} \ \langle \text{states} \rangle \ \langle \text{transitions} \rangle \\
\langle \text{Andstate} \rangle & \to \textbf{And} \ \langle \text{states} \rangle \ \langle \text{transitions} \rangle \\
\langle \text{Basicstate} \rangle & \to \textbf{Basic} \\
\langle \text{states} \rangle & \to \langle \text{state} \rangle \ | \ \langle \text{states} \rangle \ \langle \text{state} \rangle \\
\langle \text{state} \rangle & \to \langle \text{Orstate} \rangle \ | \ \langle \text{Andstate} \rangle \ | \ \langle \text{Basicstate} \rangle
\end{array}
$$

Fig. 1. The BNF for the hierarchy tree of control states and their transitions

An *Or* or an *And* control state, s, has *children*, $children(s)$. For a control state s, $children^*(s)$ is the set of all control states that are children of s either directly or by transitivity. We denote $children^+(s) = children^*(s) \cup s$. Similarly, we use the *parent*, *ancestor*, and *descendant* relations with their usual meanings. An *Or* control state s has a *default* control state, $default(s)$, which is one of its children. A *Basic* control state can be designated as *stable* or *non-stable*.[2]

A transition t has a *source* control state, $src(t)$, and a *destination* control state, $dest(t)$. Additionally, it can have four optional parts: (i) an *event trigger*, $trig(t)$, which is a conjunction of events, $pos\_trig(t)$, and negations of events, $neg\_trig(t)$; (ii) a *guard condition*, $cond(t)$, which is a boolean expression over a set of variables; (iii) a sequence of *assignments*, $asn(t)$; and (iv) a set of *generated events*, $gen(t)$.

The *least common ancestor* of two control states s and s', $lca(s, s')$, is the lowest control state (closest to the leaves of the hierarchy tree) in the hierarchy tree such that: $s, s' \in children^*(lca(s, s'))$. Given a transition t, we assume a

---

[1] Normally, a control state has a name, but we do not need it in our formalization.
[2] For example, a stable control state can be used to model non-pseudo control states of *compound transitions* in UML StateMachines [14] or **pause** commands in Esterel [7].

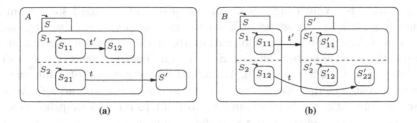

Fig. 2. Interrupting transitions

parsing mechanism that associates t with control state $lca(src(t), dest(t))$. Two control states s and s' are *orthogonal*, $s \perp s'$, if neither is an ancestor of the other and $lca(s, s')$ is an *And* control state. We call two transitions t and t' orthogonal, $t \perp t'$, if $src(t) \perp src(t')$ and $dest(t) \perp dest(t')$. The *arena* of a transition t, $arena(t)$, is the lowest *Or* control state in the hierarchy tree such that: $src(t), dest(t) \in children^*(arena(t))$. The *source scope* of a transition t, $ss(t)$, specifies the highest control state that t exits upon execution. If $src(t) \in children^+(dest(t))$, then $ss(t)$ is $dest(t)$, and if $dest(t) \in children^+ (src(t))$, then $ss(t)$ is $src(t)$. Otherwise, $ss(t)$ is the highest control state such that: $src(t) \in children^+(ss(t))$ and $dest(t) \notin children^+(ss(t))$. Similarly, the *destination scope* of a transition t, $ds(t)$, is defined.

A transition t is an *interrupt for* transition t', $t \not\downarrow t'$, if the sources of the transitions are orthogonal, and one of the following conditions holds: (i) the destination of t' is orthogonal with the source of t, and the destination of t is not orthogonal with the sources of either transitions (Fig. 2(a)); or (ii) the destination of neither transition is orthogonal with the sources of the two transitions, but the destination of t is a descendant of the destination of t' (Fig. 2(b)). (In Fig. 2, a dashed line separates the children of an *And* control state, and an arrow without a source signifies the default control state of an *Or* control state.) We use the *interrupt for* relation to model the notion of *preemption* [7,5].[3] For a set of transitions τ, its set of *interrupted transitions*, $interr(\tau) \subset \tau$, consists of transitions t' such that for each $t' \in interr(\tau)$ there is a $t \in \tau$ and $t \not\downarrow t'$.

2.2   BSML Semantics

Initially, a model resides in the default control state of each of its *Or* control states, its variables have their initial values, and its events are not present. Fig. 3 depicts the structure of a big step, operationally. A big step is the reaction of a model to an *environmental input*, which consists of an alternating sequence of small steps and *snapshots*. An environmental input, e.g., I in Fig. 3, consists of a set of environmental input events, $I.events$, and a set of variable assignments, $I.asns$. In some BSMLs, a sequence of small steps are grouped together

---

[3] For example, in Esterel [7], the concurrent execution of a statement and an `exit` statement is modelled by the *interrupt for* relation according to condition (i) above, and the concurrent execution of two `exits` is modelled by condition (ii) above.

into a *combo step*, which hides some of the effects of its small steps from one another (e.g., [15, 16]). A snapshot is a collection of *snapshot elements*, each of which is a collection of related information about the execution of a model. For example, there is a snapshot element, S_c, which maintains the set of *current* control states that a model resides in. We follow the convention of using sp itself, or sp with a superscript, as the name of a snapshot; e.g., sp and sp'. Also, we follow the convention of always using a subscript to name a snapshot element. To access a snapshot element in a snapshot, we annotate the snapshot element name with the superscript of the snapshot; e.g., S_c and S_c' access the snapshot element S_c in snapshots sp and sp', respectively.

The execution of a transition in a small step includes *exiting* a set of control states and *entering* a set of control states. The *exited control states* of transition t, $exited(t) = children^+(ss(t))$, specify the control states that could be exited upon execution of t, based on the current control states, S_c, which the model resides in. The *entered control states* of transition t, $entered(t)$, specifies exactly the control states that are entered upon execution of t. A control state s belongs to $entered(t)$ if $s \in children^+(ds(t))$ and one of the following three conditions holds: (i) $dest(t) \in children^+(s)$; (ii) there exists a control state $s' \in entered(t)$ such that, (a) either s' is an *And* control state and $s \in children(s')$, or s' is an *Or* control state and $s = default(s')$, and (b) $lca(s, dest(t))$ is not an *Or* control state; or (iii) there exists a control state $s' \in entered(t)$ such that, (a) either s' is an *And* control state and $s \in children(s')$, or s' is an *Or* control state and $s = default(s')$, and (b) $s' \in children^+(dest(t))$. For example, in Fig. 2(b), $dest(t) = S_{22}'$, $ds(t) = S'$, and $entered(t) = \{S', S_1', S_2', S_{11}', S_{22}'\}$. Therefore, the execution of a small step τ removes the set of control states $\bigcup_{t \in \tau} exited(t)$ from S_c, and adds the set of control states $\bigcup_{t \in (\tau - interr(\tau))} entered(t)$ to it.

Semantic Deconstruction. Fig. 4 shows our deconstruction of BSML semantics into eight semantics aspects, and their semantic options [1, 2], as a feature diagram [17]. The Sans Serif and SMALL CAPS fonts represent the semantic aspects and the semantic options, respectively. The feature diagram in Fig. 4 enumerates the BSML semantics that arise from our deconstruction.[4] A simple subtree in the feature diagram is an *and* choice: if the parent is chosen, all of its children, except for the *optional* children that are distinguished by a small circle attaching to them must be chosen. An arced subtree in the feature diagram is an *exclusive or* choice: if the parent is chosen, exactly one of its children can be chosen, which might be an optional feature. For example, a BSML semantics must subscribe to exactly one semantic option of the Big-Step Maximality.

Semantic Aspects. The Big-Step Maximality semantic aspect specifies when a big step concludes, meaning the model can sense the next environmental input. Similarly, the Combo-Step Maximality semantic aspect specifies when a combo step concludes, and the effect of the execution of the small steps of the combo

---

[4] There are few semantic dependencies between the choices of semantic options [1, 2], but we do not consider them here, and assume that they are satisfied.

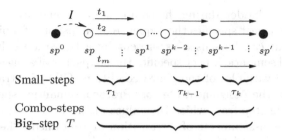

Fig. 3. Steps

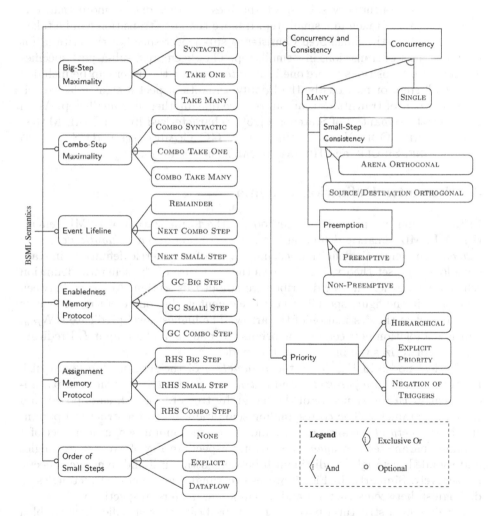

Fig. 4. Semantic aspects and their semantic options

step that has been hidden during the combo step becomes available. The Event Lifeline semantic aspect specifies the sequence of snapshots of a big step in which a generated event can be sensed as present by a transition.[5] The Enabledness Memory Protocol semantic aspect specifies the snapshots of a big step from which the values of the variables of the guard condition (GC) of a transition are obtained. Similarly, the Assignment Memory Protocol semantic aspect specifies the snapshots of a big step from which the values of the variables in the right-hand side (RHS) of the assignments of a transition are obtained. The Order of Small Steps semantic aspect determines how potential small steps at a snapshot are ordered. The Concurrency and Consistency semantic aspect consists of three sub-aspects. The Concurrency sub-aspect specifies whether one or more than one transition can be taken in a small step. If more than one transition can be taken in a small step, the Small-Step Consistency sub-aspect specifies the criteria for including a set of transitions in a small step. The Preemption sub-aspect specifies whether two transitions where one is an *interrupt for* the other can be included in a small step, or not. Lastly, the Priority semantic aspect assigns relative priority to a pair of transitions that can replace one another in a small step. As an example, the semantics of Statemate [16] is characterized by the TAKE MANY, COMBO TAKE ONE, NEXT COMBO STEP, GC COMBO STEP, RHS COMBO STEP, NONE, SINGLE, and HIERARCHICAL semantic options.

3   Semantic Definition Schema

In this section, we present our method for the formalization of BSML semantics. A BSML semantic definition is an instantiation of our *semantic definition schema*. The semantic definition schema is a set of parametric definitions in standard logic and set theory. Fig. 5 shows the structure of the semantic definition schema, whose elements we describe throughout this section. An arrow between two nodes in the figure specifies that the element in the source of the arrow uses the element in the destination of the arrow. The highest level predicate is N_{Big}, which is a relation between two snapshots sp^0 and sp, and an input I. Predicate N_{Big} characterizes the big steps of the model.

The leaf nodes in Fig. 5 are the *parameters* of the schema. We distinguish between a *structural parameter* and a *dynamic parameter*. A structural parameter deals with the structure of the hierarchy tree of a model, as opposed to a dynamic parameter. The corresponding semantic aspect of a structural parameter is a *structural* semantic aspect, and the corresponding semantic aspect of a dynamic parameter is a *dynamic* semantic aspect. In Fig. 4, we use rectangles and rounded rectangles to distinguish between structural and dynamic aspects, respectively. Similarly, In Fig. 5, we use rectangles and rounded rectangles to distinguish between structural and dynamic parameters, respectively.

A value for a structural parameter is a predicate that specifies how enabled transitions together can form a small step. A value for a dynamic parameter is a set of snapshot elements, which is usually a singleton. A snapshot element x_1

---

[5] Our deconstruction does not include asynchronous events, which use buffers.

is characterized by its type, and three predicates, which are each parameters: (i) reset_x_1, which specifies how x_1 changes at the beginning of a big step when an environmental input is received; (ii) next_x_1, which specifies how the value of x_1 is changed when a small step is executed; and (ii) en_x_1, which specifies the role of x_1 in determining a transition as enabled. We denote the set of all snapshot elements that are used by a BSML semantics as $SpEl = \{x_1, x_2, \cdots, x_n\}$.

The remainder of this section is organized as follows. Section 3.1 describes the common, non-parametric elements of the semantic definition schema. Sections 3.2 and 3.3 present the possible values for the structural and dynamic parameters, respectively. Section 3.4 describes the scope of our formalization.

3.1   Common Elements

Fig. 6 shows the semantic definition schema. Definitions in lines 1-5 specify how a big step is formed from small steps. Line 1 specifies predicate N_{Big}, which creates a big step by sensing the environmental input I at snapshot sp^0 (via predicate *reset*), taking k small steps (via predicate N), and concluding the big step at snapshot sp', when there are no further small steps to be taken, i.e., when $enabled(root, sp') = \emptyset$. The *reset* predicate in line 2, is the conjunction of the "reset" predicates of the snapshot elements of a BSML semantics; it specifies the effect of receiving the environmental input I. Line 5 specifies the operation of a small step through the N_{small} predicate, which itself is the conjunction of the "next" predicates of the snapshot elements of a BSML semantics. The effect of executing a small step is captured in the destination snapshot of the small step. The N_{small} predicates are chained together via the N relation to create a sequence of small steps, as shown in lines 3 and 4.

Definitions in lines 6-9 determine the set of potential small steps at a snapshot by walking over the hierarchy tree of a model, according to the BNF in Fig. 1, in a bottom-up way. At a snapshot sp, $enabled(root, sp)$ provides a set of sets of transitions, one of which is non-deterministically chosen as the next small step. For readability, we have used a pair of brackets "[ ]" to separate the syntactic parameter of the predicates from the snapshot parameter sp. Parameter Tr is the set of transitions of an *And* or *Or* control state. Line 9 specifies how transitions of the children of an *And* control state can be executed in a small step: the static parameter ‖, which is associated with the Concurrency semantic aspect, specifies whether one or more than one transition can be executed in a small step.

Line 14 defines the *merge* operator, used in lines 6 and 8, which depends on static parameters C, P, and Π. At each level of the hierarchy tree of a model, the merge operator decides how to choose from the set of sets of enabled transitions at the lower level of the tree (parameter $\mathbb{T}$), and the transitions at the current level of the tree (parameter T'). Parameter $\mathbb{T}$ is in a special font because its type is set of sets of transitions, as opposed to a set of transitions such as T'. The result of a merge operation is a new set of sets of transitions. A transition belonging to a set of transitions $T_1 \in \mathbb{T}$ is included in the corresponding new set of transitions for T_1, unless it is replaced with a transition in the current level. Similarly, a transition $t \in T'$ in the current level is included in a new set

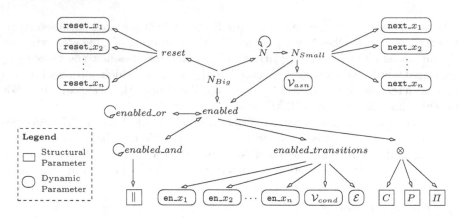

Fig. 5. The structure of the semantic definition schema

---

1. $N_{Big}(sp^0, I, sp') \equiv reset(sp^0, I, sp) \wedge (\exists k \geq 0 \cdot N^k(sp, sp'))$
   $\wedge\ enabled(root, sp') = \emptyset$

2. $reset(sp^0, I, sp) \equiv \bigwedge\limits_{1 \leq i \leq n} \mathbf{reset\_}x_i(sp^0, I, sp)$

3. $N^0(sp, sp') \equiv sp = sp'$

4. $N^{k+1}(sp, sp') \equiv \exists \tau, sp'' \cdot N_{Small}(sp, \tau, sp'') \wedge N^k(sp'', sp')$

5. $N_{Small}(sp, \tau, sp') \equiv \bigwedge\limits_{1 \leq i \leq n} \mathbf{next\_}x_i(sp, \tau, sp') \wedge \tau \in enabled(root, sp)$

---

6. $enabled([\mathbf{Or}, \langle s_1, s_2, \cdots, s_m \rangle, Tr], sp) = enabled\_or([\langle s_1, s_2, \cdots, s_m \rangle]) \otimes$
   $\qquad enabled\_transitions([Tr], sp)$

7. $enabled\_or([\langle s_1, s_2, \cdots, s_m \rangle], sp) = enabled([s_1], sp) \cup$
   $\qquad enabled\_or([\langle s_2, \cdots, s_m \rangle], sp)$

8. $enabled([\mathbf{And}, \langle s_1, s_2, \cdots, s_m \rangle, Tr], sp) = enabled\_and([\langle s_1, s_2, \cdots, s_m \rangle], sp) \otimes$
   $\qquad enabled\_transitions([Tr], sp)$

9. $enabled\_and([\langle s_1, s_2, \cdots, s_m \rangle], sp) = enabled([s_1], sp) \parallel$
   $\qquad enabled\_and([\langle s_2, \cdots, s_m \rangle], sp)$

10. $enabled\_transitions([Tr], sp) = \{t : Tr|\ evaluate([cond(t)], \mathcal{V}_{cond}) \wedge$
    $\qquad ([src(t)] \in S_c) \wedge ([neg\_trig(t)] \cap \mathcal{E} = \emptyset)$
    $\qquad ([pos\_trig(t)] \subseteq \mathcal{E}) \bigwedge\limits_{1 \leq i \leq n} \mathbf{en\_}x_i([t], sp)\}$

11. $enabled([\mathbf{Basic}], sp) = \emptyset$

12. $enabled\_or(\langle\rangle, sp) = \emptyset$

13. $enabled\_and(\langle\rangle, sp) = \emptyset$

Where *evaluate* evaluates a variable expression with respect to a snapshot element, and operators $\parallel$ and $\otimes$ are concurrency and merger operators, respectively.

---

14. $\mathbb{T} \otimes T' = \{\ T_1 - T_1' \cup T''|\ T_1 \in \mathbb{T} \wedge T_1' \subseteq T_1 \wedge T'' \subseteq T' \wedge$
    $(\forall t' : (T_1 \cup T') \cdot t' \in (T' - T'') \Leftrightarrow \exists t \in (T_1 - T_1' \cup T'') \cdot \neg C(t', t) \wedge \neg P(t', t)) \wedge$
    $(\forall t : (T_1 \cup T') \cdot t \in T_1' \Leftrightarrow \exists t' \in T'' \cdot \neg C(t, t') \wedge \neg P(t, t')) \wedge \Pi(\mathbb{T}, T', T_1, T_1', T'')\ \}$

Fig. 6. Semantic definition schema

of transitions unless it is replaced by a transition at the current or lower level. A new set of transitions is maximal in that no more transitions can be added to it without violating the Small-Step Consistency, Preemption, or Priority semantics, represented by parameters C, P, and Π, respectively.

Line 10 specifies if a transition t is enabled, by checking whether: $cond(t)$ is true with respect to the values of the variables, $src(t)$ is in the set of current control states, which the model resides in, $trig(t)$ is satisfied with respect to the statuses of events, and the "en" conditions of all snapshot elements are satisfied. Lines 11-13 are the base cases of the recursive definitions.

The dynamic parameters $\mathcal{V}_{asn}$, $\mathcal{V}_{cond}$, $\mathcal{E}$ are the names of snapshot elements in $SpEl$ that determine: the values of variables for evaluating the RHS of assignments, the values of variables for evaluating the GC of transitions, the statuses of events for evaluating the triggers of transitions, respectively. The value of each of these parameters is determined by the choice of a semantic option for its corresponding semantic aspect. Parameter $\mathcal{V}_{asn}$ is used in the formalization of the Assignment Memory Protocol, which, for the sake of brevity, we do not consider its formalization in this paper.

3.2   Structural Parameters

A value for a structural parameter is a predicate that specifies an aspect of how a small step is formed. In this section, we describe the possible values for parameter $\|$, and parameters C, P, and Π of the merge operator $\otimes$.

Table 1 specifies the values for the *concurrency* operator $\|$, based on the semantic options of the Concurrency semantic sub-aspect. The SINGLE semantics allows exactly one transition per small step, where as the MANY semantics allows all of the children of an *And* control state to have transitions in a small step.

Table 2 specifies the values for parameters C and P of the merge operator, which are determined by the Small-Step Consistency and Preemption semantic sub-aspects, respectively. These two semantic sub-aspects are relevant only for the MANY concurrency semantics. When the SINGLE concurrency semantics is chosen, both C and P are *false*. For two distinct t and t' to be included in a small step, the ARENA ORTHOGONAL semantics requires their arenas to be orthogonal, and the SOURCE/ DESTINATION ORTHOGONAL semantics requires the transitions themselves to be orthogonal. For two transitions t and t' where one is an *interrupt for* another, the NON-PREEMPTIVE semantics allows them to be taken in the same small step, but the PREEMPTIVE semantics does not.

Table 1. Concurrency semantics

Semantic Option	Parameter Value
SINGLE	$\mathbb{T} \| \mathbb{T}' = \mathbb{T} \cup \mathbb{T}'$
MANY	$\mathbb{T} \| \mathbb{T}' = \{T_1 \cup T_1' \mid T_1 \in \mathbb{T} \wedge T_1' \in \mathbb{T}'\}$

Table 2. Small-Step Consistency and Preemption semantics

Semantic Option	Parameter Value
Small-Step Consistency	
ARENA ORTHOGONAL	$C(t,t') \equiv arena(t) \perp arena(t')$
SOURCE/DESTINATION ORTHOGONAL	$C(t,t') \equiv t \perp t'$
Preemption	
NON-PREEMPTIVE	$P(t,t') \equiv (t \not\downarrow t') \vee (t' \not\downarrow t)$
PREEMPTIVE	$P(t,t') \equiv false$

Table 3. Priority semantics

Semantic Option	Parameter Value
NO PRIORITY	$\Pi(\mathbb{T}, T', T_1, T_1', T'') \equiv true$
CHILD ARENA	$\Pi(\mathbb{T}, T', T_1, T_1', T'') \equiv T_1' = \emptyset$

Table 3 specifies two possible values for parameter Π. For the sake of brevity, we consider only two HIERARCHICAL semantic options, but there are more Priority semantic options [1,2]. The CHILD ARENA semantics assigns a higher priority to a transition whose arena is lower in the hierarchy tree.

As an example, for the semantics that follow the MANY, ARENA ORTHOGONAL, PREEMPTIVE, and NO PRIORITY semantic options, the merge operator can be simplified to $\mathbb{T} \otimes T' = \mathbb{T} \cup \{\{t\} | t \in T'\}$.

3.3 Dynamic Parameters

A value for a dynamic parameter is a set of snapshot elements, possibly a singleton, which accomplish the semantics of a corresponding semantic option. For a snapshot element $x_1 \in SpEl$, the $\text{reset\_}x_1(sp^0, I, sp)$ predicate specifies the effect of receiving environmental input I in snapshot sp^0 on snapshot element x_1, which is captured in snapshot sp. The $\text{en\_}x_1(sp, t)$ predicate specifies if transition t is enabled with respect to snapshot element x_1. If $\text{en\_}x_1$ is not specified, then it is $true$. The $\text{next\_}x_1(sp, \tau, sp')$ predicate specifies the effect of executing small step τ in snapshot sp, which is captured in snapshot sp'. We annotate the name of the snapshot element that represents a semantic option with a subscript that is the same as the name of the semantic option.

In this section, for the sake of brevity, we consider the values of the dynamic parameters for the Event Lifeline semantic aspect only. The corresponding snapshot elements for the semantic options of other semantic aspects are defined similarly and independent of each other, except for the combo-step semantic options (cf., the formalization of the NEXT COMBO STEP semantics below).

Event Lifeline. There are three semantic options for the Event Lifeline semantic aspect. The REMAINDER, NEXT COMBO STEP, and NEXT SMALL STEP

$\mathbf{reset\_}E_{\text{REMAINDER}}(sp^0, I, sp) \equiv E_{\text{REMAINDER}} = I.events$

$\mathbf{next\_}E_{\text{REMAINDER}}(sp, \tau, sp') \quad \equiv E'_{\text{REMAINDER}} = E_{\text{REMAINDER}} \cup gen(\tau)$

$\mathbf{reset\_}E_{\text{NEXT COMBO STEP}}(sp^0, I, sp) \equiv E_{\text{NEXT COMBO STEP}} = I.events$

$\mathbf{next_}E_{\text{NEXT COMBO STEP}}(sp, \tau, sp') \quad \equiv E'_{\text{NEXT COMBO STEP}} = $ if $EndC$ then

$$E_{Collect} \cup gen(\tau)$$

else

$$E_{\text{NEXT COMBO STEP}}$$

$\mathbf{reset\_}E_{Collect}(sp^0, I, sp) \qquad \equiv E_{collect} = \emptyset$

$\mathbf{next_}E_{Collect}(sp, \tau, sp') \qquad \equiv E'_{collect} = $ if $EndC$ then

$$\emptyset$$

else

$$E_{Collect} \cup gen(\tau)$$

$EndC \qquad\qquad\qquad\qquad \equiv (\nexists \tau' \cdot \tau' \in enabled(root, sp' \oplus Cs))$

$\mathbf{reset\_}E_{\text{NEXT SMALL STEP}}(sp^0, I, sp) \equiv E_{\text{NEXT SMALL STEP}} = I.events$

$\mathbf{next\_}E_{\text{NEXT SMALL STEP}}(sp, \tau, sp') \quad \equiv E'_{\text{NEXT SMALL STEP}} = gen(\tau)$

Fig. 7. Snapshot elements for Event Lifeline semantics

semantics require a generated event to be present after it is generated in the remainder of the big step, in the next combo step, and in the next small step, respectively. Fig. 7 presents the snapshot elements for formalizing each semantic option. The value of parameter $\mathcal{E}$, in Fig. 6, is $E_{\text{REMAINDEER}}$, $E_{\text{NEXT COMBO STEP}}$, or $E_{\text{NEXT SMALL STEP}}$, based on the chosen Event Lifeline semantics.

In the NEXT COMBO STEP semantics, the last small step of a combo step must be identified so that the statuses of events are adjusted at the end of the combo step. The $EndC$ predicate in Fig. 7 identifies the last small step of a combo step. Its definition relies on the set of snapshot elements, Cs, which is the set of snapshot elements that specify the notion of combo step in a semantics. For example, if the NEXT COMBO STEP semantic option alone is chosen, then $Cs = \{E_{\text{NEXT COMBO STEP}}, E_{Collect}\}$. If the GC COMBO STEP semantic option is also chosen, then Cs also includes its corresponding snapshot elements. The *override* operator, $\oplus$, replaces the corresponding snapshot elements of its first parameter, which is a snapshot, with the snapshot elements in the second parameter. Thus, $sp' \oplus Cs$ is a new snapshot, replacing the corresponding snapshot elements of sp' with the ones in Cs from snapshot sp. Without Cs, the definitions of the snapshot elements of two combo-step semantic options become cyclic.

3.4   Scope of Formalization

We call a BSML semantics a *forward-referencing* semantics if the enabledness of a transition depends on the execution of other transitions in the current or future small steps. For example, in the Event Lifeline semantics, another semantic option is that an event generated by a transition in a future small step is sensed as present by the current small step [1,2]. Our current semantic definition schema does not cover the forward-referencing semantics because they convolute the role of structural and dynamic parameters.

4   Related Work

Our work is related to *tool-support generator frameworks* (TGFs) that take the definition of a notation, including its semantics, as input, and generate tool support, such as model checking and simulation capability, as output [18, 19, 20, 21, 22, 23, 24, 25]. TGFs differ in the *semantic input formats* (SIF) they use, and the procedure by which they obtain tool support for a notation. By being able to specify the semantics of various notations, an SIF is comparable with our semantic definition schema. An SIF can be an existing formalism, such as higher-order logic [19], structural operational semantic format [20], or a new formalism, such as template semantics [21]. While TGFs and their SIFs strive for flexibility and extensibility, to accommodate for new notations, we have strived for creating a semantic definition framework that produces semantic definitions whose elements can be identified as high-level semantic concepts. We believe that the former approach is in the spirit of *descriptive* semantics, where as ours is in the spirit of *prescriptive* semantics. This is because we observe that TGFs often aim for almost open-ended extensibility and flexibility, and aim to support an unclear, broad range of semantics, which leads to a general, descriptive style of semantic definition. If an SIF is used in a prescriptive way, then there should exist a clear scope of notations in mind so that the formalism can be used in an active way to define a semantics prescriptively. But such a clear scope contradicts the open-ended extensibility and flexibility goals of a TGF. We suggest that for the SIF of a TGF to produce prescriptive semantics a task similar to what we undertook for BSMLs in our previous work [1, 2] should be carried out first. This task also serves to define a suitable SIF itself, as well as the scope of the flexibility and extensibility of the TGF.

The mechanism by which we define our semantics is influenced by that of template semantics [21]. In template semantics, a semantics is defined by: (i) instantiating values for the *template parameters* of its snapshot elements, and (ii) choosing, or defining, a set of *composition operators*. In particular, (i) we have adopted lines 1-5 in Fig. 6 from the definition of *macro step* in template semantics; and (ii) we have adapted the notion of snapshot elements in template semantics to model the dynamic parameters of a BSML semantics. We do not need the notion of a composition operator because the characteristics of a composition operator are manifested in our structural parameters. Compared to the template parameters of template semantics, the parameters of our semantic definition schema correspond to higher level semantic concerns, while having fewer dependencies among them.

Our semantic definition schema can be compared with general semantic definition methods that organize a semantic definition into a hierarchy of concepts, such as *modules* and *sub-modules*, in *Action Semantics* [26], or *theories* that are related by *linkings*, in *Unifying Theories of Programming* [13]. These methods promote modularity and orthogonality in semantic definition. In comparison, we have developed a specialized framework for BSML semantics whose concepts are parameters that correspond to our semantic aspects.

Lastly, our work is comparable to that of Huizing and Gerth [27]. Huizing and Gerth taxonomize and specify the semantics of events in BSMLs, covering the semantic options of our Event Lifeline semantic aspect in this paper. In comparison, we consider additional semantic aspects.

5   Conclusion and Future Work

We presented a prescriptive, parametric semantic definition framework for defining the semantics of big-step modelling languages (BSMLs). We showed how the semantics of a wide range of BSMLs, as identified in our previous work [1, 2], can be formally specified by our semantic definition schema. Because of the high level semantic aspects and the orthogonality of their corresponding semantic parameters in the semantic definition schema, we believe that our framework is a prescriptive way to define a BSML semantics, which produces an understandable semantic definition for the various stakeholders of the semantics. A key contribution of our formalization is a parameterization that matches the structural parameters into Concurrency and Consistency and Priority semantic aspects.

In our previous work [1,2], we analyzed the *advantages* and *disadvantages* of each semantic option in isolation, but not as a whole when considered together. We plan to use our formal semantic definition schema to identify useful BSML *semantic properties*, and the class of BSML semantics that satisfy each of them. We are also interested in developing a tool-support generator framework that respects the structure of our semantic definitions, so that we can inspect, or verify, the correctness of the implementation with respect to a semantic definition.

References

1. Esmaeilsabzali, S., Day, N.A., Atlee, J.M., Niu, J.: Semantic criteria for choosing a language for big-step models. In: RE 2009, pp. 181–190 (2009)
2. Esmaeilsabzali, S., Day, N.A., Atlee, J.M., Niu, J.: Deconstructing the semantics of big-step modelling languages. Submitted to Requirements Engineering Special Issue of RE 2009 (October 2009)
3. Harel, D.: Statecharts: A visual formalism for complex systems. Science of Computer Programming 8(3), 231–274 (1987)
4. von der Beeck, M.: A comparison of statecharts variants. In: Langmaack, H., de Roever, W.-P., Vytopil, J. (eds.) FTRTFT 1994 and ProCoS 1994. LNCS, vol. 863, pp. 128–148. Springer, Heidelberg (1994)
5. Maraninchi, F., Rémond, Y.: Argos: an automaton-based synchronous language. Computer Languages 27(1/3), 61–92 (2001)
6. Alur, R., Henzinger, T.A.: Reactive modules. Formal Methods in System Design 15(1), 7–48 (1999)
7. Berry, G., Gonthier, G.: The Esterel synchronous programming language: Design, semantics, implementation. Science of Computer Programming 19(2), 87–152 (1992)
8. Heninger, K.L., Kallander, J., Parnas, D.L., Shore, J.E.: Software requirements for the A-7E aircraft. Technical Report 3876, United States Naval Research Laboratory (1978)

9. Heitmeyer, C., Jeffords, R., Labaw, B.: Automated consistency checking of requirements specifications. ACM TOSEM 5(3), 231–261 (1996)
10. Ashcroft, E.A., Wadge, W.W.: Generality considered harmful: A critique of descriptive semantics. Technical Report CS-79-01, University of Waterloo, Cheriton School of Computer Science (1979)
11. Ashcroft, E.A., Wadge, W.W.: R/ for semantics. ACM TOPLAS 4(2), 283–294 (1982)
12. Pnueli, A., Shalev, M.: What is in a step: On the semantics of statecharts. In: Ito, T., Meyer, A.R. (eds.) TACS 1991. LNCS, vol. 526, pp. 244–264. Springer, Heidelberg (1991)
13. Hoare, T., Jifeng, H.: Unifying Theories of Programming. Prentice Hall, Englewood Cliffs (1998)
14. OMG: OMG Unified Modeling Language (OMG UML), Superstructure, v2.1.2, Formal/2007-11-01 (2007)
15. Leveson, N.G., Heimdahl, M.P.E., Hildreth, H., Reese, J.D.: Requirements specification for process-control systems. TSE 20(9), 684–707 (1994)
16. Harel, D., Naamad, A.: The Statemate semantics of statecharts. ACM TOSEM 5(4), 293–333 (1996)
17. Kang, K.C., Cohen, S.G., Hess, J.A., Novak, W.E., Peterson, A.S.: Feature-oriented domain analysis (FODA) feasibility study. Technical Report CMU/SEI-90-TR-21, SEI, Carnegie Mellon University (1990)
18. Pezzè, M., Young, M.: Constructing multi-formalism state-space analysis tools: Using rules to specify dynamic semantics of models. In: ICSE 1997, pp. 239–249 (1997)
19. Day, N.A., Joyce, J.J.: Symbolic functional evaluation. In: Bertot, Y., Dowek, G., Hirschowitz, A., Paulin, C., Théry, L. (eds.) TPHOLs 1999. LNCS, vol. 1690, pp. 341–358. Springer, Heidelberg (1999)
20. Dillon, L.K., Stirewalt, K.: Inference graphs: A computational structure supporting generation of customizable and correct analysis components. IEEE TSE 29(2), 133–150 (2003)
21. Niu, J., Atlee, J.M., Day, N.A.: Template semantics for model-based notations. IEEE TSE 29(10), 866–882 (2003)
22. Lu, Y., Atlee, J.M., Day, N.A., Niu, J.: Mapping template semantics to SMV. In: ASE 2004, pp. 320–325 (2004)
23. Baresi, L., Pezzè, M.: Formal interpreters for diagram notations. ACM TOSEM 14(1), 42–84 (2005)
24. Gao, J., Heimdahl, M.P.E., Wyk, E.V.: Flexible and extensible notations for modeling languages. In: Dwyer, M.B., Lopes, A. (eds.) FASE 2007. LNCS, vol. 4422, pp. 102–116. Springer, Heidelberg (2007)
25. Prout, A., Atlee, J.M., Day, N.A., Shaker, P.: Semantically configurable code generation. In: Czarnecki, K., Ober, I., Bruel, J.-M., Uhl, A., Völter, M. (eds.) MODELS 2008. LNCS, vol. 5301, pp. 705–720. Springer, Heidelberg (2008)
26. Mosses, P.D.: Action Semantics. Cambridge Tracts in Theoretical Computer Science, vol. 26. Cambridge University Press, Cambridge (1992)
27. Huizing, C., Gerth, R.: Semantics of reactive systems in abstract time. In: Huizing, C., de Bakker, J.W., Rozenberg, G., de Roever, W.-P. (eds.) REX 1991. LNCS, vol. 600, pp. 291–314. Springer, Heidelberg (1992)

A Modular Model Composition Technique

Pierre Kelsen and Qin Ma

Laboratory for Advanced Software Systems
University of Luxembourg
6, rue Richard Coudenhove-Kalergi
L-1359 Luxembourg
{Pierre.Kelsen,Qin.Ma}@uni.lu

Abstract. Model composition is a technique for building bigger models from smaller models, thus allowing system designers to control the complexity of a model-driven design process. However many current model composition techniques are themselves complex in the sense that they merge the internal elements of the participating models in non-trivial ways. In this paper we apply some of the ideas from modular programming to reduce the complexity of model compositions. Indeed we propose a model composition technique with a modular flavor that treats the participating models as black boxes. Our technique has several desirable features: it is simple, it does not require a separate language for expressing the composition, and the understanding of the resulting composed model is made easier by the modular nature of the model composition.

1 Introduction

Models are the primary artifacts in a model-driven software development process. Models help in dealing with the complexity of the underlying domains by abstracting away irrelevant details. The models themselves can become quite large, at least if we try to represent complex problem or solution domains. Thus we need techniques for tackling model complexity.

One such technique is model composition. By composing large models from smaller models the large models should become easier to understand and to maintain. Most current model composition techniques permit the specification of rather complex composition operations. This is shown in the fact that many techniques are based on a separate language for specifying the composition (such as weaving models in AMW [1] or the Epsilon Merging Language in [10]). Because these model compositions can be complex, separate model transformations need to be defined to perform them: in [1], for instance, this transformation is generated from the weaving model. Furthermore a system specified by using complex model compositions is difficult to understand.

The main contribution of this paper is a model composition technique that has the following desirable features:

- it is simple: the composition is specified by mapping elements of one distinguished model (called a fragment) to elements of the other models;

D.S. Rosenblum and G. Taentzer (Eds.): FASE 2010, LNCS 6013, pp. 173–187, 2010.
© Springer-Verlag Berlin Heidelberg 2010

- it is modular: the participating models in the composition are equipped with an interface: only the elements in the interface can be mapped to by the fragment
- no additional language is required to express compositions
- it is formally defined

The presentation of this paper is as follows: in the next section we present a running example that will serve to illustrate the concepts in this paper. In section 3 we introduce formal definitions of models, metamodels and model conformance. We then introduce the notion of fragment metamodels in section 4. In section 5 we equip models with an interface that will support modularity via information hiding. We present our model composition technique in section 6. We show that this technique yields hierarchies of models in section 7. The final two sections discuss the contributions and put them into the context of existing work (section 8) and present concluding remarks (section 9).

2   A Running Example: The EP Language

In this paper we illustrate our model composition technique using the EP modeling language. EP is a language that allows the specification of the structure and behavior of a software systems at a platform-independent level [6,8,7]. The central concepts are *events* - modeling elements that are used to model behavior - and *properties* - which are use to model the structure of the state. A metamodel of the EP language is given in figure 1. We will also use a model conforming to this metamodel for illustrative purposes: the model describes a document management system. This model will be first introduced in section 6.

3   Basic Definitions: Models and Metamodels

To formally define our model composition technique, we first need to give formal definitions of metamodels, models and model conformance. We extend the definitions of [2] by formalizing both models and metamodels as graphs, and the mapping between a model to its metamodel as graph morphism.

Conventions

1. In the following formal narrations, for any pair p, we use $\mathsf{fst}(p)$ to denote its first element and $\mathsf{snd}(p)$ to denote its second element.
2. For any function f, we use $\mathsf{range}(f)$ to denote its co-domain.

3.1   Metamodels

A metamodel consists of a set of classes, a set of associations and a set of inheritance relations; all sets are assumed to be finite.

Definition 1 (Metamodel). *A metamodel $\mathcal{M} = (N, E, H)$ is a tuple:*

- N *is a set of nodes, representing the set of classes.*
- $E \subseteq (N \times \mu) \times (N \times \mu)$, *where* $\mu = Int \times \{Int \cup \{\infty\}\}$. *It represents the set of associations, with the two N's being the types of association ends, and the two μ's being the corresponding multiplicities. We refer to the first end of the edge the source, and the second the target.*
- $H \subseteq N \times N$ *denotes the inheritance relation among classes, where for a given $h \in H$, $\mathsf{fst}(h)$ inherits from (i.e. is a sub-type of) $\mathsf{snd}(h)$.*

We note that the above definition of a metamodel makes the simplifying assumption that the metamodel does not contain additional constraints beyond those expressed by association and inheritance relationships or multiplicity constraints. An example of a metamodel is that of the EP-language given in figure 1 (ignore for the moment the fragmentation edges indicated by the parallel lines intersecting the associations).

3.2 Models

Models are built by instantiating the constructs, i.e. classes and associations, of a metamodel.

Definition 2 (Model). *A model is defined by a tuple $M = (N, E, \mathcal{M}, \tau)$ where:*

- $\mathcal{M}$ *is the metamodel in which the model is expressed.*
- N *is a set of nodes. They are instances of nodes in the metamodel $\mathcal{M}$, i.e. $N_{\mathcal{M}}$.*
- $E \subseteq N \times N$ *is a set of edges. They are instances of edges in the metamodel $\mathcal{M}$, i.e. $E_{\mathcal{M}}$. Edges in models are often referred to as links.*
- τ *is the typing function: $(N \rightarrow N_{\mathcal{M}}) \cup (E \rightarrow E_{\mathcal{M}})$. It records the type information of the nodes and links in the model, i.e. of which metamodel constructs the nodes and links are instances.*

3.3 Model Conformance

Not all models following the definitions above are valid, or "conform to" the metamodel: typing and multiplicity constraints need to be respected.

Definition 3 (Model conformance). *We say a model $M = (N, E, \mathcal{M}, \tau)$ conforms to its metamodel $\mathcal{M}$ or is well-formed when the following two conditions are met:*

1. *type compatible: $\forall e \in E$, $\tau(\mathsf{fst}(e)) \leq \mathsf{fst}(\mathsf{fst}(\tau(e)))$ [1] and $\tau(\mathsf{snd}(e)) \leq \mathsf{fst}(\mathsf{snd}(\tau(e)))$. Namely, the types of the link ends must be compatible with (being sub-types of) the types as specified in the corresponding association ends.*

---

[1] $\leq$ denotes the subtyping relation.

2. *multiplicity compatible:* $\forall n \in N, e_{\mathcal{M}} \in E_{\mathcal{M}},$
   if $\tau(n) \leq \mathsf{fst}(e_{\mathcal{M}}),$
   then $\sharp\{e \mid e \in E \text{ and } \tau(e) = e_{\mathcal{M}} \text{ and } \mathsf{fst}(e) = n\} \in \mathsf{snd}(\mathsf{snd}(e_{\mathcal{M}}))$ [2];
   if $\tau(n) \leq \mathsf{snd}(e_{\mathcal{M}}),$
   then $\sharp\{e \mid e \in E \text{ and } \tau(e) = e_{\mathcal{M}} \text{ and } \mathsf{snd}(e) = n\} \in \mathsf{snd}(\mathsf{fst}(e_{\mathcal{M}})).$
   Namely, the number of link ends should conform to the specified multiplicity in the corresponding association end.

As an example of model conformance consider the model named *Log* in the upper right part of figure 4: it conforms to the metamodel of the EP-language given in figure 1 (if we ignore the interface definition).

4   Fragment Metamodels

Our model composition approach will make use of partial models as the glue to unite the participant models. These partial models, which will be called *fragments*, have external links to other models. At the level of the metamodel we need to indicate which associations can be instantiated into external links of fragments. For this purpose we introduce the notion of fragmentation edges.

Definition 4 (Fragmentation edges of a metamodel). *A fragmentation edge a of a metamodel* $\mathcal{M} = (N, E, H)$ *satisfies the following conditions:*

1. $a \in E.$
2. $\mathsf{snd}(\mathsf{fst}(a)) = (\_, \infty),$ *where* $\_$ *represents any integer whose value is irrelevant for this definition.*

In other words an association edge in the metamodel is a fragmentation edge if the maximum multiplicity of its source is not constrained. The intuition behind this definition is as follows: if an association a from node A to node B is a fragmentation edge then any B-instance can be the target of an arbitrary number of links (instances of this association) from A-instances. Thus if we add to existing models external links (instances of association a) from a fragment this will not violate the multiplicity constraint of the association. In a later section (section 6) this observation will be instrumental in proving that the result of the composition with a fragment is a model conforming to the original metamodel.

Figure 1 gives an example of a metamodel for the executable modeling language EP (from [7,8]) together with nine fragmentation edges indicated by parallel lines crossing the associations. These fragmentation edges have been identified in accordance with the above definition. For instance the association named *target* from *ImpactEdge* (right side of diagram) to *LocalProperty* (at the top of the diagram) has an unconstrained source multiplicity (indicated by '*') - it is therefore marked as a fragmentation edge.

The central concept of our model composition technique is that a *fragment* which is essentially a partial model that has some external links that are typed

---

[2] $\sharp$ returns the size of a set.

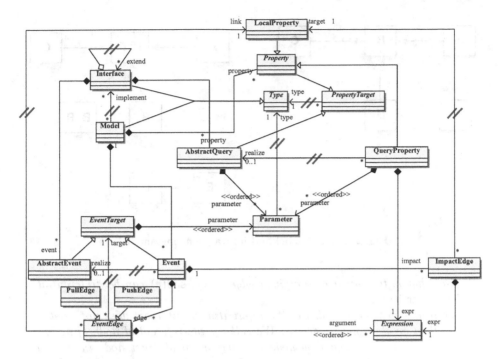

Fig. 1. A metamodel and its fragmentation edges

by fragmentation edges. Because of these external links fragments of a model conforming to a metamodel MM do not conform to MM. In order to be able to treat fragments also as models (which is desirable in a model-driven approach) we introduce the notion of a *fragment metamodel*. The basic idea is to replace the external links of a fragment by links to *referential nodes* which represent a node in another model. At the level of metamodels this is achieved by replacing the endpoint of each fragmentation edge by a new class having two subclasses: one subclass represents normal instances of the original endpoint class while the other subclass represents referential nodes. A simple example of a fragment metamodel is given in figure 2. On the left side of that figure a metamodel is shown with two fragmentation edges. On the right side the corresponding fragment metamodel is given. A more involved example is shown in figure 3. This example will be discussed in more detail at the end of this section.

After this informal discussion we define fragment metamodels formally.

Definition 5 (Fragment metamodel). *The fragment metamodel $\mathcal{M} = (N, E, H)$ is a metamodel, written $\mathcal{M}_F = (N_F, E_F, H_F)$. It is constructed as follows:*

1. $N \subseteq N_F$, $H \subseteq H_F$.
2. $\forall e \in E$,
   if e is not a fragmentation edge of $\mathcal{M}$,
   then $e \in E_F$;

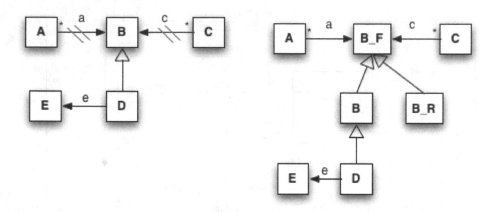

Fig. 2. A metamodel and its fragment metamodel

else (that is the target of the given edge e, i.e. snd(e) *can be "referential"),
let n =* snd(e),
(a) *if n is not yet cloned, i.e. the referential counterpart does not exist yet,
then create a new node* n_R. *We call* n_R *the referential node of n. Moreover, also create a new node* n_F *(n_F is an abstract node in the sense
that no instances can be made from it), and let $(n, n_F) \in H_F$ and
$(n_R, n_F) \in H_F$.
else i.e. n is already cloned, i.e.* n_F, n_R *exist, then do nothing.*
(b) *Create a new edge* e_R *called the referential edge of e of the following form
$($fst$(e), (n_F,$ snd$($snd$(e))))$, $e_R \in E_F$.*

The fragment metamodel of the example from figure 1 is given in figure 3. We
highlight all the changes with respect to the original metamodel in figure 1: The
target class of a fragmentation edge in the original metamodel is now extended
into a set of three classes indicated by the dashed contours, in which two new
classes, namely, the referential counterpart class following the naming convention
"XXXR" where "XXX" is the original name, and the common abstract super
class with name "XXXF", are added. Moreover, the targets of fragmentation
edges in the original metamodel are modified accordingly, leading to the newly
added abstract super classes.

Definition 6 (Fragment). *A fragment is a model that conforms to a fragment
metamodel. Moreover, there is at least one referential instance (or place-holder).*

5   Model Interfaces

One way to reduce the complexity of the model composition is information hiding. This has been used successfully at the programming level and was introduced
in the seminal paper of David Parnas [12]. The basic idea of information hiding is
to separate the code into disjoint pieces called modules that expose only a small

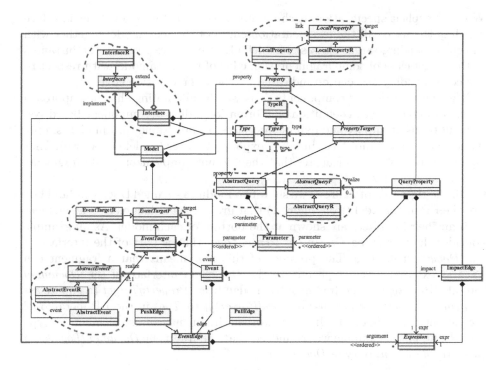

Fig. 3. A fragment metamodel of the EP metamodel

subset of their internal elements to the other modules via interfaces. Modular programming offers several advantages: modules can be developed and tested independently, they can be reused more easily and they can be changed in more flexible ways.

In this section we apply the principle of information hiding to models. We do this by equipping the models with an interface which will be defined below.

Definition 7 (Modules). *A module is a model with an interface.*

A module interacts with its context via its interface. Module interfaces are specified in terms of a set of pairs of form $(a, i : C)$, where C is the name of a metamodel class, i denotes an instance of C in the module, and a is the name of a metamodel association of which C is (a sub-class of) the target class. Note that i is optional. In case of absence, all instances in the module that are of type C are considered.

Definition 8 (Module interface). *An interface of a module specifies a set of pairs of form $(a, i : C)$, where i is optional. Moreover, a is a fragmentation edge of the metamodel in which the module is expressed and $C \leq \mathsf{snd}(a)$.*

Without explicit specification, each module is equipped with a default interface which is the set of all the fragmentation edges of the metamodel together with the corresponding target classes. The default interface exposes all the instances of the target class of some fragmentation edge of the metamodel with respect to the corresponding association indicated by the fragmentation edge.

If we view models as components, it is worthwhile noting that our approach differs from the classical definition of information hiding in component-based systems in terms of import and export interfaces. In our framework models simply do not have import interfaces but only export interfaces (as defined above). That is, models cannot access features that they do not "implement"; only fragments have this capability.

On the right side of figure 4, we show two modules - named Document and Log - of the EP metamodel (from figure 1) that are part of a document management system: their interfaces are shown at the bottom of each model. As an example consider the pair (*type, Document : Interface*) that is part of the interface of the *Document* module. The presence of this pair means that a fragment can have as external link a type link to the *Document* interface of the *Document* module. Here *type* is the fragmentation edge from *PropertyTarget* (a superclass of *Property*, itself a superclass of *LocalProperty*) to *Type* in the EP-metamodel (see at the top of figure 1). In other words a fragment can use elements of type *Document*; in the example we see indeed that the fragment *DocumentLog* uses a property *document* of type *Document*.

6   Model Integration

We call our model composition technique *model integration*. We perform model integration using a set of modules and a fragment by mapping all the referential edges of the fragment to instances of some participant modules. Moreover, the mapping should meet two conditions (which will be more precisely defined in definition 9):

1. typing is respected, in the sense that the type of the target of the mapped referential edge should be a sub-type of the type of the referential instance;
2. interfaces of the modules are respected, in the sense that if an instance is not exposed with respect to an association in the interface, it is forbidden to map a referential edge to it that is typed by the referential counterpart of the association.

An example of a model integration scenario is shown in figure 4. In this example the fragment (shown at left) has five external links into the Log module and one external link into the Document module. The referential instances of the fragment, which are the source nodes of the dashed arrows, are all mapped to some type compatible instances that are exposed in the interfaces of the participant models.

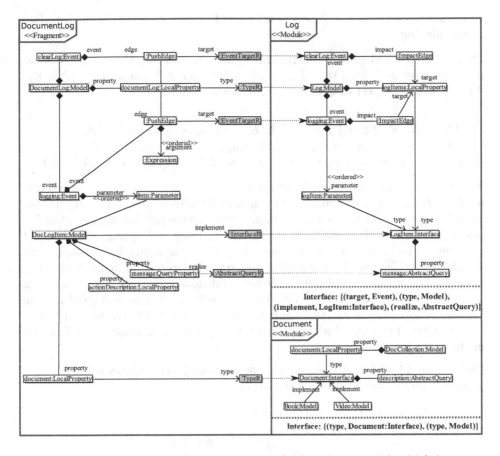

Fig. 4. Model integration of a fragment (left) and two modules (right)

Module integration is formally defined as follows.

Definition 9 (Integration Mapping). *An integration mapping of a fragment F over a set of modules $\{M_1 : I_1, \ldots, M_k : I_k\}$ having a common metamodel $\mathcal{M}$ is a function mapping each referential edge $e_r = (n, n_r)$ of the fragment to some instance n_i of some model M_i such that*

1. *if the type of n_r is the referential class node of a class node $n_{\mathcal{M}}$ in the metamodel $\mathcal{M}$, then the type of n_i is a subtype (direct or indirect) of $n_{\mathcal{M}}$.*
2. *if $\tau_F(e_r)$ is the referential association edge of an association $e_{\mathcal{M}}$ in the metamodel $\mathcal{M}$, we have $(e_{\mathcal{M}}, n_i : n_{\mathcal{M}}) \in I_i$.*

To illustrate this definition consider the fragment *DocumentLog* in figure 4. The integration mapping over modules *Log* and *Document* is indicated by the dotted edges. For instance the referential edge (: *PushEdge*, : *EventTargetR*) (at top of figure) is mapped to element *clearLog* of type *Event*. This is consistent with the definition since first *EventTargetR* is a referential class of *EventTarget* and

Event is a subtype of *EventTarget* and second *(target,Event)* is in the interface of module *Log*.

Definition 10 (Module integration: syntax). *An integration is defined over a set of valid modules* $\{M_1 : I_1, \ldots, M_k : I_k\}$, *via a fragment* $F = (N_F, E_F, \mathcal{M}_F, \tau_F)$, *with respect to a mapping function* ρ, *where:*

1. I_i *is the interface of module* M_i, $i = 1, \ldots, k$.
2. $M_i = (N_i, E_i, \mathcal{M}_i, \tau_i), i = 1, \ldots, k$, *have the same metamodel* $\mathcal{M}$.
3. *The metamodel of* F *i.e.* $\mathcal{M}_F$ *is the fragment metamodel of* $\mathcal{M}$.
4. ρ *is an integration mapping of* F *over module set* $\{M_1 : I_1, \ldots, M_k : I_k\}$.

To define the semantics of model integration, we define the result of integrating models $M_1, \ldots, M_k$ conforming to metamodel $\mathcal{M}$ with fragment F to be another model M conforming to the same metamodel $\mathcal{M}$ as the participating models M_i. Informally this result model is defined by identifying (collapsing) the endpoint of a referential edge with the instance which the referential edge is mapped to. To illustrate this, consider the module integration depicted in figure 4: the edge named *target* from : *PushEdge* to referential node : *EventTargetR* and the dotted edge from : *EventTargetR* to *clearLogEvent* will be collapsed into an edge from : *PushEdge* to *clearLogEvent* named *target*. This transformation is repeated for all referential edges leaving the fragment. This is expressed formally in the following definition:

Definition 11 (Model integration: semantics). *The semantics of an integration returns a model* $M = (N, E, \mathcal{M}, \tau)$, *where:*

1. $N = (\bigcup_{i=1,\ldots,k} N_i) \cup (N_F \setminus N_r)$, *and*

$$\tau(n) = \begin{cases} \tau_i(n) & n \in M_i \\ \tau_F(n) & n \in N_F \end{cases}$$

2. $E = (\bigcup_{i=1,\ldots,k} E_i) \cup \{v(e_F) \mid e_F \in E_F\}$, *where* $\tau(e_i) = \tau_i(e_i)$ *for all* $e_i \in E_i$, *and*
   (a) *if* $\tau_F(e_F) \in E^O_{\mathcal{M}_F}$, *then* $v(e_F) = e_F$ *and* $\tau(v(e_F)) = \tau_F(e_F)$;
   (b) *otherwise, i.e.* $\tau_F(e_F) \in E^R_{\mathcal{M}_F}$,
       i. *if* $\mathsf{snd}(e_F) \notin N_r$, *then* $v(e_F) = e_F$;
       ii. *otherwise* $v(e_F) = (\mathsf{fst}(e_F), \rho(\mathsf{snd}(e_F), e_F))$.
       And in both cases $\tau(v(e_F)) = \mathsf{ori}(\tau_F(e_F))$.

It follows from this definition that the result model of model integration is a well defined model according to Definition 2. The following theorem shows that it is also a valid one, i.e., it conforms to the same metamodel as the models that participate in the module integration.

Theorem 1. *The result model* $M = (N, E, \mathcal{M}, \tau)$ *of an integration over a set of disjoint* $M_i = (N_i, E_i, \mathcal{M}, \tau_i)$, $1 \leq i \leq k$, *via* $F = (N_F, E_F, \mathcal{M}_F, \tau_F)$, *with respect to* ρ, *is a valid model conforming to the metamodel* $\mathcal{M}$.

Proof. See [9].

7 Integration Hierarchies

By repeatedly applying model integration steps we can build up, starting from a set of disjoint modules, a hierarchy of modules which we now formally define.

Definition 12 (Module Hierarchy). *A module hierarchy is a directed acyclic graph whose nodes are either modules or fragments, such that:*

1. *all sink nodes (i.e., nodes with no outgoing edges) and source nodes (i.e., nodes without incoming edges) are modules;*
2. *each node that is a fragment has as successors a set of modules and has an associated integration mapping over these modules;*
3. *each node that is a module has either no successors (representing a unit module), or it has as successor a single fragment (representing a model that is derived by integrating the fragment with its successor modules).*

The following theorem holds.

Theorem 2. *All the models that correspond to the module nodes in a module hierarchy are valid models conforming to the original metamodel.*

Proof. See [9].

The system model is represented by the union of all the top models, i.e., those corresponding to the source nodes in the hierarchy. Moreover, the system model is also a valid model conforming to the original metamodel.

Theorem 3. *The union of all the models that correspond to the source nodes in a module hierarchy is a valid model conforming to the original metamodel.*

Proof. This theorem holds as a corollary of Theorem 2, if we consider that there exists a special empty fragment that integrates all these top models.

We introduce a more compact representation of module hierarchies called integration hierarchies.

Definition 13 (Integration hierarchy). *The integration graph for a module hierarchy is obtained by collapsing each edge in the module hierarchy graph that leads from a module node to a fragment node into the fragment node.*

In figure 5 we give an example of an integration hierarchy for a document management system. The three nodes at the bottom represent disjoint models representing the graphical user interface (Gui), the document business domain (Document) and the logging (Log). One level up in the figure the DocumentGui fragment integrates the Gui and Document models: it represents the graphical user interface adapted to managing documents. At the same level the DocumentLog fragment integrates the Document and Log models; it provides logging facilities for the Document model. At the top level the fragment named DMS integrates the lower level models into a complete document management system.

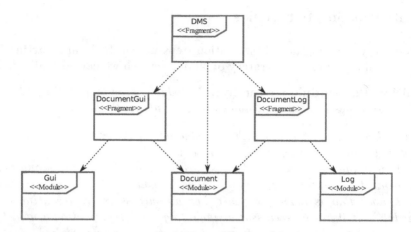

Fig. 5. Model integration of a fragment (left) and two modules (right)

At this point we would like to briefly explain why our approach facilitates model comprehension. First note that the base models (at the lowest level of the integration hierarchy) are self-contained. We can express this using terminology of component-based systems by saying that our models have only an export interface but not an import interface. At higher levels we hook up a fragment to the export interfaces of lower level models. The fragment uses a language (the fragment metamodel) very similar to the metamodel of the participant models. Furthermore the composition mechanism itself is quite simple: it consists in simply identifying referential nodes of the fragment with instances in the interface of the participant modules (as described in the previous section).

8   Discussion and Related Work

We start by reviewing the main contributions of this paper. These are, as claimed in the introduction, the following features of the composition technique: (a) it is simple, (b) it is modular, (c) it does not require an additional language to express composition, and (d) it is formally defined. As far as simplicity is concerned we note that the input to the composition are the fragment, a set of modules, and a mapping of the referential edges in the fragment to instances of the models. The actual composition (expressed in definition 11) simply collapses the referential edge with the target instance, a straightforward transformation. The modularity of our approach is based on the idea of equipping models with interfaces hiding some of the elements inside the model from the view of the fragment. The resulting concept of a module was presented in section 5. Because of the simplicity of the composition mechanism (described above) we do indeed not require a separate language for expressing the composition. Finally we have given formal definitions of the concepts related to model integration, underlining its formal foundation.

We now consider related work. Only fairly recently a common set of definitions for model composition was proposed and a set of requirements for model composition languages and tools was derived [2]. The definitions in that paper are based on examining three model composition frameworks: the Glue Generator Tool [2,3], the Epsilon Merging Language [10], and the Atlas Model Weaver [1]. The model composition techniques expressible in these frameworks may be called white-box model composition techniques: they are usually based on having full access to the modelling elements within each model. They also differ from our approach by allowing composition operations of high complexity to be specified. Of course this also means that these techniques are more expressive than ours: in particular they do not restrict participating models to conform to the same metamodel.

A model composition technique with a more modular flavor that treats the component models as black boxes was defined in [11]: their approach, named the Collaborative Component Based Model approach (CCBM) leverages software component principles and focuses on the specification of how models collaborate with each other. The Collaborative Component Based Model approach achieves black-box reuse of unmodified models and preserves them. Thus, in CCBM, models are units of reuse and integration is modular and incremental, just as for software components in Component Based Software Engineering (CBSE) [4].

In our paper we propose a model composition technique similar in spirit to the CCBM approach described above. It is also not based on transforming the component models but rather provides additional plumbing - the fragments - that connects the component models without changing them. Our approach differs from the CCBM approach in two ways: first the glue models used for composing models have a metamodel (the fragment metamodel) closely related to the metamodel of the participant models while in the CCBM approach another language (JPDD) is used for specifying the glue between the participant models. Furthermore their composition mechanism is less general in the sense that it only addresses how operations of the participant models collaborate.

Another work [13] addresses the problem of information hiding at the level of metamodels that are instances of MOF. Besides its focus on metamodels this work differs from our approach in the way it expresses information hiding: it assumes that each metamodel has import and export interfaces. Metamodel composition is expressed by binding elements in import interfaces to elements in export interfaces. In our framework, on the other hand, models have only export interfaces. Composition is realized by combining export interfaces via fragments.

The authors of [5] develop a theory of model interfaces and interface composition in the context of dealing with soft references across XML models, i.e., untyped, string-based references between XML documents. Their definition of model interfaces is heavily influenced by the assumption that models are stored as XML files: their interfaces are based on the attribute names of the XML models and are not applicable to the more general setting underlying our approach.

9 Conclusion

In this paper we have presented a modular technique for composing models conforming to the same metamodel. It differs from most existing model composition techniques in three important ways: first, information hiding is realized by each model offering an export interface (using terminology from component-based systems) but no import interface. This means that models are really self-contained: they cannot access features that they do not "implement". Second, a separate language for expressing the composition is not required since the composition only requires mapping referential nodes in the fragment to instances in the participating models. Third, for the reason just given the composition itself is quite simple. All of these differences help in reducing the coupling between the participant models and the composed model, thus facilitating the comprehension and maintenance of the composed model.

In this paper we have only taken into account metamodels that are expressed visually using the class diagram notation. Further textual constraints (expressed for instance in OCL) have not been taking into account. Considering additional constraints not expressed visually will likely lead to a more complicated definition of fragmentation edges. This will be the subject of future work.

Another line of future investigations concerns the model comprehension aspects of our model composition technique. The benefits for model comprehension are addressed rather summarily in the present paper (at the end of section 7). Future work will address this question in more detail. In particular we are interested in the reverse process of building model hierarchies. Suppose we have an existing model. Can we decompose it into a model hierarchy, thereby facilitating the comprehension of the initial model?

References

1. Atlas Model Weaver Project (2005), http://www.eclipse.org/gmt/amw/
2. Bézivin, J., Bouzitouna, S., Del Fabro, M., Gervais, M.P., Jouault, F., Kolovos, D., Kurtev, I., Paige, R.F.: A Canonical Scheme for Model Composition. In: Rensink, A., Warmer, J. (eds.) ECMDA-FA 2006. LNCS, vol. 4066, pp. 346–360. Springer, Heidelberg (2006)
3. Bouzitouna, S., Gervais, M.P.: Composition Rules for PIM Reuse. In: 2nd European Workshop on Model Driven Architecture with Emphasis on Methodologies and Transformations (EWMDA 2004), pp. 36–43 (2004)
4. Heineman, G.T., Councill, W.T.: Component-Based Software Engineering: Putting the Pieces Together. Addison-Wesley Professional, Reading (2001)
5. Hessellund, A., Wasowski, A.: Interfaces and metainterfaces for models and metamodels. In: Czarnecki, K., Ober, I., Bruel, J.-M., Uhl, A., Völter, M. (eds.) MODELS 2008. LNCS, vol. 5301, pp. 401–415. Springer, Heidelberg (2008)
6. Kelsen, P.: A declarative executable model for object-based systems based on functional decomposition. In: 1st International Conference on Software and Data Technologies (ICSOFT 2006), pp. 63–71 (2006)

7. Kelsen, P., Qin, M.: A Formal Definition of the EP Language. Technical Report TR-LASSY-08-03, Laboratory for Advanced Software Systems, University of Luxembourg (2008),
http://democles.lassy.uni.lu/documentation/TR_LASSY_08_03.pdf
8. Kelsen, P., Qin, M.: A Lightweight Approach for Defining the Formal Semantics of a Modeling Language. In: Czarnecki, K., Ober, I., Bruel, J.-M., Uhl, A., Völter, M. (eds.) MODELS 2008. LNCS, vol. 5301, pp. 690–704. Springer, Heidelberg (2008)
9. Kelsen, P., Qin, M.: A Modular Model Composition Technique. Technical Report TR-LASSY-09-01, Laboratory for Advanced Software Systems, University of Luxembourg (2009),
http://democles.lassy.uni.lu/documentation/TR_LASSY_09_01.pdf
10. Kolovos, D.S.: Epsilon Project, http://www.cs.york.ac.uk/~dkolovos
11. Occello, A., Dery-Pinna, A.-M., Riveill, M., Kniesel, G.: Managing Model Evolution Using the CCBM Approach. In: 15th Annual IEEE International Conference and Workshop on the Engineering of Computer Based Systems (ECBS-MBD workshop), pp. 453–462. IEEE Computer Society, Los Alamitos (2008)
12. Parnas, D.L.: On the Criteria to Be Used in Decomposing Systems into Modules. CACM 15(12), 1053–1058 (1972)
13. Weisemöller, I., Schürr, A.: Formal Definition of MOF 2.0 Metamodel Components and Composition. In: Czarnecki, K., Ober, I., Bruel, J.-M., Uhl, A., Völter, M. (eds.) MODELS 2008. LNCS, vol. 5301, pp. 386–400. Springer, Heidelberg (2008)

A Verifiable Modeling Approach to Configurable Role-Based Access Control

Dae-Kyoo Kim, Lunjin Lu, and Sangsig Kim

Department of Computer Science and Engineering
Oakland University
Rochester, MI 48309, USA
{kim2,l2lu,skim2345}@oakland.edu

Abstract. Role-based access control (RBAC) is a popular access control model for enterprise systems due to its economic benefit and scalability. There are many RBAC features available, each providing a different feature. Not all features are needed for an RBAC system. Depending on the requirements, one should be able to configure RBAC by selecting only those features that are needed for the requirements. However, there have not been suitable methods that enable RBAC configuration at the feature level. This paper proposes an approach for systematic RBAC configuration using a combination of feature modeling and UML modeling. The approach describes feature modeling and design principles for specifying and verifying RBAC features and a composition method for building configured RBAC. We demonstrate the approach by building an RBAC configuration for a bank application.

1 Introduction

RBAC [1] is an efficient and scalable access control model that governs access based on user roles and permissions. RBAC consists of a set of features (components), each providing a different access control function. There have been many RBAC features proposed. The NIST RBAC standard [1] presents features of core RBAC, hierarchical RBAC, static separation of duties, and dynamic separation of duties. Researchers have proposed other features such as temporal access control [2] and privacy-aware policies [3]. Not all these features are needed for an RBAC system. Depending on the requirements, one should be able to configure RBAC features by selecting only those that are needed for the requirements. For example, in commercial database management systems, Informix Online Dynamic Server 7.2 does not support static separation of duties, while Sybase Adaptive Server release 11.5 does. Informix, however, supports dynamic separation of duties, while Oracle Enterprise Server Version 8.0 does not [4]. If the requirements involve time-dependent access control (e.g., periodicity, duration), the temporal feature can be chosen.

In this paper, we present a modeling approach that enables systematic and verifiable configuration of RBAC features. This approach is motivated to reduce the development overheads and complexity of application-level RBAC systems

D.S. Rosenblum and G. Taentzer (Eds.): FASE 2010, LNCS 6013, pp. 188–202, 2010.

(where access control is tightly coupled with application functions) by separating access control from application functions and configuring RBAC features on a need basis. Configured RBAC is used as a base for the functional design of the application. In the approach, RBAC features and their relationships are captured by feature modeling [5]. Rigorous design principles based on the Unified Modeling Language (UML) [6] are presented for specifying RBAC features in a form that facilitates their reuse. The design principles also serve as verification points to ensure the correctness of RBAC feature specifications. The approach defines a composition method for building configured RBAC by composing the features that are necessary for the given requirements. We demonstrate the approach by configuring RBAC for a bank application and show how the configured RBAC can be instantiated to the application.

The rest of the paper is organized as follows. Section 2 gives an overview of related work. Section 3 describes RBAC feature modeling. Section 4 describes the formal basis of design principles for RBAC features. Section 5 presents RBAC feature specifications built upon the design principles. Section 6 describes the composition method for RBAC features. Section 7 demonstrates how RBAC features can be configured for a bank application. Section 8 concludes the paper.

2   Related Work

There is some work on using UML to describe access control models. The work can be categorized into two approaches. One is using the UML notation to describe the structure of an access control model and its constraints. Shin and Ahn [7] use UML class diagrams to describe the structure of RBAC and the Object Constraint Language (OCL) [8] to define RBAC constraints. Our previous work [9] uses object diagrams to visualize RBAC constraints. Priebe *et al.* [10] view an access control model as a design pattern and use the Gang-of-Four (GoF) pattern template [11] to describe RBAC. The other approach uses UML profiles, an extension mechanism in the UML, to define access control concepts. Jurjens [12] proposed a UML profile called UMLsec for modeling and evaluating security aspects for distributed systems based on the multi-level security model [13]. Similarly, Lodderstedt *et al.* proposed a UML profile called SecureUML [14] for defining security concepts based on RBAC. Doan *et al.* [15] extend the UML, not by a profile, but by directly incorporating security aspects of RBAC and MAC into UML model elements.

Composition of RBAC features in this work is related to model composition in aspect-oriented modeling (AOD) (e.g., [16,17,18,19]). In AOD, cross-cutting concerns are designed as design aspects that are separated from functional aspects (called primary models). Clarke and Walker [16] proposed composition patterns to compose design aspects described in UML templates with a primary model through parameter binding. Straw *et al.* [19] proposed a set of composition directives (e.g., creating, adding) for aspect composition. Similar to Clarke and Walker's work, Reddy *et al.* [17] use sequence diagram templates for specifying behaviors of design aspects and use tags for behavior composition. An aspect may include position fragments (e.g., begin, end) which constrain the location of fragment interactions to be inserted in a sequence diagram. The composition method in their work, however, is not rigorously defined, and thus it is difficult to verify resulting models. Their position fragments influenced join points in our work. Song *et al.* [18] proposed a composition method for composing a design aspect with an application design. They verify composed behaviors described in OCL by discharging a set of proof obligations. However, their verification is limited to OCL expressions, and the entire composed model cannot be verified.

3   RBAC Feature Modeling

Feature modeling is a design method for modeling commonality and variability of an application family [5]. A feature model consists of mandatory features capturing commonality and optional features capturing variability. Features are organized into a tree-like hierarchy. Fig. 1 shows a simplified feature model for RBAC.

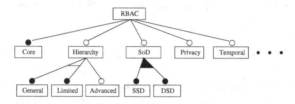

Fig. 1. RBAC Feature Model

We design an RBAC feature in the way that it encapsulates those and only those properties that pertain to the functions of the feature. In Fig. 1, filled circles represent mandatory features, while empty circles represent optional features. The empty triangle underneath the *Hierarchy* feature denotes an *alternative* group constraining that only one of the *General* and *Limited* features can be selected from the group. The filled triangle beneath the *SoD* feature denotes an *or* group constraining that at least one of the *SSD* and *DSD* features must be selected from the group.

The *Core* feature captures the essential RBAC functions that all RBAC systems must possess. The *Hierarchy* feature enables roles to be structured in a hierarchy in which permissions are inherited bottom-up and users are inherited top-down. A hierarchy can be either *General* or *Limited*. A general hierarchy allows a role to have more than one descendant, while a limited hierarchy is limited to only one descendant. The optional *Advanced* feature provides administrative functions for managing roles in a hierarchy. The *SoD* feature enforces *Separation of Duty* (SoD) constraints which divide responsibility for accessing sensitive information. SoD constraints are divided into *Static Separation of Duty* (SSD) and *Dynamic Separation of Duty* (DSD). The model can be extended with consideration of other features (e.g., [2,3]).

4 Partial Inheritance

The *Core* feature forms the basis of all configurations, and other features (henceforth, referred to as component features) add additional properties to *Core* or redefine its existing properties. This establishes inheritance relationships between *Core* and component features. However, unlike the traditional inheritance where all properties are inherited, component features may inherit only those that are needed for their functions. Partial inheritance for class diagrams and sequence diagrams is defined below.

An operation *op* with name o, formal parameter types $p_1, \ldots, p_n$, and return value type r is denoted $o(p_1, \ldots, p_n) \vdash r$. Let $Pre(op)$ and $Post(op)$ be pre-condition and post-condition of *op*. Let $Inv(c)$ be invariant of a class c and $T_1 \subseteq T_2$ denote that T_1 is a subtype of T_2. An operation $op_p = o_p(p_1, \ldots, p_n) \vdash r$ in class c_p is said to redefine an operation $op_c = o_c(p'_1, \ldots, p'_m) \vdash r'$ in class c_c iff O1: $o_p = o_c$, O2: $n = m$, O3: $\forall\, i \in 1..n, p'_i \subseteq p_i$, O4: $r \subseteq r'$, O5: $Pre(op_c) \wedge Inv(c_p) \Rightarrow Pre(op_p)$, O6: $Pre(op_c) \wedge Post(op_p) \Rightarrow Post(op_c)$ [20].

The cardinality of a relationship *rel* at an end e is an interval of positive integers and it is denoted as $bounds(rel(e))$. The containment relationship between intervals are defined as usual. That is, $\langle l_1, u_1 \rangle \subseteq \langle l_2, u_2 \rangle$ iff $l_1 \geq l_2$ and $u_1 \leq u_2$. The intersection of two intervals $\langle l_1, u_1 \rangle$ and $\langle l_2, u_2 \rangle$ is $\langle l_1, u_1 \rangle \cap \langle l_2, u_2 \rangle = \langle max(l_1, l_2), min(u_1, u_2) \rangle$. The set of traces of a sequence diagram *SD* is denoted $\mathcal{T}(SD)$. A trace s is a sub-sequence of another trace t, denoted $s \triangleright t$ iff s can be obtained from t by removing zero or more events. We say a class c_p in a component feature f_p is inherited from f_c if c_p has the same name as a class c_c in f_c and we call c_c the parent of c_p.

Definition 1. A component feature f_p partially inherits the *Core* feature f_c iff

1. At least one class in f_p is inherited from f_c.
2. Each group of inherited classes preserves all relationships between their parents. A relationship rel_c in f_c is preserved iff there is a relationship rel_p in f_p that has the same name and the same ends as rel_c and for all relationship end e, $bounds(rel_p(e)) \subseteq bounds(rel_c(e))$.
3. For each inherited class c_c and its parent c_p, $\exists_{-Y} \bullet Inv(c_p) \Rightarrow \exists_{-Y} \bullet Inv(c_c)$ where Y is the set of properties shared by c_c and c_p and $\exists_{-Y} \bullet P$ is defined as $\exists z_1. \cdots \exists z_n \bullet P$ and $\{z_1, \cdots, z_n\}$ contains all those variables in P that are not in Y.
4. For each inherited class c_c and its parent c_p, each inherited operation op_p in c_p redefines the corresponding operation op_c in c_c.
5. If a sequence diagram SD_c in f_c and a sequence diagram SD_p in f_p have the same name, then every trace of SD_c is a sub-sequence of some trace of SD_p: $\forall\, t \in \mathcal{T}(SD_c) \bullet \exists\, s \in \mathcal{T}(SD_p) \bullet (t \triangleright s)$.

5 Specifying RBAC Features

RBAC features are specified based on partial inheritance using the UML. Due to the limited space, we present only the *Core*, *General* hierarchy and *DSD* features where *General* and *DSD* are designed to be partial inheritance of *Core*.

Core feature. The *Core* feature defines the properties that are required by all RBAC systems. Fig. 2 shows the structure and behaviors of the *Core* feature. The symbol "|" in the diagram denotes parameters to be instantiated after configuration. Although the operations in the class diagram are self-descriptive, their semantics should be defined clearly. We use the Object Constraint Language (OCL) [8] to define operation semantics. The following defines the semantics of *addActiveRole()*:

context Session:: addActiveRole(r:Role)
  pre : true
  post: **let** auth:OclMessage=User^authorizedRoles() **in**
  Auth: auth.hasReturned() and auth.result() = ars and
  Cond: **if** ars → includes(r) **then** active_in = active_in@pre → including(r)
        else active_in = active_in@pre **endif**

The postcondition specifies that an invocation of the operation results in invoking *authorizedRoles()* which returns a set of authorized roles for the user, and the requested role is activated only if it is included in the authorized roles. *Auth* and *Cond* are labels to be used later in this section for proving design correctness.

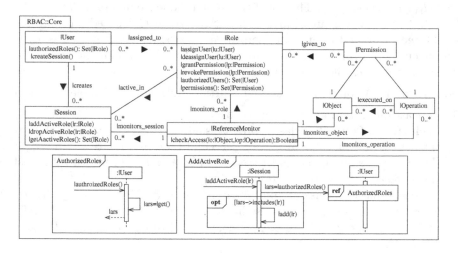

Fig. 2. RBAC *Core* Feature

General hierarchy feature. General hierarchy allows a role to have one or more immediate ascendants and descendants for inheriting user memberships and permissions from multiple sources. Fig. 3 shows the *General* hierarchy feature. Based on Definition 1, it contains only the properties that are needed for role hierarchy. The *General* hierarchy feature redefines several operations in the *Core* feature which are in bold. For example, *authorizedRoles()* and *createSession()* in the *User* class are redefined to include the roles that are inherited by the directly assigned roles. *addActiveRole()* in the *Session* class is redefined to activate inherited roles when the requested role is activated in a session. The new semantics of *addActiveRole()* is defined as follows:

context Session:: addActiveRole(r:Role)
  pre : true
  post: **let** auth:OclMessage=User^authorizedRoles(),
        desc: OclMessage = Role^descendants() **in**
  Auth: auth.hasReturned() and auth.result() = ars and
  Desc: desc.hasReturned() and desc.result() = descnd and
  Cond: **if** ars $\rightarrow$ includes(r) **then** active_in = active_in@pre $\rightarrow$ including(r)
        and descnd $\rightarrow$ forAll(d| active_in = active_in@pre $\rightarrow$ including(d)
        else active_in = active_in@pre **endif**

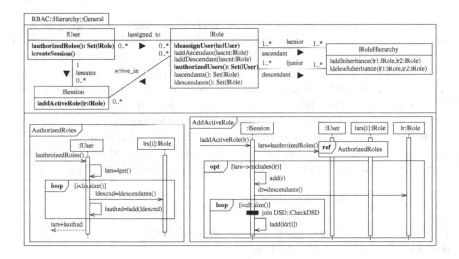

Fig. 3. *General* Hierarchy Feature

deassignUser() and *authorizedUser()* in the *Role* class are redefined to consider whether inherited roles should be also deassigned when a directly assigned role is deassigned, and whether the user can activate only the directly assigned roles or also inherited roles.

In the analysis of feature behaviors, an interference is found between the *General* hierarchy feature and the *DSD* feature when inherited roles also exist in DSD relations. To avoid the interference, inherited roles should be checked against DSD constraints before they can be activated in the same session. To handle this, we use a join point to designate where in interaction DSD constraints should be checked. The filled rectangle in the **loop** fragment in the *AddActiveRole* sequence diagram denotes a join point. The syntactic definition of join points is defined as follows based on the UML metamodel:

follows <Construct>
in <FragmentOperator> **join** [<Qualification>]::<Joint>
precedes <Construct>

<Construct> ::= Message | InteractionUse | CombinedFragment | "None"
<Joint> ::= Message | Interaction | InteractionUse | CombinedFragment
<FragmentOperator> ::= InteractionOperator
<Qualification> ::= Feature | Feature:<Qualification>

Given the syntax, a join point can be defined between messages, fragments, or combinations of both. If a behavior should be placed at the beginning of a sequence, the *None* construct is used in the *follows* condition. Similarly, *None* is used if a behavior should be placed at the end of a sequence. The *Qualification* construct represents the ownership of the joining construct. That is, the join point is effective only when the feature specified in the qualification is in use.

DSD feature. The *DSD* feature enforces DSD relations constraining that two conflicting roles cannot be activated within the same session. Fig. 4 shows the *DSD* feature. In the figure, the *DSDRole* class represents a single DSD relation, and the *cardinality* attribute specifies the number of roles to which a user can be assigned in an DSD relation. The *DSDRoleSet* class represents the set of DSD relations. The multiplicity n on the *Role* class denotes the DSD cardinality which must match the value of *cardinality*. *createSession()* in the *User* class and *addActiveRole()* in the *Session* class are redefined to take into account DSD constraints. The new semantics of *addActiveRole()* is defined below, checking if the requested role has an DSD relation with any active role in the session:

context Session:: addActiveRole(r:Role)
   pre : true
   post: let auth:OclMessage=User^authorizedRoles(),
   dsd: OclMessage = Role^DSDRoles(),
   violateDSD: active_in → exists (ar|ar.constrained_by_DSD → includes(r)) **in**
   Auth: auth.hasReturned() and auth.result() = ars and
   DSD: dsd.hasReturned() and dsd.result() = dr and
   Cond: **if** ars → includes(r) **then** active_in = active_in@pre → including(r)
        and not violateDSD **else** active_in = active_in@pre **endif**

To verify the correctness of the specifications, their conformance to Definition 1 must be checked. The partial inheritance between *Core* and *DSD* can be verified as follows by discharging the proof obligations in the definition:

- The first proof obligation is proved by the presence of the inherited classes *User*, *Role*, and *Session* in the *DSD* feature and the fact that the relationships *assigned_to*, *creates*, and *active_in* have the same ends and multiplicities.
- There are two classes (*User*, *Session*) in the *DSD* feature that have the same set of properties as the corresponding classes in the *Core* feature, and the second proof obligation can be proved by $Inv(User_{DSD}) \Rightarrow Inv(User_{Core})$

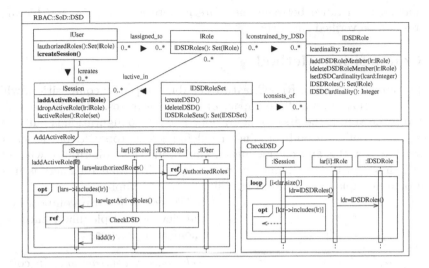

Fig. 4. *DSD* Feature

and $Inv(Session_{DSD}) \Rightarrow Inv(Session_{Core})$, which are both trivially true since there is no invariant defined for the *User* and *Session* classes in both *Core* and *DSD*.

- The third proof obligation must be discharged for every operation redefined in the inherited classes. As an example, *addActiveRole()* in the *DSD* feature redefines that of the *Core* feature, since they both have the same name, the same parameter type, and no return type. This satisfies the constraints *O1*, *O2*, *O3*, and *O4*. Based on the OCL semantics of the *addActiveRole()* operations, *O5* and *O6* can be proved by (1) $(true \land true) \Rightarrow true$, which is trivially true, and (2) $(true \land (Auth_{DSD} \land DSD_{DSD} \land Cond_{DSD})) \Rightarrow Auth_{Core} \land Cond_{Core}$. The second condition is proved as follows: Let $a = (ars \rightarrow includes(r))$, $b = (active\_in = active\_in \bullet pre \rightarrow including(r))$, $d = (active\_in = active\_in \bullet pre)$, and $e = violateDSD$. Let $Cond_{DSD} = ((a \Rightarrow (b \land \neg e)) \lor d)$ and $Cond_{Core} = ((a \Rightarrow b) \lor d)$. It suffices to prove that $(Auth_{DSD} \land Cond_{DSD}) \Rightarrow (Auth_{Core} \land Cond_{Core})$ since $(Auth_{DSD} \land DSD_{DSD} \land Cond_{DSD}) \Rightarrow (Auth_{DSD} \land Cond_{DSD})$. Since $(b \land \neg e) \rightarrow b$, we have $(a \Rightarrow (b \land \neg e)) \Rightarrow (a \Rightarrow b)$ which implies $Cond_{DSD} \Rightarrow Cond_{Core}$ which in turn implies $(Auth_{DSD} \land Cond_{DSD}) \Rightarrow (Auth_{Core} \land Cond_{Core})$. Other operations can be proved similarly.
- The fourth proof obligation is concretized as $\forall t \in \mathcal{T}(AddActiveRole_{Core}) \bullet \exists s \in \mathcal{T}(AddActiveRole_{DSD}) \bullet (t \rhd s)$ for the *AddActiveRole* sequence diagram. There are two traces involved in $\mathcal{T}(AddActiveRole_{Core})$, $<addActiveRole(), authorizedRoles()>$ and $<addActiveRole(), authorizedRoles(), add(r)>$. The first one exists in $\mathcal{T}(AddActiveRole_{DSD})$ and the second one is a subsequence of $<addActiveRole(), authorizedRoles(), getActiveRoles(), DSDRoles(), DSDRoles(), add()>$ which also exists in $\mathcal{T}(AddActiveRole_{DSD})$. Thus, the proof obligation is discharged.

The partial inheritance between the *Core* feature and the *General* hierarchy features can be verified similarly.

6   Composition Method

The partial inheritance of RBAC features enables step-wise composition, which allows verification of immediate impact of selected features. The *Core* feature is selected by default as the first configuration. The nth configuration is built upon the $(n-1)^{th}$ configuration by adding or redefining the properties of the selected feature. We view this approach a special kind of multiple inheritance where the elements having the same name get composed rather than renamed as in the traditional multiple inheritance. Fig. 5 illustrates the approach.

We define feature composition in the view of multiple inheritance as refinement as follows.

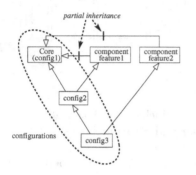

Fig. 5. Multiple Inheritance of Configurations

Relationship composition. In composition of class diagrams CD_1 and CD_2, relationship a_1 from CD_1 is composed with relationship a_2 from CD_2 if a_1 and a_2 have the same name and same relationship ends. The composed relation denoted $a_1 \oplus a_2$ has the same name and relationship ends as a_1 and a_2 and $bounds((a_1 \oplus a_2)(e)) = bounds(a_1(e)) \cap bounds(a_2(e))$ for each relationship end e. This ensures that the resulting end has the maximal bound interval that conforms to the end of both a_1 and a_2.

Operation composition. Operation $o(p_1, \ldots, p_n) \vdash r$ is said to match with operation $o'(p'_1, \ldots, p'_m) \vdash r'$ iff (1) $o = o'$, (2) $n = m$, (3) $\forall\, i \in 1..n, p'_i \subseteq p_i \vee p_i \subseteq p'_i$, (4) $r \subseteq r' \vee r' \subseteq r$. The composition of two matching operations op_1 and op_2 is denoted $op_1 \oplus op_2$. Let $op_1 = o(p1_1, \ldots, p1_n) \vdash r_1$ and $op_2 = o(p2_1, \ldots, p2_n) \vdash r_2$. We require that $op_1 \oplus op_2$ be an operation $(o(p'_1, \ldots, p'_n) \vdash r')$ that satisfies

P1 $\forall\, i \in 1..n, p'_i = lub(p1_i, p2_i)$ where *lub* is the least upper bound operation;
P2 $r' = glb(r_1, r_2)$ where *glb* is the greatest lower bound operation;
P3 $Pre(op_1) \wedge Pre(op_2) \wedge Inv(c') \Rightarrow Pre(op')$;
P4 $Pre(op_1) \wedge Pre(op_2) \wedge Post(op') \Rightarrow Post(op_1) \wedge Post(op_2)$.

P1 ensures that composed operations can take any parameter valid for component operations. P2 postulates that the return value of composed operations be of the type that conforms to the return type of component operations. Consistent with P1 and P2, P3 enforces that the precondition of composed operations must not be stronger than that of component operations. P4 constrains that the postcondition of composed operations must not be weaker than that of component operations.

Class composition. Class c_1 in class diagram CD_1 is composed with class c_2 in class diagram CD_2 if they have the same name. Let $OP(c)$ be the set of operations in class c. Class $c' = c_1 \oplus c_2$ is the composition of c_1 and c_2 iff

C1 $Inv(c') \Rightarrow Inv(c_1) \wedge Inv(c_2)$;
C2 $\forall\, op \in OP(c_1) \cup OP(c_2) \bullet \exists\, op' \in OP(c') \bullet name(op) = name(op')$;
C3 $op_1 \oplus op_2 \in OP(c')$ iff $op_1 \in OP(c_1)$, $op_2 \in OP(c_2)$ and op_1 matches op_2.

C1 ensures that the invariant of the classes that are composed is preserved in the resulting class. C2 requires that the resulting class have the operations of both the classes composed. C3 ensures that only matching operations can be composed. We are now ready to define composition operations on class diagrams. Let $\mathcal{E}(CD)$ be the set of classes and relationships of class diagram CD.

Definition 2. An operation $\oplus$ on class diagrams is a composition operation iff

- $\forall\, e_1 \in \mathcal{E}(CD_1) \bullet [\forall\, e_2 \in \mathcal{E}(CD_2) \bullet (name(e_1) \neq name(e_2)$
  $\Rightarrow e_1 \in \mathcal{E}(CD_1 \oplus CD_2)]$ and $\forall\, e_2 \in \mathcal{E}(CD_2) \bullet [\forall\, e_1 \in \mathcal{E}(CD_1) \bullet (name(e_1) \neq$
  $name(e_2)) \Rightarrow e_2 \in \mathcal{E}(CD_1 \oplus CD_2)]$;
- $\forall\, e_1 \in \mathcal{E}(CD_1) \bullet \forall\, e_2 \in \mathcal{E}(CD_2) \bullet (name(e_1) = name(e_2)$
  $\Rightarrow \exists\, e' \in \mathcal{E}(CD_1 \oplus CD_2) \bullet c' = c_1 \oplus e_2)$

An operation on sequence diagrams $\oplus$ is a composition operation if each trace of $SD_1 \oplus SD_2$ can be obtained by interleaving a trace of SD_1 and a trace of SD_2 and all traces of SD_1 and SD_2 are used. The interleave of two traces of events is the set of traces obtained by interleaving the two traces in all possible ways. Let x, y be events and μ, ν traces. The following definition of the interleave operator $|||$ is adapted from [21].

$$\epsilon \,|||\, \mu = \mu$$
$$\mu \,|||\, \epsilon = \mu$$
$$x\,\mu \,|||\, x\nu = \{x\} \times ((\mu \,|||\, x\nu) \cup (x\,\mu \,|||\, \nu) \cup (\mu \,|||\, \nu))$$
$$x\,\mu \,|||\, y\nu = \{x\} \times (\mu \,|||\, y\nu) \cup \{y\} \times (x\,\mu \,|||\, v)\ \text{for } x \neq y$$

Note that the above definition allows us to replace two consecutive occurrences of the same event by a single occurrence if they arise from different traces that are interleaved.

Definition 3. A composition operation $\oplus$ on sequence diagrams is defined iff

1. $\forall\, t \in \mathcal{T}(SD_i) \bullet \exists\, t' \in \mathcal{T}(SD_1 \oplus SD_2) \bullet (t \rhd t')$ for $i = 1, 2$;
2. $\forall\, t' \in \mathcal{T}(SD_1 \oplus SD_2) \bullet \exists\, t_1 \in \mathcal{T}(SD_1) \bullet \exists\, t_2 \in \mathcal{T}(SD_2) \bullet t' \in (t_1 \,|||\, t_2)$ where $t_1 \,|||\, t_2$ is the set of traces obtained from interleaving t_1 and t_2 in all possible ways.

7   Configuring RBAC

To demonstrate RBAC configuration, we use a banking application taken from [22]. The application requires the following RBAC policies:

R1: A teller can modify deposit accounts.

R2: A customer service representative can create or delete deposit accounts.

R3: An accountant can create general ledger reports.

R4: An accounting manager can modify ledger-posting rules.

R5: A loan officer can create and modify loan accounts.

R6: The customer service representative role is senior to the teller role.

R7: The accounting manager role is senior to the accountant role.

R8: A user may be assigned the customer service representative role and the loan officer role, but they cannot be activated simultaneously.

R1-5 describe general authorization requirements for roles, which can be addressed by the *Core* feature. R6-7 describe role hierarchies, which can be satisfied by the *General* hierarchy feature. R8 describes a dynamic SoD requirement to be addressed by the *DSD* feature. The selection is assumed to be in the order of *Core*, *General* hierarchy, and *DSD*, but it can be in any order by partial inheritance. The *Core* feature itself forms the first configuration by the composition method.

7.1   Second Configuration

The second configuration is built by composing the *Core* and *General* hierarchy features, which involves 1) adding the *RoleHierarchy* class and its associated relationships to the *Core* feature, 2) composing the co-existing classes of *User*, *Session*, and *Role*, and 3) composing the matching operations in other classes (e.g., *authorizedRoles()*, *addActiveRole()*). Based on the composition method, two operations are composed by conjoining preconditions and postconditions. Due to partial inheritance, the composition of the *addActiveRole()* operations results in the same operation as that of the *General* hierarchy feature. Thus, the composed operation satisfies the constraints $P1 - 4$ in Section 6.

The *AddActiveRole* sequence diagrams are composed by adding the *ars[i]:Role* and *r:Role* lifelines to the *AddActiveRole* sequence diagram in *Core* for checking authorized descendant roles. The **loop** fragment from the *General* hierarchy feature is added to check violation of DSD policies in the descendant roles. The fragment is enabled only when the *DSD* feature is used. Note that the composition results in the same sequence diagram as the one in the *General* hierarchy feature. This is because of the constraint 4 in Definition 1 requiring that a component feature include every trace of the *Core* feature, which is consistent with Definition 3. Thus, the resulting configuration also conforms to the composition method. This is true for every sequence diagram in the second configuration, provided that component features conform to Definition 1. The *AuthorizedRole* operations can be composed similarly.

7.2   Third Configuration

The final configuration is built by composing the second configuration *Config2* with the *DSD* feature. The composition is carried out by 1) adding the *DSDRole*

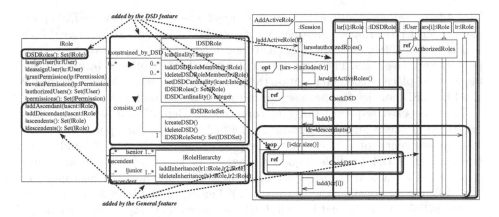

Fig. 6. Partial Composition of *Config2* with *DSD* Feature

and *DSDRoleSet* classes and their associated relationships to *Config2*, and 2) composing the co-existing classes of *User*, *Role*, and *Session*. Fig. 6 shows the *DSD* properties added to the *Config2* class diagram.

The composition of the *addActiveRole()* operations in *Config2* and the *DSD* feature results in an operation with the following semantics which checks DSD policies for the requested role and its inherited roles to active roles:

context Session:: addActiveRole(r:Role)
  pre : true
  post: **let** auth:OclMessage=User^authorizedRoles(),
  desc: OclMessage = Role^descendants(),
  dsd: OclMessage = Role^DSDRoles(),
  violateDSD: active_in → exists (ar|ar.constrained_by_DSD → includes(r)) **in**
  Auth: auth.hasReturned() and auth.result() = ars and
  Desc: desc.hasReturned() and desc.result() = descnd and
  DSD: dsd.hasReturned() and dsd.result() = dr and
  Cond: **if** ars → includes(r) **then**
        (active_in = active_in@pre → including(r) and
        descnd → forAll(d| active_in = active_in@pre → including(d)) and
        not violateDSD **else** active_in = active_in@pre **endif**

The resulting semantics conforms to the definition of operation composition in Section 6 as follows:

- *P*1 and *P*2 are trivially true, since the composed operation has the same name and parameter type (*Role*) and no return type as that of *Config2* and the *DSD* feature.
- *P*3 is true since (*true* ∧ *true* ∧ *true*) ⇒ *true*.
- *P*4 is true by *true* ∧ *true* ∧ $Auth_{Config3}$ ∧ $Desc_{Config3}$ ∧ $DSD_{Config3}$ ∧ $Cond_{Config3}$ ⇒ ($Auth_{Config2}$ ∧ $Desc_{Config2}$ ∧ $Cond_{Config2}$) ∨ ($Auth_{DSD}$ ∧ DSD_{DSD} ∧ $Cond_{DSD}$) where *Config3* signifies the third configuration.

The *AddActiveRole* sequence diagram in *Config2* is redefined to enforce DSD policies. The *getActiveRoles()* message, the *CheckDSD* fragment, and the *ar[i]:Role* and *:DSDRole* lifelines of the *DSD* feature are added to *Config2* to check DSD policies for active roles. The composition also introduces another *CheckDSD* fragment at the place of the join point on the *Session* lifeline, which is responsible for checking DSD policies for the descendant roles of the requested role.

The composed sequence diagram conforms to Definition 3 as follows: Every trace of the sequence diagram in *Config2* with the join point expanded is a sub-sequence of a trace of the sequence diagram in Fig. 6; and every trace of the *AddActiveRole* sequence diagram of the *DSD* feature is a sub-sequence of a trace of the sequence diagram in Fig. 6. Thus, the postulate (1) is satisfied. Now consider the postulate (2). Let $m_0 = addActiveRole(r)$, $m_1 = autorizedRoles()$, $m_2 = getActiveRoles()$, $m_3 = add(r)$, $m_4 = descendants()$, $m_5[i] = add(dr[i])$ and $n = dr.size()$. Then the traces of the sequence diagram in Fig. 6 are of these forms: $m_0 m_1$, $m_0 m_1 m_2 \sigma_0$, $m_0 m_1 m_2 \sigma_0 m_3 m_4 \sigma_1$, $m_0 m_1 m_2 \sigma_0 m_3 m_4 \sigma_1 m_5[1] \sigma_2$, ..., $m_0 m_1 m_2 \sigma_0 m_3 m_4 \sigma_1 m_5[1] \ldots m_5[i-1] \sigma_i$ for $2 \leq i \leq n$ and $m_0 m_1 m_2 \sigma_0 m_3 m_4 \sigma_1 m_5^1 \ldots m_5[i-1] \sigma_i \ldots \sigma_n m_5[n]$ where each σ_j for $0 \leq j \leq n$ is a trace of the *CheckDSD* sequence diagram. The traces that end with σ_j result from violations of the *DSD* constraint. Each of the above traces can be obtained by interleaving a trace of the *AddActiveRole* sequence diagram of *Config2* with the join point expanded and a trace of the *AddActiveRole* sequence diagram in the *DSD* feature.

Fig. 7 shows partial instantiation of the third configuration in the context of the bank application. The instantiation is carried out based on a mapping between RBAC elements and application concepts. For example, *Object* and

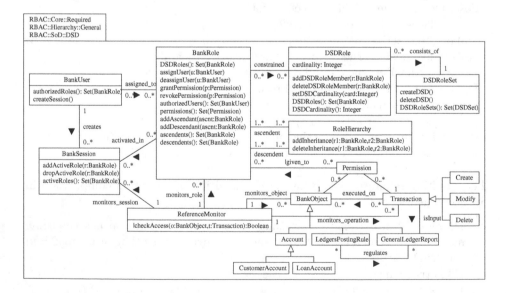

Fig. 7. Instantiation of RBAC Configured with *Core*, *General* hierarchy, and *DSD*

Operation in RBAC are mapped, respectively, to the hierarchy of bank objects such as *Account* and *LedgersPostingRule* and transaction operations such as *Create* and *Modify*. The instantiation lends itself as an initial design model for the application addressing access control concerns.

8 Conclusion

We have described a feature-based modeling approach for configuring RBAC to support the need-based development of access control systems. This approach enables fine-grained configuration of RBAC at the feature level in a systematic manner, which helps to lower development complexity and reduce potential errors by excluding unnecessary features. The composition method allows one to rigorously verify RBAC configurations. We have developed a prototype tool that supports feature selection and composition and instantiation of configurations. The tool is developed as an eclipse plug-in on top of Rational Rose Architects (RSA). We have also used the approach for Mandatory Access Control (MAC) and Discretionary Access Control (DAC). We found the approach less appealing for these models because of their low variability. However, our pilot study shows that the approach is useful for building hybrid models of RBAC and MAC which are often used in the military domain to support polices at different levels of security per role. Configuring a hybrid model requires a comprehensive analysis of both domains to identify possible conflicts in combined use of heterogeneous features.

References

1. Ferraiolo, D., Sandhu, R., Gavrila, S., Kuhn, D.R., Chandramouli, R.: Proposed NIST Standard for Role-Based Access Control. ACM Trans. on Information and Systems Security 4(3) (2001)
2. Bertino, E., Bonatti, P., Ferrari, E.: TRBAC: A Temporal Role-based Access Control Model. ACM Trans. on Information and Systems Security 4(3), 191–223 (2001)
3. Ferraiolo, D., Kuhn, D.R., Chandramouli, R.: Role-Based Access Control, second edition. Artech House (2007)
4. Ramaswamy, C., Sandhu, R.: Role-Based Access Control Features in Commercial Database Management Systems. In: Proc. of the 21st NIST-NCSC Conference (1998)
5. Kang, K., Cohen, S., Hess, J., Nowak, W., Peterson, S.: Feature-Oriented Domain Analysis (FODA) Feasibility Study. Technical Report CMU/SEI-90TR-21 (1990)
6. The Object Management Group (OMG): Unified Modeling Language: Superstructure. Version 2.1.2 formal/07-11-02, OMG (November 2007), http://www.omg.org
7. Shin, M., Ahn, G.: UML-Based Representation of Role-Based Access Control. In: Proc. of IEEE Int. Workshop on Enabling Technologies, pp. 195–200 (2000)
8. Warmer, J., Kleppe, A.: The Object Constraint Language Second Edition: Getting Your Models Ready for MDA. Addison Wesley, Reading (2003)
9. Kim, D., Ray, I., France, R., Li, N.: Modeling Role-Based Access Control Using Parameterized UML Models. In: Wermelinger, M., Margaria-Steffen, T. (eds.) FASE 2004. LNCS, vol. 2984, pp. 180–193. Springer, Heidelberg (2004)

10. Priebe, T., Fernandez, E., Mehlau, J., Pernul, G.: A Pattern System for Access Control. In: Proc. of Conf. on Data and Application Security, pp. 22–28 (2004)
11. Gamma, E., Helm, R., Johnson, R., Vlissides, J.: Design Patterns: Elements of Reusable Object-Oriented Software. Addison-Wesley, Reading (1995)
12. Jurjens, J.: UMLsec: Extending UML for Secure Systems Development. In: Proc. of the 5th Int. Conf. on the UML, Dresden, Germany, pp. 412–425 (2002)
13. Harrison, M., Ruzzo, W., Ullman, J.: Protection in Operating Systems. Communications of the ACM 19(8), 461–471 (1976)
14. Lodderstedt, T., Basin, D.A., Doser, J.: SecureUML: A UML-Based Modeling Language for Model-Driven Security. In: Proc. of the 5th Int. Conf. on the UML, Dresden, Germany, pp. 426–441 (2002)
15. Doan, T., Demurjian, S., Phillips, C., Ting, T.: Research Directions in Data and Applications Security XVIII. In: Proc. of the 18th IFIP TC11/WG 11.3 Annual Conf. on Data and Applications Security, Catalonia, Spain, pp. 25–28 (2004)
16. Clarke, S., Walker, R.: Composition Patterns: An Approach to Designing Reusable Aspects. In: Proc. of Int. Conf. on Software Engineering, pp. 5–14 (2001)
17. Reddy, R., Solberg, A., France, R., Ghosh, S.: Composing Sequence Models using Tags. In: Proc. of MoDELS Workshop on Aspect Oriented Modeling (2006)
18. Song, E., Reddy, R., France, R., Ray, I., Georg, G., Alexander, R.: Verifiable Composition of Access Control and Application Features. In: Proc. of the 10th ACM Symp. on Access Control Models and Technologies, Stockholm, Sweden, pp. 120–129 (2005)
19. Straw, G., Georg, G., Song, E., Ghosh, S., France, R., Bieman, J.: Model Composition Directives. In: Proc. of the 7th Int. Conf. on the UML, Lisbon, Portugal (2004)
20. Brady, A.F.: A Taxonomy of Inheritance Semantics. In: Proc. of the 7th Int. Workshop on Software Specification and Design, Redondo Beach, California, pp. 194–203 (1993)
21. Störrle, H.: Semantics of interactions in UML 2.0. In: Proceedings of IEEE Symposium on Human Centric Computing Languages and Environments
22. Chandramouli, R.: Application of XML Tools for Enterprise-Wide RBAC Implementation Tasks. In: Proc. of Workshop on Role-based Access Control (2000)

Incremental Consistency Checking of Dynamic Constraints

Iris Groher, Alexander Reder, and Alexander Egyed

Johannes Kepler University
Altenbergerstr. 69, 4040 Linz, Austria
{iris.groher,alexander.reder,alexander.egyed}@jku.at

Abstract. Software design models are routinely adapted to domains, companies, and applications. This requires customizable consistency checkers that allow engineers to dynamically adapt model constraints. To benefit from quick design feedback, such consistency checkers should evaluate the consistency of such changeable constraints incrementally with design changes. This paper presents such a freely customizable, incremental consistency checker. We demonstrate that constraints can be defined and re-defined at will. And we demonstrate that its performance is instant for many kinds of constraints without manual annotations or restrictions on the constraint language used. Our approach supports both model and meta-model constraints and was evaluated on over 20 software models and 24 types of constraints. It is fully automated and integrated into the IBM Rational Software Modeler tool.

Keywords: consistency checking, dynamic constraints, incremental checking.

1 Introduction

Design constraints are an important means of evaluating the correctness (consistency) of a model. While it is acceptable to tolerate design errors [1], engineers should be aware of them to avoid follow-on errors – or risk having to revisit and fix the follow-on errors at a later time. Violations of design constraints should thus be detected quickly, preferably instantly, and continuously tracked throughout the software life cycle – ideally in a non-intrusive manner that does not obstruct the natural workflow of the engineer.

This stands in stark contrast to the often individualistic nature in which modeling languages are used. Today, it is common practice to adapt modeling languages to specific domains, companies, and even applications under development. The benefits range from increased utility to better automation. Design constraints are not immune to this push to individualism. It implies that *engineers must be allowed to define new or adapt existing design constraints at will* – ideally without having to know the internals of the consistency checker. Even more importantly, feedback on design correctness should be provided incrementally with model changes without any manual overhead (since the learning curve would hinder its adoption) or observable computation delay (since noticeable delays obstruct the engineers' work flow).

D.S. Rosenblum and G. Taentzer (Eds.): FASE 2010, LNCS 6013, pp. 203–217, 2010.

Unfortunately, few existing approaches to consistency checking are readily extendable to allow the incremental, on-the-fly definition of new constraints or the customization of existing constraints without having to restart the consistency checker. The few approaches that support the addition of new constraints are either not incremental or require the engineers to manually annotate constraints in ways that are beyond their ability – a manual, error-prone process that provides some performance benefits but fails to scale for large design models [2], severely restricts the expressiveness of constraints via a limited constraint language [3] or requires the engineer to manually re-write a constraint for as many times as there are model changes affecting it [4]. Also, many existing approaches are typically tied to a specific modeling language and/or constraint language.

This paper presents an approach to the incremental consistency checking of dynamically definable and modifiable design constraints. Engineers can define constraints in a language of their choice (e.g. we have done so for Java, C#, and OCL [5]) and for any modeling language of their choice (e.g. we have used UML 1.3, UML 2.1, Matlab/Stateflow, and a domain specific language [6]). Our approach works for both model and meta-model constraints, neither of which must be manually annotated or rewritten. In which can be defined, redefined, or deleted at will throughout the development life cycle. Meta model constraints refer to constraints that hold for all instances of a certain type of model element. For example, in a home automation system, we could define a meta constraint that every light has to be connected to at least one light switch. Model constraints, on the other hand, refer to specific model elements. As such, we could add a constraint for a specific light to have at least two such switches.

We observed that engineers are willing and capable of defining both meta model and model constraints but we also observed that it is not reasonable to assume that (1) engineers are capable of defining how incremental changes affect such constraints and (2) all such constraints are known ahead time. Rather, they are discovered incrementally during modeling and the engineer should be able to add or change them as necessary. For example, in the middle of the design, an engineer could introduce the model-view-controller pattern [7] into our home automation system and desire to automatically enforce the constraints associated with that pattern. We could also change the constraint that every light has to be connected to a light switch in a way that a light either has to be connected to a light switch or to a motion sensor.

Today constraint changes typically require the complete re-evaluation of a design model which is equivalent to restarting of the constraint checker. We will see that our approach is capable of keeping up with the engineer in real time *for both constraint and model changes* for *scalable constraints*. Scalable constrains refer to constraints that are local, i.e. their evaluation does not require traversing large parts of the model. For scalable constraints our approach performs much better than existing approaches and for non-scalable constraints our approach performs no worse. Our approach is fully tool supported and integrated with the modeling tool IBM Rational Software Modeler [8]. The computational efficiency and scalability of our approach and tool were evaluated through the empirical analysis or 20 industrial software models and 24 different constraints.

2 Illustrative Example

In the following, we illustrate our approach on a simple home automation system [9]. In homes there are a wide range of electrical and electronic devices such as lights, thermostats, electric blinds, fire and smoke detection sensors, white goods such as washing machines, as well as entertainment equipment. The home automation system connects those devices and enables inhabitants to monitor and control them from a single GUI. The home network also allows the devices to coordinate their behavior in order to fulfill complex tasks without human intervention.

Fig. 2 presents a simple structural model of a home automation system. The *MyHouse* building consists of two floors, *Cellar* and *GroundFloor*. Two rooms, *WorkRoom* and *LivingRoom*, are located on the floors, each containing a light. The lights are connected to a light switch and to a motion sensor respectively. The sequence diagram in Fig. 3 describes the process of turning on the light in the work room. The user first gets a list of available devices in the room and presses the light switch. The light switch invokes the *turnOn* method on the light object. Stereotypes denote the different devices present in the house. Stereotypes are a common way of adding domain-specific extensions to UML.

Fig. 3 describes four sample constraints (using an OCL-like syntax) for the home automation system model. Constraint C1 is a standard UML consistency rule, constraints C2 and C3 are domain-specific meta model constraints, and C4 is an application-specific model constraint (we will discuss later the difference between application and domain/meta model constraints). C1 describes how UML sequence diagrams relate to UML class diagrams. It states that the name of a message must match a method in the receiver's class. The constraint is a general-purpose meta model constraint because it holds for all messages in sequence diagrams across all UML models. If the constraint is evaluated on the 2nd message in the sequence diagram in Fig. 3 (the *press* message) then the condition first computes the set of methods defined in the base class of the receiver object. The receiver object is *lightSwitch* and its base class is *LightSwitch*. The set of methods defined in the *LightSwitch* class is {*press()*}. The condition returns true because the set of methods contains a method with the name equal the message name *press*.

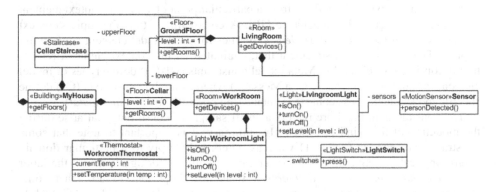

Fig. 1. Home automation system model

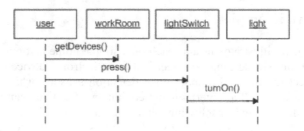

Fig. 2. Sequence diagram – User turns the work room light on

C2 and C3 describe domain-specific, meta model constraints. C2 ensures that every light is connected to at least one light switch. Clearly, this constraint no longer applies to any UML model. The condition computes the number of the switches attached to a light which must be greater than zero. C3 ensures that staircases only connect floors at neighboring levels. It compares the level number of the upper floor to the level number of the lower floor. Finally, C4 describes a domain-specific, model level constraint. It holds only for the model element *WorkroomThermostat* defined in the model in Fig.2. The constraint ensures that the current temperature is above 5 degrees *for that room only*.

C1	**Name of message must match an operation in receiver's class** methods = message.receiver.base.methods return (methods->name->contains(message.name))
C2	**Every light must at least be connected to one light switch** return light.switches.size > 0
C3	**Staircase must only connect floors at neighboring levels** return staircase.upperFloor.level = staircase.lowerFloor.level + 1
C4	**Thermostat in the work room must always be above 5 degrees** return workroomThermostat.currentTemp > 5

Fig. 3. Sample constraints

A constraint is typically defined from a particular point of view – a context element – to ease its design and maintenance [10]. A **constraint** is thus the tuple <context element, condition>. The *context element* defines for what model element a constraint applies. The condition is a statement that, evaluated on the context element, returns true if consistent or else false. Meta model constraints (C1-C3) define types of model elements as context elements (e.g., a Message) whereas model constraints (C4) define specific model elements as context elements (the class *WorkroomThermostat*).

The constraints in Fig.4 are merely a small sample of constraints that arise during the modeling of that kind of system. In summary, it is important to note that some constraints are generic (e.g., C1) whereas others only apply to a particular domain and/or application (e.g., C2). The former can be built into design tools but the latter not (*these have to be user definable!*). It is also important to note that some constraints are written from the perspective of the meta model (C1, C2, and C3) while others are written from the perspective of the application model (C4). With this freedom to define constraints arbitrarily, it is obvious that incremental consistency checking not only has to deal with model changes but also constraint changes (C2-C4 could change at any time). Next, we discuss how our approach is able to do both.

3 Dynamic Constraints

3.1 Background

In previous work, we have demonstrated that our approach provides instant design feedback for *changeable models but non-changeable constraints* without requiring manual annotations of any kind [2, 13]. The instant checking of meta model constraints was achieved by observing the consistency checker to see what model elements it accessed during the validation of a constraint. To that extend, we built a *model profiler* to monitor the interaction between the consistency checker and the modeling tool.

It is important to note that our approach treats every evaluation of a meta model constraint separately. We thus distinguish between a *constraint* and its *instances*. The constraint defines the condition (Fig. 4) and its context. It is instantiated for every model element it must evaluate (the ones identified through the context). For example, the meta model constraint that checks whether a light is connected to at least one light switch is instantiated for every light in the model – and each instance checks the validity of the constraint for its light only. For the house model presented in Fig.2 with its two light switches, our approach thus maintains two constraint instances, one for *WorkroomLight* and one for *LivingroomLight*. All instances are evaluated separately as they may differ in their findings. The instance evaluated for *LivingroomLight* is currently inconsistent because it is attached to a motion sensor instead of a light switch.

The role of the model profiler is thus to observe which model elements are accessed by which constraint instances. The model elements accessed by a constraint instance during its evaluation are referred to as the *scope* of a constraint instance. Only these model elements are relevant for computing the truth value of the constraint instance. And, more importantly, only changes to these model elements can trigger the re-evaluation of its constraint instance. Since the scope is maintained separately for every constraint instance, we are thus able to precisely identify what constraint instances to re-evaluate on what context elements *when the model changes*. In [10], we showed that our scope is complete in that it contains at least the model elements that affect a constraint instance's truth value. It is not necessarily minimal in that it may contain more elements than needed - thus also causing some, but fairly few unnecessary re-evaluations of constraint instances.

Both the monitoring of constraint instances during constraint checking and the deciding what constraints to re-evaluate are done fully automatically. Since our approach never analyzes the constraints, any constraint language can be used. This gives the engineers considerable freedom in how to write constraints. Furthermore, since our approach does not require constraints to be annotated, this greatly simplifies the writing of constraints.

3.2 Contribution of This Work

The research community at large has focused on a limited form of consistency checking by assuming that only the model but not the constraints change (the latter are pre-defined and existing approaches typically require a complete, exhaustive re-evaluation of the entire model if a constraint changes!). *The focus of this work_is on how to support dynamically changeable constraints* – that is constraints that may be added, removed, or modified at will *without losing the ability for instant, incremental consistency checking and without requiring any additional, manual annotations*. Such dynamic constraints arise naturally in many domain-specific contexts (cf. the example in the home automation domain described in Section 2). In addition to meta model constraints, this work also covers application-specific model constraints that are written from the perspective of a concrete model at hand (rather than the more generic meta model). We will demonstrate that model constraints can be directly embedded in the model and still be instantly and incrementally evaluated together with meta model constraints based on the same mechanism. For dynamic constraints, any constraint language should be usable. We demonstrate that our approach is usable with traditional kinds of constraint languages (e.g., OCL [5]) and even standard programming languages (Java or C#). Furthermore, our approach is independent of the modeling language used. We implemented our approach for UML 1.3, UML 2.1, Matlab/Stateflow and a modeling language for software product lines [6].

3.3 Meta Model and Model Constraints (+ Their Instances)

Fig. 4 illustrates the relationships between the meta model/model constraints and their instances.

Constraint = < condition, context element>
Meta Model Constraint: context element is element of meta model
Model Constraint: context element is element of model

Meta model constraints are written from the perspective of a meta model element. Many such constraints may exist in a meta model. Their conditions are written using the vocabulary of the meta model and their context elements are elements of the meta model. For example, the context element of constraint C1 in Fig. 3 is a UML Message (a meta model element). This implies that this constraint must be evaluated for every instance of a Message in a given model. In Fig.3 there are three such messages. Model constraints, on the other hand, are written from the perspective of a model element (an instance of a meta model element). Hence, its context element is a model element. For example, C4 in Fig. 3 applies to the *WorkroomThermostat* only – a specific model element.

  Fig. 4 shows that for every meta model constraint a number of constraint instances are instantiated (top right) – one for each instance of the meta model element the context element refers to. On the other hand, a model constraint is instantiated exactly once – for the model element it defines.

Constraint Instance = <constraint, model element >

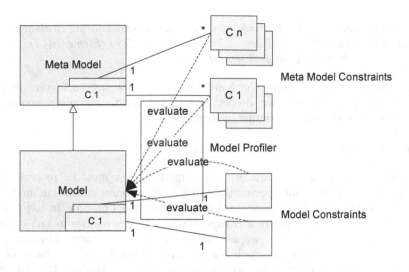

Fig. 4. Relationship between meta model and model constraint definitions and constraints

While the context elements differ for model and meta model constraints, their instances are alike: the instances of meta model constraints and the instances of model constraints have model elements as their context element. The only difference is that a meta model constraint results in many instances whereas a model constraint results in exactly one instance. Since the instances of both kinds of constraints are alike, our approach treats them in the same manner. Consequently, the core of our approach, the model profiler with its scope elements and re-evaluation mechanism discussed above, functions identical for both meta model constraints and model constraints as is illustrated in Fig. 4. The only difference is in how constraints must be instantiated. This is discussed further below in more detail.

As discussed above, we support the definition of both meta model and model constraints in Java, C#, and OCL. These languages are vastly different but our approach is oblivious of these differences because it cares only about a constraint's evaluation behavior and not its definition. The key to our approach is thus in the model profiling which happens during the evaluation of a constraint. During the evaluation, a constraint accesses model elements (and their fields). For example, if C1 defined in Fig. 3 is evaluated on message *turnOn()* in Fig.3 (a constraint instance denoted in short as *<C1, turnOn>*), the constraint starts its evaluation at the context element – the message. It first accesses the receiver object *light* and asks for the base class of this object, *WorkroomLight*. Next, all methods of this class are accessed ({*isOn, turnOn, turnOff, setLevel*}) and their names are requested. This behavior is observed and recorded by the model profiler. We define the model elements accessed during the evaluation of a constraint as a *scope* of that constraint. Our approach then builds up a simple database that correlates the constraint instances with the scope elements they accessed (<Model Element, Constraint Instance> pairs) with the simple implication that a constraint instance must be re-evaluated if and only if an element in its scope changes:

ScopeElements(Constraint Instance)=Model Elements accessed during Evaluation
ReEvaluatedConstraints(ChangedElement) = all CI where ScopeElements(CI)
includes ChangedElement

Next, we discuss the algorithm for handling model changes analogous to the discussion above. Thereafter, we discuss the algorithm for handling constraint changes which is orthogonal but similar in structure.

3.4 Model Change

If the model changes then all affected constraint instances must be re-evaluated. Above we discussed that our approach identifies all affected constraint instances through their scopes, which are determined through the model profiler. In addition to the model profiler, we also require a change notification mechanism to know when the model changes. Specifically, we are interested in the creation, deletion, and modification of model elements which are handled differently. Fig. 5 presents an adapted version of the algorithm for processing model changes published in [10]. If a new model element is created then we create a constraint instance for every constraint that has a type of context element equal to the type of the created model element. The constraint is immediately evaluated to determine its truth value. If a model element is deleted then all constraint instances with the same context element are destroyed. If a model element is changed then we find all constraint instances that contain the model element in their scope and re-evaluate them. A model change performed by the user typically involves more than one element to be changed at the same time (e.g. adding a class also changes the *ownedElements* property of the owning package). We start the re-evaluation of constraints only after all changes belonging to a group are processed, i.e. similar to the transactions concept known in databases. Since the model constraints and meta model constraints are alike, our algorithm for handling model changes remains the same. This algorithm is discussed in [10] in more detail.

```
processModelChange(changedElement)
 if changedElement was created
  for every definition d where type(d.contextElement)=type(changedElement)
    constraint = new <d, changedElement>
    evaluate constraint
 else if changedElement was deleted
  for every constraint where constraint.contextElement=changedElement
    destroy <constraint, changedElement>
 for every constraint where constraint.scope contains changedElement
  evaluate <constraint, changedElement>
```

Fig. 5. Adapted algorithm for processing a model change instantly (adapted from [10])

3.5 Constraint Change

With this paper, we introduce the ability to dynamically create, delete, and modify constraints (both meta model and model constraints). The algorithm for handling a constraint change is presented in Fig. 6. If a new constraint is created then we must instantiate its corresponding constraints:

1)   for meta model constraints, one constraint is instantiated for every model element whose type is equal to the type of the constraint's context element. For example, if the meta model constraint C1 is created anew (Fig. 3) then it is instantiated three times – once for each message in Fig.3 (*<C1, getDevices>*, *<C1, press>*, *<C1, turnOn>*) because C1 applies to UML messages as defined in its context element.

2)   for model constraints, exactly one constraint is instantiated for the model element of the constraint's context element. For example, if the model constraint C4 is defined anew (Fig. 3) then it is instantiated once for the *WorkroomThermostat* as defined in Fig.2 (*<C4, workroomThermostat>*) because this constraint specifically refers to this model element in its context.

Once instantiated, the constraints are evaluated immediately to determine their truth values and scopes. If a constraint is deleted then all its instances are destroyed. If a constraint is modified all its constraints are re-evaluated assuming the context element stays the same. If the context element is changed or the constraint is changed from a meta model to a model constraint or vice versa, then the change is treated as the deletion and re-creation of a constraint (rather than its modification).

```
processConstraintChange(changedDefinition)
if changedDefinition was created
 for every modelElement of type/instance changedDefinition.contextElement
   constraint = new <changedDefinition, modelElement>
   evaluate constraint
else if changedDefinition was deleted
 for every constraint of changedDefinition, destroy constraint
else if condition of changedDefinition was modified
 for every constraint of changedDefinition, evaluate constraint
else
 for every constraint of changedDefinition, destroy constraint
 for every modelElement of type/instance changedDefinition.contextElement
   constraint = new <changedDefinition, modelElement>
   evaluate constraint
```

Fig. 6. Algorithm for Processing a Constraint Change Instantly

4 Model Analyzer Tool

Our approach was implemented as a plugin for the IBM Rational Software Modeler [8]. The incremental change tracker for the IBM Rational Software Modeler is partly provided by Eclipse EMF [11] though we also implemented this approach for non-EMF technologies such as the Dopler product line tool suite [6] and IBM Rational Rose [12]. Fig. 7 depicts two screenshots of the tool. The right shows the IBM Rational Software Modeler. An inconsistency is highlighted in red. The tool displays the deployed constraints (bottom left) and constraints (bottom right shows the constraints for the selected constraint). The left shows a constraint in more detail. A constraint is defined by its name, context element, and OCL/Java code.

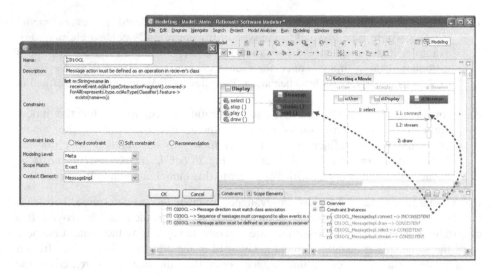

Fig. 7. Snapshot of the Model Analyzer tool

5 Validation

We empirically validated our approach on 24 constraints covering mostly the coherence between UML class, sequence, and state diagrams including well-formedness rules, consistency rules, completeness rules, and general "good practice" rules. The constraints defined in Fig. 3 are examples of the kinds of constraints included in this study. In total, the constraints were evaluated on 20, mostly third-party models with the models ranging in sizes between a few hundred elements to over 100,000 elements.

5.1 Scalability Drivers

To determine the computational complexity of our approach we need to distinguish between the initial cost of creating/changing a constraint and the incremental cost of maintaining it thereafter (with model changes). The initial cost for meta model constraints is a factor of the number of instances per constraint (*#C*) times the number of scope elements they will access during their evaluation (*#SE*). In other words, a new meta model constraint requires the instantiation of #C instances, and each instance must then be evaluated which results in #SE model elements to be looked at. A changed condition of a meta model constraint does not require the re-instantiation of constraints but requires their re-evaluation only. Since the cost of instantiating a meta model constraint is small and a constant (it is the same for every constraint irrespective of the complexity of the condition), we ignore it. The computational complexity for creating and modifying meta model constraints is thus *O(#C * #SE)*. In the case of model constraints we need to create and modify a single instance per constraint (*O(#SE)*).

The computational cost of constraint changes is different from the computational cost of model changes. A constraint as a whole is not re-evaluated with model changes. Rather, some of its instances *may be*. Changing the model thus affects a subset of the instances of *all* meta model constraints: This subset *#A* must then be re-evaluated by accessing in average the same number of scope elements #SE as above. The computational complexity of re-evaluating the consistency after a model change is thus $O(\#A * \#SE)$. We will demonstrate next that #C increases linearly with the size of the model (but not the number of constraints), #A increases linearly with the number of constraints (but not the size of the model), and #SE is essentially constant (affected by neither the size of the model nor the number of constraints). We will also demonstrate that this cost still allows for quick, instant evaluations of models.

Our approach scales well for local constraints. Local constraints refer to constraints that must investigate a small number of model elements to determine their truth values. Our approach performed much better than traditional approaches for local constraints and no worse for global constraints. The 24 constraints we evaluated in our study were all local constraints.

Fig. 8 shows the evaluation times associated with creating/modifying meta model constraints and maintaining them thereafter. We see that the cost of creating or modifying a constraint increases linearly with the size of the model. The figure depicts the evaluation time in milliseconds for changing a single meta model constraint. Still, the cost is reasonable *because it is a onetime cost only and we see that this one-time cost is less than 1 second for most constraints (note the error bar which indicates this onetime cost for all 24 constraints with a confidence interval of 95%)*. Since constraints do not get changed nearly as often as the model, this cost is acceptable and causes minor delays only.

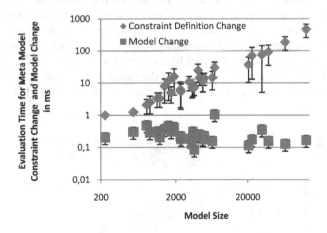

Fig. 8. Eval. time for Meta Model Constraint Changes and corresponding Model Changes

More important is the cost of maintaining a constraint with model changes. *Model changes are recurring (not onetime) and frequent (happen within seconds)*. Its cost must thus be much smaller than the cost of changing a constraint for our approach to be reasonable. After instantiation and evaluation, a new constraint is evaluated exactly like discussed in [10]. Each constraint has a chance for it to be affected by a model change. In practice, however, few constraints and few of its instances are affected.

Fig. 8 shows the evaluation time associated with maintaining a *single meta model constraint* with model changes. Since a model change affects only very few instances of a constraint, we see that the evaluation time is in average less than 1ms per model change and constraint. This obviously implies that the evaluation time of a model change increases linearly with the number of constraints but given its little cost, we could maintain hundreds of constraints (of similar complexity) with ease.

The evaluation efficiency of constraint changes is affected by the size of the model whereas the evaluation efficiency of model changes is affected by the number of constraints. Both cases are several orders magnitude more efficient than traditional batch processing, especially in large models.

Fig. 9 shows the evaluation times associated with creating/modifying model constraints and maintaining them thereafter. Model constraints were also evaluated on the same set of 20 UML models; however, since many of these models did not contain model constraints, we added them through random seeding. The seeded model constraints where derived from the meta model constraints and their complexity is thus analogous to them (and thus directly comparable). In our experience, model constraints are no more complex than meta model constraints – the findings presented next are thus applicable under this assumption. We see that the cost of creating or modifying a model constraint stays constant with the size of the model. The figure depicts the evaluation time in milliseconds for changing a single model constraint. *Note that Fig. 9 shows the evaluation time associated with maintaining a single model constraint* with model changes. Since, in average, a model constraint accesses a small number of scope elements only, the probability that a model change affects one of these scope elements is small. The larger the model, the smaller the probability gets. This obviously implies that the evaluation time of a model change decreases linearly with the size of the model. However, our experience is that unlike meta model constraints, the number of model constraints is expected to increase linearly with the size of the model. Thus, a larger model likely contains more model constraints than a smaller model. The data in Fig. 9 shows that the number of model elements is allowed to increase linearly with the model size for the cost of a model change to become constant (as in Fig. 8).

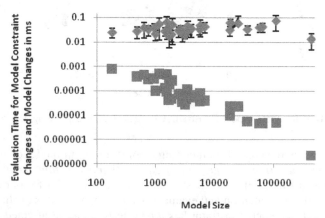

Fig. 9. Evaluation time for Model Constraint Changes and corresponding Model Changes

5.2 Memory Consumption

The memory consumption required for storing the scopes of constraints is the same as presented in [10]. The memory cost grows linear with the size of the model and the number of constraints. It is thus reasonable.

5.3 Threats to Validity

We evaluated our approach on 24 constraints. All of them were scalable which is a good indication that many constraints in general are scalable. However, this does not proof that all constraints are scalable. The works of [13, 14] show that certain kinds of model checking can be exponentially (non linear) expensive. In such cases, our approach would still perform better (certainly no worse) then batch or type-based triggered checkers [2, 3, 8].

It is important to observe that the third-party model we used in our evaluation did not contain model constraints. We therefore used random seeding of meta model constraint instances to evaluate the scalability of model constraints. We believe that this is valid because in our experience, model constraints are no more complex/elaborate than the meta model constraints, which were used for seeding.

6 Related Work

Existing approaches can be characterized based on how they evaluate a model when the constraint or model changes. We see a division between those that perform batch consistency checking and those that perform change-triggered consistency checking. It is also worthwhile distinguishing those that check the model directly [2, 3, 8] and those that check the model after transforming it to a third, usually formal representation [13, 15, 16]. The latter group is more problematic for incremental checking because they also require incremental transformation in addition to checking. And, finally, we see a division between those that allow constraints to be defined/modified at will and those that require constraints to be pre-defined. Most approaches do allow constraints to be added/removed, however, they also require the design model to be recheck in their entirety rather than checking the impact of the constraint change. The approach presented in [17] requires only parts of OCL constraints to be re-evaluated after model changes but works for model constraints only.

Modeling tools such as the IBM Rational Software Modeler [8] or ArgoUML [2] allow engineers to define custom constraints. They even have a notion of incremental checking but both require the engineer to annotate constraints with model element types where the constraint is re-evaluated if any instance of those types changes. We refer to these kinds of approaches as type-based triggering mechanisms because the manual annotation essentially defines what type of change should trigger what types of constraint re-evaluations. This mechanism is essentially a coarse-grained filter that improves the performance of batch consistency checking, however, this mechanism still does not scale because the bigger the model, the more instances of the triggering types it contains.

xLinkIt [3], a XML-based environment for checking the consistency of XML documents, is perhaps the only other technology in existence today that is capable of incremental consistency checking without additional manual overhead. However, the scalability data published in [3] shows a non-instant performance and thus the technology is likely not usable in our context where we care to provide design feedback instantly in real time. Moreover, xLinkIt defines a constraint language that is limited in its expressiveness. This is necessary because the approach analyzes the constraint itself to calculate its triggering conditions which is a complex task.

Incremental consistency checking requires reasoning over design changes rather than reasoning over the entire model state. An explicit emphasis on changes is not new. For example, version control systems such as CVS [18] or SVN [19] deal with changes and they are capable of identifying some form of constraint violations. However, version control systems can at most enforce static, syntactic checks (often referred to as conflicts where multiple stakeholders manipulated the same element) but cannot ensure the rich set of semantic constraints in existence today. More recent work on operations-based model checking [4] shows that there is an increasing emphasis on change during consistency checking. However, their work also appears to require manual annotations to relate changes to constraints (or constraints are required to be re-written from the perspective of changes).

Related to detecting inconsistencies is fixing inconsistencies. This latter issue is out of scope of this paper but it has been demonstrated in [20, 21] it is possible to use the technology for detecting inconsistencies for fixing them at a later time.

7 Conclusion

This paper introduced an approach for the instant checking of dynamic constraints. Engineers can define and modify both meta model and model constraints whenever and wherever necessary and immediately benefit from their instant checking. Engineers need to provide the constraints only – no annotations or any other manual overhead are required. The results of our evaluation demonstrate that our approach is scalable even for large models with tens of thousands of model elements. Our approach provides instant or near-instant error feedback regardless of model and constraint changes.

Acknowledgement. This research was funded by the Austrian FWF under agreement P21321-N15.

References

[1] Fickas, S., Feather, M., Kramer, J.: Proceedings of ICSE 1997 Workshop on Living with Inconsistency, Boston, USA (1997)
[2] Robins, J., et al.: ArgoUML, http://argouml.tigris.org/
[3] Nentwich, C., Capra, L., Emmerich, W., Finkelstein, A.: xlinkit: a consistency checking and smart link generation service. ACM Transactions on Internet Technology (TOIT) 2, 151–185 (2002)

[4] Blanc, X., Mounier, I., Mougenot, A., Mens, T.: Detecting model inconsistency through operation-based model construction. In: 30th International Conference on Software Engineering, Leipzig, Germany, pp. 511–520 (2008)

[5] Object Constraint Language (OCL), http://www.omg.org/spec/OCL/2.0/

[6] Dhungana, D., Rabiser, R., Grünbacher, P., Lehner, K., Federspiel, C.: DOPLER: An Adaptable Tool Suite for Product Line Engineering. In: 11th International Software Product Line Conference, Kyoto, Japan, pp. 151–152 (2007)

[7] Gamma, E., Helm, R., Johnson, R., Vlissides, J.: Design Patterns Elements of Reuseable Object-Oriented Software. Addison Wesley, Reading (1994)

[8] IBM RSM, http://www.ibm.com/software/products/de/de/swmodeler

[9] Voelter, M., Groher, I.: Product Line Implementation using Aspect-Oriented and Model-Driven Software Development. In: 11th International Software Product Line Conference, Kyoto, Japan, pp. 233–242 (2007)

[10] Egyed, A.: Instant Consistency Checking for the UML. In: 28th International Conference on Software Engineering, Shanghai, China, pp. 381–390 (2006)

[11] Eclipse Modeling Framework, http://www.eclipse.org/modeling/emf/

[12] Egyed, A., Balzer, R.: Integrating COTS Software into Systems through Instrumentation and Reasoning. Automated Software Engineering 13, 41–64 (2006)

[13] Czarnecki, K., Pietroszek, K.: Verifying feature-based model templates against well-formedness OCL constraints. In: 5th International Conference on Generative Programming and Component Engineering, Portland, USA (2006)

[14] Larsen, K.G., Nyman, U., Wąsowski, A.: On Modal Refinement and Consistency. In: Caires, L., Vasconcelos, V.T. (eds.) CONCUR 2007. LNCS, vol. 4703, pp. 105–119. Springer, Heidelberg (2007)

[15] Engels, G., Güldali, B., Soltenborn, C., Wehrheim, H.: Assuring Consistency of Business Process Models and Web Services Using Visual Contracts. In: Applications of Graph Transformations with Industrial Relevance, Kassel, Germany, pp. 17–31 (2007)

[16] Campbell, L., Cheng, B., McUmber, W., Stirewalt, K.: Automatically Detecting and Visualising Errors in UML Diagrams. Requirements Engineering Journal 7, 264–287 (2002)

[17] Jordi, C., Ernest, T.: Incremental integrity checking of UML/OCL conceptual schemas. Journal of System Software 82, 1459–1478 (2009)

[18] Concurrent Versions System, http://www.nongnu.org/cvs/

[19] Subversion, http://subversion.tigris.org/

[20] Egyed, A.: Fixing Inconsistencies in UML Design Models. In: 29th International Conference on Software Engineering, Minneapolis, USA, pp. 292–301 (2007)

[21] Küster, J.M., Ryndina, K.: Improving Inconsistency Resolution with Side-Effect Evaluation and Costs. In: Engels, G., Opdyke, B., Schmidt, D.C., Weil, F. (eds.) MODELS 2007. LNCS, vol. 4735, pp. 136–150. Springer, Heidelberg (2007)

Proving Consistency and Completeness of Model Classes Using Theory Interpretation

Ádám Darvas and Peter Müller

ETH Zurich, Switzerland
`peter.mueller@inf.ethz.ch`

Abstract. Abstraction is essential in the formal specification of programs. A common way of writing abstract specifications is to specify implementations in terms of basic mathematical structures. Specification languages like JML offer so-called model classes that provide interfaces to such structures. One way to reason about specifications that make use of model classes is to map model classes directly to structures provided by the theorem prover used for verification. Crucial to the soundness of this technique is the existence of a semantic correspondence between the model class and the related structure. In this paper, we present a formal framework based on theory interpretation for proving this correspondence. The framework provides a systematic way of determining the necessary proof obligations and justifies the soundness of the approach.

1 Introduction

Abstraction is essential in the formal specification of programs because it allows one to write specifications in an implementation-independent way, which is indispensable for information hiding. Furthermore, abstraction facilitates the readability and maintainability of specifications. A common way of writing abstract specifications is to specify implementations in terms of well-known mathematical structures, such as sets and relations. This technique is applied, for instance, in VDM [10], Larch [8], and OCL [19]. While these approaches describe the mathematical structures in a language that is different from the underlying programming language, another approach is that of the Java Modeling Language (JML) [13], which simplifies the development of specifications by describing the structures through *model classes* [2]. Model classes are immutable and are used only for specification purposes. They provide object-oriented interfaces for essential mathematical structures through their side-effect free (*pure*) methods.

Specifications can be written in an abstract way by expressing properties in terms of model classes and their operations. Fig. 1 shows a class `SingletonSet` specified in JML using the model class `JMLObjectSet` (presented in Fig. 2), which represents a mathematical set of objects. To use the model class, we declare the public specification-only model field `_set`. The field represents the abstraction of an instance of type `SingletonSet` as specified by the private **represents** clause: a singleton set containing the object referenced by the private field `value`. Given

D.S. Rosenblum and G. Taentzer (Eds.): FASE 2010, LNCS 6013, pp. 218–232, 2010.

```
class SingletonSet {
private Object value;
//@ public model JMLObjectSet _set;
//@ private represents _set <- new JMLObjectSet(value);

    //@ ensures _set.has(o);
public void setValue(Object o)
    { value = o; }
}   // other constructors and methods are omitted for brevity
```

Fig. 1. Specifying class `SingletonSet` using model class `JMLObjectSet`. JML annotation comments start with an at-sign (@).

model field `_set` and `JMLObjectSet`'s public pure method `has`, which checks for set membership, one can specify `SingletonSet`'s `setValue` method in an abstract way, in particular, without referring to the private field `value`.

While model classes provide a powerful means for writing abstract specifications, they pose a problem for static verification: program verifiers have to encode specification expressions in the logic of the underlying theorem prover, in particular, calls to the pure methods of model classes.

Previous work proposes to map model classes and their methods directly to structures and function symbols provided by the theories of the underlying theorem prover [1,11,12,4]. Calls to model-class methods are encoded as applications of these function symbols. For instance, if `JMLObjectSet`'s method `has` is mapped to symbol '$\in$' denoting set membership of a particular structure, then every call to `has` is encoded as an application of '$\in$'. Such an encoding leads to proof obligations that are handled well by theorem provers, which typically provide theories with numerous theorems for elementary structures.

Crucial to the soundness of this technique is to ensure that the mapping is *faithful*, that is, the semantics of related model classes and structures match. However, previous work mostly discusses the mapping of method signatures, but ignores their contracts. With this approach, for instance, the meaning of method `has` is given by the definition of symbol '$\in$' of the given theory, and not by the contract of `has`. This is problematic if there is a mismatch between the contract and the semantics of the operation given by the theorem prover: (1) program verifiers might produce results that come unexpected for one who relies on the contract, (2) results may vary between different theorem provers, which define certain operations slightly differently, and (3) the result of runtime assertion checking might differ from that of static verification if the model-class implementation used by the checker is based on contracts.

Our previous work takes the contracts of model classes into account and describes the main ideas behind an approach that checks if the mapping of a model class to a mathematical structure is faithful [4]. In this paper, we present a formal framework for checking the faithfulness of mappings. This framework defines precisely the proof obligations needed to show faithfulness and guarantees soundness. Our framework applies the concept of *theory interpretation* [22,24,5], which allows one to compare the "strength" of two theories, T and T', whose language (*i.e.*, set of nonlogical symbols) possibly differ. A theory interpretation of T in T' is based on a syntactic notion, a *standard translation* Φ between the terms and formulas of T and T'. Φ is a *standard interpretation of T in T'* if $\Phi(\phi)$ is a theorem of T' for each theorem ϕ of T. A theorem important for our purposes is that if there is a standard interpretation of T in T', and T' is consistent, then T is consistent.

Our approach applies the concept of theory interpretation in three stages. In the first stage, we specify the mapping of a model class to an existing theory of the underlying theorem prover. In the second stage, we attempt to formally prove that the specified mapping of a model class defines a standard interpretation of the theory formed by the specification of the model class in the theory of the corresponding structure. If the proof attempt succeeds then *consistency* of the model-class specification is guaranteed. Although consistency is only relative to the consistency of the target theory, theorem provers are unlikely to contain inconsistent theories. We will refer to this stage as the *consistency proof*.

In the third stage, we attempt to "reverse" the specified mapping and attempt to prove that the reverse mapping defines a standard interpretation of the target theory in the specification of the model class. If the proof attempt succeeds then *completeness* of the model-class specification is guaranteed. Again, completeness is only relative to the corresponding theory, but theorem provers typically define theories with rich sets of properties. In contrast to our earlier work, we define a condition that ensures the existence of a suitable reverse mapping. We will refer to the third stage as the *completeness proof*.

We have presented the main idea of faithfulness proofs earlier [4]. However, the precise conditions that are necessary to ensure soundness are subtle, and our previous work did not contain a soundness argument. The advantage of building our approach on the well-studied concept of theory interpretation is that the correctness of our approach is guaranteed by the correctness of the concept. In particular, theory interpretation takes the universes of structures into account, which is crucial for the soundness of the mapping of model classes [3] and is not present in previous work.

Although we use JML as specification language and Isabelle [18] as theorem prover in this paper, the presented approach is applicable to any combination of specification language and theorem prover, for instance, Eiffel [17] and PVS [20].

Outline. The next section introduces a model class that will serve as running example and the specification means for mapping model classes. Sections 3, 4, and 5 present the formal details of faithfulness proofs: the way universe predicates are defined, the consistency proof, and the completeness proof. In Sec. 6, we discuss related work and conclude. We refer the reader to the PhD dissertation of Darvas [3] for a case study of the presented approach, an extension to mappings whose target structure is defined inductively, and practical considerations for the case when related model classes and structures do not match perfectly.

```
//@ mapped_to("Isabelle", "HOL/Set", "α set");
/*@ immutable pure @*/ public class JMLObjectSet {
  //@ mapped_to("Isabelle", "{}");
  public JMLObjectSet() { ... }

  //@ mapped_to("Isabelle", "insert e {}");
  public JMLObjectSet(Object e) { ... }

  //@ mapped_to("Isabelle", "elem : this");
  public boolean has(Object elem) { ... }

  //@ mapped_to("Isabelle", "this = s2");
  public boolean equals(Object s2) { ... }

  /*@ ensures (\forall Object e;
                 \result.has(e) == (this.has(e) || e == elem)); @*/
  //@ mapped_to("Isabelle", "insert elem this");
  public JMLObjectSet insert(Object elem) { ... }

  //@ mapped_to("Isabelle", "this - (insert elem {})");
  public JMLObjectSet remove(Object elem) { ... }

  //@ mapped_to("Isabelle", "this Un s2");
  public JMLObjectSet union(JMLObjectSet s2) { ... }

  //@ mapped_to("Isabelle", "this - s2");
  public JMLObjectSet difference(JMLObjectSet s2) { ... }
}
```

Fig. 2. Signatures and mappings of `JMLObjectSet`'s constructors and methods that we consider in this paper. Implementations are omitted.

2   Encoding of Model Classes

Model Class `JMLObjectSet`. The class is part of JML's model library and encodes sets of objects: it provides the usual operations of mathematical sets; equality over the set-elements is based on Java's reference equality ("=="). Fig. 2 presents those constructors and methods that are discussed in the sequel.

The class is specified to be pure (meaning that all instance methods are pure) and immutable. It is specified by invariants and method specifications. The invariants of model classes are special in that they do not restrict the state space of model-class instances as invariants usually do. Instead, they give equational laws about their operations, thus they play a similar role as method specifications. Therefore, for brevity, we omit the handling of invariants here, but see [3].

A sample method specification is given in Fig. 2 for method `insert`. The proposed mapping of the class and its operations to one of Isabelle's set structures is given by `mapped_to` clauses that we introduce below.

Specifying the Mapping. In the first stage of a faithfulness proof, one specifies the mapping of the model class at hand. In our previous work [4], we introduced the mapped_to clause for this purpose. The mapping of a model class is specified by a mapped_to clause attached to the class. The first argument of the clause specifies the target theorem prover, the second the target theory, and the third the specific type (if any) in the theory to which the model class is mapped. Similarly, a method can be mapped to a term of the target theory of a given theorem prover by a mapped_to clause attached to it. The term must be well-typed and may only mention logical and nonlogical symbols of the target theory and parameters (including the explicit receiver) of the specified constructor or method. Only one clause per target theorem prover may be specified both for a model class and for a method.

For instance, in Fig. 2 class JMLObjectSet is mapped to type α *set* in the HOL/Set theory of Isabelle; and method has is mapped to the term *elem* : *this*, meaning that the method corresponds to Isabelle's set membership operator ":".

We permit one to write arbitrarily complex terms in mapped_to clauses, which allows us to support model methods with functionality that is not directly provided by the target prover. This flexibility is necessary to handle, for example, JMLObjectSet's remove method, which removes a single element of a set. Theory HOL/Set does not provide a corresponding operation but provides set difference, which allows one to express the meaning of method remove.

As different theorem provers provide different theories with different symbols and semantics, we allow mappings to multiple provers. Thus, the faithfulness proof has to be carried out in every target prover specified in mapped_to clauses.

Contexts and Auxiliary Functions. The contexts in which the consistency and the completeness proofs are carried out are not the same. The context of the former is that of the target theory T, for instance, Isabelle's HOL/Set theory. The context of the latter will be denoted by $\widehat{M}$, which is the logical encoding of model class M's specification. The encoding allows one to carry out the completeness proof in a formal system, like Isabelle or PVS [20]. Note that merely analysing the encoded specification in context $\widehat{M}$ would not be sufficient for the sound use of the mapped_to clause for verification purposes, because only consistency of the specification could be shown; its semantic correspondence to target theory T could not be justified.

We introduce function γ that encodes JML specification expressions in context $\widehat{M}$. The function takes a JML expression and yields a first-order term or formula (denoted by *FOL*) in $\widehat{M}$. Its signature is $\gamma: Expr \rightarrow FOL_{\widehat{M}}$. Note that γ takes no argument for the state. This is because instances of model classes behave like mathematical values rather than heap-allocated objects. The definition of the function for a small but representative subset of JML is the following [3]:

$$
\begin{aligned}
\gamma(E \circledast F) &\triangleq \gamma(E)\ Tr(\circledast)\ \gamma(F),\ \text{if } \circledast \in \{\texttt{\&\&}, \texttt{||}, \texttt{==>}, \texttt{==}, \texttt{!=}, \texttt{+}, \texttt{-}, \texttt{/}, \texttt{\%}\} \\
\gamma(\texttt{v}) &\triangleq v & \gamma(\texttt{new } \texttt{C}(E)) &\triangleq \widehat{C}(\gamma(E)) \\
\gamma(\texttt{!}E) &\triangleq \neg\gamma(E) & \gamma((\texttt{\textbackslash forall } T\ x.\ E)) &\triangleq \forall\ x.\ \gamma(E) \\
\gamma(E.\texttt{m}(F)) &\triangleq \widehat{m}(\gamma(E), \gamma(F)) & \gamma((\texttt{\textbackslash exists } T\ x.\ E)) &\triangleq \exists\ x.\ \gamma(E)
\end{aligned}
$$

An application of a binary JML operator ⊛ is encoded by an application of the corresponding operator in the underlying logic yielded by function Tr to the encoding the two operands. Tr is a function that maps the binary operators of JML to their equivalents in first-order logic (*i.e.*, $\wedge$, $\vee$, $\Rightarrow$, $=$, $\neq$, etc.). Calls to methods and constructors are encoded by applications of uninterpreted function symbols. We will use the convention that a method m is encoded by symbol $\widehat{m}$. Note that the encoding of old-expressions (used in postconditions to refer to values in the pre-state of the specified method) is not given. This is because old-expressions are not meaningful in model-class specifications.

Next, we introduce function ν. A standard translation Φ of T in T' is a pair (U, ν), where U is a closed unary predicate, the *universe predicate*, and ν is a function that maps all nonlogical symbols of T to a λ-expression of T' [5]. Given U and ν, the translation of terms and formulas of T can be defined in a straightforward way [5].

Following this notation, we use function ν to map methods and constructors to λ-functions of the target theory. As mapped_to clauses contain exactly that information, function ν essentially captures the content of these clauses. For instance, in model class JMLObjectSet we have:[1]

$$\nu(\texttt{remove}) \;\equiv\; \lambda\{\; this, elem.\; this - (insert\; elem\; \{\})\,\}$$

The purpose of the universe predicate and the way it is specified in model classes is described in the next section.

3   Specifying the Universe

When relating two theories, it is possible that the set of possible elements (the *universe*) of the source and the target theory differ. In such cases, the scope of quantifiers and, therefore, the semantics of quantified formulas possibly differs in the two theories. The concept of theory interpretation solves this problem by introducing the unary universe predicate U, which yields true if and only if its argument denotes an element of the target structure that is meant to be in the scope of quantifiers, and thereby, in the scope of translation Φ. Given the universe predicate, translation Φ "relativizes" quantifiers:

$$\Phi(\forall x.\; \phi) \;\triangleq\; \forall x.\; U(x) \Rightarrow \Phi(\phi) \quad \text{and} \quad \Phi(\exists x.\; \phi) \;\triangleq\; \exists x.\; U(x) \wedge \Phi(\phi)$$

The dissertation of Darvas [3, Example 9.1] demonstrates the need for relativization in the context of mapping model classes to mathematical theories.

To allow users to specify the set of operations that should form the universe predicate of a model class, we introduce the **constructing** modifier that may be attached to constructors and methods. The universe predicate is the same for the consistency and for the completeness proofs, only the context in which the predicate is expressed differs: When proving consistency, the context is that of the target theory T; when proving completeness, the context is $\widehat{M}$. Accordingly, we will denote the predicates by U_T and $U_{\widehat{M}}$.

---

[1] As a second argument, ν should take the name of the target theorem prover. For simplicity, we omit this argument as the target prover will be Isabelle in the sequel.

Given a model class M with l methods and constructors marked with modifier **constructing**, the resulting universe predicate is a disjunction with l disjuncts. The disjunct of the universe predicate $U_{\widehat{M}}(x)$ for a **constructing** method m with one implicit and n explicit parameters, and precondition P is:

$$\exists s, e_1, \ldots, e_n.\ U_{\widehat{M}}(s) \wedge U_{\widehat{M}}(e_1) \wedge \ldots \wedge U_{\widehat{M}}(e_k) \wedge$$
$$\gamma(P) \wedge \widehat{equals}(x, \widehat{m}(s, e_1, \ldots, e_n))$$

where $k \leq n$ and where we assume for simplicity that parameters $e_1, \ldots, e_k$ are of the enclosing type, while the others are not. The construction of predicate U_T is analogous in the context of T:

$$\exists s, e_1, \ldots, e_n.\ U_T(s) \wedge U_T(e_1) \wedge \ldots \wedge U_T(e_k) \wedge$$
$$\Phi_M(P) \wedge \Phi_M(x.\texttt{equals}(s.\texttt{m}(e_1, \ldots, e_n)))$$

where Φ_M is the translation function between JML expressions and the target context. The function is precisely defined in the next section.

The treatment of constructors is analogous. As an example, if the parameter-less constructor and method **insert** of model class **JMLObjectSet** are marked as **constructing** then we get the following universe predicates:

$$U_{\widehat{M}}(x) \triangleq \widehat{equals}(x, \widehat{JMLObjectSet}()) \vee (\exists s, e.\ U_{\widehat{M}}(s) \wedge \widehat{equals}(x, \widehat{insert}(s, e)))$$
$$U_T(x) \triangleq x = \{\} \vee (\exists s, e.\ U_T(s) \wedge x = (insert\ e\ s))$$

If no method is marked as **constructing** then the universe predicate is *true*. This is the case when the source and the target universe is the same.

4 Proving Consistency of a Model Class

In the second stage of the faithfulness proof, we prove consistency of the mapping: we show that there is a standard interpretation of M's theory in theory T. To do so, first we define the translation of JML expressions in the context of T based on **mapped_to** clauses. The resulting translation function will be denoted by Φ_M. Second, we attempt to prove that Φ_M is a standard interpretation.

Definition of Φ_M. The function takes a JML expression and yields a term or formula in the target context. Its signature is $\Phi_M \colon Expr \rightarrow FOL_T$ and its definition is presented in Fig. 3. For simplicity, the definition for method and constructor calls, for keyword `\result`, and for keyword **this** in the postcondition of constructors is presented for methods with one explicit parameter p. Note that terms $\nu(\texttt{m})(this, p)$ and $\nu(\texttt{C})(p)$ denote the terms that are defined by the **mapped_to** clause of the corresponding method and constructor.

Proving that Φ_M is a Standard Interpretation. To prove that translation function Φ_M is a standard interpretation of M's theory in theory T, we need to prove that three sufficient obligations hold [5].

Axiom Obligation. The obligation requires that the translation of every axiom of M is a theorem of T. The "axioms" of a model class are its method specifications.

$$\Phi_M(E \circledast F) \quad\triangleq\quad \Phi_M(E)\ Tr(\circledast)\ \Phi_M(F), \text{ if } \circledast \in \{\&\&, ||, ==>, ==, !=, +, -, /, \%\}$$

$$\Phi_M(!E) \quad\triangleq\quad \neg\,\Phi_M(E)$$

$$\Phi_M(E.\mathtt{m}(F)) \quad\triangleq\quad \nu(\mathtt{m})(\Phi_M(E), \Phi_M(F))$$

$$\Phi_M(\mathtt{new}\ \mathtt{C}(E)) \triangleq \nu(\mathtt{C})(\Phi_M(E))$$

$$\Phi_M(\backslash\mathtt{result}) \quad\triangleq\quad \nu(\mathtt{m})(\mathit{this}, p), \qquad\qquad\qquad \text{where m is the enclosing method}$$

$$\Phi_M(\mathtt{this}) \quad\triangleq\quad \nu(\mathtt{C})(p), \quad \text{if } \mathtt{this} \text{ occurs in the postcondition of constructor C}$$

$$\Phi_M(\mathtt{v}) \quad\triangleq\quad v, \text{ if v is a parameter or literal other than } \backslash\mathtt{result} \text{ and } \mathtt{this} \text{ in}$$
$$\text{postconditions of constructors}$$

$$\Phi_M((\backslash\mathtt{forall}\,T\ x.\ E)) \quad\triangleq\quad \forall\,x.\ \; U_T(x) \;\Rightarrow\; \Phi_M(E)$$

$$\Phi_M((\backslash\mathtt{exists}\,T\ x.\ E)) \quad\triangleq\quad \exists\,x.\ \; U_T(x) \;\wedge\; \Phi_M(E)$$

where the ⟨shaded⟩ parts are added only if the quantified
variable is of a model type.

Fig. 3. Definition of translation Φ_M

Their translation is straightforward, only the free variables have to be bound by universal quantifiers since these quantifications are implicit in method specifications. The specification of a method of class C with one explicit parameter p of type T, precondition P, and postcondition Q is translated to:

$$\Phi_M((\backslash\mathtt{forall}\ C\ \mathtt{this}.\ (\backslash\mathtt{forall}\ T\ p.\ P \Longrightarrow Q)))$$

which is equivalent to:

$$\forall\ \mathit{this}, p.\ (U_T(\mathit{this}) \Rightarrow (\ U_T(p) \Rightarrow\ \Phi_M(P \Longrightarrow Q))),$$

where the ⟨shaded⟩ part is only added if p is of a model type. The formulas are turned into lemmas and have to be proved in the target theory.

Universe Nonemptiness Obligation. The obligation requires that the universe of the translation is nonempty: $\exists\,x.\ U_T(x)$. This is usually trivial to prove. For instance, for class `JMLObjectSet`, picking $\{\}$ for x trivially discharges the obligation for the universe predicate presented on the facing page.

Function Symbol Obligation. The obligation requires that for each symbol f of the source theory, the interpretation of f is a function whose restriction to the universe takes values in the universe. When applying the obligation to methods of model classes, the only difference is that preconditions have to be taken into account. We have to prove for each model-class method m with n explicit parameters and precondition P that the following holds in the target theory:

$$\forall t, x_1, \ldots, x_n.\ U_T(t) \Rightarrow U_T(x_1) \Rightarrow \ldots \Rightarrow U_T(x_k) \Rightarrow$$
$$\Phi_M(P(t, x_1, \ldots, x_n)) \Rightarrow U_T(\Phi_M(t.m(x_1, \ldots, x_n))) \tag{1}$$

where $k \leq n$ and where we assume that $x_1, \ldots, x_k$ are of model types, while the others are not. The proof obligations for constructors are analogous.

The second stage of the faithfulness proof is successfully completed if the three obligations can be proven. Based on the concept of theory interpretation, we can then conclude that the specification of the model class at hand is consistent provided that the target theory is consistent.

Having proved consistency of the specification of a model class ensures that it can be safely used for reasoning about client code. However, the consistency proof does not ensure that specified `mapped_to` clauses can be used for verification purposes [4]. Assume method m of a model class was mapped to symbol f, which was specified to possess properties that m did not. The verification of specifications that rely on m may lead to results that are not justified by the model-class specifications because, after having mapped method m to symbol f, the method would be endowed with all the additional properties that f possessed. The results may also diverge between different theorem provers, which define certain operations slightly differently. Furthermore, the results of runtime assertion checking might diverge from the results of static verification if the model class implementation used by the runtime assertion checker is based on the model class contract.

To fix this issue, we need to show that method m indeed possesses all endowed properties. Thus, proving completeness of a model class with respect to a theory does not just show that the specification of the class is strong enough relative to the theory, but is crucial for the sound use of `mapped_to` clauses during the verification of client code.

5   Proving Completeness of a Model Class

In the third stage of the faithfulness proof, we prove completeness of the mapping, that is, we show that there is a standard interpretation of theory T in M's theory. To do so, first we define function Φ_S that translates terms and formulas of the target theory in the context of the model class. Second, we attempt to prove that Φ_S is a standard interpretation.

Issues of Reverse Mappings. The `mapped_to` clauses provide the basis for the translation of JML expressions to terms and formulas of the target context. However, for the completeness proof, we need a translation in the other direction. In the following, we show that translation Φ_S may not be an arbitrary translation for which we can show that it is a standard interpretation. The translation should be one that is derived from the mapping prescribed by `mapped_to` clauses. That is, we need a way to *reverse* the specified mapping, which is not trivial.

Assume that in the above example not only m, but another method n was mapped to symbol f. When proving completeness of the mapping, we would need to show that not only m, but also n possesses all properties that f has. Otherwise, n might be endowed with properties that it does not possess when the method is mapped to f.

For instance, consider symbol *insert* of theory `HOL/Set`, which is mapped to both by method `insert` and by the one-argument constructor of model class `JMLObjectSet`. Therefore, the translation of a formula that contains an application of the symbol should consider mapping the symbol both to the method and to the constructor. Although this seems to be doable by defining Φ_S such that all possible reverse mappings of a symbol must be taken into account, clearly, such a translation would not be *standard* anymore (as ν would not be a function). Furthermore, since $\nu(\texttt{JMLObjectSet(e)})(e) \equiv insert\ e\ \{\}$,[2] the translation of the general term *insert x Y* to the constructor is only valid *under the condition* that Y corresponds to the empty set. This condition would need to be added to the translated formula, again showing that the translation would not be standard. Consequently, the concept of theory interpretation would not apply.

Moreover, the problem is not merely that the resulting reverse translation would not be standard: the conditions under which certain mappings are valid may alter the semantics and satisfiability of the original formula. It is well-known that a condition over a universally bound variable has to be added as the premise of an implication, otherwise the condition has to be added as a conjunct. However, if a condition contains both an existentially and a universally quantified variable then the condition can be added neither as a premise, nor as a conjunct.

To sum up, the general reversal of translation Φ_M would not be standard, would considerably change the structure of translated formulas, and (in certain cases) would alter the semantics of translated formulas. Thus, it would be difficult to reason that the resulting translation is indeed the one we are looking for.

Our Pragmatic Approach. To resolve the problem, we take a pragmatic approach and pose a requirement on the user-defined mappings. In practice, the requirement typically does not constrain the way model classes may be written and mapped, but it ensures that the "reverse" translation of Φ_M is a standard translation and can be easily derived from Φ_M.

Besides the requirement, a number of proof obligations will be posed on the operations of the model class at hand. In the remainder of this section, we formalize the requirement, the translation Φ_S, and the necessary proof obligations.

Requirement. The requirement we pose on specified `mapped_to` clauses is that each symbol of the target theory T should be mapped to by at least one model method *unconditionally*. Formally:

For each n-ary function and predicate symbol f of T and variables $x_1, \ldots, x_n$ there is at least one method m or constructor C, and expressions $e_1, \ldots, e_k$ with free variables $x_1, \ldots, x_n$ such that either
$\Phi_M(e_1.m(e_2, \ldots, e_k)) = f(x_1, \ldots, x_n)$ or
$\Phi_M(\textbf{new}\ C(e_1, e_2, \ldots, e_k)) = f(x_1, \ldots, x_n)$ holds. $\qquad$ (2)

Although the requirement does not hold for arbitrary mappings, it typically holds for model classes. Conditional mappings are typically needed when a model class

---

[2] We will write `JMLObjectSet(e)` to refer to the one-argument constructor even when only a method or constructor name is expected, like the argument of function ν.

$$\Phi_S(Var) \triangleq Var$$

$$\Phi_S(f(t_1,\ldots,t_n)) \triangleq \begin{cases} \gamma(e_1.\mathtt{m}(e_2,\ldots,e_k)), & \text{if there is a method } \mathtt{m} \text{ and} \\ & \text{expressions } e_1,\ldots,e_k \text{ such that:} \\ & \Phi_M(e_1.\mathtt{m}(e_2,\ldots,e_k)) = f(t_1,\ldots,t_n) \\ \gamma(\mathtt{new}\ \mathtt{C}(e_1,e_2,\ldots,e_k)), & \text{if there is a constructor } \mathtt{C} \text{ and} \\ & \text{expressions } e_1,\ldots,e_k \text{ such that:} \\ & \Phi_M(\mathtt{new}\ \mathtt{C}(e_1,e_2,\ldots,e_k)) = f(t_1,\ldots,t_n) \end{cases}$$

$$\Phi_S(t_1 = t_2)) \triangleq \Phi_S(t_1) = \Phi_S(t_2), \text{ if } t_1 \text{ and } t_2 \text{ are not of model type;}$$
$$\text{otherwise handled the same way as predicate symbols}$$

$$\Phi_S(\neg\,\phi) \quad \triangleq \neg\Phi_S(\phi) \qquad \Phi_S(true) \triangleq true \qquad \Phi_S(false) \triangleq false$$

$$\Phi_S(\phi_1 \circ \phi_2) \triangleq \Phi_S(\phi_1) \circ \Phi_S(\phi_2), \text{ if } \circ \in \{\wedge, \vee, \Rightarrow\}$$

$$\Phi_S(\forall x.\ \phi) \quad \triangleq \forall x.\ \boxed{U_{\widehat{M}}(x)} \Rightarrow \Phi_S(\phi) \qquad \Phi_S(\exists x.\ \phi) \triangleq \exists x.\ \boxed{U_{\widehat{M}}(x)} \wedge \Phi_S(\phi)$$

where the shaded parts are added only if the quantified
variable is of the type to which the model class was mapped.

Fig. 4. Definition of translation Φ_S

offers methods that are redundant in the sense that they are equivalent to some compound expression consisting of calls to more basic methods. For instance, method `remove` is equivalent to set difference with a singleton set as second argument. Such methods make the use of model classes more convenient, whereas mathematical structures typically avoid this redundancy.

The requirement would not hold, for instance, if class `JMLObjectSet` provided method `remove`, but not method `difference`.

Definition of Φ_S. The reverse translation Φ_S is a transformer between terms and formulas of context T and $\widehat{M}$. Its signature is $\Phi_S\colon FOL_T \to FOL_{\widehat{M}}$. Given requirement (2), it can be easily defined. The definition of translation Φ_S for the standard syntax of first-order logic is presented in Fig. 4. Translation Φ_S is identical to translation Φ described in the literature [22,5], except that the translation of function and predicate symbols is not based on function ν but on the reversal of translation Φ_M, as expressed by the condition.

If there are multiple methods or constructors that satisfy the condition then any of them can be selected since their equivalence has to be formally proven, as we will see below.

Note that the translation of operator "=" is different if the operands are of model types and if they are of some other type. In the former case, the definition over function and predicate symbols apply: to which model method the operator is mapped depends on the user-specified mapping. In practice, it is typically (but not necessarily) the `equals` method.

If the operands are not of model type, then "=" is translated to "=" (or the equivalent symbol of the target prover). Although this is in line with the definition of function Φ, it might not be the desired translation: one might want to define equality over the elements of a model class by the `equals` method of the specific element type at hand, and not by reference equality. For brevity, we omit this issue here and refer to the dissertation of Darvas [3] for a solution.

Proof Obligations. The requirement on mappings prescribes that there should be at least one unconditional mapping for each symbol of T. However, it does not rule out methods with mappings that can be reversed only conditionally, such as the reverse mapping of symbol *insert* to the one-argument constructor. Therefore, what remains to be shown is that the functionalities of methods that are mapped to the same symbol of T are equivalent provided that the condition (if any) under which their mapping can be reversed holds.

For instance, we need to prove that the functionality of a call to the one-argument constructor `JMLObjectSet(e)` is equivalent with that of method `insert` provided that the receiver object of the method denotes the empty set.

This kind of proof obligations can be formalized as follows. Assume that for some symbol f, method m fulfills requirement (2). Then for each method n that is also mapped to symbol f (even if n also fulfills the requirement), we have to show that the following holds in context $\widehat{M}$:

$$\forall x_1, \ldots, x_p, \, y_1, \ldots, y_q.$$
$$\Phi_S(t_m^1 = t_n^1) \wedge \ldots \wedge \Phi_S(t_m^k = t_n^k) \;\Rightarrow\; \widehat{m}(x_1, \ldots, x_p) \stackrel{eq}{=} \widehat{n}(y_1, \ldots, y_q)$$

where (1) symbol $\stackrel{eq}{=}$ denotes operator "=" if the operands are not of model type, otherwise an application of the hat-function to which symbol "=" is translated by Φ_S (*i.e.*, typically function $\widehat{equals}$); and (2) the $t_m^i = t_n^i$ equalities are derived by applying translation function Φ_M on methods m and n, and taking pairwise the i-th arguments of the resulting function applications. Formally:

$$\Phi_M(x_1.m(x_2, \ldots, x_p)) = f(t_m^1, \ldots, t_m^k)$$
$$\Phi_M(y_1.n(y_2, \ldots, y_q)) = f(t_n^1, \ldots, t_n^k)$$

Proving that Φ_S is a Standard Interpretation. It remains to prove that Φ_S is a standard interpretation. The procedure is the same as for translation Φ_M: we have to show that the three sufficient obligations hold for the standard translation Φ_S.

First, the context and theory in which the obligations are to be proven needs to be constructed. As noted above, the context is denoted by $\widehat{M}$, and the theory is formed by the axiom system that is extracted from the specification of model class M. In the sequel, we will call this theory the *model theory* and assume that method signatures in M only refer to the enclosing type and type `Object`. In practice, this is typically the case for methods and constructors that correspond to the operations of the mathematical structure that M represents.

The model theory is obtained in three simple steps for a model class M:

1. Two new types are declared: *Object* and M.
2. Each method m of M is turned into a function symbol $\widehat{m}$ and its signature is declared based on m's signature using the two newly declared types.

3. Each method specification of M is turned into an axiom. For the specification of method m with parameter p, precondition P, and postcondition Q, the axiom is: $\forall\ this, p.\ \gamma(P \texttt{ ==> } Q[\texttt{this}.m(p)/\texttt{\textbackslash result}])$.
   For a constructor C, the substitution to perform on Q is $C(p)/\texttt{this}$.

Once the model theory is created, we have to show that the formulas that correspond to the three sufficient obligations for Φ_S are theorems of the model theory. The obligations are analogous to those of the consistency proof. To prove the axiom obligation, we have to show that for every axiom and definition ϕ of T, formula $\Phi_S(\phi)$ is a theorem of the model theory.

The universe nonemptiness obligation requires one to prove that universe $U_{\widehat{M}}$ is nonempty: $\exists x.\ U_{\widehat{M}}(x)$. As for the consistency proof, the obligation is typically trivially provable. The function symbol obligation is analogous to the corresponding obligation (1) on page 225 for the consistency proof. Predicate P corresponds to the domain restriction (if any) of the function at hand.

The third stage of the faithfulness proof is successfully completed if the three obligations can be proven. Based on the concept of theory interpretation, we can then conclude that all theorems of the target theory follow from the specification of the model class. That is, the specification is complete relative to the target theory. As discussed before, completeness allows a program verifier to prove properties in the target theory without creating results that cannot be explained by the model class specification. Moreover, failing to prove completeness typically indicates that the model-class specification is not complete. By adding the missing cases, the quality of the model-class specification improves.

6   Related Work and Conclusion

The concept of theory interpretation has already been used for formal program development. For instance, Levy applied theory interpretation to formally show the correctness of compiler implementations [14]; the work of Maibaum et al. (e.g., [15]) and the Specware tool [23] applies the concept together with other formal machinery for the construction of formal specifications and their refinement into programs; and the theorem prover Ergo applies the concept to maximize theory reuse [9].

The idea of using function symbols that are understood by the back-end theorem prover directly on the specification level is already present in ESC/Java [7], which uses such function symbols instead of pure-method calls in specifications. However, the meaning of the symbols is hidden on the specification level, and the tool does not give support for showing consistency of their definitions.

Similarly, Caduceus [6] allows one to declare predicates that can be defined or axiomatized either on the source level or in the back-end prover [16]. However, there is no consistency proof for the user-provided definitions and axioms.

Schoeller et al. developed a model library for Eiffel [21]. They address the faithfulness issue by equipping methods of model classes with specifications that directly correspond to axioms and theorems taken from mathematical textbooks. A shortcoming of this approach is that the resulting model library has to follow exactly the structure of the mimicked theory. This limits the design decisions one can make when composing the model library and it is unclear how one can support multiple theorem provers. Our approach allows more flexibility by allowing mapped_to clauses to contain arbitrary terms of the target context.

Charles [1] proposes the introduction of the native keyword to JML with the meaning that methods marked as native introduce uninterpreted function symbols that can be defined on the level of the underlying theorem prover. Furthermore, the native keyword may also be attached to classes meaning that such classes get mapped to corresponding data types of the underlying prover.

Charles' approach differs from ours in two ways. First, our approach ensures faithfulness of the mapping. There is no attempt to do so in the work of Charles. Second, mapped_to clauses allow one to specify the mapping on the specification language level. Furthermore, properties of model classes are specified in JML, which typically provides easier understanding (for programmers) of the semantics than definitions given directly on the level of a theorem prover.

Leavens et al. [12] identify the problem of specifying model classes as a research challenge. They propose two possible solution approaches that are related to our work and summarize the open problems for both of them. One approach considers automatic translations between model classes and mathematical structures, and the authors argue why such translations are difficult. We deal with these problems by specifying the mapping manually and proving faithfulness of the mapping. The other approach is similar to the work by Schoeller and Charles.

Conclusion. We presented a formal framework for faithfulness proofs based on theory interpretation. Proving faithfulness of model classes ensures consistency of model class specifications, prevents unexpected results from program verifiers, and also improves the overall quality of model class specifications.

Acknowledgments. We are grateful to Peter H. Schmitt for directing us to the concept of theory interpretation as the appropriate framework for our approach. We thank Reiner Hähnle, Gary T. Leavens, and the anonymous reviewers for helpful comments. This work was funded in part by the IST-2005-015905 MOBIUS project.

References

1. Charles, J.: Adding native specifications to JML. In: FTfJP (2006)
2. Cheon, Y., Leavens, G.T., Sitaraman, M., Edwards, S.: Model variables: cleanly supporting abstraction in design by contract. Software: Practice and Experience 35(6), 583–599 (2005)
3. Darvas, Á.: Reasoning About Data Abstraction in Contract Languages. Ph.D. thesis, ETH Zurich (2009)
4. Darvas, Á., Müller, P.: Faithful mapping of model classes to mathematical structures. IET Software 2(6), 477–499 (2008)

5. Farmer, W.M.: Theory interpretation in simple type theory. In: Heering, J., Meinke, K., Möller, B., Nipkow, T. (eds.) HOA 1993. LNCS, vol. 816, pp. 96–123. Springer, Heidelberg (1994)
6. Filliâtre, J.C., Hubert, T., Marché, C.: The Caduceus verification tool for C programs, tutorial and Reference Manual (2007)
7. Flanagan, C., Leino, K.R.M., Lillibridge, M., Nelson, G., Saxe, J.B., Stata, R.: Extended static checking for Java. In: PLDI, vol. 37, pp. 234–245. ACM Press, New York (2002)
8. Guttag, J.V., Horning, J.J.: Larch: Languages and Tools for Formal Specification. Texts and Monographs in Computer Science. Springer, Heidelberg (1993)
9. Hamilton, N., Nickson, R., Traynor, O., Utting, M.: Interpretation and instantiation of theories for reasoning about formal specifications. In: ACSC, Australian Computer Science Communications 19, pp. 37–45 (1997)
10. Jones, C.B.: Systematic software development using VDM. Prentice Hall, Englewood Cliffs (1986)
11. Leavens, G.T., Cheon, Y., Clifton, C., Ruby, C., Cok, D.R.: How the design of JML accommodates both runtime assertion checking and formal verification. Science of Computer Programming 55(1-3), 185–205 (2005)
12. Leavens, G.T., Leino, K.R.M., Müller, P.: Specification and verification challenges for sequential object-oriented programs. Formal Aspects of Computing 19(2), 159–189 (2007)
13. Leavens, G.T., Baker, A.L., Ruby, C.: JML: A notation for detailed design. In: Behavioral Specifications of Businesses and Systems, pp. 175–188. Kluwer Academic Publishers, Dordrecht (1999)
14. Levy, B.: An Approach to Compiler Correctness Using Interpretation Between Theories. Ph.D. thesis, University of California, Los Angeles (1986)
15. Maibaum, T.S.E., Veloso, P.A.S., Sadler, M.R.: A theory of abstract data types for program development: bridging the gap? In: Nivat, M., Floyd, C., Thatcher, J., Ehrig, H. (eds.) CAAP 1985 and TAPSOFT 1985. LNCS, vol. 185, pp. 214–230. Springer, Heidelberg (1985)
16. Marché, C.: Towards modular algebraic specifications for pointer programs: a case study. In: Comon-Lundh, H., Kirchner, C., Kirchner, H. (eds.) Jouannaud Festschrift. LNCS, vol. 4600, pp. 235–258. Springer, Heidelberg (2007)
17. Meyer, B.: Eiffel: The Language. Prentice Hall, Englewood Cliffs (1992)
18. Nipkow, T., Paulson, L.C., Wenzel, M.T. (eds.): Isabelle/HOL. LNCS, vol. 2283. Springer, Heidelberg (2002)
19. Object Constraint Language, OMG Available Specification, Version 2.0 (2006), http://www.omg.org/docs/formal/06-05-01.pdf
20. Owre, S., Shankar, N.: A brief overview of PVS. In: Mohamed, O.A., Muñoz, C., Tahar, S. (eds.) TPHOLs 2008. LNCS, vol. 5170, pp. 22–27. Springer, Heidelberg (2008)
21. Schoeller, B., Widmer, T., Meyer, B.: Making specifications complete through models. In: Reussner, R., Stafford, J.A., Szyperski, C. (eds.) Architecting Systems with Trustworthy Components. LNCS, vol. 3938, pp. 48–70. Springer, Heidelberg (2006)
22. Shoenfield, J.R.: Mathematical Logic. Addison-Wesley, Reading (1967)
23. Srinivas, Y.V., Jüllig, R.: Specware: Formal support for composing software. In: Mathematics of Program Construction, pp. 399–422. Springer, Heidelberg (1995)
24. Turski, W.M., Maibaum, T.S.E.: The Specification of Computer Programs. Addison-Wesley, Reading (1987)

Automatic Cross Validation of Multiple Specifications: A Case Study*

Carlo Ghezzi, Andrea Mocci, and Guido Salvaneschi

Politecnico di Milano
DeepSE Group, Dipartimento di Elettronica e Informazione
p.za Leonardo da Vinci 32, 20133 Milano (MI) Italy
{ghezzi,mocci,salvaneschi}@elet.polimi.it

Abstract. The problem of formal software specification has been addressed and discussed since the infancy of software engineering. However, among all the proposed solutions, none is universally accepted yet. Many different formal descriptions can in fact be given for the same software component; thus, the problem of determining the consistency relation among those descriptions becomes relevant and potentially critical. In this work, we propose a method for comparing two specific kinds of formal specifications of containers. In particular, we check the consistency of intensional behavior models with algebraic specifications. The consistency check is performed by generating a behavioral equivalence model from the intensional model, converting the algebraic axioms into temporal logic formulae, and then checking them against the model by using the NuSMV model checker. An automated software tool which encodes the problem as model checking has been implemented to check the consistency of recovered specifications of relevant Java classes.

1 Introduction and Motivations

Given a software component, its *specification* is a description of its functionality, guaranteed by its provider, upon which clients can rely [1]. Although the problem of formally and precisely specifying software has been discussed through all the history of software engineering, none of the proposed solutions has been universally accepted yet. For almost every specification methodology, it is possible to distinguish between a *syntactic part*, which describes the component's signature, and a *semantic part*, which describes the behavior of the component in terms of visible effects for the clients. The difficult problems are in the semantic part.

Different descriptions can in fact be given for the same software component. A possible classification of specifications distinguishes between *operational* and *descriptive* specifications [2]. An operational specification describes the desired behavior by providing a model implementation of the system, for example by using abstract automata. Examples of operational specifications are state machine models (e.g. [3]). Another different specification style is through descriptive

---

* This research has been partially funded by the European Commission, Programme IDEAS-ERC, Project 227977-SMScom.

D.S. Rosenblum and G. Taentzer (Eds.): FASE 2010, LNCS 6013, pp. 233–247, 2010.

specifications, which are used to state the desired properties of a software component by using a declarative language, for example by using logic formulae. Examples of such notations are *JML* [4] or *algebraic specifications* [5]. Different specification styles (and languages) may differ in their expressiveness and very often their use depends on the preference and taste of the specifier, the availability of support tools, etc. Moreover, sometimes different specifications for the same piece of software are provided to describe different viewpoints. Living with multiple specifications of the same entity, however, can be dangerous. In particular, a question naturally arises about their *consistency* or even their *equivalence*. Intuitively, let us consider two specifications A and B. We say that A is consistent with B if all the behaviors specified by A are also specified by B. The equivalence problem can be stated as mutual consistency, that is, we consider A and B equivalent if and only if A is consistent with B and vice-versa. In general, it is not possible to formally state a precise definition of consistency without instantiating the specific formalisms used to express A and B. Another relevant problem of software specification is that its production might be as expensive as coding. This difficulty is why specifications are often partial, given informally, or they are completely absent. To address this issue, recent research [6, 7, 8] has proposed several techniques for automatic recovery.

This paper casts the general problem of automatically comparing two formal specifications of stateful components into two instance specification languages. It proposes an automated methodology to check *algebraic specifications* against *intensional behavior models* [9] by using symbolic model checking [10]. For both specification techniques, inference methods and tools are available: algebraic specifications can be recovered with a tool named HEUREKA [8] and intensional behavior models can be inferred by our recent work SPY [7]. However, the possibility to extract the specifications is not essential to the proposed approach; it will be used only to leverage an empirical evaluation of the contribution based on recovered specifications. Even if the specification comparison methodology is not restricted to any particular kind of software components, the specifications styles are particularly suitable for classes implementing containers. For this reason, we will consider containers as the case study entities for which we apply our specification consistency method. Containers are rather complex abstract data types, implemented by components with infinite states. For instance, consider a set of strings. Let strings be defined over a finite alphabet I; their cardinality is $|I^*| = |\mathbb{N}|$. If we now consider containers implementing sets of strings in I^*, their cardinality is $|\wp(\mathbb{N})|$. Thus, when dealing with containers, we are possibly dealing with components with a number of states which may be non-denumerable. To avoid intrinsic unmanageable complexity, in this paper we address the problem of specification consistency with a specific limitation. We do not aim at finding a proof of consistency of two specifications, which may require complex formalisms and would hardly be automated. Instead, we cast the problem by providing an automatic way of comparing the behavioral information prescribed by the specifications under a finite subset of the behaviors of the component, and we guarantee that under that limit the specifications are either consistent or not. Intuitively, the proposed approach instantiates an intensional behavior model as a finite state machine (a *BEM*, *Behavioral Equivalence Model*), whose states represent behaviorally equivalent classes of component instances, and algebraic specifications are finitized and translated into temporal logic formulae. Algebraic specifications play the role of properties to be verified against a limited and partial model of the component. This approach has been implemented and extensively tested; in particular, we verified the consistency of specifications recovered from relevant number of classes coming from the JAVA library.

A justification for the analysis of such complex specifications by instantiating them to finite models can be found in the so-called *small scope hypothesis* [11]. This hypothesis is fundamental when dealing with large state spaces; intuitively, it states that *most bugs have small counterexamples*. Within our context, the hypothesis can be formulated as follows: if the specifications are not consistent, a counterexample which shows the inconsistency is likely to be found in small and partial models of the specifications. Conversely, if the analysis does not show any counterexample, in theory we cannot conclude anything about their consistency, but in practice it is *very unlikely* that the two specifications are inconsistent.

This paper is organized as follows. Section 2 illustrates algebraic specifications and intensional behavior models and details the problem of comparing those two specification techniques. Section 3 describes the proposed approach for checking algebraic specifications against intensional behavior models. Section 4 provides empirical evaluation of the methodology. Section 5 discusses related work in the state of the art. Finally, Section 6 outlines conclusions and future work.

2   Specifying Containers

This section illustrates two different techniques, intensional behavior models and algebraic specifications, that can be used to specify the behavior of stateful components. Both techniques focus on software components implementing containers. Such components are designed according to the principle of *information hiding*, that is, clients cannot access the data structures internal to the component, but they must interact with it by using a set of methods which define the *interface* of the component. To illustrate the two specification techniques, we refer to the *Deque* container, which is inspired by the *ArrayDeque* class of the JAVA library. Essentially, the class is a double-ended queue, that is, a queue that also supports LIFO removal through the *pop* operation. Figure 1 illustrates the interface of this data abstraction when strings are used as contained objects.

```
public class Deque {
    public Deque() { .. } public void push(String elem) { .. }
    public String pop() { .. } public String deq() { .. }
    public Integer size() { .. }
}
```

Fig. 1. The public interface of *Deque*

sorts : $Deque, String, Boolean, Integer$
operations :
$deque$: $\rightarrow Deque$
$push$: $Deque \times String \rightarrow Deque$; $size$: $Deque \rightarrow Integer$
$deq.state$: $Deque \rightarrow Deque$; $deq.retval$: $Deque \rightarrow String \cup \{Exception\}$
$pop.state$: $Deque \rightarrow Deque$; $pop.retval$: $Deque \rightarrow String \cup \{Exception\}$
axioms : $\forall x \in Deque \; e, f \in String$
$\quad\quad pop.state(push(x,e)) = x; pop.retval(push(x,e)) = e$
$\quad\quad pop.state(Deque()) = Deque(); pop.retval(Deque(), e) \rightsquigarrow Exception$
$\quad\quad deq.state(push(push(x,e),f)) = push(deq(push(x,e)),f)$
$\quad\quad deq.state(push(Deque(),e)) = Deque()$
$\quad\quad deq.state(Deque()) = Deque(); deq.retval(push(Deque(),e)) = e$
$\quad\quad deq.retval(push(push(x,e),f)) = deq.retval(push(x,e))$
$\quad\quad deq.retval(Deque()) \rightsquigarrow Exception$
$\quad\quad size(Deque()) = 0; size(push(x,e)) = size(x) + 1$

Fig. 2. An algebraic specification of the Deque data abstraction

According to the classification scheme of [1], a method can be a *constructor*, an *observer* or a *modifier*. A constructor is a method that produces a new instance of the class. An observer is a method that returns a values expressing some information about the internal state of the object (e.g., the size of a container), while a modifier is a method that changes the internal state of the object. In practice, a method can play both roles of observer and modifier. It is therefore useful to distinguish between *impure* and *pure* observers; that is, observers that modify the internal state or not, respectively. In the case of the *Deque* data abstraction on Fig. 1, the method *Deque()* is a constructor; method *size()* is a pure observer, method *push(String)* is a modifier and methods *pop()* and *deq()* are both observers and modifiers.

Section 2.1 briefly introduces algebraic specifications, while Section 2.2 illustrates intensional behavior models. Thus, we proceed to introduce how those models can be compared.

2.1   Algebraic Specifications

Algebraic specifications (*ASs*), initially investigated in [5], are nowadays supported by a variety of languages, such as [12]. ASs model a component's hidden state implicitly by specifying axioms on sequences of operations. An algebraic specification $\Sigma = (\Pi, E)$ is composed of two parts: the *signature* Π and the *set of axioms* E. Formally, a signature $\Pi = (\alpha, \Xi, F)$ is a tuple where α is the sort to be defined by the specification, Ξ is the set of the external sorts, and F is a set of functional symbols f_i, describing the signatures of operations. Each functional symbol has a *type*, that is, a tuple $t \in (\{\alpha\} \cup \Xi)^+$. The length n_t of each t specifies the arity of the functional symbol; the first $n_t - 1$ elements specify the domain of the functional symbol while the last element denotes its range; we denote each functional symbol as $f_i : \xi_1, \ldots, \xi_{n_t-1} \rightarrow \xi_{n_t}$ (where $\xi_i \in (\{\alpha\} \cup \Xi)$)

to clearly distinguish domain and range. Each axiom is a universally quantified formula expressing an equality among terms in the algebra. Fig. 2 shows the AS for our illustrating example, the *Deque* described in Fig. 1. The notation used in this specification explicitly manages the case of impure observers by using two different implicitly defined operations, one for the returned value (e.g., the *pop.retval* operation) and one for the sort to be defined (e.g., the *pop.state* operation). Moreover, we model exceptions as particular values of the codomain of observers. In the case of impure observer, we specify the exception as a particular returned value and we state that its occurrence does not modify the internal state. For example, see the definition of the impure observer *pop* in Figure 2.

In this paper, we consider a particular class of ASs, called *linear specifications*. An algebraic specification is linear when its signature is linear. A signature defining a sort α is *linear* if the following conditions hold: (i) there is exactly one constant $f :\to \alpha$; (ii) Every non-costant function is in the form $f : \alpha, \xi_2, \ldots, \xi_{n_t-1} \to \xi_{n_t}$, with $\xi_{i<n_t} \in \varXi$ and $\xi_{n_t} \in (\{\alpha\} \cup \varXi)$. For simplicity, we also require axioms to not include hidden functions and conditional axioms. The set of axioms defines the properties that the specified data abstraction should exhibit. Formally, the concept of *algebra* is used to assign semantics to signatures and specifications. An algebra is composed of a set, the *carrier set* of the algebra, and a family of functions on that set. An algebra A is a $\varPi$-algebra, that is, it satisfies the signature $\varPi$, if it gives an interpretation of the sorts and the functional symbols in the signature. Moreover, an algebra A is also a $\varSigma$-*Algebra*, that is, it satisfies the whole specification $\varSigma$, if A gives an interpretation of the signature $\varPi$ which also satisfies the set of axioms. The actual semantics prescribed by the set of axioms depends on the semantics given by the equality relation of them. Given a possible implementation of the data abstraction adhering to a specification $\varSigma$, which is by definition a $\varSigma$-algebra, the equality relation expressed with the set of axioms can be interpreted as a specification of which sets of instances are in the same *abstract state* [1]. Different definitions of this concept exist in the literature. The most commonly used is based on the concept of *behavioral equivalence* [13]. Given two objects o_1 and o_2 instances of a class C, o_1 and o_2 are *behaviorally equivalent* if for any sequence of operations t of C ending with an observer, the objects $o_1.t$ and $o_2.t$ obtained by invoking t are themselves behaviorally equivalent. For observers returning primitive types, they are behaviorally equivalent if their values are the same.

HEUREKA [8] is a tool for recovering ASs for JAVA classes. HEUREKA leverages on the concept of behavioral equivalence to infer which sequence of method invocations produce instances that are likely to be behaviorally equivalent. Thus, the equations produced by this step are generalized into likely algebraic axioms.

2.2   Intensional Behavior Models

Another possible way to specify the behavior of stateful components is by using *behavior models*. Essentially, a behavior model is a finite state automaton where each state is labeled with observer return values and each transition represents a modifier invocation. *Behavioral equivalence models (*BEM*)* [7] are particular

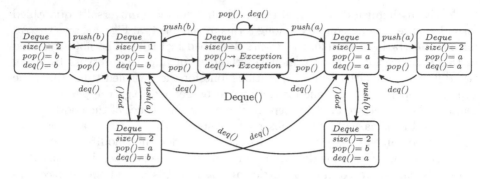

Fig. 3. A BEM of the Deque container

kind of behavior models, where each state represents a set of behaviorally equivalent instances of a data abstraction. A BEM is defined by choosing a finite set of actual parameters for each method. Figure 3 shows a possible BEM for the *ArrayDeque* data abstraction when *a* and *b* are used as actual parameters for the *push* method. Thus, each transition modeling the behavior of the *push* method is labeled with either *push(a)* or *push(b)*. Each state is labeled with observer return values. Obviously, a finite state machine cannot describe every possible behavior of the *Deque* data abstraction, even if we limit the inserted elements to two possible strings. For example, the BEM of Figure 3 models the behavior of the data abstraction only up to size 2.

To overcome this limitation, we proposed *intensional behavior models* [9], and a corresponding recovery technique, called SPY [7]. The key idea is to intensionally describe every possible BEM of the data abstraction. Since BEMs are finite-state automata, they can be viewed as graphs, with nodes labeled with observer return values. *Attributed graph transformation systems (GTS)* [14] can be used to intensionally describe the generation of a set of attributed graphs. In this way, we can specify how to generate all possible BEMs corresponding to all possible instances of the container class of interest.

A GTS is composed of a set of rules, as in a classic Chomsky grammar. In a GTS, rules describe how a graph is modified by their application. Each rule is described by three graphs, the *negative application condition (NAC)*, the *left hand side graph (LHS)*, and the *right hand side graph (RHS)*, and a set of attribute conditions *AC*. Figure 4 describes the intensional behavior model of the *Deque* data abstraction. A rule can be applied when the following conditions hold for a source graph. The *LHS* describes which topological conditions must be matched by a subgraph of the source graph to make the rule applicable. The application of the rule replaces such subgraph with the subraph described by the *RHS*. *NAC*s express conditions that must not be matched for the rule to be applied. Both *LHS* and *NAC* nodes and arcs are labeled with variables on the domain of attributes. The *AC* set is composed of binary predicates on variables defined on the *LHS* attribute variables.

For example, Figure 4(a) describes the rule for the constructor of the *Deque* data abstraction. Consider an initial empty graph. The *LHS* of the constructor

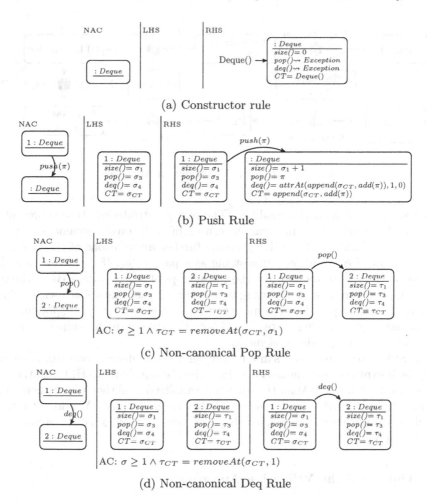

Fig. 4. Deque Intensional Behavior Model

rule is trivially matched because the graph is empty and the *LHS* is empty, and the *NAC* is not matched since the empty graph does not contain any *Deque* node. Thus, the constructor rule is applicable. The *RHS* graph describes how the matching subgraph must be modified if the rule is applied; in the case of the constructor rule, it introduces an initial *Deque* node representing the empty deque. As for the *push* rule of Figure 4(b), note that integer numbers are used to establish a correspondence between nodels of *LHS* and *RHS*. If the applicability conditions are verified, the rule transforms the source graph into a new graph. The resulting graph is built by replacing the *LHS* subgraph with *RHS*. Numbered nodes in the *LHS* are replaced by identically numbered nodes in *RHS*. Attributes are modified according to functions labeling nodes in the *RHS*. Referring to the *push* rule in Figure 4(b), the application of *RHS* adds a new state representing the state obtained after a *push* application, and a

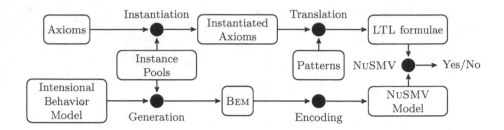

Fig. 5. Outline of the Validation Approach

transition labeled with the modifier. The newly introduced state represents a new set of behaviorally equivalent instances built through sequences of applications of operations. The *NAC* prevents further applications of the *push* rule with the same *LHS* and the same string as a parameter. If we have two String objects on the graph representing the instance pool to generate a BEM, the rule can be applied two times, generating two states representing a stack with a single element. It is then possible to apply the rule in Figure 4(d), corresponding to a *pop* method, by matching states 1 and 3 of the rule with the empty stack and the stack containing a single element.

The SPY [7] tool implements intensional behavior model recovery from dynamic analysis. It exploits the same notion of behavioral equivalence as HEUREKA. It first starts by recovering a BEM for the class to be analized, and then tries to generalize its transitions by recovering intensional behavior model rules. We do not include details on the recovery approach in this paper; the reader who is interested in more details can refer to [7].

2.3 Outline of the Validation Approach

We now provide an intuitive description of the foundations of the proposed validation approach. The aim of the proposed method is to validate an AS against an intensional behavior model, both modeling the behavior of a container. Figure 5 describes a workflow of the proposed approach through its constituent steps. In an ideal world, given a specification Σ and an intensional behavior model I, it would be desirable to check that the (possibly *infinite*-state) BEM generated by I satisfies the specification Σ, that is, the set of states, together with the transition function and the state labelling are a Σ-algebra. However, we already emphasized that containers have a state space that may be infinite, and in general not even denumerable, as in the case of the *Deque* data abstraction over the set of all possible strings on a finite alphabet.

We therefore limit the analysis as follows. First, we require the analyzer to provide interpretations of the external sorts in the ASs; we require that those sorts, together with the operations among them, have a finite carrier set. Those external sorts define the so-called *instance pools*, that is, the set of actual parameters for methods, that are used to generate a BEM from the intensional behavior model. As already stated, limiting the instance pools to be finite does not imply that the container has a finite number of states; for this reason, we also limit the rule application to generate a finite-state BEM. In this case, verifying the consistency of the specification Σ to such a finite-state model, boils down to verifying that the algebra determined by those limitations is a Σ-algebra. Since we want to verify that the algebra determined by the BEM is a Σ-algebra, we must precisely interpret the symbols of the specification with the mathematical definition of the BEM. Let us consider a linear specification $\Sigma = (\Pi, E)$. A BEM over the same signature Π is a tuple $\mathcal{B}_\Pi = \langle Q, I, \delta, q_0, \Psi \rangle$, composed of a set of states Q, an initial state q_0, an input set I, a transition function δ, and a set Ψ of state labelling functions representing observer return values. The input set of the BEM is the set of instantiated modifiers $I = \bar{\mathcal{M}}_\Pi$. Moreover, the set Ψ is composed as follows: for every observer functional symbol $f_o : \alpha, \xi_1, \ldots, \xi_{n_t-1} \to \xi_{n_t} \in F$, there is a $\Psi_{f_o} : Q \times \bar{\mathcal{O}}_\Pi \to \xi_{n_t}$, which is a state labelling function representing return values for the set of instantiated observers $\bar{\mathcal{O}}_\Pi$.

The sets of instantiated modifiers $\bar{\mathcal{M}}_\Pi$ and observers $\bar{\mathcal{O}}_\Pi$ are defined as follows. Let us consider the provided instance pools, $IP(\xi_i)$, for each external sort $\xi_i \in \Xi$. Thus, the sets of instantiated modifiers and observer return values are defined as tuples whose first element is the functional symbol and the other elements are elements from the instance pools. For a given modifier $f_m : \alpha, \xi_1, \ldots, \xi_{n_t-1} \to \alpha \in F$, the possible invocations of the modifier with the specified instance pools are: $\bar{\mathcal{M}}_{f_m} = \{\langle f_m, e_1, \ldots, e_{n_t} \rangle | e_i \subset IP(\xi_i)\}$. As of the push method, the instantiated modifiers with $IP(String) = \{a, b\}$, are $\langle push, a \rangle$ and $\langle push, b \rangle$. The whole set of possible modifier invocations, that is, the input set of the BEM, is the union of the instantiated modifiers for each modifier: $\bar{\mathcal{M}}_\Pi = \bigcup_{f_m} \bar{\mathcal{M}}_{f_m}$. Similarly, we define instantiated observer set $\bar{\mathcal{O}}_{f_o}$ for a given observer f_o and the whole set of possible observer invocations $\bar{\mathcal{O}}_\Pi$. We are now ready to define $A(\mathcal{B}_\Pi)$, that is, the Π-algebra over the BEM:

- The carrier sets for each external sort $\xi_i \in \Xi$ are the instance pools $IP(\xi_i)$;
- The carrier set for the defined sort α is the set of states Q;
- For each functional symbol $f \in F$ of the signature Π, we defined the interpretation $f^{A(\mathcal{B}_\Pi)}$ as follows:
  - Since Π is linear, there is only one constructor f_c, for which $f_c^{A(\mathcal{B}_\Pi)} = q_0$;
  - For every modifier $f_m : \alpha, \xi_1, \ldots, \xi_{n_t-1} \to \alpha \in F$, $f_m^{A(\mathcal{B}_\Pi)} = \delta|_{I \in \bar{\mathcal{M}}_{f_m}}$;
  - For every observer $f_o : \alpha, \xi_1, \ldots, \xi_{n_t-1} \to \xi_{n_t} \in F$, $f_o^{A(\mathcal{B}_\Pi)}(q, e_1, \ldots e_{n_t-1}) = \Psi_{f_o}(q, \langle e_1, \ldots e_{n_t-1} \rangle)$.

At this point, the core of our approach relies on validating the axioms of the specification Σ over the BEM Π-algebra $A(\mathcal{B}_\Pi)$. Given the interpretations provided by the BEM Π-algebra, axioms can be rewritten accordingly, and they become simple properties of the transition and labeling function of the BEM. Let us consider the simple BEM on Figure 3, and consider the following axiom: $\forall s \in Deque, e \in String : pop(push(s, e)).state = s$. With the chosen instance pools and the given interpretation, the axiom becomes: $\forall s \in Q, e \in IP(String) : \delta(\delta(s, \langle push, e \rangle), \langle pop \rangle) = s$. Since $IP(String)$ is finite, the axiom can be instantiated for every external sort: $\forall s \in Q, \delta(\delta(s, \langle push, a \rangle), \langle pop \rangle) = s \wedge \delta(\delta(s, \langle push, b \rangle), \langle pop \rangle) = s$.

The last step is the precise definition of the validity of axioms in our model. The only quantified values in this case can be elements of the specified sort, that is, states of the BEM. Theoretically, it would be possible to verify directly those axioms by proving that for every possible valuation of variables in the model. However, since the BEM is finite, the interpreted functions might be partial, and thus most of the axioms could be not verified just because the model is finite. Instead, we would like to verify that in all the cases on which the interpreted functions are defined on the BEM, the axioms hold. For example, the axiom above cannot hold in any finite BEM of the *Deque*, since there does not exist a finite BEM where the *push* operation is defined in every state. Thus, our problem reduces to verifying the axioms in all the valuations of the variables for which the transition function δ is defined, and we consider the axiom holding precisely in these cases. Fortunately, an explicit management of this problem can be avoided by a proper encoding of the BEM, which will be clear in the following section.

3   Validating Axioms through Model Checking

In the previous section, consistency of an algebraic specification with an intensional behavior model has been reduced to determining if the axioms of an algebraic specification Σ are verified in the BEM Π-algebra $A(\mathcal{B}_\Pi)$. Axioms can be interpreted as properties of the transition relation δ and the observer labeling functions Ψ_{f_o}. In this section, we will show how this problem can be reduced to checking temporal logic formulae derived from the algebraic axioms, as they are interpreted in the BEM Π-algebra $A(\mathcal{B}_\Pi)$, against a Kripke structure derived by the BEM. To prove this, we encode the BEM as a Kripke structure and the property over the infinite traces as an LTL formula. The approach is realized in two steps, which correspond to the structure of this section:

1. *Formal* BEM *encoding:* the BEM is encoded into a Kripke structure;
2. *Axiom rewriting:* algebraic axioms are translated into temporal formulae expressed in LTL, by following certain translation patterns.

Formal Bem Encoding. A BEM is encoded into a Kripke structure which can be directly used to generate an equivalent model in the input language of the NuSMV model checker. A Kripke structure is similar to a nondeterministic finite state automaton, where each state is labeled with a set of atomic propositional formulae Φ. Formally, the Kripke structure is composed of a *Frame* $\mathcal{F}$ and an evaluation function V. The frame is a tuple $\mathcal{F} = \langle S, S_0, \mathcal{R} \rangle$, where S is a set of states, $S_0 \subseteq S$ are the inital states of the frame, and $\mathcal{R} \subseteq S \times S$ is the reachability relation between states. The evaluation function $V : \Phi \to \wp(S)$ essentially defines which atomic formulae are true in which states. In fact, for each formula $\phi \in \Phi$, $V(\phi)$ is the set of states where ϕ is true. Our encoding of a BEM as a Kripke structure prescribes that each state of the frame corresponds to a state of the BEM together with an operation, that is, to a pair $\langle q, i \rangle$ with

$q \in Q \wedge i \in I$. Formally, the set $\mathcal{S}$ of states of the frame is defined as $\mathcal{S} = \{\langle q, i \rangle : q \in Q \wedge i \in I \wedge \exists q' \in Q : \delta(q, i) = q'\}$; the set of initial states is defined as $S_0 = \{\langle q, i \rangle : \langle q, i \rangle \in S \wedge q = q_0\}$. In other words, each state on the frame models a state of the BEM where an existing transition, corresponding to a given modifier, is enabled. Thus, we encode the reachability relation as follows: $\langle q, i \rangle \mathcal{R} \langle q', i' \rangle \Leftrightarrow \delta(q, i) = q'$. This encoding is a classic way to translate a deterministic transition-labeled automaton into a Kripke structure where non-determinism models the possible operation choice. Practically, from each state of the frame, the next reachable states always represent the state reached by applying a given transition on the BEM, but they differ with respect to the next possibly enabled operation.

In almost any existing model checker, the frame is defined by means of some temporal logic axioms or some operational constructs, whose semantics implicitly defines the structure of the frame, that is, its states and its reachability relation. Thus, the encoding is based on the direct use of the set of atomic formulae Φ and axioms based on them. We can split the set of atomic formulae Φ in three different sets to encode the Kripke structure defined above:

- Φ_S, the set of atomic formulae representing states of the BEM;
- Φ_I, the set of atomic formulae representing enabled transitions;
- Φ_O, the set of atomic formulae representing observer return values.

Φ_S has the same cardinality as the set of states Q of the BEM. It contains a set of mutually exclusive propositions, each being true iff the current state of the frame models a given state of the BEM. If we define a representation bijection $\mu_S : \Phi_S \rightarrow Q$, then $\forall \phi_S \in \Phi_S : V(\phi_S) = \{\langle \mu_S(\phi_S), i \rangle \in \mathcal{S}\}$. The same encoding is applied to transitions (i.e., instantiated modifiers). That is, if we define a representation bijection $\mu_I : \Phi_I \rightarrow I$, then the evaluation function V is defined as follows: $\forall \phi_I \in \Phi_I : V(\phi_I) = \{\langle q, \mu_I(\phi_I) \rangle \in \mathcal{S}\}$. Finally, we must encode observer return values with ad-hoc propositional formulae. Consider any observed pair of instantiated observer and return value present in the BEM: $\langle \bar{o}, e_{n_t} \rangle$, such that $\bar{o} \in \bar{\mathcal{O}}_{f_o} \wedge \exists q \in Q : \Psi_{f_o}(q, \bar{o}) = e_{n_t}$. For any of these pairs, we define a specific propositional formula, defined by a representation bijection μ_O. Then, $\forall \phi_O \in \Phi_O : \mu_O(\phi_O) = \langle \bar{o}, e_{n_t} \rangle \Rightarrow V(\phi_O) = \{\langle q, i \rangle \in \mathcal{S} : \Psi_{f_o}(q, \bar{o}) = e_{n_t}\}$. In practice, we encode each observer - return value pair in the BEM as an atomic formula in the Kripke structure. At this point, we have defined every possible atomic formula used in the encoding of the BEM. As stated above, we need to encode the frame structure described previously as a set of axioms. For space reasons, we omit the actual encoding; the reader can find them in [15].

Rewriting Axioms as LTL Formulae. To explain the rationale behind the translation of algebraic axioms into LTL formulae, consider the axiom $\forall x \in Deque, e \in String : pop.state(push(x, e)) = x$ and its equivalent property on the δ function derived by interpreting the BEM: $\forall s \in Q, e \in IP(String) : \delta(\delta(s, \langle push, e \rangle), \langle pop \rangle) = s$. Consider all the possible infinite traces of the BEM, that is, all the ω-words defined in the alphabet $\bar{\mathcal{M}}_\Pi$, and the generalized transition function $\delta^* : Q \times \bar{\mathcal{M}}_\Pi^* \rightarrow Q$. Suppose that the axiom above holds in the model. Given any infinite trace $x \in \bar{\mathcal{M}}_{\Pi}^{\omega}$, if the axiom holds, then for every finite prefix $\bar{x}$ of x such that $\bar{x} = \bar{x}_0 \langle push, a \rangle \langle pop \rangle$ or $\bar{x} = \bar{x}_0 \langle push, b \rangle \langle pop \rangle$, then the state reached by the sequence of operations $\bar{x}_0$ is the same as the one reached by $\bar{x}$, that is, $\delta^*(q_0, \bar{x}_0) = \delta^*(q_0, \bar{x})$. In practice, the traces we are interested in all the ones generated by the transitions where the δ function of the BEM has been defined. The encoding we defined above guarantees that the traces generated by the Kripke structure are exactly those. Each state of the frame encodes both the current state of the BEM, that is, a formula in Φ_S, and the current operation applied, that is, a formula in Φ_I, together with formulae encoding the current return values of observers. Thus, a property about the traces of the BEM model like the one we defined for the axiom above, can be written as an LTL formula. In the case above, the corresponding LTL formula is: $\forall \phi_S \in \Phi_S : G(\phi_S \wedge \mu_I(\langle push, a \rangle) \wedge X(\mu_I(\langle pop \rangle)) \Rightarrow X^2 \phi_S) \wedge G(\phi_S \wedge \mu_I(\langle push, b \rangle) \wedge X(\mu_I(\langle pop \rangle)) \Rightarrow X^2 \phi_S)$. A pattern for axioms in this form is the the following:

Pattern 1. *Any axiom in the following form:* $\forall x \in \alpha : m_j(\ldots m_1(m_0(x)) \ldots) = x$ *where* $m_i, n_i \in \bar{\mathcal{M}}_{\Pi}$, *is translated to the following LTL formula:* $\forall \phi_s \in \Phi_S :$ $G(\phi_s \wedge \mu_I^{-1}(m_0) \wedge X(\mu_I^{-1}(m_1)) \wedge \ldots \wedge X^j(\mu_I^{-1}(m_j)) \Rightarrow X^{j+1} \phi_s)$

Please note that a formal proof of the correspondence expressed by this pattern cannot be included for space limitations. However, the reader can find proofs in [15]. We identified several patterns for translating algebraic axioms to LTL formulae, based on the approach described above, but for space reasons we are not able to show all the patterns.

4   Evaluation

Both the NUSMV encoding of the BEM and the algebraic axiom translation have been implemented as a software tool. We now proceed to empirically evaluate the performance of the encoding and model checking as prescribed by the proposed approach. In Section 1, we illustrated one of the possible applications of our validation approach in the context of specification recovery. In this paper, we proposed a solution to an instance of the general problem of automatic comparison of recovered formal specifications of containers, that is, the problem of checking algebraic specifications against intensional behavior models. Moreover, the tools and the extracted specifications are particularly suitable for classes implementing containers. Thus, an empirical assessment may compare algebraic specifications and intensional behavior models as recovered from the respective extraction tools, for relevant containers such as the ones implemented in the JAVA library. We selected a set of container classes implemented in the *java.util* package of the JAVA library, and extracted both algebraic specifications with HEUREKA and the intensional behavior models with SPY. We report here two different evaluation experiments. For both the experiments, we generated a random set of instance pools to instantiate the algebraic axioms and generate a BEM of the class to be analyzed. In the first experiment, we used the same set

Table 1. Empirical Results

Class		Experiment I				Experiment II			
		Axioms		Performance		Axioms		Performance	
		Ver.	Not Ver.	Time (mm:ss)	Mem. (MB)	Ver.	Not Ver.	Time (mm:ss)	Mem. (MB)
ArrayDeque	Exh.	20	0	00:04.30	63.68	10	3	00:04.30	52.4
32 states	BMC	1	0	00:11.4	74.40	0	1	00:01.12	44.40
PriorityQueue	Exh.	13	0	00:03.50	30.01	7	4	00:02.10	23.01
37 states	BMC	1	0	00:14.40	57.92	0	0	–	–
Stack	Exh.	11	0	00:07.90	68.68	4	0	00:02.90	40.58
157 states	BMC	1	0	00:09.40	60.92	1	0	00:09.40	60.92
TreeMap	Exh.	21	0	07:06.00	274.87	12	6	04:06.00	204.87
64 states	BMC	1	0	01:00.20	269.26	0	0	–	–
TreeSet	Exh.	23	0	03:05.20	69.64	13	7	01:35.20	49.64
33 states	BMC	3	0	41:42.50	511.12	1	0	12:21.53	317.14

of test cases as inference basis for both the extraction methods. The inference basis was manually checked to be relevant in the sense that it included all the interesting behaviors of the component; the testing approach was similar to the simpler one used to assess the SPY method [7]. The rationale behind this choice is that we expect the two specifications to be coherent. Instead, the second experiment uses on purpose two different inference bases. We choose to use the same inference basis of the first experiment for the intensional model, and instead use a smaller inference basis for HEUREKA. The smaller inference basis has been chosen to not include some behaviors of the component. We expect that some of the recovered algebraic axioms could be wrong; thus, some of the properties expressed by these axioms should not be verified by the model checker. The reason for this choice is simply to verify that our approach is able to detect inconsistency behind recovered specifications. Table 1 shows empirical results of the validation approach for both the experiments. The first column include the name of the checked class and immediately below the number of states of the generated BEM. The second column contains the number of axioms that have been checked, showing verified and not verified axioms. The last two columns include the total time and memory needed for the verification. The experiments have been performed in a Intel® Core Duo™ machine at 2.16 Ghz with 2 Gb of RAM. In the general case, we tried to verify each axiom with the exhaustive search, based on BDDs [10]. For each class, the first row of the table illustrates the empirical results for axioms for which the exhaustive verification was possible under reasonable amounts of time (i.e., within an hour of execution time). In some cases, expecially with patterns involving two sequences of operations, exhaustive search could be too expensive in terms of execution time and memory consumption, up to unfeasibility with the used resources. For such axioms, we used the *Bounded Model Checking (BMC)* [16] feature of NuSMV, based on SAT solving techniques. Essentially, BMC limits the search up to a given depth. Results of the first experiment on Table 1 show that every axiom has been verified in the intensional behavior model, that is, that the specification recovered by HEUREKA does not contradict the model inferred by SPY. Instead, the results of the second experiment show that some of the axioms were not verified, and thus our approach is able to detect inconsistencies between algebraic specifications and intensional behavior models.

5   Related Work

This paper proposed a methodology to cross-validate intensional behavior models and algebraic specifications by using model checking. The use of model checking is justified because it is inherently a methodology for cross-validation of specifications. In fact, model checking consists in general in the problem of checking if an operational description satisfies a set of properties expressed in temporal logic. Both the operational description and the temporal logic properties can be considered as specifications, and the process of model checking can be seen as a method to validate their consistency. In particular, a recent advance [17] introduces *multi-valued model checking*, which explicitly manages situations like uncertainty and inconsistency. Other related works come from the algebraic specification community; for example, HETCASL [18] is a framework for the formal analysis of heterogeneous algebraic specifications by means of theorem proving. Several related state-of-the-art techniques come from requirements engineering community, that is, from methodologies involving discovery and management of inconsistent requirements within the context of multiple viewpoints or requirement-related artifacts. A recent advance [19] proposed goal model checking over operational descriptions derived from scenarios. Finally, some relevant related works include techniques for model comparison to support software evolution analysis, such as [20]. However, those techniques are used to compare the same software artifacts during their evolution, and not to compare different software artifacts.

6   Conclusions

We illustrated a method for comparing specifications of classes implementing containers by using model checking. In particular, we proposed a model-checking based technique to check the consistency of intensional behavior models against algebraic specifications. In fact, the former can be used to generate a particular finite-state model, the behavioral equivalence model, while the latter plays the role of a set of properties to be verified. To perform model checking, we provided a formal encoding of the BEM as a Kripke structure and a practical encoding in the source code of the NuSMV model checker. Moreover, we identified a comprehensive set of patterns to translate algebraic specifications to LTL formulae. We showed that it is possible to check algebraic specifications against intensional behavior models in reasonable amounts of time and occupied memory.

References

1. Guttag, J.V., Liskov, B.: Program Development in Java: Abstraction, Specification and Object-Oriented Design. Addison-Wesley, Reading (2001)
2. Ghezzi, C., Jazayeri, M., Mandrioli, D.: Fundamentals of Software Engineering. Prentice Hall PTR, Upper Saddle River (2002)
3. Harel, D., Gery, E.: Executable object modeling with statecharts. In: ICSE 1996: 18th International Conference on Software Engineering (1996)
4. Leavens, G.T., Baker, A.L., Ruby, C.: JML: A notation for detailed design. In: Behavioral Specifications of Businesses and Systems, pp. 175–188. Kluwer, Dordrecht (1999)
5. Guttag, J.V., Horning, J.J.: The algebraic specification of abstract data types. Acta Informatica 10(1) (1978)
6. Ernst, M.D.: Dynamically Discovering Likely Program Invariants. Ph.D. thesis, University of Washington, Seattle, Washington (August 2000)
7. Ghezzi, C., Mocci, A., Monga, M.: Synthesizing intensional behavior models by graph transformation. In: ICSE 2009: Proc. of 31st Int. Conf. on Soft. Eng. (2009)
8. Henkel, J., Reichenbach, C., Diwan, A.: Discovering documentation for Java container classes. IEEE Trans. Software Eng. 33(8), 526–543 (2007)
9. Baresi, L., Ghezzi, C., Mocci, A., Monga, M.: Using graph transformation systems to specify and verify data abstractions. In: Proc. of GT-VMT 2008 (2008)
10. Burch, J.R., Clarke, E.M., McMillan, K.L., Dill, D.L., Hwang, L.J.: Symbolic model checking: 10^{20} states and beyond. Inf. Comput. 98(2)
11. Jackson, D.: Software Abstractions: Logic, Language, and Analysis. MIT Press, Cambridge (2006)
12. Mosses, P.D. (ed.): CASL Reference Manual. LNCS (IFIP Series), vol. 2960. Springer, Heidelberg (2004)
13. Doong, R., Frankl, P.G.: The ASTOOT approach to testing object-oriented programs. ACM Trans. on Soft. Eng. and Meth. 3(2) (1994)
14. Ehrig, H., Ehrig, K., Prange, U., Taentzer, G.: Fundamentals of Algebraic Graph Transformation. EATCS Monographs in TCS. Springer, Heidelberg (2005)
15. Spy Checker Website (2009), http://home.dei.polimi.it/mocci/spy/check/
16. Biere, A., Cimatti, A., Clarke, E., Zhu, Y.: Symbolic model checking without BDDs. In: Cleaveland, W.R. (ed.) TACAS 1999. LNCS, vol. 1579, pp. 193–207. Springer, Heidelberg (1999)
17. Chechik, M., Devereux, B., Easterbrook, S., Gurfinkel, A.: Multi-valued symbolic model-checking. ACM Tr. Softw. Eng. Methodol. 12(4) (2003)
18. Mossakowski, T., Maeder, C., Lüttich, K.: The heterogeneous tool set, hets. In: Grumberg, O., Huth, M. (eds.) TACAS 2007. LNCS, vol. 4424, pp. 519–522. Springer, Heidelberg (2007)
19. Uchitel, S., Chatley, R., Kramer, J., Magee, J.: Goal and scenario validation: a fluent combination. Requir. Eng. 11(2), 123–137 (2006)
20. Ivkovic, I., Kontogiannis, K.: Tracing evolution changes of software artifacts through model synchronization. In: ICSM 2004. IEEE Computer Society, Los Alamitos (2004)

An Automata-Theoretic Approach to Hardware/Software Co-verification

Juncao Li[1], Fei Xie[1], Thomas Ball[2], Vladimir Levin[2], and Con McGarvey[2]

[1] Department of Computer Science, Portland State University
Portland, OR 97207, USA
{juncao,xie}@cs.pdx.edu
[2] Microsoft Corporation
Redmond, WA 98052, USA
{tball,vladlev,conmc}@microsoft.com

Abstract. In this paper, we present an automata-theoretic approach to Hardware/ Software (HW/SW) co-verification. We designed a co-specification framework describing HW/SW systems; synthesized a hybrid Büchi Automaton Pushdown System model for co-verification, namely Büchi Pushdown System (BPDS), from the co-specification; and built a software tool for deciding reachability of BPDS models. Using our approach, we succeeded in co-verifying the Windows driver and the hardware model of the PIO-24 digital I/O card, finding a previously undiscovered software bug. In addition, our experiments have shown that our co-verification approach performs well in terms of time and memory usages.

1 Introduction

Computer systems are pervasive, ranging from embedded control to banking to education. Users demand high-confidence in these systems, and high-confidence is traditionally achieved by extensive testing which is becoming increasingly cost-prohibitive. As a result, formal verification such as model checking [1] is playing a greater role in verifying the correctness of these systems. In practice, engineers typically attempt to verify hardware and software independently. In order to verify complete systems, the correctness of the Hardware/Software (HW/SW) interfaces must be established.

HW/SW co-verification, verifying hardware and software together, is essential to establishing the correctness of HW/SW interfaces. One major challenge in co-verification is the integration of hardware and software representations within the same formal model. Hardware and software verification utilize different models. For verification of software implementations, one of the most popular models has been pushdown systems whose semantics closely resemble the semantics of software programs which are often infinite systems. Hardware designs are finite-state and often modeled as some kind of finite-state state machines. However, for co-verification it is not desired to model both hardware and software as pushdown systems or finite state machines (see related work).

In this paper, we present an automata-theoretic approach to HW/SW co-verification. The foundation of this approach is a hybrid Büchi Automaton Pushdown System as a unifying model for HW/SW co-verification, namely the Büchi Pushdown System (BPDS). It synchronizes a single Pushdown System (PDS) that has an unbounded stack

D.S. Rosenblum and G. Taentzer (Eds.): FASE 2010, LNCS 6013, pp. 248–262, 2010.

and a Büchi Automaton (BA). The co-verification flow as supported by this approach is shown in Figure 1. The main components of this flow include:

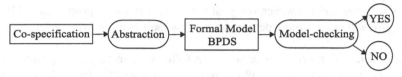

Fig. 1. Co-verification flow

- *Co-specification.* Co-specification is essential in order to present system designs at proper levels of details. We developed a co-specification framework that describes the hardware model, the software model, and the HW/SW interface.
- *Co-verification model.* We designed a formal co-verification model, BPDS, to capture hardware and software designs, as well as their concurrent executions and interactions. The core contribution is our process for constructing a BPDS by synchronizing a BA that abstracts hardware and a PDS that abstracts software.
- *Model-checking BPDS.* We developed a method for checking reachability properties of a BPDS and analyzed its complexities. To evaluate the effectiveness of our approach, we implemented an automatic verification tool for BPDS.

Another component of this flow is abstraction, which we will elaborate in another paper.

Related work. Kurshan, et al. presented a co-verification framework that models hardware and software designs using finite state machines [2]. Xie, et al. extended this framework to hardware and software implementations and improves its scalability via component-based co-verification [3]. However, finite state machines are limited in modeling software implementations, since they are not suitable to represent software features such as a stack.

Another approach to integrating hardware and software within the same model is exemplified by Monniaux in [4]. He modeled a USB Open Host Controller Interface (OHCI) device using a C program and instrumented the device driver, another C program, in such a way as to verify that the USB OHCI controller driver correctly interacts with the device. The hardware and software were both modeled by C programs, thus formally Pushdown Systems (PDS). However, straightforward composition of the two PDSs to model the HW/SW concurrency is problematic, because it is known, in general, that verification of reachability properties on concurrent PDS with unbounded stacks is undecidable [5]. Based on an approximation of the OHCI HW/SW interface, Monniaux merges the C program models of both hardware and software into one sequential program, formally a single PDS. Monniaux's approach has three key drawbacks: (1) programming languages such as C do not have semantics for concurrency, so the concurrent nature of hardware is not fully modeled; (2) the HW/SW concurrency is not accurately modeled; (3) the complexity of checking the resulting PDS is often unnecessarily high, due to the way hardware and concurrency is modeled in the PDS.

Schwoon used a combination of PDS and BA to verify Linear Temporal Logic (LTL) properties of PDS and his approach has been implemented in the Moped tool [6]. A LTL formula is first negated and then represented as a BA. Moped combines the BA and PDS in such a way that the BA monitors the state transitions of the PDS, so the model-checking problem is to compute if the BA has an accepting run. Schwoon's goal was to verify software only; however, our goal is to co-verify safety properties of HW/SW systems. We will discuss more details about Schwoon's work in Section 3.1.

Outline. The rest of this paper is organized as follows. In Section 2, we present our co-specification framework, which is illustrated by a Windows PCI device driver example. In Section 3, we introduce our co-verification model, BPDS. In Section 4, we describe how to construct a BPDS by synchronizing a BA and a PDS. In Section 5, we discuss how to conduct reachability analysis on a BPDS. In Section 6, we present the evaluation and experimental results. In Section 7, we conclude and discuss future work.

2   Co-specification

Co-specification describes the HW/SW system to be verified. The essential parts include the hardware model, the software model, and the HW/SW interface. The level of detail varies due to (1) platform differences, e.g., embedded system or PC; (2) verification foci, e.g., verifying software by providing hardware models, verifying hardware using software models, or verifying both. As an example, we show how to specify the HW/SW interface for the verification of a device driver implementation and its device model. The goal of this specification is to verify if the driver implementation is correct in terms of the HW/SW interface properties. In order to facilitate the understanding of our modeling approach, we first introduce a simple Windows PCI driver example.

2.1   A Windows PCI Driver Example

Device drivers check device status or send commands to devices by reading or writing device registers, and receive notification of state changes from devices through interrupts. In Windows [7], device drivers are organized through driver stacks. Each layer of a driver stack services a specific type of device in the corresponding hardware stack. Usually, different driver layers have different I/O interfaces. In this paper, we utilize PCI (Peripheral Component Interconnect) device drivers as an example. PCI drivers read/write device registers using functions such as READ_REGISTER_UCHAR, WRITE_REGISTER_UCHAR, READ_PORT_UCHAR, WRITE_PORT_UCHAR, etc. Depending on whether a driver uses memory or port mapped I/O to represent its device interface registers in virtual memory, the functions are different.

Figure 2 shows excerpts from an Open System Resources (OSR) sample driver for a PCI device, Sealevel PIO-24 digital I/O card. The card has three 8-bit ports (namely, A, B, and C) for input or output. When the interrupt is enabled and Port A has an input, the card fires a data-ready interrupt. The driver reads data when the data-ready interrupt fires and outputs data by writing to the port registers. DioEvtDeviceControl is the callback function that handles device control commands and DioIsr is the Interrupt Service Routine (ISR).

```
VOID DioEvtDeviceControl( ... ) {

  switch(IoControlCode) {

  // Waits for an interrupt to occur, and when it does,
  // ISR/DPC will read the contents of PortA.
  case IOCTL_WDFDIO_READ_PORTA_AFTER_INT:

  // If PortAInput is true, the interrupt is enabled
  if (devContext->PortAInput == FALSE) {
    status = STATUS_INVALID_DEVICE_STATE;
  } else {
    // Store the I/O request to CurrentRequest
    devContext->CurrentRequest = Request;

    // Tell ISR: we're waiting for an interrupt
P1:   devContext->AwaitingInt = TRUE;
    ...
    return;
  }
  break;
  ...
  }
  ...
}
```

```
BOOLEAN DioIsr( ... ) {

  // Check if we have an interrupt pending
  data = READ_REGISTER_UCHAR(
      devContext->BaseAddress +
          DIO_INTSTATUS_OFFSET );
  if(data & DIO_INTSTATUS_PENDING) {

    // Are we waiting for this interrupt
P2:   if(devContext->AwaitingInt) {
      // Read the contents of PortA
      data = READ_REGISTER_UCHAR(
          devContext->BaseAddress +
              DIO_PORTA_OFFSET );
      // Store it in our device context
      // DPC will send the data to users
      devContext->PortAValueAtInt = data;
      devContext->AwaitingInt = FALSE;
    }

    // Request our DPC
P3:   WdfInterruptQueueDpcForIsr( Interrupt );
    // Tell WDF, and hence Windows, this is our interrupt
    return(TRUE);
  }
  return(FALSE);
}
```

Fig. 2. Excerpts from OSR sample driver code for PIO-24 digital I/O card

2.2 Language Features for Co-specification

In our example, the C program of the driver is the software model. Next, we focus on the hardware model and the HW/SW interface.

We specify the hardware model and hardware-related parts of the HW/SW interface using the Verilog hardware description language [8]. There are two major reasons behind using Verilog for models related to hardware. First, Verilog is a popular language for hardware design. Lots of existing hardware has been designed using Verilog. Second, Verilog supports the concurrent semantics of hardware. A key feature is parallel assignments (a.k.a. nonblocking assignments that use the operator "<=" in the examples), which capture the simultaneous updates of register states through state transitions.

The **hardware model** describes behaviors of the device as state transitions. Different from the commonly used clock-driven semantics of Verilog, a state transition of our hardware model represents an arbitrarily long but finite sequence of clock cycles. This preserves hardware design logic that is externally visible to software, but hides details only necessary for synthesizable Register Transfer Level (RTL) design. Figure 3 shows the hardware model of the PIO-24 digital I/O card. The model simply fires an interrupt when it is in an interrupt-enabled state and Port A has an input. We define rand as a function that returns a non-deterministic value in the given range. There are three tasks: reset, environment, and random. The environment task is executed non-deterministically to simulate inputs from the environment to the device, e.g., the physical *reset* event that clears all registers. Depending on the properties to be verified, hardware models may be extended to exhibit more behaviors. Our model in Figure 3 has been simplified to one aspect of the device to illustrate the device/driver interactions.

```
begin hardware model                              ...
  // declare registers                            Ctrl <= rand(8'h0, 8'hFF) & 8'h9B;
  reg [7:0] PortA, IntConfg;                       IntConfg <= rand(8'h0, 8'h07);
  ...                                              IntStatus <= rand(8'h0, 8'h01);
  // declare the tasks                           end endtask
  task reset; begin // clears all registers
    PortA <= 8'h0;                                // initial state of the device: non-deterministically initialized
  ...                                             initial random;
  end endtask                                     // non-deterministically execute the environment
  // model the inputs from the environment        if( rand(0,1) ) begin
  task environment; begin                           // low level triggers the interrupt
    // non-deterministically reset the hardware      if( (IntConfg == 8'h04) && ((PortA & 8'h01)==0) )
    if(rand(0,1)) reset;                             begin
    // if the interrupt is enabled but not fired,      IntStatus <= 1; // set the interrupt status
    // non-deterministically input to PortA.            INTR <= 1; // set the interrupt pending status to SW
    else if((IntConfg & 8'h4) && (IntStatus==0))     end
        PortA <= rand(8'h0, 8'hFF);                  // high level triggers the interrupt
                                                     if( (IntConfg == 8'h05) && ((PortA & 8'h01)==1) )
  end endtask                                        begin IntStatus <= 1;   INTR <= 1; end
  ...                                                ...
  // assign non-deterministic value to registers   end
  task random; begin                              else environment;
    PortA <= rand(8'h0, 8'hFF);               end hardware model
```

Fig. 3. Hardware model for PIO-24 digital I/O card device

The **interface specification** describes the HW/SW interface. Hardware and software run asynchronously and only communicate through their interface. The HW/SW interface includes two parts: shared interface states and interface events. Interface states are state variables provided either by hardware or software and accessible to both; interface events have two types: hardware or software. A hardware interface event happens when hardware updates the software interface states, and vice versa. A typical example of hardware interface events is an interrupt which causes context switches in software. However, it is possible that in a HW/SW system, software provides shared memory for hardware to access. In this case, a hardware interface event (e.g., write to the shared memory) will not cause any context switch in software. In summary, interface events identify the situations when both software and hardware must transit synchronously.

Modern system designs usually have software and hardware aligned as layers in a stack, different layers of software work with their corresponding layers of hardware together to deliver certain functionalities. For example, PCI bus and USB bus are different HW/SW layers in a PC system. Interface specification needs to describe the HW/SW interface behaviors in order to hide the implementation details of other hardware and software layers that lie in between the hardware and software layers to be verified.

For the PIO-24 digital I/O device/driver, the device provides interface registers for the driver to operate the device. In order for the driver to access the interface registers, the Windows OS maps the device interface registers into virtual memory through a technique called Memory Mapped I/O (MMIO). When the driver writes to/reads from a mapped memory address by calling register operation functions, the corresponding interface register will be updated by the OS. How the register should be updated depends on the HW/SW interface protocol. We need to specify (1) the virtual memory alignment for the mapped interface registers, so a specific memory address is related to the proper interface register; (2) how interface registers should be updated when the driver accesses the registers, i.e., when software interface events happens. On the other side, the device communicates with the driver through interrupts, i.e., hardware interface events. When hardware fires an interrupt, the Windows OS sets its internal interrupt pending status to be true and schedules the driver-provided ISR to service the interrupt.

Figure 4 shows the HW/SW interface specification for the PIO-24 digital I/O device/driver: (1) resource mappings for the driver. The PIO-24 device is mapped as MMIO. The resource mapping type indicates the set of interface register functions used by the driver; (2) interface declaration, which declares the device interface registers with their sizes and mapped address offsets in virtual memory, software interface events when the driver writes/reads a specific interface register, and hardware interface events when hardware fires interrupts; (3) implementation of software interface events. Each interface register is associated with two software interface event functions: read and write. The functions describe device interface state transitions when read/write events happen on the registers. Hardware interface events are defined by connecting the interrupts to the corresponding ISRs that are implemented in the driver model.

```
begin interface
  // resource mappings: Memory Mapped I/O
  use MMIO;

  // interface declaration
  // syntax: <offset(byte), length(byte)> -->
  //           name, read_event, write_event;
  <0x00, 1> --> PortA, read_PortA(), write_PortA(VAR);
  ...
  <0x04, 1> --> IntConfg, read_IntConfg(),
                write_IntConfg(VAR);
  <0x05, 1> --> IntStatus, read_IntStatus(),
                write_IntStatus(VAR);
  interrupt INTR: // interrupt pending status
    void FireISR(); // the ISR connected to this interrupt
```

```
// implementation of software interface events
write_IntConfg(val) {
  if( ((val==4) && (PortA & 8'h1)!=0) ||
      ((val==5) && (PortA & 8'h1)==0) ||
      (val==6) || (val==7) || (val==0) )
    IntConfg <= val;
}
read_IntStatus() { // clear the interrupt status when read
  reg [7:0] retreg;
  retreg <= IntStatus;
  IntStatus <= 0;
  return retreg; // return the register value to software
}
...
end interface
```

Fig. 4. Interface specification for PIO-24 digital I/O card device/driver

3 Co-verification Model: Büchi Pushdown System

We propose a hybrid Büchi Automaton Pushdown System, namely Büchi Pushdown System (BPDS) to represent both hardware and software in co-verification. Before we present BPDS, we first review the fundamentals of Büchi Automata (BA) and Pushdown Systems (PDS).

3.1 Background

Büchi Automata as Hardware Models. A **Büchi Automaton** $\mathcal{B}$, as defined in [9], is a non-deterministic finite state automaton accepting infinite input strings. Formally, $\mathcal{B}$ is a tuple $(\Sigma, Q, \delta, q_0, F)$, where Σ is the input alphabet, Q is the finite set of states, $\delta \subseteq (Q \times \Sigma \times Q)$ is the set of state transitions, $q_0 \in Q$ is the initial state, and $F \subseteq Q$ is the set of final states. $\mathcal{B}$ accepts an infinite input string if and only if it has a run over the string to visit at least one of the final states infinitely often. A run of $\mathcal{B}$ on an infinite string s is a sequence of states visited by $\mathcal{B}$ when taking s as the input. We use $q \xrightarrow{\sigma} q'$ to denote a transition from state q to q' with the input symbol σ.

Pushdown Systems as Software Models. A **Pushdown System**, as defined in [6], is a tuple $\mathcal{P} = (G, \Gamma, \Delta, \langle g_0, \omega_0 \rangle)$ where G is a finite set of global states (a.k.a. control locations), Γ is a finite stack alphabet, and $\Delta \subseteq (G \times \Gamma) \times (G \times \Gamma^*)$ is a finite set of transition rules. $\langle g_0, \omega_0 \rangle$ is the initial configuration. A PDS transition rule is written as $\langle g, \gamma \rangle \hookrightarrow \langle g', \omega \rangle$, where $((g, \gamma), (g', \omega)) \in \Delta$. A configuration of $\mathcal{P}$ is a pair $\langle g, \omega \rangle$, where $g \in G$ is a global state and $w \in \Gamma^*$ is a stack content. The set of all configurations is denoted by $Conf(\mathcal{P})$. If $\langle g, \gamma \rangle \hookrightarrow \langle g', \omega \rangle$, then for every $v \in \Gamma^*$ the configuration $\langle g, \gamma v \rangle$ is an immediate predecessor of $\langle g', \omega v \rangle$ and $\langle g', \omega v \rangle$ is an immediate successor of $\langle g, \gamma v \rangle$. The reachability relation $\Rightarrow$ is the reflexive and transitive closure of the immediate successor relation. Given a set $C \subseteq Conf(\mathcal{P})$, the forward reachability analysis, $post^*(C)$, computes the successors of elements of C. Schwoon [6] has designed algorithms to check both reachability and LTL properties on PDS. For computing $post^*$ on $\mathcal{P}$, the time and space complexities are both $(|G| + |\Delta|)^3$. The Moped tool implements all these algorithms.

3.2 Büchi Pushdown System

We synthesize a BPDS $\mathcal{BP}$ by building the synchronization of a BA $\mathcal{B}$ and a PDS $\mathcal{P}$. Let $\mathcal{B} = (\Sigma, Q, \delta, q_0, F)$ represent hardware, where Σ is the power set of the set of propositions that may hold on a configuration of $\mathcal{P}$ (i.e. a symbol of Σ is a set of propositions). In other words, the state transition of $\mathcal{B}$ is constrained by the current configuration of $\mathcal{P}$. We extend the definition of a pushdown system as $\mathcal{P} = (I, G, \Gamma, \Delta, \langle g_0, \omega_0 \rangle)$ representing software, where I is the power set of the set of propositions that may hold on a state of $\mathcal{B}$, G is a finite set of global states, Γ is a finite stack alphabet, and $\Delta \subseteq (G \times \Gamma) \times I \times (G \times \Gamma^*)$ is a finite set of transition rules. We write $\langle g, \gamma \rangle \xrightarrow{\tau} \langle g', w \rangle$ as a rule $((g, \gamma), \tau, (g', w)) \in \Delta$. $\langle g_0, w_0 \rangle$ is the initial configuration. It is important to note that we extend the pushdown system so that the transition rules in Δ are all labeled by $\tau \in I$, i.e., the state transition of $\mathcal{P}$ is constrained by the current state of $\mathcal{B}$.

To define the BPDS, $\mathcal{BP}$, for co-verification, we first define two labeling functions:

- $L_{\mathcal{P}2\mathcal{B}} : (G \times \Gamma) \to \Sigma$, which associates a configuration of $\mathcal{P}$, $\langle g, \gamma \rangle \in (G \times \Gamma)$, with the set of propositions that hold on it.
- $L_{\mathcal{B}2\mathcal{P}} : Q \to I$, which associates a state of $\mathcal{B}$ with the set of propositions that hold on it.

$\mathcal{BP} = ((G \times Q), \Gamma, \Delta', \langle (g_0, q_0), w_0 \rangle, F')$ is constructed by taking the Cartesian product of $\mathcal{B}$ and $\mathcal{P}$: $\langle (g, q), \gamma \rangle \hookrightarrow_{\mathcal{BP}} \langle (g', q'), \omega \rangle \in \Delta'$, where $q \xrightarrow{\sigma} q' \in \delta, \sigma \subseteq L_{\mathcal{P}2\mathcal{B}}(\langle g, \gamma \rangle)$ and $\langle g, \gamma \rangle \xrightarrow{\tau} \langle g', w \rangle \in \Delta, \tau \subseteq L_{\mathcal{B}2\mathcal{P}}(q)$. A configuration of $\mathcal{BP}$ is referred to as $\langle (g, q), \omega \rangle \in (G \times Q) \times \Gamma^*$. The set of all configurations is denoted as $Conf(\mathcal{BP})$. The labeling functions defines how $\mathcal{B}$ and $\mathcal{P}$ synchronize with each other. $\langle (g_0, q_0), w_0 \rangle$ is the initial configuration. $\langle (g, q), \omega \rangle \in F'$ if $q \in F$.

If $\langle (g, q), \gamma \rangle \hookrightarrow_{\mathcal{BP}} \langle (g', q'), \omega \rangle \in \Delta'$, then for every $v \in \Gamma^*$ the configuration $\langle (g, q), \gamma v \rangle$ is an immediate predecessor of $\langle (g', q'), \omega v \rangle$, and $\langle (g', q'), \omega v \rangle$ is an immediate successor of $\langle (g,q), \gamma v \rangle$. A trace of $\mathcal{BP}$ is a sequence of configurations $\langle (g_0, q_0), \omega_0 \rangle, \langle (g_1, q_1), \omega_1 \rangle, \ldots, \langle (g_i, q_i), \omega_i \rangle, \ldots$ such that $\langle (g_i, q_i), \omega_i \rangle$ is an immediate predecessor of $\langle (g_{i+1}, q_{i+1}), \omega_{i+1} \rangle$, where $i \geq 0$. The reachability relation, $\Rightarrow_{\mathcal{BP}}$, is the reflexive and transitive closure of the immediate successor relation. Given a set $C \subseteq Conf(\mathcal{BP})$, the forward reachability analysis, $post^*(C)$, computes the successors of elements of C. In this paper, we are concerned with the reachability properties of $\mathcal{BP}$, i.e., given a configuration c and the initial configuration $c_0 = \langle (g_0, q_0), \omega_0 \rangle$, we want to check if $c \in post^*(\{c_0\})$.

4 Constructing BPDS from Co-specification

In this section, we discuss how to construct a BPDS model from the co-specification presented in Section 2. We assume that the hardware and software models in the co-specification are amenable to abstraction into BA and PDS. Without loss of generality, we describe the state space of the BPDS model using Boolean variables. Before we discuss how to construct the BPDS model, we introduce two tools for conducting predicate abstractions of hardware and software, respectively. The predicate abstraction tools help scale the verification but only preserve the safety properties of a system design, so we restrict the generated BPDS model for reachability analysis. It is important to note that (1) this approach is only one example on constructing BPDS and (2) the BPDS model proposed in Section 3 is not restricted to safety properties only.

4.1 Background

Predicate Abstraction of RTL Designs. Jain, et al. have presented a predicate abstraction algorithm for verifying RTL designs in Verilog [10]. The algorithm computes the abstraction of a Verilog module given certain predicates. The VCEGAR toolkit based on this algorithm generates hardware abstractions in the form of Boolean expressions (see example in Figure 6). This is one representation of state transition relations.

Predicate Abstraction of C Programs. Ball, et al. have shown Boolean programs to be effective abstractions of C programs in the SLAM project [11]. A Boolean program, conceptually a PDS, is essentially a C program in which the only data type available is Boolean. Given predicates, C2BP, the abstraction tool of SLAM, builds Boolean programs from C programs.

4.2 From Co-specification to BPDS

There are four steps to construct a BPDS model from the co-specification: (1) instrumenting the software model based on the HW/SW interface; (2) predicate abstraction of the instrumented software model using C2BP based on manually provided predicates; (3) instrumenting the hardware model based on the HW/SW interface; (4) predicate abstraction of the instrumented hardware model using VCEGAR based on manually provided predicates. The PDS (as a result of C2BP) and the BA (as a result of VCEGAR) are readily synchronized due to the instrumentation, thus forming a BPDS model.

```
UCHAR READ_REGISTER_UCHAR                   VOID WRITE_REGISTER_UCHAR
      (PUCHAR Register) {                         (PUCHAR Register, UCHAR Value) {
switch(Register) {                          switch(Register) {
  case BASE_ADDRESS+0x0: return read_PortA();   case BASE_ADDRESS+0x0: write_PortA(Value); return;
  ...                                           ...
  case BASE_ADDRESS+0x4: return read_IntConfg();  case BASE_ADDRESS+0x4: write_IntConfg(Value); return;
  case BASE_ADDRESS+0x5: return read_IntStatus();  case BASE_ADDRESS+0x5: write_IntStatus(Value); return;
  default: abort "Register address error."; return 0;  default: abort "Register address error."; return;
  }                                             }
}                                           }
```

Fig. 5. Redirecting read/write register calls to software interface events

At the software side, the instrumentation has three steps. First, we add the signatures of the software interface events into the driver program. Since the header of a software interface event is declared the same way as a C function, the signature of the interface event is simply its type signature. Second, we instrument the driver program to redirect the calls to the register read/write functions to the corresponding software interface events. Third, we instrument the driver to respond to the hardware interface events. Figure 5 shows an example instrumenting the PIO-24 digital I/O card driver, where the calls to two register read/write functions are replaced by calls to software interface events. As discussed in Section 2.2, the OS maintains a variable (*INTR* in the interface specification example) to indicate the interrupt pending status. When hardware fires an interrupt, i.e., a hardware interface event happens, the interrupt pending status is set true, so the OS schedules the ISR. We instrument the driver with a guarded expression at each program statement so that "if the interrupt pending status is true, non-deterministically call ISR". As a result, the context switch to ISR is simulated in the sequential software model. In a uni-processor system, the completeness of this approach is based on the assumption that the ISR cannot be switched out during execution. This is true for most Windows device drivers such as the PIO-24 digital I/O card driver. It is easy and theoretically sound to extend the instrumentation to support multiple ISRs with different priorities, because the number of ISRs in a system are finite. In the last step of software abstraction, we use C2BP to generate Boolean programs from the instrumented C programs. We convert the Boolean programs to PDS using Moped [6].

At the hardware side, we first convert the hardware model and the implementation of software interface events into Verilog modules. The non-deterministic function (rand) used in Figure 3 is not directly supported by Verilog. Since input variables of Verilog modules are treated as non-deterministic by VCEGAR, we construct non-deterministic functions using input variables. Second, we utilize VCEGAR to generate the predicate abstraction of the state transition relation for the hardware design (in the form of Verilog modules). Third, we then construct the BA as follows: (1) the alphabet Σ is the power set of the set of propositions induced by the software interface events; (2) the set of states Q are defined by the Boolean variables from the predicate abstraction; (3) the transition relation δ is the predicate abstraction, whose transitions are labeled with input symbols from Σ; (4) the set of final states F is set to Q, since we are interested in reachability only. As an example, Figure 6 shows the abstraction of the software interface events read_IntStatus and write_IntConfg, as hardware state transitions.

```
// predicates for read_IntStatus              // predicates for write_IntConfg
decl b0; // stands for {IntStatus == 1}       decl b0; // stands for {(4 & IntConfg) == 0}
decl b1; // stands for {retreg==1}            decl b1; // stands for {(1 & PortA) == 0}
                                              decl b2; // stands for {val == 5}

read_IntStatus
begin                                         write_IntConfg
   TRANS ( !next(b0) )                        begin
   TRANS ( (!b0 & !next(b1))                     TRANS ( (!b1 & b0 & b2 & next(b0))  |  (b1 & b0 & b2 & !next(b0))
          |  (b0 & next(b1)) )                        |  (!b0 & b2 & !next(b0))  |  (!b2) )
end                                           end
```

Fig. 6. Abstraction of software interface events as state transitions in the form of Boolean expressions (`TRANS`). The transitions are labeled corresponding to their software events respectively.

The constructed BPDS $\mathcal{BP}$ contains a PDS $\mathcal{P}$ representing software, a BA $\mathcal{B}$ representing hardware, and their synchronization, where $\mathcal{P}$ is from software abstraction, $\mathcal{B}$ is from hardware abstraction, and the synchronization by interface events is from the abstraction of the HW/SW interface (through instrumentation). The interface events have two directions, from $\mathcal{P}$ to $\mathcal{B}$ (referred to as software interface events) and from $\mathcal{B}$ to $\mathcal{P}$ (referred to as hardware interface events). In the formal model, the transitions of $\mathcal{B}$ are labeled corresponding to the software interface events and the transitions of $\mathcal{P}$ are labeled corresponding to the hardware interface events. Thus, we are able to synchronize $\mathcal{B}$ and $\mathcal{P}$. Before software abstraction, the signatures of software interface events are merged into the program, so $\mathcal{P}$ already contains the signatures. During the state transitions of $\mathcal{P}$, a software interface event happens when its dedicated stack symbol is reached. The BA transition that is enabled will be executed with the next PDS transition. The PDS transition also needs to be enabled by the current state of $\mathcal{B}$. For example, when $\mathcal{P}$ inputs from $\mathcal{B}$, the transition will depend on the state of $\mathcal{B}$. A hardware interface event happens when $\mathcal{B}$ transits to a state, which may cause a context switch in $\mathcal{P}$. Because $\mathcal{P}$ is a sequential PDS, we model the context switch by calling the function that services the hardware event, which is done during the step of software instrumentation.

Because the transitions of hardware and software are normally asynchronous except at their synchronization points, non-deterministic delays of either $\mathcal{B}$ or $\mathcal{P}$ should be allowed in the BPDS. Conceptually, the delays are introduced as self-loop transitions on the states of $\mathcal{B}$ or $\mathcal{P}$ where no interface event happens. When an interface event happens, both hardware and software have to transit synchronously.

5   Reachability Checking of BPDS

We have developed a tool, CoVer, for checking reachability properties of BPDS. As shown in Figure 7, CoVer has two components: (1) BPDS2PDS, which converts a BPDS model $\mathcal{BP}$ into a PDS model $\mathcal{P}'$; and (2) Moped [6], which checks reachability properties of $\mathcal{P}'$. Different from the PDS $\mathcal{P}$ in $\mathcal{BP}$, the new PDS model $\mathcal{P}'$ is a standard PDS in the sense that $\mathcal{P}'$ does not have inputs. The properties to be checked are provided to Moped through labeling states in the software PDS $\mathcal{P}$ and/or the hardware BA $\mathcal{B}$.

First, we present the conversion algorithm, BPDS2PDS, and argue that the conversion preserves the reachability properties of $\mathcal{BP}$. Second, we analyze the complexity of the conversion, the size of $\mathcal{P}'$ compared to $\mathcal{BP}$, and the verification complexity.

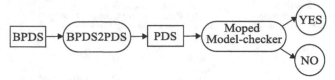

Fig. 7. CoVer: reachability checking of BPDS

5.1 Converting BPDS to PDS

The conversion works in such a way that the transition rules of $\mathcal{B}$ and $\mathcal{P}$ are selected and merged in $\mathcal{P}'$ depending on whether or not an interface event happens. We represent hardware transition rules as the union of two groups as $\delta = R_{model} \cup R_{evt}$. R_{model} is the set of rules that are not associated with software interface events. R_{evt} is the set of rules associated with software interface events. We define two functions: (1) $\mathrm{HW}_{evt}(\tau)$ checks if the transition label τ of a rule in $\mathcal{P}$ is true for a hardware interface event. If yes, this rule services the hardware interface event, for instance, calling the ISR; (2) $\mathrm{SW}_{evt}(\gamma)$ checks if γ is the stack symbol of a software interface event.

Algorithm 1 converts $\mathcal{BP}$ (given δ as rules of $\mathcal{B}$ and Δ as rules of $\mathcal{P}$) into a PDS $\mathcal{P}'$ with its rules as Δ'. Algorithm 1 explores the rules of $\mathcal{P}$ and $\mathcal{B}$ to build new PDS rules of $\mathcal{P}'$ based on the synchronization of $\mathcal{P}$ and $\mathcal{B}$. It terminates when all rules in δ and Δ are processed. For each transition rule in Δ, the algorithm has three choices: (1) if the transition handles a hardware interface event, the transition is merged with its corresponding transition in $\mathcal{B}$ to form a transition of $\mathcal{P}'$; (2) if it is a software interface event, the transition is merged with its corresponding transition in $\mathcal{B}$ as well. Hardware and software should always be synchronous on interface events; (3) when no interface event happens, the loop between lines 15-18 merges the transition of $\mathcal{P}$ with transitions of $\mathcal{B}$. Because hardware and software are asynchronous, the transition labels of $\mathcal{P}$ and

---

Algorithm 1. BPDS2PDS($\delta = R_{model} \cup R_{evt}, \Delta$)

1: $\Delta' \leftarrow \emptyset$
2: **for all** $\langle g, \gamma \rangle \xrightarrow{\tau} \langle g', \omega \rangle \in \Delta$ **do**
3:    **if** $\mathrm{HW}_{evt}(\tau)$ **then**
4:       {*If this PDS rule handles a hardware interface event*}
5:       **for all** $q \xrightarrow{\sigma} q' \in R_{model}$ **and** $\sigma \subseteq L_{\mathcal{P}2\mathcal{B}}(\langle g, \gamma \rangle)$ **and** $\tau \subseteq L_{\mathcal{B}2\mathcal{P}}(q)$ **do**
6:          $\Delta' \leftarrow \Delta' \bigcup \{\langle (g, q), \gamma \rangle \hookrightarrow \langle (g', q'), \omega \rangle\}$
7:       **end for**
8:    **else if** $\mathrm{SW}_{evt}(\gamma)$ **then**
9:       {*Else if this is a software interface event*}
10:       **for all** $q \xrightarrow{\sigma} q' \in R_{evt}$ **and** $\sigma \subseteq L_{\mathcal{P}2\mathcal{B}}(\langle g, \gamma \rangle)$ **and** $\tau \subseteq L_{\mathcal{B}2\mathcal{P}}(q)$ **do**
11:          $\Delta' \leftarrow \Delta' \bigcup \{\langle (g, q), \gamma \rangle \hookrightarrow \langle (g', q'), \omega \rangle\}$
12:       **end for**
13:    **else**
14:       {*For transitions with no interface event*}
15:       **for all** $q \xrightarrow{\sigma} q' \in R_{model}$ **do**
16:          $\Delta' \leftarrow \Delta' \bigcup \{\langle (g, q), \gamma \rangle \hookrightarrow \langle (g', q'), \gamma \rangle\}$
17:          $\Delta' \leftarrow \Delta' \bigcup \{\langle (g, q), \gamma \rangle \hookrightarrow \langle (g', q), \omega \rangle\}$
18:       **end for**
19:    **end if**
20: **end for**
21: **return** Δ'

$\mathcal{B}$ trivially hold on each other. There are four types of rules that can be generated for $\mathcal{P}'$ in the third condition: (1) $\mathcal{P}$ self-loops on its current state while $\mathcal{B}$ transits, which occurs in line 16; (2) $\mathcal{B}$ self-loops on its current state while $\mathcal{P}$ transits, which occurs in line 17; (3) Both $\mathcal{B}$ and $\mathcal{P}$ self-loop; (4) Both $\mathcal{B}$ and $\mathcal{P}$ transit. Rule (3) is trivial and can be eliminated. Rule (4) equals to consecutive transitions by Rules (1) and (2), because hardware and software execute asynchronously when no interface event happens.

$\mathcal{P}'$ **preserves the reachability property of** $\mathcal{BP}$. (1) The state space of $\mathcal{P}'$ equals to that of $\mathcal{BP}$; (2) The initial state of $\mathcal{P}'$ is the initial state of $\mathcal{BP}$; (3) We do not utilize the final states F' (the BA constraints) of $\mathcal{BP}$ in the reachability checking; (4) In Algorithm 1, it is clear that $\mathcal{P}'$ preserves all the transitions of both $\mathcal{B}$ and $\mathcal{P}$. Self-loop transitions are introduced for states of both $\mathcal{B}$ and $\mathcal{P}$ to model the asynchronous transitions between hardware and software. They do not affect the correctness of reachability checking.

5.2 Complexity Analysis

Algorithm 1 generates $O(|\Delta| \times |\delta|)$ PDS rules and has a time complexity of $O(|\Delta| \times |\delta|)$. The number of rules in $\mathcal{P}'$ is equal to the number of rules of $\mathcal{BP}$, because we add a rule to $\mathcal{P}'$ only if there is a corresponding rule in $\mathcal{BP}$. $\mathcal{P}'$ and $\mathcal{BP}$ have the same configurations because their state space is identical. We use Schwoon's $post^*$ algorithm [6] (implemented in Moped) to solve the reachability problems of $\mathcal{P}'$, so the time and space model-checking complexities on $\mathcal{P}'$ are $O((|G \times Q| + |\Delta \times \delta|)^3)$.

6 Evaluation

We first show an overall evaluation of our co-verification framework, where we succeeded in verifying the Windows driver and the hardware model of the PIO-24 digital I/O card, finding a previously undiscovered software bug – an "invalid read" bug. Then we discuss our experiments on evaluating the model-checking performance of our BPDS model. All experiments were run on a workstation with Intel Xeon 3GHz dual core CPU and 2GB physical memory.

For PIO-24, we abstract the hardware model (269 lines), the driver program (1724 lines), and the interface specification into a BPDS model. The verification detects a bug using 12 predicates and 4165 peak live Binary Decision Diagram (BDD) nodes in 0.02 seconds. The falsifying path that combines the execution of both hardware and software leads to a violation where a Deferred Procedure Call[1] (DPC) finishes the input request in success without actually reading the data from the device. As shown in Figure 2, the "invalid read" bug occurs when `DioIsr` interrupts `DioEvtDeviceControl` at P1, where `CurrentRequest` and `AwaitingInt` become inconsistent. `DioIsr` will not execute the `if` block at P2 because `AwaitingInt` is FALSE. Later the DPC is requested at P3. The DPC sends data back to the application that generated the I/O request if `CurrentRequest` is not null, but the data is never actually read from the device. It is important to note that this bug cannot be detected when using a sequential model because the inconsistency of variable states only happens in HW/SW concurrent

---

[1] We omit the DPC implementation due to page limitation.

executions, as represented in our approach. Furthermore, because our approach to co-verification includes both hardware and software models, certain kinds of false bugs will not appear. For example, if the device's status is always interrupt-disabled as the driver reaches P1, the above described "invalid read" bug cannot happen. On the other hand, the verification of this property costs one person about 6 hours' manual efforts to construct the BPDS model. In order to avoid this overhead, the abstraction/refinement process needs to be fully automated (see Section 7).

We present an evaluation of the BPDS model based on synthetic programs derived from the template T shown in Figure 8 and hardware models derived from the template H shown in Figure 9. T is similar to the evaluation template used in [12] and later in [6]. The difference is that T operates a hardware counter which has global state. The templates allow us to generate a Boolean program $T(N)$ and its corresponding hardware model $H(N)$ for $N > 0$. $T(N)$ and $H(N)$ together have four global variables[2], where there are three variables (a, b, and c) representing the states of the hardware counter. $T(N)$ has $2N + 2$ procedures including software interface events: main as program entry point, rd_reg as a software interface event that returns the value of the most significant bit of the counter, N software interface events of the form inc_reg<i>, and N procedures of the form level<i> that call rd_reg and inc_reg<i>, where $0 < i \leq N$. For $0 < j < N$, the instances of <stmt> in the body of procedure level<j> are replaced by a call to procedure level<j+1>. The instances of <stmt> in the body of procedure level<N> are replaced by skip. $H(N)$ provides hardware transitions corresponding to the N software interface events inc_reg<i>, where the transitions increase the hardware counter by one. To further increase the complexity of the model for purposes of testing, we define an environment model that non-deterministically left-shifts the hardware counter by one bit. Templates T and H cover common scenarios where software operates hardware via interface events.

We compare the two approaches that model hardware using BA or using PDS. When using PDS, we model both hardware and software using a sequential program, similar to Monniaux's approach [4]. We model the environment and interface events as procedures such as environment() and inc_reg<i>(). The procedure environment is called after each software interface event to simulate the input from environment.

Table 1 shows the statistics on the co-verification models generated from Figure 8 and Figure 9, where the counter's size varies from 3 to 5 bits (i.e., the number of Boolean variables used by the counter). We force the reachability checking to be exhaustive, so the results represent the worst case performance. Statistics show that the PDS hardware model adds significant overhead to co-verification compared to the BA hardware model. For example, when $N = 4000$ and the counter has 5-bit size, the PDS hardware model generates 148k transition rules and has 22383 peak live BDD nodes, compared to 76k transition rules and 2115 peak live BDD nodes for the BA hardware model.

Table 2 shows the statistics on the model when interrupt checking is enabled. Compared to the result in Table 1, we use one more global variable to track whether an interrupt has fired. Similar to the procedure environment(), the ISR (not shown) calls interface events to left-shift the counter by one bit. The statistics show that although the

---

[2] Actually, we use three groups of templates. They differ in the size of the counter. For a counter with 3, 4, or 5 bits, we have 4, 5, or 6 global variables.

```
// a, b, c represent        void level<i>()        bool rd_reg()         // Using PDS as hardware model
// the hardware counter     begin                  begin                 void inc_reg<i>()
decl g, a, b, c;              decl t;                 return c;           begin
void main()                   t := 0;              end                     if (!a) then
begin                         if(g) then                                       a := 1;
  level1();                     while(!t) do        // Büchi automaton        elsif (!b) then
  level1();                       inc_reg<i>();      // as hardware model        a,b := 0,1;
  if (!g) then                    t := rd_reg();    void inc_reg<i>()         elsif (!c) then
    reach: skip;                od                  begin                       a,b,c := 0,0,1;
  else                        else                    skip;                   else
    skip;                       <stmt>; <stmt>;     end                         a,b,c := 0,0,0;
  fi                          fi                                            fi
end                           g := !g;                                    end
                            end
```

Fig. 8. Boolean program template T for evaluating the BPDS model

```
decl a,b,c;

inc_reg<i>                                              // Run non-deterministically    // Using PDS as
begin                                                   environment                    // hardware model
  TRANS ( (!a & !b & !c & next(a) & !next(b) & !next(c)) begin                          bool environment()
       | (!a & !b & c & next(a) & !next(b) & next(c))      TRANS( (b & next(a)) |       begin
       | (!a & b & !c & next(a) & next(b) & !next(c))             (!b & !next(a)) )      10: if(*) then
       | (!a & b & c & next(a) & next(b) & next(c))       TRANS( (c & next(b)) |            a,b,c := b,c,0;
       | (a & !b & !c & !next(a) & next(b) & !next(c))            (!c & !next(b)) )         goto 10;
       | (a & !b & c & !next(a) & next(b) & next(c))      TRANS( !next(c) )              fi
       | (a & b & !c & !next(a) & next(b) & next(c))    end                            end
       | (a & b & c & !next(a) & !next(b) & !next(c)) )
end
```

Fig. 9. Hardware model template H for evaluating the BPDS model

Table 1. Comparison of co-verification statistics with BA and PDS hardware models (hardware does not interrupt software, and the size of global counter varies from 3 to 5 bits)

Table 2. Statistics when interrupt checking is enabled (one more Boolean variable is used to track the interrupt status)

N	Time usage with BA HW model (Sec)			Time usage with PDS HW model (Sec)		
	3 bits	4 bits	5 bits	3 bits	4 bits	5 bits
1k	0.42	0.72	1.28	2.47	8.08	35.62
2k	0.91	1.47	2.64	5.09	16.31	71.83
3k	1.42	2.33	4.08	8.14	25.42	109.33
4k	1.91	3.11	5.50	10.75	33.70	144.22

N	Time usage (Sec)			Peak live BDD nodes		
	3 bits	4 bits	5 bits	3 bits	4 bits	5 bits
1k	1.67	3.31	6.98	2335	5129	10325
2k	3.70	6.97	14.42	2335	5129	10337
3k	6.12	11.19	22.76	2335	5129	10325
4k	8.30	15.61	30.41	2335	5129	10337

full HW/SW concurrency is checked, as expected the verification complexities grow in the same order of magnitude as Table 1, where the complexities depend on the numbers of both global states and rules (the sizes of the program and hardware design). It can be inferred from Table 1 and Table 2 that using PDS as the hardware model without interrupt checking performs even worse than when using BA as the hardware model with interrupt checking. The time usage of Algorithm 1 that converts a BPDS to a PDS representation is very low. In our experiments, the maximum time usage is 0.45 seconds.

7   Conclusion and Future Work

In this paper, we have presented an automata-theoretic approach to co-verification. The core of this approach is a formal model for co-verification, the Büchi Pushdown System (BPDS). We have designed a co-specification framework for HW/SW interfaces and demonstrated a process of constructing a BPDS from the abstraction of hardware, software, and their interface specification. A BPDS can be converted to a PDS with the same complexities, so reachability analysis algorithms for PDS can be readily utilized to analyze BPDS. The evaluation has shown that BPDS is an effective model for co-verification. For the next step, we plan to automate the abstraction/refinement process of co-verification by integrating the abstraction/refinement engine of SLAM (C2BP for abstraction and Newton [11] for refinement) and the VCEGAR engine. One challenge for this integration is how to automatically propagate the predicates discovered by one engine across the HW/SW boundary to the other engine.

Acknowledgement. This research received financial support from National Science Foundation of the United States (Grant #: 0916968).

References

1. Clarke, E.M., Grumberg, O., Peled, D.: Model checking. MIT Press, Cambridge (1999)
2. Kurshan, R.P., Levin, V., Minea, M., Peled, D., Yenigün, H.: Combining software and hardware verification techniques. FMSD 21(3), 251–280 (2002)
3. Xie, F., Yang, G., Song, X.: Component-based hardware/software co-verification for building trustworthy embedded systems. JSS 80(5), 643–654 (2007)
4. Monniaux, D.: Verification of device drivers and intelligent controllers: a case study. In: Proc. of EMSOFT, pp. 30–36 (2007)
5. Ramalingam, G.: Context-sensitive synchronization-sensitive analysis is undecidable. ACM Trans. Program. Lang. Syst. 22(2), 416–430 (2000)
6. Schwoon, S.: Model-Checking Pushdown Systems. PhD thesis (2002)
7. Solomon, D.A.: Inside Windows NT, 2nd edn. Microsoft Press, Redmond (1998)
8. IEEE: IEEE Standard for Verilog (IEEE Std 1364-2005). IEEE (2005)
9. Kurshan, R.P.: Computer-Aided Verification of Coordinating Processes: The Automata-Theoretic Approach. Princeton University Press, Princeton (1994)
10. Jain, H., Kroening, D., Sharygina, N., Clarke, E.M.: Word-level predicate-abstraction and refinement techniques for verifying RTL Verilog. IEEE TCAD 27(2), 366–379 (2008)
11. Ball, T., Bounimova, E., Cook, B., Levin, V., Lichtenberg, J., McGarvey, C., Ondrusek, B., Rajamani, S.K., Ustuner, A.: Thorough static analysis of device drivers. In: Proc. of EuroSys, pp. 73–85 (2006)
12. Ball, T., Rajamani, S.K.: Bebop: A symbolic model checker for boolean programs. In: Proc. of SPIN, pp. 113–130 (2000)

Shape Refinement through Explicit Heap Analysis[*]

Dirk Beyer[1,2], Thomas A. Henzinger[3],
Grégory Théoduloz[4], and Damien Zufferey[3]

[1] Simon Fraser University, B.C., Canada
[2] University of Passau, Germany
[3] IST Austria (Institute of Science and Technology Austria)
[4] EPFL, Switzerland

Abstract. Shape analysis is a promising technique to prove program properties about recursive data structures. The challenge is to automatically determine the data-structure type, and to supply the shape analysis with the necessary information about the data structure. We present a stepwise approach to the selection of instrumentation predicates for a TVLA-based shape analysis, which takes us a step closer towards the fully automatic verification of data structures. The approach uses two techniques to guide the refinement of shape abstractions: (1) during program exploration, an explicit heap analysis collects sample instances of the heap structures, which are used to identify the data structures that are manipulated by the program; and (2) during abstraction refinement along an infeasible error path, we consider different possible heap abstractions and choose the coarsest one that eliminates the infeasible path. We have implemented this combined approach for automatic shape refinement as an extension of the software model checker BLAST. Example programs from a data-structure library that manipulate doubly-linked lists and trees were successfully verified by our tool.

1 Introduction

Proving the safety of programs that use dynamically-allocated data structures on the heap is a major challenge due to the difficulty of finding appropriate abstractions. For cases where the correctness property intimately depends on the shape of the data structure, researchers have over the last decade designed abstractions that are collectively known as shape analysis. One approach that has been particularly successful is based on the representation of heaps by three-valued logical structures [17]. The abstraction is specified by a set of predicates over nodes (unary and binary) representing core facts (e.g., points-to and field predicates) and derived facts (e.g., reachability). The latter category of predicates is called instrumentation predicates. Instrumentation predicates are crucial to control the precision of the analysis. First, they can keep track of relevant properties; second, they allow for more precise successor computations; and third, when used as abstraction predicates, they can control node summarization.

---

[*] Supported in part by the Canadian NSERC grant RGPIN 341819-07, by the SFU grant PRG 06-3, by the Swiss National Science Foundation, and by Microsoft Research through its PhD scholarship program.

D.S. Rosenblum and G. Taentzer (Eds.): FASE 2010, LNCS 6013, pp. 263–277, 2010.

In our previous work, we combined shape analysis with an automatic abstraction-refinement loop [4]. If a chosen abstraction is too coarse to prove the desired correctness property, a spurious counterexample path is identified, i.e., a path of the abstract program which witnesses a violation of the property but has no concrete counterpart. We analyzed such counterexample paths in order to determine a set of additional pointers and field predicates which, when tracked by the abstraction, remove the spurious counterexample. These core predicates are then added to the analysis, and a new attempt is made at proving the property. A main shortcoming of that work is that the refinement loop never automatically discovers the shape class (e.g., doubly-linked list, binary tree) that is suitable for proving the desired property, and it never adds new instrumentation predicates to the analysis. Consequently, programs can only be verified if all necessary shape classes and instrumentation predicates are "guessed" by the verification engineer when an abstraction is seeded. In the absence of such a correct guess, the method will iteratively track more and more core predicates, until either timing out or giving up because no more relevant predicates can be found.

In this work, we focus on the stepwise refinement of a TVLA-based shape analysis by automatically increasing the precision of the shape classes via instrumentation predicates. Suppose that counterexample analysis (e.g., following [4]) indicates that we need to track the heap structure to which a pointer p points, in order to verify the program. We can encounter two situations: (1) we do not yet track p and we do not know to which kind of data structure p points; or (2) we already track the shape of the heap structure to which p points but the tracked shape class is too coarse and may lack some necessary instrumentation predicates. We address situation (1) by running an explicit heap analysis in order to identify the shape of the data structure from samples, and situation (2) by selecting the coarsest refinement from a lattice of plausible shape classes. Our implementation provides such plausible shape classes by default for standard data structures like lists and trees, but also supports a flexible way to extend the existing shape classes.

Example. We illustrate our method on a simple program that manipulates doubly-linked lists (cf. Fig. 1(a)). First, two (acyclic) doubly-linked lists of arbitrary length are generated (`alloc_list`); then the two lists are concatenated; finally, the program checks if the result is a valid doubly-linked list (`assert_dll`). Our algorithm automatically verifies that no assertion in this program is violated. The algorithm starts with a trivial abstraction, where no predicates are tracked, and the reachability analysis using this abstraction finds an abstract error path. The algorithm checks whether this abstract error path corresponds to a concrete error path of the program by building a path formula (i.e., a formula which is satisfiable iff the path is a concrete error path). The path formula of the first abstract error path is unsatisfiable; therefore, this is an infeasible error path (also called spurious counterexample), and the abstraction is refined using an interpolation-guided refinement process. The following atoms occur in interpolants for the first path formula: pointer equalities among `l1`, `l2`, and `p`; `l1->succ = p`; and `l2->pred = p`. Since the interpolants mention pointers of a recursive data structure, we need to observe them via a shape analysis tracking `l1`, `l2`, and `p` (and their aliases).

But it is not enough to know which pointers to analyze; we also need to know their data structures, in order to determine the shape abstraction (so-called shape class), because different data structures require different instrumentation predicates. Since it is

```
1  typedef struct node {
2    int data;
3    struct node *succ, *prev;
4  } *List;
5  List alloc_list() {
6    List r = (List) malloc(...);
7    List p = r;
8    if (r == 0) exit(1);
9    while (*) {
10     List t = (List) malloc(...);
11     if (t == 0) exit(1);
12     p->succ = t; t->pred = p;
13     p = p->succ;
14   }
15   return r;
16 }
17 void assert_dll(List p) {
18   while ((p != 0) && (p->succ != 0)) {
19     assert(p->succ->pred == p);
20     p = p->succ;
21   }
22 }
23 void main() {
24   List l1 = alloc_list();
25   List l2 = alloc_list();
26
27   List p = l1;
28   while (p->succ != 0) p = p->succ;
29   p->succ = l2; l2->pred = p;
30
31   assert_dll(l1);
32 }
```

(a) Example C program

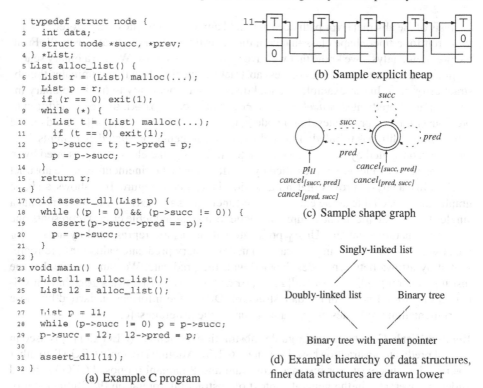

(b) Sample explicit heap

(c) Sample shape graph

(d) Example hierarchy of data structures, finer data structures are drawn lower

Fig. 1. Example program, two list abstractions, and hierarchy of data structures

the first time we encounter this data structure, our algorithm uses an explicit heap analysis to collect explicit heap samples that would occur during program execution. We graphically illustrate an explicit heap that is collected by the explicit heap analysis in Fig. 1(b). A node (rectangle with three boxes) represents one structure element; the first box represents the integer value for the field data; the second and third box represent the pointer values of the fields succ and prev, respectively. An arrow represents a pointer valuation. A symbol $\top$ in a box represents an unknown value. When a threshold is hit (e.g., once we have collected explicit heaps with at least 5 nodes each), we stop the explicit heap analysis, and extract the shape class from the explicit heap samples by checking which data structure invariants they satisfy. In the example heap, all nodes satisfy the invariant for acyclic singly-linked lists for each field individually, and the invariant for doubly-linked lists (for every node n, the predecessor of the successor of n is n itself), but not the invariant for binary trees (acyclic graph formed by the two field pointers). Knowing that the data structure is not a tree, and because both fields pred and succ occur in interpolants, we restrict the search for a shape abstraction to those suitable for doubly-linked lists. We refine the shape abstraction by choosing the coarsest shape class for doubly-linked lists, i.e., in addition to points-to predicates, we track two binary predicates for the fields pred and succ, and no instrumentation predicates.

The refined abstraction is still not fine enough to prove the program safe, because we find a new abstract error path. Its path formula is unsatisfiable, but the interpolant-based analysis of the abstract error path does not yield any new predicates. Therefore, we have to search for a finer shape class that contains instrumentation predicates as well. From the previous analysis we know that we have a doubly-linked list. We use a binary search to find, in the given lattice, the coarsest abstraction specification that eliminates the abstract error path. In our example, the tool discovers the necessity to track the unary instrumentation predicates $cancel[\texttt{succ}, \texttt{pred}]$ and $cancel[\texttt{pred}, \texttt{succ}]$ in addition to previously tracked predicates. For a node v, the predicate $cancel[f_1, f_2](v)$ holds if the following condition is fulfilled: if the field f_1 of an element represented by v points to an element represented by some node v', then the field f_2 of the element represented by v' points back to the element represented by v. After this last refinement step, the abstract reachability analysis proves that no assertion is violated. Figure 1(c) shows a shape graph that is reachable at the entry point of function $\texttt{assert\_dll}$. A node represents a single structure element, and a summary node (drawn as a double circle) represents one or more structure elements. Unary predicate valuations are represented by arrows (or the absence of arrows) from predicates to nodes; binary predicate valuations are represented by arrows between nodes, labeled with the predicate. We can observe that the instrumentation predicates $cancel[\texttt{succ}, \texttt{pred}]$ and $cancel[\texttt{pred}, \texttt{succ}]$ have a valuation of 1 for all nodes in the data structure. Due to the information carried by those instrumentation predicates, we are able to prove the program safe.

Related Work. Counterexample-guided abstraction refinement (CEGAR) [7] is used in several predicate-abstraction based verifiers [6,1,3]. Attempts to apply CEGAR to other abstract domains exist. For instance, Gulavani and Rajamani proposed CEGAR-based widening operators in the general context of abstract interpretation [9]. Refinement of shape analysis in particular has also been studied: Loginov et al. proposed a technique to learn new instrumentation predicates from imprecise verification results [13]. In our previous work [4], we studied how to combine nullary predicate abstraction and shape analysis, and how to refine shape analysis by discovering new core predicates.

Our current work is also in the tradition of combining symbolic and explicit analyses for program verification. In particular, combinations of symbolic abstraction methods with concrete program execution (testing) to build safety proofs have received much attention recently. Such techniques have been applied in the context of predicate abstraction-based model checkers to accelerate the state construction and guide the refinement [8,2,12,18], and in the context of constraint-based invariant generation [10]. We explored in previous work the use of precision adjustment to switch between explicit and symbolic steps during a reachability analysis [5]. To the best of our knowledge, no existing technique uses explicit heaps to guide the refinement of a shape abstraction.

2   Preliminaries

2.1   Programs

In this exposition, we consider flat programs (i.e., programs with a single function). Our tool implementation supports interprocedural analysis [15, 11, 16]. We formalize programs using control-flow automata. A *control-flow automaton* (CFA) is a directed, labeled graph (L, E), where the set L of nodes represents the control locations of the program (program-counter values), and the set $E \subseteq L \times Ops \times L$ of edges represents the program transfers. Each edge is labeled with a program operation that can be either an assignment or an assume predicate. The program operations are based on a set X of identifiers to identify program variables, and a set F of identifiers to identify fields. Variable identifiers and field identifiers can be either of type *integer* (denoted by int) or of type *pointer* to a (possibly recursive) structure (denoted by a C struct type). A *structure* is a set of field identifiers. We use a C-like syntax to denote program operations; in particular, *p->field* denotes the content of the field *field* in the structure pointed to by variable *p*. A *program* (G, l_0) consists of a CFA $G = (L, E)$ and an initial control location $l_0 \in L$. A *program path* t of length n is a sequence $(op_1 : l_1); \ldots; (op_n : l_n)$ of operations, such that $(l_{i-1}, op_i, l_i) \in E$ for all $1 \leq i \leq n$. A program path is *feasible* if there exists a concrete program execution with matching locations. The *verification problem* (G, l_0, l_{err}) is constituted by a program (G, l_0) and an error location l_{err}. The answer to the verification problem is SAFE if there exists no feasible path t that ends in location l_{err}, and UNSAFE otherwise. In the following two subsections we present the two abstract domains that our model-checking algorithm uses to compute an over-approximation of reachable states: explicit-heap abstraction and shape abstraction.

2.2 Explicit-Heap Abstraction

Explicit heap analysis stores concrete instances of data structures in its abstract states. Each abstract state represents an explicit, finite part of the memory. An *abstract state* $H = (v, h)$ of explicit heap analysis consists of the following two components: (1) the variable assignment $v : X \rightarrow \mathbb{Z}_\top$ is a total function that maps each variable identifier (integer or pointer variable) to an integer (representing an integer value or a structure address) or the special value $\top$ (representing the value 'unknown'); and (2) the heap assignment $h : \mathbb{Z} \rightharpoonup (F \rightarrow \mathbb{Z}_\top)$ is a partial function that maps every valid structure address to a field assignment, also called *structure cell* (memory content). A field assignment is a total function that maps each field identifier of the structure to an integer, or the special value $\top$. We call H an *explicit heap*. The initial explicit heap $H_0 = (v_0, \emptyset)$, with $v_0(x) = \top$ for every program variable x, represents all program states. Given an explicit heap H and a structure address a, the *depth* of H from a, denoted by $depth(H, a)$, is defined as the maximum length of an acyclic path whose nodes are addresses and where an edge from a_1 to a_2 exists if $h(a_1)(f) = a_2$ for some field f, starting from $v(a)$. The *depth* of H, denoted by $depth(H)$, is defined as $\max_{a \in X} depth(H, a)$.

The *explicit-heap abstraction* is a mapping $\Theta : L \rightarrow 2^X$, which assigns to each program location a subset of variables from X. Only the variables in the subset are tracked by the explicit heap analysis, i.e., the variable assignment of an abstract heap at location l maps every variable not in $\Theta(l)$ to $\top$. The abstract post operator reflects the effect of applying an operation on the explicit heap, provided it affects a data structure pointed to by a variable in the explicit-heap abstraction. Figure 1(b) graphically depicts an explicit heap (v, h) with $v = \{l1 \mapsto 1\}$ and $h = \{1 \mapsto \{data \mapsto \top, prev \mapsto 0, succ \mapsto 2\}, 2 \mapsto \{data \mapsto \top, succ \mapsto 3, prev \mapsto 1\}, 3 \mapsto \{data \mapsto \top, succ \mapsto 4, prev \mapsto 2\}, 4 \mapsto \{data \mapsto \top, succ \mapsto 5, prev \mapsto 3\}, 5 \mapsto \{data \mapsto \top, prev \mapsto 4, succ \mapsto 0\}\}$.

2.3   Shape Abstraction

Shape abstraction *symbolically* represents instances of data structures in its abstract states. We use a shape abstraction that is based on three-valued logic [17]. The notions of shape class, tracking definition, and shape-class generator are taken from *lazy shape analysis* [4]. We model the memory content by a set V of *heap nodes*. Each heap node represents one or more structure cells. Properties of the heap are encoded by predicates over nodes. The number of nodes that a predicate constrains is called the arity of the predicate, e.g., a predicate over one heap node is called *unary predicate* and a predicate over two heap nodes is called *binary predicate*. A *shape class* $\mathbb{S} = (P_{core}, P_{instr}, P_{abs})$ consists of three sets of predicates over heap nodes: (1) a set P_{core} of core predicates, (2) a set P_{instr} of instrumentation predicates with $P_{core} \cap P_{instr} = \emptyset$, where each instrumentation predicate $p \in P_{instr}$ has an associated *defining formula* φ^p over predicates, and (3) a set $P_{abs} \subseteq P_{core} \cup P_{instr}$ of abstraction predicates [17]. We denote the set of shape classes by S. A shape class $\mathbb{S}$ *refines* a shape class $\mathbb{S}'$, written $\mathbb{S} \preccurlyeq \mathbb{S}'$, if (1) $P'_{core} \subseteq P_{core}$, (2) $P'_{instr} \subseteq P_{instr}$, and (3) $P'_{abs} \subseteq P_{abs}$. The partial order $\preccurlyeq$ induces a lattice of shape classes. We require the set P_{core} of core predicates to contain the (special) unary predicate sm. For a heap node v, the predicate $sm(v)$ has the value *false* if v represents exactly one structure cell, and the value $1/2$ if v represents one or more structure cells. In the latter case, the heap node is called *summary node*. In the following, we make use of the following two families of core predicates. A *points-to predicate* $pt_x(v)$ is a unary predicate that is *true* if pointer variable x points to a structure cell that is represented by v, and *false* otherwise. A *field predicate* $fd_\phi(v)$ is a unary predicate that is *true* if field assertion ϕ holds for all structure cells that are represented by heap node v, and *false* otherwise. A field assertion is a predicate over the field identifiers of a structure. Therefore, field predicates represent the data content of a structure, rather than the shape of the structure. A *shape graph* $s = (V, val)$ for a shape class $\mathbb{S} = (P_{core}, P_{instr}, P_{abs})$ consists of a set V of heap nodes and a valuation val in three-valued logic of the predicates of $\mathbb{S}$: for a predicate $p \in P_{core} \cup P_{instr}$ of arity n, $val(p) : V^n \rightarrow \{0, 1, 1/2\}$.

The *shape abstraction* is a function $\Psi : L \rightarrow 2^S$ that maps each control location to a set of shape classes (different shape classes can be used to simultaneously track different data structures). The Ψ-abstraction, i.e., the result of applying a shape abstraction Ψ, is an abstract state, called shape region. A *shape region* $G = \{(\mathbb{S}_1, S_1), ..., (\mathbb{S}_n, S_n)\}$ consists of a set of pairs $(\mathbb{S}_i, S_i)$ where $\mathbb{S}_i$ is a shape class and S_i is a set of shape graphs for $\mathbb{S}_i$. The abstract post operator for shape graphs is defined as in TVLA [17].

Tracking definitions and shape-class generators. Instead of directly considering shape classes, we separate two aspects of shape classes. First, a tracking definition provides information about which pointers and which field predicates need to be tracked on a syntactic level. Second, given a tracking definition, a shape-class generator determines which predicates are actually added to the shape class.

A *tracking definition* $D = (T, T_s, \Phi)$ consists of (1) a set T of *tracked pointers*, which is the set of variable identifiers that may be pointing to some node in a shape graph; (2) a set $T_s \subseteq T$ of *separating pointers*, which is the set of variable identifiers for which we want the corresponding predicates (e.g., points-to, reachability) to be abstraction predicates (i.e., precisely tracked, no value $1/2$ allowed); and (3) a set Φ of field assertions. A tracking definition $D = (T, T_s, \Phi)$ *refines* a tracking definition $D' = (T', T'_s, \Phi')$, if $T' \subseteq T$, $T'_s \subseteq T_s$ and $\Phi' \subseteq \Phi$. We denote the set of all tracking definitions by $\mathcal{D}$. The coarsest tracking definition $(\emptyset, \emptyset, \emptyset)$ is denoted by D_0.

A *shape-class generator* (SCG) is a function $m : \mathcal{D} \to \mathcal{S}$ that takes as input a tracking definition and returns a shape class, which consists of core predicates, instrumentation predicates, and abstraction predicates. While useful SCGs contain points-to and field predicates for pointers and field assertions from the tracking definition, and the predicate sm, other predicates need to be added by appropriate SCGs. An SCG m *refines* an SCG m' (denoted by $m \sqsubseteq m'$) if $m(D) \preccurlyeq m'(D)$ for every tracking definition D. We require that the set of SCGs contains at least the coarsest element m_0, which is a constant function that generates for each tracking definition the shape class $(\emptyset, \emptyset, \emptyset)$. Furthermore, we require each SCG to be monotonic: given an SCG m and two tracking definitions D and D', if $D \preccurlyeq D'$, then $m(D) \preccurlyeq m(D')$.

A *shape type* $\mathbb{T} = (\sigma, m, D)$ consists of a structure type σ, an SCG m, and a tracking definition D. For example, consider the type `struct node {int data; struct node *succ;};` and the tracking definition $D = (\{l1, l2\}, \{l1\}, \{data = 0\})$. To form a shape type for a singly-linked list, we can choose an SCG that takes a tracking definition $D = (T, T_s, \Phi)$ and produces a shape class $\mathbb{S} = (P_{core}, P_{instr}, P_{abs})$ with the following components: the set P_{core} of core predicates contains the default unary predicate sm for distinguishing summary nodes, a binary predicate $succ$ for representing links between nodes in the list, a unary points-to predicate for each variable identifier in T, and a unary field predicate for each assertion in Φ. The set P_{instr} of instrumentation predicates contains for each variable identifier in T a reachability predicate. The set P_{abs} of abstraction predicates contains all core and instrumentation predicates about separating pointers from T_s. More precise shape types for singly-linked lists can be defined by providing an SCG that adds more instrumentation predicates (e.g., cyclicity).

A *shape-abstraction specification* is a function $\widehat{\Psi}$ that assigns to each control location a set of shape types. The specification $\widehat{\Psi}$ defines a shape abstraction Ψ in the following way: a pair $(l, \{\mathbb{T}_1, \ldots, \mathbb{T}_k\}) \in \widehat{\Psi}$ yields a pair $(l, \{\mathbb{S}_1, \ldots, \mathbb{S}_k\}) \in \Psi$ with $\mathbb{S}_i = \mathbb{T}_i.m(\mathbb{T}_i.D)$ for all $1 \le i \le k$. (We use the notation $X.y$ to denote the component y of a structure X.) Given a program P, the initial shape-abstraction specification $\widehat{\Psi}_0$ is defined as the set $\{(\sigma, m_0, D_0) \mid \sigma$ is a structure type occurring in $P\}$; the initial shape region G_0 consists of one pair $(\emptyset, \emptyset)$ for every shape type in $\widehat{\Psi}_0$. Region G_0 does not constrain the state space; it represents all program states.

3 Shape Analysis with Abstraction and Refinement

We introduce a new verification algorithm that is based on abstraction *and* refinement. Shape types can be refined in two different ways: either we refine the shape type's tracking definition, or we refine the shape type's SCG. In both cases, the resulting shape class is guaranteed to be finer, because SCGs are monotonic. Previous work has shown how tracking definitions can be refined, by extracting information from infeasible error paths using interpolation [4]. Our approach is based on this algorithm, and proposes a novel technique to refine SCGs, by combining information from two sources. The first source of information is explicit heaps and is used to restrict the refinement to SCGs that are designed to support the kind of data structure (e.g., doubly-linked list, binary tree) that the program manipulates. When we discover pointers to data structures for the first time, we run an explicit heap analysis of the program until we encounter explicit heaps with a depth that exceeds a given threshold. The explicit heaps that have been computed are queried for data structure invariants, and are then abstracted to shape graphs. The second source of information is infeasible error paths. We simulate shape analysis with different SCGs along the path to determine the coarsest SCG that is able to eliminate the infeasible path. A library of SCGs that supports standard data structures like lists and trees is available in BLAST.

3.1 Model-Checking Algorithm (*ModelCheck*)

Our analysis algorithm operates on an abstract reachability tree (ART), whose nodes contain two abstract states: one abstract state models the heap memory explicitly (using explicit heaps), and the other abstract state models the heap memory symbolically (using shape graphs). Formally, an abstract reachability tree (ART) [3] is a tree that fulfills the following properties. Every node n is a tuple $n = (l, H, G)$ which consists of a control-flow location l, an explicit heap H, and a shape region G. The root node $n_0 = (l_0, H_0, G_0)$ consists of the initial control-flow location l_0, the initial explicit heap H_0, and the initial shape region G_0. An edge (n, n') in the ART means that node n' is the abstract successor of node n, i.e., the edge $((l, H, G), (l', H', G'))$ exists in the ART if l' is a successor location of l in the CFA, H' is the abstract explicit-heap successor of explicit heap H, and G' is the abstract shape successor of shape region G. A node n is covered if there exists another node n' in the ART for the same location and all concrete states represented by n are represented by n'.

Algorithm *ModelCheck* (Alg. 1) takes as input a program P, an error location l_{err} of P, and a lattice M of SCGs. The algorithm tries to prove (or disprove) that l_{err} is not reachable in any concrete program execution. It keeps track of the current abstraction, i.e., an explicit-heap abstraction and shape-abstraction specification. In addition, it maintains a mapping from program types to sets of enabled SCGs (subsets of M). Only enabled SCGs are considered during refinement. In a first step, the algorithm initializes the abstractions for each control location of the input program P with trivial abstractions. All SCGs are initially enabled, and the ART A is initialized as a tree with a single node representing the initial program states. Then a check-refine loop is executed until either the program is declared safe or a feasible path to the error location is found.

In each iteration, we first call procedure *BuildART* to extend the given ART A for the given program P and the current abstractions Θ and $\widehat{\Psi}$, towards a resulting ART that is closed under abstract successors. Procedure *BuildART* (not shown in pseudocode) takes as input a program P, an error location l_{err}, an ART A, an explicit-heap abstraction Θ, and a shape abstraction specification $\widehat{\Psi}$. If the procedure stops, it returns a pair (A, n) consisting of the ART and its last processed (leaf) node. It operates on the ART nodes and performs a waitlist-based reachability analysis to explore the abstract state space that Θ and $\widehat{\Psi}$ define. Children of nodes are computed until every leaf of the ART is covered, i.e., the ART is *complete*. The procedure stops if one of the following conditions is fulfilled: (a) The reachability analysis encounters a node n whose location

---

Algorithm 1. $ModelCheck(P, l_{err}, M)$

Input: a program P, an error location l_{err} of P,
        a lattice M of SCGs with finite height
Output: either an ART to witness safety,
        or an error path to witness the existence of a feasible error path
Variables: an explicit-heap abstraction Θ, a shape-abstraction specification $\widehat{\Psi}$, an ART A,
        a mapping E from types to sets of enabled SCGs
  for each location l of P **do**
    $\widehat{\Psi}(l) := \widehat{\Psi}_0$; $\Theta(l) := \emptyset$;
  for each pointer type σ in P **do**
    $E(\sigma) := M$
  $A = \{(l_0, H_0, G_0)\}$;
  while *true* **do**
    $(A, n) := BuildART(P, l_{err}, A, \Theta, \widehat{\Psi})$;
    if n is not an error node **then** // ART A is safe, i.e., A contains no error node
      if A is complete **then**
        print "Yes. The program is safe. Certificate:" A; **stop**;
      else // threshold exceeded, switch off explicit tracking
        $(A, \Theta, \widehat{\Psi}, E) := Abstract(A, n, \Theta, \widehat{\Psi}, M, E)$;
    else // n is an error node, i.e., $n = (l_{err}, \cdot, \cdot)$
      let t be the path in A from the root to n
      if $PathFormula(t)$ is satisfiable **then** // t is feasible; the error is really reachable
        print "No. The program is unsafe. Counterexample path:" t; **stop**;
      else // t is infeasible due to a too coarse abstraction
        $(A, \Theta, \widehat{\Psi}, E) := Refine(A, n, \Theta, \widehat{\Psi}, M, E)$;

---

is the error location. Then the last computed node contains the error location. (b) The reachability analysis completes the ART, i.e., all leaf nodes of the ART are covered and the ART does not contain any node with the error location — the ART is *safe*, and complete. (c) The depth of the last explicit heap that the procedure has computed exceeds a given threshold. The last computed node contains an explicit heap suitable for abstraction.

Algorithm *ModelCheck* distinguishes the different outcomes of *BuildART* based on the ART properties safe and complete. (1) If the ART is safe and complete, the overall algorithm can stop and report that the program is safe. (2) If the ART is safe but not complete, then the threshold for the explicit heap analysis was reached at node n, in other words, the explicit heap analysis has collected enough information to guide the refinement of the shape-abstraction specification. Procedure *Abstract* is called to analyze explicit heaps to restrict enabled SCGs, refine SCGs in the shape-abstraction specification, and replace explicit heaps in the ART by shape graphs. (3) If n represents an error location and the path from the root of A to n is feasible, then the overall algorithm can stop and report an error. (4) If n represents an error location but the path from the root of A to n is infeasible, then the path was encountered due to a too coarse abstraction, and procedure *Refine* will try to find a more suitable abstraction. Procedure *Refine* may fail due to the absence of a suitable, fine-enough SCG in the lattice of SCGs. Note that Algorithm *ModelCheck* may not terminate, in case it produces finer and finer abstractions to rule out longer and longer infeasible error paths.

Algorithm 2. $Abstract(A, n, \Theta, \widehat{\Psi}, M, E)$

Input: an ART A, an ART node n, an abstraction consisting of Θ and $\widehat{\Psi}$,
     a set M of SCGs, and a type-to-SCGs mapping E
Output: an ART, an abstraction consisting of Θ and $\widehat{\Psi}$, and a type-to-SCGs mapping E
    let $n = (l, H, G)$
    let pointer $p \in \Theta(l)$ s.t. $depth(H, p) > k$
    let $\sigma = type(p)$; choose $(\sigma, m, D) \in \widehat{\Psi}(l)$
    // evaluate invariants on explicit heap, and update abstractions
    $E(\sigma) := E(\sigma) \cap SCGsFromExplicit(H, p)$
    let m' be the coarsest SCG in $E(\sigma)$
    replace (σ, m, D) by (σ, m', D) in $\widehat{\Psi}(l)$
    remove all x from $\Theta(l)$ s.t. $type(x) = type(p)$
    // remove explicit heap info and update shape graphs in ART
    for each node $n = (l, H, G)$ in A **do**
      $n' = (l, H_0, G')$ with $G' = HeapToShape(H, \widehat{\Psi}(l))$
      replace n by n' in A
    return $(A, \Theta, \widehat{\Psi}, E)$

3.2 Algorithm for Abstraction from Explicit Heaps (*Abstract*)

When the explicit heap analysis has generated sufficiently large explicit heaps, Algorithm *Abstract* (Alg. 2) is called to extract information from explicit heaps in order to choose a suitable SCG, and explicit heaps are abstracted to shape graphs. The algorithm takes as input an ART A, a leaf node n of the ART, the current abstraction specified by an explicit-heap abstraction Θ and a shape-abstraction specification $\widehat{\Psi}$, a lattice of SCGs, and a mapping E from types to sets of enabled SCGs. Upon termination, the algorithm returns the updated ART, abstraction, and mapping.

The algorithm first determines a pointer to the data structure whose depth exceeds the threshold k. Function $SCGsFromExplicit$ analyzes an explicit heap and returns all relevant SCGs: Every SCG is annotated with a set of invariants that must be fulfilled by explicit heaps for the SCG to be relevant (e.g., all SCGs generating instrumentation predicates for trees are annotated with the tree-ness invariant). For each SCG m, function $SCGsFromExplicit$ evaluates the invariants of m on explicit heap H, and if all those invariants are fulfilled, the function enables m for its structure type. Then the abstraction is updated: pointer p and all other pointers of the same type are removed from the explicit-heap abstraction, and we refine the SCG of the chosen shape type to be the coarsest enabled SCG for the structure type. After the refinement of the SCG, we erase the explicit heap in the ART node, and replace the corresponding shape region by the result of abstracting the explicit heap to shape graphs (function $HeapToShape$). The result of $HeapToShape$ has a single shape graph for each shape class that results from applying the newly refined SCG to the current tracking definitions. For example, the shape graph represented in Fig. 1(c) is a possible abstraction of the explicit heap represented in Fig. 1(b). In the next iteration of reachability, the construction of the ART continues from the newly computed shape graphs. Note that converting an explicit heap to a shape graph is significantly less expensive than obtaining the shape graph via abstract post computations, and is similar to dynamic precision adjustment [5].

Algorithm 3. $Refine(A, n, \Theta, \widehat{\Psi}, M, E)$

Input: an ART A, an ART node n, an abstraction consisting of Θ and $\widehat{\Psi}$,
   a set M of SCGs, and a type-to-SCGs mapping E
Output: an ART, an abstraction consisting of Θ and $\widehat{\Psi}$, and a type-to-SCGs mapping E
Variables: an interpolant map Π
   let $t = (op_1 : l_1); \ldots ; (op_k : l_k)$ be the program path from n to the root of A;
   $\Pi := ExtractInterpolants(t)$;
   for $i := 1$ to k **do**
       choose (σ, m, D) from $\widehat{\Psi}(l_i)$, with $D = (T, T_s, P)$
       // Step 1: Refine the tracking definitions
       for each atom $\phi \in \Pi(l_i)$ **do**
           if some pointer p occurs in ϕ, and $type(p)$ matches σ **then**
               add p and all elements of $alias(p)$ to $D.T$
               add p to $D.T_s$
           if pointer p is dereferenced in ϕ **then**
               add to $D.P$ the field assertion corresponding to ϕ
       // Step 2: Start explicit heap analysis or refine the SCG
       for each pointer p in $D.T$ **do**
           if $p \notin \Theta(l_i)$ and $m = m_0$ **then**
               // p was not analyzed before, switch to explicit heap analysis mode
               add p to $\Theta(l_i)$
           if $p \notin \Theta(l_i)$ and $m \neq m_0$ **then**
               // in shape analysis mode: binary-search refinement
               $m' := FineTune(t, m, E(\sigma))$
               if $m = m'$ **then** // the binary search cannot refine; extend the search
                   add to $E(\sigma)$ every $m'' \in M$ s.t. $m \not\sqsubseteq m''$
                   $m' := FineTune(t, m, E(\sigma))$
               replace (σ, m, D) by (σ, m', D) in $\widehat{\Psi}(l_i)$
       if $\Theta(l_i)$ or $\widehat{\Psi}(l_i)$ was changed **then**
           remove from A all nodes with location l_i and their children
   if $\widehat{\Psi}$ and Θ did not change **then**
       print "Refinement failed on path:" t; **stop**;
   return $(A, \Theta, \widehat{\Psi}, E)$

3.3 Algorithm for Shape Refinement (*Refine*)

When an infeasible error path is found in the ART, it is due to a shape abstraction that
is not fine enough. Algorithm *Refine* tries to produce a finer shape abstraction such that
the infeasible error path does not occur in the ART built using the refined abstraction.
Algorithm *Refine* (Alg. 3) takes as input an ART A, a leaf node n of the ART, the
current abstraction specified by an explicit heap abstraction Θ and a shape-abstraction
specification $\widehat{\Psi}$, a lattice of SCGs, and a mapping from types to set of enabled SCGs.
The algorithm assumes that the location of n is the error location and that the path from
the root of A to n is infeasible. Upon termination, a refined ART, a refined abstraction,
and a (possibly updated) mapping from types to set of enabled SCGs is returned.

The first step of the algorithm analyzes the infeasible error path. We compute the
(inductive) interpolants of the (unsatisfiable) path formula corresponding to the path

from the root to node n, for every location on the path (*ExtractInterpolants*). We use the interpolants to check whether we can find new pointers or field assertions to track by analyzing all atoms occurring in interpolants. If we find a pointer that we have to track, we add it to the set of tracked separating pointers, and add all its aliases to the set of tracked pointers. If it is the first time we encounter a pointer, we need to know which kind of data structure it is pointing to in order to enable only a subset of SCGs. To discover this information, we cannot rely exclusively on syntactical type information. For example, the types for doubly-linked lists and binary trees (without parent pointers) have the same syntactical structure. We enable an explicit heap analysis of the data structure by adding the pointer to the abstraction of the explicit heap analysis, and the SCG is the trivial SCG m_0. If we considered the pointer before, then the explicit analysis was switched on, and we refined the SCG to a non-trivial SCG. In this case, the explicit heap analysis need not be run again because it will not provide new information. Instead, we decide to fine-tune the SCG by using a binary-search-like exploration of the lattice of enabled SCGs. If the fine-tuning fails to yield a finer SCG, it may still be the case that there exists a fine-enough SCG in the lattice of all SCGs that is prevented to be found because the explicit heap analysis over-restricted the set of enabled SCGs. In this case, we extend the set of enabled SCGs to include all SCGs from the set M of SCGs that are not coarser than the current SCG.

Procedure *FineTune* takes as input an infeasible program path t, the current SCG m and a lattice M of SCGs. The procedure searches for the coarsest SCG m' such that m' *rules out* path t, i.e., the abstract strongest postcondition of the program path represents no states when SCG m is replaced by m' in the shape-abstraction specification. Note that we only compute shape regions along the given path t at this point, not along any other program path. To make the search more efficient, we try to prune in each iteration approximately half of the candidate SCGs. Because of the monotonicity of SCGs, if a given SCG cannot rule out t, then no coarser SCG can. The algorithm maintains a set C of candidates. The set C is initialized with all SCGs in M that are finer than m. We repeat the following steps until no more SCGs can be removed from C. We select a subset S of SCGs as small as possible such that the set of SCGs coarser than some SCG in S contains as many elements as the set of SCGs finer than some SCG in S. If no SCG in S rules out t, we remove from C all SCGs coarser or equal to a SCG in S; otherwise, we keep in C only those SCGs that are coarser or equal to some SCG in S that rules out t. When the loop terminates, if $C = \emptyset$, then the fine-tuning failed and we return m; otherwise, we choose one SCG m' in C that generates the fewest predicates when applied to the current tracking definition, and return m'.

4   Experimental Evaluation

Implementation. Our new algorithm is implemented as an extension of BLAST 3.0, which integrates TVLA for shape transformations and the FOCI library [14] for formula interpolation. In addition to the algorithm discussed in this paper, our implementation supports nullary-predicate abstraction and refinement based on interpolants.

The SCG library provided with BLAST supports singly-linked lists, doubly-linked lists, and trees with and without parent pointers. The library is based on well-known instrumentation predicates from the literature [17]: for singly-linked lists, reachability (unary) and cyclicity (unary); for doubly-linked lists, reachability (unary and binary), cyclicity (unary), and cancellation (unary, holds for a given node when the node pointed to by the forward pointer has its backward pointer pointing to the given node); for trees (with and without parent pointers), down pointer and its transitive closure (binary), downward reachability (unary), downward acyclicity (binary), and in addition, for trees with a parent pointer, cancellation for left and right (unary, holds for a given node when the node pointed to by the left, respectively right, pointer has its parent pointer pointing to the given node).

The library of SCGs is implemented in BLAST using a domain-specific language (DSL), in order to decouple the specification of SCGs from the verification and refinement engine. Should the verification engineer need to verify a program that uses a data structure that is not yet supported in BLAST's default SCG lib, the DSL makes it easy to add support for different data structures and other instrumentation predicates. Each DSL entry corresponds to a data structure. Instead of specifying all SCGs in the lattice, the DSL entry specifies the most refined SCG, and coarser SCGs are derived by considering subsets of predicates. Moreover, a refinement relation between different data structures is specified separately.

Example Programs. We evaluate our technique on the open source C library for data structures GDSL 1.4 [1]. We consider non-trivial low-level functions operating on doubly-linked lists and trees. Each function is inserted in client code, non-deterministically simulating valid uses of the function. The client code inputs arbitrary valid data structures to the function, and on return, checks that a given property is preserved. The benchmarks cancel_* and acyclic_* operate on doubly-linked lists, and check, respectively, for the preservation of the structure of a doubly-linked list (i.e., the backward pointer of the node pointed to by a given node's forward pointer points back to the given node, and vice versa), and for acyclicity following forward pointers. The benchmarks bintree_* and treep_* operate on binary trees, and check, respectively, for the preservation of acyclicity following left and right pointers, and for the validity of parent pointers with respect to left and right pointers.

Results. All examples could be proved safe by BLAST after a few refinement steps. Table 1 reports the execution time of BLAST on a GNU/Linux machine with an Intel Core Duo 2 6700 and 4 GB of memory. The first part of the table reports the results with the most refined (maximal) SCGs used for all pointers in the program, and therefore no refinement is needed. The first column reports the kind of data structure and the number of instrumentation predicate families used by the SCG. The second column reports the verification time. The second part of the table reports the results when refinement is used. The first column of this part of the table reports the SCG and number of enabled instrumentation predicates families (compared to maximum). The second column reports the number of each kind of refinements: the first kind (td) corresponds to the refinement of a tracking definition (i.e., a new pointer or a new field predicate is discovered), and the second kind (scg) corresponds to the refinement of SCGs (i.e., new instrumentation predicates are introduced). The information in the first and second columns is identical for both configurations with refinement. To evaluate the impact of

---

[1] Available at http://home.gna.org/gdsl/

Table 1. Runtime of BLAST on functions from the GDSL library, using (a) maximal SCG, or shape refinement with (b) program annotations or (c) explicit heap analysis to determine the SCG

Program	Maximal SCG		SCG / #instr. pred. families/max	With refinement		
	SCG	Time		#refines	Annotation	Explicit
cancel_list_link	dll/3	10.04 s	dll / 1/3	1 td, 1 scg	12.65 s	13.76 s
cancel_list_insert_after	dll/3	23.62 s	dll / 1/3	1 td, 1 scg	24.41 s	26.82 s
cancel_list_insert_before	dll/3	30.90 s	dll / 3/3	2 td, 2 scg	69.01 s	77.22 s
cancel_list_remove	dll/3	4.42 s	dll / 2/3	1 td, 1 scg	28.49 s	29.05 s
acyclic_list_link	dll/3	11.57 s	sll / 2/2	1 td, 1 scg	6.32 s	6.49 s
acyclic_list_insert_after	dll/3	24.21 s	sll / 2/2	1 td, 1 scg	23.57 s	26.06 s
acyclic_list_insert_before	dll/3	34.53 s	dll / 3/3	2 td, 2 scg	80.81 s	88.21 s
acyclic_list_remove	dll/3	4.23 s	sll / 2/2	1 td, 2 scg	96.77 s	99.75 s
bintree_rotate_left	tree+p/5	>9000 s	tree / 2/4	3 td, 2 scg	414.28 s	521.31 s
bintree_rotate_right	tree+p/5	>9000 s	tree / 2/4	3 td, 1 scg	419.24 s	437.30 s
bintree_rotate_left_right	tree+p/5	>9000 s	tree / 2/4	2 td, 2 scg	7023.41 s	7401.74 s
treep_rotate_left	tree+p/5	>9000 s	tree+p / 2/5	4 td, 2 scg	180.58 s	66.63 s
treep_rotate_right	tree+p/5	>9000 s	tree+p / 2/5	4 td, 2 scg	402.70 s	384.19 s
treep_rotate_left_right	tree+p/5	>9000 s	tree+p / 2/5	4 td, 2 scg	1175.14 s	1189.42 s

the explicit heap analysis on performance, we replace in one experimental setting the procedure *Abstract* by a procedure that enables the suitable set of SCGs based on our knowledge of the data structures, encoded as annotations for BLAST in the code. Therefore, the third column reports verification times for the experiments when using annotations to determine the type of data structures (explicit heap analysis disabled), and the fourth column, when using the explicit heap analysis to infer the type of data structures. We run the explicit heap analysis until five different samples of data structures containing (at least) four structure nodes are collected. In all examples, both tracking definitions and SCGs are refined. In most examples, the finest SCG is not needed (only a subset of available predicates is used). Note that for three out of four acyclic_* benchmarks, a shape class for singly-linked lists (considering only the forward pointer) is sufficient to prove safety.

The explicit heap analysis correctly identifies the data-structure in every example. The run time for explicit-heap based refinement is comparable to annotation-guided refinement. The variations between the two result from two sources: (1) the overhead of performing the explicit heap analysis, and (2) the abstraction from explicit heaps to shape graphs and the subsequent ART extension. On all examples, the explicit heap analysis accounts for a negligible fraction of the execution time. Most of the runtime is consumed by (symbolic) shape operations in TVLA. On the one hand, some shape-graph computations are saved. But on the other hand, depending on how large the ART is when *Abstract* is executed, many explicit heaps may abstract to the same shape graph, subsequently causing an overhead. Infeasible error paths may also have different lengths resulting in different interpolation and refinement timings. On small examples, the refinement contributes most of the total execution time (up to nearly 50%): most of the time is spent in the path simulations of *FineTune*. On larger examples, most of the time is spent in the final iteration of the reachability analysis, in particular, while computing abstract shape successors using TVLA. Overall, we conclude that the explicit heap analysis provides reliable information for the refinement, for a reasonable overhead.

Our refinement strategy outperforms the direct use of the most refined SCG on large examples (involving trees), because the refinement allows for the use of significantly less instrumentation predicates, compared to the most refined SCGs. On smaller examples, though, the run time can be larger if refinement is used, due to the high portion of time spent on refinement and the high number of instrumentation predicates we need, compared to the most refined case. The final reachability analysis sometimes takes significantly less time if the most refined SCG is used; one particular case is the two list_remove examples. The reason is that the SCG discovered by our refinement strategy (which only tracks the forward pointer) happens to generate more different shape graphs than the most refined SCG (which tracks both pointers), although the former generates less predicates than the latter.

References

1. Ball, T., Rajamani, S.K.: The SLAM project: Debugging system software via static analysis. In: Proc. POPL, pp. 1–3. ACM, New York (2002)
2. Beckman, N., Nori, A.V., Rajamani, S.K., Simmons, R.J.: Proofs from tests. In: Proc. ISSTA, pp. 3–14. ACM, New York (2008)
3. Beyer, D., Henzinger, T.A., Jhala, R., Majumdar, R.: The software model checker BLAST. Int. J. Softw. Tools Technol. Transfer 9(5-6), 505–525 (2007)
4. Beyer, D., Henzinger, T.A., Théoduloz, G.: Lazy shape analysis. In: Ball, T., Jones, R.B. (eds.) CAV 2006. LNCS, vol. 4144, pp. 532–546. Springer, Heidelberg (2006)
5. Beyer, D., Henzinger, T.A., Théoduloz, G.: Program analysis with dynamic precision adjustment. In: Proc. ASE, pp. 29–38. IEEE, Los Alamitos (2008)
6. Chaki, S., Clarke, E.M., Groce, A., Jha, S., Veith, H.: Modular verification of software components in C. IEEE Trans. Softw. Eng. 30(6), 388–402 (2004)
7. Clarke, E.M., Grumberg, O., Jha, S., Lu, Y., Veith, H.: Counterexample-guided abstraction refinement for symbolic model checking. J. ACM 50(5), 752–794 (2003)
8. Gulavani, B.S., Henzinger, T.A., Kannan, Y., Nori, A.V., Rajamani, S.K.: SYNERGY: A new algorithm for property checking. In: Proc. FSE, pp. 117–127. ACM, New York (2006)
9. Gulavani, B.S., Rajamani, S.K.: Counterexample-driven refinement for abstract interpretation. In: Hermanns, H., Palsberg, J. (eds.) TACAS 2006. LNCS, vol. 3920, pp. 474–488. Springer, Heidelberg (2006)
10. Gupta, A., Majumdar, R., Rybalchenko, A.: From tests to proofs. In: Kowalewski, S., Philippou, A. (eds.) ACAS 2009. LNCS, vol. 5505, pp. 262–276. Springer, Heidelberg (2009)
11. Henzinger, T.A., Jhala, R., Majumdar, R., McMillan, K.L.: Abstractions from proofs. In: Proc. POPL, pp. 232–244. ACM Press, New York (2004)
12. Kröning, D., Groce, A., Clarke, E.M.: Counterexample-guided abstraction refinement via program execution. In: Davies, J., Schulte, W., Barnett, M. (eds.) ICFEM 2004. LNCS, vol. 3308, pp. 224–238. Springer, Heidelberg (2004)
13. Loginov, A., Reps, T.W., Sagiv, M.: Abstraction refinement via inductive learning. In: Etessami, K., Rajamani, S.K. (eds.) CAV 2005. LNCS, vol. 3576, pp. 519–533. Springer, Heidelberg (2005)
14. McMillan, K.L.: Interpolation and SAT-based model checking. In: Hunt Jr., W.A., Somenzi, F. (eds.) CAV 2003. LNCS, vol. 2725, pp. 1–13. Springer, Heidelberg (2003)
15. Reps, T.W., Horwitz, S., Sagiv, M.: Precise interprocedural data-flow analysis via graph reachability. In: Proc. POPL, pp. 49–61. ACM, New York (1995)
16. Rinetzky, N., Sagiv, M., Yahav, E.: Interprocedural functional shape analysis using local heaps. Technical Report TAU-CS-26/04, Tel-Aviv University (2004)
17. Sagiv, M., Reps, T.W., Wilhelm, R.: Parametric shape analysis via 3-valued logic. ACM Trans. Program. Lang. Syst. 24(3), 217–298 (2002)
18. Yorsh, G., Ball, T., Sagiv, M.: Testing, abstraction, theorem proving: Better together! In: Proc. ISSTA, pp. 145–156. ACM, New York (2006)

Memory Leaks Detection in Java by Bi-abductive Inference

Dino Distefano and Ivana Filipović

Queen Mary University of London

Abstract. This paper describes a compositional analysis algorithm for statically detecting leaks in Java programs. The algorithm is based on separation logic and exploits the concept of bi-abductive inference for identifying the objects which are reachable but no longer used by the program.

1 Introduction

In garbage collected languages like Java the *unused memory* is claimed by the garbage collector, thus relieving the programmer of the burden of managing explicitly the use of dynamic memory. This claim is only partially correct: technically, the garbage collector reclaims only allocated portions of memory which have become unreachable from program variables, and often, this memory does not entirely correspond to the unused memory of the system. For instance, it is quite common that memory is allocated, used for a while, and then no longer needed nor used by the program. However, some of this memory cannot be freed by the garbage collector and will remain in the state of the program for longer than it needs to be, as there are still references to it from some program variables. Even though this phenomenon, typical of Java and other garbage collected languages like Python, defines a different form of "memory leakage" than in traditional languages like C, its results are equally catastrofic. If an application leaks memory, it first slows down the system in which it is running and eventually causes the system to run out of memory. Many memory-leak bugs have been reported (e.g., bug #4177795 in the Java Developer's Connection[13]) and experiments have shown that on average 39% of space could be saved by freeing reachable but unneeded objects [24,22].

There are two main sources of memory leaks in Java code [20,14,18]:

- *Unknown or unwanted object references.* As commented above, this happens when some object is not used anymore, however the garbage collector cannot remove it because it is pointed to by some other object.
- *Long-living (static) objects.* These are objects that are allocated for the entire execution of the program.

These two possibilities appear in different forms. For example, a common simple error, such as forgetting to assign null to a live variable pointing to the object

D.S. Rosenblum and G. Taentzer (Eds.): FASE 2010, LNCS 6013, pp. 278–292, 2010.

not needed anymore, leads to a memory leak. Such a leak can have serious consequences if the memory associated to it is substantial in size. Some more sophisticated examples discussed in literature are:

- *Singleton pattern, Static references and Unbounded caches.* The Singleton pattern [8] ensures that a class has *only one* instance and provides a global access point to it. Once the singleton class is instantiated it remains in memory until the program terminates. However, the garbage collector will not be able to collect any of its referants, even when they have a shorter lifetime than the singleton class [18]. Most caches are implemented using the Singleton pattern involving a static reference to a top level Cache class.
- *Lapsed listener methods.* Listeners are commonly used in Java programs in the Observer pattern [8]. Sometimes an object is added to the list of listeners, but it is not removed once it is no longer needed [20]. Here, the collection of listeners may grow unboundedly. The danger with such listener lists is that they may grow unboundedly causing the program to slow down since events are propagated to continuously growing set of listeners. Swing and AWT are very prone to this kind of problems.
- *Limbo.* Memory problems can arise also from objects that are not necessarily long-living but that occupy a consistent amount of memory. The problem occurs when the object is referenced by a long running method but it is not used. Until the method is completed, the garbage collector is not able to detect that the actual memory occupied by the object can be freed [7].

In this paper we propose a static analysis algorithm able to detect, at particular program points, the objects that are reachable from program variables but not further used by the program. This allows the possibility to free the unnecessary occupied memory. Our technique is based on the concept of *footprint*: that is, the part of memory that is actually used by a part of the program. Calculating the footprint of a piece of code singles out those allocated objects that are really needed from those that are not. The synthetization is done using *bi-abduction* [2], a recent static analysis technique which has been shown useful for calculating the footprint of large systems. Because it is based on bi-abduction our analysis is *compositional* (and therefore it has potential to scale for realistic size programs as shown in [2]) and it allows to reason about leaks for incomplete piece of code (e.g., a class or a method in isolation from others). This paper shows how bi-abduction is a valuable notion also in the context of garbage collection.

Throughout the paper we consider a running example given in Figure 1. The program uses a bag of integers and two observers for each bag, that register when an object is added to or removed from the bag, and consequently perform certain actions. The leaks here are due to live variables not being assigned null when they are no longer needed. Also, with the Observer pattern, a common mistake is not to remove the observers when they are no longer used. This is also illustrated by the example.

```
public class Driver {
        public static void main( String [] args ) {
1.              BufferedReader br = new BufferedReader(new InputStreamReader(System.in));
2.              System.out.print("Enter numbers [-1 to finish]");
3.              IntegerDataBag bag = new IntegerDataBag();    //new bag is allocated
4.              IntegerAdder adder = new IntegerAdder( bag );   //the observers are added
5.              IntegerPrinter printer = new IntegerPrinter( bag ); //to the bag
6.              Integer number = -1;
7.              try{ number = Integer.parseInt(br.readLine()); }
                    catch (IOException ioe) {
                        System.out.println("IO error trying to read input!");
                        System.exit(1);
                    }
8.              while (number >= 0) { //reading the input
                    try {           //and filling the bag
                        bag.add(number);
                        number = Integer.parseInt(br.readLine());
                    } catch (IOException ioe) {
                        System.out.println("IO error trying to read input!");
                        System.exit(1);
                    }
                }
9.              bag.printBag();
10.             ArrayList rlist = new ArrayList();
11.             rlist = bag.reverseList();  //after this point bag is no longer used
12.             IntegerDataBag revbag = new IntegerDataBag();   //new bag
13.             IntegerAdder adderr = new IntegerAdder(revbag);  //and its observers
14.             IntegerPrinter printerr = new IntegerPrinter(revbag); //but observers
15.             Iterator i = rlist.iterator();   //are not used
16.             while (i.hasNext()){
                    revbag.add((Integer) i.next());
                }
18.             Integer s=revbag.sum();
19.             Integer m=revbag.mult();
20.             System.out.print("The sum and the product are: "+s+" "+m+"\n");
        }
}
```

Fig. 1. Running example - Driver.java

2   Informal Description of the Algorithm for Discovering Memory Leaks

Our algorithm for memory leak detection is two-fold. It runs two shape analyses[1]: a *forward* symbolic execution of the program and a *backwards* precondition calculation. The memory leak at each program point is obtained by comparing the results of the two analyses. More precisely:

1. For each method of each class (apart from the main method) we calculate its specifications. The specifications describe the minimal state necessary to run the method safely (i.e., without NullPointerException).

---

[1] Shape analyses, introduced in [21], are program analyses that establish deep properties of the program heap such as a variable point to a cyclic/acyclic linked list.

2. Using the results obtained in the previous step, we calculate the precondition of each subprogram of the main method. Here, the subprogram is defined with respect to the sequential composition. The calculation of the precondition of each subprogram is done in a backwards manner, starting from the last statement in the program. The results are saved in a table as (program location, precondition) pairs.

3. Using the forward symbolic execution, intermediate states at each program point are calculated and added to the results table computed in step 2.

4. The corresponding states obtained in steps 2 and 3 are compared, and as the preconditions obtained by the backwards analysis are sufficient for safe execution of the program, any excess state that appears in the corresponding precondition obtained by the forward analysis, is considered a memory leak.

3 Basics

3.1 Programming Language

The programming language we consider here is a while java-like language [4].

$$
\begin{aligned}
s ::= {} & x = E \mid x.\langle C : t\ f \rangle = E \mid x = E.\langle C : t\ f \rangle \mid x = \mathsf{new}\ C(v) \mid \mathsf{return}\ E \\
& \mid \mathsf{invoke}\ x.\langle C : t\ m \rangle(v) \mid x = \mathsf{invoke}\ y.\langle C : t\ m \rangle(v) \mid \mathbf{if}\ B\ \mathbf{then}\ c \\
& \mid \mathbf{while}\ B\ \mathbf{do}\ c \\
c ::= {} & s \mid c; c
\end{aligned}
$$

Let $\mathsf{FN}, \mathsf{CN}, \mathsf{TN}$ and MN be countable sets of field, class, type and method names respectively. A signature of an object field/method is a triple $\langle C : t\ f \rangle \in \mathsf{CN} \times \mathsf{TN} \times (\mathsf{FN} \cup \mathsf{MN})$ indicating that the field f in objects of class C has type t. We denote a set of all signatures by Sig. Here, $E \in \mathsf{Pvar} \cup \{\mathsf{nil}\}$ and Pvar is a countable set of program variables ranging over $x, y, \ldots$, while v denotes a list of actual parameters. Basic commands include assignement, update and lookup of the heap, allocation, return from a method and method invocation. Programs consist of basic commands, composed by the sequential composition.

3.2 Storage Model and Symbolic Heaps

Let $LVar$ (ranged over by $x', y', z', \ldots$) be a set of logical variables, disjoint from program variables $PVar$, to be used in the assertion language. Let $Locs$ be a countably infinite set of locations, and let $Vals$ be a set of values that includes $Locs$. The storage model is given by:

$$
Heaps \overset{def}{=} Locs \rightharpoonup_{\mathsf{fin}} Vals \qquad Stacks \overset{def}{=} (PVar \cup LVar) \to Vals
$$
$$
States \overset{def}{=} Stacks \times Heaps,
$$

where $\rightharpoonup_{\mathsf{fin}}$ denotes a finite partial map.

Program states are symbolically represented by special separation logic formulae called *symbolic heaps*. They are defined as follows:

E	$::=$	$x \mid x' \mid \mathsf{nil}$	*Expressions*
Π	$::=$	$E{=}E \mid E{\neq}E \mid \mathsf{true} \mid p(\overline{E}) \mid \Pi \wedge \Pi$	*Pure formulae*
S	$::=$	$s(\overline{E})$	*Basic spatial predicates*
Σ	$::=$	$S \mid \mathsf{true} \mid \mathsf{emp} \mid \Sigma * \Sigma$	*Spatial formulae*
H	$::=$	$\exists \boldsymbol{x}'.\,(\Pi \wedge \Sigma)$	*Symbolic heaps*

Expressions are program or logical variables x, x' or nil. Pure formulae are conjunctions of equalities and inequalities between expressions, and abstract pure predicates $p(\overline{E})$ describe properties of variables ($\overline{E}$ denotes a list of expressions). They are not concerned with heap allocated objects. Spatial formulae specify properties of the heap. The predicate emp holds only in the empty heap where nothing is allocated. The formula $\Sigma_1 * \Sigma_2$ uses the separating conjunction of separation logic and holds in a heap h which can be split into two *disjoint parts* H_1 and H_2 such that Σ_1 holds in H_1 and Σ_2 in H_2. In symbolic heaps some (not necessarily all) logical variables are existentially quantified. The set of all symbolic heaps is denoted by SH. In the following we also use a special state fault, different from all the symbolic heaps, to denote an error state. S is a set of basic spatial predicates. The spatial predicates can be arbitrary abstract predicates [19]. In this paper, we mostly use the following instantiations of the abstract predicates $x.\langle C : t\ f\rangle \mapsto E$, $\mathsf{ls}(E, E)$ and $\mathsf{lsn}(E, E, E)$. The *points-to* predicate $x.\langle C : t\ f\rangle \mapsto E$ states that the object denoted by x points to the value E by the field f. We often use the notation $x.f \mapsto E$ when the class C and type t are clear from the context. Also, if the object has only one field, we simplify notation by writing $x \mapsto \_$. Predicate $\mathsf{ls}(x, y)$ denotes a possibly empty list segment from x to y (not including y) and it is defined as:

$$\mathsf{ls}(x, y) \iff (x = y \wedge \mathsf{emp}) \vee (\exists x'.x \mapsto x' * \mathsf{ls}(x', y))$$

Predicate $\mathsf{lsn}(O, x, y)$ is similar to $\mathsf{ls}(x, y)$, but it also keeps track of all the elements kept in the list. This is done by maintaining a set O of all the values.

$$\mathsf{lsn}(O, x, y) \iff (x = y \wedge \mathsf{emp} \wedge O = \emptyset) \vee$$
$$(\exists x', o', O'.\mathit{union}(o', O') = O \wedge x \mapsto o', x' * \mathsf{lsn}(O', x', y))$$

Here *union* is an abstract predicate indicating the union of its arguments. We do not write the existential quantification explicitly, but we keep the convention that primed variables are implicitly existentially quantified. Also, we use a field splitting model, i.e., in our model, objects are considered to be compound entities composed by fields which can be split by $*$[2]. Notice that if S_1 and S_2 describe the same field of an object then $S_1 * S_2$ implies false. A fundamental rule which gives the bases of local reasoning in separation logic is the following:

$$\frac{\{H_1\}\ C\ \{H_2\}}{\{H_1 * H\}\ C\ \{H_2 * H\}}\ \text{Frame Rule}$$

---

[2] An alternative model would consider the granularity of $*$ at the level of objects. In that case, objects cannot be split by $*$ since they are the smallest unit in the heap.

where C does not assign to H's free variables [17]. The frame rule allows us to circumscribe the region of the heap which is touched by C, (in this case H_1), perform local surgery, and combine the result with the frame, i.e. the part of the heap not affected by the command C (in this case H).

3.3   Bi-abduction

The notion of *bi-abduction* was recently introduced in [2]. It is the combination of two dual notions that extend the entailment problem: *frame inference* and *abduction*. Frame inference [1] is the problem of determining a formula $\mathfrak{F}$ (called the *frame*) which is needed in the conclusions of an entailment in order to make it valid. More formally,

Definition 1 (Frame inference). *Given two heaps H and H' find a frame $\mathfrak{F}$ such that $H \vdash H' * \mathfrak{F}$.*

In other words, solving a frame inference problem means to find a description of the extra parts of heap described by H and not by H'.

Abduction is dual to frame inference. It consists of determining a formula $\mathfrak{A}$ (called the *anti-frame*) describing the pieces of heap missing in the hypothesis and needed to make an entailment $H * \mathfrak{A} \vdash H'$ valid. In this paper we use abduction in the very specific context of separation logic.

Bi-abduction is the combination of frame inference and abduction. It consists in deriving at the same time frames and anti-frames.

Definition 2 (Bi-Abduction). *Given two heaps H and H' find a frame $\mathfrak{F}$ and an anti-frame $\mathfrak{A}$ such that $H * \mathfrak{A} \vdash H' * \mathfrak{F}$*

Many solutions are possible for $\mathfrak{A}$ and $\mathfrak{F}$. A criterion to judge the quality of solutions as well as a bi-abductive prover were defined in [2]. In this paper we use bi-abduction to find memory leaks in Java programs.

4   Detecting Memory Leaks

Algortihm 1 computes allocated objects that can be considered memory leaks, at particular program points. Firstly, the program is labelled using the *LabelPgm*() function (described in more details below). Secondly, the specs of all the methods in the program are computed using the function *CompSpecs*(). Using these specs, *ForwardAnalysis*() performs symbolic execution of the program (see Section 4.1). The result of the analysis are assertions, obtained by symbolically executing the program which represent an over-approximation of all the possible states the program can be at each location. These assertions, together with the program locations to which they correspond, are recorded in an array *LocPre*. Next, *BackwardAnalysis*() is performed, again using the calculated specs of the methods. At each program point an assertion is obtained, that represents a preconditions for a subprogram starting at that program location. These results are written in an array *LocFp* indexed by the locations. Finally, for each program

Table 1. Algorithm 1 LeakDetectionAlgorithm(Prg)

$Plocs := LabelPgm(1, Prg);$
$Mspecs := CompSpecs();$
$LocPre := ForwardAnalysis(Mspecs);$
$LocFp := BackwardAnalysis(Mspecs);$
forall $loc \in Plocs$ **do**
    $Pre := LocPre(loc);$
    $Fp := LocFp(loc);$
    $MLeak(loc) := \{R \mid H_1 \vdash H_2 * R \wedge H_1 \in Pre \wedge H_2 \in Fp\}$
end for

---

point, the results, i.e. the preconditions obtained in these two ways are compared by solving a frame inference problem. The solution frame corresponds to the memory leaked at that location.

Labelling program points. The program is labeled only at *essential* program points. A program point is considered essential only if

- it is a basic command not enclosed within a **while** or **if** statement,
- or, if it is the outer-most **while**-statement or the outer-most **if**-statement.

This means that we do not consider essential those statements within the body of **while** and **if** statements, either basic or compound. Function $LabelPgm$,

$$LabelPgm(i, s) = (i : s) \qquad LabelPgm(i, s; c) = (i : s); LabelPgm(i + 1, c)$$

takes a program and an integer, and returns a labelled program. We labelled our running example (Fig. 1) according to the labelling algorithm. Memory leaks are sought for only at the essential program locations. The rationale behind this choice can be understood as follows. If a new unnamed cell is assigned in each iteration to a variable then the garbage collector can claim the object before the iteration during the execution of the loop (if there are no references to it). For example this is the case of the `Integer.parseInt(br.readLine())` in the body of the while loop at location 8 in Fig. 1. The other possibility is when objects used in the body of the **while**-loop are potentially used in each iteration and could become a memory leak only upon the exit from the loop; for example a data structure is created, traversed or manipulated during the execution of the loop. Such structure is not a leak as long as the loop is executing (for example the `bag` in the body of the loop at location 8). Only if the structure is not used anymore after the loop has terminated, but the variable holding the structure is not set to null, then it is considered to be a leak and should be detected.

4.1   Forward and Backward Shape Analyses

Our algorithm is based on two existing shape analyses [3,2] which can be seen as attempts to build proofs for Hoare triples of a program. We provide brief and rather informal summary of both.

Forward Shape analysis. The forward shape analylsis consists of three main steps: symbolic execution, heap abstraction and heap rearrangement. Symbolic execution implements a function $\mathsf{exec} : Stmts \times \mathsf{SH} \to \mathcal{P}(\mathsf{SH}) \cup \{\mathsf{fault}\}$. It takes a statement and a heap and returns a set of resulting heaps after the execution of the statement or the special element fault indicating that there is a possible error. For example, the result of the execution of a statement $x.\langle C\colon t\ f\rangle = E_2$, which assigns value E_2 to the field f of object x, in a heap $\mathsf{H} * x.\langle C\colon t\ f\rangle \mapsto E_1$ is $\mathsf{H} * x.\langle C\colon t\ f\rangle \mapsto E_2$.

Abstraction implements the function $\mathsf{abs} : \mathsf{SH} \to \mathsf{SH}$ which helps to keep the state space small. abs is applied after the execution of any command.

The rules of symbolic execution work at the level of the object fields which is the most basic entity considered in the analysis. In other words, the rules manipulate only points to predicate $\mapsto$, but they cannot be applied to composite abstract predicates or inductive predicate like $\mathsf{ls}(x, y)$. In case the field object that needs to be accessed by symbolic execution is hidden inside one of these composite/inductive predicates, rearrangement is used to expose this field. Rearrangement implements function $\mathsf{rearr} : Heaps \times Vars \times Sig \to \mathcal{P}(\mathsf{SH})$.

Forward shape analysis can be defined as the composition of rearrangement, symbolic execution and abstraction $\mathcal{F} = \mathsf{abs} \circ \mathsf{exec} \circ \mathsf{rearr}$. The forward analysis is *sound* since it computes, at any program point, an over-approximation of the set of all states in which the program can be in any possible run [3]. Complete formal description of the forward shape analysis used here, as well as the tool jStar implementing it, can be found in [3,4].

Compositional backward shape analysis. Backward analysis is achieved using bi-abduction which allows to construct shape analysis in a compositional fashion. Given a class composed of methods $m_1(\boldsymbol{x_1}), \dots, m_n(\boldsymbol{x_n})$ the proof search automatically synthesizes preconditions $P_1, \dots, P_n$, and postconditions $Q_1, \dots, Q_n$ such that the following are valid Hoare triples:

$$\{P_1\}\, m_1(\boldsymbol{x_1})\, \{Q_1\}, \dots, \{P_n\}\, m_n(\boldsymbol{x_n})\, \{Q_n\}.$$

The triples are constructed by symbolically executing the program and by composing existing triples. The composition (and therefore the construction of the proof) is done in a bottom-up fashion starting from the leaves of the call-graph and then using their triples to build other proofs for methods which are on a higher-level in the call-graph. To achieve that, the following rule for sequential composition —called the Bi-Abductive Sequencing Rule— is used [2]:

$$\frac{\{P_1\}\, C_1\, \{Q_1\} \qquad \{P_2\}\, C_2\, \{Q_2\}}{\{P_1 * \mathfrak{A}\}\, C_1; C_2\, \{Q_2 * \mathfrak{F}\}}\ Q_1 * \mathfrak{A} \vdash P_2 * \mathfrak{F} \tag{BA-seq}$$

This rule is also used to construct a proof (triple) of a method body in compositional way. In that case the specifications that are used refer to commands (e.g., statements) or (previously proved) methods in case of a method call. BA-seq can be used to analyze the program either composing specifications "going forward"

```
1: OneFieldClass x = new OneFieldClass();  ║  {emp}c₁{x ↦ _}
2: OneFieldClass y = new OneFieldClass();  ║  {emp}c₂{y ↦ _}
3: x.update(val)                           ║  {x ↦ _}c₃{x ↦ val}
```

Fig. 2. Example code (left) and statements specifications (right)

or "going backward". Here, we use it as a core rule for the definition of our backward analysis.[3] A tool implementing bi-abductive analysis exists [2].

Forward and Backward analyses in action. In this section we exemplify forward and backward analysis by applying them to an example. Let us consider a program consisting of three labelled commands shown on the left of Fig. 2. For succinctness, let us denote the statements above as c_1, c_2 and c_3. The specifications of the statements are given on the right of the figure. In forward analysis, the program is executed symbolically, starting from an empty state. During the execution the memory is accumulated in the program state and a post-state of each statement is a pre-state of the following statement. Let us first consider what assertions at each program point we get by executing the forward analysis.

$$\{\mathsf{emp}\}c_1\{x \mapsto \_\}c_2\{x \mapsto \_ * y \mapsto \_\}c_3\{x \mapsto val * y \mapsto \_\}$$

We observe that the preconditions for the corresponding program points are:

$$1 : \mathsf{emp} \qquad 2 : x \mapsto \_ \qquad 3 : x \mapsto \_ * y \mapsto \_.$$

Let us now consider what happens when we combine the triples using the Bi-Abductive Sequencing Rule in a backwards manner. Firstly, the triples of the last two labelled statements in the program are combined, and a new triple for the subprogram consisting of these two statements is obtained. That triple is used further to be combined with the previous statement in the program, and so on, until the beginning of the program is reached. If we apply the rule to specifications for c_2 and c_3, we get

$$\frac{\{\mathsf{emp}\}\,c_2\,\{y \mapsto \_\} \qquad \{x \mapsto \_\}\,c_3\,\{x \mapsto val\}}{\{x \mapsto \_\}\,c_2; c_3\,\{x \mapsto val * y \mapsto \_\}} \quad y \mapsto \_ * x \mapsto \_ \vdash x \mapsto \_ * y \mapsto \_$$

Here, $\mathfrak{A} = x \mapsto \_$ and $\mathfrak{F} = y \mapsto \_$. Now, we combine the obtained triple for $c_2; c_3$ with the triple for c_1.

$$\frac{\{\mathsf{emp}\}\,c_1\,\{x \mapsto \_\} \qquad \{x \mapsto \_\}\,c_2; c_3\,\{x \mapsto val * y \mapsto \_\}}{\{\mathsf{emp}\}\,c_1; c_2; c_3\,\{x \mapsto val * y \mapsto \_\}} \quad \mathsf{emp} * \mathfrak{A} \vdash x \mapsto \_ * y \mapsto \_ * \mathfrak{F}$$

Here, $\mathfrak{A} = \mathsf{emp}$ and $\mathfrak{F} = \mathsf{emp}$. In this case, the preconditions for the corresponding program points are

$$1 : \mathsf{emp} \qquad 2 : x \mapsto \_ \qquad 3 : x \mapsto \_$$

---

[3] In the special case of while-loop the rule is used in a forward way combined with the abstraction mechanism which ensure convergence of the analysis [2].

Note that in the backward analysis state is accumulated in the postcondition. However, this does not pose any problem as it is the precondition that describes what state is necessary for safely running the program. The postcondition describes what is accumulated after the execution is finished (when starting from the inferred precondition).

Soundness of the algorithm. Our algorithm is sound in the sense that it only classifies as leaks a subset of those parts of memory which are allocated but not used anymore. This is stated in the following result.[4]

Theorem 1. *The* LeakDetectionAlgorithm *only identifies real leaks.*

5 Examples

In this section we illustrate how our algorithm works on several examples. Firstly, we revisit our running example given in Fig. 1 and show in detail how our algorithm operates on actual code. Then, we examine two more examples that reflect other causes of memory leaks discussed in introduction.

For the sake of succinctness, we use a special predicate $\forall_* x \in X.p(x)$, which states that property p holds for each element x of X separately. For instance, if $X = \{x_1, \ldots, x_n\}$ then $\forall_* x \in X.p(x)$ stands for $p(x_1) * \ldots * p(x_n)$.

5.1 Running Example

Our algorithm first applies the two analyses to our example. Here, we compare the results obtained by the forward and backward analyses and infer which portion of the program state can be considered a memory leak. The results of the analyses and all the necessary specification of the underlying classes in our example can be found in a technical report [5].

At label 1 of the program, the precondition obtained in both forward and backward analysis is emp, and so there is no memory leak before the execution of the program has started, as expected. In fact, class Driver does not leak any memory upto label 9. There, forward analysis finds that the symbolic state

$$\exists O. \ br \mapsto \_ * bag.list \mapsto x' * bag.observers \mapsto y' * ls(x', nil) * lsn(O, y', nil) * \\ (\forall_* o \in O.o.bag \mapsto bag)$$

describes a precondition for label 9. This precondition is a result of the symbolic execution of the program up-to that point, and so, it reflects the actual program state. That is: this precondition contains all the memory allocated and reachable in the execution of the program so far. Backward analysis, on the other hand, calculates that the precondition at this point is

$$bag.list \mapsto x' * ls(x', nil).$$

---

[4] The proof is reported in [5].

Backward analysis pinpoints the exact memory necessary for safe execution of the program. So the subprogram starting at label 9 needs nothing more and nothing less than this precondition in order to execute safely (without crashing).

Our algorithm now uses frame inference to compare these two preconditions and concludes that the state

$$\exists O.\ br \mapsto \_ * bag.observers \mapsto y' * lsn(O, y', nil) * (\forall_* o \in O.o.bag \mapsto bag)$$

is *not* necessary for the execution of the rest of program, and hence, it is a leak.

During the execution of the program memory accumulates unless it is explicitelly freed, by say, setting certain variables to null and waiting for the garbage collector to reclaim the objects that are no longer refered to by variables. In our running example, no memory is freed, and the most dramatic memory leak appears towards the end of the program. At label 18, forward analysis produces the following symbolic state as precondition:

$$\exists O, O'.\ br \mapsto \_ * bag.list \mapsto x' * bag.observers \mapsto y' * ls(x', nil) * lsn(O, y', nil)*$$
$$(\forall_* o \in O.o.bag \mapsto bag) * rlist \mapsto z' * ls(z', nil) * revbag.list \mapsto u'*$$
$$revbag.observers \mapsto v' * ls(u', nil) * lsn(O', v', nil) * (\forall_* o \in O'.o.bag \mapsto bag).$$

However, the backward analysis finds that the precondition corresponding to the same label is

$$revbag.list \mapsto x' * ls(x', nil).$$

This leaves a substantial ammount of memory to lie around in the program state, while it is not needed by the program:

$$\exists O, O'.\ br \mapsto \_ * bag.list \mapsto x' * bag.observers \mapsto y' * ls(x', nil) * lsn(O, y', nil)*$$
$$(\forall_* o \in O.o.bag \mapsto bag) * rlist \mapsto z' * ls(z', nil)$$
$$*revbag.observers \mapsto v' * lsn(O', v', nil) * (\forall_* o \in O'.o.bag \mapsto bag).$$

```
                                           {MyClass.myContainer ↦ x'  ∧  x' = nil}
                                           MyClass myObj = new Myclass();
{emp}                                      {myObj.myContainer ↦ x'  ∧  x' = nil}
myClass()                                  myObj.leak(100000);
{this.myContainer ↦ x'}                    {MyClass.myContainer ↦ x' * ls(x', nil)}
                                           {MyClass.myContainer ↦ x' * ls(x', nil)}
{this.myContainer ↦ x' * ls(x', nil)}      System.gc();
leak(i)                                    {MyClass.myContainer ↦ x' * ls(x', nil)}
{this.myContainer ↦ x' * ls(x', nil)}      //do some other computation
                                           //not involving myContainer
                                           {p*MyClass.myContainer ↦ x'*ls(x', nil)}
```

Fig. 3. Specifications (left) and forward analysis (right) of MyClass

5.2   Examples on Other Sources of Leakage

We now illustrate two examples demonstrating some of the possible causes of memory leaks discussed in the introduction. The following example illustrates a memory leak caused by a static reference. Here, we have a huge static object LinkedList which is allocated when the program starts executing. Even though it is not used anymore after a certain point in the program, because it is not explicitely set to null and it is referenced by a static variable, the garbage collector will not be able to reclaim its memory

```
public class Myclass {
  static LinkedList myContainer = new LinkedList();
  public void leak(int numObjects) {
    for (int i = 0; i < numObjects; ++i) {
      String leakingUnit = new String("this is leaking object: " + i);
      myContainer.add(leakingUnit);}
  }
  public static void main(String[] args) throws Exception {
    { Myclass myObj = new Myclass();
      myObj.leak(100000); // One hundred thousand }
    System.gc();
    // do some other computation not involving myObj
  }
}
```

Specifications of the methods and forward analysis applied to the main() method are given in Fig. 3. Here, p denotes a predicate describing the postcondition of the program and not mentioning any memory given by $MyClass.myContainer \mapsto x'* ls(x', nil)$. Since the code does not use any memory referenced by myContainer upon the exit from the local block, the backward analysis finds that myContainer is last used inside this block. Hence our algorithm discovers that at the end of this local block the memory referenced by myContainer is leaked.

In the last example we consider the phenomenon of Limbo, discussed in the introduction. The code of program and the forward analysis of main() (assuming

```
public static voin main(String args[]){          {emp}
int big_list = new LinkedList();                 int big_list = new LinkedList();
//populate the list                              {big_list ↦ x' ∧ x' = nil}
populate(big_list);                              populate(big_list);
// Do something with big_list                    {big_list ↦ x' * ls(x', nil)}
int result=compute(big_list);                    intresult = compute(big_list);
//big_list is no longer needed but               {big_list ↦ x' * ls(x', nil)}
//it cannot be garbage collected.                for(;;)handle_input(result);
//Its reference should be set                     {big_list ↦ x' * ls(x', nil)}
//to null explicitly.
for (;;) handle_input(result);  }
```

Fig. 4. Example of Limbo: code (left), and forward analysis (right)

that for handling input no memory is needed) are reported in Fig. 4. The program first allocates a very big list and does some computation over its elements. Then, it starts handling some input, which might last for very long (possibly forever). At the end of `main()`, the memory referenced by the list would be garbage collected, but as the input handling might last very long, this could lead to running out of memory. Our backward analysis discovers that the last point where `big_list` is used is `int result=compute(big_list)`. There our algorithm discovers that the code leaks the memory referenced by this variable.

6   Related Work

The paper [15] introduces a backwards static analysis which tries to disprove the assumption that the last statement has introduced a leak. If a contradiction is found, then the original assumption of the leak was wrong. Otherwise, the analysis reports a program trace that leads to the assumed error. Like ours, this analysis allows to check incomplete code. However, it can only detect memory objects that are not referenced anymore, therefore this analysis is not suitable for detecting the kind of leaks (Java leaks) we are concerned with in this paper. The same limitation applies to the techniques described in [12,9]. Similarly, the static analyses described in [6,26] aim at detecting leaks caused by objects not reachable from program variables. Therefore they cannot detect the kind of leaks we aim at with our analysis. The paper [22] introduces a static analysis for finding memory leaks in Java. This technique is tailored for arrays of objects. On the contrary, our framework works for different kind of data structures representable by abstract predicates.

A static analysis for detecting unused (garbage) objects is introduced in [25]. This analysis is similar to ours in its aim. However, the two approaches are substantially different. The authors use finite state automata to encode safety properties of objects (for example "the object referenced by y can be deallocated at line 10"). The global state of program is represented by first-order logical structures and these are augmented with the automaton state of every heap-allocated object. This shape analysis is *non* compositional and works globally. Our technique instead is compositional (since based on bi-abduction) and exploits local reasoning (since based on separation logic). Compositional shape analyses based on bi-abduction and separation logic have a high potential to scale as demonstrated in [2]. Moreover, their approach employs an automaton for each property at a program point, whereas our approach simultaneously proves properties for many objects at all essential program points in a single run of the algorithm.

Different from static approaches as the above and ours there are dynamic techniques for memory leak detection [10,16,11,23]. The main drawback with dynamic techniques is that they cannot give guarantees. Leaks that do not occur in those runs which is checked will be missed and remain hidden in the program.

7   Conclusion

Allocated but unused objects reachable from program variables cannot be reclaimed by the garbage collector. These objects can be effectively considered memory leaks since they often produce the same catastrophic problems that leaks have in languages like C: applications irreversibly slow down until they run out of memory. In this paper we have defined a static analysis algorithm which allows the detection of such allocated and unused objects which cannot be freed by the garbage collector. Our technique exploits the effectiveness of separation logic to reason locally about dynamic allocated data structures and the power of bi-abductive inference to synthesize the part of allocated memory truly accessed by a piece of code. The paper shows how separation logic based program analyses and bi-abduction can be combined to reason statically about memory leaks in garbage collected languages. We have shown the effectiveness of our technique on examples involving different sources of leakage among which the Observer pattern, that is one of the most used design patterns in real life.

All the technology for implementing this algorithm exists, and this will be our natural next step.

Acknowledgments. Distefano was supported by a Royal Academy of Engineering research fellowship. Filipović was supported by EPSRC.

References

1. Berdine, J., Calcagno, C., O'Hearn, P.: Symbolic execution with separation logic. In: Yi, K. (ed.) APLAS 2005. LNCS, vol. 3780, pp. 52–68. Springer, Heidelberg (2005)
2. Calcagno, C., Distefano, D., O'Hearn, P., Yang, H.: Compositional shape analysis by means of bi-abduction. In: POPL, pp. 289–300 (2009)
3. Distefano, D., O'Hearn, P., Yang, Y.: A local shape analysis based on separation logic. In: Hermanns, H., Palsberg, J. (eds.) TACAS 2006. LNCS, vol. 3920, pp. 287–302. Springer, Heidelberg (2006)
4. Distefano, D., Parkinson, J.: jstar: towards practical verification for java. In: OOP-SLA, pp. 213–226 (2008)
5. Distefano, D., Filipović, I.: Memory Leaks Detection in Java by Bi-Abductive Inference. Technical Report, Queen Mary University of London (January 2010)
6. Dor, N., Rodeh, M., Sagiv, M.: Checking cleanness in linked lists. In: Palsberg, J. (ed.) SAS 2000. LNCS, vol. 1824, pp. 115–135. Springer, Heidelberg (2000)
7. Flanagan, B.: Java in a Nutshell. O'Really, Sebastopol (1996)
8. Gamma, E., Helm, R., Johnson, R., Vlissides, J.: Design Patterns: Elements of Reusable Object-Oriented Software. Addison-Wesley, Reading (1995)
9. Hackett, B., Rugina, R.: Region-based shape analysis with tracked locations. In: POPL, pp. 310–323 (2005)
10. Hastings, R., Joyce, B.: Purify: Fast detection of memory leaks and access errors. In: Proceedings of the Winter USENIX Conference (1992)
11. Hauswirth, M., Chilimbi, T.: Low-overhead memory leak detection using adaptive statistical profiling. In: ASPLOS, pp. 156–164 (2004)

12. Heine, D., Lam, M.: A practical flow-sensitive and context-sensitive c and c++ memory leak detector. In: PLDI, pp. 168–181 (2003)
13. The java developer's connection. Internet page, http://bugs.sun.com/bugdatabase
14. Livshits, V.: Looking for memory leaks, http://www.oracle.com/technology/pub/articles
15. Orlovich, M., Rugina, R.: Memory leak analysis by contradiction. In: Yi, K. (ed.) SAS 2006. LNCS, vol. 4134, pp. 405–424. Springer, Heidelberg (2006)
16. Mitchell, N., Sevitsky, G.: An automated and lightweight tool for diagnosing memory leaks in large java applications. In: Cardelli, L. (ed.) ECOOP 2003. LNCS, vol. 2743, pp. 351–377. Springer, Heidelberg (2003)
17. O'Hearn, P., Reynolds, J., Yang, H.: Local reasoning about programs that alter data structures. In: Fribourg, L. (ed.) CSL 2001 and EACSL 2001. LNCS, vol. 2142, p. 1. Springer, Heidelberg (2001)
18. Pankajakshan, A.: Plug memory leaks in enterprise java applications. Internet page, http://www.javaworld.com/javaworld/jw-03-2006/jw-0313-leak.html
19. Parkinson, M., Bierman, G.: Separation logic, abstraction and inheritance. In: POPL, pp. 75–86 (2008)
20. Poddar, I., Minshall, R.: Memory leak detection and analysis in webshere application server (part 1 and 2). Internet page, http://www.ibm.com/developerworks/websphere/library/techarticles/0608_poddar/0608_poddar.html
21. Sagiv, M., Reps, T., Wilhelm, R.: Solving shape-analysis problems in languages with destructive updating. ACM Trans. Program. Lang. Syst. 20(1), 1–50 (1998)
22. Shaham, R., Kolodner, E., Sagiv, M.: Automatic removal of array memory leaks in java. In: CC, pp. 50–66 (2000)
23. Shaham, R., Kolodner, E., Sagiv, M.: Heap profiling for space-efficient java. In: PLDI, pp. 104–113 (2001)
24. Shaham, R., Kolodner, E., Sagiv, M.: Estimating the impact of heap liveness information on space consumption in java. In: MSP/ISMM, pp. 171–182 (2002)
25. Shaham, R., Yahav, E., Kolodner, E., Sagiv, M.: Establishing local temporal heap safety properties with applications to compile-time memory management. Sci. Comput. Program. 58(1-2), 264–289 (2005)
26. Xie, Y., Aiken, A.: Context- and path-sensitive memory leak detection. In: ESEC/SIGSOFT FSE, pp. 115–125 (2005)

Analyzing the Impact of Change in Multi-threaded Programs

Krishnendu Chatterjee[1], Luca de Alfaro[2], Vishwanath Raman[2], and César Sánchez[3]

[1] Institute of Science and Technology, Vienna, Austria
[2] Computer Science Department, University of California, Santa Cruz, USA
[3] IMDEA-Software, Madrid, Spain

Abstract. We introduce a technique for debugging multi-threaded C programs and analyzing the impact of source code changes, and its implementation in the prototype tool DIRECT. Our approach uses a combination of source code instrumentation and runtime management. The source code along with a test harness is instrumented to monitor Operating System (OS) and user defined function calls. DIRECT tracks all concurrency control primitives and, optionally, data from the program. DIRECT maintains an abstract global state that combines information from every thread, including the sequence of function calls and concurrency primitives executed. The runtime manager can insert delays, provoking thread interleavings that may exhibit bugs that are difficult to reach otherwise. The runtime manager collects an approximation of the reachable state space and uses this approximation to assess the impact of change in a new version of the program.

1 Introduction

Multi-threaded, real-time code is notoriously difficult to develop, since the behavior of the program depends in subtle and intricate ways on the interleaving of the threads, and on the precise timing of events. Formal verification provides the ultimate guarantee of correctness for real-time concurrent programs. Verification is however very expensive, and quite often infeasible in practice for large programs, due to the complexity of modeling and analyzing precisely and exhaustively all behaviors. Here, we aim for a more modest goal: we assume that a program works reasonably well under some conditions, and we provide techniques to analyze how the program behavior is affected by software modifications, or by changes in the platform and environment in which the program executes. Our techniques perform *sensitivity analysis* of the code with respect to its environment, and *impact analysis* for software changes [2]. These analyses assist software designers to answer two important questions: (1) *Is the program robust?* Can small changes in platform, compiler options and libraries affect the program's behavior in an important way? (2) *Does a program change introduce unexpected behaviors?*

We propose to instrument a program and run it one or multiple times. At certain points in the program, called *observable statements,* the instrumentation code collects information about the state of the execution, which we call *global state.* Observable statements include OS primitives such as lock and semaphore management, scheduling and timer calls. To perform sensitivity analysis the program is run again, but this time

D.S. Rosenblum and G. Taentzer (Eds.): FASE 2010, LNCS 6013, pp. 293–307, 2010.

the instrumentation code simulates changes in the platform. To perform change impact analysis, the versions of source code before and after a change are instrumented and run to compare the set of collected global states. These uses are described in Section 3.

We present the tool DIRECT, which implements these analyses for real-time embedded code written in C, including programs that run on embedded platforms with only limited memory available. The instrumentation stage is implemented relying on the CIL toolset [14]. The effectiveness of DIRECT is shown via two case studies: a C version of dining philosophers, and an implementation of the network protocol 'adhoc' for Lego robots. Specifically, we show how DIRECT can be used to (a) expose a bug in a new version of the adhoc protocol, (b) debug a deadlock in a naive implementation of dining philosophers, (c) compare different fork allocation policies in dining philosophers with respect to resource sharing and equity. We also report on how sensitivity analysis increases thread interleavings and hence the number of unique global states that can be observed for a fixed program and test.

Related work. Change impact analysis is well studied in software engineering [2]. For example, [15,16,17] consider change impact analysis of object-oriented programs written in Java. They use static analysis to determine changes in the implementation of classes and methods and their impact on test suites, to aid users understand and debug failing test cases. Change impact analysis is related to program slicing [19] and incremental data-flow analysis [10]. While there is a large body of work analyzing change impact from the perspective of testing and debugging of imperative, object-oriented and aspect-oriented programs, there is not much literature in change impact analysis for multi-threaded programs. There is work analyzing the impact of change on test selection and minimization [6] and in using runtime information to compute the impact set of a change [9]. Several research efforts study the impact of change based on revision histories. For example, [7] use machine learning techniques to mine source code repositories, trying to predict the propensity of a change in source code to cause a bug.

CHESS [12] explores the problem of coverage in multi-threaded programs attempting to expose bugs by exhaustive thread interleaving. Our work differs from [12] in that we study the impact of change between two versions of a program, whereas CHESS explores only the state space of a single program. Moreover, CHESS borrows techniques from model-checking and it is not easily applicable to the online testing of embedded systems. ConTest [5] explores testing multi-threaded Java programs by placing sleep statements conditionally, producing different interleavings via context switches. ConTest is a Java testing tool, that requires test specification that include the expected outcome. DIRECT does not require test specifications and it is designed to study the impact of change between two versions of a program, while [5] focuses on a single program and test. Moreover, DIRECT targets embedded C programs.

The work closest to ours is [3], that uses runtime, static and source code change information to isolate sections of newly added code that are likely causes of observed bugs. However, [3] does not address concurrent programs, and requires programmer interaction or test specifications to detect "faulty" behavior. In [3] program changes are tracked using information from a version control system. DIRECT accumulates the information at runtime, alleviating the need to rely on sometimes expensive static analysis. This way, we readily obtain a fully automatic tool for embedded systems.

2   Definitions

In this section we present a model of multi-threaded C programs. We consider interleaving semantics of parallel executions, in which the underlying architecture runs a single thread at any given time. This semantics is conventional for most current embedded platforms. The extension to real concurrency (with multi-cores or multi-processors) is not difficult but rather technical, and it is out of the scope of this paper. We now present the formal definitions of our model.

Programs and statements. The dynamics of a program P consist of the execution of a set $T = \{T_i \mid 0 \leq i \leq m\}$ of threads; we take $[T] = \{1, 2, \ldots, m\}$ as the set of indices of the threads in P. Let $Stmts$ be the set of statements of P. We distinguish a set of *observable* statements. This set includes all user defined function calls within the user program, as well as all the operating system (OS) calls and returns, where the OS may put a thread to sleep, or may delay in a significant way the execution of a thread. In particular, observable statements include invocations to manage locks and semaphores, such as *mutex_lock*, *semaphore_init* and *thread_delay*. We associate with each statement a unique integer identifier, and we denote by $S \subset \mathbb{N}$ the set of identifiers of all observable statements. We use F to denote the set of all user-defined *functions* in the program and we define $\mathcal{F} : S \mapsto \{\perp\} \cup F$ to be the map that for every statement $s \in S$ gives the function being invoked in s, if any, or $\perp$ if s is not a function call. Finally, we define the *scope* of a statement s to be the user-defined function that contains s, and represent the scope of s as $sc(s)$.

Runtime model. The program is first instrumented with a test harness, and then compiled into a self-contained executable that implements the functionality of the original program together with the testing infrastructure. A *run* is an execution of such a self-contained executable. A *thread state* is a sequence of observable statements $(s_0, s_1, \ldots, s_n)$ where s_n represents an observable statement, and $s_0, s_1, \ldots, s_{n-1}$ the function invocations in the call stack (in the order of invocation) at the time s_n is executed. Precisely, a thread state $\sigma = (s_0, s_1, \ldots, s_n) \in S^*$ is such that each s_0, $\ldots$, s_{n-1} is a call statement and for all $0 < i \leq n$, the scope of s_i is s_{i-1}, that is: $sc(s_i) = \mathcal{F}(s_{i-1})$. In particular, $sc(s_0)$ is the function in which the thread is created, typically *main*. A *block* of code is the sequence of instructions executed between two consecutive thread states. A *joint state* of the program P is a tuple $(k, \sigma_0, \sigma_1, \ldots, \sigma_m, t)$ where,

1. $k \in [T]$ is the thread index of the current active thread,
2. for $0 \leq i \leq m$, the sequence $\sigma_i \in S^*$ is the thread state of the thread T_i, and
3. t is defined as follows: let $\sigma_k = (s_0^k, s_1^k, \ldots, s_n^k)$ be the thread state of the current active thread. If s_n^k is not an OS function call then t is *user*, if s_n^k is an OS function call, then t is *call* immediately preceding the execution of statement s_n^k, and is *ret* when the OS function returns.

We refer to the joint states of the program as *abstract global states* or simply as global states. The set of all global states is represented by $\mathcal{E}$.

We illustrate these definitions using Program 1. This program consists of two threads: T_0 that executes *infa* (on the left); and T_1 that executes *infb* (on the right). Each thread

Program 1. A simple application with two threads

```
1    void infa(void)   {
2       while (1) {
3          if (exp) {
4             mutex_lock(b);
5             mutex_lock(a);
6             // critical section
7             mutex_unlock(a);
8             mutex_unlock(b);
9          } else {              21    void infb(void) {
10            mutex_lock(c);     22       while (1) {
11            mutex_lock(a);     23          mutex_lock(a);
12            // critical section 24          mutex_lock(b);
13            mutex_unlock(a);   25          // critical section
14            mutex_unlock(c);   26          mutex_unlock(b);
15         }                     27          mutex_unlock(a);
16      }                        28       }
17   }                           29    }
```

is implemented as an infinite loop in which it acquires two mutexes before entering its critical section. The calls *mutex_lock* and *mutex_unlock* are the OS primitives that request and release a mutex respectively. For simplicity, assume that the identifier of a statement is its line number. Let s_0 be the statement that launched thread T_0. The state of thread T_0 executing statement *mutex_lock(b)* at line 4 in function *infa* is $(s_0, 4)$. Similarly, the thread state of T_1 that corresponds to line 23, is $(s_1, 23)$, where s_1 is the statement that launched thread T_1. An example of a global state is $(1, (s_0, 4), (s_1, 23), call)$, produced when thread T_1 is in thread state $(s_1, 23)$ and the OS function call at line 23 is about to be executed, indicating mutex a is yet to be acquired, with T_0 being at $(s_0, 4)$. A possible successor is $(1, (s_0, 4), (s_1, 23), ret)$, produced when thread T_1 is in thread state $(s_1, 23)$, the OS function call at line 23 has returned, indicating mutex a has been acquired, with T_0 remaining at $(s_0, 4)$.

3   Sensitivity Analysis and Change Impact Analysis

Changes involved during software development and maintenance of concurrent programs can induce subtle errors by adding undesirable executions or disallowing important behaviors. Our goal is to facilitate the discovery of the changes in the behavior of the system due to changes in the source code, or in the execution platform, compiler or libraries. We consider the following sources of differences:

1. *Changes in platform.* When a program is run on a different platform, the execution of each code block may vary due to changes in the target processor.
2. *Changes in compiler options and libraries.* When included libraries or compiler options change, the execution time of each code black may vary.
3. *Source code changes.* Changes in the source code can affect resource interactions and scheduling of the various threads beyond the running time of code blocks.

The goal of DIRECT is to enable the analysis of the above changes, in terms of program behavior. DIRECT operates in two stages. First the system is exercised one or multiple times and the reached states are collected. These runs are called the *reference runs* and the union G of all the reached states is called the *reference set*. Then, a new run R of the program is obtained after the program is affected by some of the above changes. This new run is called the *test run*. The reference set G can be thought of as an approximation of the reachable state space in lieu of a formal specification. If during R a global state e is observed that was not seen in G, DIRECT outputs e along with a trace suffix leading to e. By examining the trace, developers can gain insight into how code changes or environment changes can lead to behavior changes.

Changes in platform, compiler options, and libraries. To analyze the effect of changes in platform, compiler options and libraries, the reference set G and the test run R are obtained from the same program source. G is generated by running the original program with an instrumentation that just collects events. A test run is obtained using DIRECT to modify in an appropriate fashion the duration of the code blocks. This comparison performs *sensitivity analysis,* aimed at discovering the effect of minor timing changes with respect to the reference set. DIRECT can be instructed to modify the block duration in three ways:

- *Proportional delays,* to approximate the effect of changes in platform.
- *Random delays,* to simulate the effect of interrupt handling, included libraries and other characteristics of the hardware.
- *Constant delays,* to simulate the effect of the different latencies of OS calls.

Delay changes can lead to behavior changes in multiple ways. For example, a delay may cause a sleeping thread to become enabled, so that the scheduler can choose this thread to switch contexts. For each of the three delay insertion mechanisms given above, DIRECT can do *selective sensitivity analysis,* where a subset of the threads in the program are subjected to delay insertion.

Changes in source code. To analyze the effects of source code changes, the test run R is obtained using the new version, with or without the injection of delays. For change impact analysis DIRECT compares every global state seen in the test run R of the modified program against the reference set G collected for the original program. Only events in R that correspond to statements of the original program are compared against the set G; events in R corresponding to statements introduced in the new program are trivially not in G. Since we use the set G as an approximation to a formal specification, we are interested in reporting new interleavings with respect to statements that were present in the original program due to source code changes. The instrumentation introduced by DIRECT keeps track of the corresponding statements in the two programs, making a behavioral comparison possible.

Changes in the source code typically involve some change in the logic of the program, brought about by insertion of new code, deletion of code or relocation of some sections of code. In order to analyze the impact of such change between two versions P and P' of a program, it is necessary to relate observable statements corresponding to sections of the code that did not change from P to P'.

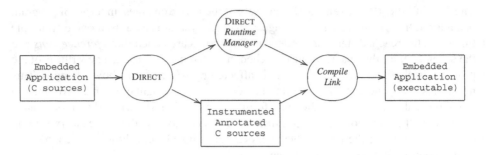

Fig. 1. DIRECT tool flow

Consider again Program 1. If the expression exp in the if condition at line 3 is not always false a deadlock can occur if Thread T_0 acquires resource a and then Thread T_1 acquires resource b. T_1 cannot release resource b until it completes its critical section, which requires resource a held by T_0. One fix for this problem consists in switching the order in which the mutexes a and b are acquired by T_0. Taking line numbers as the identifiers of all observable statements, we notice that the calls to acquire resources a and b are statements 5 and 4 before the change and 4 and 5 after the change. To analyze the impact of this code change, it is necessary to preserve the integer identifiers of these statements during program transformation, even though these statements have moved in the course of the transformation.

4   Implementation

We discuss now the relevant implementation issues.

4.1   Program Instrumentation

Fig. 1 shows the program instrumentation flow of DIRECT. DIRECT relies on the CIL toolset [14] to parse and analyze the program under consideration, and to insert instrumentation in the code. The instrumented version of the program is compiled and linked with a runtime manager to produce the final executable. The application can then be run just like the original user program. The runtime manager is a custom piece of software that gains control of the user application before and after each observable global state. The instrumentation step performs two tasks:

- replace observable statements with appropriate calls to the resource manager, allowing the tracking of visible statements and the insertion of delays.
- wrap every call to a user defined function with invocations to the run-time manager that keep track of the call stack.

Instrumenting observable statements. DIRECT reads a configuration file that specifies the set of functions to track at runtime. This set typically includes OS primitives such as mutex and semaphore acquisitions and releases, and other timing and scheduling-related primitives. Each observable statement s is replaced by a call to a corresponding

---

Program 2. man_mutex_lock replaces mutex_lock in the source code

---

```
void man_mutex_lock  (int statement_id, resource_t a)  {
   // Gets the current thread id from the set of registered threads.
   int thread_id = self_thread_id();

   // Injects pre-call delays for sensitivity analysis.
   injectDelay(thread_id, Pre);

   // Generates \ProgramEvent before the OS function call.
   registerJointState(thread_id, statement_id, call);

   // Calls the actual OS primitive.
   mutex_lock(a);

   // Injects post-call delays for sensitivity analysis.
   injectDelay(thread_id, Post);

   // Generates \ProgramEvent after the OS function call.
   registerJointState(thread_id, statement_id, ret);

   // Stores the start time of the subsequent block of code.
   storeBlockStartTime(thread_id);
}
```

---

function in the runtime manager. The function in the runtime manager performs the following tasks:

1. First, an optional delay can be introduced to simulate a longer run-time for the code block immediately preceding the observable statement.
2. The internal representation of the thread state is updated, due to the occurrence of the observable statement s.
3. The original observable statement s (such as an OS call) is executed.
4. An optional delay can be introduced, to simulate a longer response time from the OS, or the use of modified I/O or external libraries.
5. Finally, the internal representation of the thread state is again updated, indicating the completion of the statement s.

Note that DIRECT updates the thread state twice: once before executing s, another when s terminates. Distinguishing these two states is important. For example, when the thread tries to acquire a lock, the call to *mutex_lock* indicates the completion of the previous code block and the lock request, while the completion of *mutex_lock* indicates that the thread has acquired the lock. Program 2 illustrates the implementation of the runtime manager function *man_mutex_lock* that replaces the OS primitive *mutex_lock*. The first argument in all calls to runtime manager functions that replace OS functions is $s \in S$. The subsequent arguments are the actual arguments to be passed to the OS primitive.

Tracking thread states. DIRECT also tracks the call stack to perform context-sensitive analysis, distinguishing calls to the same function that are performed in different stack configurations. To this end, DIRECT wraps each function call in a *push-pop* pair. If i is the integer identifier of the call statement, the *push* instrumentation call adds i to the call stack, and the *pop* call removes it.

Preserving accurate timing. The instrumentation code, by its very existence, causes perturbations in the original timing behavior of the program. To eliminate this undesirable effect, DIRECT freezes the real-time clock to prevent the runtime processing overhead from affecting the timing of the application code. The current version of DIRECT implements this freezing as a modified version the Hardware Abstraction Layer (HAL) in the eCos synthetic target running on Ubuntu 8.04. In this manner, the exposed bugs are not caused by artificial interleavings created by the effect of the runtime manager, and they are more likely to correspond to real bugs.

Tracking corresponding pieces of code. To perform change impact analysis, it is important to identify the common, unchanged portions of P and P'. A transformation from P to P' may involve (a) sections of new code that are inserted, (b) sections of code that are deleted, and (c) sections of code that have moved either as a consequence of insertions and deletions or as a consequence of code re-organization.

DIRECT deals with these variations by first generating a text dump summarizing the CFG of P and P'. The key problem in tracking code changes is that of variations in coding style; syntactically identical program fragments may still be very different based on the use of indentation, line breaks, space characters and delimiters. Our CFG summaries preserve instructions (assignments and function calls) exactly, but summarize all other statements (blocks, conditionals, goto statements etc.) This summarization is done to remove artifacts such as labels introduced by CIL that may change from P to P', but have no bearing on tracking

```
<Block>
<Loop>
<If>
<Block>
    cyg_mutex_lock(& a);
    cyg_mutex_lock(& b);
    cyg_mutex_unlock(& b);
    cyg_mutex_unlock(& a);
<Block>
    cyg_mutex_lock(& c);
    cyg_mutex_lock(& a);
    cyg_mutex_unlock(& a);
    cyg_mutex_unlock(& c);
```

Fig. 2. A summary snippet

statements. Fig. 2 shows the summary generated for the program fragment on the left of Program 1. Given two CFG summaries, DIRECT identifies sections of code that have been preserved using a text difference algorithm [18,13,4]. Given two text documents D and D', this algorithm extracts a list of space, tab and newline delimited words from each document. The list of words are compared to produce a set of insertions, deletions and moves that transform D to D'. We use the set of moves generated by the algorithm to relate the set of statements in P that are also in P'.

Tracking additional components of the program joint state. DIRECT supports the following extensions to the joint state of a program.

- *Resource values.* Resources are often managed and synchronized using concurrency control primitives. Since DIRECT captures these control primitives the precise values of the resources can be accessed by the runtime manager with total precision. Let R be the set of all *resources*, including mutexes and semaphores. Every resource has an associated *value*, that has the range $\{0, 1, 2, \ldots, \max(r)\}$, where $\max(r) = 1$ for all mutexes and $\max(r) > 0$ for all counting semaphores.

- *Global variables.* DIRECT can also track global variables, but these values are not tracked whenever they change but only when an observable statement is reached.
- *Extending observable statements.* Users can expand on the set of OS primitives or library functions to track.
- *Block execution times.* Average block execution times of each block in each thread can be tracked to later perform proportional delay injection.

4.2 Detecting New Events Efficiently

To perform sensitivity and change impact analysis, it is crucial to test efficiently whether an observed event is a member of a given state set. Time efficiency is needed to scale to large programs. Space efficiency is especially important in the study of embedded software. Even though the set of states represented can be very large, an embedded software implementation can only use a very limited amount of memory. To achieve the desired efficiency, DIRECT stores the set of reachable states as a Bloom filter [11], a probabilistically correct data-type that implements sets of objects, offering two operations: insertion and membership checking.

Bloom filters guarantee that after inserting an element, checking membership of that element will return true. However, a membership query for an element that has not been inserted in the Bloom filter is only guaranteed to respond false (the correct answer) with a high probability. That is, Bloom filters allow some false positive answers for membership queries. This fact implies that DIRECT may (rarely) miss new global states, but that every new global state found by DIRECT is guaranteed to be new.

The performance of Bloom filters depends on the use of good (independent) hash functions, which are difficult to design. DIRECT uses double-hashing [8] to obtain k (good) hash functions from 2 (good) hash functions. Therefore, the cost of an operation is virtually that of the computation of two hash-functions, so all operations run in almost constant time.

5   Case Studies

We report two case studies: a solution to the dining philosophers problem and an adhoc protocol for legOS, adapted to run in an eCos [1] environment.

5.1   An Adhoc Protocol

We analyzed a multi-threaded implementation of an ad-hoc network protocol for Lego robots. As illustrated in Fig. 3, the program is composed of five threads, represented by ovals in the figure, that manage four message queues, represented by boxes. Threads *user* and *generator* add packets to the *input* queue. Thread *router* removes packets from the *input* queue, and dispatches them to the other queues. Packets in the *user* queue are intended for the local hardware device and hence are consumed by the *user* thread. Packets in the *broadcast* queue are intended for broadcast, and they are moved

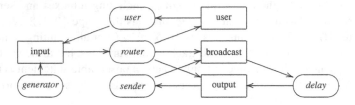

Fig. 3. Scheme of an ad-hoc network protocol implementation

Program 3. A snippet of code from the packet router thread

```
1    semaphore_wait(&bb_free_sem);
2    semaphore_wait(&bb_mutex);
4    // code that forms a new packet and copies it into
5    // the free slot in the broadcast queue
     ...
40   semaphore_post(&bb_mutex);
     ...
50   semaphore_post(&bb_els_sem);
     ...
```

---

to the *output* queue by the *delay* thread, after a random delay, intended to avoid packet collisions during broadcast propagation. Packets in the *output* queue are in transit to another node, so they are treated by the *sender* thread. Notice that if the *sender* fails to send a packet on the network, it reinserts the packet back in the *broadcast* queue (even if it is not a broadcast packet), so that retransmission will be attempted after a delay. Each queue is protected by a mutex, and two semaphores that count the number of empty and free slots, respectively. The reference implementation has no non-blocking resource requests. Program 3 shows a snippet of the router code. It first checks whether the broadcast queue is free by trying to acquire the semaphore *bb_free_sem* at line 1. If the semaphore is available, the router acquires a mutex, *bb_mutex* that controls access to the broadcast queue, before inserting a packet in the queue. Then, the router posts the semaphore *bb_els_sem* indicating that the number of elements in the queue has increased by one.

A very subtle bug is introduced by replacing the call to acquire the semaphore *bb_free_sem* by a non-blocking call. The change is itself quite tempting for a developer as this change improves CPU utilization by allowing the router not to block on a semaphore, continuing instead to process the input queue while postponing to broadcast the packet. Program 4 shows the snippet of code that incorporates this change. The bug is exhibited when the the block of code that should execute when the semaphore is successfully acquired, terminates prematurely. Specifically, the call to post the semaphore *bb_els_sem* at line 51 should only occur when the call at line 1 to acquire *bb_free_sem* succeeds. This bug goes undetected as long as the call to acquire *bb_free_sem* always succeeds. Two other threads, besides the router, access the semaphore *bb_free_sem*: the delay thread and the send thread. Notice that as long as the send thread succeeds, it does not try to place the packet back on the broadcast queue and the bug goes undetected. If

Program 4. The router thread after changing to a non-blocking call (trywait)

```
1    if (semaphore_trywait(&bb_free_sem)) {
2        semaphore_wait(&bb_mutex);
4        // code that forms a new packet and copies it into
5        // the free slot in the broadcast queue
         ...
40       semaphore_post(&bb_mutex);
41   }
     ...
51   semaphore_post(&bb_els_sem);
     ...
```

the send thread fails to send the packet, acquires *bb_free_sem* and causes the broadcast queue to fill up, the router fails to get *bb_free_sem*, exposing the bug that eventually leads to a deadlock, where packets can no longer be routed. In one of our tests for this program, we model failure to send a packet using randomization; each attempt to send a packet has an equal chance at success and failure. This test exposed the bug. Specifically, the new global state observed corresponds to an invocation to post *bb_els_sem* at line 51 in Program 4. In the Appendix, we show the last two global states in the suffix of states that lead to this new state. The global state immediately preceding the new state is one where the non-blocking semaphore request in the packet router fails. DIRECT reports a trace to the new global state (the bug) and tools to visualize this trace.

5.2 Dining Philosophers

Program 5 shows an implementation of a philosopher in a proposed solution to the dining philosophers problem analyzed using DIRECT. The numbers on the left are identifiers of observable statements. A naive implementation lets each philosopher pick up her left fork first leading to a deadlock; each philosopher is holding her left fork and none can get an additional fork to eat. Table 1, shows the tail-end of the sequence of states of a system with 5 dining philosophers. Each line shows a global state containing the index of the active thread, the state of each thread, the resource values, the set of resources held by the active thread and whether the event corresponds to a function call or return. The transition from state 5 to state 6 is the one where the fifth philosopher (thread T_4) acquires her left fork. As evidenced in state 6 all resources have been allocated with each philosopher holding one fork. This state inevitably leads to a deadlock, shown in the final state, where all philosophers are waiting at statement 3, that corresponds to a request for the second fork in Program 5. When we fix the deadlock using monotonic locking and run the program again, we notice that the new state is one where the fifth philosopher is denied her first fork, avoiding the deadlock.

We found that the sequences of states generated serve another useful purpose, namely analyzing waiting times for philosophers and checking whether the fork allocation policies are philosopher agnostic. We analyzed the sequence of states generated after fixing the deadlock. We noticed that a simple analysis on the sequence shows that the observable statement 4 where the philosophers have acquired both forks, occurs half the number of times for the first and last philosophers compared to the others. If we change

Program 5. Dining philosopher

```
void philosopher(int philosopher_id) {
  int first_fork, second_fork;

  // fork assignment policy
  first_fork = philosopher_id;
  second_fork = (philosopher_id + 1) % N_PHILS;

  if (first_fork > second_fork) {
    first_fork = second_fork;
    second_fork = philosopher_id;
  }
  while (1) {
0   thread_delay(20);        // thinking phase

    // eating phase
1   semaphore_wait(&forks[first_fork]);   // pick first fork
2   thread_delay(2);                      // pause
3   semaphore_wait(&forks[second_fork]);  // pick second fork
4   thread_delay(20);                     // eating phase
5   semaphore_post(&forks[second_fork]);  // replace second fork
6   thread_delay(2);                      // pause
7   semaphore_post(&forks[first_fork]);   // replace first fork
  }
}
```

the implementation so that all the even numbered philosophers pick their left fork first and the odd numbered philosophers pick their right fork first, they all get to eat virtually the same number of times. The latter implementation may cause livelocks under certain schedulers, but is equitable to the philosophers when compared to monotonic locking. The asymmetry in the implementation for the last philosopher turns out to be the culprit. Since the last philosopher always wishes to pick up her right fork first which is also the first fork that the first philosopher needs, they end up waiting for each other to finish. The last philosopher cannot pick up her left fork till she gets her right fork and vice versa for the first philosopher. This asymmetry favors the other philosophers. In fact, philosophers T_0 and T_4 acquire their first fork roughly half the number of times that the others do, and have the largest wait times for their forks when compared to the others.

5.3 Increasing Coverage with Random Delays

An interesting question in change impact analysis is that of coverage. Given a program, a test and a platform, how do we generate as many global states as possible? The larger the number of states that the tool exercises, the more likely it is that a state observed in a test run, that does not occur in any reference run, point to a potential bug or otherwise interesting new global state. Towards this end, DIRECT provides the mechanism of injecting random delays, in user specified ranges, that increases context switching

Table 1. A sequence leading to a deadlock in a naive implementation of dining philosophers

State no.	Thread index	T_0	T_1	T_2	T_3	T_4	Res values	Res held	(c)alls/ (r)ets
1	3	$(0,2)$	$(0,2)$	$(0,2)$	$(0,1)$	$(0,0)$	$(0,0,0,1,1)$	$()$	c
2	3	$(0,2)$	$(0,2)$	$(0,2)$	$(0,1)$	$(0,0)$	$(0,0,0,0,1)$	(3)	r
3	3	$(0,2)$	$(0,2)$	$(0,2)$	$(0,2)$	$(0,0)$	$(0,0,0,0,1)$	(3)	c
4	4	$(0,2)$	$(0,2)$	$(0,2)$	$(0,2)$	$(0,0)$	$(0,0,0,0,1)$	$()$	r
5	4	$(0,2)$	$(0,2)$	$(0,2)$	$(0,2)$	$(0,1)$	$(0,0,0,0,1)$	$()$	c
6	4	$(0,2)$	$(0,2)$	$(0,2)$	$(0,2)$	$(0,1)$	$(0,0,0,0,0)$	(4)	r
...	...								
16	4	$(0,3)$	$(0,3)$	$(0,3)$	$(0,3)$	$(0,2)$	$(0,0,0,0,0)$	(4)	r
17	4	$(0,3)$	$(0,3)$	$(0,3)$	$(0,3)$	$(0,3)$	$(0,0,0,0,0)$	(4)	c

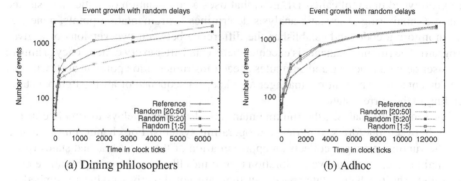

(a) Dining philosophers   (b) Adhoc

Fig. 4. Number states observed as running time increases, with and without random delays

between threads, producing new states. We studied the effect of injecting random delays in the ranges $[1..5]$, $[5..20]$ and $[20..50]$ clock ticks in all threads for the two case studies presented in this section. We plot the results in Figure 4a and Figure 4b, where the x-axis represents run durations in clock ticks and the y-axis reports the log of the number of unique states observed. In this study, we ran each program for a set of durations. In each run, we first measured the number of unique states without random delay injection; the *Reference* line in the graphs. For each duration, we then ran the same application, injecting random delays and took the union of the set of states seen in the reference run and the set of states seen with random delay injection. The size of these sets, for each run duration, are shown by the points along the lines labeled with random delays in the graphs. For dining philosophers, we noticed that the number of *new* states in the reference run is zero after 200 clock ticks, but using random delays we see an increase in the number of new states for each run duration as shown in Figure 4a. Since code blocks take longer to execute with delay injection, the total number of global states diminishes with longer delays, reducing the number of unique states seen. This phenomenon is also witnessed by the increase in states seen with smaller delay ranges. For the adhoc protocol, we noticed that the number of new states observed in the reference run decreases as the duration of the runs increase, but the number of new states are consistently higher with random delay injection just as in the case of dining philosophers. We also observed that in this case, changing the range of the random delays does not produce any significant change in the number of new states seen, unlike in the case of dining philosophers. These results on our case studies give us strong evidence that random delay injection is a good mechanism to increase the number of observed states for a given program and test. We note here that the techniques proposed in CHESS [12] or [5] can be used in addition to random delay injection to get a better approximation of the reachable state space.

6   Conclusions

This paper reports on techniques for the change impact and sensitivity analysis of concurrent embedded software written in the C programming language. These techniques are prototyped in a tool called DIRECT, that uses a combination of static analysis and runtime monitoring. The static analysis determines instrumentation points, generates the monitoring code, and establishes the difference between two versions of a given program. The runtime manager is executed before and after every concurrency primitive and user defined function, and computes at each instrumentation point an abstraction of the current state. The runtime manager also keeps a sequence of abstract global states leading to the current state.

For sensitivity analysis, the runtime manager also inserts delays to simulate differences between platforms, libraries and operating systems. For change impact analysis, the runtime manager collects an approximation of the set of reached states of the original program. Exhaustive exploration techniques like [12,5] can approximate more accurately the reachable state space, but they are not directly suitable for embedded systems, and to perform (online) change impact analysis. The states reached during the executions of the new version are then compared against the set of reached states of the original program. The prototypes were developed in a modified version of the eCos environment in which the instrumented code was executed with the real-time clock stopped, so that the execution of the runtime manager incurred no additional delay. We presented two case studies to illustrate how the techniques described in this paper can help capture bugs in concurrency programs.

There are some limitations of the work presented here that we plan to study in future research. First, we would like to apply DIRECT to large programs to see how well our techniques scale with program size. Second, the indication of a new global state may not correspond to a real bug but just a false positive. While we did not encounter such false positives in our case studies, we plan to study the number of false positives as the program size increases and steps to minimize them. Finally, the current sensitivity analysis can only insert delays in execution blocks. We would like to extend it with the ability to accelerate blocks (negative delays), whenever it is safe to do so.

We also plan to extend the techniques reported here in two directions. First, we will use DIRECT in real embedded systems, where the illusion of instantaneous execution time of the manager that we obtained via simulation is not accurate. Second, we will explore the design of schedulers that try to maximize the set of global states reached. Unlike in CHESS [12] we plan to proceed in several rounds, where the scheduler of the next round is obtained using the set of global states obtained in the previous runs with some static analysis.

References

1. ecos homepage, http://ecos.sourceware.org/
2. Arnold, R.S.: Software Change Impact Analysis. IEEE Computer Society Press, Los Alamitos (1996)
3. Bohnet, J., Voigt, S., Döllner, J.: Projecting code changes onto execution traces to support localization of recently introduced bugs. In: Proc. of the 2009 ACM Symposium on Applied Computing (SAC 2009), pp. 438–442. ACM, New York (2009)
4. Burns, R.C., Long, D.D.: A linear time, constant space differencing algorithm. In: Performance, Computing, and Communication Conference (IPCCC 1997), pp. 429–436. IEEE International, Los Alamitos (1997)
5. Edelstein, O., Farchi, E., Goldin, E., Nir, Y., Ratsaby, G., Ur, S.: Framework for testing multi-threaded Java programs. Concurrency and Computation: Practice and Experience 15(3-5), 485–499 (2003)
6. Harrold, M.J.: Testing evolving software. Journal of Systems and Software 47(2-3), 173–181 (1999)
7. Kim, S., James Whitehead, J.F., Zhang, Y.: Classifying software changes: Clean or buggy? IEEE Transactions on Software Engineering 34(2), 181–196 (2008)
8. Knuth, D.E.: The Art of Computer Programming, 2nd edn. Sorting and Searching, vol. 3. ch. 6.4. Addison-Wesley, Reading (1998)
9. Law, J., Rothermel, G.: Whole program path-based dynamic impact analysis. In: ICSE 2003, pp. 308–318 (2003)
10. Marlowe, T.J., Ryder, B.G.: An efficient hybrid algorithm for incremental data flow analysis. In: Proc.of the 17th ACM SIGPLAN-SIGACT Symposium on Principles of Programming Languages (POPL 1990), pp. 184–196. ACM, New York (1990)
11. Mitzenmacher, M., Upfal, E.: Probability and Computing. Cambridge University Press, Cambridge (2005)
12. Musuvathi, M., Qadeer, S., Ball, T., Basler, G., Nainar, P.A., Neamtiu, I.: Finding and reproducing Heisenbugs in concurrent programs. In: OSDI 2008, pp. 267–280 (2008)
13. Myers, E.W.: An O(ND) difference algorithm and its variations. Algorithmica 1(2), 251–266 (1986)
14. Necula, G.C., McPeak, S., Rahul, S.P., Weimer, W.: CIL: Infrastructure for C program analysis and transformation. In: Horspool, R.N. (ed.) CC 2002. LNCS, vol. 2304, pp. 213–228. Springer, Heidelberg (2002)
15. Ren, X., Chesley, O.C., Ryder, B.G.: Identifying failure causes in Java programs: An application of change impact analysis. IEEE Trans. Softw. Eng. 32(9), 718–732 (2006)
16. Ren, X., Shah, F., Tip, F., Ryder, B.G., Chesley, O.: Chianti: a tool for change impact analysis of Java programs. SIGPLAN Not. 39(10), 432–448 (2004)
17. Ryder, B.G., Tip, F.: Change impact analysis for object-oriented programs. In: PASTE 2001: Proceedings of the 2001 ACM SIGPLAN-SIGSOFT workshop on Program analysis for software tools and engineering, pp. 46–53. ACM, New York (2001)
18. Tichy, W.F.: The string-to-string correction problem with block move. ACM Trans. on Computer Systems 2(4) (1984)
19. Tip, F.: A survey of program slicing techniques. J. Prog. Lang. 3(3) (1995)

Evaluating Ordering Heuristics for Dynamic Partial-Order Reduction Techniques

Steven Lauterburg, Rajesh K. Karmani, Darko Marinov, and Gul Agha

Department of Computer Science
University of Illinois, Urbana, IL 61801, USA
{slauter2,rkumar8,marinov,agha}@illinois.edu

Abstract. Actor programs consist of a number of concurrent objects called actors, which communicate by exchanging messages. Nondeterminism in actors results from the different possible orders in which available messages are processed. Systematic testing of actor programs explores various feasible message processing schedules. Dynamic partial-order reduction (DPOR) techniques speed up systematic testing by pruning parts of the exploration space. Based on the exploration of a schedule, a DPOR algorithm may find that it need not explore some other schedules. However, the potential pruning that can be achieved using DPOR is highly dependent on the order in which messages are considered for processing. This paper evaluates a number of heuristics for choosing the order in which messages are explored for actor programs, and summarizes their advantages and disadvantages.

1 Introduction

Modern software has several competing requirements. On one hand, software has to execute efficiently in a networked world, which requires concurrent programming. On the other hand, software has to be reliable and dependable, since software bugs could lead to great financial losses and even loss of lives. However, putting together these two requirements—building concurrent software while ensuring that it be reliable and dependable—is a great challenge. Approaches that help address this challenge are in great need.

Actors offer a programming model for concurrent computing based on message passing and object-style data encapsulation [1, 2]. An actor program consists of several computation entities, called actors, each of which has its own thread of control, manages its own internal state, and communicates with other actors by exchanging messages. Actor-oriented programming systems are increasingly used for concurrent programming, and some practical actor systems include Actor-Foundry, Asynchronous Agents Framework, Axum, Charm++, Erlang, E, Jet-lang, Jsasb, Kilim, Newspeak, Ptolemy II, Revactor, SALSA, Scala, Singularity, and ThAL. (For a list of references, see [16].)

A key challenge in testing actor programs is their inherent nondeterminism: even for the same input, an actor program may produce different results based on the *schedule* of arrival of messages. Systematic exploration of possible message

D.S. Rosenblum and G. Taentzer (Eds.): FASE 2010, LNCS 6013, pp. 308–322, 2010.

arrival schedules is required both for testing and for model checking concurrent programs [3–5, 7, 10–12, 18, 21, 22]. However, the large number of possible message schedules often limits how many schedules can be explored in practice. Fortunately, such exploration need not enumerate all possible schedules to check the results. *Partial-order reduction (POR)* techniques speed up exploration by pruning some message schedules that are equivalent [7, 10, 12–14, 18, 22]. *Dynamic partial-order reduction (DPOR)* techniques [10, 18, 19] discover the equivalence dynamically, during the exploration of the program, rather than statically, by analyzing the program code. The actual dynamic executions provide more precise information than a static analysis that needs to soundly over-approximate a set of feasible executions. Effectively, based on the exploration of some message schedules, a DPOR technique may find that it need not explore some other schedules.

It turns out that pruning using DPOR techniques is highly sensitive to the order in which messages are considered for exploration. For example, consider a program which reaches a state where two messages, m_1 and m_2, can be delivered to some actors. If a DPOR technique first explores the possible schedules after delivering m_1, it could find that it need not explore the schedules that first deliver m_2. But, if the same DPOR technique first delivers m_2, it could happen that it cannot prune the schedules from m_1 and thus needs to perform the entire exhaustive exploration. We recently observed this sensitivity in our work on testing actor programs [16], and Godefroid mentioned it years ago [12]. Dwyer et al. [8] evaluate the search order for different exploration techniques. However, we are not aware of any prior attempt to analyze what sorts of message orders lead to better pruning for DPOR.

This paper addresses the following questions:

- What are some of the natural *heuristics* for ordering scheduling decisions in DPOR for message-passing systems?
- What is the impact of choosing one heuristic over another heuristic?
- Does the impact of these heuristics depend on the DPOR technique?
- Can we predict which heuristic may work better for a particular DPOR technique or subject program?

The paper makes two contributions. First, it presents eight ordering heuristics (Sect. 5) and evaluates them on seven subject programs (Sect. 6). We compare the heuristics for two DPOR techniques: one based on dynamically computing persistent sets [10, 12] and the other based on dCUTE [18] (Sect. 2). As our evaluation platform, we use the Basset system [16]. The results show that different heuristics can lead to significant differences in pruning, up to two orders of magnitude. Second, the paper summarizes the advantages and disadvantages of various heuristics. In particular, it points out what types of programs, based on the communication pattern of the actors, may benefit the most from which heuristics. This provides important *guidelines* for exploring actor programs in practice: based on the type of the program, the user can instruct an exploration tool to use a heuristic that provides better pruning, resulting in a faster exploration and more efficient bug finding.

2   Actor Language and Execution Semantics

For illustrative purposes, we describe an imperative actor language *ActorFoundry* that is implemented as a Java framework [15]. A class that describes an actor behavior extends `osl.manager.Actor`. An actor may have local state comprised of primitives and objects. The local state cannot be shared among actors. An actor can communicate with another actor in the program by sending asynchronous messages using the library method `send`. The sending actor does not wait for the message to arrive at the destination and be processed. The library method `call` sends an asynchronous message to an actor but blocks the sender until the message arrives and is processed at the receiver. An actor definition includes method definitions that correspond to messages that the actor can accept and these methods are annotated with `@message`. Both `send` and `call` can take arbitrary number of arguments that correspond to the arguments of the corresponding method in the destination actor class. The library method `create` creates an actor instance of the specified actor class. It can take arbitrary number of arguments that correspond to the arguments of the constructor. Message parameters and return types should be of the type `java.io.Serializable`. The library method `destroy` kills the actor calling the method. Messages sent to the killed actor are never delivered. Note that both `call` and `create` may throw a checked exception `RemoteCodeException`.

We informally present semantics of relevant ActorFoundry constructs to be able to more precisely describe the algorithms in Sect. 3. Consider an Actor-Foundry program P consisting of a set of actor definitions including a *main* actor definition that receives the initial message. $send(a, msg)$ appends the contents of the message msg to the message queue of actor a. We will use Q_a to denote the message queue of actor a. We assume that at the beginning of execution the message queue of all actors is empty.

The ActorFoundry runtime first creates an instance of the main actor and then sends the initial message to it. Each actor executes the following steps in a loop: remove a message from the queue (termed as an *implicit receive* statement from here on), decode the message, and process the message by executing the corresponding method. During the processing, an actor may update the local state, create new actors, and send more messages. An actor may also throw an exception. If its message queue is empty, the actor blocks waiting for the next message to arrive. Otherwise, the actor *nondeterministically* removes a message from its message queue. The nondeterminism in choosing the message models the asynchrony associated with message passing in actors. An actor executing a `create` statement produces a new instance of an actor.

An actor is said to be *alive* if it has not already executed a `destroy` statement or thrown an exception. An actor is said to be *enabled* if the following two conditions hold: the actor is alive, and the actor is not blocked due to an empty message queue or executing a `call` statement.

A variable pc_a represents the program counter of the actor a. For every actor, pc_a is initialized to the implicit receive statement. A scheduler executes a loop inside which it *nondeterministically* chooses an enabled actor a from the set $\mathcal{P}$.

It executes the next statement of the actor a, where the next statement is obtained by calling $statement\_at(pc_a)$. During the execution of the statement, the program counter pc_a of the actor a is modified based on the various control flow statements; by default, it is incremented by one.

The concrete execution of an internal statement, i.e., a statement not of the form **send**, **call**, **create**, or **destroy**, takes place in the usual way for imperative statements. The loop of the scheduler terminates when there is no enabled actor in $\mathcal{P}$. The termination of the scheduler indicates either the normal termination of a program execution, or a deadlock state (when at least one actor in $\mathcal{P}$ is waiting for a **call** to return).

3   Automated Testing of ActorFoundry Programs

To automatically test an ActorFoundry program for a given input, we need to explore all *distinct*, feasible execution paths of the program. A path is intuitively a sequence of statements executed, or as we will see later, it suffices to have just a sequence of messages received. In this work, we assume that the program always terminates and a test harness is available, and thus focus on exploring the paths for a given input. A simple, systematic exploration of an ActorFoundry program can be performed using a *naïve* scheduler: beginning with the initial program state, the scheduler nondeterministically picks an enabled actor and executes the next statement of the actor. If the next statement is implicit receive, the scheduler nondeterministically picks a message for the actor from its message queue. The scheduler records the ids of the actor and the message, if applicable. The scheduler continues to explore a path in the program by making these choices at each step. After completing execution of a path (i.e., when there are no new messages to be delivered), the scheduler backtracks to the last scheduling step (in a depth-first strategy) and explores alternate paths by picking a different enabled actor or a different message from the ones chosen previously.

Note that the number of paths explored by the naïve scheduler is exponential in the number of enabled actors and the number of program statements in all enabled actors. However, an exponential number of these schedules is equivalent. A crucial observation is that actors do not share state: they exchange data and synchronize only through messages. Therefore, it is sufficient to explore paths where actors interleave at message receive points only. All statements of an actor between two implicit receive statements can be executed in a single *atomic* step called a *macro-step* [2, 18]. At each step, the scheduler picks an enabled actor and a message from the actor's message queue. The scheduler records the ids of the actor and the message, and executes the program statements as a macro-step. A sequence of macro-steps, each identified by an actor and message pair (a, m), is termed a *macro-step schedule*. At the end of a path, the scheduler backtracks to the last macro-step and explores an alternate path by choosing a different pair of actor and message (a, m).

Note that the number of paths explored using a macro-step scheduler is exponential in the number of deliverable messages. This is because the scheduler,

```
scheduler(P)
  pc_{a_1} = l_0^{a_1}; pc_{a_2} = l_0^{a_2}; ...; pc_{a_n} = l_0^{a_n};
  Q_{a_1} = []; Q_{a_2} = []; ...; Q_{a_n} = [];
  i = 0;
  while (∃a ∈ P such that a is enabled)
    (a,msg_id) = next(P);
    i = i + 1;
    s = statement_at(pc_a);
    execute(a, s, msg_id);
    s = statement_at(pc_a);
    while (a is alive and s ≠ receive(v))
      if s is send(b, v)
        for all k ≤ i
          such that b == path_c[k].receiver
          and canSynchronize(path_c[k].s, s)
          // actor a' "causes" s
          path_c[k].S_p.add((a', _));
        execute(a, s, msg_id);
        s = statement_at(pc_a);
  compute_next_schedule();
```

```
compute_next_schedule()
  j = i - 1;
  while j ≥ 0
    if path_c[j].S_p is not empty
      path_c[j].schedule =
        path_c[j].S_p.remove();
      path_c = path_c[0 ... j];
      return;
    j = j - 1;
  if (j < 0) completed = true;
```

```
next(P)
  if (i ≤ |path_c|)
    (a,msg_id) = path_c[i].schedule;
  else
    (a,msg_id) = choose(P);
    path_c[i].schedule = (a,msg_id);
    path_c[i].S_p.add((a, _));
  return (a,msg_id);
```

Fig. 1. Dynamic partial-order reduction algorithm based on persistent sets

for every step, executes all permutations of actor and message pairs (a, m) that are enabled before the step. However, messages sent to different actors may be independent of each other, and it may be sufficient to explore all permutations of messages for a *single* actor instead of all permutations of messages for *all* actors [18].

The independence between certain events results in equivalent paths, in which different orders of independent events occur. The equivalence relation between paths is exploited by dynamic partial-order reduction (DPOR) algorithms to speed-up automatic testing of actor programs by pruning parts of the exploration space. Specifically, the equivalence is captured using the *happens-before relation* [9, 18], which yields a partial order on the state transitions in the program. The goal of DPOR algorithms is to explore only one linearization of each partial order or equivalence class.

We next describe two stateless DPOR algorithms for actor programs: one based on dynamically computing persistent sets [10] (adapted for testing actor programs), and the other one used in dCUTE [18].

DPOR based on Persistent Sets

Flanagan and Godefroid [10] introduced a DPOR algorithm that dynamically tracks dependent transitions and computes persistent sets [12] among concurrent processes. They presented the algorithm in the context of shared-memory programs. Figure 1 shows our adaptation of their algorithm for actor programs, which also incorporates the optimization discussed by Yang et al. [23].

The algorithm computes persistent sets in the following way: during the initial run of the program, for every scheduling point, the scheduler *nondeterministically* picks an enabled actor (call to the *choose* method, which is underlined) and adds all its pending messages to the persistent set S_p. It then explores all permutations of messages in the persistent set. During the exploration, if the scheduler

```
scheduler(P)
    pc_{a_1} = l_0^{a_1}; pc_{a_2} = l_0^{a_2}; ...; pc_{a_n} = l_0^{a_n};
    Q_{a_1} = []; Q_{a_2} = []; ...; Q_{a_n} = [];
    i = 0;
    while (∃a ∈ P such that a is enabled)
        (a, msg_id) = next(P);
        i = i + 1;
        s = statement_at(pc_a);
        execute(a, s, msg_id);
        s = statement_at(pc_a);
        while (a is alive and s ≠ receive(v))
            if s is send(b, v)
                for all k ≤ i
                    such that b == path_c[k].receiver
                    and canSynchronize(path_c[k].s, s)
                    path_c[k].needs_delay = true;
            execute(a, s, msg_id);
            s = statement_at(pc_a);
        compute_next_schedule();
```

```
compute_next_schedule()
    j = i − 1;
    while j ≥ 0
        if path_c[j].next_schedule ≠ (⊥, ⊥)
            (a, m) = path_c[j].schedule;
            (b, m') = path_c[j].next_schedule;
            if a == b or path_c[j].needs_delay
                path_c[j].schedule =
                    path_c[j].next_schedule;
                if a ≠ b
                    path_c[j].needs_delay = false;
                path_c = path_c[0 ... j];
                return;
        j = j − 1;
    if (j < 0) completed = true;

next(P)
    if (i ≤ |path_c|)
        (a, msg_id) = path_c[i].schedule;
    else
        (a, msg_id) = choose(P);
        path_c[i].schedule = (a, msg_id);
        path_c[i].next_schedule = next(a, msg_id);
    return (a, msg_id);
```

Fig. 2. Dynamic partial-order reduction algorithm for the dCUTE approach

encounters a **send**(a, v) statement, say at position i in the current schedule, it analyzes all the receive statements executed by a earlier in the same execution path (represented as $path\_c$). If a receive, say at position $k < i$ in the schedule, is not related to the send statement by the happens-before relation (checked in the call to method $canSynchronize$), the scheduler adds pending messages for a new actor a' to the persistent set at position k. The actor a' is "responsible" for the send statement at i, i.e., a receive for a' is enabled at k, and it is related to the send statement by the happens-before relation.

DPOR in dCUTE

Figure 2 shows the DPOR algorithm that is a part of the dCUTE approach for testing open, distributed systems [18]. (Since we do not consider open systems here, we ignore the input generation from dCUTE.) It proceeds in the following way: during the initial run of the program, for every scheduling point, the scheduler *nondeterministically* picks an enabled actor (call to the *choose* method, which is underlined) and explores permutations of messages enabled for the actor. During the exploration, if the scheduler encounters a send statement of the form **send**(a, v), it analyzes all the receive statements seen so far in the same path. If a receive statement is executed by a, and the send statement is not related to the receive in the happens-before relation, the scheduler sets a flag at the point of the receive statement. The flag indicates that all permutations of messages to some other actor a' (different from a) need to be explored at the particular point. The exploration proceeds in a nondeterministic fashion again from there on. A more detailed discussion of the algorithm can be found in [18].

Note that the algorithms discussed above re-execute the program from the beginning with the initial state in order to explore a new program path. The algorithms can be easily modified to support checkpointing and restoration of intermediate states, since these operations do not change DPOR fundamentally.

4   Illustrative Example

To illustrate key DPOR concepts and how different message orderings can affect the exploration of actor programs, we use a simple example actor program that computes the value of π. It is a porting of a publicly available [17] MPI example, which computes an approximation of π by distributing the task among a set of worker actors.

Figure 3 shows a simplified version of this code in ActorFoundry. The Driver actor creates a *master* actor that uses a given number of *worker* actors to carry out the computation. The Driver actor sends a start message to the master actor which in turn sends messages to each worker, collects partial results from them, reduces the partial results, and after all results are received, instructs the workers to terminate and terminates itself.

Figure 4 shows the search space for this program with master actor M and two worker actors A and B. Each state in the figure contains a set of messages. A message is denoted as X_Y where X is the actor name and Y uniquely identifies the message to X. We assume that the actors are created in this order: A, B, M. Transitions are indicated by arrows labeled with the message that is received, where a transition consists of the delivery of a message up to the next delivery.

The *boxed* states indicate those states that will be visited when the search space is explored using a DPOR technique, and when actors are chosen for exploration according to *the order in which the receiving actors are created*. Namely, the search will favor exploration of messages to be delivered to A over those to be delivered to B or M, so if in some state (say, the point labeled K) messages can be delivered to both A and B, the search will first explore the delivery to A and only after that the delivery to B. To illustrate how this ordering affects how DPOR prunes execution paths, consider the state at point G. For this state, the algorithm will first choose to deliver the message B_1. While exploring the search space that follows from this choice, all subsequent sends to actor B are causally dependent on the receipt of message B_1. This means that DPOR does not need to consider delivering the message M_A before B_1. This allows pruning the two paths that delivering M_A first would require. Similar reasoning shows that DPOR does not need to consider delivering B_2 before A_2 at points S and T, and that it does not need to consider delivering B_1 at point K. In total, this ordering prunes *10 of 12* paths, i.e., with this ordering, only 2 of 12 paths are explored.

The *shaded* states indicate those states that will be visited when the search space is explored using the same DPOR, but when actors are chosen for exploration according to *the reverse-order in which the receiving actors are created*. This means that the search will favor exploration of messages to be delivered to M over those to be delivered to B or A. This reverse-ordering causes DPOR to prune execution paths differently. Consider the state at point H. For this

```
class Master extends Actor {                  class Worker extends Actor {
  ActorName[] workers;                          int id;
  int counter = 0;                              int nbWorkers;
  double result = 0.0;                          public Worker(int id, int nb) {
  public Master(int N) {                          this.id = id;
    workers = new ActorName[N]                     this.nbWorkers = nb;
    for (int i = 0; i < N; i++)                 }
      workers[i] =                              @message void intervals(ActorName master, int n) {
        create(Worker.class, i, N);              double h = 1.0 / n; double sum = 0;
  }                                              for (int i = id; i <= n; i += nbWorkers) {
  @message void start() {                          double x = h * (i - 0.5);
    int n = 1000;                                  sum += (4.0 / (1.0 + x*x));
    for (ActorName w: workers)                   }
      send(w,"intervals", self(), n);            send(master, "sum", h * sum);
  }                                            }
  @message void sum(double p) {                @message void stop() {destroy("done");}
    counter++;                               }
    result += p;
    if (counter == workers.length) {         class Driver extends Actor {
      for (ActorName w: workers)               static void main(String[] args) {
        send(w,"stop");                          ActorName master =
      destroy("done");                             create(Master.class, args[0]);
    }                                            send(master, "start");
  }                                            }
}                                            }
}
```

Fig. 3. ActorFoundry code for the pi example

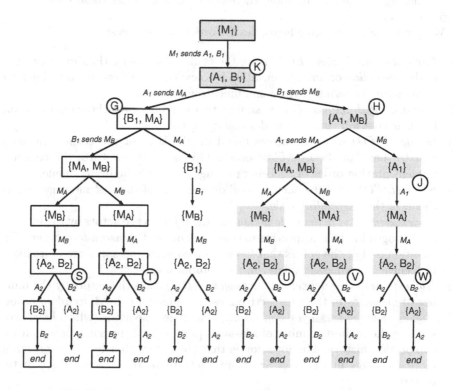

Fig. 4. State space for the pi example with two worker actors

state, the algorithm will first choose to deliver the message M_B. Following this path, it comes to point J, where the delivery of message A_1 results in message M_A being sent. This send to actor M is *not* causally dependent on the receipt of message M_B. This means that the DPOR also needs to consider delivering the message A_1 before M_B at point H. As the search continues, it discovers that it does not need to consider delivering A_2 before B_2 at points U, V, and W; and also it does not need to consider delivering A_1 at point K. In total, the reverse-ordering prunes *9 of 12* paths, which is one fewer than when the messages are selected in the order in which the receiving actors are created. As shown in Sect. 6, this difference in the number of paths pruned increases as the number of worker actors increases.

5 Heuristics

The example in Sect. 4 illustrates the idea that scheduling decisions may affect the efficiency of DPOR techniques. In the algorithms presented in Sect. 3, the scheduling choices are represented by the calls to the *choose* method (underlined). Observe that these DPOR algorithms first collect all possible messages for an actor at a given state, and then explore some orders for processing this set of messages. The key question, therefore, is how to order these messages for a given state.

We present eight possible heuristics for ordering messages:

1. *Earliest created actor (ECA)* sorts the enabled actors by their creation time in the *ascending* order. The intuition is to capture the "asymmetry" between some actors in terms of the communication pattern.
2. *Latest created actor (LCA)* is similar to ECA but sorts the enabled actors by their creation time in the *descending* order.
3. *Queue (FIFO)* sorts the actors based on the time of the *earliest* message sent to them, in the *ascending* order. This heuristic captures the common implementation order of choosing messages from a scheduling queue.
4. *Stack (LIFO)* sorts the actors based on the time of the *last* message sent to them, in the *descending* order.
5. *Lowest number of deliverable messages (LDM)* sorts the actors by the number of messages in their respective message queue, in the *ascending* order. The intuition is that the actors that have received more messages are more likely to receive more messages later in the computation.
6. *Highest number of deliverable messages (HDM)* sorts the actors by the number of messages in their respective message queue, in the *descending* order.
7. *Highest average messages sent (HMS)* prioritizes the actors which have been sending the highest number of messages per received message, based on the exploration history. The intuition is that the actors that have been sending more messages in the past are more likely to send more messages in the future.

8. *Send graph reachability (SGR)* is based on information collected during prior executions. Specifically, it maintains a directed graph where nodes represent actors and edges indicate that a message was sent from the first node to the second at some point in the exploration. Now, consider two messages: one to actor A, and one to actor B. If actor B is reachable in the graph from actor A and no such path exists from actor B to actor A, then SGR will prioritize actor A over actor B. The intuition is that actor B is less likely to cause a message to be sent to actor A.

These eight heuristics capture some intuition based on the functioning of the DPOR algorithms and on the patterns of communication in actor programs. While our list of heuristics is not complete by any means, we believe that it is sufficiently representative to help us answer the questions raised by our study (Sect. 1).

6 Evaluation

To evaluate the different heuristics for dynamic partial-order reduction, we conducted experiments using two different DPOR techniques. The heuristics and DPOR techniques are implemented in the Basset framework [16]. Basset provides an extensible environment for exploration of Java-based actor programs. It is built on top of Java PathFinder (JPF), a popular explicit state model checker for Java bytecode [20].

We first describe the subject programs used to quantitatively evaluate the heuristics. We then present experimental results comparing the different heuristics for the two DPOR techniques. All experiments are performed using Sun's JVM 1.6.0_16-b01 on a 2.80GHz Intel Core2 Duo running Ubuntu release 9.04.

6.1 Subject Programs

Our experiments use the seven actor programs listed in Table 1. All of these subjects are either originally written using the ActorFoundry library [1, 2] or ported to that environment.

The `pi` subject is the example described in Sect. 4. However, the results shown here are for a configuration using five worker actors. Two of the subjects implement more complex algorithms previously used in the dCUTE study [18]: `leader` is an implementation of a leader election algorithm; and `shortpath` is an implementation of the Chandy-Misra's shortest path algorithm [6]. The `shortpath` subject appears twice in the results: once for a graph with 4 nodes (`shortpathA`), and again for a graph with 5 nodes (`shortpathB`). Note that the two graphs are dissimilar. The `fibonacci` subject computes the n-th element in the Fibonacci sequence. `quicksort` is an implementation of a distributed sorting algorithm that use a standard divide-and-conquer strategy to carry out the computation. `pipesort` is a modified version of the sorting algorithm used in the dCUTE study [18]. `chameneos` is an implementation of the `chameneos-redux` benchmark from the Great Language Shootout (http://shootout.alioth.debian.org).

Table 1. Comparison of different ordering heuristics. (The best result is bold.)

Heur.	Subject	dCUTE # of Paths	time [sec]	Persistent # of Paths	time [sec]	Subject	dCUTE # of Paths	time [sec]	Persistent # of Paths	time [sec]
ECA	chameneos	3821	300	19683	1474	pipesort size=4	**288**	**22**	**288**	**23**
LCA		**216**	**19**	**216**	**20**		5970	441	5970	453
FIFO		972	75	3240	267		1794	128	1791	138
LIFO		2031	142	4899	320		1080	77	1080	78
LDM		753	67	3375	279		384	33	384	32
HDM		3821	312	19683	1626		2072	154	1480	126
HMS		3691	301	19683	1639		307	25	307	26
SGR		3821	280	19683	1422		**288**	**24**	**288**	**24**
ECA	fib(5)	684	65	327	31	quicksort size=6	7038	514	3822	327
LCA		**16**	**5**	**16**	**5**		**32**	**6**	**32**	**6**
FIFO		68	9	40	7		572	48	368	31
LIFO		81	12	81	13		243	26	243	25
LDM		508	51	261	28		6390	512	2502	206
HDM		526	59	263	31		5118	424	2804	250
HMS		82	12	66	10		195	21	183	21
SGR		684	70	327	34		7038	514	3822	325
ECA	leader	101	9	101	9	shortpath graph A	516	32	392	25
LCA		188	16	188	15		680	43	640	33
FIFO		122	12	119	12		**360**	**24**	**238**	**18**
LIFO		125	11	125	11		859	48	750	36
LDM		133	12	133	12		585	42	492	33
HDM		**88**	**9**	**88**	**9**		562	39	419	30
HMS		141	14	126	12		540	35	453	32
SGR		101	9	101	10		516	33	392	25
ECA	pi 5 workers	**120**	**25**	**120**	**22**	shortpath graph B	7216	397	2658	127
LCA		945	142	19845	2921		7462	570	1865	109
FIFO		**120**	**22**	**120**	**22**		**3488**	**244**	**528**	**41**
LIFO		945	149	19845	2833		6472	489	2638	167
LDM		**120**	**23**	**120**	24		7326	509	1178	71
HDM		706	120	3424	614		13438	1111	2756	273
HMS		945	179	19845	3542		3618	268	783	44
SGR		153	29	567	77		7940	493	3349	186

6.2   Results and Observations

Table 1 shows the results of experiments comparing the different heuristics for both the DPOR based on persistent sets and the one used for dCUTE. For each heuristic, we tabulate the total number of paths executed and the total exploration time in seconds. The results suggest that the efficiency of the two DPOR techniques is greatly dependent on the order in which messages are selected for exploration.

Recall the four research questions posed in Sect. 1. The first question is discussed in Sect. 5 where we describe some intuitive ordering heuristics to guide

DPOR algorithms. We address the remaining three questions now by making observations on the results in Table 1.

1. What is the impact of choosing one heuristic over another heuristic?

The table shows that for 6 out of 8 experiments, one of the heuristics (but not necessarily the same) performs the best, i.e., there is no tie for the best performing heuristic. In the case of `pipesort` the tie between ECA and SGR is due to the relationship between the two heuristics. Specifically, ECA is the tie-breaking heuristic for SGR.

SGR performs the same as ECA for 6 out of 8 experiments. However, for the remaining two experiments, SGR performs worse than ECA. This suggests that the SGR heuristic, despite its usage of additional information, does not offer any advantage over ECA.

We also observe that the difference between the best and the worst heuristic can be very large. For example, for the `quicksort` subject sorting an array of size 6 and dCUTE DPOR, the best heuristic (LCA) has 2 orders of magnitude (more precisely, 220X) fewer executions than the worst performing heuristic (ECA). Note that both these heuristics are natural orders on the scheduling queue. In fact, the dCUTE DPOR algorithm as originally presented [18] employs the ECA ordering. The second best performing heuristic (HMS) for `quicksort` still explores 6 times as many executions as the best heuristic. For the other subjects, the ratio between the number of executions in the worst and the best case ranges from 2X (for `leader`) to 91X (for `chameneos`).

In general, the exploration time strongly correlates with the number of executed paths. This observation suggests that the better heuristics do not have a significant computation cost, and thus their reduction in the number of executions directly translates into savings in the exploration time. There are exceptions: for the subject `shortpathB`, the exploration time does not correlate with the number of paths executed as closely as other experiments. We believe that this is due to our experiments using Basset which is built on top of JPF and uses checkpointing and restoring to explore different paths, rather than re-execution. Hence, the time may relate more to the number of states visited instead of the number of executions, or stated differently, the time may depend more strongly on the length of executions instead of the number of executions.

2. Does the impact of these heuristics depend on the DPOR technique?

Although the results differ between the two DPOR algorithms for the experiments, the results exhibit a *similar ranking* of heuristics for both algorithms. In other words, for a given subject, heuristics that perform well for one DPOR technique tend to perform well for the other. Similarly, a heuristic that performs poorly typically does so for both DPOR algorithms.

It is evident from the table that for all 8 experiments, the best heuristic exactly matches for both DPOR algorithms. Moreover, even the worst heuristic matches for 7 out of 8 experiments.

3. Can we predict which heuristic may work better for a particular DPOR technique or subject program?

We found that which heuristic performs the best relates to the communication patterns employed by the program. For example, in a *pipelined computation*, it is more efficient to schedule first the actors that represent the early stages in the pipeline. On the other hand, in a *divide-and-conquer tree*, it is more efficient to schedule child actors before the parent actor.

Indeed, the ECA heuristic is the best performing heuristic for `pipesort`. ECA prioritizes actors in the early stages of a pipeline, and this enables the DPOR algorithms to collect all possible messages for actors in the later stages of the pipeline.

For 3 out of 8 subjects, the LCA heuristic performs the best among all heuristics. Two of these subjects—`fib` and `quicksort`—employ a divide-and-conquer approach. The remaining subject, `chameneos`, has a request-reply pattern between a broker and many clients. LCA allows the DPOR algorithm to collect all possible messages sent from the clients to the broker before exploring all the permutations of this set of messages.

For subjects with arbitrary graphs and communication patterns, the FIFO heuristic outperforms the remaining heuristics. For instance, the input graphs for `shortpathA` and `shortpathB` are dissimilar, and the effectiveness of several heuristics varied between the two experiments. Yet, the FIFO heuristic is the most effective heuristics for both inputs.

We performed some additional experiments for `shortpath` (not shown in the table) to identify how much the choice of heuristic depends on the program *input* rather than program *code*. In particular, the input to `shortpath` is a graph, and the messages exchanged depend on the topology of this graph. We considered seven more graphs (all with four or five nodes) in addition to the two for which the results are shown. While there is some variation of the results, in all the cases, FIFO is the best heuristic, either by itself, or together with some other heuristics (e.g., for a graph that is a list, there is only one execution path for any heuristic). These results are not conclusive, but they strongly suggest that the choice of heuristic depends on the program (and its communication pattern) more than on the input. Ideally, we would like to evaluate how `shortpath` performs for all graphs of a given size (but some explorations time out after an hour even for graphs of size just four). We would also like to evaluate sensitivity of heuristics to the inputs for other programs. We leave that as future work.

In summary, the results suggest the following set of guidelines for selecting a heuristic before the exploration of a program. (1) If there is no well-defined topology and communication pattern in the program (or if this communication pattern is not known a priori), then the default heuristic should be FIFO, since it is never the worst and sometimes is even the best heuristic. (2) If the communication pattern is a pipeline, then ECA should be used. (3) If the communication pattern is a divide-and-conquer tree, then LCA should be used.

7 Conclusions

Systematic exploration of message schedules is a viable approach to address the important but challenging problem of testing actor programs. Dynamic partial-order reduction (DPOR) techniques can significantly speed up systematic exploration, but they are highly sensitive to the order in which messages are explored. We described and compared several heuristics that can be used for ordering messages. Our results show up to two orders of magnitude difference in the number of executions explored. Moreover, our analysis of the results discovered guidelines that, based on the type of program, can aid selection of a good heuristic before the exploration. There has been recent work on combining DPOR techniques with stateful exploration [24, 25], and we plan to evaluate the effectiveness of heuristics for such approaches. Similarly, we plan to evaluate the impact of heuristics on DPOR algorithms based on sleep sets [12].

Acknowledgments. The authors would like to thank Mirco Dotta, Stoyan Gaydarov, and Bobak Hadidi for their help in preparing evaluation subjects, and Samira Tasharofi for discussions and other assistance during the course of this project. This material is based upon work partially supported by the National Science Foundation under Grant Nos. CCF-0916893, CNS-0851957, CCF-0746856, and CNS-0509321.

References

1. Agha, G.: Actors: A model of concurrent computation in distributed systems. MIT Press, Cambridge (1986)
2. Agha, G., Mason, I.A., Smith, S.F., Talcott, C.L.: A foundation for actor computation. Journal of Functional Programming 7(1), 1–72 (1997)
3. Artho, C., Garoche, P.L.: Accurate centralization for applying model checking on networked applications. In: 21st IEEE/ACM International Conference on Automated Software Engineering, ASE 2006, pp. 177–188. IEEE Comp. Society, Los Alamitos (2006)
4. Arts, T., Earle, C.B.: Development of a verified Erlang program for resource locking. In: Formal Methods in Industrial Critical Systems (2001)
5. Barlas, E., Bultan, T.: NetStub: A framework for verification of distributed Java applications. In: 22nd IEEE/ACM International Conference on Automated Software Engineering, ASE 2007, pp. 24–33. ACM, New York (2007)
6. Chandy, K.M., Misra, J.: Distributed computation on graphs: Shortest path algorithms. Comm. ACM (1982)
7. Clarke, E.M., Grumberg, O., Peled, D.A.: Model Checking. MIT Press, Cambridge (1999)
8. Dwyer, M.B., Person, S., Elbaum, S.G.: Controlling factors in evaluating path-sensitive error detection techniques. In: Proceedings of the 14th ACM SIGSOFT International Symposium on Foundations of Software Engineering, FSE 2006, pp. 92–104. ACM, New York (2006)

9. Fidge, C.J.: Partial orders for parallel debugging. In: Workshop on Parallel and Distributed Debugging, pp. 183–194 (1988)
10. Flanagan, C., Godefroid, P.: Dynamic partial-order reduction for model checking software. In: Proceedings of the 32nd ACM SIGPLAN-SIGACT Symposium on Principles of Programming Languages, POPL 2005, pp. 110–121. ACM, New York (2005)
11. Fredlund, L.Å., Svensson, H.: McErlang: A model checker for a distributed functional programming language. In: Proceedings of the 12th ACM SIGPLAN International Conference on Functional Programming (ICFP), pp. 125–136 (2007)
12. Godefroid, P. (ed.): Partial-Order Methods for the Verification of Concurrent Systems. LNCS, vol. 1032. Springer, Heidelberg (1996)
13. Jaghoori, M.M., Sirjani, M., Mousavi, M.R., Khamespanah, E., Movaghar, A.: Symmetry and partial order reduction techniques in model checking Rebeca. Acta Informatica (2009)
14. Kahlon, V., Wang, C., Gupta, A.: Monotonic partial order reduction: An optimal symbolic partial order reduction technique. In: Bouajjani, A., Maler, O. (eds.) Computer Aided Verification. LNCS, vol. 5643, pp. 398–413. Springer, Heidelberg (2009)
15. Karmani, R.K., Shali, A., Agha, G.: Actor frameworks for the JVM platform: A comparative analysis. In: Proceedings of the 7th International Conference on the Principles and Practice of Programming in Java (2009)
16. Lauterburg, S., Dotta, M., Marinov, D., Agha, G.: A framework for state-space exploration of Java-based actor programs. In: 24th IEEE/ACM International Conference on Automated Software Engineering, ASE 2009. IEEE, Los Alamitos (2009)
17. Pi original source code webpage,
    http://www-unix.mcs.anl.gov/mpi/usingmpi/examples/simplempi/main.htm
18. Sen, K., Agha, G.: Automated systematic testing of open distributed programs. In: Baresi, L., Heckel, R. (eds.) FASE 2006. LNCS, vol. 3922, pp. 339–356. Springer, Heidelberg (2006)
19. Vakkalanka, S.S., Gopalakrishnan, G., Kirby, R.M.: Dynamic verification of MPI programs with reductions in presence of split operations and relaxed orderings. In: Gupta, A., Malik, S. (eds.) CAV 2008. LNCS, vol. 5123, pp. 66–79. Springer, Heidelberg (2008)
20. Visser, W., Havelund, K., Brat, G., Park, S., Lerda, F.: Model checking programs. Automated Software Engineering 10(2), 203–232 (2003)
21. Yabandeh, M., Knežević, N., Kostić, D., Kuncak, V.: CrystalBall: Predicting and preventing inconsistencies in deployed distributed systems. In: NSDI 2009: Proceedings of the 6th USENIX symposium on Networked systems design and implementation, pp. 229–244. USENIX Association (2009)
22. Yang, J., Chen, T., Wu, M., Xu, Z., Xuezheng Liu, H.L., Yang, M., Long, F., Zhang, L., Zhou, L.: MODIST: Transparent model checking of unmodified distributed systems. In: NSDI 2009: Proceedings of the 6th USENIX symposium on Networked systems design and implementation, pp. 213–228. USENIX Association (2009)
23. Yang, Y., Chen, X., Gopalakrishnan, G., Kirby, R.M.: Distributed dynamic partial order reduction based verification of threaded software. In: Bošnački, D., Edelkamp, S. (eds.) SPIN 2007. LNCS, vol. 4595, pp. 58–75. Springer, Heidelberg (2007)
24. Yang, Y., Chen, X., Gopalakrishnan, G., Kirby, R.M.: Efficient stateful dynamic partial order reduction. In: Havelund, K., Majumdar, R., Palsberg, J. (eds.) SPIN 2008. LNCS, vol. 5156, pp. 288–305. Springer, Heidelberg (2008)
25. Yi, X., Wang, J., Yang, X.: Stateful dynamic partial-order reduction. In: Liu, Z., He, J. (eds.) ICFEM 2006. LNCS, vol. 4260, pp. 149–167. Springer, Heidelberg (2006)

A Lightweight and Portable Approach to Making Concurrent Failures Reproducible

Qingzhou Luo[1], Sai Zhang[2], Jianjun Zhao[1], and Min Hu[1]

[1] School of Software, Shanghai Jiao Tong University
{seriousam,zhao-jj,minhu_fox}@sjtu.edu.cn
[2] Computer Science & Engineering Department, University of Washington
szhang@cs.washington.edu

Abstract. Concurrent programs often exhibit bugs due to unintended interferences among the concurrent threads. Such bugs are often hard to reproduce because they typically happen under very specific interleaving of the executing threads. Basically, it is very hard to fix a bug (or software failure) in concurrent programs without being able to reproduce it. In this paper, we present an approach, called ConCrash, that automatically and deterministically reproduces concurrent failures by recording logical thread schedule and generating unit tests. For a given bug (failure), ConCrash records the logical thread scheduling order and preserves object states in memory at runtime. Then, ConCrash reproduces the failure offline by simply using the saved information without the need for JVM-level or OS-level support. To reduce the runtime performance overhead, ConCrash employs a static data race detection technique to report potential possible race conditions, and only instruments such places. We implement the ConCrash approach in a prototype tool for Java and experimented on a number of multi-threaded Java benchmarks. As a result, we successfully reproduced a number of real concurrent bugs (e.g., deadlocks, data races and atomicity violation) within an acceptable overhead.

1 Introduction

The increasing popularity of concurrent programming has brought the issue of concurrent defect analysis to the forefront. Concurrent programs often exhibit wrong behaviors due to unintended interferences among the concurrent threads. Such concurrent failures or bugs - such as data races and atomicity violations - are often difficult to fix without being able to reproduce them. However, in a multi-threaded concurrent program, the number of possible interleavings is huge, and it is not practical to try them all. Only a few of the interleavings or even one specific interleaving actually produce the failure; thus, the probability of reproducing a concurrent failure is extremely low. A traditional method of reproducing concurrent failure is to repeatedly execute the program with the hope that different test executions will project in different interleavings. Unfortunately this approach is proved to be neither efficient nor reproducible in practice. Firstly, execution result of a concurrent program depends on the underlying operating system or the virtual machine for thread scheduling - it does not try to explicitly control the thread schedules; therefore, executions often end up with the same interleaving many times,

D.S. Rosenblum and G. Taentzer (Eds.): FASE 2010, LNCS 6013, pp. 323–337, 2010.

which means getting an access to the buggy interleaving is always a time-consuming task. Moreover, many concurrent applications (like servers) often run a long time and serve for specific users. So it would be extremely hard to reproduce such environmental dependent bugs in off-line testing.

The high cost of reproducing concurrent failures has motivated the development of sophisticated and automated analysis techniques, such as [6–8, 10, 11, 14, 16, 18, 19]. Of particular interest for our work is the ReCrash approach proposed by Artzi et al [5]. ReCrash monitors every execution of the target (sequential) program, stores partial copies of method arguments, and converts a failing program execution into a set of deterministic unit tests, each of which reproduces the problem that causes the program to fail. The ReCrash approach is designed for sequential programs. However, the non-determinism in a multi-threaded concurrent program might disallow the unit tests generated by ReCrash to reproduce a concurrent failure.

The work described in this paper aims to reduce the amount of time a developer spends on reproducing a concurrent failure. A key element in designing such an approach is the ability to provide a deterministic thread executing order of a non-deterministic execution instance. In this paper, we propose ConCrash, an automated concurrent failure reproducing technique for Java. ConCrash handles all threads and concurrent constructs in Java, except for windowing events, I/O inputs and network events which are topics of our future work.

The ConCrash approach adapts the concept of *logical thread schedule* as described in [7]. It monitors each critical event to capture the thread execution order during one execution of a multi-threaded program. When the concurrent program fails, ConCrash saves both information about thread scheduling and current object states in memory and automatically generates an *instrumentation scheme* and a set of *JUnit tests*. The *instrumentation scheme* records the thread schedule information during the failing execution as pure text, and then enforces the exact same schedule when replaying the execution, while the JUnit tests captures the failed method invocation sequences. The ConCrash approach can be used on both client and developer sides. When a concurrent failure occurs, the user could send an *instrumentation scheme* as well as generated *JUnit tests* to developers. While developers could use a ConCrash-enabled environment to replay the thread execution order, step through execution, or otherwise investigate the root cause of the failure.

Unlike most of the existing replay techniques like [7], our ConCrash approach does not depend on JVM modification or existing OS-level support for replay. Instead, ConCrash instruments the compiled class files by modifying their bytecode. To reduce the runtime performance overhead, ConCrash also employs a static data race detection technique [14] to find potential possible race conditions, and only instruments such places. While starting to reproduce a failure, ConCrash eliminates the nondeterminacy of the program caused by JVM scheduler by transforming the compiled nondeterministic multi-threaded program into a deterministic sequential program without changing the semantics.

We implement the ConCrash approach in a prototype tool for Java and experimented on a number of multi-threaded Java benchmarks. We successfully reproduced a number of real concurrent bugs (e.g., deadlocks, data races, atomicity violation) within an acceptable overhead. The main contributions of this paper are:

- A lightweight and portable technique that efficiently captures and reproduces multi-threaded concurrent failures, which can be integrated with various static analysis tools.
- Implementation of a prototype tool for Java. For the sake of applicable in long-running multi-threaded programs, we employ and extend a testing framework to support automatic generation of multi-threaded JUnit test cases.
- An empirical evaluation that shows the effectiveness and efficiency of ConCrash approach on Java benchmarks and real-world applications.

The rest of this paper is organized as follows. In Section 2, we give an overview of the ConCrash approach using a simple motivating example. We describe the details of the ConCrash approach in Section 3. In Section 4, we describe the implementation issues of ConCrash approach for Java and the results of our experiments, respectively. Related work is discussed in Section 5 followed by conclusion and future work.

2   Motivating Example

In this section, we use a real-world program to give an overview of our approach. Consider the two-threaded program snippet taken from *hedc* benchmark [14] in Fig. 1.

Two threads executing the code of MetaSearchResearch.java and Task.java have one shared variable thread_. There could be an unsynchronized assignment of null to field thread_ (line 55 in Task.java), which could cause the program to crash with a NullPointerException (line 53 in MetaSearchResult.java) if the Task completes just as another thread calls Task.cancel().

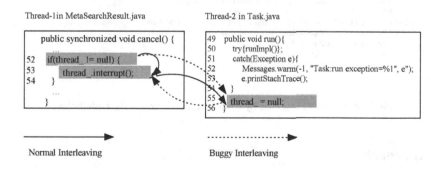

Fig. 1. A Motivating Example

In this case, it would be nearly impossible to reproduce the failure by repeatedly executing the original program due to the huge volume of different thread execution orders. Moreover, since in typical OS and JVM design, the thread scheduler is nearly deterministic, executing the same program many times does not help, because the same interleaving is usually created. Actually, in our experiment environment (Section 4), executing the original program for more than 300 times could reproduce only one failure.

Suppose that the motivating example is running in a ConCrash-enabled environment. ConCrash first uses an existing static data race detection technique [14] to pre-process this program to find all possible race conditions (it is a one time cost). ConCrash then instruments the program at the reported race conditions. In this example, line 53 in MetaSearchResult.java and line 55 in Task.java are reported to be potential race conditions and ConCrash instruments these two statements to monitor the thread execution logical order. For each method invoked, ConCrash also maintains a state copy of the method receiver and arguments.

As soon as the (instrumented) program crashes, ConCrash will generate *an instrumentation scheme* and a set of *JUnit tests*. The user could send the *scheme* and *tests* with the initial bug report to developers. Upon receiving such a scheme and tests, the developer could use ConCrash (we provide an instrumentation tool in ConCrash design) to instrument the original program to resume the original thread schedule order. After that, the developer could run tests under a debugger to easily reproduce the failure and locate its cause.

For this motivating example, one of the generated JUnit test case is shown in Fig. 2. In lines 2 - 6 of Fig. 2, ConCrash first reads the current object (thisObject) from a trace file to resume the state. ConCrash then reads other thread objects from the recorded file (lines 7 and 8), and synchronizes them to restart at a certain checkpoint before the crash occurs (lines 9 and 10). Finally, ConCrash invokes the crashed method (and loads augments if there is any) on the deterministic replay program version.

```
1. public void test_MetaSearchResult_cancel_3() throws Throwable {
2.      //Read object from trace file
3.      //adpated from ReCrash implementation
4.      TraceReader.setMethodTraceItem(3);
5.      MetaSearchResult thisObject =
6.          (MetaSearchResult)TraceReader.readObject(0);
        // Resume thread execution orders
7.      ThreadEntity te = TraceReader.getStackTraceItem().threadEntity;
8.      Monitor.restartThreads(te.checkPoints,3);
9.      Monitor.waitForThreads();
        // Method invocation
10.     thisObject.cancel();
11. }
```

Fig. 2. A generated test case by ConCrash to reproduce the hedc failure

3   Approach

In this section we discuss our ConCrash approach in detail. The overview of our approach is shown in Fig. 3. Our approach consists of three stages: getting instrumentation sites (Section 3.1), instrumenting original program to generate record & replay version (Section 3.2), and generating JUnit test cases after a crash (Section 3.3).

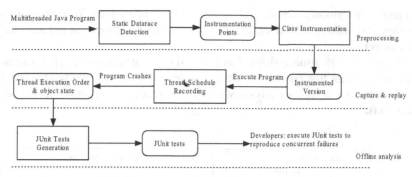

Fig. 3. An overview of the ConCrash approach

3.1 Stage One: Getting Instrumentation Sites

It is obviously not practical to instrument every statement in a program, because that would incur a huge slow down rate. Based on a recent study [12], most concurrent bugs can be categorized as *data race*, *atomicity violation* and *dead lock*. While *data race* bugs always have certain execution orders of raced statements, *dead lock* and *atomicity violation*[1] bugs also have specific orders of lock acquire/release operations. After recording such orders we would be able to replay those defects. We next present different strategies for handling these different types of concurrent bugs.

3.1.1 Statements Involved in Data Races

A data race condition is defined as two accesses to a shared variable in different threads without holding a common lock, at least one of which is a write. A data race condition often causes non-predictable behavior of a program and is usually considered as a defect. We are concerned about the execution order of the two accesses in a data race pair and employ a static race detection tool called Chord [14] to detect possible data race pairs. Chord reads the source code of a program and bytecode, performs four stage analysis and outputs the results in files. Though it reports some false positives, the experiments show that Chord is applicable for static race detection for most programs. We take the result of Chord as a part of our instrumentation sites.

►**Example.** In Fig. 1 Chord reports all those three shadowed lines as potential data race pairs. Then we instrument the program before the shadowed lines in the next stage.   ◄

3.1.2 Lock Acquire and Release Operations

Atomicity violation bugs [10] are caused by concurrent non-atomic execution of a code region which was intended to run atomically. Admittedly a large part of atomicity violation are caused by data races, however, being data race free would not guarantee atomicity violation free. When the remote and local accesses in a atomicity violation are all well synchronized, it will not count for a data race. To address such problems,

---

[1] Here we refer to the part of *atomicity violations* that do not count for *data races*.

we also record the global order of lock acquire/release operations. With this information we should be able to reproduce atomicity violation bugs which are not reported by data race detection tools.

A *critical event* [7] is usually defined as a shared variable access or a synchronization event. Here we adapt this concept to the union set of the above two instrumentation sites. In our record and replay analysis, we only consider the temporal execution order of those points.

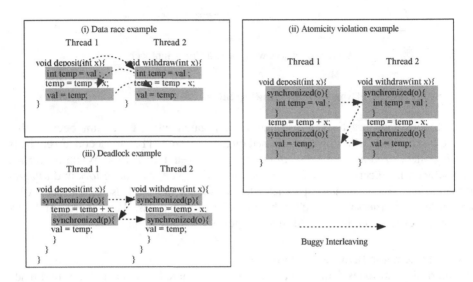

Fig. 4. Three different types of concurrency bugs and our instrumentation sites

▶**Example.** Fig. 4 is a frequently used example in concurrency testing. In the first data race example, our instrumentation points consist of the four shadowed statements involved in the race. With execution order information among these statements we would be able to reproduce this data race bug. In the other two examples, the order of acquire/release lock operation is recorded, which consists of all the synchronized operations in shadowed lines. With the exact order of acquiring or releasing a lock the other two bugs could be also reproduced in following stages.   ◀

3.1.3   Test Case Generation Points

Like ReCrash [5], we instrument a part of all the methods in the program at their entry and exit points. The purpose of this instrumentation is to get a copy of receiver object and method invocation arguments, which are used to generate test cases after a program crash. Each **T**est **C**ase **G**eneration **P**oint information (*TCGP* in short) is pushed into a stack at the entry point of a method. It is then popped at the exit point after successful execution of the method. See Fig. 5 for an example. A large part among all methods, like non-public methods and simple getter/setter methods are excluded because they are considered less likely to expose a bug, and also because of the concern about runtime performance.

We extend this technique to apply in multi-threaded program, that is, in each test case generation point we also make a copy of the *TCGP* stack of all other live threads. In the generated test cases this information is used to recreate all threads to simulate the crash scenario.

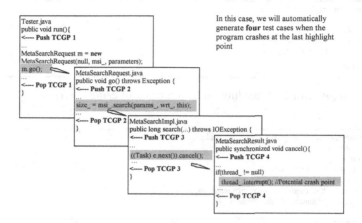

Fig. 5. An example of test case generation points

3.2 Stage Two: Instrumenting the Original Program to Generate Record and Replay Version

After getting all instrumentation sites from the previous stage, we instrument the byte-code of a program at those sites to capture the logical thread schedule order for deterministic record and replay.

3.2.1 Logical Thread Schedule
Capturing the actual physical thread schedule information is neither feasible nor useful in our approach. Rather than doing so, we record the 'Lamport clock' of the thread as a logical thread schedule. As shown in [7], a logical thread schedule is used to record the begin and the end time stamps of a few of consecutive *critical events* in one thread, as the form *<FirstCriticalEvent, LastCriticalEvent>*. The interval in every tuple is the logical running time of the thread before a thread switch occurs.

3.2.2 Thread Execution Order Record and Replay
The Java record/replay algorithm in [7] could produce sufficient trace information to deterministically replay a multi-threaded program execution. Based on this algorithm [7], rather than extending a specific JVM, we instrument on bytecode level. From the view point of bytecode level, the different types of *critical event* can be divided into `putfield`, `getfield` instructions and `monitorenter`, `monitorexit` instructions. Our instrumentation is based on these individual bytecode instructions. Details of this technique can be found in following algorithms.

```
     Input: number_of_interval, global_clock, local_clock
 1   RecordOnStmt():
 2   Enter monitor
 3   Get thread_entity for current thread
 4   gc_copy = global_clock
 5   if thread_entity.local_clock < global_clock then
 6        Update FirstCriticalEvent and LastCriticalEvent array for current thread number_of_interval =
          number_of_interval + 1
 7   end
 8   Execute critical event
 9   global_clock = global_clock + 1
10   thread_entity.local_clock = gc_copy

11   Exit monitor
```

Algorithm 1. Recording execution order of *critical events*

```
     Input: number_of_interval, global_clock, local_clock
 1   ReplayOnStmt():
 2   Enter monitor
 3   Get thread_entity for current thread
 4   gc_copy = global_clock
 5   while global_clock < FirstCriticalEvent[number_of_interval] do
 6        Wait for the execution of other threads
 7   end
 8   Execute critical event
 9   global_clock = global_clock + 1
10   if global_clock >= LastCriticalEvent[number_of_interval] then
11        number_of_interval = number_of_interval + 1
12   end
13   thread_entity.local_clock = gc_copy
14   Notify all other threads

15   Exit monitor
```

Algorithm 2. Algorithm for replaying *critical events*

3.2.3   Discussions about Effects of Instrumentation

Instrumentation is intrusive, which means that it could potentially affect the behavior of the original threads. However, the instructions we added only operate on their own data structures, and therefore would not change the control flow of the original program. The main impact is that it could possibly change the time slice allocated to a thread by the scheduler. Thus, as our algorithm only captures the linear order of shared variable (data race pairs) accesses and lock acquire/release operations of the original program, this linear order is also a legal order of the execution of the original program. Proof with details can be found in [9]. Time and space overhead of the instrumented program will be discussed in Section 4.

3.3   Stage Three: Generating JUnit Test Cases after a Crash

Testing long running multi-threaded programs is always a difficult task because of its inherent non-determinism and its expensive tracing overhead. ConCrash extends a unit test case generation framework to support multi-threaded application, which utilizes logical thread schedule information to deterministically trigger program crashes.

Specifically, we augment the unit tests generation technique in [5] to handle concurrent features. In ConCrash, the method call stack data is captured and used for tests generation when a crash happens. Whenever a method is called, it pushes the receiver object and parameters onto stack and then pop this information after normal exit of the method. After a crash happens, ConCrash can simply generate test cases by passing the same receiver object and method parameters, which are serialized to the disk before.

As ReCrash only monitors the execution of the main thread, if an exception is thrown in the run() method of another thread it would not be recorded. Instead ConCrash also supports concurrent features in Java by wrapping each run() method in a try block to capture exceptions thrown by each individual thread.

▶**Example.** As seen in Fig. 6, two JUnit test cases are automatically generated after crash. Inside the method invocation Monitor.restartThreads(te.TCGP_stack, 2) another thread is created to simulate the behavior of thread 1 based on the time schedule. We use the argument TCGP_stack to pass all the necessary information. For example, in the search test case, thread 1 will be recreated and executed Task.run() afterwards concurrently with thread 2, while in another test case SohoSynoptic.run-Impl() will be invoked. All the classes loaded in the two test cases are the replay version of the program, which forces them to execute with the same logical order when a crash happened.   ◀

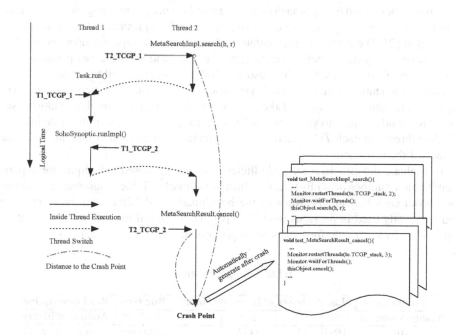

Fig. 6. An example of multi-threaded JUnit test cases generation

The last issue we care about is how to recreate all corresponding threads in the generated test cases. Since JUnit does not support multi-threaded test cases up to now, we use a WrapperThread to achieve the goal. By using Java Reflection APIs, the WrapperThread has the ability to dynamically invoke the specified method when needed. After loading information such as method name and arguments from trace files, a `WrapperThread` is started at specific *TCGP*.

3.3.1 Discussions about the Effectiveness of Generated Test Cases

To our intuition, the closer the start point of a test case to the fault locality, the more useful it is in the debugging process. As shown in Fig. 6 we use a term *Distance to the Crash Point* to indicate the distance for the test case to reach the crash point. Due to the selective instrumentation of `ConCrash`, a small set of test cases which are too far away from the crash point could possibly fail in reproducing that crash. In the worst case there is only one alive thread *t* at one *TCGP*, but after that a lot of new threads are created. If *t* crashes sometime later, then the test case generated at that specific *TCGP* could not be able to reproduce that crash, since it does not know which thread would be created in future. Our approach, though not sound, is demonstrated to be practically useful. In our experiment in Section 4, we show that the 'nearest' test cases are strongly guaranteed to reproduce crashes.

4   Implementation and Evaluation

We have implemented our approach for concurrent Java programs using the Chord static datarace detection tool [14], ReCrash tool [5], XStream [3] framework, and Soot analysis toolset [2]. The current implementation of our approach supports Java version 1.6. The preprocessing stage (includes identifying data race and lock/release operations) are built on top of Soot and Chord. We also use Soot to instrument all the class files containing instrumentation sites. By modifying `reCrashJ` [1] we implement `ConCrash` to support multi-threaded features. Like `reCrashJ`, the `ConCrash` implementation uses the stored shadow stack to generate a suite of JUnit tests. Each test in the suite invokes all alive threads at each *TCGP* and loads the receiver and method arguments from the serialized shadow stack.

To evaluate the effectiveness and efficiency of our proposed technique, we experimented on a number of multi-threaded Java benchmarks. Table 1 summarizes the details about each benchmark. Most of the benchmarks and failures are representative and frequently used in previous work [10] [6] [18] [14]. All the failures could not be reproduced by `ReCrash`, for it does not support multi-threaded applications.

Table 1. Subject Programs

Programs	#Loc	#Classes	#Methods	#Threads	Bug type	Brief description
XtangoAnimator	2088	31	220	3	Deadlock	Animation library
ftp	21897	118	1114	3	Data race	Apache ftp server
raytracer	1308	21	72	3	Data race	Ray tracing program
Hedc	29948	136	1552	6	Data race	Web crawler
Shop	299	3	11	3	Atomicity	Simulated shop
Pingpong	303	4	12	3	Data race	Simulated ball game

4.1   Procedure

We focus on the crash reproducibility and performance overhead of ConCrash in the evaluation. For each subject program, we first use Chord and Soot to get all instrumentation sites, then instrument the program and deploy it into a ConCrash-enabled environment.

Most of the bugs in the subject programs happen in very rare situations: 100 times of normal execution will not manifest those bugs. We seed a few sleep() operations in the program in the recording phase to trigger specific bugs. As demonstrated in [9], the thread schedule of seeded version is also a legal schedule of the original program, which guarantees the buggy schedule we capture could also happen in production run. When the program crashes within an exception, ConCrash outputs an instrumentation scheme which captures the thread execution orders (when failure occurs), and a set of JUnit tests. We then construct the replay version by using the instrumentation scheme, and then run all generated JUnit tests on it.

To measure the recording overhead we run each benchmark for a certain task for 100 times and compare the execution time of the original program with the execution time of the recorded version. The average time cost is taken between all the runs. At the same time the size of trace files are also recorded.

4.2   Results

The results for the experiments of concurrent crash reproducibility and performance overhead are shown in Tables 2 and 3, respectively. The experiments were done on a 3.00 GHz machine with 1GB memory and Sun JVM 1.6.0 in Windows XP system. In Table 2, we list the number of instrumentation sites and the crash type for each buggy program. To evaluate the effectiveness of ConCrash, we count the number of generated JUnit test cases with regard to the reproducible ones and reproduce rate. In Table 3 we compare the running time of the original program with instrumented ones. The time was measured in realtime execution time, and network related benchmarks (like **ftp** and **hedc**) were set in a local network to reduce the effects of web transmission. Slow down rate and the size of the trace files are also considered.

Table 2. Crash reproducibility study result

Programs	#Instrumentation sites data race/lock release		Exception type	# generated test cases	# reproducible test cases
XtangoAnimator	N.A.[1]	49	CustomException	1	1
ftp	51	61	NullPointerException	4	2
raytracer	52	17	AssertionError	1	1
Hedc	19	394	NullPointerException	4	3
Shop	10	3	ArrayOutOfIndex	3	2
Pingpong	4	0	NullPointerException	2	2

[1]Chord does not terminate after 10 hours in **XtangoAnimator**

4.2.1   Failure Reproducibility

We can observe from Table 2 that ConCrash was able to reproduce all three kinds of typical concurrent crashes (atomicity violation, deadlock, and data race) in the subject programs investigated.

In most cases, the generated tests of ConCrash could reproduce concurrent failures. As mentioned before, we do not record for every operation but rather for a small part of them. The failed cases are always because of the long distance between the *TCGP* to the crash point. However, our results showed that in our experiments all the failures could be reproduced by the last two closest test cases.

Table 3. Performance overhead study

Programs	Original(ms)	Instrumented(ms) data race/lock release/All			Slow down	File size(kb)
XtangoAnimator	367.1	N.A.	439	439	19.6%	1.52
ftp	3206	3946	4009	4565	42.4%	45.2
raytracer	47	75	51	78	66%	1.4
Hedc	1501.4	1676.5	1701.6	1731.3	15.3%	27.9
Shop	278.1	335.8	309.3	367.1	32%	3.1
Pingpong	315.6	367.2	N.A.[1]	367.2	16.3%	2.34

[1] There is no lock acquire/release operations in **Pingpong**

4.2.2   Performance Overhead

We compare the execution time of the original program and ConCrash-instrumented version in Table 3. All the applications are set for a certain task, except for **ftp** we wrote a test harness program to start a new user and download a specific file. The data is then collected in 100 times' **normal** runs for each program. We also provide a comparison between different instrumentation strategies. Our results showed ConCrash has a run-time overhead from 15% to 66%. We believe such overhead is acceptable for real-world use, though there is still improvement space if more selective instrumentation strategies are adapted. We also believe that the performance of ConCrash could be further improved with the integration of better data race/atomicity violation detection tools.

The size of the trace files is relatively small - 45kb for the largest benchmark, including both schedule files and JUnit tests. It could be easily sent via Internet to developers when a crash happens.

4.3   Threats to Validity

Like any empirical evaluation, this study also has limitations which must be considered. Although we have experimented with several well-known multi-threaded Java benchmarks, in which the largest one is over 30KLOC, they are smaller than traditional Java software systems. For this case, we can not claim that these experiment results can be necessarily generalized to other programs. On the other hand, the systems and crashes we chose to investigate might not be representative. Though we experimented on reproducing several typical concurrent failures, such as data race, deadlock, and atomicity violation, we still can not claim ConCrash could reproduce an arbitrary concurrent crash.

Another threat is that we have not conducted any readability study about the generated test case on software developers (though the readability of the test case is secondary to reproducibility). For this reason, we might not be able to claim ConCrash can be applied to real-world development process.

The final threat to internal validity maybe mostly lies with possible errors in our tool implementation and the measure of experiment results. To reduce these kind of threats, we have performed several careful checks.

4.4 Discussion

When designing the ConCrash approach, we choose bytecode level instrumentation to make concurrent failure be deterministically reproduced. If we use OS-level support or JVM-level capture and replay, ConCrash would have to be deployed on a specific environment, which will deteriorate the portability of our approach. In current ConCrash implementation, no other program or configuration is needed, and the pre-instrumentation also permits the high comparability of ConCrash-enabled environment.

When using Chord to report potential data races, the coverage of Chord (or other analysis techniques used for preprocessing) might affect the precision/effectiveness of the ConCrash approach. Investigating the tradeoffs would be one of our future directions.

Current implementation of ConCrash uses shallow (depth-1) copying strategy as default mode like [5]. However, in some cases (e.g., the Hedc benchmark) an argument is side-effected, between the method entry and the crash point, in such a way that will prevent the crash from reproducing.

5 Related Work

In this section, we discuss some closely related work in the areas of multi-threaded program analysis, testing, and debugging. We also compare several similar tools in Table 4.

Much research has been done on testing and debugging multi-threaded programs. Researchers have proposed analysis techniques to detect deadlocks [15], data races [14], and atomicity violations [10]. The problem of generating different interleavings for the purpose of revealing concurrent failures [15] and record/replay techniques [7, 13, 17, 20] have also been examined. Moreover, systematic and exhaustive techniques, like model checking [11], have been developed recently. These techniques exhaustively explore all interleavings of a concurrent program by systematically switching threads at synchronization points.

Choi et al. [7], presented the concept of logical thread schedule and proposed an approach to deterministically replay a multi-threaded Java program. They are able to reproduce race conditions and other non-deterministic failures. However, Their method relies on the modification of the underlying JVM, while our method uses bytecode level instrumentation to capture the thread execution orders. Moreover, our approach generates a series of JUnit tests, which help developers to debug the program.

Recently, Park *et al.* [17] also proposed the idea of deterministic replay of concurrency bugs. They used the feedback of previous failed replay attempt of the program to reproduce concurrency bugs. They also presented five sketching methods for recording the execution of concurrent programs, while our approach employs a static analysis tool as frontend to identify recording points. ConCrash tries to reproduce concurrency failures with JUnit tests at those points, which is also different from their feedback approach.

The most similar work to us is the ReCrash approach [5] proposed by Artzi *et al.*. ReCrash generates tests by utilizing partial snapshots of the program states captured on each method execution in the case of a failure. The empirical study shows that ReCrash is easy to implement, scalable to large program, and generate simple but helpful tests. Our work on ConCrash aims to handle concurrent failures. We use the concept of logical thread schedule to capture the execution order, making the behavior of multi-threaded program deterministic when reproducing the concurrent failure.

Table 4. A comparison between closely related testing tools for concurrent programs

Items	Instrumentation level	Running environment[1]	Deterministic replay in multi-threaded programs	Unit test cases generation
ReCrash [5]	byte code	both	No	Yes[2]
DejaVu [7]	JVM	developer site	Yes	No
RaceFuzzer [19]	byte code	developer site	No[3]	No
ConTest [9]	source code	developer site	Yes	No
ConCrash	byte code	both	Yes	Yes

[1] Running environment consists of user site and developer site
[2] ReCrash's generated test cases could not be applied in multi-threaded programs
[3] Depends on RaceFuzzer's random scheduler

6 Conclusions and Future Work

In this paper, we presented a lightweight and portable approach, called ConCrash, to making concurrent failures reproducible. ConCrash records the logical thread scheduling order and preserves object states in memory at runtime. When a crash occurs, it reproduces the failure offline by simply using the saved information without the need for JVM-level or OS-level support. To reduce the runtime overhead, ConCrash uses an effective existing data race detection technique to report all potential race conditions, and only instruments such places plus lock acquire/release points. We implemented the ConCrash approach in a prototype tool for Java. Our experiments on several well-known multi-threaded Java benchmarks indicate that ConCrash is effective in reproducing a number of typical concurrent bugs within an acceptable overhead.

We recommend the ConCrash approach be an integrated part of the existing ReCrash technique. As our future work, we would like to examine alternative techniques like dynamic program slicing [4] to improve the performance of ConCrash. We also intend to investigate the cost/effectiveness tradeoffs when reproducing concurrent failures at the application level.

Acknowledgements. We thank anonymous reviewers for useful comments. We also thank Shan Lu and STAP group members for their valuable discussions. This work was supported in part by National Natural Science Foundation of China (NSFC) (Grant No. 60970009).

References

1. reCrashJ implementation, http://groups.csail.mit.edu/pag/reCrash/
2. Soot Homepage, http://www.sable.mcgill.ca/soot/
3. XStream Project Homepage, http://xstream.codehaus.org/
4. Agrawal, H., Horgan, J.R.: Dynamic program slicing. In: PLDI 1990, pp. 246–256 (1990)
5. Artzi, S., Kim, S., Ernst, M.D.: Recrash: Making software failures reproducible by preserving object states. In: Vitek, J. (ed.) ECOOP 2008. LNCS, vol. 5142, pp. 542–565. Springer, Heidelberg (2008)
6. Choi, J.D., Lee, K., Loginov, A., O'Callahan, R., Sarkar, V., Sridharan, M.: Efficient and precise datarace detection for multithreaded object-oriented programs. In: PLDI 2002, pp. 258–269 (2002)
7. Choi, J.D., Srinivasan, H.: Deterministic replay of Java multithreaded applications. In: SPDT 1998, pp. 48–59 (1998)
8. Choi, J.D., Zeller, A.: Isolating failure-inducing thread schedules. SIGSOFT Softw. Eng. Notes 27(4), 210–220 (2002)
9. Edelstein, O., Farchi, E., Nir, Y., Ratsaby, G., Ur, S.: Multithreaded Java program test generation. IBM Systems Journal 41(1), 111–124 (2002)
10. Flanagan, C., Freund, S.N.: Atomizer: a dynamic atomicity checker for multithreaded programs. In: POPL 2004, pp. 256–267 (2004)
11. Freund, S.N.: Checking concise specifications for multithreaded software. Journal of Object Technology 3, 81–101 (2004)
12. Lu, S., Park, S., Seo, E., Zhou, Y.: Learning from mistakes: a comprehensive study on real world concurrency bug characteristics. SIGARCH Comput. Archit. News 36(1), 329–339 (2008)
13. Musuvathi, M., Qadeer, S., Ball, T., Basler, G., Arumuga Nainar, P., Neamtiu, I.: Finding and reproducing heisenbugs in concurrent programs. In: OSDI 2008, pp. 267–280 (2008)
14. Naik, M., Aiken, A., Whaley, J.: Effective static race detection for Java. In: PLDI 2006, pp. 308–319 (2006)
15. Naik, M., Park, C., Sen, K., Gay, D.: Effective static deadlock detection. In: ICSE 2009, pp. 386–396 (2009)
16. O'Callahan, R., Choi, J.D.: Hybrid dynamic data race detection. SIGPLAN Not. 38(10), 167–178 (2003)
17. Park, S., Zhou, Y., Xiong, W., Yin, Z., Kaushik, R.H., Lee, K., Lu, S.: PRES: probabilistic replay with execution sketching on multiprocessors. In: SOSP 2009, pp. 177–192 (2009)
18. von Praun, C., Gross, T.R.: Object race detection. In: OOPSLA 2001, pp. 70–82 (2001)
19. Sen, K.: Race directed random testing of concurrent programs. In: PLDI 2008, pp. 11–21. ACM, New York (2008)
20. Steven, J., Chandra, P., Fleck, B., Podgurski, A.: jRapture: A capture/replay tool for observation-based testing. SIGSOFT Softw. Eng. Notes 25(5), 158–167 (2000)

Efficient Runtime Assertion Checking of Assignable Clauses with Datagroups

Hermann Lehner and Peter Müller

ETH Zurich, Switzerland
{hermann.lehner,peter.mueller}@inf.ethz.ch

Abstract. Runtime assertion checking is useful for debugging programs and specifications. Existing tools check invariants as well as method pre- and postconditions, but mostly ignore **assignable** (or **modifies**) clauses, which specify the heap locations a method is allowed to assign to. A way to abstract from implementation details is to specify **assignable** clauses using datagroups, which represent sets of concrete memory locations.

Efficient runtime checking of **assignable** clauses with datagroups is difficult because the members of a datagroup may change over time and because datagroups may get very large, especially for recursive data structures. We present the first algorithm to check **assignable** clauses in the presence of datagroups. The key idea is to compute the set of locations in a datagroup lazily, which requires data structures that reflect when the contents of a datagroup change during the execution of a method. We implemented our approach in a prototypical runtime assertion checker for the Java Modeling Language (JML); our experiments show that the runtime overhead is moderately small.

1 Introduction

To verify interesting program properties, it is important to know the side effects of a method. To this end, frame properties define which heap locations a method may modify, and, more importantly, that everything else in the heap stays unchanged. In JML, a method specification expresses such frame properties by the use of the **assignable** clause. This clause declares the heap locations that may be updated during method execution.

To achieve information hiding, we can mention *datagroups* in **assignable** clauses to abstract away from concrete locations [7,8]. For any field of an object, we can specify which datagroup(s) it belongs to. A datagroup is *static* if it only contains fields of the same object. Otherwise, the datagroup is *dynamic*.

Dynamic datagroups are crucial to specify frame properties for aggregate or recursive data structures. In our example in Fig. 1, we introduce a class `Store` that manages items. Dynamic datagroups allow us to specify that method `add` changes at most the internal data structure of the store.

To check a program against its specification, we can either use a static verification tool or we equip the code with runtime assertion checks that fail if an illegal operation is about to happen. Both approaches have already been taken to check **assignable** clauses, however datagroups pose a problem on both sides.

D.S. Rosenblum and G. Taentzer (Eds.): FASE 2010, LNCS 6013, pp. 338–352, 2010.

```
class Item {
  JMLDataGroup footprint;                    // 0

  boolean selected;                          // 1

  String name; //@ in footprint;             // 2

  int price; //@ in footprint;               // 3

  /*@ assignable this.footprint, other.selected; */
  void copy(Item other){
    this.name = other.name;
    this.price = other.price;
    other.selected = false;
  }
}

class Node {
  JMLDataGroup struct;                       // 0

  Node left; //@ in struct;                  // 1
  /*@ maps left.struct into struct; */

  Node right; //@ in struct;                 // 2
  /*@ maps right.struct into struct; */

  Item data;                                 // 3

  /*@ assignable this.struct; */
  void replace(Node old, Node new){ [...] }
}

class Store {
  JMLDataGroup struct;                       // 0

  Node root; //@ in struct;                  // 1
  /*@ maps root.struct into struct; */

  /*@ assignable this.struct; */
  void add(Item i){ [...] }
}
```

Fig. 1. A store that contains items, using a tree as internal data structure. `Store` and `Node` objects contain a field `struct`, whose datagroup contains the fields `left` and `right` of the same object, and the `struct` datagroup of the children. The `struct` datagroup allows us to refer to all locations of the data structure without exposing implementation details. The number behind each field declaration will be used later when we explain our algorithm.

Many static verification tools [1,3,5,9,10,11] support **assignable** clause to some extent; some partly support static datagroups, but no static verification tool currently supports dynamic datagroups. To precisely reason about dynamic datagroups, a verification environment produces proof obligations that have to be discharged manually, as checking the containment in a dynamic datagroup is essentially a reachability problem, which is not handled well by SMT solvers. Existing static analyses can only provide an over-approximation that is too imprecise to be useful.

The situation for runtime assertion checkers (RAC) is similar: The RAC for JML presented in Cheon's dissertation [4] does not provide checks for **assignable** clauses. Ye [12] adds limited support for static datagroups only. JML's semantics is to determine upon method invocation the set of locations in the datagroups. The number of locations in a dynamic datagroup is unknown at compile time and can grow as fast as the heap itself. Therefore, a naïve implementation of the semantics would lead to a large memory and time overhead.

We present an algorithm to efficiently check **assignable** clauses at runtime. The motivation for such checks is twofold: First, we can use a RAC to check a program's validity with little effort and small annotation overhead before starting to prove its correctness in an interactive theorem prover. In this way, we find bugs early and reduce the risk of getting stuck in an expensive manual proof. Second, if we use an automatic verification tool, we often get spurious error messages because of under-specification or deficiencies of the prover. In this case, we can use RAC to see if the program really violates the specification for the given input values. In order to achieve our goal we attack the problem from three sides.

(1) We provide efficient implementations of two operations that are heavily used in our algorithm: checking if an **assignable** clause mentions a certain location or datagroup, and collecting all static datagroups that contain a location. We introduce new data structures for assignable maps and for static datagroups based on bitset operations to achieve this goal.

(2) We reduce memory consumption by introducing the concept of *lazy unfolding* of dynamic datagroups to avoid unnecessary overhead. Instead of unfolding the datagroups of an **assignable** clause in the pre-state of the method, we track the changes to dynamic datagroups during method execution and only store the difference between the pre-state and the current state. We can decide at compile time, which operations trigger a change to the dynamic datagroups and instrument the code at that point to store the changes.

(3) We optimize time complexity by caching the result of checking whether a location is assignable, as this information can be reused within the same method.

2   Prerequisites

In this section, we introduce the notations and semantics of locations, method call stacks, **assignable** clauses, and datagroups.

Locations. At runtime, a field of an object is called a *location*. For convenience, we define a function $obj(\cdot)$ that yields the object of a location. For example, $obj(o.f)$ yields o.

Method Call Stack. We introduce the binary relation $m_1 \hookrightarrow m_2$ which states that method m_2 is called by m_1 at runtime. We also introduce the reflexive transitive closure: $m_1 \hookrightarrow^* m_2$, meaning, m_1 is m_2 or m_1 is a direct or transitive caller of m_2.

Assignable Clauses. We can specify the frame of a method using the clause `assignable` $l_1, \ldots, l_n$;, where l_i has the form $o.f$ to refer to a field of an object. JML provides several other forms to specify assignable locations, but these are not relevant for this paper.

The semantics of an `assignable` clauses is defined as follows. The fields mentioned in the clause are evaluated to a set of locations. This evaluation is performed in the pre-state of the method, that is, upon method invocation. The `assignable` clause only restricts assignment to locations that already existed in the pre-state of the method.

Let $\mathcal{A}_m$ be the set of locations from the `assignable` clause of method m. Furthermore, let $\mathcal{F}_m^{\triangleleft}$ be the set of locations that have been freshly allocated *during* the execution of m. The little triangle $\triangleleft$ indicates that this set contains the locations that have been freshly allocated in m and all methods directly or transitively called by m.

Let's assume a method m that is called by m' (i.e., $m' \hookrightarrow m$). According to the JML semantics, a location is assignable in m if it is either freshly allocated or it is in the set of locations evaluated from the `assignable` clause of m and it was already assignable in m'. We can write this condition as follows:

$$\mathcal{A}_m^{\text{eff}} = \mathcal{F}_m^{\triangleleft} \cup (\mathcal{A}_m \cap \mathcal{A}_{m'}^{\text{eff}}).$$

An important consequence of JML's semantics is that a runtime assertion checker needs to consider the `assignable` clauses of all methods on the call stack to determine whether a location is assignable. An alternative to this expensive check would be to enforce for each call that the `assignable` clause of the callee denotes a subset of the locations that are assignable in the caller. However, such a requirement would be overly conservative since it rejects certain calls based on the `assignable` clause of the callee rather than its actual behavior. Therefore, our checker actually inspects the call stack when necessary.

Datagroups. Datagroups are sets of locations. Every field of a program defines its own datagroup that initially contains only the field itself.

If we are not interested in the value of the field but only its datagroup, JML provides a special type `JMLDataGroup` to indicate that the field just serves as a declaration of the corresponding datagroup.

To add all locations in the datagroup of a location $o.f$ to a datagroup of the same object o, JML uses the **in** clause at the field declaration. In the class `Item` in Fig. 1, the two fields `name` and `price` are declared to be in the datagroup of the field `footprint`. We declare `footprint` of type `JMLDataGroup`, since we are interested in its datagroup, but not its value.

To add all locations in the datagroup of a location $o.f$ to a datagroup of another object p, JML uses the **maps** ... **into** clause. For instance in class `Node` in Fig. 1, we add `left.struct` to the datagroup of `struct`. The field `left` is called a *pivot field*, as an update of `left` changes the contents of datagroup `struct`. Since `left.struct` also has a datagroup itself, we essentially nest datagroups in our example. Adding locations from other objects makes a datagroup *dynamic*; the set of locations in the datagroup now depends on the program state.

Upon evaluation of an **assignable** clause in method m, the semantics states that each datagroup mentioned in the **assignable** clause is evaluated to a set of locations. We call this process *unfolding* of the datagroup. Datagroups that contain nested datagroups do not evaluate to nested sets of locations, but result in one single set of locations which is added to the set $\mathcal{A}_m$.

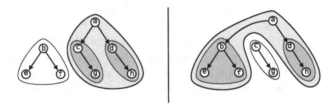

Fig. 2. A set of `Node` objects. Shapes depict the `struct` datagroups. Objects within the shape contain fields that the datagroup contains. Arrows depict references. Left: The situation in the pre-state of a call to `a.replace(c,b)`. Right: The post-state of the call.

Fig. 2 shows the dynamic datagroup of `a.struct` in light gray. One can see that `a.struct` also contains all locations that are mentioned in nested datagroups, depicted by a darker gray. The left picture shows the initial state where the pivot field `a.left` points to node c, the right picture depicts the datagroup of `a.struct` after executing the statement `a.left = b`. White shapes depict datagroups that are not in `a.struct`. This example illustrates that dynamic datagroups may contain different locations in different program states.

3   Checking Assignable Clauses with Static Datagroups

In a first step, we present an algorithm to check **assignable** clauses in the presence of *static* datagroups only. This part of the algorithm serves as a basis for checking **assignable** clauses with dynamic datagroups, as presented in the next section.

3.1   Data Structures

Our goal is to check **assignable** clauses in the presence of static datagroups in constant time. The following operations are involved in the check for field updates and we want them to perform in constant time: (1) lookup of all assignable fields of a given object without unfolding datagroups, (2) lookup of all datagroups that contain a location, and (3) the decision if the intersection between two sets of fields of an object is empty.

Field Identifiers. We assign a number to each field of a class such that at runtime, in the presence of inheritance, every field of an object has a unique number. In Fig. 1 we show these numbers in comments behind field declarations.

Assignable Locations. As explained in Sec. 2, the evaluation of **assignable** clauses leads to a set of locations. We give this set some structure and represent it as a map from objects to bitsets, in which the keys of the map are the objects of the locations, and each bit of the bitset correspond to a field of that object. Furthermore, as opposed to the semantical description of datagroups in Sec. 2, we do not unfold the static datagroups mentioned in such sets and instead deal with unfolding of datagroups on demand.

For method `copy` of class `Item` in Fig. 1, we represent the set $\mathcal{A}_{\texttt{copy}}$ by $\{\texttt{this} \mapsto [\checkmark \cdot \cdot \cdot], \texttt{other} \mapsto [\cdot \checkmark \cdot \cdot]\}$, where the fields receive their indices in the bitset in order of presence, as shown in the code, i.e., the first bit in the bitset of object `this` represents field `footprint` and the second bit in the bitset of object `other` represents field `selected`.

To retrieve the bitset of a given object o in a set $\mathcal{A}$, we write $\mathcal{A}[o]$. For example, $\mathcal{A}_{\texttt{copy}}[\texttt{other}]$ yields $[\cdot \checkmark \cdot \cdot]$. If the map does not contain o, $\mathcal{A}[o]$ yields an empty bitset. To store object o with bitset bs in $\mathcal{A}$, we write $\mathcal{A}[o] \leftarrow bs$.

This design allows us to perform the operation (1) in constant time, as we can use `HashMaps` as the underlying data structure.

Fresh Locations. If an object is newly created, all locations of that object are *fresh*. To represent the set of fresh locations $\mathcal{F}^{\triangleleft}$, we need to save only the set of newly allocated objects, which implicitly gives us the set of fresh locations. The query $\mathcal{F}^{\triangleleft}[o]$ simply yields *true* if the object o is freshly allocated in the current method execution, and *false* otherwise.

Static Datagroups. For each field, we use a bitset to represent the datagroup(s) the field belongs to. That is, we equip every class with an array of bitsets. For class `Item`, we represent the static datagroups by the following array.

$$
\begin{array}{ll}
\texttt{footprint} & \left[\begin{matrix} [\checkmark \cdot \cdot \cdot] \\ [\cdot \checkmark \cdot \cdot] \\ [\checkmark \cdot \checkmark \cdot] \\ [\checkmark \cdot \cdot \checkmark] \end{matrix}\right. \\
\texttt{selected} & \\
\texttt{name} & \\
\texttt{price} &
\end{array}
$$

To access the datagroups that *statically* contain field f of class c, we write $\mathcal{D}^{\text{st}}[c@f]$. For instance, $\mathcal{D}^{\text{st}}[\texttt{Item@name}]$ yields $[\checkmark \cdot \checkmark \cdot]$, which means that **name** is in the datagroup of `footprint` (the first bit) and of course in its own data-group (the third bit). For simplicity, we may also write $\mathcal{D}^{st}[o.f]$ to get the static datagroups of field f of class c, where o is of type c.

We set up the data structures for static datagroups such that we can perform the second and third operation described at the beginning of this section in constant time. Operation (2) involves an array access, and operation (3) involves computing the intersection of two bitsets, which is possible in constant time.

3.2   Code Instrumentation

An **assignable** clause restricts assignments throughout a method execution. This implies that checks of the **assignable** clause need to be performed through-out a method execution and not only in pre- and post-states. In the following, we present the code instrumentation to build up the necessary data structures and to check the validity of a field update. The relevant statements are: field updates (as these might violate the **assignable** clause), object creation (to track fresh locations), method invocation (to evaluate **assignable** clauses in the pre-state of a method and merge assignable sets), and method return (to update the assignable sets from the caller).

Field Update. Updating a field is the only way to violate an **assignable** clause. Before an update of a location $o.f$ in a method m called by m', we need to check if $o.f$ (hereafter referred to as loc) is in the set $\mathcal{A}_m^{eff}$. According to the semantics defined in Sec. 2, this is the case if either (1) the object of the location o has been freshly allocated during the execution of m and therefore is a member of the set $\mathcal{F}_m^{\triangleleft}$, or (2) loc is assignable in m' and the **assignable** clause of m either mentions the location itself or at least one datagroup that contains loc. Therefore, we need to check:

$$loc \in \mathcal{F}_m^{\triangleleft} \ \lor \ loc \in (\mathcal{A}_m \cap \mathcal{A}_{m'}^{eff}).$$

As explained in Sec. 3.1, we use maps of bitsets to represent sets of assignable lo-cations and we do not unfold the datagroups. Checking if loc is in a set of fresh locations $\mathcal{F}_m^{\triangleleft}$ is performed by $\mathcal{F}_m^{\triangleleft}[o]$. Checking if loc is in a set of assignable locations $\mathcal{A}_m$ is performed by $\mathcal{A}_m[o] \cap \mathcal{D}^{st}[loc] \neq \emptyset$. That is, we get the bitset representing the fields of object o in $\mathcal{A}_m$ and intersect it with the bitset rep-resenting the datagroups that contain loc. If the intersection of the two bitsets is not empty, either $\mathcal{A}_m$ contains loc or it contains at least one datagroup that contains loc. We maintain the set $\mathcal{A}_{m'}^{eff}$ explicitly, as we explain below. This gives us the the following assertion that needs to hold at runtime:

$$\mathcal{F}_m^{\triangleleft}[o] \ \lor \ (\mathcal{A}_m \cap \mathcal{A}_{m'}^{eff})[o] \cap \mathcal{D}^{st}[loc] \neq \emptyset$$

All of these operations can be performed in constant time, which means that we can check the **assignable** clauses for field updates in constant time in the presence of static datagroups only.

Object Creation. On creation of a new object o in method m, all locations of o are fresh in m and in every transitive caller m_i of m. According to the semantics of fresh sets, we would have to add all fields of o to $\mathcal{F}_m^\lhd$ as well as to each $\mathcal{F}_{m_i}^\lhd$. Since any caller of m can observe newly allocated locations only *after* m returns, we add o only to $\mathcal{F}_m^\lhd$ and update the callers later.

Because of this simplification, the instrumentation of object creation can be performed in constant time and produces a memory overhead linear in the number of newly allocated objects.

Method Invocation. On invocation of method m, we evaluate the **assignable** clause of m to the set $\mathcal{A}_m$. For all location $o.f$ in the **assignable** clause, we enable the bit that represents f in the bitset $\mathcal{A}_m[o]$. To do this, we perform the following update: $\mathcal{A}_m[o] \leftarrow \mathcal{A}_m[o] \cup \mathcal{B}(f)$ where $\mathcal{B}(f)$ is the bitset in which only the bit for field f is enabled. Furthermore, we compute the intersection $\mathcal{A} = (\mathcal{A}_m \cap \mathcal{A}_{m'}^{\text{eff}})$ because we need this set at every field update within the method and because this set does not change during method execution. We call this computation *merging* of assignable locations because we merge caller and callee. Our data structures allow efficient merging as follows: for each object that is a key in the maps of both $\mathcal{A}_m$ and $\mathcal{A}_{m'}^{\text{eff}}$, we compute the intersection of the corresponding bitsets, $bs = \mathcal{A}_m[o] \cap \mathcal{A}_{m'}^{\text{eff}}[o]$. If $bs \neq \emptyset$, we add it to the resulting set $\mathcal{A}[o] \leftarrow bs$, otherwise we just drop it.

The time and memory overhead at method invocation is linear in the number of objects that contain assignable fields.

Method Return. Before a method m may return to its caller m' the set of fresh locations $\mathcal{F}_m^\lhd$ needs to be added to $\mathcal{F}_{m'}^\lhd$.

This operation can be done with time overhead linear in the number of objects in $\mathcal{F}_m^\lhd$ and does not increase the memory overhead as $\mathcal{F}_m^\lhd$ will be consumed by the garbage collector.

4   Checking Assignable Clauses with Dynamic Datagroups

We extend the algorithm for checking **assignable** clauses to deal with *dynamic* datagroups, that is, datagroups that contain fields from other objects and therefore depend on the heap. We optimize our algorithm to cope well with situations that match the following two observations we made.

(1) A dynamic datagroup typically contains many locations through nested datagroups in recursive or aggregate data structures, whereas a location is typically only in a few datagroups of other objects. In our example in Fig. 1, the datagroup **struct** in class **Store** contains the field **root** and the fields **struct**, **left**, and **right** of all n nodes in the store, that is, $3 \times n$ locations. By contrast, the field **struct** of a node is dynamically contained in no more than $log_2(n)$ datagroups, namely in the datagroups **struct** of all ancestors, assuming that the tree is balanced.

(2) `assignable` clauses are often quite unspecific, yet useful. This implies that the set of assignable locations is often very large although only a few locations actually get assigned to. An example supporting this observation is method `add` in class `Store`. As we do not want to reveal the internal data structure of the store, we specify that `add` is only allowed to assign to the datagroup `struct` of the store, i.e., the `root` field of the store and all `struct`, `left`, and `right` fields of the nodes. In other words, method `add` cannot change the content of any existing item, but may for instance balance the tree.

Because of these two observations, we do not unfold datagroups into sets of locations in the pre-state of a method as described in the semantics, which is potentially very expensive in both time and space. This decision raises three issues:

(1) We have to spent more effort to check if a field is assignable, as the information is not directly available.

(2) We can no longer merge sets of assignable locations of callers and callees upon method invocations. If we had to merge two sets that contain partially overlapping dynamic datagroups we would have to unfold the datagroups to find out which locations are in the intersection. Since we decide not to unfold datagroups, we cannot merge anymore.

(3) As the content of dynamic datagroups may change over time, we need to keep track of all changes in dynamic datagroups in order to reconstruct the assignable locations as of the pre-state of the method.

In the following sections, we explain how we can efficiently cope with these issues.

4.1   Data Structures

We do not change any of the existing data structures for checking assignable clauses, but add data structures to represent dynamic datagroups. We design our data structures such that it is possible to quickly find all datagroups that dynamically contain a location.

Dynamic Datagroups. To represent dynamic datagroups, we add an array of sets of locations to each object to store for each field of the object a set of datagroups that dynamically contain the field. We call these *back-links*, from the location back to the datagroup. For the object g of class `Node` (see Fig. 2), we therefore represent the dynamic datagroups by the following array, in which only the entry for field `struct` contains a back-link.

$$
\begin{array}{ll}
\texttt{struct} & \left[\begin{array}{l} \{\texttt{c.struct}\} \\ \{\} \\ \vdots \end{array}\right] \\
\texttt{left} & \\
\vdots &
\end{array}
$$

To access the set of datagroups that *dynamically* contain location loc in heap h over one pivot field, we write $\mathcal{D}_h^{\mathrm{dyn}}[loc]$. Furthermore, we write $\mathcal{D}_h^{*\mathrm{dyn}}[loc]$ for the reflexive transitive closure of $\mathcal{D}_h^{\mathrm{dyn}}[loc]$. Implicitly, we also unfold static datagroups to calculate those sets. Since we evaluate dynamic datagroups in the pre-state of a method, we introduce the notation $h_0(m)$ to refer to the pre-heap of method m.

In our example in Fig. 2, $\mathcal{D}^{dyn}_{h_0(\text{replace})}[\text{g.struct}]$ yields the set $\{\text{c.struct}\}$, whereas $\mathcal{D}^{*dyn}_{h_0(\text{replace})}[\text{g.struct}]$ yields the set $\{\text{g.struct}, \text{c.struct}, \text{a.struct}\}$.

Assignable Stack. Since we no longer merge **assignable** clauses, we now have to check for each field update whether the updated location is assignable in each method on the call stack. To enable this check, we provide access to the sets of assignable and fresh locations for all methods on the call stack by passing a stack of assignable maps to the callee (rather than one merged assignable map).

Using stacks results in a memory footprint for storing assignable locations that grows linearly in the number of methods on the call stack.

4.2   Code Instrumentation

In order to support dynamic datagroups, we need to change the code instrumentation for field updates and method invocations, whereas object creation and method return stay unchanged.

Field Update. We reuse the efficient check of field updates for **assignable** clauses with static datagroups, but have to do additional work. Again, we need to check before updating a location $o.f$ (referred to as loc) in method m, if it is in $\mathcal{A}^{\text{eff}}_m$. Without merging assignable sets of locations, we do the following: for every method m_i that is in the call stack of m, we check that the location loc is either fresh in m_i or contained in the assignable set of locations of m_i. More formally:

$$\forall m_i \cdot m_i \hookrightarrow^* m \implies loc \in \mathcal{F}^{\triangleleft}_{m_i} \lor loc \in \mathcal{A}_{m_i}.$$

Since we do not update the set of fresh locations for all transitive callers of m, we need to add some extra logic to find out if loc is fresh in m_i. This is the case if loc has been freshly allocated during execution of m_i, that is, either in m_i itself or some callee of m_i. We can express this by $\exists m_k \cdot m_i \hookrightarrow^* m_k \land \mathcal{F}^{\triangleleft}_{m_k}[o]$. Although this looks more complicated, it actually allows us to simplify the implementation considerably.

Since we do not unfold dynamic datagroups, we need to perform some computation to check if loc is assignable. loc is in $\mathcal{A}_{m_i}$, if we find a datagroup dg that both dynamically contains the location loc, and is mentioned in the **assignable** clause. We write this as $\exists dg \cdot dg \in \mathcal{D}^{*dyn}_{h_0(m_i)}[loc] \land dg \in \mathcal{A}_{m_i}$. We reuse our technique from the static datagroups to replace $dg \in \mathcal{A}_{m_i}$ by $\mathcal{A}_{m_i}[obj(dg)] \cap \mathcal{D}^{st}[dg] \neq \emptyset$, see Sec. 3.2.

The time complexity for finding a datagroup that dynamically contains loc is linear in the size of $\mathcal{D}^{*dyn}[loc]$ multiplied by the number of methods on the call stack. However, we can dramatically speed up this lookup by introducing caches for finding dynamic datagroups, see Sec. 5. So in summary, we check the following assertion at runtime:

$$\forall m_i \cdot m_i \hookrightarrow^* m \implies$$
$$\exists m_k \cdot m_i \hookrightarrow^* m_k \land \mathcal{F}^{\triangleleft}_{m_k}[o] \quad \lor$$
$$\exists dg \cdot dg \in \mathcal{D}^{*\text{dyn}}_{h_0(m_i)}[loc] \land \mathcal{A}_{m_i}[obj(dg)] \cap \mathcal{D}^{\text{st}}[dg] \neq \emptyset$$

Updating a Pivot Field. Whenever we update a pivot field of a datagroup, we change the content of the datagroup. This is a problem because upon a method call, we do not unfold the datagroups mentioned in the **assignable** clause of the callee, even though the semantics of **assignable** clauses prescribes that the set of assignable locations is to be determined in the pre-state of the method. Consequently, any change to a datagroup mentioned in an **assignable** clause needs to be tracked in order to be able to reconstruct the situation in the pre-state of a method.

We apply a technique that we call *lazy unfolding*. If we update a pivot field of a datagroup that is contained in an assignable map, we perform two operations. (1) We add the old location that was contained in the datagroup via the pivot field before the update directly to the assignable map. By doing this, the location stays assignable although it is not in the datagroup anymore. (2) We add additional information to the assignable map, stating that the back-link of the new location that is contained in the datagroup via the pivot field after the update should not be considered when we check whether a location is assignable. By doing this, we can cut away parts of datagroups in assignable maps.

Note that this information needs to be stored per assignable map and not per datagroup as every assignable map is evaluated in a different state, and thus has a different set of assignable locations for the same datagroup.

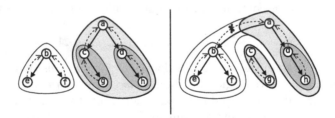

Fig. 3. The same situation as in Fig. 2. Dashed arrows depict the back-links from locations to datagroups. The cross depicts the back-link that has been invalidated in the assignable map of method **replace**.

Fig. 3 shows how the lazy unfolding works in our running example. On the left side, we see again the situation in the pre-state, the locations in the gray shapes are assignable. On the right side, we see the datagroups after the update a.left = b. To preserve the assignable locations of the pre-state, we add c.struct explicitly to the assignable map, which preserves the assignability of the locations of objects c and d. Furthermore, we mark the back-link from b.struct to a.struct in the assignable map as invalid, which essentially renders the locations of objects b, e, and f not assignable. Looking at the locations in the gray shapes, one can see that we effectively preserved the assignability of locations in the pre-state on the left-hand side although the datagroup changed in the meantime.

Method Invocation. On invocation of method m, we evaluate the `assignable` clause of m to the set $\mathcal{A}_m$ as described in Sec. 3.2, but we do not merge the assignable sets of the caller and the callee. Instead, we add the sets of assignable and fresh locations from method m to the stack of assignable maps.

5 Introducing Caches

As we have shown in the last section, the time overhead to check if a location loc is assignable depends on the height of the call stack and on the size of the set of dynamic datagroups $\mathcal{D}^{*\mathrm{dyn}}[loc]$. For every update of location loc, we check if loc is assignable in all assignable maps on the stack. This involves to compute the set $\mathcal{D}^{*\mathrm{dyn}}[loc]$ and to check for each datagroup in that set whether it is mentioned in the assignable map or not. That is, we spend a considerable effort to check if a location is assignable.

In this process of checking, we gain a lot of additional information. We learn which datagroups in $\mathcal{D}^{*\mathrm{dyn}}[loc]$ are mentioned in what assignable map, and we also learn which datagroups in $\mathcal{D}^{*\mathrm{dyn}}[loc]$ are not assignable. We can reuse all this information since the set of locations of an `assignable` clauses is computed in the pre-state and does not change during method execution.

We equip each assignable map with a cache that stores all the additional information from the queries since the method invocation. The information in the cache is valid for this assignable map as long as the corresponding method executes. Caches become especially useful if we assign to the same set of locations several times in a method, for instance when doing a computation in a loop.

6 Evaluation

6.1 Experimental Results

As a proof of concept, we implemented the algorithm described in this paper to check `assignable` clauses in Java programs.

To test the efficiency of our algorithm, we chose a doubly-linked list, where the nesting of datagroups is as deep as the number of nodes in the list: every node is equipped with a `struct` datagroup that contains the `next` and `previous` fields and dynamically contains the `struct` field of the successor node.

We performed experiments with different list operations to measure the performance of our algorithm[1]. The most interesting experiment has been to reverse large doubly-linked list, which involves operations on every node of the list and changes the structure of the dynamic datagroups completely. In fact, every pivot

---

[1] On a desktop computer with a single core 3.4 GHz CPU.

field gets assigned to, which leads to a complete unfolding of the datagroup. This is the worst case scenario for our algorithm, which tries to avoid unfolding as much as possible.

Surprisingly, we need only a bit more than one seconds to add 10'000 nodes to a list and reverse it with the runtime assertion checker enabled. We spend around 80% of the time to add the nodes, and 20% of the time to reverse the list. The memory footprint is around 20MB before reversing the list and grows to 25MB during reversing because of the caches that get filled in the process. If we switch off runtime assertion checking for the same example, the program terminates within half a second and uses around 2.5MB. When repeating the experiment with 20'000 nodes, time and memory consumption doubles for both versions.

For the doubly-linked list, the runtime overhead of our checker is a factor of 2 and the memory overhead is a factor of 10. For the main applications of run-time assertion checking (to prepare static verification and to reproduce possibly spurious verification errors), we consider this overhead acceptable, especially for recursive data structures such as our doubly-linked list. We expect the overhead to be significantly smaller for non-recursive aggregate structures, where dynamic datagroups are not nested as deeply.

6.2   Theoretical Results

Our algorithm depends mainly on the following factors: the size of the set of dynamic datagroups that contain a location ($|\mathcal{D}^{\bullet dyn}|$), the size of the assignable sets ($|\mathcal{A}|$), and the size of the call stack ($|cs|$),

Time Complexity. Field update is the only operation that may generate a significant time overhead. The check if a location is assignable has a time complexity of $\mathcal{O}(|\mathcal{D}^{\bullet dyn}| \times |cs|)$ if the result is not cached in any assignable map, and $\mathcal{O}(|cs|)$ if the result is cached in all assignable maps. That is, the caches have a big impact on the performance if we have a deep nesting of **assignable** clauses. We also see that we do not have a good solution for recursive method calls, where $|cs|$ gets big.

In our running example, $|\mathcal{D}^{\bullet dyn}|$ is logarithmic to the number of nodes in the tree, which leads to a very good performance.

Memory Overhead. The data structures that produce a significant memory overhead are the ones for storing the sets of assignable locations, including caches. That is, the memory overhead depends on the number of assignable locations mentioned in the **assignable** clauses, the amount of lazy unfolding and of course the number of methods on the call stack. We get an overhead of $\mathcal{O}(|\mathcal{A}| \times |cs|)$, where the size of $\mathcal{A}$ depends on how much unfolding happened already.

In our running example, if we have a method with an **assignable** clause stating 'a.struct' $|\mathcal{A}|$ initially contains only the location a.struct and our memory overhead is very small. For each left or right pointer that we assign to in a method, we add one more location to that set, and, if we completely reorder the whole tree, end up in a complete unfolding of the datagroup.

7 Related Work

Cheon's runtime assertion checker for JML [4] provides data structures to represent **assignable** clauses and datagroups but does not generate checks for it. Ye uses those data structures in his thesis [12] to implement an **assignable** clause checker in the presence of static datagroups only. The checks have a time overhead linear in the size of the set of locations from the **assignable** clause, whereas our algorithm for static datagroups works in constant time.

The CHASE tool [3] provides a simple means to discover common specification mistakes, but is not designed to be sound. It performs a purely syntactic check on **assignable** clauses, ignores aliasing, and does not support datagroups.

Spoto and Poll [10] formalized a trace semantics for a sound reasoning on **assignable** clauses. Their approach takes aliasing into account, but datagroups are not supported. They conclude that JML's **assignable** clause may be unsuited for a precise and correct static analysis.

The LOOP tool [11] generates PVS proof obligations for a given JML annotated Java program. It is mainly used to prove non-trivial properties of JavaCard applications. LOOP can deal with **assignable** clauses, but datagroups are not taken into account.

KRAKATOA [9] is a verification tool for Java. The specification language of KRAKATOA is similar to JML and contains an *assigns* clause to specify a list of locations that can be assigned. Again, it is not possible to apply information hiding by using datagroups.

The KEY system [1] allows one to verify Java programs against JML specifications. KEY handles **assignable** clauses, but not datagroups.

ESC/JAVA2 supports most JML annotations, including **assignable** clauses and datagroups. However, ESC/JAVA2 fails to give a precise and correct answer on **assignable** clauses that mention datagroups.

Spec#[2] does not provide datagroups, but instead uses a hierarchical heap model to provide abstraction; if a *modifies* clause allows modification of an object o then all (committed) objects that have o as (transitive) owner can be modified as well. This is similar to declaring a datagroup in each object that contains the locations of that object and all (transitively) owned objects. Therefore, we expect that our algorithm, especially the idea of lazy unfolding, can also be applied to Spec#.

8 Conclusion

We presented an algorithm to check **assignable** clauses in the presence of static and dynamic datagroups. Our algorithm performs well, in particular, on recursive data structures with large and deeply nested dynamic datagroups by introducing the concept of lazy unfolding of datagroups. We provide the foundation to close a big gap in the runtime assertion checker of JML. The algorithm has been tested against recursive data structures with a prototypical implementation of a runtime assertion checker.

We plan to prove correctness of our algorithm by adding an operational semantics to our JML formalization in Coq [6] that includes the runtime assertion checks and show that the algorithm enforces the semantics of **assignable** clauses. Moreover, we intend to contribute our algorithm to the OpenJML project and to use that implementation for larger experiments.

Acknowledgments. We are grateful to Alex J. Summers and the anonymous reviewers for helpful comments.

References

1. Ahrendt, W., Baar, T., Beckert, B., Bubel, R., Giese, M., Hähnle, R., Menzel, W., Mostowski, W., Roth, A., Schlager, S., Schmitt, P.H.: The KeY tool. In: SS (2004)
2. Barnett, M., Leino, K.R.M., Schulte, W.: The Spec# programming system: An overview. In: Barthe, G., Burdy, L., Huisman, M., Lanet, J.-L., Muntean, T. (eds.) CASSIS 2004. LNCS, vol. 3362, pp. 49–69. Springer, Heidelberg (2005)
3. Cataño, N., Huisman, M.: Chase: A static checker for JML's assignable clause. In: Zuck, L.D., Attie, P.C., Cortesi, A., Mukhopadhyay, S. (eds.) VMCAI 2003. LNCS, vol. 2575, pp. 26–40. Springer, Heidelberg (2002)
4. Cheon, Y.: A Runtime Assertion Checker for the Java Modeling Language. PhD thesis, Iowa State University (2003)
5. ESC/Java2, http://secure.ucd.ie/products/opensource/ESCJava2
6. Kägi, A., Lehner, H., Müller, P.: A formalization of JML in the Coq proof system. Technical report, ETH Zurich (2009),
   http://www.pm.inf.ethz.ch/people/lehnerh/jmlcoq
7. Leino, K.R.M.: Data groups: Specifying the modification of extended state. In: OOPSLA, pp. 144–153 (1998)
8. Leino, K.R.M., Poetzsch-Heffter, A., Zhou, Y.: Using data groups to specify and check side effects. In: PLDI, pp. 246–257 (2002)
9. Marché, C., Paulin-Mohring, C., Urbain, X.: The Krakatoa tool for certification of Java/JavaCard programs annotated with JML annotations. JLAP 58, 89–106 (2004)
10. Spoto, F., Poll, E.: Static analysis for JML's assignable clauses. In: Ghelli, G. (ed.) FOOL (2003)
11. van den Berg, J., Jacobs, B.: The LOOP compiler for Java and JML. In: Margaria, T., Yi, W. (eds.) TACAS 2001. LNCS, vol. 2031, pp. 299–312. Springer, Heidelberg (2001)
12. Ye, C.: Improving JML's assignable clause analysis. Technical report, Iowa State University (2006)

Performance Modeling and Analysis of Context-Aware Mobile Software Systems*

Luca Berardinelli, Vittorio Cortellessa, and Antinisca Di Marco

Dipartimento di Informatica
Università dell'Aquila
Via Vetoio, 67010 Coppito (AQ), Italy
{luca.berardinelli,vittorio.cortellessa,
antinisca.dimarco}@di.univaq.it

Abstract. Context-awareness is becoming a first class attribute of software systems. In fact, applications for mobile devices need to be aware of their context in order to adapt their structure and behavior and offer the best quality of service even in case the (software and hardware) resources are limited. Although performance is a key non-functional property for such applications, existing approaches for performance modeling and analysis fail to capture the characteristics related to the context, thus resulting not suited for this domain.

In this paper we introduce a framework for modeling and analyzing the performance of context-aware mobile software systems. The framework allows to model: the software architecture, the context management, the adaptable behaviors and the performance parameters. Such models can then be transformed into performance models for analysis purposes. We tailor an integrated environment for modeling these elements in UML, and we show how to use it for performance analysis purposes. The modeling environment description and the performance analysis are driven by an example in the eHealth domain.

1 Introduction

The rapid evolution of portable devices and their increasing pervasiveness in everyday life have motivated, in the last few years, a growing interest for methodologies, techniques and tools that allow to effectively develop and analyze software systems running on such devices.

The main characteristics of portable devices are: mobility and limitation of hardware resources. Both features obviously claim for specific requirements of the deployed software systems that have to be taken into account along the whole software lifecycle.

Mobility can either physical or logical [18]. Physical mobility regards the transfers of a portable device among a certain number of physical locations. Logical mobility takes into account the re-deployment actions that certain software components can be subject to.

The limitation of hardware resources has brought to develop specific releases of software products for portable devices that require limited amounts of resources. However,

---

* This work has been supported by the Italian Project PACO (Performability- Aware Computing: Logics, Models, and Languages) funded by MIUR.

D.S. Rosenblum and G. Taentzer (Eds.): FASE 2010, LNCS 6013, pp. 353–367, 2010.

some resources not only are limited, but their available amounts can change during the device usage. Hence, more recently this limitation has been tackled by providing to software the ability of adapting to changes in the environment.

Mobility and context-awareness (and, as a consequence, adaptation) obviously have a large impact on the performance of software systems. Their bad effects on performance are today passively accepted as unavoidable fees to pay in the domain of advanced portable systems. As opposite, if opportunely managed, they can become powerful instruments in the hands of software developers to maintain an acceptable level of user-perceived performance even in presence of changes and degradations in the surrounding environment [16].

Goal of this paper is to introduce a framework to model and analyze performance of context-aware mobile software systems. The framework is aimed at producing UML models that embed, besides mobility and context-awareness facets, the parameters that allow an automated model-based performance analysis of the system. The elements that build up a context-aware mobile software system model are: the software architecture, the context management, the adaptable behaviors and the performance parameters.

Within this framework different types of mobility and context-awareness can be modeled and, if needed, combined. The rationale behind an uniform modeling of such aspects is that the runtime behavior of a mobile/adaptable software system can be driven both by a mobility event and a change in its computational environment that lead to changes in the software itself, namely adaptation actions. However, besides the specific characteristics of mobility and context-awareness, the interdependencies between them can be captured, and the cross-effects on the system performance can be taken into account. Thus certain types of analysis that were not feasible with specific models (for mobility or context-awareness) can be carried out in our integrated framework. The framework is based on an existing UML tool (i.e. MagicDraw) and on existing UML profiles, such as the UML profile for Modeling and Analyzing Real-Time Embedded Systems (MARTE) [17].

The paper is organized as follows: Section 2 introduces some related work and places our contribution with respect to the existing literature, in Section 3 we present our framework under the guideline of a reference example in the eHealth domain, in Section 4 we show how different types of awareness can be merged together into an unique model, Section 5 shows the results of performance analysis experiments and highlights the potential of our approach, and finally in Section 6 we conclude the paper and discuss possible future work.

2   Related Work

Several approaches have been introduced in the last few years to manage mobility and adaptation at the middleware level. Among these, very relevant work has been done within the framework of the MUSIC project [13]. The MUSIC middleware monitors the context and the resources to catch their changes and adapts the application to fulfill the users' QoS requirements. The approach uses QoS predictors and utility functions to support the adaptation process. The adaptation is based on the concept of service plan [15], i.e. a platform-independent specification containing information on service configurations, its dependencies on the environment and its QoS.

All the MUSIC contributions can be used at run time given that the application has been developed to be context-aware and QoS validated. As assessed in [15], the information the MUSIC middleware needs is specified in the service plan, but such information is collected at the design time. As opposite to MUSIC project, we provide a support to model and analyze performance properties of such systems before their implementation and deployment. For example, with our framework it would be possible to automatically generate the (MUSIC) service plan and provide the QoS models that work as predictors in the MUSIC adaptation process.

Another interesting project is DiVA [2], which aims at providing an integrated framework for managing dynamic variability in adaptive systems. DiVA exploits both Model-Driven and Aspect-Oriented technologies to define an architectural model (including base, variant and adaptation models) at design time. The composition and validation at runtime of alternative models allow: (i) the choice of the system configuration that best adapts to the changed execution context, and (ii) the deployment and execution of the chosen configuration supported by a reflective middleware. However, such approach does not provide any support for non-functional analysis.

Grassi et al. in [8] have proposed a modeling framework for QoS-aware self-adaptive software applications that present several similarities with our framework. Such framework, based on the definition of an intermediate pivot language (i.e. D-KLAPER), is aimed at providing instruments to transform software models into non-functional models and analyze QoS characteristics while changes in the application and/or its environment may occur.

Our work improves the approach in [8] for several aspects: (i) context-awareness and mobility are based in our approach on a set of attributes whose evolution is modeled through Statecharts, whereas in [8] a set of triggers has to be specified in isolation; (ii) the previous difference allows us to introduce dependencies among events that cannot apparently modeled with D-KLAPER; (iii) we have implemented our approach in UML, so to prove that such language has the potential to represent triggers and (simple) adaptation mechanisms, whereas this part of D-KLAPER still does not find any correspondence in UML. However, on the other side, the work in [8] also presents some advantages, such as: (i) to explicit represent adaptation actions, (ii) to take into account the non-functional costs of such actions, (iii) to generate a Markov Reward Model that allows to study non-functional properties even in non steady states of the system.

Finally, our idea of managing all context- and mobility-related aspects with statecharts is very close to the concept of *modes*. Modes has been proposed in [11] to extend the Darwin ADL for modeling Service Oriented Computing systems. Modes are also language primitives in the Architecture&Analysis Description Language (AADL) [1] for modeling Real-Time&Embedded Systems. In both cases they can be used to model the structural evolution of software architecture at runtime. Besides components, AADL allows the modal specification of all its modeling elements like system, connectors and properties. Thus, our logical mobility and hardware managers can be modeled as AADL component's modes whereas the overall context manager as system's modes. In AADL, it is also possible to model the physical mobility by means of system's modes. However, in this case, it can't be associated to a system user as we do associating the manager to UML Actors. Therefore, differently to AADL, our UML-based modeling approach can be (i) "sized" for different definitions of context and (ii) used as a general "modal-based" modeling approach for software system of multiple domain.

3   Modeling Performance-Annotated Context-Aware Software Systems

In this section we describe our approach for designing UML models of context-aware software systems that embed performance annotations. The description is driven by a reference example in the eHealth domain. In [4] an extended description of our approach has been reported, where more technical details are provided and a general scope of the approach is illustrated.

The envisaged eHealth service supports the doctor's everyday activities, such as the retrieval of mixed media information on his patients that combines text with or without different kinds of images referring to their personal data, their medical histories and patient-related diseases. The results can be displayed on the doctor's handheld device.

The UML model we devise is organized in three views:

The **Service View** (SV) represents the services provided by the software system as perceived and used by external actors (Use Case Diagram, UCD) along with their behavioral specifications (Sequence Diagram, SD). A *Physical Mobility Manager* (Statechart, SC) is assigned to each nomadic user that exploits the system services while moving with his mobile device [9][6].

The **Component View** (CV) represents a software architecture (Component Diagram, CD) integrated with mobility annotations that allow to distinguish logically mobile from fixed software artifacts. A *Logical Mobility Manager* is associated to each component whose implementation is (even partially) mobile [9] .

The **Deployment View** (DV) represents: (i) the current/allowed allocation of software artifacts on execution environments (e.g. handheld devices) that can physically move across different places (*Dynamic* Deployment Diagram, dynDD), and (ii) several detailed hardware device specifications (*Hardware* Deployment Diagram, hwDD). A *Hardware Configuration Manager* is associated to each resource whose state (that may represent its current amount) may vary at runtime.

To enable model-based performance analysis the UML model has to be annotated with additional information coming from several profiles. We have adopted the UML Profile for Modeling and Analysis of Real-Time Embedded Systems (MARTE) [17] and the UML Profile for Mobile Systems [9]. In addition, we have defined a Context Modeling profile to model the *managers* that handle the different types of awareness. The driving criterion in our profiling task has been to re-use existing profiles wherever possible[1].

---

[1] Hereafter we denote with typewritten words model variables whereas with the *italicized* ones the stereotypes of profiles. Note, however, that the UML diagrams have been suitably tailored to fit the page limitation and to preserve their readability, whereas a machine-readable complete UML model of our eHelath example can be downloaded at *http://www.di.univaq.it/cortelle/docs/eHealthSystemModelASE.rar*.

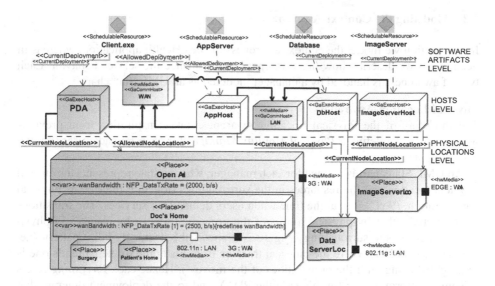

Fig. 1. The Dynamic Deployment Diagram

3.1   Modeling the Software Architecture

The retrieval of patient related information (that hereafter we refer as RequestPatientIn-foPages) is supposed to be the most frequently invoked service (basing on the user profile). In our modeling approach, each service is provided by a component-based system whose architectural description is given by a Component Diagram (CD). The CD identifies the software components, their interconnections and the executable artifacts implementing them. Moreover, it specifies which component is mobile and the perfor-mance parameters needed for the analysis.

In Figure 1 the *dynamic* DD of the application is shown. It is inspired by the diagram introduced in [9], as it basically contains two types of information: (i) the allocation of the software artifacts (*SchedulableResources*) on the execution environments (*GaEx-ecHost*) through deployment relationships (*CurrentDeployment, AllowedDeployment*) that go from the Software Artifact level to the Hosts level, and (ii) the positioning of the execution hosts (e.g. PDA) on different physical locations using associations (*Cur-rentLocation, AllowedLocation*) that go from the Hosts level to the Physical Locations level. The dynamic nature of dynDD derives from the need to change the current and allowed relationships between levels whenever logical and/or physical mobility events take place.

Looking at Figure 1 we deduce that the RequestPatientInfoPages service is avail-able if the user PDA is able to connect to a WAN network (*hwMedia*). Different *Places* can provide different types of network connections (i.e. typed Ports of *Places*), but some of them might not be exploitable by the service (such as the white-colored port 802.11n:LAN at Doctor's Home) due to particular design choices and/or hardware limitations.

3.2   Modeling the Context-Awareness

In this section we model the context-awareness of the eHealth application, whereas in Section 3.3 we describe how this awareness can influence the service behavior. Each type of awareness is handled by a manager modeled as an UML Statechart.

Physical Location-Awareness
The modeling of the Physical Location Awareness takes inspiration from previous works [6][9]. We define a *Physical Mobility Manager* for each nomadic user (i.e. the doctor in our case).

An UML Statechart is defined for each manager, where a state represents the current physical location and the resources in the surroundings (together referred as physical configuration, *PhyConfig*) at the time when users demand for services. The transitions are triggered either by physical moves of the nomadic users or by changes in physical resources in the surroundings. Figure 2(a) shows the doctor mobility pattern (i.e. the one of his PDA) where the physical transfer from his home to the patient's one is highlighted along with the probabilities of the moves[2]. Hence each *PhyConfig* refers to some platform device (in this case the PDA), and to the deployment diagram that embeds it. A *PhyConfig* state determines the ends of the *Current-* and *AllowedNodeLocations* relationships among mobile execution hosts and places on dynDD (Figure 1.

Logical Location-Awareness
Logical mobility is informally defined as the *capability to dynamically change the bindings between code fragments and the location where they are executed* [7]. We adopt the solution proposed in [9] that is based on an UML Statechart called *Logical Mobility Manager*. In a Logical Mobility Manager a state corresponds to the current allocation (*CurrentDeployment*) of the software components (*MobileCode*) to the proper execution platforms (*GaExecHost* in Figure 1). State transitions represent the possible re-deployments of mobile software artifacts through the communication channels (*HwMedia* in Figure 1) to other platform devices (*AllowedDeployment*).

For example, when the client artifact (i.e. client.exe in Figure 1) actually runs on the PDA, it can migrate back and forth to the application host due to some design reason (e.g. performing heavy tasks on the server side when resources on the PDA are scarce).

Hardware Platform Awareness
The third dimension of the context-awareness, as defined in this paper, takes into account the detailed hardware specification of the execution environment. We illustrate in Figure 2 the *Hardware Configuration Managers* for hardware resources whose internal configuration *HwConfig* can influence the service behavior (see [4] for a detail of these resources).

Figure 2(b) illustrates the CPU, BATTERY and DISPLAY managers as separate UML Statecharts that model the states and transitions of corresponding hardware components. Each state specifies a set of *nfpConstraints* (based on variables defined on the configured hardware component) [17] to be held in the current configuration *HwConfig*.

---

[2] For each state the probabilities of the outgoing transitions at most sum to 1, where the gap to 1 implicitly corresponds to the probability of the self-transition.

In addition, a remote firing transition (i.e. BATTERY2LowPowerDowngrade) is illustrated to highlight how the remaining BATTERY capacity (`currCapacity`) can influence the configuration of the CPU by firing a remote transition that limits its clock frequency (`currFrequency`).

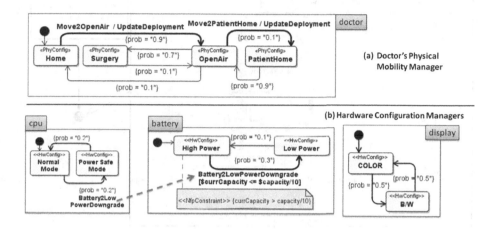

Fig. 2. Physical and Hardware Configuration Managers

3.3 Modeling the Service Behaviors

The eHealth modeling is completed by the specification of service's behaviors.

The left side of Figure 3 shows an UML Sequence Diagram associated to the RequestPatientInfoPages service. When the doctor, once logged in, invokes the distributed service, the server-side components are in charge of retrieving data from a local (i.e. connected by LAN) database and, if suited, from a remote (i.e. connected by WAN) image server for patients' x-rays or disease-related images. Finally the result is displayed on the client.

The service behavior can be determined by the current context conditions defined by the values of the managers' model variables. Figure 3 represents indeed an Interaction Overview Diagram (IOD) that models the behavior alternatives and the conditions that determine the current behavior, as expressed at the topmost branching point of the figure. Hence, the same service can have multiple implemented behaviors whose activation is driven by the logics expressed within the managers.

Besides the StandardBehavior described above, the right side of Figure 3 reports a box for a ResourceConstrained behavior that will be executed in case of scarce resources and that excludes the interactions with the image server (i.e. the white lifeline and the bold labeled messages in Figure 3)[3].

---

[3] For sake of readability, in Section 5 we simplify the conditions for the activation of Resource-Constrained behavior by basing only on the display characteristics.

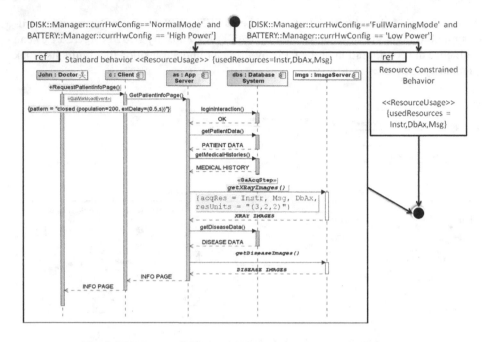

Fig. 3. The context-aware RequestPatientInfoPages service behavior

3.4   Adding Performance Annotations

The eHealth model described so far also contains additional information related to performance. Such information is necessary to obtain performance models through automated model-to-model transformations [5]. In particular, the previously illustrated diagrams include:

- The workload (*GaWorkloadEvent*) for each service (Figure 3).
- The resource demand vector (GaAcqStep) that represents the amount of resources that an operational step needs to be completed (Figure 3); in particular, a resource demand vector provides values (i.e. *resUnits* tag of *GaAcqStep*[4]) for the ordered list (*acqRes*) of available *logical resources* (i.e. Instr, DbAx, and Msg *ResourceUsage* in Figure 3) necessary to execute the step.
- The multiplicity, service time and scheduling policy of each *hardware resource* such as CPUs, DISKs and NETWORKs (e.g. wanBandwidth in Figure 1).

Resource demand vectors represent the platform-independent annotations related to performance, in that they are abstract quantifications of resource consumption. In order to associate these annotations to platform specifications and build a solvable performance model (following the approach in [19]), the characteristics of platform devices have to be also specified (see [4]).

In a context-aware domain the platform device characteristics can change depending on the context. In our case, for example, the available network connections can

---

[4] We assume that the resource units are implicitly released at the end of each step.

have different non functional properties that affect the quality of the service provision. In particular, the RequestPatientInfoPages performance can be affected by the network bandwidth `wanBandwidth` (Figure 1) whose value is bound to the *CurrentNodeLocation* association and varies when the doctor moves across the other allowed physical locations (i.e. *AllowedNodeLocation*).

4   An Unique Model for Mobility and Context-Awareness

On the basis of the modeling approach introduced above, all considered awareness (in this paper the physical location-, the logical location- and the hardware platform-awareness) must be properly combined. Each of them can be defined in isolation or, through remote firing, can affect the other ones. For sake of performance analysis they can be considered together or in isolation, depending on the facets of interest of the software system. For example, one can investigate only the performance degradation due to an extremely high physical mobility of users without considering at all the states of resources on portable devices.

Therefore the types of statecharts that model the evolution of context dimensions, as the ones described in Section 3, can be lumped when necessary for analysis purposes in one statechart that models the runtime evolution of a mobile context-aware software system.

Each state of such statechart (that we call *superstate*) represents a possible context, and it is obtained from the combination of a certain number of states (in this paper three states), one for each statechart modeling a context dimension evolution (in this paper physical mobility, logical mobility, hardware platform evolution). Obviously not all the combinations are allowed, for example a certain configuration of hardware devices cannot allow a certain deployment of software components to devices. Therefore, in order to build a consistent unique model, only superstates that are feasible combinations of states have to be considered.

Once this set of superstates has been defined, a list of provided services and their corresponding behaviors have to be associated to each state. In fact, if multiple behaviors for some services are available, then the behavior to be adopted must be specified in each superstate where the service can be provided. We remark that this type of association does not need human processing, as it can be automated by parsing an Interaction Overview Diagram (see Figure 3). The latter, in fact, represents the behavior alternatives guarded by predicates over model variables. A superstate is uniquely characterized by the values assumed from model variables. Hence, the model variable values that determine a certain superstate drives the choice towards the appropriate behavior alternative among the ones modeled in the Interaction Overview Diagram.

Transitions have to be defined in this unifying statechart. Being each superstate obtained by lumping a certain number of states of respective statecharts, the transitions outgoing these latter states have to be opportunely combined (along with their probabilities) to build up transitions outgoing the superstate. The Harel's theory on statecharts [10], along with the Hermanns et al.'s work on stochastic statecharts [14], provide sufficient results to automate this step in most cases.

In Figure 4 we report the unifying statechart obtained by lumping some of the awareness managers introduced in Section 3.2. In particular, we have considered the doctor's

Physical Mobility Manager and the PDA Display Hardware Configuration Manager (Figure 2). This choice allows, on one end to keep the example as simple as possible, and on the other end to keep into account two different types of awareness, as we will show in Section 5.

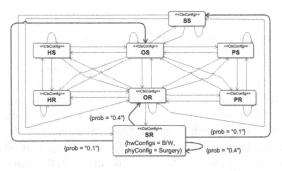

Fig. 4. The eHealth system unifying statechart

The lumping process of these two managers brings to an unifying statechart where all eight potential superstates are feasible (i.e. the cartesian product of the manager state spaces). In Figure 4 each superstate is a different context *CtxConfig*, and is labeled with two letters: the first one recalls the state of the Physical Mobility Manager it comes from (i.e. H for Home, O for OpenAir, S for Surgery and P for PatientHome), the second one recalls the behavior adopted in the state as a consequence of the Display state (i.e. S means StandardBehavior, that is adopted when the display is in Color state, whereas R means ResourceConstrainedBehavior, adopted when the display is in B/W). For sake of illustration the SR superstate has been completely represented, along with example probabilities on its outgoing transitions.

5   Performance Analysis

Several interesting experiments can be conducted on the model that we have built to study the system performance vs different model parameters. For example, the utilization of a certain platform device can be analyzed while varying the intensity of traffic due to user mobility, or the response time of a certain service can be analyzed in different superstates (or across superstates).

In fact, as outlined in Section 3.4, our model embeds all the performance parameters necessary to apply an automated transformation that generates a performance model, such as a Stochastic Petri Net or a Queueing Network. In this specific case we have used the approach illustrated in [5] [5].

In Figure 5 an Execution Graph [19] of the RequestPatientInfoPages service has been reported as obtained through a model transformation of the Sequence Diagram in Figure 3. An Execution Graph is a platform-independent model that represents the software dynamics along with its requests of resources. In Figure 5 square blocks represent the basic operations that the components perform to provide the service. Beside each block a demand vector is shown that reports (from the annotations of the Sequence Diagram) the amount of logical resources that are required to complete the block (see Section 3.4). In particular: (i) Instr represents the number of high-level instructions to be executed from a CPU, (ii) DbAx represents the number of mass memory blocks to be acceded on

---

[5] For sake of space we do not enter into technical details of such transformations; readers interested can refer to [3] for a recent survey on this topic.

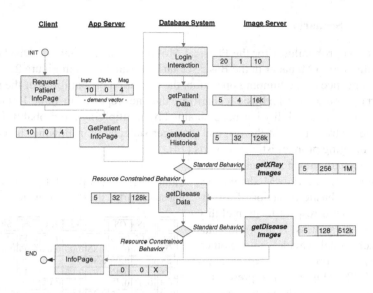

Fig. 5. Execution Graph of RequestPatientInfoPages service

DISK (each block is sized 32 bytes), and (iii) Msg represents the number of bytes to be exchanged on the network (i.e. WAN/LAN).

Decision points have been generated in Figure 5 to embed the (bold labeled) blocks that are executed only in the StandardBehavior (similar labeling of the Sequence Diagram). The topmost labels indicates the names of the components that execute the underlying blocks.

The last block before the end of the graph represents the return of patient data to the doctor's PDA. The demand vector of such block cannot be uniquely identified, in that it brings over the WAN (connecting PDA and AppHost) the data retrieved. These data are different depending on the behavior executed. Therefore an X value is placed in the Msg field of this block demand vector, and X holds either 272kB or 1.772MB in case of, respectively, Resource Constrained and Standard Behavior[6].

The platform characteristics that we have considered in all experiments are reported in [4].

We have considered three scenarios for our software system, namely: Basic, High Mobility and Powerful Display. In the Basic scenario we devise a low mobility of the doctor (and hence of his PDA) that for most of time operates in the Surgery room, and an equal probability for the display to be color or b/w (i.e. equal probability for the two service behaviors). In the High Mobility scenario we introduce frequent doctor's relocations with respect to the Basic scenario. In the Powerful Display scenario, reported in [4], we instead introduce, with respect to the Basic scenario, a much higher probability for the Display to be in Color state (i.e. higher probability of adopting a StandardBehavior).

---

[6] These X values are obtained by summing up the amount of bytes of Msg fields of blocks executed in the two different behaviors.

5.1   A Basic Scenario

The transition probabilities for the Physical Mobility Manager and the Display Hardware Configuration Manager in the Basic scenario are annotated in Figure 2.

In consequence of the lumping operation, the transition probabilities of the unifying statechart of Figure 4 for the Basic scenario are the ones reported in Table 1. It is easy to observe that each probability has been obtained by multiplying the probabilities of the corresponding transitions in the original manager statecharts, following the canonical theory of merging probabilistic statecharts [14].

The statechart shown in Figure 4 can be interpreted as a Markov Model that describes the stochastic behavior of a software system with respect to its mobility and context-awareness. Hence, the solution of such model provides, among other, the steady-state probabilities of each superstate [20]. This result represents a measure of how often the system will be in a certain superstate, and it is therefore a crucial parameter for many types of non-functional analysis. The solution of such Markov Model in the Basic scenario leads to the steady-state probabilities reported in Table 2.

We have considered the response time of the RequestPatientInfoPages service as the performance index of interest in our experiments. Minimum, maximum and average values of such index are evaluated overall the superstates for each scenario. Note, however, that since scenarios differ from each other only for transition probabilities (while keeping software and platform characteristics unchanged), the minimum and maximum response times are invariant across scenarios. As opposite, the average response time is computed as the weighted sum of response time in each superstate, where the weights are the steady-state probabilities. Therefore different values of average response time are obtained in different scenarios.

Table 1. Transition probabilities for the unifying statechart in the Basic scenario

	HS	OS	SS	PS	HR	OR	SR	PR
HS	0.05	0.45			0.05	0.45		
OS	0.05	0.05	0.35	0.05	0.05	0.05	0.35	0.05
SS		0.05	0.45			0.05	0.45	
PS		0.45		0.05		0.45		0.05
HR	0.05	0.45			0.05	0.45		
OR	0.05	0.05	0.35	0.05	0.05	0.05	0.35	0.05
SR		0.05	0.45			0.05	0.45	
PR		0.45		0.05		0.45		0.05

Table 2. Steady-state probabilities of superstates in the Basic scenario

HS	OS	SS	PS
0.0067	0.0608	0.4250	0.0067

HR	OR	SR	PR
0.0067	0.0608	0.4250	0.0067

In order to obtain the response time in each superstate the Execution Graph shown in Figure 5 has to be synthesized to obtain an unique demand vector for each Execution Host [19]. For example, the demand vectors of the four blocks executed by Database System in Figure 5 have to be summed up to obtain the demand of resources addressed to DbHost where Database System is deployed. Thereafter, each synthesized demand vector has to be combined with the corresponding platform characteristics specified in [4] to obtain the amount of time spent in each platform device to complete the service.

Summarizing, on the basis of the Steady-state probabilities of superstates (Table 2), the Demand vectors synthesized from the Execution Graph (Figure 5), and the Platform characteristics (see [4]), the response time values of RequestPatientInfoPages service in the Basic scenario are reported in Table 3, where values are expressed in seconds.

Since minimum and maximum values are invariant with respect to the scenario, the two leftmost values reported in Table 3 also hold for the other two scenarios. For these values we have reported in the bottommost row of Table 3 the superstate name where this value is achieved. A

Table 3. Response time values in the Basic scenario

		Max	Min	Average
Response Time		82.069	1.17	14.59
Superstate		OS	SR	-

maximum response time of 82.069 seconds is obtained when the doctor's PDA is in OpenAir and its display works in color (i.e. OS state), whereas a minimum response time of 1.17 seconds is obtained when the doctor's PDA is in Surgery and its display works in black and white (i.e. SR state).

The average response time obviously depends on the steady-state probabilities. In particular, as it can be observed in Table 2, in this case most of time is spent in Surgery (i.e. either SS or SR state) where the network bandwidth is quite large ([4]). Therefore the average response time is much closer to its lower bound than its upper bound.

5.2 High Mobility Scenario

The transition probabilities of the Physical Mobility Manager in the High Mobility scenario are reported in Table 4, whereas the probabilities for the Display Hardware Configuration Manager are the ones adopted in the Basic scenario.

Table 4. Transition probabilities for Physical Mobility Manager in the High Mobility scenario

		Home	OpenAir	Surgery	PatientHome
Home		0.5	0.5		
OpenAir		0.25	0.25	0.25	0.25
Surgery			0.5	0.5	
PatientHome			0.5		0.5

Table 5. Steady-state probabilities of superstates in the High Mobility scenario

HS	OS	SS	PS	HR	OR	SR	PR
0.1	0.2	0.1	0.1	0.1	0.2	0.1	0.1

Similarly to the Basic scenario, after the lumping operation and the solution of the corresponding Markov Model, the steady-state probabilities of the High Mobility scenario are reported in Table 5.

For this scenario we have obtained an average response time of RequestPatientInfoPages service of $RT = 26.32$ seconds.

This value of the response time is quite larger than the one obtained in the Basic scenario, and this is mainly due to the following reason. In this scenario the doctor moves more often than in the Basic scenario, and therefore it experiences very different network bandwidths in a quite homogeneous distribution.

From a qualitative viewpoint this result is quite obvious, but we like to remark that our approach allows to quantify such differences among performance indices, and hence it represents a powerful instrument in the hands of software designers to support their decisions. For example, sensitivity analysis can be conducted on response time while varying the probability of moving among pairs of locations.

6   Conclusions

We have introduced a framework for modeling and analyzing the performance of context-aware mobile software systems. Context-awareness is intended to be a composite concept, with different types of awareness concurring to its definition. No assumption underlies our framework about the types of awareness that can be modeled, as each awareness is simply represented by a statechart whose states and transitions are based on model variables.

Three main aspects represent the potential of our framework: (i) the rigorous definition in UML 2 of all necessary instruments to build a model of such an application is mostly based on reusing existing profiling, thus it does not represent "yet another profile" for context, but a promising approach to the modeling of context-related concepts, (ii) the process of lumping statecharts together in an unique stochastic model for context-awareness and mobility represents a powerful unifying approach to the more general modeling and analysis of non-functional properties, (iii) the existing mature approaches for automation in the performance model generation and solution allow to conceive, even in this specific domain, the performance analysis a viable and effective activity in the daily practice of software designers. Besides, our definition of context is extensible and/or shrinkable because any set of system attributes can enter the context as long as a manager statechart is defined for it.

This work opens the view on a plethora of problems that can be faced and solved on the basis of the promising results shown here.

First of all the validation of such approach against real case studies would lead feedback on its actual usability and effectiveness to capture performance issues.

Performance models that represent the resource contention should be addressed (possibly using existing model transformation approaches) in order to conduct a sensitivity study of such models vs. increases of system workload (i.e. a large number of users). Yet other types of performance indices could be useful in this domain, such as the utilization of certain devices across contexts.

However our models at the moment have some limitations on which we are working. First, certain scenarios involving remote firing transitions are complex to be managed in the lumping operation. We are working on parallel compositions of stochastic processes to remove this complexity. Besides, due to intrinsic constraints of UML 2, in our models the managers cannot change state during the execution of a service, but only between one invocation and another. We are trying to introduce this characteristic in our framework without needing a heavyweight extension of the UML metamodel. Moreover we are looking at more complex forms of adaptation that, for example, completely replace the internal structure and behavior of a certain component if needed [12].

We retain that such type of analysis, as well as the analysis of other non-functional attributes like reliability, can be of great support to the decision of system modelers. As shown also in our example, the validation of certain non-functional properties over a system model allows not only to qualitatively validate possible modelers' intuitions, but also to quantitatively study the trends of non-functional metrics depending on context changes.

References

1. Architectural and Analysis Description Language, http://www.aadl.info/
2. DynamIc VAriability in complex, adaptive systems, Research Project, http://www.ict-diva.eu/

3. Balsamo, S., Di Marco, A., Inverardi, P., Simeoni, M.: Model-based performance prediction in software development: A survey. IEEE Transactions on Software Engineering, 295–310 (2004)
4. Berardinelli, L., Cortellessa, V., Di Marco, A.: An Unified Approach to Model Non-Functional Properties of Mobile Context-Aware Software. Technical Report 003-2009, Computer Science Department, University of L'Aquila (2009), http://www.di.univaq.it/cortelle/docs/report-003-2009.pdf
5. Cortellessa, V., Mirandola, R.: PRIMA-UML: a performance validation incremental methodology on early UML diagrams. Science of Computer Programming 44(1), 101–129 (2002)
6. Di Marco, A., Mascolo, C.: Performance analysis and prediction of physically mobile systems. In: WOSP, p. 132. ACM, New York (2007)
7. Fuggetta, A., Picco, G.P., Vigna, G.: Understanding code mobility. IEEE Transactions on software engineering 24(5), 342–361 (1998)
8. Grassi, V., Mirandola, R., Randazzo, E.: Model-Driven Assessment of QoS-Aware Self-Adaptation. In: Software Engineering for Self-Adaptive Systems, p. 222. Springer, Heidelberg (2009)
9. Grassi, V., Mirandola, R., Sabetta, A.: A UML profile to model mobile systems. LNCS, pp. 128–142. Springer, Heidelberg (2004)
10. Harel, D.: Statecharts: A visual formalism for complex systems. Science of computer programming 8(3), 231–274 (1987)
11. Hirsch, D., Kramer, J., Magee, J., Uchitel, S.: Modes for software architectures. In: Gruhn, V., Oquendo, F. (eds.) EWSA 2006. LNCS, vol. 4344, pp. 113–126. Springer, Heidelberg (2006)
12. Inverardi, P., Mancinelli, F., Nesi, M.: A declarative framework for adaptable applications in heterogeneous environments. In: Proceedings of the 2004 ACM symposium on Applied computing, pp. 1177–1183. ACM, New York (2004)
13. IST-MUSIC Project. Middleware Support for Self-Adaptation in Ubiquitous and Service-Oriented Environments, http://www.ist-music.eu/
14. Jansen, D.N., Hermanns, H.: QoS modelling and analysis with UML-statecharts: the StoCharts approach. SIGMETRICS Perform. Eval. Rev. 32(4), 28–33 (2005)
15. Lundesgaard, S.A., Lund, K., Eliassen, F.: Service Plans for Context-and QoS-aware Dynamic Middleware. In: ICDCS Workshops 2006, p. 70 (2006)
16. Mikic-Rakic, M., Malek, S., Medvidovic, N.: Architecture-driven software mobility in support of QoS requirements. In: Proceedings of the 1st international workshop on Software architectures and mobility, pp. 3–8. ACM, New York (2008)
17. Object Management Group, Inc. UML Profile for MARTE, ptc/08-06-09 (2008)
18. Picco, G.P., Murphy, A.L., Roman, G.C.: LIME: Linda meets mobility. In: ICSE, pp. 368–377. ACM, New York (1999)
19. Smith, C.U., Williams, L.G.: Performance Solutions: a practical guide to creating responsive, scalable software. Addison-Wesley, Boston (2002)
20. Tjims, H.C.: Stochastic models: an algorithmic approach. IMA Journal of Management Mathematics

A Process to Effectively Identify "Guilty" Performance Antipatterns*

Vittorio Cortellessa[1], Anne Martens[2], Ralf Reussner[2], and Catia Trubiani[1]

[1] Università degli Studi dell'Aquila, L'Aquila, Italy
[2] Karlsruhe Institute of Technology, 76131 Karlsruhe, Germany
{vittorio.cortellessa,catia.trubiani}@univaq.it,
{martens,reussner}@ipd.uka.de

Abstract. The problem of interpreting the results of software performance analysis is very critical. Software developers expect feedbacks in terms of architectural design alternatives (e.g., split a software component in two components and re-deploy one of them), whereas the results of performance analysis are either pure numbers (e.g. mean values) or functions (e.g. probability distributions). Support to the interpretation of such results that helps to fill the gap between numbers/functions and software alternatives is still lacking. Performance antipatterns can play a key role in the search of performance problems and in the formulation of their solutions. In this paper we tackle the problem of identifying, among a set of detected performance antipatterns, the ones that are the real causes of problems (i.e. the "guilty" ones). To this goal we introduce a process to elaborate the performance analysis results and to score performance requirements, model entities and performance antipatterns. The cross observation of such scores allows to classify the level of guiltiness of each antipattern. An example modeled in Palladio is provided to demonstrate the validity of our approach by comparing the performance improvements obtained after removal of differently scored antipatterns.

Keywords: Software Performance Engineering, Antipatterns, Feedback, Performance Analysis.

1 Introduction

The problem of interpreting the results of performance analysis and providing feedback to software designers to overcome performance issues is probably the most critical open issue today in the field of software performance engineering. A large gap in fact exists between the representation of analysis results and the feedback expected by software designers. The former usually contains numbers (such as mean response time and throughput variance), whereas the latter should embed architectural design suggestions useful to overcome performance problems (such as modifying the deployment of certain software components).

---

* This work has been partly supported by the italian project PACO (Performability-Aware Computing: Logics, Models, and Languages) funded by MIUR.

D.S. Rosenblum and G. Taentzer (Eds.): FASE 2010, LNCS 6013, pp. 368–382, 2010.

A consistent effort has been made in the last decade to introduce automation in the generation of performance models from software models [1], whereas the reverse path from analysis results back to software models is still based on the capabilities of performance experts to observe the results and provide solutions. Automation in this path would help to introduce performance analysis as an integrated activity in the software life cycle, without dramatically affecting the daily practices of software engineers.

Strategies to drive the identification of performance problems and to generate feedback on a software model can be based on different elements that may depend on the adopted model notation, on the application domain, on environmental constraints, etc. Our approach rests on the capability to automatically detect and solve *performance antipatterns*. In general, antipatterns [3] document common mistakes (i.e. "bad practices") made during software development as well as their solutions: what to avoid and how to solve the problems. In particular, performance antipatterns [11] describe recurring software performance problems and their solution.

In Figure 1 the process that we propose is reported: the goal is to modify a software system model in order to produce a new model where the performance problems of the former one have been removed. Boxes in the figure represent data, and segments represent steps.

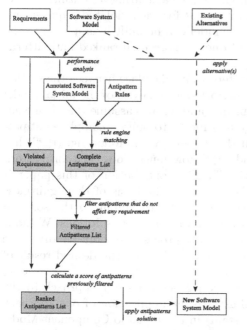

Fig. 1. Performance analysis interpretation

The left hand side of Figure 1, represented with solid arrows, is the part of the process that is based on antipatterns and is the object of this paper. Other techniques can be used to solve performance problems and are represented on the right hand side of Figure 1. In this side a list of *existing alternatives* can contain a number of options for what could be changed in the software system model. From this list, alternatives can be chosen to directly create a new software system models [9]. Alternatives to apply can be chosen randomly, manually by software architects based on their experience, or based on heuristics. These techniques are out of the scope of this paper, thus the right-hand path is represented with dashed arrows in Figure 1.

The inputs of our process are: a *software system model* and a set of performance *requirements*. The software system model contains all information required for an automated transformation into a performance analysis model, that basically is: resource demands of software services, control flow, allocation of software services to hardware processors, workload and operational profile of the system. The requirements represent what end-users expect from the system and thus represent the target performance properties to be fulfilled.

First, the performance indices of the current software system model are determined in a *performance analysis* step. We obtain two types of results from this step: (i) an *annotated system model*, which is the current software model annotated with performance results, and (ii) a list of *violated requirements* as resulting from the analysis. If no requirement is violated by the current software system then the process terminates here. *Antipattern rules* represent a system-independent input that enters the process at the second step. They formalise known performance antipatterns so that they can be automatically detected by a rule engine (see, for example, [10,12])([1]). Antipattern rules are applied to the annotated model to detect all performance antipatterns and list them in a *complete antipatterns list*.

Then we compare the complete antipatterns list with the violated requirements. We obtain a *filtered antipatterns list*, where antipatterns that do not affect any violated requirement have been filtered out. In the following step, on the basis of relationships observed before, we estimate how guilty an antipattern is with respect to a violated requirement by calculating a guiltiness score. As a result, we obtain a *ranked antipatterns list* for each violated requirement. Finally, a new improved software system model can be built by applying to the current software system the solutions of one or more high-ranked antipatterns for each violated requirement.

In this paper we focus on the process steps that take place between the shaded boxes of Figure 1. We assume that the performance analysis of the initial model has identified a list of violated requirements, and we also assume that a rule engine has parsed the current software system model to build a complete antipatterns list [4]. The questions tackled in this paper are the following: (i) "What are the most guilty antipatterns?" and (ii) "How much does each antipattern contribute to each requirement violation?". The contribution of this paper is a technique to rank antipatterns in the model on the basis of their guiltiness for violated requirements. Such ranked list will be the input to the solution step that can use it to give priorities to certain antipattern solutions. Without such ranking technique the antipattern solution process can only blindly move among antipattern solutions without eventually achieving the desired result of requirements satisfaction.

The paper is organized as follows. Section 2 describes our approach to the antipattern ranking, in section 3 we illustrate the application of our approach to a case study (i.e. a web reporting system) in the Palladio Component Model (PCM) [2], Section 4 focuses on the open issues of the proposed approach, Section 5 presents the related work, and finally in Section 6 conclusions are provided.

---

[1] We have introduced a technique based on first-order logic to specify such rules [5].

2   Our Approach for Antipattern Ranking

In this section we provide a detailed description of our approach shown in the shaded boxes of Figure 1. The input data for our approach are a set of *violated requirements* (Section 2.1) and a *complete antipatterns list* for the system under study (Section 2.2). In the first step, we filter out antipatterns that do not affect any requirements and obtain a matrix of *filtered antipatterns* (Section 2.3). In the second step, we assign a guiltiness score for the filtered antipatterns with respect to each violated requirement (Section 2.4). The resulting *ranked antipatterns list* for each requirement can be used to decide which antipattern solution(s) to apply in order to obtain an improved software system model.

2.1   Violated Requirements

The performance requirements that, upon the model analysis, result to be violated represent very likely the effects (to be removed) of some antipatterns, therefore we focus on them.

System requirements are classified on the basis of the performance indices they address and the level of abstraction they apply. Here we consider requirements that refer to the following performance indices [8]([2]):

- *Response time* is defined as the time interval between a user request of a service and the response of the system. Usually, upper bounds are defined in "business" requirements by the end users of the system.
- *Utilisation* is defined as the ratio of busy time of a resource and the total elapsed time of the measurement period. Usually, upper bounds are defined in "system" requirements by system engineers on the basis of their experience, scalability issues, or constraints introduced by other concurrent software systems sharing the same hardware platform.
- *Throughput* is defined as the rate at which requests can be handled by a system, and is measured in requests per time. Throughput requirements can be both "business" and "system" requirements, depending on the target it applies; for the same motivation it can represent either an upper or a lower bound.

Various levels of abstraction can be defined for a requirement: system, processor, device (e.g., CPU, Disk), device operation (e.g., read, write), software component, basic and composed services. In the following, by "basic service" we denote a functionality that is provided by a component without calling services of other components. By "composed service", we denote a functionality that is provided by a component and involves a combination of calls to services of other components. Both types of services can be offered to the end user at the system boundary, or be internal and only used by other components.

However, we do not consider all possible combinations of indices and levels of abstraction. Our experience on system requirements leads us to focus on the most frequent types of requirements, that concern: *utilisation* of processors, *response time* and/or *throughput* of basic and composed services.

---

[2] Note that the values of all these indices depend on the system workload.

Table 1 contains simplified examples of performance requirements and their observed values. Each requirement is represented by: (i) an identifier (ID), (ii) the type of requirement ($Requirement$) that summarizes the performance index and the target system element, (iii) the required value of the index ($Required\ Value$), (iv) the maximum system workload for which the requirement must hold ($System\ Workload$), and (v) the observed value as obtained from the performance analysis ($Observed\ Value$). In Table 1 three example requirements are reported. The first one refers to the utilisation index (i.e., U): it requires that processor $Proc_1$ is not utilised more than 70% under a workload of 200 reqs/sec, while it shows an observed utilisation of 64%. The second one refers to the response time index (i.e., RT) and the third one refers to the throughput index (i.e., T) of certain software services. Requirements R_2 and R_3 are violated, whereas R_1 is satisfied.

Table 1. Example of Performance Requirements

ID	Requirement	Required Value	System Workload	Observed Value
R_1	$U(Proc_1)$	0.70	$200\frac{reqs}{sec}$	0.64
R_2	$RT(CS_y)$	2 sec	$50\frac{reqs}{sec}$	3.07 sec
R_3	$T(BS_z)$	$1.9\frac{reqs}{sec}$	$2\frac{reqs}{sec}$	$1.8\frac{reqs}{sec}$
...	...	...	...	...

Table 2. Details of Violated Requirements

ID	Involved Entities
R_2	$Comp_x.BS_a, Comp_y.BS_b, Proc_2$
R_3	$Comp_w.BS_z, Proc_3$
...	...

Violated requirements are further detailed by specifying the system entities involved in them. For utilisation requirements, we only consider as involved the processor for which the requirement is specified. For example, if a utilisation requirement has been specified for processing node $Proc_2$, we consider only $Proc_2$ to be involved. For requirements on services (i.e. response time and throughput requirements), all services that participate in the service provisioning are considered as involved. For example, if a violated requirement is specified for a service S_1, and S_1 itself calls services S_2 and S_3, we consider all three services S_1, S_2 and S_3 to be involved. Furthermore, all processing nodes hosting the components that provide involved services are considered as involved ([3]). Namely, if the component providing service S_1 is deployed on a processing node $Proc_1$, and the component(s) providing S_2 and S_3 are deployed on a processor $Proc_2$, we additionally consider $Proc_1$ and $Proc_2$ to be involved. With this definition we want to capture the system entities that are most likely to cause the observed performance problems.

In Table 2, the involved services of two violated requirements are reported: R_2 involves all basic services participating in the composed service CS_y (i.e., BS_a, BS_b) prefixed by the names of components that provide them (i.e., $Comp_x$, $Comp_y$ respectively), whereas R_3 only involves the target basic service BS_z

---

[3] The allocation of services to processing nodes is part of the Software System Model (see Section 1).

similarly prefixed. The list of involved entities is completed by the processors hosting these components.

2.2 Complete Antipatterns List

We assume that a rule engine has parsed the annotated system model and has identified all performance antipatterns occurring in it. All detected performance antipatterns and the involved system entities are collected in a *Complete Antipatterns List*. An example of this list is reported in Table 3(a): each performance antipattern has an identifier (*ID*), the type of antipattern (*Detected Antipattern*), and a set of system entities such as processors, software components, composed and basic services, that are involved in the corresponding antipattern (*Involved Entities*). In [11] a list of types of antipatterns is reported.

Note that the detection process takes into account only the annotated software system model and the antipattern rules and thus it is independent of the violated requirements.

Table 3. Example: Antipatterns Lists

(a) Complete Antipatterns List

ID	Detected Antipattern	Involved Entities
PA_1	Blob	$Comp_x$
PA_2	Concurrent Processing Systems	$Proc_1$ $Proc_2$
PA_3	Circuitous Treasure Hunt	$Comp_l.BS_z$
...	...	...

(b) Filtered Antipatterns List.

		R_1	R_2	...	R_j
				Requirements	
Anti-patterns	PA_1		$Comp_x$		
	PA_2	$Proc_1$			
	...				
	PA_x				$e_1, .., e_k$

2.3 Filtering Antipatterns

The idea behind the step that filters the list of detected antipatterns is very simple. For each violated requirement, only those antipatterns with involved entities in the requirement survive, whereas all other antipatterns can be discarded.

A *filtered* list is shown in Table 3(b): rows represent performance antipatterns taken from the complete list (i.e. Table 3(a)), and columns represent violated performance requirements (i.e. Table 2). A non-empty (x, j) cell denotes that the performance antipattern PA_x is a candidate cause for the violation of the requirement R_j. In particular, the (x, j) cell contains the intersection set of system entities $\{e_1, .., e_k\}$ that are involved in the antipattern PA_x and the violated requirement R_j. We will refer to this set as $involvedIn(PA_x, R_j)$ in the following. Antipatterns that do not have any entity in common with any violated requirement do not appear in this list.

This filtering step allows to reason on a restricted set of candidate antipatterns for each requirement. In Section 2.4 we illustrate how to use a filtered antipattern list to introduce a rank for each antipattern that allows to estimate its guiltiness vs. a requirement that has been violated.

2.4 Ranking Antipatterns

The goal of ranking antipatterns is to introduce an order in the list of filtered antipatterns for each requirement, where highly ranked antipatterns are the most promising causes for the requirement violation. The key factor of our ranking process is to consider the entities involved in a violated requirement. We first assign a score to each entity, and then we rank an antipattern on the basis of a combination of the scores of its involved entities, as follows.

In Table 4 we have summarized all equations that we introduce to assign scores to system entities involved in a violated requirement. As outlined in Section 2.1, the requirements that we consider in this paper are: utilisation of processors, response time and throughput of composed and basic services.

Table 4. How to rank performance antipatterns

Type	Equation
Utilisation	$score_{i,j} = (observedUtil_i - requiredUtil_j)$
Response time	$score_{i,j} = \dfrac{ownComputation_i}{maxOwnComputation_j} \cdot \dfrac{observedRespTime_j - requiredRespTime_j}{observedRespTime_j}$
Throughput	$score_{i,j} = \begin{cases} \dfrac{requiredThrp_j - observedThrp_j}{requiredThrp_j} & \text{if } workload_i > observedThrp_i \\ & \text{or } isClosed(systemWorkload) \\ 0 & \text{else} \end{cases}$

Utilisation. The violation of an utilisation requirement can only target (in this paper scope) a processor. For each violated requirement R_j, we introduce a utilisation score to the involved processor $Proc_i$ as reported in the first row of Table 4. $score_{i,j}$ represents a value between 0 and 1 that indicates how much the $Proc_i$ observed utilisation ($observedUtil_i$) is higher than the required one ($requiredUtil_j$).

Response time. The violation of the response time in composed services involves all services participating to that end-user functionality. For each violated requirement R_j, we introduce a response time score to the involved service S_i as reported in the second row of Table 4. We quantify how far the observed response time of the composed service CS_j ($observedRespTime_j$) is from the required one ($requiredRespTime_j$). Additionally, in order to increase the guiltiness of services that mostly contribute to the response time of the composed service, we introduce the first multiplicative factor of the equation. We denote with $ownComputation_i$ the observed computation time of a service S_i participating in the composed service CS_j. If service S_i is a basic service, $ownComputation_i$ equals the response time $RT(S_i)$ of service S_i. However, composite services can also consist of other composite services. Thus, if service S_i is a composite service that calls services S_1 to S_n with probability $P(S_1)$ to $P(S_n)$, $ownComputation_i$ is the response time of service S_i minus the weighted response time of called services:

$$ownComputation_i = RT(S_i) - \sum_{1 \leq c \leq n} P(S_c)RT(S_c)$$

We divide by the maximum own computation over all services participating in CS_j, which we denote by $maxOwnComputation_j$. In this way, services with higher response time will be more likely retained responsible for the requirement violation.

The violation of the response time in basic services involves just the referred service. The same equation can be used, where in this case the first multiplicative factor is equal to 1 as $ownComputation_i$ corresponds to $maxOwnComputation_j$.

Throughput. The violation of the throughput in composed services involves all services participating to the end-user functionality. For each violated requirement R_j, we introduce a throughput score to each involved service S_i as reported in the third row of Table 4. We distinguish between open and closed work-loads here. For an open workload ($isOpen(systemWorkload)$), we can identify bottleneck services S_i that cannot cope with their arriving jobs ($workload_i > observedThrp_i$). To these services a positive score is assigned, whereas all other services are estimated as not guilty for this requirement violation and a score of 0 is assigned to them. For closed workloads ($isClosed(systemWorkload)$), we always observe job flow balance at the steady-state and thus for all services $workload_i = observedThrp_i$ holds. Thus, we cannot easily detect the bottleneck service and we assign a positive score to all involved services. For the positive scores, we quantify how much the observed throughput of the overall composed service ($observedThrp_j$) is far from the required one ($requiredThrp_j$).

The violation of the throughput in basic services involves just this one service. We can use the previous equation as it is, because the only involved service is the one under stress.

Combining the scores of entities. Finally, we rank the antipatterns filtered for each violated requirement R_j. To each antipattern PA_x that shares involved entities with a requirement R_j is assigned a guiltiness degree $GD_{PA_x}(R_j)$ that measures the guiltiness of PA_x for R_j. We consider system entities involved in both PA_x and R_j, as reported in the filtered antipatterns matrix $involvedIn(PA_x, R_j)$. We define the guiltiness degree as the sum of the scores of all involved entities:

$$GD_{PA_x}(R_j) = \sum_{i \in involvedIn(PA_x, R_j)} score_{i,j}$$

Thus the problematic entities that have a high score contribute to consistently raise the overall score of the antipatterns they appear in.

3   Experimenting the Approach

In this section we report the experimentation of our approach on a business reporting system case study. First, we describe the example system and the performance analysis with the Palladio approach [2]. Then, we propose the stepwise application of our approach.

3.1   The Business Reporting System (BRS)

The system under study is the so-called Business Reporting System (BRS), which lets users retrieve reports and statistical data about running business processes from a data base. Figure 2 shows an overview of the software system model, visualized in an UML-like diagram, and some labels indicate the detected antipatterns ([4]).

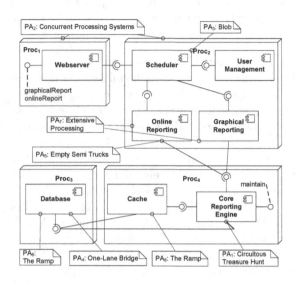

Fig. 2. Case Study: BRS Software System Model

The BRS is a 4-tier system consisting of several software components, as described in the following. The WebServer handles user requests for generating reports or viewing the plain data logged by the system. It delegates the requests to a Scheduler, which in turn forwards the requests. User management functionality (login/logout) is directed to the UserMgmt, whereas report and view requests are forwarded to the OnlineReporting or GraphicalReporting, depending on the type of request. Both components make use of a CoreReportingEngine for the common report generation functionality. The CoreReportingEngine accesses the Database, for some request types using an intermediate Cache.

The system supports seven use cases: users can login, logout and request both reports or views, each of which can be both graphical or online; administrators can invoke the maintenance service. Note that in Figure 2, we only depict those services we specified requirements for.

The PCM model of BRS contains the static structure, the behaviour specification of each component annotated with resource demands and a resource environment specification. For performance analysis, the PCM software system model is transformed automatically into an Extended Queueing Network model suited for simulation with SimuCom [2]. SimuCom is a discrete-event simulator and collects arbitrarily distributed response time, throughput and utilisation for all services of the system.

---

[4] All detailed Palladio models and the description of performance antipatterns have been omitted for brevity here, but can be accessed at palladio-approach.net/_AntipatternGuiltiness as well as the configuration of the BRS model (i.e. workload, usage profile, etc.).

3.2 Our Approach in Practice

The results of the performance analysis of the BRS model are reported in Table 5, where the focus is on performance requirements and their observed values. ID's of violated requirements are typed as bold (i.e. R_2, R_5, R_6, R_7, R_9). In the following, we will concentrate on solving the shaded R_5 requirement in order to illustrate our approach.

Table 5. BRS - Performance requirement analysis

ID	Requirement	Required Value	Observed Value
R_1	$U(Proc_1)$	0.50	0.08
R_2	$U(Proc_2)$	0.75	0.80
R_3	$U(Proc_3)$	0.60	0.32
R_4	$U(Proc_4)$	0.40	0.09
R_5	$RT(CS_{graphical Report})$	2.5 sec	4.55 sec
R_6	$T(CS_{graphical Report})$	0.5 req/sec	0.42 req/sec
R_7	$RT(CS_{online Report})$	2 sec	4.03 sec
R_8	$T(CS_{online Report})$	2.5 req/sec	2.12 req/sec
R_9	$RT(BS_{maintain})$	0.1 sec	0.14 sec
R_{10}	$T(BS_{maintain})$	0.3 req/sec	0.41 req/sec

Table 6. BRS - Violated Requirements

ID	Involved Entities
R_2	$Proc_2$
R_5	$WebServer, Scheduler,$ $UserMgmt, GraphicalReport,$ $CoreReportingEngine,$ $Database, Cache$
R_6	$WebServer, Scheduler,$ $UserMgmt, GraphicalReport,$ $CoreReportingEngine,$ $Database, Cache$
R_7	$WebServer, Scheduler,$ $UserMgmt, OnlineReport,$ $CoreReportingEngine,$ $Database, Cache$
R_9	$CoreReportingEngine$

The violated requirements are further detailed with their involved system entities in Table 6. Following our approach, the detected performance antipatterns occurring in the software system are collected in the *Complete Antipatterns List*, as shown in Table 7. These antipatterns have been also annotated in Figure 2 on the system model.

Table 7. BRS- Complete Antipatterns List

ID	Detected Antipattern	Involved Entities
PA_1	Circuitous Treasure Hunt	Database.getSmallReport, Database.getBigReport $Proc_3$, CoreReportingEngine.getReport, $Proc_4$
PA_2	Concurrent Processing Systems	$Proc_1$, $Proc_2$
PA_3	Blob	Scheduler, $Proc_2$
PA_4	One-Lane Bridge	Database, $Proc_3$
PA_5	Empty Semi Trucks	OnLineReporting.viewOnLine, $Proc_2$, $Proc_4$ CoreReportingEngine.prepareView, CoreReportingEngine.finishView
PA_6	Ramp	Database, $Proc_3$
PA_7	Extensive Processing	GraphicalReporting, OnLineReporting, $Proc_2$
PA_8	Ramp	Cache, $Proc_4$

The combination of violated requirements and detected antipatterns produces the ranked list of BRS antipatterns shown in Table 8. It represents the result of our antipatterns ranking process, where numerical values are calculated according to the equations reported in Table 4, whereas empty cells contain a value 0 by default, that is no guiltiness.

Table 8. BRS - Ranked Antipatterns List

		Requirements				
		R_2	R_5	R_6	R_7	R_9
Anti-patterns	PA_1		0.558	0.122	0.633	
	PA_2	0.054				
	PA_3	0.054	0.051	0.135	0.032	
	PA_4		0.616	0.161	0.689	
	PA_5	0.054				
	PA_6		0.616	0.161	0.689	
	PA_7	0.054	0.125	0.135	0.06	
	PA_8		0.003	0.015	0.03	

Table 8 can be analyzed by columns or by rows. Firstly, by columns, we concentrate on a certain requirement, for example R_5, and we look at the scores of antipatterns. Our approach indicate which antipatterns are more guilty for that requirement violation (i.e., PA_4 and PA_6) and which is the less guilty one (i.e., PA_8). As another example, four antipatterns affect the requirement R_2, but none of them is apparently more guilty than the other ones. So, in this case our approach is able to identify the antipatterns involved without providing a distinction between them. Yet for the requirement R_9 no detected antipattern has a non-zero guiltiness. This means that the violation of R_9 cannot be associated to any known antipattern. In such a case, further performance improvements could be obtained manually, or the requirement has to be relaxed as it is infeasible.

Observing the table by rows, instead, we can distinguish either the antipatterns that most frequently enter the violation of requirements (i.e. PA_3 and PA_7 in this case) or the ones that sum up to the highest total degree of guiltiness (i.e. PA_4 and PA_6 in this case). Different types of analysis can originate from these different views of the ranked list, however for sake of space in what follows we perform an analysis by columns on requirements R_5 and R_7.

In order to satisfy R_5, on the basis of information in Table 8 we have decided to separately solve one-by-one the following antipatterns: PA_4, PA_6, and as counterexample, PA_8.

PA_4 is a "One-Lane Bridge" in the Database. To solve this antipattern, we increase the level of parallelism in the Database, thus at the same time multiple threads can access concurrently. PA_6 is a "Ramp" in the Database. Here, the data access algorithms have to be optimised for larger amounts of data. This can be solved with a reduced resource demand of the database. In our example, we assumed that the resource demand is halved. PA_8 is a "Ramp" in the Cache. The latter accumulates more and more information over time and is slowed down. This can be solved with a reduced resource demand of the Cache. In our example, we assumed again that the resource demand is halved.

The results of the *new* software systems (i.e., BRS_{PA_x}, the BRS initial system with PA_x solved) are collected in Table 9. It can be noticed that the high

Table 9. RT($CS_{graphicalReport}$) across different software system models

ID	Requirement	Required Value	Observed Value			
			BRS	BRS_{PA_4}	BRS_{PA_6}	BRS_{PA_8}
R_5	RT($CS_{graphicalReport}$)	2.5 sec	4.55 sec	2.14 sec	2.06 sec	4.73 sec

guiltness degrees of PA_4 and PA_6 have provided a relevant information because their removal consistently improves the response time. After the removal of PA_8, instead, the requirement R_5 is still violated because it has been removed a cause that affects much less the violated requirement considered.

In Figure 3 we summarize our experiments on the requirement R_5. The target performance index of R_5 (i.e. the response time of the *graphicalReport* service) is plotted on the y-axis, whereas on the x-axis the degree of guiltiness of antipatterns is represented. The horizontal bottommost line is the requirement threshold, that is the response time required, whereas the horizontal topmost line is the observed value for the original BRS system before any modification. Single points represent the response times observed after the separate solution of each performance antipatterns, and they are labeled with the ID of the antipattern that has been solved for that specific point. Of course, the points are situated, along the x-axis, on the corresponding guiltiness degree of the specific antipattern.

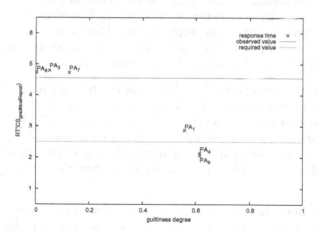

What is expected to observe in such representation is that the points approaches (and possibly go below) the required response time while increasing their guiltiness degree, that is while moving from left to right on the diagram. This would confirm that solving a more guilty antipattern helps much more than solving a less guilty one, thus validating our guiltiness metric.

Fig. 3. RT($CS_{graphicalReport}$) vs the guiltness degree of antipatterns

All antipatterns with non-zero guiltiness have been solved, one by one, to study their influence on the requirement R_5. Figure 3 very nicely validates our hypothesis, in that very guilty antipatterns more dramatically affect the response time, and their solution leads towards the requirement satisfaction. The same considerations made above can be reiterated for the other requirements ([5]).

---

[5] Figures summarizing our experiments on requirements R_2, R_6 and R_7 are reported in palladio-approach.net/_AntipatternGuiltiness.

4   Discussion

The experimentation in Section 3 shows promising results for the example that we have considered and the types of requirements introduced. This is a proof of concept that such a ranking approach can help to identify the causes of performance problems in a software system. The experimentation phase has been very important to refine our approach, in fact by observing the performance analysis results we have fine tuned the equations that represent the antipattern ranking.

However, this is only a first step in this direction, and several issues are yet to be addressed. We discuss some of them in this section, as they also represent the main topics of our current and future work in this field.

Refinement of scores and ranking. Although we have obtained promising results in our experiments, the score model can certainly be improved and needs more experimentation on models of different application domains. First, other types of requirements, among the one listed in Section 2, may need appropriate formulas for scoring the entities involved in them. Second, nested requirements could be pre-processed to eliminate from the list of violated requirements those that are dominated from other ones. Third, more experience could lead to refine the antipattern scoring on the basis of, let say, the application domain (e.g. web-based application) or the adopted technology (e.g. Oracle DBMS). For example, a detected "Circuitous Treasure Hunt" might be of particular interest in database-intensive applications, whereas a detected "Concurrent Processing Systems" might be more important for web-based applications. Finally, to achieve more differentiation in the scoring process for guilty performance antipatterns, negative scores to the entities involved in satisfied requirements can be devised.

Lack of model parameters. The application of this approach is not limited (in principle) along the software lifecycle, but it is obvious that an early usage is subject to lack of information because the system knowledge improves while the development process progresses. Lack of information, or even uncertainty, about model parameter values can be tackled by analyzing the model piecewise, starting from complete sub-models. This type of analysis can bring insight on the missing parameters.

Lack of performance indices. In the same situation as above, performance analysis could not produce all indices needed to apply the process. For example, internal indices of subsystems that are not yet designed in details cannot be collected. In this case we can plan a successive (possibly goal-oriented) analysis to collect the lacking performance indices.

Influence of operational profile. Different operational profiles usually give rise to different analysis results that, in turn, may result in different antipatterns identified in the system. This is a critical issue and, as usually in performance analysis experiments, the choice of the operational profile(s) must be carefully conducted.

Influence of other software layers. The performance model that we have considered here only takes into account the software application and the hardware platform. Between these two layers there are other components, such as middleware and operating system, that can embed performance antipatterns. The approach shall be extended to these layers for a more accurate analysis of the system.

5 Related Work

In this section we discuss the related work that deals with automated approaches to improve the performance of software systems based on analysis results.

Xu et al. [12] present a semi-automated approach to find configuration and design improvement on the model level. Based on a Layered Queueing Network model, two types of performance problems are identified in a first step: bottleneck resources and long paths. Then, rules containing performance knowledge are applied to solve the detected problems. The approach is notation-specific, because it is based on LQN rules, and also it does not incorporate heuristics to speed-up the search of solutions, as suggested in this paper.

Parsons et al. [10] present a framework for detecting performance antipatterns in Java EE architectures. The method requires an implementation of a component-based system, which can be monitored for performance properties. It uses the monitoring data to construct a performance model of the system and then searches for EJB-specific performance antipatterns in this model. This approach cannot be used for performance problems in early development stages, but it is limited to implemented and running EJB systems.

Diaz Pace et al. [7] have developed the ArchE framework. ArchE assists the software architect during the design to create architectures that meet quality requirements. Currently, only rules to improve modifiability are supported. A simple performance model is used to predict performance metrics for the new system with improved modifiability.

In our previous work [6], we have proposed an approach for automated feedback generation for software performance analysis. The approach relies on the manual detection of performance antipatterns in the performance model. There is no support to rank and solve antipatterns. More recently, in [4] we have presented an approach to automatically detect performance antipatterns based on model-driven techniques.

In another previous work we have proposed a complementary approach to improve software performance for component-based software systems based on metaheuristic search techniques [9]. We proposed to combine random moves, as shown on the right hand side of Figure 1, and heuristic rules to search the given design space.

6 Conclusion

In this paper we have shown an approach to rank possible causes of performance problems (i.e. antipatterns) depending on their guiltiness for violated requirements. This work, as shown in Figure 1, is embedded in a wider research area that is the interpretation of performance analysis results and the generation of feedback.

The approach presented here is being integrated with the other work that we have conducted up today in this area. In particular, upstream in Figure 1 we have built a parser (based on XML technologies) that retrieve all antipatterns in a software model. Such parser produces the complete antipattern list that is one of the input of the process presented here. We are tackling the same problem, in parallel, with a model-driven approach. Downstream in Figure 1 we are facing the problem of using the ranked antipattern list to decide the most promising model changes that can rapidly lead to remove performance problems. In this direction several interesting issues have to be faced, such as the simultaneous solution of multiple antipatterns. This research direction can benefit from techniques introduced in model co-evolution.

Finally, we are working to the combination of antipattern-driven approaches, that is the leftmost side of Figure 1, and meta-heuristic approach that run on the rightmost side of the same figure.

References

1. Balsamo, S., Di Marco, A., Inverardi, P., Simeoni, M.: Model-based Performance Prediction in Software Development: A Survey. IEEE TSE 30(5), 295–310 (2004)
2. Becker, S., Koziolek, H., Reussner, R.: The Palladio component model for model-driven performance prediction. Journal of Systems and Software 82, 3–22 (2009)
3. Brown, W.J., Malveau, R.C., McCormick III, H.W., Mowbray, T.J.: AntiPatterns: Refactoring Software, Architectures, and Projects in Crisis. Wiley and Sons, Chichester (1998)
4. Cortellessa, V., Di Marco, A., Eramo, R., Pierantonio, A., Trubiani, C.: Approaching the model-driven generation of feedback to remove software performance flaws. In: 35th Euromicro Conference, pp. 162–169. IEEE Press, New York (2009)
5. Cortellessa, V., Di Marco, A., Trubiani, C.: Performance Antipatterns as Logical Predicates. In: 15th International Conference on Engineering of Complex Computer Systems. IEEE Press, New York (to appear, 2010)
6. Cortellessa, V., Frittella, L.: A Framework for Automated Generation of Architectural Feedback from Software Performance Analysis. In: Wolter, K. (ed.) EPEW 2007. LNCS, vol. 4748, pp. 171–185. Springer, Heidelberg (2007)
7. Díaz Pace, A., Kim, H., Bass, L., Bianco, P., Bachmann, F.: Integrating Quality-Attribute Reasoning Frameworks in the ArchE Design Assistant. In: Becker, S., Plasil, F., Reussner, R. (eds.) QoSA 2008. LNCS, vol. 5281, pp. 171–188. Springer, Heidelberg (2008)
8. Jain, R.: The Art of Computer Systems Performance Analysis: Techniques for Experimental Design, Measurement, Simulation, and Modeling. Wiley and Sons, Chichester (1991)
9. Martens, A., Koziolek, H., Becker, S., Reussner, R.: Automatically improve software models for performance, reliability and cost using genetic algorithms. In: Joint WOSP/SIPEW International Conference. ACM Press, New York (to appear, 2010)
10. Parsons, T., Murphy, J.: Detecting Performance Antipatterns in Component Based Enterprise Systems. Journal of Object Technology 7(3), 55–90 (2008)
11. Smith, C.U., Williams, L.G.: More New Software Performance Antipatterns: Even More Ways to Shoot Yourself in the Foot. In: Computer Measurement Group Conference (2003)
12. Xu, J.: Rule-based Automatic Software Performance Diagnosis and Improvement. In: Workshop on Software Performance, pp. 1–12. ACM Press, New York (2008)

Author Index